COMPUTING WITH LOGIC

Logic Programming with Prolog

David Maier

Oregon Graduate Center

David S. Warren

State University of New York at Stony Brook

The Benjamin/Cummings Publishing Company, Inc.

Menlo Park, California • Reading, Massachusetts
Don Mills, Ontario • Wokingham, U.K. • Amsterdam
Sydney • Singapore • Tokyo • Madrid • Bogota
Santiago • San Juan

Sponsoring Editor: Alan Apt
Production Editor: Laura Kenney
Copyeditor: Jonas Weisel
Technical Art: Graphic Typesetting Service
Cover Designer: Gary Head
Cover Photo: A. Gescheidt, © The Image Bank
Compositor: Graphic Typesetting Service

The basic text of this book was designed using the Modular Design System, as developed by Wendy Earl and Design Office Bruce Kortebein.

The programs presented in this book have been included for their instructional value. They have been tested with care but are not guaranteed for any particular purpose. The publisher does not offer any warranties or representations, nor does it accept any liabilities with respect to the programs.

Library of Congress Cataloging-in-Publication Data

Maier, David, 1953–
Computing with logic.

Includes bibliographies and index.
1. Prolog (Computer program language) 2. Logic programming. I. Warren, David S. II. Title.
QA76.73.P76M349 1988 005.13'3 87–23856
ISBN 0-8053-6681-4

BCDEFGHIJ-DO-898

The Benjamin/Cummings Publishing Company, Inc.
2727 Sand Hill Road
Menlo Park, CA 94025

In Memory of Otto Carl Frederick Krueger
and
For Sarah Ruth Maier
The gardener and his fruit
D. M.

For Paula, Tessa, and Jonah
How can I keep from singing?
D. S. W.

Preface

This text is appropriate for a senior or first-year graduate course on logic programming. It concentrates on the formal semantics of logic programs, automatic theorem-proving techniques, and efficient implementation of logic languages. It is also an excellent reference for the computer professional wishing to do self-study on the fundamentals of logic programming. We have included numerous examples to illustrate all the major concepts and results. No other text deals with implementation in as much detail. Other discussions of implementation techniques do not explain and develop the relationship between interpreter (or compiler) behavior and resolution theorem proving. We stress that connection throughout.

Logic Programming

A course just on logic programming is a reasonable endeavor for several reasons. First, logic programs offer a different way of thinking about problem solving. They have both a declarative and a procedural meaning, so that a person can think about the correctness of a program apart from its operational behavior. Second, logic programming languages have a "stronger" and more natural formal semantics than most other programming languages. They are, therefore, a good vehicle for studying language semantics and meaning-preserving program transformations. Third, logic programming languages are very-high-level languages. They are almost specification languages (languages for specifying what problem is to be solved apart from the means of solution). But for logic programming languages, these specifications can be executed directly. Fourth, detailed knowledge of how these languages are implemented will allow a programmer to program more efficiently and effectively in them. Fifth, the implementation techniques and strategies can be applied to improving the efficiency of other high-level and run-time-intensive languages.

Logic languages, particularly Prolog and its concurrent and parallel variants, have gotten much publicity in connection with their use in proposed "fifth generation" systems, which rely heavily on artificial intelligence and knowledge representation techniques. There are many reasons for the interest. For one, the structure of Prolog resembles that of rule-based expert systems and knowledge bases (databases with inferential components). Rule-based systems typically employ more varied inference strategies than Prolog, but Prolog provides a foundation for understanding the semantics of other kinds of rules and is itself a good language for writing rule processors with various search strategies. Prolog is well suited for symbolic manipulation and information representation tasks. Construction and extraction of data structures are the principal mechanisms for computation in Prolog, and often the same code can be used to do both operations. Also, code can easily be treated as data in Prolog, through the use of "metaprogramming" features, making it a natural choice for writing tools that generate or modify other programs. The integration of data and procedure in Prolog is almost seamless. Whether a particular relationship is represented as a table or a function, or some mixture of the two, is largely irrelevant to other parts of a program that use the relationship. This transparency gives great flexibility in deciding how to represent a particular chunk of knowledge in Prolog. Finally, the declarative semantics of "pure Prolog" make it amenable to implementation on parallel machines, since the meaning of a program is not bound up with a particular model of computation.

The only background absolutely necessary for this book is a first course in data structures. A previous course in compilers is useful for understanding the parsing and symbol table issues. Also, a course with abstract mathematical content that involves theorems (such as finite structures, automata theory, or abstract algebra) is helpful for the more formal material, but we have tried to be self-contained for the topics in mathematical logic.

How to Use This Book

There is more material here than will comfortably fit in a semester. The material on model elimination and on the connection of Datalog to relational algebra can be skipped with no effect on continuity. If Prolog programming is covered in another course, Chapters 8 and 12 are not essential. Also, the chapters on formal logic are fairly independent of the chapters on implementation. A course on formal foundations of logic programming could omit Chapters 3, 6, 10, and 11. A course stressing implementation techniques could leave out portions of Chapters 2, 5, and 9 after the sections on Proplog, Datalog, and Prolog semantics, respectively.

When either of us has taught the course, we have included a programming component—sometimes a course project, sometimes a number of shorter assignments. The appendix presents two ways the course might be structured to include a course project involving Prolog. Shorter programming projects require a bit more planning to integrate, since the book does not get to term structures until fairly far along in the text. One possibility is to introduce lists earlier to permit more interesting Prolog programming assignments sooner. Students in the course will need a companion text, a Prolog programming primer, if there is any substantial programming component. Ours is *not* a text for Prolog programming techniques, or Prolog for certain applications, although those might be reasonable topics for a follow-up course. (We are, however, faithful to DEC-10 Prolog and C-Prolog syntax, and all of the longer examples have actually been run.) We have tried to make the programming examples realistic. Some of the programs (such as the course requirements and fabric examples from Chapter 1 and the poker example from Chapter 7) have to be fairly large to capture a reasonable slice of the real world accurately. Such examples are too unwieldy to use in the classroom in their entirety; instructors should select subsets or alternate examples for presentation.

The material in this book is more important than Prolog programming techniques for a serious computer science student. Most of the computer science in logic programming is not in Prolog applications and programming. However, the material presented here will help a student use Prolog to its best capabilities. Programming in Prolog without knowing its logical foundations means a student probably does not grasp the true nature of the language. Prolog is an impure language—if a student does not recognize the underlying ideal, he or she cannot separate good techniques from bad techniques. A student familiar with the material in this book will be better able to give Prolog programs, or fragments of them, a declarative reading and will be better able to write programs with a declarative meaning. Such programs are not only easier to understand and debug, they almost always are executed more efficiently. A logic programmer has to direct a theorem prover to provide control over the deduction process in order to get reasonable performance. He or she must understand the deduction process to control it intelligently.

The reader may question why we use Prolog and Prolog subsets as the only examples of logic programming languages when we are trying to give a general introduction to the field. First, Prolog is currently the only *real* logic programming language, and the only one in widespread use. Second, it is the logic language for which the most advanced implementations exist. Compilers exist for few other logic programming languages. Third, the choice of language does not much affect the sections on mathematical logic. The material covered in those sections is applicable to any logic programming language. Fourth, Prolog's deduction process is simple and straightforward (top-down, left-to-right) and is hence easier to control. We will take up other logic programming languages in a planned companion volume.

This book is based on notes for a first-year graduate course offered at SUNY Stony Brook and Oregon Graduate Center. Those notes were based, in turn, on a compiler course at Stony Brook in which students implemented a Prolog compiler, and a graduate seminar at OGC in logic programming.

Acknowledgments

Thank you all—particularly our wives, Kaye Van Valkenburg and Paula Pelletier. Also our technical reviewers: John Conery, Bruce Porter, Ray Reiter, and Sharon Salveter (who tested the text in the classroom). Alan Apt, our editor, encouraged the project early on and kept us motivated through the long haul. (You can release the children now, Alan.) Harry Porter gave the whole manuscript a thorough reading, and we avoided incorporating his suggestions only when we were too lazy (or he was too pedantic). Allen Van Gelder showed us how to simplify our arguments on lifting proof trees, and Jean-Louis Lassez helped us see how most general unifiers really work in logic languages. Dick Kieburtz lent us his cottage on the Oregon coast as a comfortable place to write. Quintus helped support the second author during the final throes and gave the use of their impressive Prolog system to produce the example in Chapter 12. Kathy Hammerstrom helped route the right versions of the manuscript to the right places and prepared the table of contents. Laura Kenney patiently led us through the process of turning our manuscript into a book. Thanks to all the students in our courses who helped debug the manuscript, especially Doug Pase (a champion entomologist), Mark Grossman, Phil Miller, Gary Beaver, Bart Schaefer, Deborah Bouchette, Siroos Farahmand-nia, Todd Brunhoff, Phil White, Martin Zimmerman, Brad Needham, Jerry Peak, Hassan Hosseini, Becky Lakey, Mike Rudnick, Larry Morandi, Wroff Courtney, Paul Bober, and Malcolm Printer.

D. M.
D. S. W.

Introduction

A critical property of a programming language is its level of abstraction. We want to program in a more declarative style—saying what a program should compute, rather than how to compute it. In logic programming we define properties and relationships for the objects of interest, and the system determines how to compute with those objects. In this paradigm programming becomes setting up constraints with knowns and unknowns. The system solves for the unknowns, analogously to solving linear equations or to a spreadsheet filling in values of empty cells. There are some key differences, though, between the latter examples and the kind of constraints solving in logic programming.

1. In logic programming the constraints involve data structures and variables representing data structures, rather than algebraic equations and variables representing numbers.
2. There is usually some degree of nondeterminism involved in solving logic programming constraints. We expect constraint solving to yield sets of answers in general. In logic programming we typically have more than one rule for resolving a constraint into a set of subconstraints. Often we want the answers for all the possible ways of resolving the constraint. In a spreadsheet we expect a solution to the constraints to yield a unique value for each unknown cell.
3. There are multiple strategies for solving the constraints defined by logic programs, and many different ways have been proposed for evaluating logic programs, including parallel, data flow, and intelligent-control strategies. This choice of implementation techniques is evidence that we have abstracted away more of the machine details in logic programming languages than in more conventional programming languages.

Why is a declarative style in a programming language better than the traditional procedural style? Such a style encourages the programmer to think about the *intent* of a program, about the *static* description of relationships and properties that are to hold in a program, without having to worry about dynamic changes in the store of a computer. It de-emphasizes the role of time in understanding programs and allows parts of a program to be examined and understood in isolation. Programs in a declarative language are easier to modify because we can add further constraints without having to worry about the timing of checking those constraints. Adding a constraint does not invalidate other constraints already present, so statements are not context dependent. In a procedural language the effect of a statement depends on the statements executed before it, and the statement changes the context for all statements that follow it. For example, encountering the statement X := X + 1 means the value associated with variable X is different for statements that go before and those that come after. The semantics of a statement in a procedural language is quite complex, because that meaning is both dependent on a context and indicates a modification to the context.

Divorcing the meaning of a program from any particular computational model is important. The separation gives the freedom to pick alternative implementations of a program. The fact that there are a number of alternative implementations gives evidence that a language is at a high level of abstraction. For relational database query languages—a particularly simple sort of logic programming language—most query evaluators examine alternative execution strategies for a query and pick the one estimated to be the most time efficient. The split between meaning and the computation model means declarative languages are more amenable to optimization, because such languages can express the intent of a program apart from a particular implementation of that intent. Optimizers need not analyze programs to extract the intent from the implementation, as with say, a vectorizing compiler for FORTRAN. Of course, declarative languages have efficiency penalties. We cannot expect an evaluator always to find as efficient an execution strategy as a human programmer could.

The most widely used logic programming language is Prolog. It does not achieve all the ideals just set forth. We do need to think about control when writing a Prolog program, but at least we may ignore control for a first cut at understanding the program.

Consider what we need for an effective declarative language.

1. A clear statement of the semantics of the language, independent of operational considerations. For logic programming, the semantics is based on formal logic and model theory. For numerical equation solvers, the semantics comes from arithmetic and algebra.
2. A theory of meaning-preserving transformations on programs—that is, a deduction system. In logic programming we have rules and properties relating knowns and unknowns, and we apply transformations to them to solve for the unknowns. An example of such a transformation in the domain of algebra is that adding equals to both sides of an equality or inequality preserves the relationship.
3. Strategies for applying the transformations to yield a solution for the unknowns if it exists, and special forms for statements that support particular strategies. The special forms should make the strategy easy to express. An example is Gaussian elimination. A set of simultaneous linear equations is organized

into a matrix of coefficients. That organization allows certain solution-preserving transformations to be applied to the set of equations through scaling, row swaps, and substraction of rows. It is easy to express a sequence of these transformations that will solve the equations in terms of iterations through the matrix.

4. Suitable data structures and algorithms for implementing the strategy efficiently in a particular machine. In the Gaussian elimination example we have the choice of implementing the coefficient matrix in row-major or column-major order, or perhaps with some kind of linked structure or entry list if we expect a sparse matrix.

This book is organized into three parts, each of which covers the preceding points 1–4 for three successively more powerful logic languages. Part I is on Proplog, a logic language based on propositional logic. Part II is on Datalog, a language for predicate logic (without function symbols). Part III covers Prolog, a language based on functional logic (predicate logic including function symbols). In each part there are at least three chapters—call them A, B, and C.

Chapter A introduces the language via examples to give an intuitive semantics. It also presents a naive interpreter (constraint solver) based on the intuitive semantics.

Chapter B formalizes the semantics using the appropriate logic and models and then looks at the semantics of the full logic (since our languages are based on restricted subsets), deduction, a particular format for formulas (called clauses), and a deduction rule (called resolution) that works on clauses. The resolution rule is the basis for a procedure, known as refutation, for deciding the validity of a formula. We then look at a subclass of clauses, called Horn clauses, and specialize and refine the refutation procedure for that subclass. We show that the specialized procedure is the basis of the naive interpreter of Chapter A, demonstrating the correctness and completeness of the interpreter.

Chapter C takes a naive interpreter, known correct from Chapter B, and optimizes it using special data structures and the Procrastination Principle: put off until later work that might not have to be done, such as concatenating lists or copying data structures.

Part III, on Prolog, includes three additional chapters beyond A, B, and C. One chapter is on procedural extensions to the pure logic form of the language. The second chapter is on further optimization of the interpreter and compilation techniques, the latter being based on symbolic execution and in-line expansion of parts of the interpreter. The third chapter contains an extended example on implementing a database query language in Prolog. It illustrates areas in which Prolog has proved particularly apt: parsing, translation, code generation, and code optimizations.

Why did we choose to develop our topic and recapitulate it twice rather than doing it just once for Prolog? We use a sequence of three increasingly complex languages because we can expound certain concepts more clearly without all the complications of functional logic. We can introduce a few new ideas for each language. Often an argument or development from one language carries over to the next with little or no change. Also, for Prolog, the theorem-proving theory diverges quickly from the efficient interpreter. It is easier to point out the connections in the simpler languages.

Why did we pick the particular sublanguages of Prolog that we did? We chose Proplog because it corresponds to a natural subset of first-order logic, propositional logic, and the structures and models used there are finite and easy to reason about. We chose Datalog because of its connection with query languages for relational databases (which is where the "Data" part comes from). Relational query languages are essentially Datalog without recursion. Such languages are another major example of declarative languages. Datalog also permits us to examine the notion of a logical variable in its simplest form.

We have tried to be obvious rather than clever or succinct. There are no great mysteries to logic programming semantics or Prolog implementation. We present those topics so that any advanced computer science student or practitioner can master them.

Contents

PART I Proplog and Propositional Logic 1

Part I Introduction 1

Chapter 1 Computing with Propositional Logic 3

1.1. Representing Knowledge in Proplog 3
1.1.1. Computer Science Requirements Example 4
1.1.2. Fabric Example 8

1.2. Evaluating Proplog Programs 16
1.2.1. Bottom-up Evaluation 17
1.2.2. A Simple Bottom-up Interpreter 21
1.2.3. Top-down Evaluation 25
1.2.4. A Simple Top-down Interpreter 29

1.3. Proplog as a Declarative Component in a Procedural System 33
1.3.1. Traffic Light Example 33
1.3.2. Fabric Identification Program 36

1.4. Exercises 39

1.5. Comments and Bibliography 43

Chapter 2 Propositional Logic 45

2.1. Propositional Logic for Proplog 45
2.1.1. What Is a Logic? 46
2.1.2. Formal Syntax of Proplog 46
2.1.2.1. Parsing Proplog Programs 48
2.1.3. Semantics for Proplog 50

2.1.4. Deduction in Proplog 52

2.2. Full Propositional Logic 55
2.2.1. Syntax of Propositional Logic 55
2.2.2. Semantics for Propositional Logic 57

2.3. Deduction in Propositional Logic 59
2.3.1. Resolution in Propositional Logic 62
2.3.2. Limiting Choice in Resolution 72

2.4. Horn Clauses 78
2.4.1. If 79
2.4.2. Horn Clause Syntax 81
2.4.3. Resolution with Horn Clauses 82
2.4.4. Search Strategies 90

2.5. Negation and the Closed World Assumption 94

2.6. Exercises 99

2.7. Comments and Bibliography 104

Chapter 3 Improving the Proplog Interpreter 107

3.1. Indexing Clauses 108

3.2. Lazy Concatenation 109

3.3. Exercises 116

3.4. Comments and Bibliography 116

PART II Datalog and Predicate Logic 119

Part II Introduction 119

Chapter 4 Computing with Predicate Logic 121

4.1. Why Proplog Is Too Weak 121

4.2. Pasta or Popovers 125

4.3. A Simple Datalog Interpreter 133

4.4. Separating Noodles from Muffins 138

4.5. Answers 140

4.6. An Example of Recursion 142

4.7. Informal Semantics for Datalog 145

4.8. **Procedural Extensions to Datalog 147**
4.8.1. Negation-as-Failure 147
4.8.2. Numbers, Comparisons, and Arithmetic 151

4.9. **Datalog and Databases 153**

4.10. **Exercises 160**

4.11. **Comments and Bibliography 165**

Chapter 5 Predicate Logic 167

5.1. **Predicate Logic for Datalog 168**
5.1.1. Formal Syntax of Datalog 168
5.1.2. Semantics for Datalog 168

5.2. **Full Predicate Logic 172**
5.2.1. Syntax of Predicate Logic 174
5.2.2. Semantics for Predicate Logic 178

5.3. **Deduction in Predicate Logic 185**
5.3.1. Special Forms 189
5.3.2. If 191

5.4. **Herbrand Interpretations 192**
5.4.1. Herbrand's Theorem 194

5.5. **Resolution in Predicate Logic 196**
5.5.1. Correctness of Resolution 204
5.5.2. Completeness of Resolution 205

5.6. **Horn Clauses 209**

5.7. **Exercises 217**

5.8. **Comments and Bibliography 222**

Chapter 6 Improving the Datalog Interpreter 225

6.1. **Representations 226**

6.2. **Naive Datalog Interpreter 228**

6.3. **Delayed Copying and Application 233**

6.4. **Delayed Composition of Substitutions 236**

6.5. **Avoiding Copies Altogether 240**
6.5.1. Applying Substitutions in the Matching Routine 240
6.5.2. Structure Sharing for Code 243

6.6. Simplifying Local Substitutions 249

6.7. Binding Arrays 251
6.7.1. Looking Back 257

6.8. Implementing Evaluable Predicates 258

6.9. Exercises 261

6.10. Comments and Bibliography 262

PART III Prolog and Functional Logic 265

Part III Introduction 265

Chapter 7 Computing with Functional Logic 269

7.1. Evaluating Arithmetic Expressions Using Datalog 269

7.2. Adding Structures to Datalog 275

7.3. A Simple Prolog Interpreter 279

7.4. Evaluating Expression Trees 284

7.5. Informal Semantics for Prolog 286

7.6. Lists 287
7.6.1. List Syntax 290
7.6.2. Difference Lists 293
7.6.3. Transitive Closure with Cycles 296
7.6.4. An Extended Example: Poker 299

7.7. Exercises 308

7.8. Comments and Bibliography 312

Chapter 8 Prolog Evaluable Predicates 313

8.1. Prolog Pragmatics 313
8.1.1. Documentation Conventions 313

8.2. Input/Output 314

8.3. Call 318

8.4. Controlling Backtracking: The Cut 320

8.5. Arithmetic 323

8.6. Control Convenience 326

8.7. Metaprogramming Features 327
8.7.1. Term Testing and Comparison 328
8.7.2. Structure Manipulation 331

8.8. Lists of All Answers 334

8.9. Modifying the Program 337

8.10. Exercises 342

8.11. Comments and Bibliography 345

Chapter 9 Functional Logic 347

9.1. Functional Logic for Prolog 349
9.1.1. Formal Syntax of Prolog 349
9.1.2. Semantics for Prolog 349

9.2. Full Functional Logic 352
9.2.1. Syntax of Functional Logic 353
9.2.2. Semantics for Functional Logic 353

9.3. Deduction in Functional Logic 357
9.3.1. Special Forms and Skolem Functions 360

9.4. Herbrand Interpretations 364
9.4.1. Herbrand's Theorem 366

9.5. Resolution in Functional Logic 369

9.6. Answers 372

9.7. Model Elimination 374

9.8. Horn Clauses 376

9.9. Exercises 379

9.10. Comments and Bibliography 379

Chapter 10 Improving the Prolog Interpreter 381

10.1. Representations 381

10.2. Naive Prolog Interpreter 384

10.3. Delayed Copying and Application 388

10.4. Delayed Composition of Substitutions 389

10.5. Avoiding Copies Altogether 390

10.5.1. Applying Substitutions in the Matching Routine 390
10.5.2. Structure Sharing for Code 392
10.5.2.1. Structure Sharing for Terms 394
10.5.2.2. Copy on Use for Terms 399
10.5.2.3. Comparison of Methods 402

10.6. Binding Arrays 403

10.7. Implementing Model Elimination with Prolog Techniques 409

10.8. Exercises 412

10.9. Comments and Bibliography 415

Chapter 11 Interpreter Optimizations and Prolog Compilation 417

11.1. Activation Records 417

11.2. Including Variable Bindings in the Stack Frame 424

11.3. Backtrack Points 425

11.4. Implementing Evaluable Predicates 427

11.5. Reclaiming Deterministic Frames 429
11.5.1. Deterministic Frames with Structure Sharing 432

11.6. Indexing 433

11.7. Last Call and Tail Recursion Optimizations 437

11.8. Compiling Prolog 444
11.8.1. The Warren Prolog Engine 447
11.8.2. WPE Instructions 449
11.8.3. Allocating Binding Frames 451
11.8.4. A Complete Datalog Example 452
11.8.5. Temporary Variables 454
11.8.6. Nondeterminism 456
11.8.7. Terms in Clauses 462
11.8.7.1. Terms in the Body 463
11.8.7.2. Terms in the Head 464
11.8.8. Final Literal Optimization 466
11.8.9. Trimming Environments 470

11.9. Exercises 471

11.10. Comments and Bibliography 476

Chapter 12 An Example 479

12.1. Universal Scheme Query Languages 479

12.2. The PIQUE Query Language 485

12.3. Implementing PIQUE in Prolog 489
12.3.1. Representing the Database Scheme and Data 489
12.3.2. PIQUE Scanner 495
12.3.3. PIQUE Parser 498
12.3.4. PIQUE Translator 503
12.3.5. Optimizations of Simple Queries 511
12.3.6. Compound Queries 519
12.3.7. Programming in Prolog 522

12.4. Exercises 523

12.5. Comments and Bibliography 526

Appendix: Possible Course Projects 527

Theory and Use of Logic Programming 527

Implementation of Logic Programming Systems 528

Index: 529

PART I

Proplog and Propositional Logic

In Chapters 1–3, we will see:

1. The declarative reading of a simple logic language, Proplog.
2. Different interpretation strategies, top-down and bottom-up, for that language.
3. A semantics for the language independent of any particular computation system, using the notion of a logical model.
4. The mechanisms of refutation theorem proving using the resolution rule, along with proofs of soundness and completeness.
5. An efficient implementation of the refutation procedure as applied to Proplog.

Chapter 1 introduces Proplog and develops two interpreters based on an intuitive understanding of its semantics and inference rules. To an experienced programmer Proplog may seem hopelessly simple, but the examples demonstrate that Proplog can capture certain categories of real information. Proplog can be extended with probabilities to get the types of rules used in some diagnostic and classification expert systems. We also show how it can be the declarative component in a procedural framework, making the behavior of the containing system easy to understand and modify.

Chapter 2 formalizes the intuitive semantics of Chapter 1. There we carefully justify the inferences we made from Proplog programs in Chapter 1. We contrast the syntax with the semantics—the sequences of symbols that are statements in a language versus the abstracted properties of some world that the statements describe. The computer can manipulate only the symbols of the program statements, but what is important is what those symbols are taken to say about the world. *Truth assignments* abstract and formalize possible worlds (or maybe better, possible states of the world) and provide the semantics, or meaning, for Proplog statements and programs. Chapter 2 develops the important relationship of implication between statements. We say statement S1 implies statement S2, if in all possible worlds where S1 is true (those whose truth assignments are *models* for S1), S2 is also true. It is implication that forms the basis of our programming language; an interpreter, therefore, is a procedure that determines implication among statements. In propositional logic we can enumerate all possible models for a statement, so we can check implication directly from the semantic definition.

Such a direct check will not be possible later in the book as the logics get more expressive. For this reason (as well as for efficiency), we look at *inference rules*. An inference rule is a way of deriving a new implied statement by the syntactic manipulation of a set of statements. Such rules are the first step toward computing directly with declarative statements—they give us the ability to manipulate statements syntactically while preserving their meanings.

For Proplog programs we need a directed procedure—a procedure that, given a set of statements and an arbitrary statement, will determine whether the set implies the statement. To that end we introduce an inference rule called *resolution* and a procedure for applying it, called *refutation*. We will cast arbitrary logical formulas into a uniform format, called *conjunctive form*, to make the resolution inference rule easier to express and apply. Refutation is a complete deduction procedure for propositional logic, which means that it will always discover a way to apply the inference rules to prove an implication when the implication holds. Furthermore, for propositional logic, refutation will always terminate if controlled properly. Thus, the question of whether one group of propositional logic statements implies another is *decidable*—there is an algorithm that always halts and that can answer yes or no to an implication problem. Such a complete proof mechanism is the source of the procedural component of Proplog.

Chapter 3 considers the efficient implementation of Proplog interpreters. We concentrate on the top-down interpreter, since that approach has proven most viable for implementation of Prolog; it will be developed further in the later chapters. Not a lot of improvement can be made to the naive algorithm, since it is so simple. We can reduce some searching by grouping together statements that apply to the same goal. We introduce the Procrastination Principle, putting off work until later, in connection with lazy concatenation of lists. Both techniques will be carried through to the implementations of Datalog and Prolog.

Do not be dismayed if this introduction to Part I is a bit hard to decipher, but do come back and reread it after Chapter 3 to get the big picture.

1

Computing with Propositional Logic

This chapter introduces computing with the simplest of logics: propositional logic. We first present Proplog, a small subset of Prolog, and show how it can be used to express certain simple facts and rules. Then we consider drawing conclusions from a database of Proplog facts and rules, and we look at ways a computer system could treat such a database as a *program* for testing if a given fact can be inferred from the facts and rules. Such a system for making inferences from a database is called a Proplog *interpreter*. Two simple but somewhat inefficient interpreters for Proplog are presented as illustrations. Overall this chapter should provide a feeling for both the *declarative* and *procedural* readings of a logic language.

1.1. Representing Knowledge in Proplog

Proplog is a very restricted subset of the logic programming language Prolog. It is a self-contained subset, however, so the reader can try out the examples here with almost any Prolog interpreter or compiler. Proplog can express that some sentence or *proposition* holds conditionally or unconditionally. By "holding conditionally," we mean that the proposition is true when certain other propositions are true. Such a conditional proposition is a *rule*, while a proposition that is unconditionally true is a *fact*. The term *statement* or *clause* means either a Proplog rule or fact. Sometimes we will refer to a fact as a *unit clause*.

We begin with two extended examples, which we will draw upon extensively in these first two chapters. The first is based on the departmental requirements for an undergraduate major in computer science at SUNY Stony Brook, as given in the 1983–85 catalog. The second summarizes information on fabric weaves taken from various sewing and textile books. In using logic to represent real-world knowledge, we must isolate the entities and relationships of interest for a particular domain, and deal in an abstract world where nothing else exists. We will use statements whose truth or falsity depends only on the state for the portion of the world we are trying to capture. There will be statements about taking courses and satisfying requirements, and about a fabric having certain properties or being of a certain type. We then express relationships that have to hold among those statements—constraints on the simultaneous truth of groups of those statements. We spend a little time applying the constraints: given that certain statements are true, what other statements are constrained to be true? We are solving for an unknown that is the truth or falsity of a statement.

The notation used here may seem a trifle odd, but it is chosen to be consistent with CProlog syntax. Propositions will always begin with a lowercase letter, and subsequent words will be capitalized but not separated by a space.

1.1.1. *Computer Science Requirements Example*

Consider a set of requirements for graduation with a computer science undergraduate degree. The department requires that each student take courses to satisfy requirements in five areas: basic computer science, mathematics and applied math, advanced computer science, engineering, and natural science. The following Proplog rule expresses these area requirements:

```
aStudentHasSatisfiedTheCSRequirements :-
      aStudentHasSatisfiedTheBasicCSRequirements,
      aStudentHasSatisfiedTheMathRequirements,
      aStudentHasSatisfiedTheAdvancedCSRequirements,
      aStudentHasSatisfiedTheEngineeringRequirements,
      aStudentHasSatisfiedTheNaturalScienceRequirements.
```

These propositions, however, are bulky and tedious to read. Instead of writing out each proposition, therefore, we will select just a couple of key terms to summarize the idea of each. Thus, we abbreviate the propositions in the preceding clause to get:

```
csReq :- basicCS, mathReq, advancedCS, engReq, natSciReq.
```

This rule says that **csReq**, "a student has satisfied the CS requirements," is true if all the five area requirements are satisfied. The ':-' can be read as "if" and the ',' can be read as "and." Every Proplog statement is terminated with a period. A Proplog clause always has a single proposition to the left of ':-'. That proposition is called the *head* of the clause. A clause has zero (in the case of a fact) or more (in the case of a rule) propositions on the right, which are collectively called the *body* of the clause.

We go on to say in detail what each of the area requirements is. First, to meet the basic CS requirement, a student must take an introduction to problem solving and programming, and then three courses: Computer Organization (**compOrg**), Advanced Programming (**advProg**), and Theory of Computation (**theory**). This basic requirement is expressed by the following clause:

```
basicCS :- introReq, compOrg, advProg, theory.
```

There are two ways to satisfy the requirement for an introduction to problem solving and programming. It can be satisfied by taking the single course Introduction to Computer Science (**introCS**) or by taking the two-course sequence Introduction to Computer Science I and II (**introI** and **introII**). This choice can be expressed in Proplog by simply using two clauses:

```
introReq :- introCS.
introReq :- introI, introII.
```

The first clause states that the introduction requirement can be satisfied by taking Introduction to Computer Science. The second clause states that the same requirement also can be satisfied by taking both Introduction to Computer Science I and II. Thus, either schedule will satisfy the requirement. Two clauses with the same head allow the expression of a disjunction: an "or" of the two statements.

Continuing, we now must specify how the mathematics requirements can be met. The math requirements are divided into three subgroups: the calculus requirements, a finite math requirement, and an algebra requirement. The following clauses describe the breakdown of the requirements:

```
mathReq :- calcReq, finiteReq, algReq.

calcReq :- basicCalc, advCalc.

basicCalc :- calcI, calcII.
basicCalc :- calcA, calcB, calcC.
basicCalc :- honorsCalcI, honorsCalcII.

advCalc :- linAlg.
advCalc :- honorsLinAlg.

finiteReq :- finStructI, stat.

algReq :- finStructII.
algReq :- absAlg.
```

These clauses express that there are three ways to satisfy the basic calculus requirement: the standard calculus sequence (**calcI** and **calcII**), a more leisurely sequence for those not so well prepared (**calcA**, **calcB**, and **calcC**), or the honors sequence for those who prefer no social life (**honorsCalcI** and **honorsCalcII**). Either of the two advanced calculus courses, Linear Algebra (**linAlg**) and Honors Linear Algebra (**honorsLinAlg**), will meet that requirement. Two applied math courses, Finite Structures I (**finStructI**) and Probability and Statistics (**stat**), must be taken to satisfy the finite mathematics requirement. Finally, either the second applied math course on finite structures (**finStructII**) or the math course on abstract algebra (**absAlg**) will satisfy the algebra requirement.

The advanced computer science requirement is stated as follows:

Four other computer science courses selected from Groups 1 and 2. Two of these four courses must be selected from Group 1.
Group 1: Compilers (**compilers**), Operating Systems (**opSys**), Architecture (**arch**).
Group 2: File Structures (**fileStruct**), Databases (**dbms**), Programming Languages (**progLang**), Computer Communications (**compComm**), Artificial Intelligence (**ai**), Graphics (**graphics**), Microprocessors (**micros**), Research (**research**).

Thus a student can fulfill the advanced CS requirement either by taking all the courses in Group 1 and one course from Group 2, or by taking two courses from each group. The following Proplog clauses can be used to express this requirement:

```
advancedCS :- group1All, group2One.
advancedCS :- group1Two, group2Two.

group1All :- compilers, opSys, arch.

group2One :- fileStruct.   group2One :- dbms.
group2One :- progLang.     group2One :- compComm.
group2One :- ai.           group2One :- graphics.
group2One :- research.     group2One :- micros.

group1Two :- compilers, opSys.
group1Two :- compilers, arch.
group1Two :- arch, opSys.

group2Two :- fileStruct, dbms.       group2Two :- fileStruct, progLang.
group2Two :- fileStruct, compComm.   group2Two :- fileStruct, ai.
group2Two :- fileStruct, graphics.   group2Two :- fileStruct, micros.
group2Two :- fileStruct, research.

group2Two :- dbms, progLang.         group2Two :- dbms, compComm.
group2Two :- dbms, ai.               group2Two :- dbms, graphics.
group2Two :- dbms, micros.           group2Two :- dbms, research.

group2Two :- progLang, compComm.     group2Two :- progLang, ai.
group2Two :- progLang, graphics.     group2Two :- progLang, micros.
group2Two :- progLang, research.

group2Two :- compComm, ai.           group2Two :- compComm, graphics.
group2Two :- compComm, micros.       group2Two :- compComm, research.

group2Two :- ai, graphics.           group2Two :- ai, micros.
group2Two :- ai, research.

group2Two :- graphics, micros.       group2Two :- graphics, research.

group2Two :- micros, research.
```

The engineering requirement, which is just a single course, Digital System Design (**digSys**), is easy to express:

```
engReq :- digSys.
```

The natural science requirement can be satisfied by taking the standard introductory sequence for one of physics, chemistry, or biology.

```
natSciReq :- physicsI, physicsII.
natSciReq :- chemI, chemII.
natSciReq :- bioI, bioII.
```

This entire set of clauses is a complete and unambiguous specification of the courses that a computer science student must take to fulfill the departmental requirements for a computer science major. Each clause represents a part of the requirements. Each can be understood as saying, "One way to satisfy so-and-so requirement is to take such-and-such courses." Equivalently, and slightly more abstractly, a clause:

```
a :- b, c.
```

can be read as:

It is true that **a** if it is true that **b** and it is true that **c**.

For example, **natSciReq** is true if the natural science requirements have been met and **chemI** is true if the student in question has taken the first course in the chemistry sequence.

Let's see how we might use this specification of the requirements for a computer science major. We would like to be able to determine from a student's transcript whether he or she meets these requirements. To do so we must express the student's courses with Proplog facts. For instance, we would use the following Proplog unit clauses to identify the courses of a student named Maria Marcatello:

```
introI.       introII.
compOrg.      advProg.

theory.       compilers.
opSys.        arch.
progLang.     research.

calcA.        calcB.
calcC.        linAlg.
absAlg.       finStructI.
stat.         digSys.

physicsI.     physicsII.
```

Here the clause **introI.** means that Maria has taken, and received a passing grade in, Introduction to Computer Science I. If the conjunction of zero propositions is considered to be true, a fact can be considered a degenerate type of rule with no propositions on the right side. Thus, writing:

```
introI.
```

is a notational convenience for:

```
introI :- .
```

Now the question of whether Maria has satisfied the requirements can be determined by looking through *all* the clauses, both rules and facts. We have to see whether the proposition that Maria has satisfied the computer science requirements, **csReq**, is borne out by the facts according to the rules. For example, from the facts:

```
introI.
introII.
```

and the rule:

```
introReq :- introI, introII.
```

we can conclude that Maria has satisfied the introduction to programming requirement, **introReq.** Careful inspection reveals that Maria has satisfied all the other requirements for a computer science degree as well. In Section 1.2.1 we will demonstrate rigorously that she has satisfied these requirements.

1.1.2. *Fabric Example*

In the previous example the propositions describe events that have or have not happened in a particular world. In this example the propositions will describe properties and classification that may or may not be true of a particular piece of fabric. The rules are sufficient to classify a piece of fabric only if it is of one of the types discussed here. There are fabrics not covered that the rules would misidentify.

In woven fabric two sets of threads are interlaced at right angles. The *warp* threads (also called *ends* or *warp ends*) run the length of a piece of fabric. During the weaving process the warps are raised and lowered in different patterns, and a *fill* thread is passed back and forth between them. Fill threads are sometimes called *weft* or *woof* threads, *picks*, or, collectively, *filling*. (See Figure 1.1.) The type of weave is determined by such factors as:

1. the pattern in which the warps cross the fill
2. the relative sizes of warp and fill threads
3. the relative spacing of warp and fill threads
4. the colors of threads

The three basic groups of weaves are *plain weaves*, *twill weaves*, and *satin weaves*. In plain weaves the warp ends (or groups of ends) cross over and under

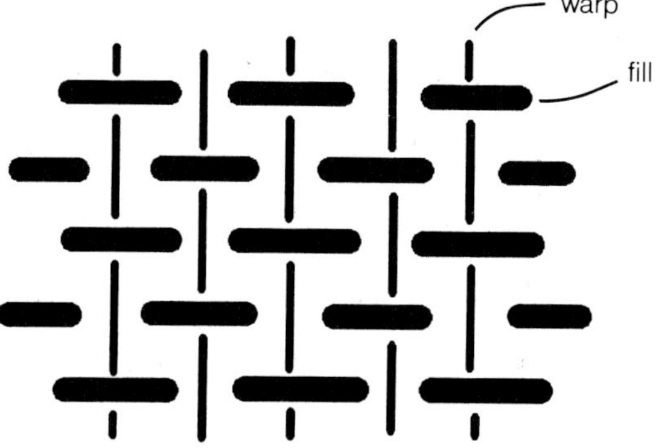

Figure 1.1 Plain weave

successive picks, and adjacent warp ends go alternate directions around the picks. (See Figure 1.1.) Thus the warp pattern repeats every two threads. In twill weaves a warp end passes over more than one pick, or *floats*, and passes under one or more picks, or *sinks*. (See Figure 1.2.) Successive warp ends have the same pattern, except they are offset by one pick for each warp end. Thus the warp pattern repeats every three or more warp ends. The successive offsets give twills a diagonal texture. Satin weave is characterized by long floats or sinks, usually for four or more threads. (See Figure 1.3.) If the float is long, the sink is for one thread; conversely, if the sink is long, the float is for one thread. Satin weaves do not have the diagonal texture of twills, but they usually have a lustrous look.

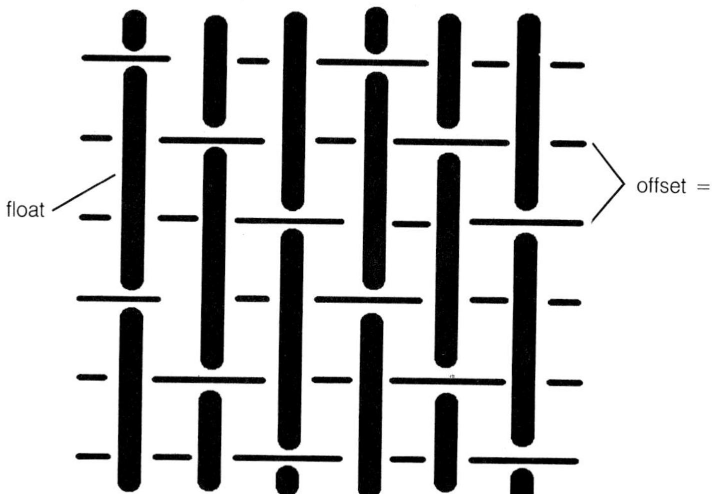

Figure 1.2 Twill weave (warp faced)

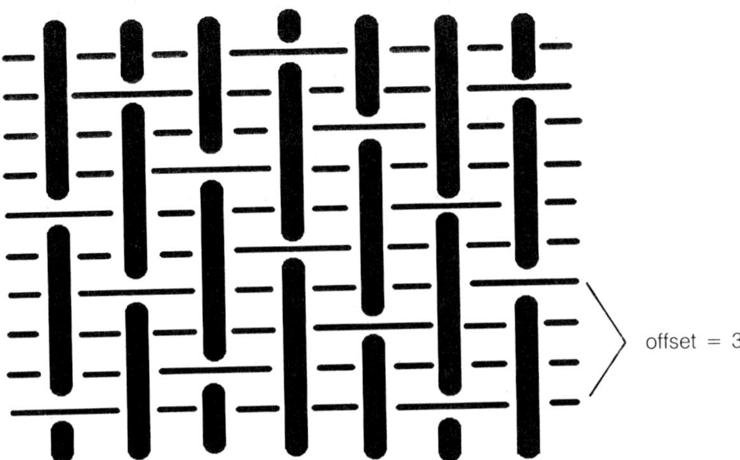

Figure 1.3 Satin weave

The basic weaves can be recognized in a number of ways based on their properties. The following rules categorize a fabric into one of the three basic weave groups:

```
plainWeave :- alternatingWarp.
twillWeave :- diagonalTexture.
twillWeave :- hasFloats, warpOffsetEQ1.
satinWeave :- hasFloats, warpOffsetGT1.
```

Note we have two rules for identifying a twill weave based on different properties. Recall that multiple rules with the same head are used to represent disjunction.

Different fabrics with ordinary plain weaves can be distinguished by the colors of threads, the spacings of threads, the texture, and the fiber. Fabric in which the number of warp ends per inch equals the number of picks per inch is called *balanced*. (See Figure 1.4.) When the threads are fine and spaced enough to let light through, *sheer* fabrics result. *Percale* is cotton fabric with a balanced weave and a smooth texture. *Organdy* is a sheer cotton fabric, while *organza* is a similar fabric of silk. All these fabrics have threads of a single color, so we introduce a derived property, **solidPlain**, to categorize them.

```
solidPlain :- plainWeave, oneColor.
percale :- solidPlain, cotton, balanced, smooth.
organdy :- solidPlain, cotton, sheer.
organza :- solidPlain, silk, sheer.
```

Patterns are woven into fabrics by having groups of contiguous warp or fill threads of different colors. *Plaids* have groups of different colored threads in both warp and fill. *Gingham* is a cotton plaid where the widths of the different groups of threads are the same.

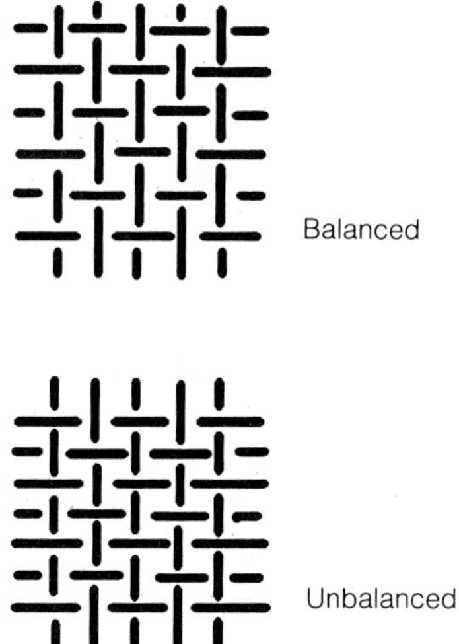

Figure 1.4

```
patternPlain :- plainWeave, colorGroups.
plaid :- patternPlain, warpStripe, fillStripe.
gingham :- plaid, equalStripe.
```

Basket weave is a variation on plain weave in which groups of two or more warp threads function as a unit. For *oxford cloth*, warp ends are grouped in twos, and picks are single. This grouping is denoted 2/1. (See Figure 1.5.) Also, in oxford cloth, the picks are thicker than the warp ends. For *monk's cloth*, the picks are also grouped in units, with the same number of threads in a pick group as in a warp

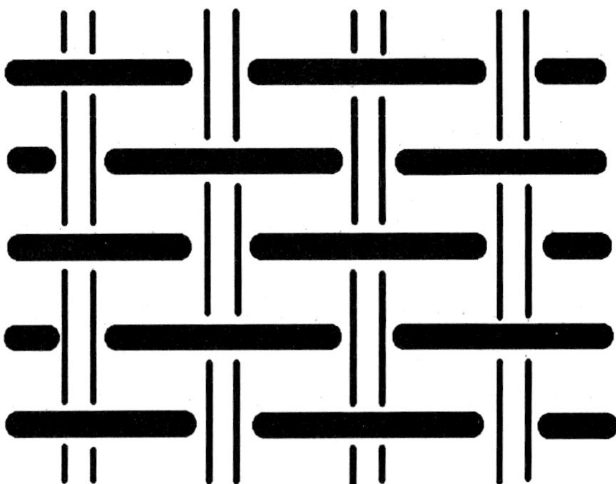

Figure 1.5 Oxford Cloth

Figure 1.6 Monk's Cloth

group. The number of threads in a group is usually two or four, and the groupings are designated 2/2 or 4/4. (See Figure 1.6.) The warp and pick threads have the same thickness. *Hopsacking* has a rough texture and an *open* weave (adjacent warp ends not touching, likewise for picks).

```
basketWeave :- plainWeave, groupedWarps.
oxford :- basketWeave, type2To1.
oxford :- basketWeave, thickerFill.
monksCloth :- basketWeave, type2To2, sameThickness.
monksCloth :- basketWeave, type4To4, sameThickness.
hopsacking :- basketWeave, rough, open.
```

Ribbed weave fabrics are a variation on plain weave with some threads thicker than others. There are several ribbed fabrics where the fill threads are all of the same thickness but thicker than the warp threads. The varieties are distinguished by the size and shape of the ribs, and the balance of warp ends to picks. *Faille* (pronounced "file") has small, flat ribs. *Grosgrain, bengaline,* and *ottoman* have more rounded ribs, and the ribs are small, medium, and heavy, respectively.

```
ribbedWeave :- plainWeave, someThicker.
crossRibbed :- ribbedWeave, thickerFill.
faille :- crossRibbed, smallRib, flatRib.
grosgrain :- crossRibbed, smallRib, roundRib.
bengaline :- crossRibbed, mediumRib, roundRib.
ottoman :- crossRibbed, heavyRib, roundRib.
```

Napped fabrics are finished by brushing with wire brushes to give a very soft texture. *Flannel* is the most common napped fabric, which is plain or twill weave cotton or wool.

```
flannel :- plainWeave, cotton, napped.
flannel :- twillWeave, cotton, napped.
flannel :- plainWeave, wool, napped.
flannel :- twillWeave, wool, napped.
```

In *leno* weave a special attachment to the loom, called a doup, crosses and uncrosses pairs of warp threads between picks. (See Figure 1.7.) *Marquisette* is a fabric with an open leno weave.

```
lenoWeave :- plainWeave, crossedWarps.
marquisette :- lenoWeave, open.
```

Pile fabrics have an extra set of warp or fill threads loosely woven to produce loops on one or both sides of the fabric. (See Figure 1.8.) Pile fabrics are distinguished as *fill pile* or *warp pile*, depending on which direction the extra threads are used. *Velvet* has a warp pile where the loops are cut. *Terry cloth* is a fill pile fabric with uncut loops on both sides. *Corduroy* and *velveteen* are also fill pile fabrics but with cut pile loops. In corduroy the loops are aligned to give ridges in the pile, whereas in velveteen they are staggered to give a solid pile.

```
fillPile :- plainWeave, extraFill.
warpPile :- plainWeave, extraWarp.
velvet :- warpPile, cut.
terry :- fillPile, uncut.
terry :- fillPile, reversible.
corduroy :- fillPile, cut, alignedPile.
velveteen :- fillPile, cut, staggeredPile.
```

Twills vary by the relative lengths of the floats and sinks in the warp ends. If the lengths are the same, the fabric is called *even*. If the lengths are not equal, the

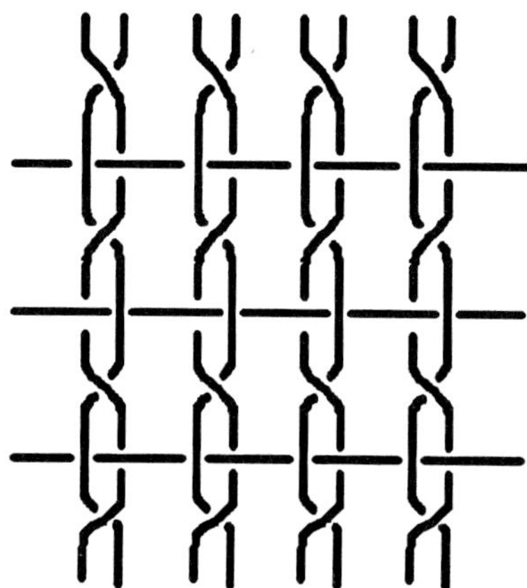

Figure 1.7 Leno

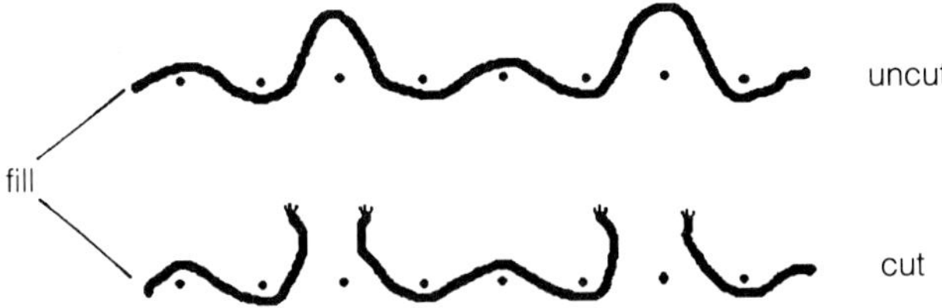

Figure 1.8 Pile: end view

fabric is *faced*: *filling-faced* if sinks are longer; *warp-faced* if the floats are longer. *Drill* and *denim* are both warp-faced twills. Denim, though, has a white filling, whereas drill has the filling the same color as the warp. *Serge* is an even twill with a heavy diagonal rib.

```
evenTwill :- twillWeave, floatEQSink.
fillingFaced :- twillWeave, floatLTSink.
warpFaced :- twillWeave, floatGTSink.
denim :- warpFaced, coloredWarp, whiteFill.
drill :- warpFaced, oneColor.
serge :- evenTwill, heavyRib.
```

For satin weaves, we get *satin* if the floats are in the warp and *sateen* if they are in the fill. Both have a smooth finish. *Moleskin* is a napped, satin weave, cotton fabric.

```
satin :- satinWeave, warpFloats, smooth.
sateen :- satinWeave, fillFloats, smooth.
moleskin :- satinWeave, cotton, napped.
```

Figure 1.9 collects all the fabric rules.

```
plainWeave :- alternatingWarp.
twillWeave :- diagonalTexture.
twillWeave :- hasFloats, warpOffsetEQ1.
satinWeave :- hasFloats, warpOffsetGT1.

solidPlain :- plainWeave, oneColor.
percale :- solidPlain, cotton, balanced, smooth.
organdy :- solidPlain, cotton, sheer.
organza :- solidPlain, silk, sheer.

patternPlain :- plainWeave, colorGroups.
plaid :- patternPlain, warpStripe, fillStripe.
gingham :- plaid, equalStripe.
```

Figure 1.9 (continued on next page)

```
basketWeave :- plainWeave, groupedWarps.
oxford :- basketWeave, type2To1.
oxford :- basketWeave, thickerFill.
monksCloth :- basketWeave, type2To2, sameThickness.
monksCloth :- basketWeave, type4To4, sameThickness.
hopsacking :- basketWeave, rough, open.

ribbedWeave :- plainWeave, someThicker.
crossRibbed :- ribbedWeave, thickerFill.
faille :- crossRibbed, smallRib, flatRib.
grosgrain :- crossRibbed, smallRib, roundRib.
bengaline :- crossRibbed, mediumRib, roundRib.
ottoman :- crossRibbed, heavyRib, roundRib.

flannel :- plainWeave, cotton, napped.
flannel :- twillWeave, cotton, napped.
flannel :- plainWeave, wool, napped.
flannel :- twillWeave, wool, napped.

lenoWeave :- plainWeave, crossedWarps.
marquisette :- lenoWeave, open.

fillPile :- plainWeave, extraFill.
warpPile :- plainWeave, extraWarp.
velvet :- warpPile, cut.
terry :- fillPile, uncut.
terry :- fillPile, reversible.
corduroy :- fillPile, cut, alignedPile.
velveteen :- fillPile, cut, staggeredPile.

evenTwill :- twillWeave, floatEQSink.
fillingFaced :- twillWeave, floatLTSink.
warpFaced :- twillWeave, floatGTSink.
denim :- warpFaced, coloredWarp, whiteFill.
drill :- warpFaced, oneColor.
serge :- evenTwill, heavyRib.

satin :- satinWeave, warpFloats, smooth.
sateen :- satinWeave, fillFloats, smooth.
moleskin :- satinWeave, cotton, napped.
```

Figure 1.9 Continued

We now use these rules to find out what you are wearing. You first notice there is a diagonal pattern to the fabric. Looking more closely, you see that the warp ends dominate on the visible side of the fabric. Furthermore, the warps are blue and the filling is white. We summarize your observations with the following Proplog facts:

```
diagonalTexture.
floatGTSink.
coloredWarp.
whiteFill.
```

With the rule:

```
twillWeave :- diagonalTexture.
```

you infer:

```
twillWeave.
```

Now you can apply the rule:

```
warpFaced :- twillWeave, floatGTsink.
```

to derive:

```
warpFaced.
```

You're rolling. The rule:

```
denim :- warpFaced, coloredWarp, whiteFill.
```

lets you conclude:

```
denim.
```

You are astonished to find out you put on your jeans this morning. In the next section we will see how a computer could relieve you of this agonizing mental effort.

1.2. Evaluating Proplog Programs

We have seen two examples of Proplog databases and suggested ways they might be used to make some simple deductions. (We use the term *database* when we want to emphasize that a program contains both rules and facts.) Now consider how to arrange things so the computer does the deduction. For example, given the courses a student has taken and the rules from the graduation requirements example, the computer should be able to determine which requirements and subrequirements have been met. Similarly, suppose we have a set of facts concerning the properties of a fabric and the rules from the fabric example. Then given a fabric as a hypothesis, the computer should be able to tell us whether the facts and rules support that hypothesis. A computer program that will make deductions from a Proplog database, or verify hypotheses against it, is called a Proplog *interpreter*. In this section we describe two simple attempts at a Proplog interpreter. One is based on "bottom-up" reasoning and the other on "top-down" reasoning. The goal of both interpreters is to treat a Proplog database as a program and run it.

Both interpreters are trying to direct the deduction process toward some end. We look at both to contrast their computational properties. No one algorithm works best for all kinds of deduction problems. In terms of constraints the bottom-up interpreter is better suited to the sort of problem in which you are given a set of knowns and you must figure out what unknowns they determine. The top-down interpreter starts with a particular unknown and tries to solve for it by looking for a set of knowns that will establish the unknown.

Later in this section we introduce *demonstration trees*. A demonstration tree summarizes how constraints (rules) propagate information about the knowns to determine unknowns. We use these trees to point out the connection between the two interpreters. Both can be seen as building demonstration trees. However, the bottom-up interpreter builds trees from leaves to the root, while the top-down interpreter works from the root to the leaves.

When studying the behavior of the top-down interpreter, we make use of another kind of tree, a *search tree*. Such a tree documents the choices the interpreter tries when extending a partial demonstration tree toward its leaves. A top-down interpreter must make sure that all choices at each point are tried eventually. That is, the search tree must be explored fully. Our top-down interpreter explores the search tree depth first; we consider breadth-first exploration in an exercise.

1.2.1. *Bottom-up Evaluation*

Consider the graduation requirements example. We can start with the facts and use the rules in a right-to-left direction to see what requirements have been met. For this approach we maintain a list of satisfied subrequirements; then, using this list and the rules, we add higher-level requirements that have been satisfied. We continue adding requirements until no new ones can be added. We can then check to see if a certain requirement or subrequirement has been deduced.

For the facts concerning Maria Marcatello's transcript, we want to know if the top-level requirement, **csReq**, is in our list of satisfied requirements. We start with her transcript as the initial list of satisfied subrequirements:

```
introI, introII, compOrg, advProg, theory, compilers, opSys, arch,
progLang, research, calcA, calcB, calcC, linAlg, absAlg,
finStructI, stat, digSys, physicsI, physicsII.
```

With this list of satisfied subrequirements, we see that each subrequirement on the right-hand side of the rule:

```
introReq :- introI, introII.
```

has been satisfied, so we can add **introReq** to the list of satisfied requirements. Similarly we see that we can add **basicCalc**, **advCalc**, **algReq**, **finiteReq**,

group1All, **group2One**, **group1Two**, **group2Two**, **engReq**, and **natSciReq**. Adding these eleven additional satisfied requirements to the list gives us the following:

```
introReq, basicCalc, advCalc, algReq, finiteReq, group1All,
group2One, group1Two, group2Two, engReq, natSciReq,

introI, introII, compOrg, advProg, theory, compilers, opSys,
arch, progLang, research, calcA, calcB, calcC, linAlg, absAlg,
finStructI, stat, digSys, physicsI, physicsII.
```

Using this augmented list of satisfied requirements, we again look at all the rules to see if we can add any new facts to the list. We do not add any fact more than once, nor do we add any fact already present in the list. (We are treating the list as a set.) For example, we can use:

```
advancedCS :- group1All, group2One.
```

to add **advancedCS** to the list of facts. We can also deduce **advancedCS** from the rule:

```
advancedCS :- group1Two, group2Two.
```

but we do not add that fact again. Making all the deductions we can from the current list, we get a new list of satisfied requirements:

```
basicCS, calcReq, advancedCS,

introReq, basicCalc, advCalc, algReq, finiteReq, group1All,
group2One, group1Two, group2Two, engReq, natSciReq,

introI, introII, compOrg, advProg, theory, compilers, opSys,
arch, progLang, research, calcA, calcB, calcC, linAlg, absAlg,
finStructI, stat, digSys, physicsI, physicsII.
```

One more iteration results in:

```
mathReq,

basicCS, calcReq, advancedCS,

introReq, basicCalc, advCalc, algReq, finiteReq, group1All,
group2One, group1Two, group2Two, engReq, natSciReq,

introI, introII, compOrg, advProg, theory, compilers, opSys,
arch, progLang, research, calcA, calcB, calcC, linAlg, absAlg,
finStructI, stat, digSys, physicsI, physicsII.
```

and another iteration gives:

```
csReq,

mathReq,

basicCS, calcReq, advancedCS,

introReq, basicCalc, advCalc, algReq, finiteReq, group1All,
group2One, group1Two, group2Two, engReq, natSciReq,

introI, introII, compOrg, advProg, theory, compilers, opSys, arch,
progLang, research, calcA, calcB, calcC, linAlg, absAlg, finStructI,
stat, digSys, physicsI, physicsII.
```

If we iterate again, we see nothing more can be added to the list, so we are done. Since **csReq** is in this final list of satisfied requirements, we conclude Maria Marcatello has completed her computer science major requirements.

This method of interpreting Proplog programs is called *bottom-up* or *forward-chaining*. It works from the facts and runs the rules right to left to deduce the higher-level propositions. This demonstration that Maria has met her requirements implicitly constitutes a tree, as shown in Figure 1.10. This tree, which we will call a *demonstration tree*, has facts on its leaves and rules on its internal nodes. An internal node is labeled by the head of a rule, and its children correspond to the propositions in the body of the rule. The bottom-up method of evaluation corresponds to building demonstration trees, starting from the leaves and growing toward the roots. (This method is "bottom-up" only because computer scientists habitually draw their trees upside-down.) Note that the height of a node above the leaves indicates at what stage in the procedure its head was added to the list of facts.

Actually, bottom-up evaluation need not give rise to a strict tree, as the nodes for **group1Two** and **group2Two** show. The result can be a *demonstration DAG* (directed acyclic graph), with multiple roots, branches that merge, and multiple components. For example, suppose the applied math department requires a concentration in mathematics, computer science, or economics:

```
concReq :- mathConc.
concReq :- csConc.
concReq :- econConc.
```

The computer science concentration requires three courses:

```
csConc :- introCS, compOrg, advProg.
```

Let's combine the rules for computer science with these applied math rules. (Say we are evaluating students aspiring to a double major.) Suppose Hector Ng has

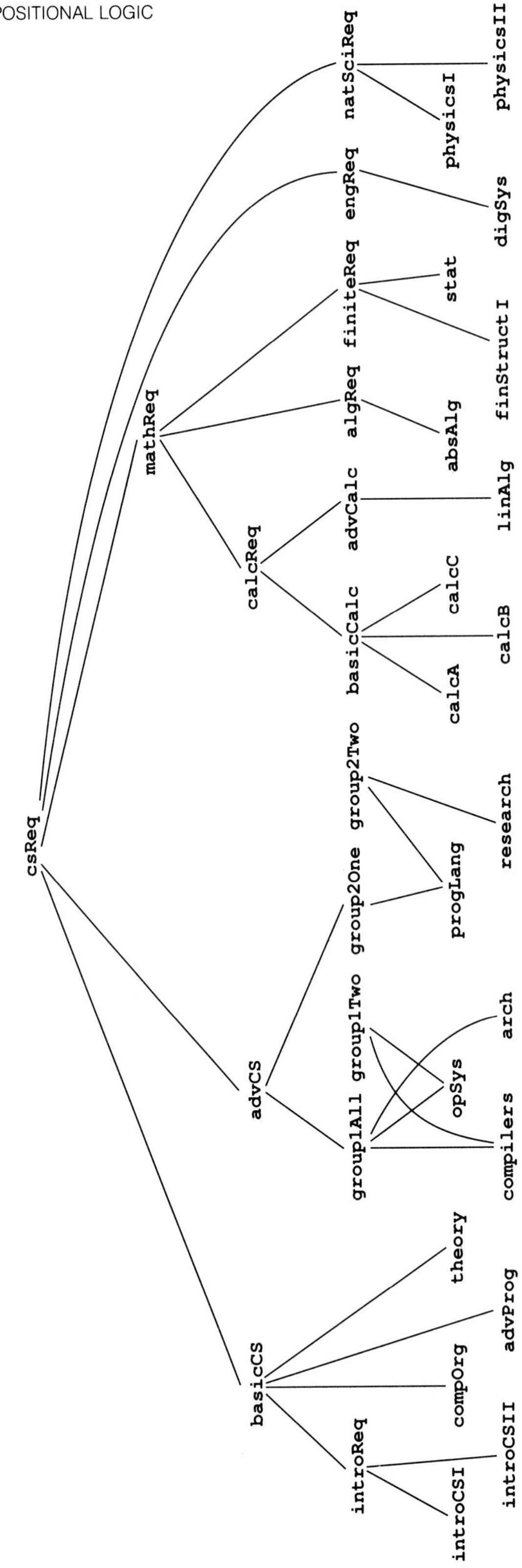

csReq
basicCS
advCS
mathReq
engReq
natSciReq
introReq
compOrg
advProg
theory
introCSI
introCSII
group1All
group1Two
group2One
group2Two
compilers
opSys
arch
progLang
research
calcReq
algReq
finiteReq
basicCalc
advCalc
calcA
calcB
calcC
linAlg
absAlg
stat
finStruct I
digSys
physicsI
physicsII

Figure 1.10

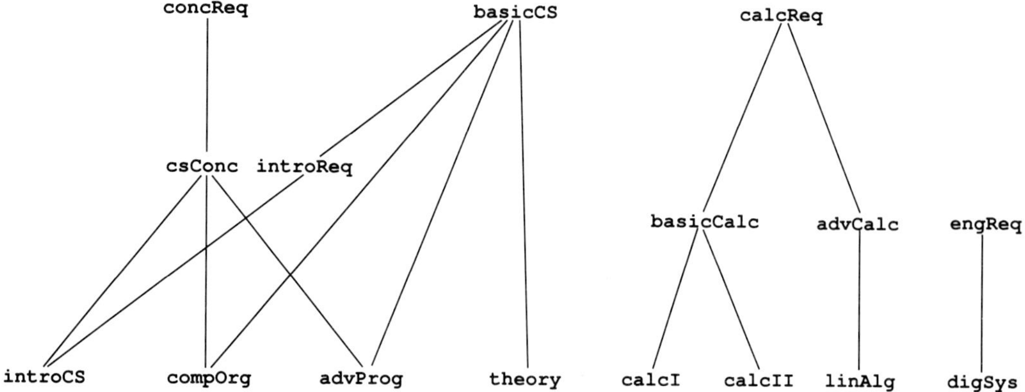

Figure 1.11

introCS, **compOrg**, **advProg**, **theory**, **calcI**, **calcII**, **linAlg**, and **digSys** on his transcript so far. The demonstration DAG from running the bottom-up procedure with the combined rules on those facts is shown in Figure 1.11. Note the graph has four roots, three disjoint components, and several multiply used facts.

1.2.2. *A Simple Bottom-up Interpreter*

We now consider how to implement an interpreter that uses the bottom-up evaluation method. The language for expressing algorithms is Pascal—more or less. We occasionally add a language feature that is not in Pascal (but we wish were), and sometimes we lapse into Pascal-like pseudocode. We represent propositions with instances of the type *symbol*, which is simply an array of characters. Assume that the clauses of the Proplog program, both rules and facts, are stored in an array and indexed from 1 to MAXCLAUSES. A clause is represented as a record with two fields. The first field, called HEAD, contains the head of a rule, or the only proposition in the clause if the clause is a fact. The second field, called BODY, contains the list of propositions that appear in the body of a clause. The body of a fact, which is empty, is represented by **nil**, the empty list, in the BODY field. The following type declarations summarize these representations:

```
type

    symbol = array [1..20] of char;

    symbollist = ↑symlistrec;

    symlistrec = record
                     SYM: symbol;
                     REST: symbollist
                 end;
```

```
clauserec = record
                HEAD: symbol;
                BODY: symbollist
            end;

clausearray = array [1..MAXCLAUSES] of clauserec;
```

EXAMPLE 1.1: The clause:

```
basicCalc :- calcA, calcB, calcC.
```

is represented with these data types, as shown in Figure 1.12, where the electrical ground symbol stands for **nil.** □

We write our bottom-up interpreter as a function that takes a list of propositions and determines whether they are all supported by the facts and rules. The interpreter returns **true** if they are all supported and **false** if not. The global variable CLAUSE, of type *clausearray*, holds the database of clauses making up the Proplog program. CURRENTLIST holds the list of propositions deduced so far by the algorithm. During each iteration of the **repeat**-loop, NEWLIST collects all the new facts that can be deduced from CURRENTLIST and the CLAUSE database. These new facts are then added to CURRENTLIST. The **for**-loop works by examining each rule and fact in CLAUSE in turn. If all the propositions in the body of the examined clause are in CURRENTLIST, then its head is added to NEWLIST, if it is not already in CURRENTLIST or NEWLIST. Note that each fact in the CLAUSE database trivially has all the propositions in its body contained in CURRENTLIST, so all facts will be added to NEWLIST on the first iteration of the **repeat**-loop.

```
var CLAUSES: clausearray;

function establishbu(GOALLIST: symbollist): boolean;
    var CURRENTLIST, NEWLIST: symbollist;
      I: integer;
    begin
      CURRENTLIST := nil; {the first iteration will add the facts}
      repeat
        NEWLIST := nil;
        for I := 1 to MAXCLAUSES do
          if satisfied(CLAUSE[I].BODY, CURRENTLIST) then
            if not member(CLAUSE[I].HEAD, CURRENTLIST) then
              if not member(CLAUSE[I].HEAD, NEWLIST) then
              addtolist(CLAUSE[I].HEAD, NEWLIST);
        concat(NEWLIST, CURRENTLIST)
      until NEWLIST = nil;
      {check if all goals have been established}
      establishbu := satisfied(GOALLIST, CURRENTLIST)
    end;
```

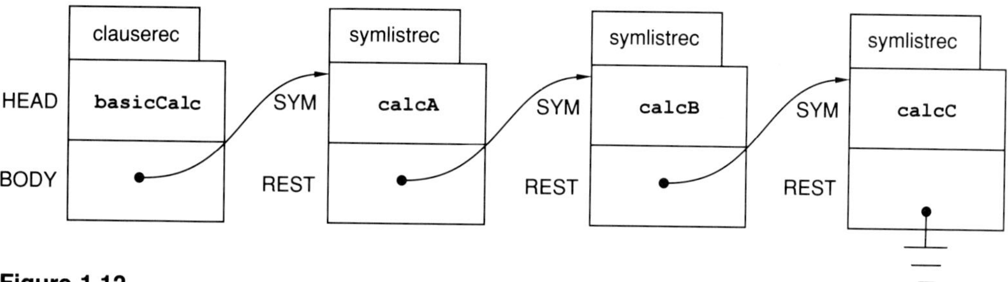

Figure 1.12

The function *establishbu* uses four subroutines. Two of the subroutines do list manipulation; the other two are predicates on lists. The procedure *addtolist* is used to add a new proposition to the beginning of a list. It updates the list that is the second argument to reference the augmented list.

```
procedure addtolist(PROP: symbol; var LIST: symbollist);
   var NEWREC: symbollist;
   begin
     new(NEWREC);
     NEWREC↑.SYM := PROP;
     NEWREC↑.REST := LIST;
     LIST := NEWREC
   end;
```

The procedure *concat* concatenates two lists by traversing the first to its end and changing its last record to reference the second list (after checking that the first list is nonempty). The procedure returns the concatenated lists by updating its second argument. Figure 1.13 shows the before-and-after configuration of two lists passed in to *concat*.

```
procedure concat(FIRST: symbollist; var SECOND: symbollist);
   var TEMP: symbollist;
   begin
     if FIRST <> nil then
       begin
         TEMP := FIRST;
         while TEMP↑.REST <> nil do
           TEMP := TEMP↑.REST;
         TEMP↑.REST := SECOND;
         SECOND := FIRST
       end
   end;
```

Function *member* has the declaration:

```
function member(PROP: symbol; LIST: symbollist): boolean;
```

and simply tests if a proposition is in a list. Its implementation is left as an exercise (Exercise 1.11). The function *satisfied* checks if each proposition in its first argument

Before:

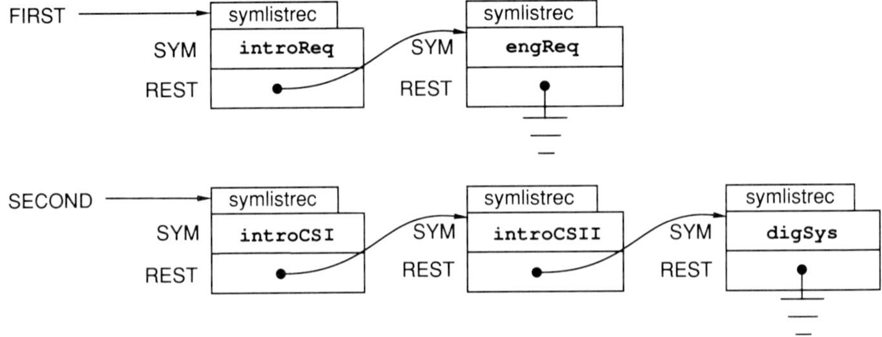

After:

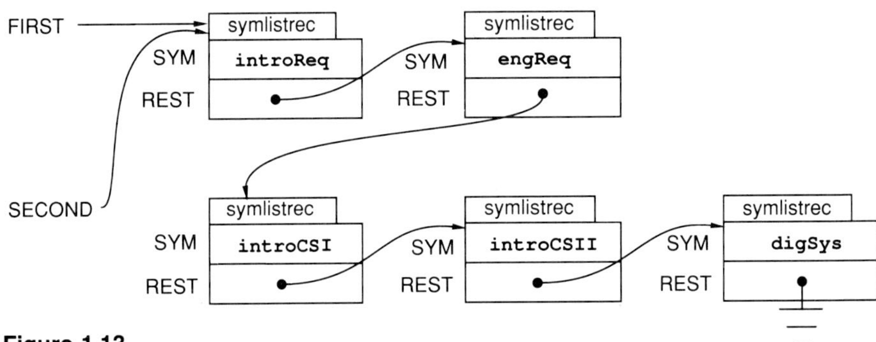

Figure 1.13

is contained in the second argument. It is used to check if the body of a clause is contained in CURRENTLIST, and also at the end of *establishbu* to see if the input goals have been satisfied.

```
function satisfied(GOALS: symbollist; KNOWN: symbollist): boolean;
    var SAT: boolean;
    begin
      SAT := true;
      while SAT and (GOALS <> nil) do
        begin
          SAT := member(GOALS↑.SYM, KNOWN);
          GOALS := GOALS↑.REST
        end;
      satisfied := SAT
    end;
```

1.2.3. *Top-down Evaluation*

Another approach to evaluating Proplog programs is to start from a given goal and work backward to the facts. The propositions needed to establish the original goal become subgoals, and we address each subgoal in turn. Each subgoal can generate its own subgoals, and so forth. If at some level all the subgoals are identical to facts in the program, we have succeeded in establishing the original goal. This approach is called a "top-down" evaluation method, because it tries to grow a demonstration tree from the root toward the leaves. The approach is also known as *backward chaining*. This top-down method will be the basis for our ultimate Prolog interpreter.

What propositions do we generate as subgoals for a given goal? Obviously, we want a set of subgoals such that if we establish each subgoal, we know that we can satisfy the goal itself. Thus, for subgoals, we choose the set of propositions that appears as the body of a rule with the given goal as the head. We are using rules here in a left-to-right fashion. If there is more than one rule with the goal as the head, we try each rule in turn. If there is a fact in the program that is the same as the given goal, we can use it, instead of a rule, to establish the goal directly.

Consider a Proplog program consisting of the rules from the fabric example along with these facts about a particular sample of fabric:

```
cotton.
napped.
floatLTSink.
hasFloats.
warpOffsetEQ1.
```

If our hypothesis is that the sample of fabric is flannel, then our initial goal is:

```
flannel.
```

The first rule with **flannel** as its head is:

```
flannel :- plainWeave, cotton, napped.
```

We take:

```
plainWeave, cotton, napped.
```

as our subgoals and try to establish each of them. Figure 1.14 shows a partial demonstration tree corresponding to this choice of subgoals. The question marks at the leaves indicate that the propositions at those nodes have not been established yet. The current goal list corresponds to the question marks on the frontier, from left to right.

A question arises as to which subgoal to work on first. In this instance we could immediately satisfy **cotton** and **napped** using facts from the program, if we wanted. However, for simplicity in the method, our interpreter will consider

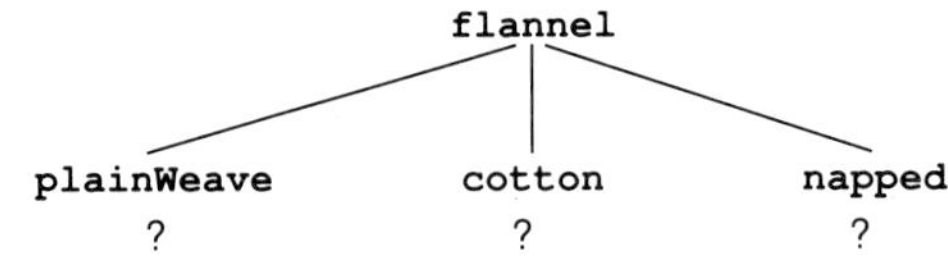

Figure 1.14

subgoals left to right. (We also had a choice as to which rule to use first in generating subgoals. We chose the first one as it appeared in the list of rules.)

We now try to establish **plainWeave**. The only rule with **plainWeave** as its head is:

```
plainWeave :- alternatingWarp.
```

We can establish **plainWeave** if we can establish **alternatingWarp**. Therefore, we remove **plainWeave** from the list of unsatisfied subgoals and add **alternatingWarp** in its place. Here again is a choice: Where to add the new subgoal in the list? We choose to put it in place of **plainWeave**:

```
alternatingWarp, cotton, napped.
```

The partial tree so far is given in Figure 1.15. At this point we have no rule or fact to use with **alternatingWarp**. We must undo our last choice of rule to get back to the list of subgoals:

```
plainWeave, cotton, napped.
```

There is no other rule that matches **plainWeave**. Thus we undo another choice and return to:

```
flannel.
```

There are other rules with **flannel** as the head. We try the next one:

```
flannel :- twillWeave, cotton, napped.
```

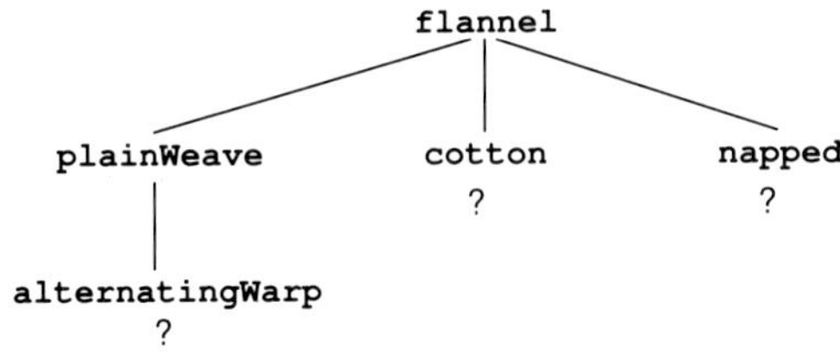

Figure 1.15

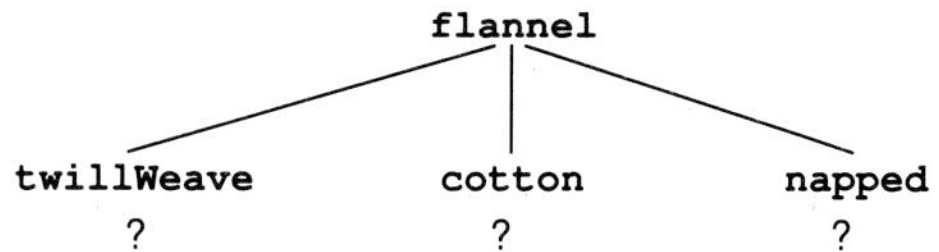

Figure 1.16

to get the list of subgoals:

```
twillWeave, cotton, napped.
```

The partial demonstration tree for this set of goals is shown in Figure 1.16. We now must establish **twillWeave**. The first rule with **twillWeave** as its head is:

```
twillWeave :- diagonalTexture.
```

The new set of subgoals is:

```
diagonalTexture, cotton, napped.
```

and the partial tree is shown in Figure 1.17. There is no match for **diagonalTexture** in the program, so we retract the last choice of rule and try the next rule with *twillWeave* as head:

```
twillWeave :- hasFloats, warpOffsetEQ1.
```

We now have the following list of subgoals:

```
hasFloats, warpOffsetEQ1, cotton, napped.
```

The corresponding tree is given in Figure 1.18.

Now the subgoal **hasFloats** is a fact in the program, so it is established directly, giving a subgoal list:

```
warpOffsetEQ1, cotton, napped.
```

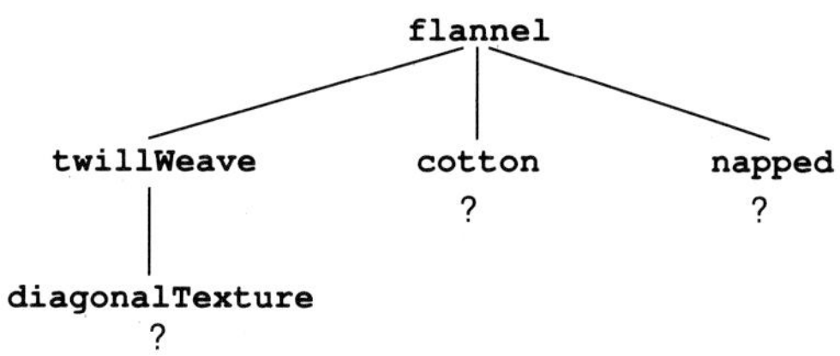

Figure 1.17

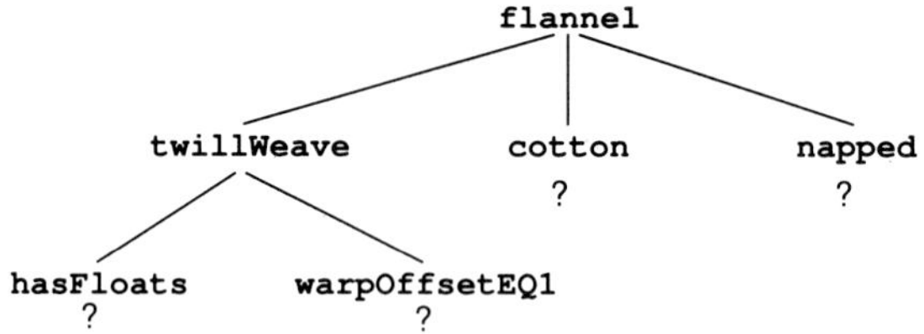

Figure 1.18

Figure 1.19 shows the new state of the demonstration tree, which had the question mark removed from the **hasFloats** node. Likewise, **warpOffsetEQ1**, **cotton**, and **napped** can all be established from goals in the program.

We are left with the empty list of subgoals, which signifies success in the top-down approach. At this point the demonstration tree is complete; it looks like the one in Figure 1.19 but without any question marks. All the subgoals generated have been established, hence the initial goal, **flannel**, is established. If the original goal could not be derived from the program, we would discover that situation when we eventually ran out of rules to try as choices at the topmost level.

Notice that this method does not generate all the conclusions derivable from the Proplog program. We can derive **fillingFaced** (How?) from the facts and rules, but it was not necessary to do so to establish **flannel**. Top-down evaluation is more "directed" than bottom-up evaluation, because it tries to establish only subgoals that might help in establishing the original goal. Bottom-up evaluation is driven by the facts—it is useful when there is no specific hypothesis but we want to see what propositions are entailed by the facts.

The directed nature of top-down evaluation does not make it obviously preferable to the bottom-up method. First, the top-down method may try to use a rule in generating subgoals that will ultimately fail, as did:

```
plainWeave :- alternatingWarp.
```

in the example. The bottom-up method never applies a rule unless its application will deduce a new fact. Second, the top-down method, as we have described it, may end up establishing the same subgoal more than once.

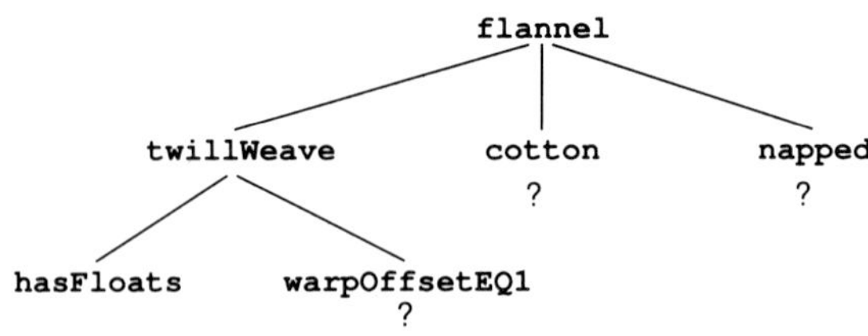

Figure 1.19

EXAMPLE 1.2: With the Proplog program:

```
a :- b, c.
b :- c, d.
c :- e.
d.
e.
```

and the goal **a**, we generate the demonstration tree shown in Figure 1.20, in which **c** and **e** are established twice. □

We always get trees, rather than DAGs, with the top-down method. The top-down procedure "throws away" previously established propositions, so a particular occurrence of a subgoal cannot be used to support more than one deduction in a derivation. For the same reason, however, it tends to require less space than bottom-up evaluation. The top-down approach (as we have described it) keeps around only a list of unestablished goals, plus a stack of recursive calls. Bottom-up maintains a list of all propositions proved so far. For Proplog, the length of that list is bounded by the size of the database of rules and facts, but in Datalog and Prolog that list can be much larger than the database. Finally, the top-down procedure can get into an infinite loop, where the bottom-up procedure always terminates.

EXAMPLE 1.3: If we change the second rule in Example 1.2 to:

```
b :- a, d.
```

we end up trying to build an infinite demonstration tree, as shown in Figure 1.21. □

1.2.4. *A Simple Top-down Interpreter*

In this section we'll present a program that implements the top-down evaluation method and uses the same representations and declarations as the bottom-up program shown earlier. The function *establishtd* is passed a list, GOALLIST, of goals to establish from a Proplog program held in a global array CLAUSE. The function makes recursive calls to itself. Each invocation attempts to solve the first subgoal

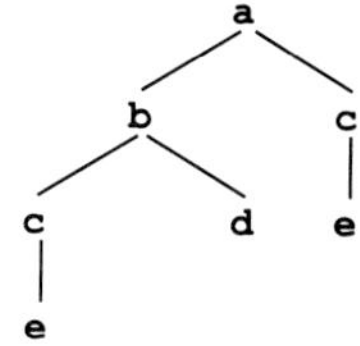

Figure 1.20

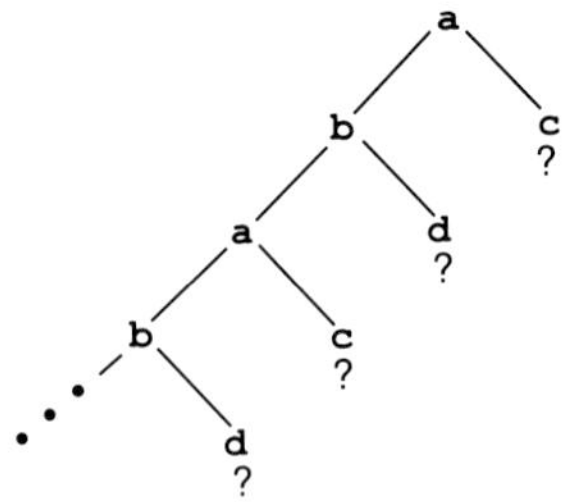

Figure 1.21

in GOALLIST by matching it against the head of a clause in the database. A **for**-loop steps through the clauses. If there is a match, *establishtd* is called recursively on a list of subgoals made up of the body of the clause followed by the remaining goals in GOALLIST. If the recursive call succeeds, the calling program does as well; *establishtd* also succeeds when called with the empty list of goals. If the recursive call fails, another rule is tried as a match for the first goal. If all the rules matching the first goal are exhausted without success, *establishtd* fails.

Note that, by the structure of the program, if one invocation of *establishtd* returns **true,** then so does the invocation that called it, the invocation that called that one, and so on up to the original invocation.

To simplify the program, we posit a **return** statement that allows us to return explicitly a value for a function and exit the function body, rather than doing an implicit return of the value at the end of the function body. The **return** statement allows us to exit the **for**-loop as soon as a solution has been found.

```
function establishtd(GOALLIST: symbollist): boolean;
    var I: integer;
    begin
      if GOALLIST = nil then return(true)
      else
        for I := 1 to MAXCLAUSES do
          if CLAUSE[I].HEAD = GOALLIST↑.SYM then
            if establishtd(copycat(CLAUSE[I].BODY, GOALLIST↑.REST)) then
              return(true);
      return(false)
    end;
```

The *establishtd* routine uses a concatenation subroutine that is slightly different from the one used in *establishbu*. In addition to being a function, it must not be destructive. That is, it makes a copy of the first list, since the first list is the body of a rule, and we had better not change the rules. Figure 1.22 shows the structure of a list returned by *copycat.*

```
function copycat(FIRST, SECOND: symbollist): symbollist;
    var COPYLAST: symbollist; {points to last node on copy of FIRST list}
    begin
```

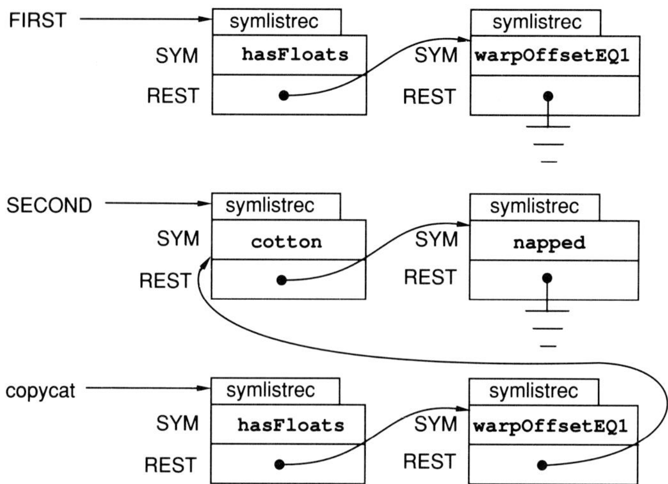

Figure 1.22

```
if FIRST = nil then copycat := SECOND
else
  begin
    new(COPYLAST);
    copycat := COPYLAST;
    COPYLAST↑.SYM := FIRST↑.SYM;
    while FIRST↑.REST <> nil do
      begin
        new(COPYLAST↑.REST);
        COPYLAST := COPYLAST↑.REST;
        FIRST := FIRST↑.REST;
        COPYLAST↑.SYM := FIRST↑.SYM
      end;
    COPYLAST↑.REST := SECOND;
  end
end;
```

Neither the bottom-up nor the top-down interpreters presented in this chapter are particularly efficient. We will look at improving the efficiency in Chapter 3.

To explore how *establishtd* works, we need to keep track of the various recursive invocations. We do so by labeling each invocation with a string of integers. The initial invocation is labeled ϵ (the empty string). If we have an invocation labeled w, then the ith recursive invocation of *establishtd* made in the **for**-loop will have label wi. Thus invocation 132 is the second recursive call to *establishtd* by the invocation that was the third recursive call by the invocation that was the first recursive call by the original invocation.

We use the example from the last section for establishing the goal **flannel** to show how *establishtd* works. We organize the invocations into the form of an

```
ε: flannel.
    1: plainWeave, cotton, napped. |
        11: alternatingWarp, | cotton, napped. ×
    2: twillWeave, cotton, napped. |
        21: diagonalTexture, | cotton, napped. ×
        22: hasFloats, warpOffsetEQ1, | cotton, napped.
            221: | warpOffsetEQ1, cotton, napped.
                2211: |cotton, napped.
                    22111: |napped.
                        221111: nil
```

Figure 1.23

outline, as shown in Figure 1.23. Each line represents one call to *establishtd*. Each invocation is preceded by its label, and *called* invocations are indented under the *calling* invocation. The list of subgoals given on each line is the argument to that invocation of *establishtd*. The vertical bar (|) shows where the concatenation took place. Thus the rule involved with each invocation can be reconstructed by taking the first goal of the next outer entry as the head, and the goals to the left of the bar as the body. When the bar is at the left of the subgoal list, a fact was used. An '×' marks the failure points, meaning the first subgoal on the line could not be matched.

The execution of *establishtd* gives rise to a type of tree different from the demonstration tree. This tree, called the *search tree*, gives the pattern of recursive calls of *establishtd* on a given goal. We show the search tree for establishing **flannel** in Figure 1.24. We have used the labels from Figure 1.23 on the nodes. Normally we would show the subgoals to be established at each node in the search tree.

From the search tree we see that *establishtd* is searching the space of partial demonstration trees depth first. Depth-first searching proceeds as follows. To extend the search from a partial demonstration tree T_1, *establishtd* looks at one way to

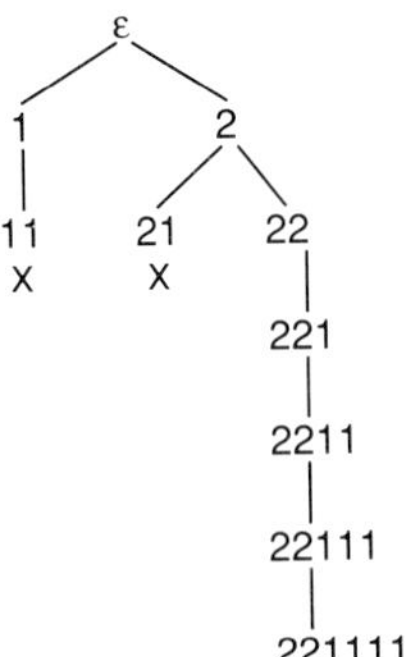

Figure 1.24

extend that tree—call it T_2. It then looks for a single way to extend T_2, and so forth, backing up to try other choices if it arrives at some tree T_i that cannot be extended. Furthermore, when extending a partial demonstration tree, *establishtd* always tries to do so at the leftmost unsolved leaf.

Other search strategies are compatible with top-down evaluation. For example, we might search depth first but always try to expand the rightmost unsolved leaf, or try to expand the leaf least recently introduced. We could do the search breadth first; for a partial demonstration tree T, we would generate all extensions of T for further consideration. (See Exercise 1.16.) Breadth-first search has the advantage of always finding a demonstration tree when one exists. For the remainder of the book, though, we concentrate on depth-first, left-to-right searching of partial demonstration trees. We choose a depth-first search because it means we have to maintain only one partial demonstration tree at a time, as opposed to multiple trees with breadth-first searching. We use left-to-right expansion of unsolved goals because it lends itself well to stack-based technology. We need maintain only a list of unsolved subgoals and a stack of past points at which there is a choice for how to expand the first subgoal on the list.

1.3. Proplog as a Declarative Component in a Procedural System

The power of Proplog is obviously limited. This section shows how to leverage it as the declarative "brains" of a system with simple procedural "brawn." A Proplog program P will control a procedural loop. During each iteration through the loop, we use P to determine, on the basis of initial conditions in the loop, what actions to carry out in the current iteration. In our first example, traffic light control, the initial conditions are the current state of the lights, the time since the last change of lights, and the presence of cars at the intersection. The actions in the loop are changes of lights. We will see that in a fairly fixed procedural framework we can achieve a wide variety of behaviors by changing only the declarative Proplog component, possibly adding new input conditions and output actions. The second example is a fabric identification program based on the Proplog rules from the beginning of the chapter. We include a second set of rules that determine information about a fabric sample for which a user is prompted. The inputs for this example are the set of fabric properties that can be established based on information entered so far by the user. The output action is to query the user for some yet undetermined attributes of the fabric.

1.3.1. *Traffic Light Example*

The task is to control the traffic signal at an intersection of two roads. At the intersection a small east-west road crosses a major north-south road. (See Figure 1.25.) The signal has lights in all directions, and we have a timer and detectors for cars in the east-west lanes to use in the control system.

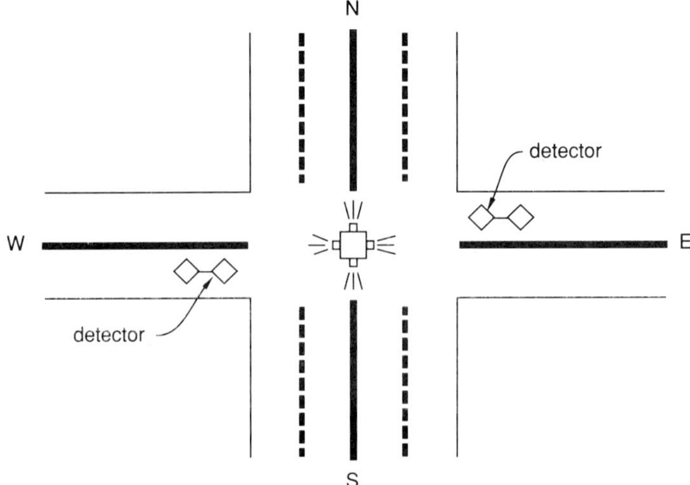

Figure 1.25

Consider the problem first without inputs from the detectors. Thus the only inputs are the current status of the various lights and the number of seconds since the timer was last reset. We decide that a yellow light should last for 5 seconds and a green for 30. We can, therefore, partition the timer inputs into three ranges of interest: fewer than 5 seconds, between 5 and 30 seconds, and more than 30 seconds. The following propositions represent the inputs. The first six refer to which lights are on; the last three concern the range of the timer.

```
greenNS
greenEW
yellowNS
yellowEW
redNS
redEW

timerLT5
timer5to30
timerGT30
```

The actions will be turning the lights on or off, and resetting the timer to zero. These actions will also be represented as propositions. For example, **greenNSon** means to turn on the green light in the north-south direction. Similarly, **redEWoff** means to turn off the red light for the east-west lanes. The proposition to reset the timer is **resetTimer**.

The procedural loop for the control system is driven off a set of Proplog rules *P* that tell which output actions are implied by various combinations of input conditions. It starts by obtaining values (**true** or **false**) for all the input conditions. It gets those values by reading sensors or remembering the states of the lights. Next the loop runs a Proplog interpreter to determine all action propositions implied by the rules plus input propositions. The final part of the loop is to perform the action corresponding to each action proposition that is established by the interpreter. The loop repeats this sequence forever.

What rules must be in *P*? Say the situation is a green light east-west and a red light north-south. Assume the timer was reset when the east-west signal turned green. We want to change the east-west signal to yellow after it has been green for more than 30 seconds. At the same time we reset the timer to time the yellow. The following rules cause this action:

```
greenEWoff :- greenEW, timerGT30.
yellowEWon :- greenEW, timerGT30.
resetTimer :- greenEW, timerGT30.
```

Note that all these actions are conditioned by the same set of input propositions. To structure our rule base better, we introduce a new proposition, **warnEW**, and change the rules to:

```
warnEW :- greenEW, timerGT30.

greenEWoff :- warnEW.
yellowEWon :- warnEW.
resetTimer :- warnEW.
```

Five seconds after the yellow east-west light, the east-west signal should go to red, and the north-south lanes should get a green light. Another proposition, **stopEW**, helps to structure the next group of rules.

```
stopEW :- yellowEW, timer5to30.

redNSoff :- stopEW.
greenNSon :- stopEW.
yellowEWoff :- stopEW.
redEWon :- stopEW.
resetTimer :- stopEW.
```

By symmetry, the rules for cycling the north-south signal from green to red are:

```
warnNS :- greenNS, timerGT30.

greenNSoff :- warnNS.
yellowNSon :- warnNS.
resetTimer :- warnNS.

stopNS :- yellowNS, timer5to30.
```

```
redEWoff :- stopNS.
greenEWon :- stopNS.
yellowNSoff :- stopNS.
redNSon :- stopNS.
resetTimer :- stopNS.
```

Notice that on many cycles of the procedural loop no action will be taken, since the timer has not advanced to a critical range. Also notice that not all the input conditions are used in the rules. The way we synchronize the north-south and east-west lights, some of those conditions are redundant. For instance, we could express the rule:

```
warnNS :- greenNS, timerGT30.
```

with:

```
warnNS :- redEW, timerGT30.
```

The new "warn" and "stop" propositions added here group together actions that occur in the same circumstances. This grouping facilitates certain changes, such as when we include propositions to deal with the detectors. We add two new input propositions, **detectEW** and **noDetectEW**, and then add one new action, **clearDetectEW**. The action **clearDetectEW** makes **detectEW** false and **noDetectEW** true. Subsequently, any car crossing a sensor embedded in the east-west lanes will flip the values of those two propositions. Since the east-west road is smaller and has less traffic, we want to change the rules in *P* to give a green east-west light only if the detector is on, and to clear the detector then. To change the trigger condition for an east-west green, we need change only the rule:

```
warnNS :- greenNS, timerGT30.
```

to:

```
warnNS :- greenNS, detectEW, timerGT30.
```

The rule:

```
clearDetectEW :- warnNS.
```

takes care of resetting the detector.

Consider another change. The east-west signal should turn back to red before 30 seconds have elapsed if no cars are present in that direction. There is a new situation in which we want to warn east-west, which the following single rule captures:

```
warnEW :- greenEW, noDectectEW.
```

In addition, we must keep clearing the detector while the east-west signal is green:

```
clearDetectEW :- greenEW.
```

(To be more realistic, we have to ensure that a car traveling east-west during green crosses the sensor between the time the detector is cleared and the next time the detector is checked. We could add another timer, and warn east-west early only if no car has crossed the sensor in, say, the 3 seconds since the detector was last cleared.)

1.3.2. *Fabric Identification Program*

Given the rules for fabric identification in Section 1.1.2, we want to produce a system in which a user can enter information about a fabric sample. The system adds that information to the clause database as facts and then tries to deduce the fabric type. If there is not enough information to make an identification, the system should prompt the user for more.

We start by distinguishing fabric attributes, such as **alternatingWarps**, **hasFLoats**, and **solidPlain**, from fabric types, such as **flannel**, **velvet**, and **terry**. User input will concern fabric attributes; the system will deduce fabric types. (We could further subdivide base attributes, such as **hasFloats**, from derived attributes, such as **solidPlain**, and let a user input only base attributes. For this example we will let the user posit derived attributes directly.)

We group attributes into properties, such that attributes in a property are mutually exclusive. Examples of properties are:

```
floatLength = (floatLTSink, floatEQSink, floatGTSink)
warpOffset = (warpOffsetEQ1, warpOffsetGT1)
weave = (plainWeave, twillWeave, satinWeave)
overallTexture = (alternatingWarp, diagonalTexture)
floats = (hasFloats)
```

Assume that the user is allowed to enter any fabric attributes before the system enters the main procedural loop. Each time through the loop the Proplog interpreter executes with the fabric rules and the attribute facts acquired so far to see if it can establish a fabric type proposition. If not, it prompts the user for more input. How should it do the prompting? A very crude way is to run down the list of attributes and ask the user for a yes-or-no answer on each. But a much better interface is possible, since if one attribute in a property is true, all other attributes in the property must be false. A slight refinement to asking yes-or-no questions is to present a menu of attributes in a property and have the user select one. We add some rules to indicate when a property is known. A group of rules for the **floatLength** property is:

```
knownFloatLength :- floatLTSink.
knownFloatLength :- floatEQSink.
knownFloatLength :- floatGTSink.
```

If the identification system can deduce **knownFloatLength**, it will not query the user about any attributes in the **floatLength** property. Assume the appropriate "known" rules are added for each property.

The main procedural loop in the identification system will really have two deduction phases—one to see if a fabric type is derivable and a second to determine what property to ask about next. The inputs to the second phase will be the truth value of propositions **knownA** and **unknownA** for each property **A**. The action propositions will have the form **askA** for each property **A**. The identification system proceeds as follows:

1. Accept any attributes from the user, and add them to the clause database as facts.
2. Interpret the identification rules along with the added facts to see what propositions are derived. If any fabric type proposition is derived, print it and quit.
3. Otherwise, figure the inputs for the second deduction phase. For each property **A**, if **knownA** was deduced in the last step, use it as a fact for this deduction phase. If **knownA** was not derived, take **unknownA** instead.
4. Use a set of "metarules" (described in the discussion following this list) to establish an action proposition **askB** for some property **B**. (Take the first such proposition to be established.)
5. Query the user to provide an attribute for property **B**, and add that attribute as a fact to the fabric-identification clauses.
6. Remove all "known" and "unknown" facts, and repeat from Step 2.

The rules for Step 4 will attempt to order the queries to the user by the information that is most useful at a given point. Obviously, it is important to know the **weave** property of the fabric sample early on, so the system should ask about the **overallTexture** and **floats** properties:

```
askOverallTexture :- unknownWeave, unknownOverallTexture.
askFloats :- unknownWeave, unknownFloats.
```

Other properties are not as useful, or possibly not relevant, unless some other attribute has been established already. For example, the system should not ask about **floatLength** until it knows the fabric has a twill weave:

```
askFloatLength :- unknownFloatLength, twillWeave.
```

We leave specifying more metarules for Exercise 1.23. In Chapter 2, we will see the **not** operator, which will let us deduce the "unknown" propositions from Proplog rules without procedural intervention.

1.4. EXERCISES

1.1. Using the rules in the fabric example, what fabrics do the following facts imply?

```
colorGroups.
warpStripe.
cut.
fillStripe.
alternatingWarp.
extraFill.
alignedPile.
```

1.2. In the fabric example, what rule or rules could be removed without impairing the ability to identify any fabrics?

1.3. What follows is the prerequisite requirements for computer science courses at Stony Brook.

Introduction to CS II requires Introduction to CS I.
Computer Organization and Advanced Programming both require Introduction to CS, or Introduction to CS I and II.
File Structures and Programming Languages both require Advanced Programming.
Theory requires Advanced Programming and Abstract Algebra (or Finite Structures II).
Compilers requires Computer Organization, Advanced Programming, and Theory.
Databases requires Advanced Programming and File Structures.
Operating Systems requires Computer Organization and Advanced Programming.
Architecture, Graphics, and Microprocessors all require Computer Organization and Digital System Design.
The prerequisite for Computer Communications is the departmental calculus requirement.
Artificial Intelligence requires Advanced Programming and Theory.

a. Write a Proplog program to express this information, using propositions such as **canTakeOpSys** and **hasTakenIntroI**.
b. Some of the prerequisites are redundant—which are they?
c. Would adding the rule:

```
canTakeOpSys :- canTakeFileStruct.
```

change the behavior of your program? How about:

```
canTakeFileStruct :- canTakeOpSys.
```

Why?

1.4. Consider the set of facts:

```
hasFloats.
warpOffsetEQ1.
warpOffsetGT1.
```

In the fabric example these facts imply both **twillWeave** and **satinWeave**. Can we add any rule to the fabric example to prevent such a contradiction?

1.5. For a Proplog program P, let a *base proposition* be a proposition in P that appears not as the head of any rule in P but only as a fact or in the body of a rule.
   a. What are the base propositions in the fabric example?
   b. Which minimal sets of base propositions imply **calcReq** in the requirements example?

1.6. Is there a way to express the statement "Every twill-weave fabric is either even, filling faced, or warp faced" in Proplog? (That is, the three properties exhaust the possibilities for twill-weave fabrics.)

1.7. Give all the demonstration trees for the goal **p** using the Proplog program:

```
p :- q, r.
p :- q, s.
q :- t.
q :- t, u.
r :- r, v.
s :- t.
t.
t :- v.
u.
v.
```

1.8. Give a Proplog program P and a goal **g** such that **g** has an infinite number of demonstration trees with respect to P.

1.9. Show how to transform a set P of Proplog clauses into an equivalent set P', such that any proposition implied by P (and hence by P') has a demonstration tree with respect to P' of height at most 1. (The height of a tree is the number of edges in the longest root-leaf path in the tree.) You may change only rules in going from P to P'.

1.10. Note that in bottom-up interpretation of Proplog, once a rule or fact from the database is used, it can provide no more information. Use that observation to produce a more efficient version of *establishbu*. (Provided that proposition symbols are represented as consecutive integers, there is an algorithm that is linear in the size of the program database. The size of the database is measured by occurrences of proposition symbols.)

1.11. Give the algorithm for the function *member* in Section 1.2.2.

1.12. Recode *establishtd* to remove the **return** statements. Assume only an implicit return at the end of the routine.

1.13. Give the search tree for *establishtd* with goal **flannel**, using the rules in the fabric example, plus the facts:

```
wool.
napped.
```

```
hasFloats.
diagonalTexture.
```

in that order.

1.14. In *establishtd*, a rule may be needed several times, because the same proposition can enter the goal list more than once. Consider the strategy of adding each established subgoal as a fact in CLAUSE. What are the advantages and disadvantages of this strategy?

1.15. Write a version of *establishtd* that checks whether a proposition is being used in an attempt to satisfy itself. That is, if in trying to establish proposition **p**, we make a recursive call to *establishtd* with **p** as the first goal in the goal list, we fail. Does your interpreter halt on all inputs?

1.16. The interpreter *establishtd* works by searching the space of (partial) demonstration trees depth first (which is not the same as saying it tries to construct a demonstration tree top down).

a. Give the algorithm for a variant of *establishtd* that searches the space of demonstration trees breadth first. This new algorithm will need to keep a *set* of goal lists, and at each invocation, will generate possibly many new lists from each list in the set, representing all the alternatives for solving the first goal on the list. For example, with the database:

```
p :- q, r.
p :- q, s.
p :- t.
q :- u, v.
q :- w.
```

the breadth-first algorithm will generate sets of goal lists as follows:

```
{p}
{q, r; q, s; t}
{u, v, r; w, r; u, v, s; w, s}
.
.
.
```

b. Show that your algorithm is more complete than *establishtd*, since it will always halt if the initial goal is implied by the database of clauses.

1.17. Consider the following function called *demo*, which uses the same type definitions as *establishbu*, but must be called initially with one goal.

```
function demo(GOAL: symbollist): boolean;
   var SUCCEEDING: boolean;
      NEWGOALS: symbollist;
```

```
begin
  for each clause C such that C.HEAD = GOAL↑.SYM do
    begin
      SUCCEEDING := true;
      NEWGOALS := C.BODY
      while SUCCEEDING and (NEWGOALS <> nil) do
        if demo(NEWGOALS) then NEWGOALS := NEWGOALS↑.REST
        else SUCCEEDING := false;
      if SUCCEEDING and (NEWGOALS = nil) then return(true)
    end;
  return(false);
end;
```

a. Consider the Proplog program:

```
p :- q, r.
p :- s.
q :- t.
q :- s.
t.
s.
```

Draw the recursive call tree for *demo* invoked with goal **p**.

b. This function is also a top-down evaluator of Proplog programs. Describe its advantages over *establishtd*.

1.18. Some expert systems represent their knowledge base with structures that resemble Proplog rules, except there are weights attached to the rules. A weight gives a probability or confidence that the head of a rule is true if the propositions in the body are true. For example:

```
souffleRises :- beatenWell, quietWhileCooking.   .9
souffleRises :- haveLuck.   .6
beatenWell :- useWhisk.   .4
beatenWell :- useMixer.   .8
quietWhileCooking :- kidsOutside.   .8
haveLuck :- knockOnWood.   .3
```

The first rule states that there is a 0.9 probability the souffle will rise if the eggs are beaten well and the house is quiet while the souffle is cooking. Propositions in the body of a rule may have some probability of being true, rather than being unconditionally true. In that case the probability of the head of the rule is the product of the probability associated with the rule with the probabilities of the propositions in the body. For example, if we start with the facts:

```
useWhisk.
kidsOutside.
```

each with 1.0 probability, we then get **beatenWell** with 0.4 probability and **quietWhileCooking** with 0.8 probability, using the third and fifth rules. Using the first rule, we get **souffleRises** with a (0.4)(0.8)(0.9) = 0.288 probability. Where there are multiple derivations of a proposition, we assign that proposition the maximum probability over all derivations. Thus, if we have the facts:

```
useMixer.
kidsOutside.
knockOnWood.
```

the derivation of **souffleRises** using the first rule gives (0.8)(0.8)(0.9) = 0.576 probability, while the second rule gives a probability of (0.3)(0.6) = 0.18. We thus take 0.576 as the probability of **souffleRises**.

Give an algorithm for determining the probability of a proposition given a database of facts (each with probability 1.0) and weighted rules.

1.19. For the traffic light example in Section 1.3.1, would a bottom-up or a top-down Proplog interpreter be a better choice?

1.20. For the traffic light example, assume detectors are added in the north-south lanes. Modify the rules so that when there is no traffic at the intersection, the red light comes on in both directions, then goes directly to green for the lanes in which a car is first detected.

1.21. Extend the traffic light example to include pedestrian signals. A walk signal must change to a wait signal 15 seconds before the corresponding light turns red.

1.22. In the fabric identification system of Section 1.3.2, some of the properties are not completely covered by the attributes given. For example, the **floats** property has only the attribute **hasFloats**, which does not cover all the possibilities. How can we modify the system to keep track of the information that the user has said no to all attributes in a property, so that we do not reask him or her about the property?

1.23. Add metarules to the fabric identification system to control user prompting for the following fabric types:

percale	**organdy**
organza	**plaid**
gingham	**oxford**
monksCloth	**hopsacking**
velvet	**terry**
corduroy	**velveteen**

1.24. How can the fabric identification system be programmed to give up when confronted with a fabric it cannot identify?

1.5. COMMENTS AND BIBLIOGRAPHY

The general idea of using Horn clauses as programs was proposed by Kowalski (and developed in his excellent book [1.1]), but in the more general context of functional logic, which we will see in later chapters. Artificial Intelligence applications have used propositional logic with weights as the basis for expert systems. For example, the expert system, MYCIN [1.2], can be understood as various procedural extensions to a top-down evaluator for an underlying propositional Horn clause logic with weights.

The requirements example was taken from the 1983–85 SUNY Stony Brook Undergraduate Catalog [1.3]. The material for the fabrics example was woven from several sources [1.4–1.6].

1.1. R. Kowalski, *Logic for Problem Solving,* North Holland, Amsterdam, 1979.

1.2. E. H. Shortliffe, *MYCIN: A Rule-Based Computer Program for Advising Physicians Regarding Antimicrobial Therapy Selection,* Ph.D. thesis, Stanford University, Stanford, CA, 1974.

1.3. *The Undergraduate Catalog,* State University of New York, Stony Brook, NY, 1983–85.

1.4. M. L. Joseph, *Introductory Textile Science,* 2d ed., Holt, Rinehart and Winston, New York, NY, 1966.

1.5. *Reader's Digest Complete Guide to Sewing,* Reader's Digest Assoc., Pleasantville, NY, 1976.

1.6. *The Vogue Sewing Book,* rev. ed., Vogue Patterns, New York, NY, 1975.

2

Propositional Logic

So far we have relied on the reader's gullability in presenting the Proplog interpreters. We have not offered much, other than intuition, as evidence that the interpreters are *sound*—that is, that they draw only valid conclusions from Proplog programs. What justifies the intuition that the interpreters are doing things the right way? We could postulate that one of our interpreters—say *establishbu*—is by definition "the right way." Then the meaning of a Proplog program is whatever *establishbu* does to it. This approach has several problems:

1. It is not good for giving a declarative reading to programs. We are just begging the question of whether the intepreter handles clauses in accordance with our understanding of them. For example, we expect that the order of clauses in a program should not affect whether a fact is derived or not, but that invariant is not immediately evident from looking at the interpreter. If we had chosen *establishtd* as our standard, the order of clauses would make a difference in behavior, and we would have to deal with the meaning of an infinite loop.
2. It is not a good basis for reasoning. Imagine the difficulty in proving other interpreters sound if such a proof has to be in terms of the code of the *establishbu* routine.
3. It does not conform with how we want to understand Proplog programs. The notion of *conditional truth* that we used to understand rules is not evident.

This chapter examines how we can give a precise meaning to Proplog programs independent of the workings of a particular interpreter.

2.1. Propositional Logic for Proplog

To argue rigorously about Proplog programs, we need a formal system that assigns precise meanings to Proplog clauses and that defines valid deductions. Propositional logic is that formal system. To see why the interpreters given are sound, and in one case complete, we will delve into mechanical theorem proving for propositional logic. We first introduce a fragment of propositional logic sufficient to deal with Proplog and then look at full propositional logic.

2.1.1. *What Is a Logic?*

A logic is a formalization of some aspect of language. Historically, most logics have been motivated by an attempt to understand natural language, such as English. Various logics have been developed to formalize and capture different aspects of everyday English.

According to the logic-based approach to language, a language formalization consists of three parts: syntax, semantics, and deduction.

The *syntax* of a language is a precise specification of the legal expressions in the language. Usually the legal expressions are certain sequences of symbols. For example, a logic for everyday English (which currently does not exist) would have a syntactic component to specify that a sequence of words such as "The dog chases the cat" is a legal English sentence, while the sequence "Dog cat the the chases" is not.

The *semantic* component of a logic captures the meaning of expressions in the language. For example, the semantic component of the hypothetical logic for English might make the meaning of a declarative sentence a function from states of the world to the set {**true**, **false**}. Consider the function that, given a world state (an abstraction of one, actually), returned the value **true** if in that state, there was a certain furry mammal running around after another kind of smaller furry mammal. The semantics might assign this function as the meaning for the sequence "The dog chases the cat."

The *deductive* component of a logic provides rules for manipulating expressions that preserve some aspect of the semantics. For example, the hypothetical logic for English might contain a "passivization" rule, which says precisely how one can interchange the subject and object of a sentence and appropriately change the verb to (or from) a past participle. (Under passivization the sentence "The dog chases the cat" becomes "The cat is chased by the dog.") One property of this transformation might be that it preserves the meaning of sentences under the semantics adopted.

The logics that we will use all have these three components. They are, however, considerably less ambitious than a complete logic of English. Logic emphasizes the importance of semantics and deduction, perhaps at the expense of a natural syntax. The approach to the study of language taken by the field of linguistics places more emphasis on syntax. In logic, precision and formality are considered critical.

2.1.2. *Formal Syntax of Proplog*

We now develop a logic for the Proplog language. Proplog is a stylization of a very simple fragment of English. We described the meanings of Proplog clauses in Chapter 1 via translations to English. For example, the clause:

```
basicCS :- introReq, compOrg, advProg, theory.
```

has the meaning:

> The basic CS requirement is met if the intro requirement is met and Computer Organization has been taken and Advanced Programming has been taken and Theory has been taken.

This long, somewhat stilted sentence is made up of simple sentences put together in a certain pattern using the words *if* and *and*. The Proplog clause is a shorthand way of writing this English sentence. The proposition symbols in Proplog stand for simple English sentences; the ':-' stands for *if*; the ',' stands for *and*. Thus the logic for Proplog can be seen as an attempt to formalize a small, stylized portion of English.

As mentioned earlier, a logic begins with a formal syntax: a precise definition of what sequences of symbols are legal expressions in the language. We must first decide what our symbols are. The most basic, nondecomposable symbols written on a page are letters, digits, and punctuation; typed on terminal, they are the ASCII characters. When we look at an English sentence, we have learned to see words as units, not as individual letters. In a similar way we view a Proplog program as a sequence of "words" rather than as a sequence of characters. These words are called *tokens*. The Proplog rule:

```
basicCS :- introReq, compOrg, advProg, theory.
```

consists of a sequence of 10 tokens: 5 tokens representing different propositional symbols, 1 ':-' token, 3 ',' tokens, and 1 '.' token. The Proplog language has conventions for how a sequence of characters represents a token. These conventions are called *lexical rules* (not to be confused with Proplog rules themselves). An example of a lexical rule for Proplog is that the two contiguous characters ':' and '-', in that order, always represent the ':-' token. Another example is that a token representing a propositional symbol is a contiguous sequence of letters and digits, the first of which is a lowercase letter. A program that takes as input a sequence of characters and produces as output the sequence of tokens that it represents is called a *lexical analyzer* or a *scanner*. We do not take the time here to specify precisely a lexical analyzer for Proplog, but it is not hard to do so.

We are left with the problem of specifying the sequences of tokens that make up legal Proplog programs. The context-free grammar in Figure 2.1 provides the specification. The all-uppercase words are nonterminals in the context-free grammar. The symbols ':-', ',', and '.' represent corresponding tokens in Proplog. The symbol 'propsym' is special; it stands for any proposition symbol token. Each 'propsym' is a sequence of letters and digits, the first of which is a lowercase letter. In the grammar, PGM generates a list of zero or more CLAUSEs. Each CLAUSE generates either a fact or a rule. PROPLIST generates the list of propositions making up the body of a rule.

EXAMPLE 2.1: Figure 2.2 shows how to generate the clause:

```
basicCs :- introReq, compOrg, advProg, theory.
```

using the grammar. The symbol $\Rightarrow$ means "derives in one step," and the symbol $\stackrel{*}{\Rightarrow}$ means "derives in zero or more steps." □

PGM $\rightarrow$ CLAUSE PGM
PGM $\rightarrow$ ϵ
CLAUSE $\rightarrow$ propsym TAIL .
TAIL $\rightarrow$: - PROPLIST
TAIL $\rightarrow$ ϵ
PROPLIST $\rightarrow$ propsym PROPTAIL
PROPTAIL $\rightarrow$, PROPLIST
PROPTAIL $\rightarrow$ ϵ

where propsym = lc (lc + uc + digit)*
    lc = any lowercase letter
    uc = any uppercase letter
    digit = any digit

Figure 2.1

2.1.2.1. Parsing Proplog Programs The grammar given in Figure 2.1 is not the most obvious one. For example, more natural productions for CLAUSE are:

CLAUSE $\rightarrow$ propsym .
CLAUSE $\rightarrow$ propsym : - PROPLIST .

The advantage of the grammar in Figure 2.1 is that it is amenable to recursive-descent parsing. We digress from the main line of development to outline such a parser.

Assume we have a procedure that implements the scanner; it is written so that a sequence of calls returns the tokens in the input stream one after another. It returns a new token, called 'end_of_file', when there are no more characters in the input stream. For the moment a token is represented simply by a value of an enumeration type. Given such a scanner, we can write a recursive-descent parser for Proplog programs, using a global variable NEXTTOKEN to hold the next token to be parsed. The following routines parse a list of propositional symbols. The rest of the parser is an exercise. (See Exercise 2.1.)

CLAUSE $\Rightarrow$ **basicCS** TAIL . $\Rightarrow$
basicCS : - PROPLIST . $\Rightarrow$
basicCS : - **introReq** PROPTAIL . $\Rightarrow$
basicCS : - **introReq**, PROPLIST . $\stackrel{*}{\Rightarrow}$
basicCS : - **introReq**, **compOrg**, **advProg**, **theory** PROPTAIL . $\Rightarrow$
basicCS : - **introReq** , **compOrg**, **advProg** , **theory** .

Figure 2.2

```
type token = record
                    TYP: (end_of_file, propsym, period, colon_dash, comma)
             end;

var NEXTTOKEN: token

{PROPLIST → propsym PROPTAIL}
procedure proplist;
    begin
      if NEXTTOKEN.TYP = propsym then
        begin
          scanner(NEXTTOKEN);
          proptail
        end
      else error
    end;

{PROPTAIL → ε
 PROPTAIL → , PROPLIST}
procedure proptail;
    begin
      if NEXTTOKEN.TYP = comma then
        begin
          scanner(NEXTTOKEN);
          proplist
        end
    end;
```

These procedures terminate normally on a legal input; otherwise, they report an error condition. An actual parser for Proplog would build data structures representing the program, as given in Section 1.2.2. To build those data structures, we must distinguish the different propsym tokens. Rather than passing around the actual symbols for propositions, we enter a proposition symbol once in an array of such symbols, and subsequently refer to it by its index in the array. Such an array is called a *symbol table*. The scanner maintains the symbol table, assigning indices to propositional symbols as they are first encountered, and looking up the indices of symbols already seen. Rather than simply returning the type of a token, the scanner also returns an index in the symbol table for tokens of type propsym. A revised definition of the token type is the variant record:

```
type token =
        record
          case TYP: (end_of_file, propsym, period, colon_dash, comma) of
            propsym: (PROPNUM: symtabindex);
            end_of_file, period, colon_dash, comma: ()
        end;
```

Symbol table indices can serve in place of actual propositional symbols in the data structures representing a program. That change reduces the space needed for storing the program and also saves time in comparing propositions, since an index comparison replaces a string comparison.

2.1.3. *Semantics for Proplog*

The semantics for Proplog is a simple one—it just designates clauses as **true** or **false**. The designation is done not in isolation but, rather, relative to some state of the world. We need not describe the whole world, since most of that information is irrelevant to the meaning of a particular program. Instead we abstract from the world just the information needed to ascribe meaning to a given program. The abstraction is based on which propositions appear in the program. A proposition is true or false in each state of the world. For example, the sentence "Theory has been taken" can be either true or false, depending on the state of the world (and an understanding of to whom it applies, in this case our hypothetical student from Chapter 1, Maria Marcatello). If Maria Marcatello took that particular course and received an acceptable grade in it, the statement is true. The world assigns a truth value, **true** or **false**, to every proposition in a program. Such a mapping of propositions to truth values is called a *truth assignment* for the propositions, or an *interpretation* for the program.

The truth values of the simple sentences, or propositions, determine whether each fact and rule is true or false. That is, a truth assignment determines a truth value for every rule and fact. For a fact, this determination is trivial: the fact is true if the proposition it represents is assigned **true**. For example, if the truth assignment assigns **true** to the proposition that Maria took the theory course, then the fact:

```
theory.
```

is assigned **true**.

Given a truth assignment, a rule is assigned **false** if the proposition in the head of the rule is assigned **false** and all the propositions in the body are assigned **true**; otherwise, the rule is assigned **true**. Assume Maria took Introduction to Computer Science I and II, and assume that she was given credit as having met the intro requirements. Then the rule:

```
introReq :- introI, introII.
```

is assigned **true**, because all the propositions involved are assigned **true**. A rule being true in this semantics means that this world does not constitute a counterexample to the rule. That is, if this rule is published as true by the computer science department and the preceding situation holds for Maria, everyone is happy. On the other hand, assume Maria has taken Introduction to Computer Science I and II, but she does not get credit for having met the intro requirements. In this case the rule is false. Maria has a clear-cut case that the department lied. Now consider the situation in which Maria took Introduction to Computer Science I but did not take Introduction to Computer Science II, so the truth assignment assigns **true** to **introI** and **false** to **introII**. Assume that the department says she has not satisfied the intro requirement: The truth assignment assigns **false** to **introReq**. This situation is not a counterexample to the rule, and we assign the rule **true**. What if the situation is the same, except Maria is given credit as having met the intro requirement? That is, the truth assignment assigns **true** to **introReq**. This situation is not a counterexample to the rule either. The rule says only that if Maria has taken both Introduction to Computer Science I and II, then she has met the intro requirement; it says nothing about the situation where she has not taken those courses. These situations are evidence that it is reasonable to assign **false** to a rule only if the head is false and all the propositions of the body are true.

We can provide more formal definitions. A *truth assignment*, TA, is a function from a set of propositions to {**true**, **false**}. Given a Proplog program P, let the *base* of P, denoted B_P, be the set of all proposition symbols appearing in P. Given a Proplog program P, and a truth assignment TA for B_P, a *meaning function* for TA, denoted M_{TA}, is a function from the clauses of P to {**true**, **false**} defined as follows: For a fact **p** in P, $M_{TA}(\mathbf{p}) = TA(\mathbf{p})$. For a rule r:

```
p :- q1, q2, ..., qn.
```

$M_{TA}(r) =$ **false** if $TA(\mathbf{p}) =$ **false** and $TA(\mathbf{q1}) = TA(\mathbf{q2}) = \cdots = TA(\mathbf{qn}) =$ **true**; otherwise $M_{TA}(r) =$ **true**.

We extend the meaning function to apply to entire programs: $M_{TA}(P) =$ **true** exactly when $M_{TA}(C) =$ **true** for every clause C in P. If $M_{TA}(P) =$ **true**, then TA is said to *satisfy* P; otherwise, it *falsifies* P. If TA satisfies P, then TA is called a *model* for P.

EXAMPLE 2.2: Consider the following Proplog program P taken from the fabric example in Section 1.1.2.

```
basketWeave :- plainWeave, groupedWarps.
oxford :- basketWeave, thickerFill.
plainWeave.
groupedWarps.
thickerFill.
```

Let P' be P with the fact **thickerFill** removed. The base for P (and also P') is:

$B_P =$ {**basketWeave, plainWeave, groupedWarps, oxford, thickerFill**}

Consider the two truth assignments, TA and TA', given in Figure 2.3. The meaning function M_{TA} assigns **false** to the first rule, **true** to the second rule, and **true** to all the facts, so $M_{TA}(P) =$ **false**. The meaning function $M_{TA'}$ assigns **true** to all the clauses in P', hence $M_{TA'}(P') =$ **true**. □

PROPOSITION	TA	TA′
basketWeave	false	true
plainWeave	true	true
groupedWarps	true	true
oxford	false	false
thickerFill	true	false

Figure 2.3

2.1.4. *Deduction in Proplog*

Deduction is the final aspect of a logic for Proplog. The deduction system captures the concept of "logical implication." For Proplog, logical implication is a relation between Proplog programs and sets of propositions. A Proplog program, P, *logically implies* a set of propositions, G, if every truth assignment of B_P that makes P true also makes all the propositions of G true.

A small point needs patching. G may contain propositions not mentioned in B_P. Thus a truth assignment on B_P might not assign a value to every proposition in G. Therefore, the base should include all propositions in P and G. We denote this augmented base by $B_{P,G}$. It turns out, however, that any proposition in G but not in B_P is not logically implied by P. (See Exercise 2.2.)

To see that this definition of implication is what we want, consider the case of the Proplog program P_{req} that contains the course requirement rules for a computer science major given in Section 1.1.1. The department publishes the Proplog rules as the true state of affairs. To see what propositions the rules imply we need only consider states of the world in which those rules are true—that is, truth assignments that make P_{req} true. We finish the program by adding P_{mm}, the set of facts that say that Maria Marcatello took certain courses. Thus we are interested only in situations (truth assignments) in which those facts are true—that is, where Maria took those courses. Now we wish to know whether, in all the still-possible states of affairs, Maria has satisfied her CS requirements. That is, for every truth assignment TA where $M_{TA}(P_{req} \cup P_{mm})$ = **true**, is TA(**csReq**) = **true**? The question is whether the Proplog program $P_{req} \cup P_{mm}$ logically implies the proposition **csReq**.

To understand the significance of logical implication, consider Maria's situation. She knows that some particular state of affairs is the real situation, but she may have incomplete knowledge of the entire state. The real world assigns a truth value to every proposition of interest. Let RTA be the truth assignment for Maria's real world. The problem is that she does not know what value RTA assigns to some propositions, such as **csReq**. How can she be absolutely sure that she really has satisfied the requirement—that is, RTA(**csReq**) = **true**? She cites the departmental bulletin, which lays out the requirements, establishing that the rules of P_{req} are true in the real world. She cites her transcript, which shows that she has indeed taken all the courses that are the facts of P_{mm}. If she can claim that $P_{req} \cup P_{mm}$ logically implies **csReq**, she can graduate, because every truth assignment that makes $P_{req} \cup P_{mm}$ true makes **csReq** true. If RTA makes the $P_{req} \cup P_{mm}$ true and $P_{req} \cup P_{mm}$

logically implies **csReq**, then *RTA* has to make **csReq** true, even though we do not know *RTA*'s value on every proposition.

Given a Proplog program *P* and a set of propositions *G*, how might we test whether *P* logically implies *G*? First note that there are only a finite number of truth assignments that need to be checked. The truth values of *P* depend only on the truth values assigned to proposition symbols in $B_{P,G}$. One way to test logical implication is simply to enumerate all the truth assignments for $B_{P,G}$. For each truth assignment, check whether it makes all the clauses of *P* true; if it does, then check to see if it makes each proposition in *G* true. If some truth assignment makes the program true but some proposition in *G* false, the logical implication does not hold.

EXAMPLE 2.3: Consider the following Proplog program, *P*, taken from the fabric example of Section 1.1.2.

```
fillPile :- plainWeave, extraFill.
warpPile :- plainWeave, extraWarp.
plainWeave.
extraFill.
```

Does *P* imply the propositions G = {**fillPile**} and G' = {**warpPile**}? Figure 2.4 gives all the truth assignments that make *P* true. All these assignments make *G* true, but the last one makes **warpPile**, and hence G', false. Thus *P* logically implies *G*, but not G'. □

The following pseudocode represents a function that tests logical implication. The program is encoded in an array, CLAUSE. In the program we have extended the meaning function to apply to lists of propositions. If *G* is such a list, $M_{TA}(G)$ = **true** exactly when $TA(\mathbf{p})$ = **true** for every proposition **p** in *G*.

```
function logically_implies(PROPLIST: symbollist): boolean;
  begin
    for each truth assignment TA for the set of symbols in CLAUSE
        or PROPLIST do
      if TA(CLAUSE) = true then
        if TA(PROPLIST) = false then return(false);
    return(true)
  end;
```

The purpose of *logically_implies* is very close to that of the *establishbu* interpreter for Proplog programs. The question immediately arises as to whether they compute the same function. Given the same Proplog program *P* and list of propositions *G*, do they always return the same value? Yes, they do. Indeed we presented truth assignments and logical implication precisely to provide a soundness criterion for Proplog interpreters.

To see this equivalence, we first show that if *establishbu* returns **true**, then so will *logically_implies*. What we prove is that in the function *establishbu* every proposition on CURRENTLIST and NEWLIST is logically implied by *P*. The proof

	TRUTH ASSIGNMENTS		
`fillPile`	true	true	true
`plainWeave`	true	true	true
`extraFill`	true	true	true
`warpPile`	true	true	false
`extraWarp`	true	false	false
G	true	true	true
G'	true	true	false

Figure 2.4

is by induction on the number of iterations of the **for**-loop in *establishbu*. CURRENTLIST begins empty, so the basis is vacuously true. A proposition gets on one of these lists only if it is a fact **p** or the head of a rule r where all the propositions in the body of the rule are in CURRENTLIST. Any truth assignment that makes P true makes **p** true, so the induction hypothesis is maintained by adding facts to NEWLIST. By the induction hypothesis, all truth assignments that make P true make all the propositions in the body of r true. Every truth assignment that makes program P true makes the rule r true, and thus must make the head of r true. So CURRENTLIST contains only propositions that are logically implied by P. Thus, if *establishbu* returns **true**, so will *logically_implies*.

We now must prove that if *establishbu* returns **false**, then so will *logically_implies*. We argue that if a proposition **p** does not appear in the final value of CURRENTLIST for *establishbu*, then **p** is not logically implied by P. To show the implication does not hold, we need only exhibit a truth assignment that makes P true and makes **p** false. Consider the truth assignment TA that assigns all the propositions in the final value of CURRENTLIST **true** and all other propositions **false**. Clearly TA assigns **p** **false**; we must show that $M_{TA}(P)$ = **true**. The only way TA can fail to make P true is by making a rule r in P false, since all the facts in P are added to CURRENTLIST during the first iteration of the **for**-loop, and hence are assigned **true** by TA. For $M_{TA}(r)$ = **false**, TA must make the head of r false and make all the propositions in the body of r true. Since TA makes the body true, by the definition of TA, all those propositions must be added to CURRENTLIST at some point. The next iteration of the **for**-loop would put the head of r on CURRENTLIST, so it would appear in CURRENTLIST when *establishbu* terminates. Thus TA will assign **true** to the head of r, so $M_{TA}(r)$ will have the value **true**. Hence TA makes P true and **p** false, and **p** is not logically implied by P.

We have shown that *establishbu* and *logically_implies* are equivalent programs.

The next question is whether the top-down Proplog interpreter *establishtd* is equivalent to *logically_implies*. It certainly seems as though they should be equivalent. They are not, however, because the top-down interpreter may go into an infinite loop and never return an answer. If *establishtd* does halt, it gives the same answer as *establishbu*. This limited equivalence can be shown most easily by comparing the demonstration trees implicitly built by the two interpreters. The details of the argument are left as an exercise. (See Exercise 2.5.)

2.2. Full Propositional Logic

This section discusses a logic larger than that needed to give a semantics to Proplog. For all of Proplog, Datalog, and Prolog, we consider extensions to a larger logic. Why? First, these languages have some artificial limitations (for computational reasons). They cannot represent statements built by arbitrarily combining propositions with *if* and *and.* They can assert that propositions are conditionally or unconditionally true but not conditionally nor unconditionally false. Propositional logic, covered in this section, does not have such limitations. It can represent arbitrary logical combinations of propositions. Second, we could expect to see interpreters some day for the larger logics we study. Such interpreters exist—they are called *theorem provers.* The technology for theorem provers is not yet such that we can use these larger logics for programming languages.

The previous section gave a logic for Proplog and portrayed it as a simple semantics for a small subset of English sentences—those of the form: ". . . if . . . and . . . and . . . ." The ellipses stand for simple (unanalyzed) sentences and the number of *and*s is arbitrary. This subset seems artificially restricted and awkward. We can include more sentences in our logic using similar semantic ideas. The additional English words to include in the logic are *or* and *not,* both as sentential operators. The extended logic also permits *and* in more general combinations. By *sentential operator,* we mean a word as it is used to link together entire sentences, rather than words, phrases, or clauses.

We want to handle such sentences as:

Maria took Programming Languages and Maria took Linear Algebra.
Maria satisfied the math requirements and it is not the case that Maria took Statistics.

As a sentential operator, we express *not* as "it is not the case that." "Maria did not take Statistics" is expressed as "It is not the case that Maria took Statistics." While some uses of the words *and, or,* and *not* are not as sentence operators, we can even handle some of those sentences by paraphrasing. Consider "Maria and Hector took Advanced Programming." Here *and* is not a sentential operator; it combines two proper nouns. But we could paraphrase the sentence to "Maria took Advanced Programming and Hector took Advanced Programming." This sentence is of the correct form, and we could use it to provide a meaning for the original form.

2.2.1. *Syntax of Propositional Logic*

We first give a few examples of statements in propositional logic. We will continue to use ',' for *and*; we use ';' for *or* and '¬' for "it is not the case that." Propositions are abbreviated as in Proplog. The '¬' binds tighter than ',', which in turns binds tighter than ';'. Parentheses override this precedence.

EXAMPLE 2.4: Here are some formulas in propositional logic, followed by their intended meanings in English.

```
compOrg, ¬digSys.
```

Maria took Computer Organization and it is not the case that Maria took Digital Systems.

```
theory; ¬(fileStruct, opSys).
```

Maria took Theory or it is not the case that Maria took File Structures and Maria took Operating Systems. □

A precise definition of the language of propositional logic must distinguish sequences of symbols that are in the language from sequences that are not. The context-free grammar in Figure 2.5 describes the syntax of propositional logic. The same lexical conventions apply as for Proplog, so 'propsym' is a special token that stands for any sequence of letters and digits beginning with a lowercase letter. In the grammar PROPEXP generates a propositional expression, which is simply a propositional formula followed by a period. PROPFORM generates propositional formulas. A *propositional formula* is either a single propositional term or a disjunction of terms. PROPTERM generates propositional terms. A *propositional term* is either a propositional factor or a conjunction of factors. PROPFACT generates a *propositional factor,* which is a propositional unit or the negation of a propositional unit. A *propositional unit*, which is generated by PROPUNIT, is a single proposition symbol or an entire propositional formula in parentheses. This grammar is more straightforward than the one for Proplog, but it is less amenable to efficient parsing.

EXAMPLE 2.5: A Proplog program cannot express that propositions are *mutually exclusive*: both cannot be true at once. Neither can it express that two propositions are *exhaustive*: between them, they cover all the cases. That is, at least one is true. Full propositional logic can express both situations. To oversimplify slightly, say that all fabric is either smooth or rough but not both. The following propositional expression asserts that **smooth** and **rough** are mutually exclusive and exhaustive:

```
¬(smooth, rough), (smooth; rough).
```

Figure 2.6 gives a derivation for this proposition under the grammar of Figure 2.5. □

PROPEXP → PROPFORM .
PROPFORM → PROPTERM
PROPFORM → PROPTERM ; PROPFORM
PROPTERM → PROPFACT
PROPTERM → PROPFACT , PROPTERM
PROPFACT → PROPUNIT
PROPFACT → ¬ PROPUNIT
PROPUNIT → propsym
PROPUNIT → (PROPFORM)

Figure 2.5

```
PROPEXP ⇒ PROPFORM . ⇒ PROPTERM .
PROPFACT , PROPTERM . ⇒ PROPFACT , PROPFACT . ⇒*
¬ PROPUNIT , PROPUNIT . ⇒*
¬ ( PROPFORM ) , ( PROPFORM ) . ⇒
¬ ( PROPTERM ) , ( PROPFORM ) . ⇒*
¬ ( PROPUNIT , PROPUNIT ) , ( PROPFORM ) . ⇒*
¬ ( smooth, rough), ( PROPFORM ) . ⇒*
¬ ( smooth, rough), ( PROPUNIT ; PROPUNIT ) . ⇒*
¬ ( smooth, rough), ( smooth; rough ) .
```

Figure 2.6

According to the grammar, while a propositional formula is a piece of a propositional expression, the only difference is a period thrown in to help the parser find the end of the expression. We deal with formulas for the remainder of this chapter.

A convenient way to look at propositional formulas is as binary trees, called *formula trees*. The interior nodes are labeled by *and*, *or*, or *not*, and the leaves by propositional symbols. The structure of the tree obviates the need for parentheses.

EXAMPLE 2.6: The propositional expression of the last example corresponds to the formula tree in Figure 2.7. □

The tree representation of propositional formulas makes it simple to define subformulas. A *subformula* of a propositional formula f is a portion of f corresponding to a subtree of the formula tree for f.

EXAMPLE 2.7: The propositional formulas:

```
¬(smooth, rough)
(smooth ; rough)
rough
```

are all subformulas of:

```
¬(smooth, rough) , (smooth ; rough)
```

corresponding to the left subtree of the root, the right subtree of the root, and the right subtree of that subtree, respectively. □

2.2.2. *Semantics for Propositional Logic*

The semantics for full propositional logic is similar to the semantics for Proplog that was developed in Section 2.1.3. The *base* of a propositional formula f, denoted B_f, is the set of all proposition symbols appearing in f. A truth assignment for f, then, assigns **true** or **false** to every proposition symbol in B_f. The meaning function

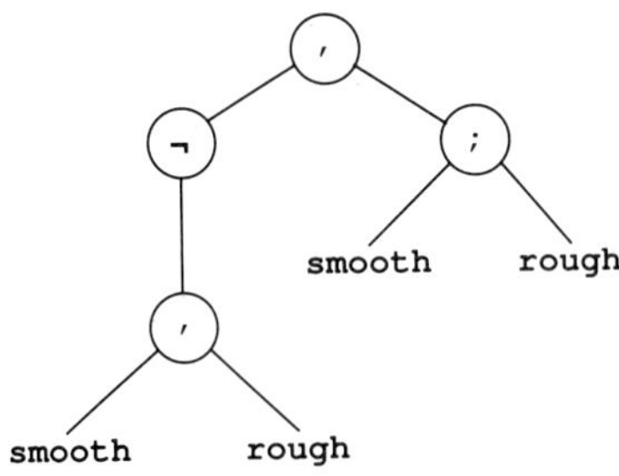

Figure 2.7

for propositional formulas under a truth assignment *TA*, denoted M_{TA} again, is defined recursively on the subformulas of a formula.

A subformula that is just a single propositional symbol **p** takes its meaning directly from the truth assignment:

$$M_{TA}(\mathbf{p}) = TA(\mathbf{p}).$$

The *and* (' , ') of two subformulas *g* and *h* is assigned **true** if both the subformulas are assigned **true**; it is assigned **false** otherwise.

$$M_{TA}(g, h) = M_{TA}(g) \textbf{ and } M_{TA}(h)$$

Here **and** is simply a Boolean operation on truth values (as are **or** and **not** in the following truth assignments). The *or* (' ; ') of two subformulas *g* and *h* is assigned **true** if one or both of the subformulas are assigned **true**; it is assigned **false** otherwise.

$$M_{TA}(g; h) = M_{TA}(g) \textbf{ or } M_{TA}(h)$$

The *not* ('¬') of a subformula *g* is assigned **true** if the subformula is assigned **false**; it is assigned **false** if the subformula is assigned **true**.

$$M_{TA}(\neg g) = \textbf{not } M_{TA}(g)$$

EXAMPLE 2.8: Consider the propositional formula *f*:

¬(smooth, rough), (smooth; rough)

used in the previous examples. The base for *f* is simply:

$$B_f = \{\textbf{smooth}, \textbf{rough}\}.$$

Under the truth assignment *TA* defined as:

$$TA(\textbf{smooth}) = \textbf{false}, TA(\textbf{rough}) = \textbf{false}$$

we have:

M_{TA}(**¬(smooth, rough), (smooth; rough)**) =
M_{TA}(**¬(smooth, rough)**) **and** M_{TA}(**smooth; rough**) =
not M_{TA}(**smooth, rough**) **and** (M_{TA}(**smooth**) **or** M_{TA}(**rough**)) =
not(M_{TA}(**smooth**) **and** M_{TA}(**rough**)) **and** (M_{TA}(**smooth**) **or** M_{TA}(**rough**)) =

not(TA(**smooth**) **and** TA(**rough**)) **and** (TA(**smooth**) **or** TA(**rough**)) =
not (false and false) and (false or false) =
not (false) and (false) =
true and false = **false** □

We extend the meaning function to apply to a set S of propositional formulas. S is assigned **true** if (and only if) every formula in S is assigned **true.** That is:

$M_{TA}(S)$ = **true** exactly when $M_{TA}(f)$ = **true** for every f in S.

Such a truth assignment is a *model* for S. The distinction between a formula and a finite set of formulas becomes much less important here than the distinction between a single Proplog clause and set (program) of clauses. A *finite* set of formulas can be transformed to a single, logically equivalent formula by simply conjoining all the formulas of the set with the ',' operator. The emphasis on finite sets is important. We can talk of infinite sets of formulas, but no single formula can be infinitely long. For a finite set of formulas G, let $conj(G)$ denote the conjunction of all the formulas in G.

2.3. Deduction in Propositional Logic

This section covers deduction in the full propositional logic. It first presents transformations on formulas that preserve some aspect of their semantics and shows how to apply such transformations to convert any formula to a special form, called *conjunctive form.* It then turns to a particular deduction method, *resolution,* that provides the core of a method for deciding logical implication.

Two formulas f and g are *logically equivalent* if they have the same truth value under all truth assignments. That is, $M_{TA}(f) = M_{TA}(g)$ for every truth assignment TA for the combined bases of f and g. As a simple example, **p** and $\neg\neg$**p** are logically equivalent. A truth assignment that assigns **true** to **p** makes both **p** and $\neg\neg$**p** true. A truth assignment that assigns **false** to **p** makes them both false. Note that this rule holds for any formula in place of the proposition **p**. If f is any formula, then:

f is logically equivalent to $\neg\neg f$.

We use the symbol '≡' for logically equivalent.

There are many other logical equivalences. For example, the commutative and associative laws for *and* and *or*:

$f,\ g \equiv g,\ f$
$(f,\ g),\ h \equiv f,\ (g,\ h)$
$f;\ g \equiv g;\ f$
$(f;\ g);\ h \equiv f;\ (g;\ h)$

One set of logical equivalences goes by the name of *DeMorgan's laws.* They are:

$\neg(f,\ g) \equiv \neg f;\ \neg g$
$\neg(f;\ g) \equiv \neg f,\ \neg g$

for any two propositional formulas *f* and *g*. (See Exercise 2.11.)

Another set of equivalences are the distributive laws:

$$f;\ (g,\ h) \equiv (f;\ g),\ (f;\ h)$$
$$f,\ (g;\ h) \equiv (f,\ g),\ (f,\ h)$$

Using equivalences such as these, we can transform a formula into another, logically equivalent formula. Note that given a formula *f*, if we replace a subformula *h* of *f* by a logically equivalent formula *h'*, the result is logically equivalent to *f*. (Why?)

A propositional formula is called a *literal* if it is of the form **p** or ¬**p** for some proposition **p**. Examples of literals are:

```
csReq
¬csReq
¬theory
introI
```

Examples of formulas that are not literals are:

```
mathReq, algReq
¬¬theory
theory; ¬algReq
```

A formula is a *clausal formula* if it consists of literals connected by *or* (';'). Examples of clausal formulas are:

```
mathReq; algReq
¬theory; mathReq; digSys
mathReq; ¬theory; ¬compOrg
dbms
¬research
```

These last two clausal formulas are trivial; they have no top-level binary operators. The following are not clausal formulas:

```
mathReq, algReq
¬theory; mathReq; digSys, research
¬(theory; research); mathReq
```

A formula is in *conjunctive form* if it consists of clausal formulas connected by *and* (','). An example of a formula in conjunctive form is:

```
(¬compilers; dbms; ¬mathReq), research, (algReq; introCS)
```

We can use the equivalences just given to transform any formula into an equivalent conjunctive formula. First, we use DeMorgan's laws to push all the '¬'s inward as far as possible. Then we eliminate double '¬'s. This step turns the formula into an equivalent one consisting of literals connected by ';'s and ','s. Finally, we use the distributive laws to distribute ';'s over ','s.

EXAMPLE 2.9: In propositional logic, one formula can express what takes several rules in Proplog. For instance, the formula:

```
advCalc; ¬(linAlg; honorsLinAlg)
```

expresses the same conditions as the two rules:

```
advCalc :- linAlg.
advCalc :- honorsLinAlg.
```

in Proplog. (Think about it.) To convert the formula to conjunctive form, first use one of DeMorgan's laws to move the '¬' inward:

```
advCalc; (¬linAlg, ¬honorsLinAlg)
```

and then distribute ';' over ',' to obtain:

```
(advCalc; ¬linAlg), (advCalc; ¬honorsLinAlg)
```
□

A formula is *valid* if every truth assignment makes it true. A valid propositional formula is called a *tautology*. The simplest example of a tautology is the formula:

p; ¬p

for any proposition **p**. A formula is *satisfiable* if there is some truth assignment that makes it true. The simplest example of a satisfiable (but not valid) formula is:

p

for any proposition **p**.

We generalize slightly the definition of "logical implication" given for Proplog and apply it to formulas. A set of formulas *S logically implies* a formula *f* if every truth assignment that makes all formulas of *S* true also makes *f* true. (The truth assignments are over the combined bases of all the formulas in *S* and formula *f*.) As an example:

p, ¬q logically implies **¬q; r**.

There are various relationships among these definitions. A formula *f* is valid if and only if the formula ¬*f* is not satisfiable. For a finite set of formulas *S* and a formula *f*, *S* logically implies *f* if and only if ¬*conj*(*S*); *f* is valid. (See Exercise 2.14.)

Algorithms exist to determine each of these properties. We simply enumerate all the truth assignments for the proposition symbols appearing in the formula(s), compute the truth value(s) for the formula(s), and check that the desired property holds for all these truth assignments. For obvious reasons this method of determining semantic relationships among propositional formulas is called the *method of truth tables*.

EXAMPLE 2.10: The formula f =

(¬smooth, ¬rough); smooth; rough

is valid, as the exhaustive consideration of truth assignments for {**smooth, rough**} given in Figure 2.8 shows. □

Consider the following Boolean function *is_satisfiable* that determines whether a formula is satisfiable or not. The type for the argument, *pform*, is a representation of propositional formulas as formula trees.

```
function is_satisfiable(FORMULA: pform): boolean;
   begin
     for each truth assignment TA for FORMULA do
       if evalform(FORMULA,TA) then return(true);
     return(false)
   end;
```

The function *evalform* takes a propositional formula and a truth assignment and determines whether or not the truth assignment is a model for the formula. Its specification is left as Exercise 2.16.

Using *is_satisfiable* as a subfunction, we can easily write functions *is_valid* and *implies,* which determine validity and logical implication, respectively. For *is_valid* to determine the validity of a propositional formula f, it simply passes $\neg f$ to *is_satisfiable*. If *is_satisfiable* returns **true**, *is_valid* returns **false**, and vice versa. Similarly, given a finite set of formulas S and a formula f, we can use *is_valid* to check whether S logically implies f: we construct the formula $\neg conj(S)$; f and pass it to *is_valid*.

Similarly, a function that determines whether a formula is valid can be the body of functions that determine satisfiability and logical implication. (See Exercise 2.17.)

2.3.1. *Resolution in Propositional Logic*

Truth tables can be used to test validity and implication, but they can quickly grow unwieldy. (See Exercise 2.18.) Their analogs in functional logic are not even finite. We want *inference rules:* operations on formulas that reduce implication to symbolic

TA(**smooth**)	*TA*(**rough**)	$M_{TA}(f)$
true	**true**	**true**
true	**false**	**true**
false	**true**	**true**
false	**false**	**true**

Figure 2.8

manipulation, and thus avoid enumeration of truth assignments. An example of such a rule is:

For formulas *f*, *g*, and *h*, if ¬*f*; *g* and ¬*g*; *h*, then ¬*f*; *h*.

So since:

```
¬(p, ¬q); (¬q; r)
```

and:

```
¬(¬q; r); ¬(q, ¬r)
```

we may conclude:

```
¬(p, ¬q; ¬(q, ¬r).
```

Inference rules form the basis for *deduction procedures* (also called *theorem provers*). A deduction procedure starts with an initial set of formulas and applies inference rules in some order to deduce new formulas implied by the initial set. The goal is to deduce a particular formula of interest, thus constructing a proof of its implication by the initial set of formulas. We are interested in two properties of a deduction procedure. The first is whether it is *complete*. If a formula is implied by a set of formulas, will the procedure always find a proof of the implication using its inference rules? The second property is the combinatorial behavior of the deduction procedure. At any point there are usually many ways to apply the inference rules to deduce new formulas. The deduction procedure uses a *search strategy* to consider the choices in turn. The number of choices at each point largely determines the cost of the search. The most efficient deduction procedures control the number of choices in some way, while maintaining completeness. One way is to employ a small set of inference rules, so there are few choices of what rule to apply next. Another way is to limit the formulas to which a rule is applied, knowing that certain deductions can be made in multiple ways. It is not necessary to try all those ways; one is sufficient.

We will concentrate on one particularly powerful deduction rule called *resolution*. It is so powerful that deduction procedures can be formulated using only this one rule. Having only one rule in the deduction procedure obviously limits choice substantially. There is no choice of which rule to use, only of formulas to which to apply it. However, the resolution rule guarantees only a limited kind of completeness. Namely, if the formula **false** is implied by the initial set of formulas (the initial formulas are unsatisfiable), then some sequence of applications of the resolution rule will generate that formula. This limitation is not so grave as it seems. Deduction procedures that use the resolution rule make use of the *refutation principle* and, consequently, are called *refutation procedures*. The refutation principle states that to prove that a set *S* of formulas implies a formula *f*, we express that implication as a new formula *g*, and try to show that the negation of *g* is unsatisfiable. The resolution rule is always sufficient to show unsatisfiability of *g*.

Many refutation procedures exist; they differ in the exact form of the resolution rule they use, the formulas chosen to apply the rule to, and the search strategy when choices exist. All the procedures are sound, but only some are complete. The search strategy of certain refutation procedures may cause them to search indefinitely without deriving the formula **false**, even when that formula is derivable with the resolution rule. Most of the material in later sections involves restricting choice in a refutation procedure. The choices can be restricted by using only special cases of the resolution rule, by limiting the formulas it is applied to, and by simplifications that can be made when the initial formulas have certain simple forms. The development culminates with a refutation procedure almost identical to the top-down interpreter of Chapter 1.

The resolution rule works not directly on arbitrary propositional formulas as defined in Section 2.2.1 but only on formulas in conjunctive form. For explaining the resolution rule, we adopt a different representation of conjunctive form formulas. We view such a formula as a set of clausal formulas, called a *clause set*. Each clausal formula is considered to be a set of literals, called a *clause*. We continue to use a semicolon to separate literals in a clause to reinforce that the set represents a disjunction of its literals. Formally, the clause is only a set, and the semicolons in it are not logical connectives. The limitation of resolution to clause sets is not a serious problem, because, as described in Section 2.2.3, any formula can be transformed into a logically equivalent one that is in conjunctive form. This conjunctive formula can then be broken into a set of formulas in clausal form. Each of these formulas can then be turned into clauses. The original formula is unsatisfiable if and only if this set of clauses is unsatisfiable. So we can use a refutation procedure to determine (un)satisfiability of any formula.

EXAMPLE 2.11: Recall the following conjunctive form formula from the last section.

```
(¬compilers; dbms; ¬mathReq), research, (algReq; introCS).
```

Its representation as a clause set is:

```
{{¬compilers; compilers; ¬mathReq},
  {research},
  {algReq; introCS}} □
```

Observe that a clause is satisfied by a truth assignment if the truth assignment makes at least one literal in the clause true. A clause set is satisfied by a truth assignment if and only if each clause is satisfied.

A clause is not exactly the same as a clausal formula. A clause can have no duplicate literals because it is a set, while a clausal formula can have duplicate literals. It is also possible for a clause to be the empty set of literals. In this case no truth assignment can make it true; the empty clause is unsatisfiable (has no satisfying truth assignment) and is equivalent to the formula **false**. As a simplification, we can exclude a clause that contains both a proposition and its negation (such as **p** and **¬p**). Such a clause is satisfied by any truth assignment and can be omitted from a clause set when deciding satisfiability.

The strategy in a deduction procedure using the refutation principle is as follows. Let f be a formula whose validity we want to test. We start with a clause set S_0 representing f, and generate a new clause set S_1 from it by adding a clause C generated through an application of the resolution rule. The resolution rule constructs C so that S_1 is unsatisfiable if and only if S_0 is unsatisfiable. We continue to modify the clause set to generate a sequence S_2, S_3, S_4, . . . of clause sets, until one is obtained that is obviously unsatisfiable. An "obviously unsatisfiable" clause set is one that contains the empty clause. In the case of propositional logic (but not all logics), the sequence of clause sets is finite. If the sequence terminates without generating an obviously unsatisfiable clause set, we can conclude that S_0 is satisfiable.

The resolution rule is a scheme to produce S_{i+1} from S_i. It generates a clause C from a clause set S such that $S \cup \{C\}$ is unsatisfiable exactly if S is. The resolution rule is simple to state. One literal is the *complement* of another if one of them is the negation of the other, such as **p** and **¬p**. The resolution rule takes two clauses from S such that one contains a literal and the other contains its complement. It constructs the new clause C, called the *resolvent,* by taking the union of the two clauses and deleting the complementary pair of literals. C will have no duplicate literals because it is a set.

EXAMPLE 2.12: Consider the following clause set S:

```
{{¬p; q; ¬r},
 {s; ¬p; ¬q; t},
 {p; q; r}}
```

The first two clauses contain a complementary pair of literals: **q** and **¬q**. One resolution step produces the resolvent:

```
{¬p; ¬r; s; t}
```
□

Terminology: The literal **q** in the last example was the literal "resolved on" in the resolution step. Call one application of the resolution rule a *resolution step*.

In a refutation procedure the resolvent C generated by a resolution step from a clause set S is added to S. If C is already a member of S, S is unchanged by this addition. The refutation procedure continues by trying another resolution step, possibly involving C. A brute-force refutation procedure tries all possible resolution steps until none will generate a new clause. The procedure computes the clause set S^* that is the closure of S under the operation of "a resolution step." S^* is the *resolution closure* of S.

EXAMPLE 2.13: Consider the following clause set S:

1. {**p**}
2. {**¬s**; **r**}
3. {**¬r**}
4. {**r**; **t**}
5. {**s**; **¬p**}

We number the clauses in S for easy reference and omit the outer set brackets. Let's find the resolution closure of S.

Resolving 1 and 5 on **p** gives:	6. {**s**}
Resolving 2 and 3 on **r** gives:	7. {¬**s**}
Resolving 2 and 5 on **s** gives:	8. {**r**; ¬**p**}
Resolving 2 and 6 on **s** gives:	9. {**r**}
Resolving 1 and 8 on **p** gives:	9. {**r**}
Resolving 3 and 4 on **r** gives:	10. {**t**}
Resolving 3 and 8 on **r** gives:	11. {¬**p**}
Resolving 3 and 9 on **r** gives:	12. {}
Resolving 1 and 11 on **p** gives:	12. {}
Resolving 5 and 7 on **s** gives:	11. {¬**p**}
Resolving 6 and 7 on **s** gives:	12. {}

At this point no resolution step will generate a new clause, so S^* consists of clauses 1–12. □

A refutation procedure detects the validity of a formula f by converting $\neg f$ to a clause set S, applying refutation steps to generate S^*, and concluding f is valid if S^* contains the empty clause. In the following discussion we show that a set of clauses is unsatisfiable if (and only if) its resolution closure contains the empty clause. The closure in the last example contains the empty clause, and the method of truth tables will confirm that the original five clauses are indeed unsatisfiable.

We wish to show that the brute-force refutation procedure is both sound and *refutation complete*. The procedure is sound if whenever the resolution closure S^* of a clause set S contains the empty clause, S is indeed unsatisfiable. The procedure is refutation complete if for every clause set S that is unsatisfiable, the procedure produces the empty clause.

Showing that a refutation procedure is sound requires proving that a resolution step preserves unsatisfiability, which will be true if the resolvent clause is logically implied by the original clauses. We claim that if a clause set S is satisfied by a truth assignment TA, then any resolvent of clauses from S is satisfied by TA. Let the clauses being resolved be $\{\mathbf{p}\} \cup D$ and $\{\neg\mathbf{p}\} \cup E$, where **p** is the literal resolved on and D and E are clauses. Since M_{TA} assigns both clauses **true**, and TA must assign one of **p** and ¬**p** **false**, it has to make (at least) one of D and E true. Therefore it must make the resolvent clause $C = D \cup E$ true. By a simple induction, any truth assignment that satisfies S satisfies S^*. If no truth assignment satisfies S^* (which is the case if it contains the empty clause), then no truth assignment can satisfy S. This argument proves soundness.

The completeness proof for our refutation procedure relies on the notion of a semantic tree for a clause set S, which is a compact form for representing all possible truth assignments for S. Let the *base* of S, B_S, be the set of all proposition symbols in S.

DEFINITION: A *semantic tree* T_S for a clause set S is a complete binary tree of depth $|B_S|$ such that:

1. For every interior node i of T_S, the edges out of i are labeled by **p** or $\neg$**p** for some proposition **p** in B_S.
2. Along every root-to-leaf path in T_S, either **p** or $\neg$**p** appears, for every proposition **p** in B_S. □

Each root-to-leaf path in a semantic tree T_S for a clause set S defines one of the possible truth assignments for S. If **p** is on the path, the truth assignment for the path maps **p** to **true**; if $\neg$**p** is on the path, the truth assignment maps **p** to **false**.

Although not required by the definition, the semantic trees we consider here have a unique proposition symbol associated with each level of the tree. Thus all nodes of level l will have edges labeled by **p** and $\neg$**p**, for some proposition **p** in B_S.

EXAMPLE 2.14: For the clause set S of the last example, $B_S = \{\mathbf{p}, \mathbf{r}, \mathbf{s}, \mathbf{t}\}$. A semantic tree T_S for S is shown in Figure 2.9. □

DEFINITION: Let T_S be a semantic tree for a clause set S. A node i in T_S is a *failure node* for a clause C in S if the path from the root of T_S to node i contains the

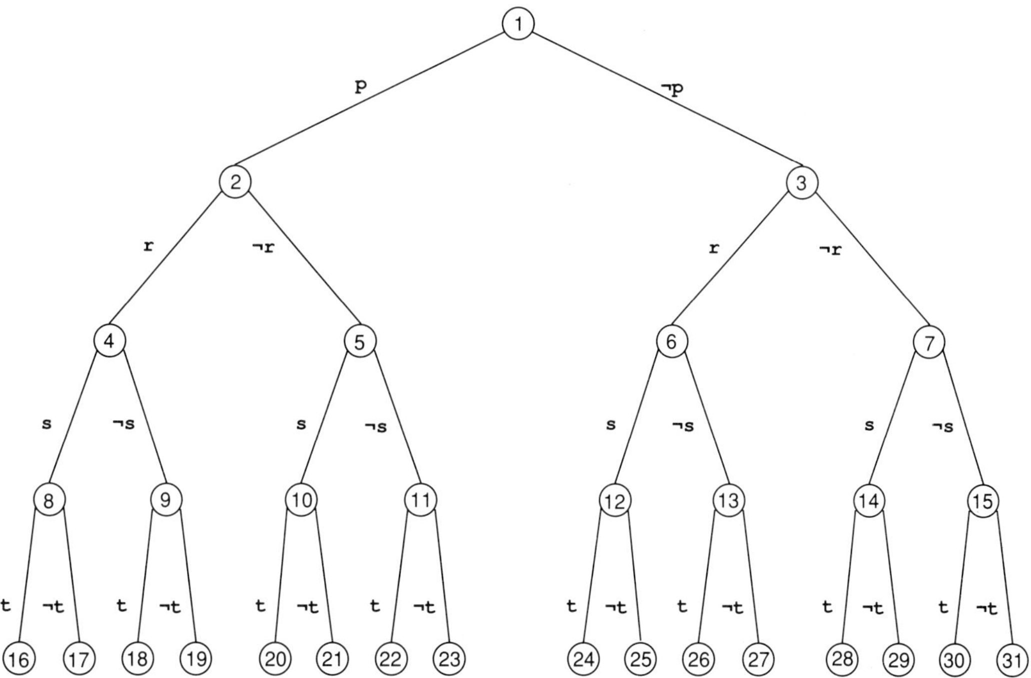

Figure 2.9

complement of every literal in C, and no ancestor of node i has this property. Node i is a *failure node* for S if it is a failure node for some clause C in S, and no clause D in S has a failure node that is an ancestor of node i. □

The idea of a failure node is that we can conclude that a certain truth assignment falsifies S by looking at only the portion of the truth assignment down to the node. Once some clause in S is assigned **false**, then there is no need to see the rest of the truth assignment.

EXAMPLE 2.15: In Figure 2.9, the failure nodes for the clause set S =

1. {**p**}
2. {¬**s**; **r**}
3. {¬**r**}
4. {**r**; **t**}
5. {**s**; ¬**p**}

are:

node 3:	clause 1 fails
node 4:	clause 3 fails
node 10:	clause 2 fails
node 11:	clause 5 fails □

DEFINITION: A semantic tree T_S for a clause set S is a *failure tree* for S if every root-to-leaf path in T_S contains a failure node. □

A clause set S is unsatisfiable if and only if every semantic tree for S is a failure tree. If some root-to-leaf path in a semantic tree T_S for S has no failure nodes, the path corresponds to a satisfying truth assignment for S. Furthermore, no other semantic tree for S can be a failure tree. (Why?) When drawing failure trees, we prune off the branches below failure nodes, so the failure nodes are exactly the leaves.

EXAMPLE 2.16: The semantic tree T_S in Figure 2.9 is a failure tree for the clause set S from the last example. That tree is redrawn in Figure 2.10 with branches below failure nodes removed. T_S is not a failure tree for the clause set S' =

1. {**p**}
2. {¬**s**; **r**}
3. {¬**r**}
4. {**r**; **t**}

because there is no failure node along the path from node 1 to node 22. That path gives rise to the truth assignment:

TA(**p**) = **true**, TA(**r**) = **false**, TA(**s**) = **false**, TA(**t**) = **true**

that satisfies S'. □

Here is the crucial definition to finish the argument for completeness of refutation.

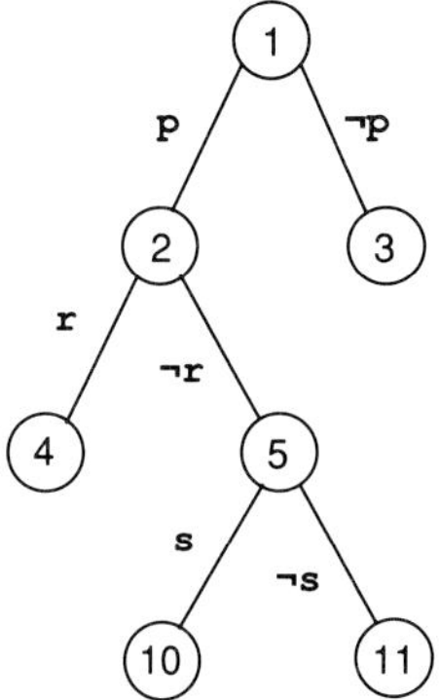

Figure 2.10

DEFINITION: Let T_S be a semantic tree for a clause set S. Node i in T_S is an *inference node* for S if both children of i are failure nodes for S. □

We make three important observations:

1. Any failure tree for a clause set S (except the tree of one node) contains an inference node. (Why?) In Figure 2.10, node 5 is the only inference node.
2. If clause set S has a failure tree of one node, then S contains the empty clause.
3. An inference node i indicates a particular resolution step whose resolvent fails at node i or above.

To elaborate on the third observation, let node i be an inference node in a semantic tree T_S for a clause set S. Let j and k be the children of node i, and assume the branch to j is labeled by **p** and the branch to k is labeled by ¬**p**. Figure 2.11 depicts this situation. S must have distinct clauses C_j and C_k that fail at nodes j and k, respectively. (Why are the clauses distinct?) Now C_j was not made false until node j, so C_j must contain the literal ¬**p**. Similarly, C_k must contain the literal **p**. Hence C_j and C_k will resolve on **p**; call the resolvent C. Every literal in C_j, except ¬**p**,

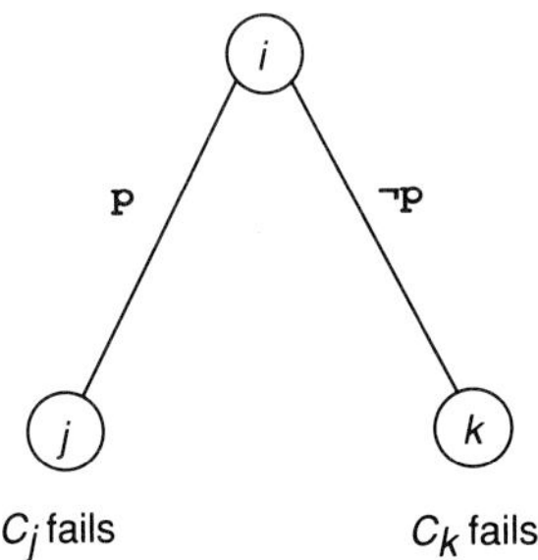

Figure 2.11

must be false by node i, if not before. Likewise, every literal in C_k, except **p**, must be false by node i. Thus C fails at or before node i.

These three observations show that the resolution closure of an unsatisfiable clause set S contains the empty clause. Let T_S be a failure tree for S with the fewest nodes, and let node i be an inference node in T_S. Let clause C be the resolvent of the indicated resolution step at node i. The clause set $S' = S \cup \{C\}$ has a smaller failure tree than S. The failure tree for S' with the fewest nodes is no larger than T_S with the children of node i removed. If the argument is repeated, each clause added to S results in a smaller failure tree. The process terminates with the one-node failure tree, so S^* must contain the empty clause.

To see that the brute-force refutation procedure is complete, we need only note in addition that the resolution closure of a clause set is finite. Hence the brute-force procedure can always compute the entire closure, producing the empty clause if the original clauses are unsatisfiable. In more general logics the resolution closure can be infinite. A refutation procedure in such a logic is still judged refutation complete if it eventually produces the empty clause when the original clauses are unsatisfiable, even if it runs forever in other cases.

EXAMPLE 2.17: Consider again the clause set S:

1. {**p**}
2. {¬**s**; **r**}
3. {¬**r**}
4. {**r**; **t**}
5. {**s**; ¬**p**}

Node 5 is an inference node in the failure tree T_S for S shown in Figure 2.10. The clauses that fail at nodes 10 and 11 are:

2. {¬**s**; **r**}
5. {**s**; ¬**p**}

We know they must resolve on **s**. Their resolvent is:

6. {**r**; ¬**p**}

which fails at node 5.

Let S_1 be S with clause 6 added. Figure 2.12 shows a failure tree T_{S_1} for S_1. This tree has the single inference node 2. The clauses that fail at nodes 4 and 5 are:

3. {¬**r**}
6. {**r**; ¬**p**}

Resolving them, we get:

7. {¬**p**}

which fails at node 2.

Let S_2 be S_1 with clause 7 added. Figure 2.13 gives a failure tree T_{S_2} for S_2. Node 1 is an inference node. The clauses that fail at nodes 2 and 3 are:

7. {**p**}
1. {¬**p**}

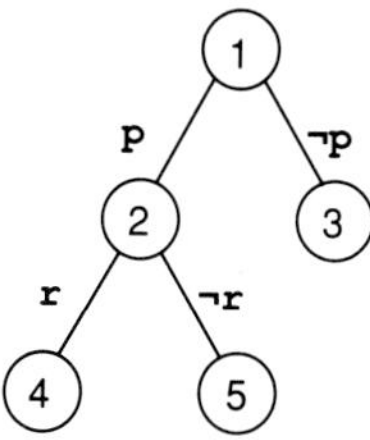

Figure 2.12

Their resolvent is the empty clause, which fails at node 1. □

The refutation principle can be used to test a logical implication—say, whether a set of formulas R logically implies a formula f. First transform R into a logically equivalent clause set S_1 and transform $\neg f$ into a clause set S_2. Next use resolution to determine whether the clause set $S = S_1 \cup S_2$ is unsatisfiable. If S is unsatisfiable, then no truth assignment makes all the clauses true. Hence every truth assignment that makes S_1 true makes S_2 false—that is, makes $\neg f$ false, and so makes f true. Therefore R logically implies f.

To determine the unsatisfiability a clause set S, a refutation procedure need not actually compute the entire resolution closure S^* of S. It need only determine whether or not the empty clause is in S^*. That computation may be shorter, since we can show that the empty clause is in the closure by simply exhibiting a sequence of resolution steps that derives it. In the last example we obtained the empty clause in only three resolution steps, while we would need at least six steps to generate the resolution closure.

A *resolution tree* summarizes the derivation of a clause by resolution from a clause set S. The leaves of the tree are labeled with clauses from S, and each interior node is labeled with a resolvent of its children. A resolution tree is called a *refutation tree* for S if its root is labeled by the empty clause. Exhibiting a refutation tree, then, is sufficient to show unsatisfiability for a clause set. The goal of an efficient refutation procedure is to find a refutation tree for a clause set without generating large portions of its resolution closure.

EXAMPLE 2.18: Figure 2.14 shows a refutation tree for the clause set S from the last example. Notice its similarity to the failure tree for S in Figure 2.10. □

As with demonstration trees, a resolution tree might actually be a DAG, since some clauses could take part in more than one resolution step.

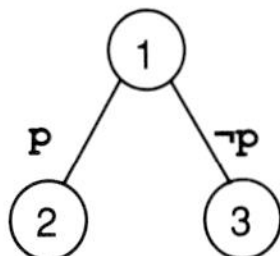

Figure 2.13

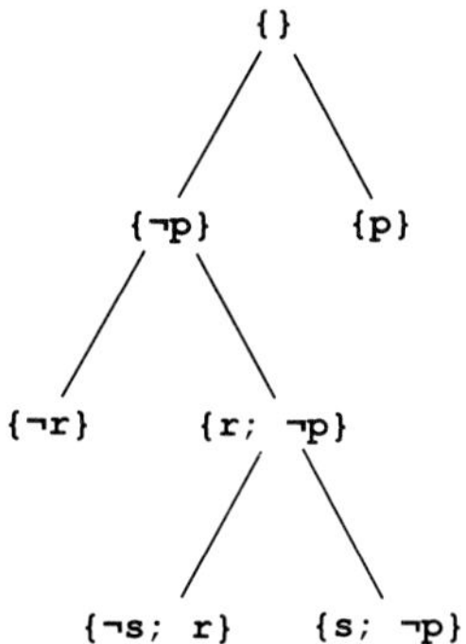

Figure 2.14

EXAMPLE 2.19: In Figure 2.15, we see a resolution DAG for the clause set S =

{**p**; ¬**r**}
{**r**}
{¬**p**; ¬**s**}
{¬**p**; **s**}

The clause {**p**} is used in two resolution steps. □

2.3.2. *Limiting Choice in Resolution*

Testing a clause set S for unsatisfiability is the same as testing if S^* contains the empty clause, which, in turn, is the same as determining if there is a refutation tree (or DAG) for S. The basic strategy of refutation procedures is searching the space of all resolution DAGs for S to find a refutation DAG. Most such programs proceed by building a partial DAG, bottom-up, and then considering all the ways to extend that DAG. However, the space of DAGs is large and often redundant. If one refu-

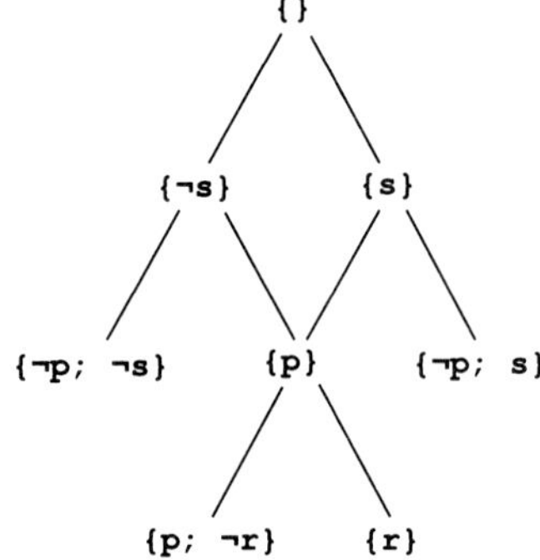

Figure 2.15

tation DAG exists, there are likely to be many. (See Exercise 2.23.) Suppose we can find a restricted subset of all resolution DAGs with the property that, if there is a refutation DAG, then there is one in the restricted subset. In this case a refutation procedure need search only the smaller space. The restriction on the smaller space has to be in a usable form. The restriction must be defined structurally, ideally tied to limiting the mechanism by which resolution DAGs are extended. Any restriction on the search space of DAGs leads to fewer extensions to consider at each stage, and thence to a more efficient deduction procedure.

There are two sources of choice when building resolution DAGs:

1. deciding which two clauses to resolve next, and
2. deciding which literals to use in the chosen clauses.

This section considers restrictions on resolution DAGs that limit both choices. While these restrictions preserve the completeness of the resolution method, we do not prove this claim.

The first restriction goes under the name *linear resolution*. Linear resolution on a clause set *S* restricts one of the clauses at each resolution step to be the resolvent from the previous resolution step. The last resolvent generated is called the *center clause*, and the other clause that enters the resolution step is the *side clause*. The side clause at each step is either one of the original clauses from *S* or a previous center clause. Evidently any previous center clause will be a descendent of the current center clause in the resolution DAG being built.

The name "linear resolution" and the terminology for clauses come from the shape of a resolution DAG under the restriction given. The DAG is almost a *vine*, which is a tree where every interior node has at least one child that is a leaf.

EXAMPLE 2.20: Let *S* be the clause set:

{¬t}
{¬s; ¬p}
{¬p; s}
{p; q}
{¬q; r}
{¬r; t}

Figure 2.16 shows a resolution DAG for *S* using linear resolution. The center clauses run up the left side of the DAG; the side clauses all enter from the right side. All the side clauses in the DAG are from *S*, except **{p, t}**, which is a descendent of the center clauses with which it is resolved. □

One way to think about linear resolution is that the center clause is a list of literals to be "resolved away." Each side clause removes one literal from the list and "introduces" zero or more other literals. For instance, if the current center clause is **{p; ¬r}**, and the side clause is **{r; s; ¬t}**, we can think of the resolution step as removing **¬r** from the center clause and introducing the literals **s** and **¬t** to get the next center clause, **{p; s; ¬t}**.

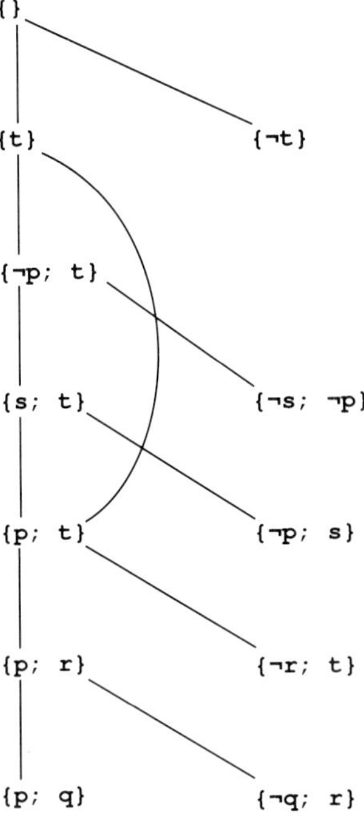

Figure 2.16

Linear resolution limits the choice of clauses to resolve at each step; one of the clauses is always fixed (except for the very first step). However, linear resolution says nothing about on which literal to resolve. *Selected literal* (*SL*) resolution is a refinement of linear resolution in which the literal to resolve upon in each step is one of the literals most recently introduced into the center clause. That literal is called the *selected literal.* One way to keep track of when literals were introduced by side clauses is to order the literals in each center clause. We will put the literals introduced by a side clause at the front (left) of the resolvent and always pick the leftmost literal in a center clause for the next resolution.

EXAMPLE 2.21: Consider SL resolution on the clause set S =

1. {**p**; **q**}
2. {¬**p**; **r**; **s**}
3. {¬**r**; **q**}
4. {¬**q**; **s**}
5. {¬**s**; **t**}
6. {¬**t**; ¬**s**}

Rather than drawing the resolution DAG, we just show successive center clauses in that DAG. Take clause 1 as the initial center clause. Its selected literal is **p**, so clause

2 is the only choice for side clause. We remove **p** from the center clause and introduce **r** and **s** to get the next center clause:

7. {**r**; **s**; **q**}

Literal **r** is now the selected one. Again the choice of side clause is dictated: clause 3. That clause removes **r** and introduces **q** to give:

8. {**q**; **s**}

(Note that we removed the second occurrence of **q**. The center clause is still treated as a set of literals, even though it is ordered.) Literal **q** is now the selected one, which means clause 4 is the next side clause. We remove **q** and (re)introduce **s** to get the resolvent:

9. {**s**}

At this point we have a choice of clause 5 and clause 6 for the next side clause. Choosing clause 5 yields:

10. {**t**}

Now clause 6 is the only choice for side clause, which gives:

11. {¬**s**}

as the new center clause. There are many choices for the next side clause: clauses 2 and 4 from *S*, as well as center clauses 7, 8, and 9. In our omniscience, we choose clause 9. The resolvent is the empty clause; we have a refutation. □

The last restriction of the resolution method we consider is a specialization of SL resolution called *model elimination*. Model elimination restricts the set of descendent clauses of the center clause that are considered as candidates for side clause. This restriction gives rise to a succinct representation of the descendent clauses of interest, while preserving completeness of the refutation procedure. Information about the descendent clauses can be embedded in the center clause. That information is sufficient to perform a resolution step between current and descendent center clauses. The primary reason for looking at model elimination is that, as we shall see in Chapter 10, it can use many of the same data structures and optimization techniques as for a Prolog implementation, yet it works on full logic, rather than a subset.

DEFINITION: Let *C* be the current center clause, and let *D* be some previous center clause (and hence a descendent of *C* in the resolution DAG). Clause *D* is a *progenitor* of *C* if either:

1. The selected literal of *C* was introduced when the selected literal of *D* was removed.
2. Clause *D* is a progenitor of a clause *E*, and *E* is a progenitor of *C*. □

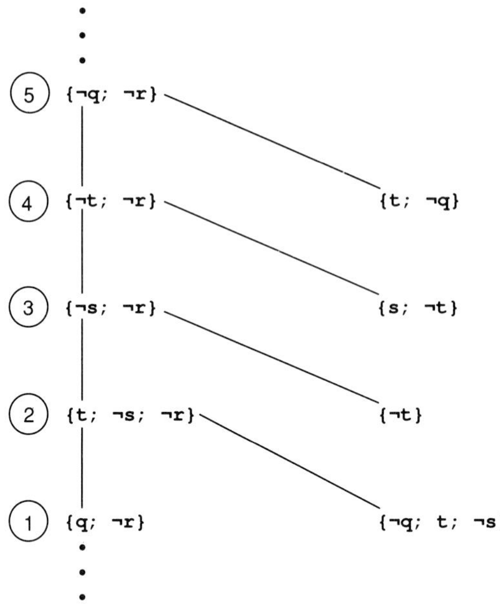

Figure 2.17

EXAMPLE 2.22: Consider the portion of a linear resolution DAG shown in Figure 2.17. Center clause 1 is a progenitor of center clauses 2–5. Literals **t** and **¬s** were introduced to replace **q**; **¬t** was introduced later when **¬s** was removed, and **¬t** was replaced by **¬q**. Clause 2 is not a progenitor of any clause. Clause 3 is a progenitor of clauses 4 and 5, and clause 4 is a progenitor of clause 5. Notice the clauses of which a given clause is a progenitor are consecutive center clauses in the resolution DAG. (See Exercise 2.25.) □

In model elimination on a clause set *S*, if *C* is the center clause under consideration, the choices for side clause are restricted to be members of *S* or progenitors of *C*. In the last example, clause 1 could be a side clause for clause 5, but clause 2 cannot be a side clause for clause 4. There is a slight change in duplicate removal in model elimination from SL resolution. When a literal is introduced by a side clause, and that literal is already present in the center clause, the introduced literal is omitted in favor of the literal already present. This change affects not which literals appear in the resolvent but their order. Thus, if {**p**; **¬q**; **r**} is the center clause and {**p**; **r**} the side clause, the resolvent is {**¬q**; **r**}. With this restriction, we observe that if clause *D* is a progenitor of clause *C*, then *D* minus its selected literal will always be a subset of *C*! Therefore, when we resolve *C* with *D* as a side clause, the effect is to eliminate the first literal from *C*. (Think about it.)

EXAMPLE 2.23: In Figure 2.18, clause 1 is a progenitor of clause 3, which will resolve with 3 on its selected literal, **¬q**. Note that clause 1 with **q** removed is a subset of

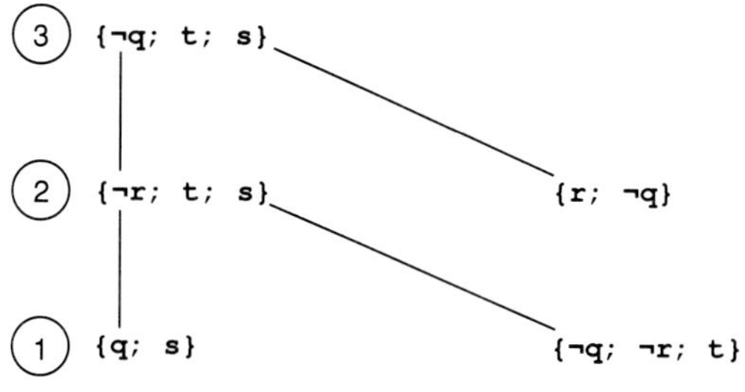

Figure 2.18

clause 3. If we resolve clauses 1 and 3 on **q**, we get { **t; s** }, which is just clause 3 with the selected literal removed. □

We can concisely represent all progenitors of a center clause *in the clause itself* with the following trick. When a selected literal is resolved away, rather than removing it from the resolvent, we *frame* it (surround it in brackets) and leave it in place in the resolvent. If the selected literal of a center clause is ever the complement of a framed literal in the clause, we just remove the selected literal. If a framed literal ever makes it to the front of a center clause, it is removed, because the clause it represents will not be a progenitor of any further center clauses. In model elimination on a clause set S, a resolution step with a side clause from S is called an *extension*, resolving with a progenitor is called *reduction*, and removing a framed literal from the front of a center clause is called *contraction*.

EXAMPLE 2.24: Consider the clause set S:

{**p**; **q**}
{**p**; ¬**q**}
{¬**p**; ¬**r**; **q**}
{¬**p**; ¬**q**}
{**r**}

Let's start with {**p**; **q**} as the initial center clause. Extending with {¬**p**; ¬**r**; **q**}, we frame **p** to get:

{¬**r**; [**p**]; **q**}

We added ¬**r** and **q** to the front but then removed the first occurrence **q**. Using extension with {**r**} yields:

{[¬**r**]; [**p**]; **q**}

Two contraction steps will remove both framed literals to give:

{**q**}

as the next center clause. Extending with {**p**; ¬**q**} as the side clause, we get:

{**p**; [**q**]}

and then using {¬**p**; ¬**q**} gives:

{¬**q**; [**p**]; [**q**]}

At this point, we could extend with one of the clauses in *S*, but we can perform a reduction step using the framed literal **q** to arrive at:

{[**p**]; [**q**]}

(Why is reduction preferable to extension?) Both the framed literals can now be removed by contraction to give the empty clause and, thus, a refutation. □

The framed literals in the model elimination method can serve another purpose. If, in searching for refutation DAGs, a program considers candidates for side clause in turn (depth first) rather than in parallel (breadth first), the search can yield an infinite resolution DAGs. Thus the program may run forever, even when a refutation DAG exists. Framed literals can be used to detect cycling in DAG building.

EXAMPLE 2.25: Suppose the current center clause is {**p**; **q**}, and the side clause is {¬**p**; **s**}. Their resolvent is {**s**; [**p**]; **q**}, which is then extended with {**p**; ¬**s**} to get {**p**; [**s**]; [**p**]; **q**}. We could forge blindly ahead, extending alternately with {¬**p**; **s**} and {**p**; ¬**s**}, ad infinitum. However, by noticing that the selected literal is the same as a framed literal, we can abandon the current path in searching for a refutation DAG and make another choice at some previous point in the search. □

2.4. Horn Clauses

We have looked at ways of narrowing the search in refutation procedures by restricting the range of choices in building resolution DAG. Even with these restrictions there is still a considerable amount of choice. If we restrict the form of the clauses themselves, we can further reduce choice. The restricted clauses considered here, which have at most one positive literal, are called *Horn clauses*. Having only one positive literal naturally limits the choice of literal on which to resolve. This restriction on the form of clauses limits their expressiveness. Horn clauses cannot capture all constraints and relationships among propositions that full propositional logic can, but they include Proplog rules and facts, which are not totally powerless.

The first subsections introduce a logical connective for *if*, which allows us to write Horn clauses in the familiar form of Proplog rules and think about them as rules: conditional relationships among propositions. The later sections prove the refutation completeness of a restricted form of resolution, *input resolution.* for sets of Horn clauses and consider particular search strategies employed by refutation procedures using input resolution. By completeness, we mean that some complete refutation procedure using input resolution exists; not every search strategy gives rise to a complete procedure. The nature of the proof is to show that any refutation tree using Horn clauses can be transformed into a refutation vine that is constructable by input resolution.

2.4.1. *If*

The language we have defined as propositional logic has only three sentence operators: *and, or,* and *not.* Among the others we might include is *if*, as in:

> Maria has satisfied the computer science intro requirements *if* Maria has taken Introduction to Computer Science.

As a symbol for "if," we will use (not surprisingly) ': -'. "If" connects two sentences, and we can extend the grammar for propositional formulas to include this connective. The precedence of ': -' is the lowest of all the operators, so it binds the least tightly. For example:

```
p;q  :-  r,s.
(p;q)  :-  (r,s).
```

represent the same formula tree. The semantics of ': -', relative to a truth assignment *TA*, is defined as follows:

$M_{TA}(g :- h)$ = **true** if $M_{TA}(g)$ = **true or** $M_{TA}(h)$ = **false**;
$M_{TA}(g :- h)$ = **false** otherwise.

Thus:

$$g :- h \equiv g; \neg h.$$

Recall that a formula in clausal form is one that is the disjunction of a set of literals such as:

oxford; monksCloth; ¬plainWeave; ¬groupedWarps; hopsacking

Any formula in clausal form can be represented by a formula involving "if" and only positive literals. (A *positive* literal is an unnegated proposition; a *negative* literal is a negated proposition.) First we group the positive and negative literals together.

```
(oxford; monksCloth; hopsacking); (¬plainWeave; ¬groupedWarps).
```

Using one of DeMorgan's laws, we move the negation outward:

```
(oxford; monksCloth; hopsacking); ¬(plainWeave, groupedWarps).
```

By the logical equivalence given earlier, we can rewrite this formula as:

```
oxford; monksCloth; hopsacking :- plainWeave, groupedWarps.
```

A propositional formula with a single "if," a disjunction of positive literals on the left, and a conjunction of positive literals on the right is in *implication form.*

Consider what a resolution step looks like when performed on clauses in implication form. A literal from the disjunction of one formula must match a literal from the conjunction of the other formula. The resolvent is formed by combining disjuncts and combining conjuncts with the matching literals removed.

EXAMPLE 2.26: We can resolve the clauses:

```
p; q :- r, s, t.
t :- p, s, u.
```

on **p**, yielding:

```
q; t :- r, s, t, u.
```

as the resolvent. □

We take a few liberties with the notation for propositional formulas to put clausal formulas with only one type of literal (positive or negative) into implication form. A clausal formula with all positive literals, such as **p; q**, is written with the ':-' omitted:

```
p; q.
```

We can construe the conjunction of no literals as always being true, so the last formula can be viewed as:

```
p; q :- true.
```

For all negative literals, we consider a disjunct of no literals to be always false, so **¬p; ¬q** is rendered as:

```
:- p, q.
```

We can think of this formula as:

```
false :- p, q.
```

We use ': -' by itself for the empty clause. The unsatisfiability of the empty clause is consistent with our conventions, since we view it as:

```
false :- true.
```

which is logically equivalent to **false**.

2.4.2. *Horn Clause Syntax*

Horn clauses are of particular interest for resolution theorem proving and Proplog. A clause is a *Horn clause* if it contains at most one positive literal.

EXAMPLE 2.27: The clauses:

```
{csReq; ¬basicCS; ¬mathReq; ¬advancedCS; ¬engReq; ¬natSciReq}
{introReq; ¬introCS}
{introCS}
{¬csReq; ¬mathReq}
{}
```

are all Horn clauses. The following clauses are not Horn:

```
{csReq; mathReq}
{introReq; ¬introCS; theory} □
```

Notice that a Horn clause written in implication form looks like a Proplog clause, except for a Horn clause with no positive literal.

EXAMPLE 2.28: The Horn clauses in the last example correspond to the following formulas in implication form:

```
csReq :- basicCS, mathReq, advancedCS, engReq, natSciReq.
introReq :- introCS.
introCS.
:- csReq, mathReq.
:- . □
```

We view a Proplog program as a set of Horn clauses, in particular, a set in which every (Horn) clause has *exactly* one positive literal. (Such clauses are called *definite.*) Intentionally, Proplog clauses and propositional formulas that look the same have the same meaning.

clause `:- y, x'`, with the literals in that order. Here x' is a list of the literals in x but not in y, in the same order as x. That is, if x and y share a literal, the copy in x is omitted. Thus a properly ordered vine corresponds to one kind of SL resolution. Notice that the vine in Figure 2.26 is not properly ordered, but the vine in Figure 2.27 is. A properly ordered refutation vine exists whenever a refutation vine exists, but we will not prove this fact rigorously. We instead appeal to the following lemma, whose proof is left as an exercise. (See Exercise 2.31.)

SEPARABILITY LEMMA: Let H be a Horn clause set. Let V be a refutation vine where the clause at the leftmost leaf is `:-` **p**, x, for x a sequence of literals. There are refutation vines V_p and V_x over H, with clauses `:-` **p** and `:-` x at the leftmost leaf, respectively. Furthermore, neither V_p nor V_x is as deep as V. □

The Separability Lemma gives rise to an inductive proof that a properly ordered refutation vine exists when any refutation vine exists. Take a refutation vine V with leftmost leaf `:-` **p**, x, and generate V_p and V_x as guaranteed by the lemma. Inductively find properly ordered refutation vines W_p and W_x with leftmost leaves `:-` **p** and `:-` x. Splice these vines into a properly ordered refutation vine W with leftmost leaf `:-` **p**, x. (See Exercises 2.32 and 2.33.)

2.4.4. *Search Strategies*

We just saw that a refutation procedure for Horn clauses can restrict itself to refutation vines and resolution on the first literal of the center clause. Such a refutation procedure searches for a refutation by building resolution vines bottom up, using a headless clause at the leftmost leaf. For a Proplog program and goal list, there is only one headless clause, but in general there are many. The refutation procedure can segregate the headless clauses and the definite clauses. It tries each headless clause in turn as the leftmost leaf, looking for one from which it can build a refutation vine with the definite clauses. Once a leftmost leaf is chosen, there is still choice left, although not so much as with general clauses. To get a fully defined deduction procedure, we have to specify the order in which the choices are considered.

We put off the choice issue for the moment. We present the basic framework of a deduction algorithm where the order of choices is left unspecified. Later we treat particular ways of considering choices, called *search strategies*. We demonstrated that restrictions placed on resolution with Horn clauses never prevent a refutation from being derived when the initial clauses are unsatisfiable. However, a particular refutation procedure using these restrictions could still fail to find a refutation, because it gets caught in an infinite portion of the search space that contains no refutation vines.

The following pseudoprogram constructs resolution vines from a set of definite Horn clauses, given an initial center clause (leftmost leaf). Since all center clauses in our restricted version of resolution are headless, each can be represented as just a list of propositions in a variable CENTERCL. We store a definite Horn clause as a record with two fields: HEAD for the positive proposition symbol, and BODY for a list of the proposition symbols that appear in negative literals. H will be a globally accessible set of all the definite Horn clauses.

```
procedure printvine(CENTERCL: symbollist);
  begin
    printlist(CENTERCL);
    if CENTERCL <> nil then
      begin
        choose a Horn clause SIDECL from H;
        if SIDECL.HEAD = CENTERCL↑.SYM then
          begin
            printclause(SIDECL);
            printvine(elimdupl(copycat(SIDECL.BODY, CENTERCL↑.REST)))
          end
      end
  end;
```

The *printvine* procedure prints out an upside-down representation of a properly ordered vine. It first prints the current center clause (CENTERCL), then a side clause (SIDECL) that resolves with the center clause on its first literal, and finally their resolvent (in the recursive call to *printvine)*. The function *copycat* concatenates two lists, copying the first. (Why is the copying necessary?) The function *elimdupl* eliminates duplicates in its argument, always keeping the first occurrence of a literal so as to get a properly ordered vine. The pseudoprogram *printvine* is not a completely specified refutation procedure, since it contains the statement "choose a Horn clause." For every properly ordered vine, there is a correct sequence of choices at this step to generate that vine.

Notice that we do not represent '¬' symbols explicitly in this program. By convention, we know that every symbol on CENTERCL represents a negative literal, and every symbol in the BODY field of a Horn clause representation is negative. We could explicitly store the '¬'s in some way, but it would just waste space and time in the algorithm.

Consider the possible traces of *printvine,* one trace for each sequence of choices. These possible traces can be represented as a tree, each path of which corresponds to a resolution vine. Call this tree an *or-tree* for the moment. An or-tree defines the search space for which a Horn-clause refutation procedure must provide a search strategy.

EXAMPLE 2.35: Figure 2.28 shows an or-tree for the following Horn clause set, using **: - p** as the initial center clause. The nodes are labeled with the successive values of CENTERCL on recursive calls to *printvine*. The edges are labeled with the choices for SIDECL. Note that two paths in the tree correspond to refutation vines and one does not.

```
p :- u.
p :- q, r.
q :- t.
t :- u.
t :- v.
r.
u. □
```

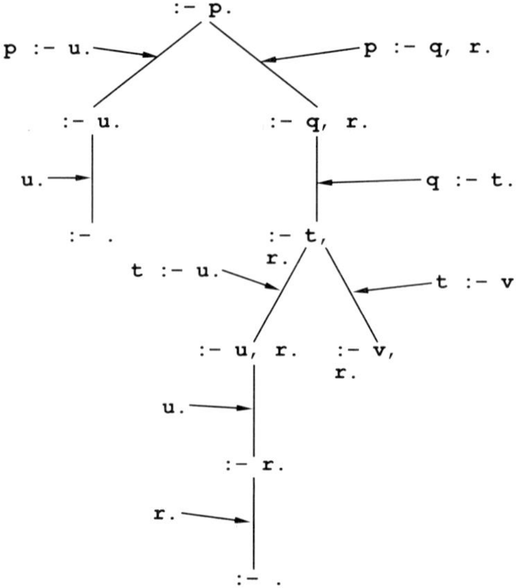

Figure 2.28

Given the observations just made, the set H of Horn clauses plus the initial CENTERCL is unsatisfiable if and only if one of the paths in the or-tree terminates at the empty clause. To get a fully defined refutation procedure based on *printvine,* we must give the details of how to search the paths in the or-tree for the clauses in H. One strategy to search the or-tree is depth first. That is, working left to right, we travel down each path in turn, looking for a leaf labeled by the empty clause. Hence, at each branch point in the or-tree, depth-first search completely explores one choice before considering another. A refutation procedure with depth-first search is obtained by refining the 'choose' pseudocode statement as a loop through all the clauses in H, with H represented as an array. We also turn the program into a Boolean function *resolvedf* (the 'df' is for depth-first) that stops if it finds a refutation.

```
function resolvedf(CENTERCL: symbollist): boolean;
  var I: integer;
  begin
    if CENTERCL = nil then return(true);
    for I := 1 to MAXCLAUSES do
      if H[I].HEAD = CENTERCL↑.SYM then
        if resolvedf(elimdupl(copycat(H[I].BODY, CENTERCL↑.REST)))
          then return(true);
    return(false)
  end;
```

A problem arises with this way of searching the or-tree. The or-tree may have infinitely long paths. It could contain both an infinite path and another path that terminates in the empty clause. If the infinite path is encountered by the depth-first search before the refutation path, the algorithm will go into an infinite loop and never find the refutation. Thus a depth-first search strategy of the or-tree as a Horn clause refutation procedure is not complete. This incompleteness is a drawback of the depth-first search strategy. Depth-first search does have some compensating advantages. Its implementation is straightforward, and it uses little space. The state of the search is captured by remembering a single path in the or-tree and the last clause tried at each branch point on that path. The space required is proportional to the longest path searched. A possible solution to the infinite search problem is to carry along framed literals in CENTERCL to indicate previous goals. The refutation procedure can then fail if the first literal is ever the same as a framed literal. (See Exercise 2.26.)

A breadth-first search strategy for the or-tree would not have the problem with completeness. Breadth-first search explores the or-tree level by level, considering all paths simultaneously to a given depth. A disadvantage of breadth-first search is the space it requires. The refutation procedure must store a center clause on each path across the entire width of the tree. Breadth-first search always finds a path to the empty clause if one exists, but it will run forever on an infinite or-tree with no refutation path.

There is an optimization we can make to *resolvedf*. The use of the function *elimdupl* seems expensive. Running through the entire center clause to check for duplicates every time is costly. Consider what happens if we simply do not check for duplicates. If a duplicate occurrence of a proposition makes its way to the front CENTERCL, some computation must have removed the first occurrence of that proposition. Whatever that computation was, it will also remove the duplicate occurrence. The result of *resolvedf* is unchanged if we simply delete the check for duplicates:

```
function resolvedf2(CENTERCL: symbollist): boolean;
  begin
    if CENTERCL = nil then return(true);
    for I := 1 to MAXCLAUSES do
      if CENTERCL↑.SYM = H[I].HEAD then
        if resolvedf2(copycat(H[I].BODY, CENTERCL↑.REST))
          then return(true);
    return(false)
  end;
```

In some cases this change may not really be an optimization. If there are many duplicates, the time saved in not checking for duplicates may be more than offset by the time it takes to do the (redundant) computation necessary to resolve away the duplicate. This situation could indeed occur. In most situations, however, duplicates are rare enough, or the redundant computation fast enough, that not checking for duplicates is the more efficient algorithm.

This algorithm brings the discussion of propositional logic full circle. We started with a formal semantics for Proplog, based on propositional logic, to provide a basis for the soundness and completeness of the naive interpreters. We looked at full propositional logic and deduction methods for it, in particular the resolution rule and the refutation principle. We then refined the deduction procedure to be more computationally tractable—first by restricting the resolution rule and second by limiting the types of clauses used. We ended up with a limited search space of resolution vines, for which we chose a particular search strategy, yielding *resolvedf2*.

Compare *resolvedf2* with the naive interpreter for top-down evaluation of Proplog programs, *establishtd*. They are equivalent, if we identify the Horn clause array H with the Proplog program CLAUSE array and CENTERCL with GOALLIST. Indeed we have shown that the top-down interpreter of Proplog programs is really a resolution theorem prover (that is, a deduction procedure using the resolution rule) for Horn clauses. We think of *establishtd* as trying to find a demonstration tree for an intial goal, while *resolvedf* searches for a refutation based on an initial headless clause, but it is actually the same activity. Negating a conjunction of propositions, such as the initial goal list, gives a Horn clause with no positive literals, such as the headless clause at the leftmost leaf. The or-tree of partial resolution vines is like the search trees introduced in Section 1.2.4. The only difference is that the search tree ends at the first path to the empty clause or the first infinite path, while the or-tree captures the entire search space. Refutation vines and demonstration trees are not so closely related. A refutation vine captures the steps in building a demonstration tree. The successive center clauses of the vine give the fringe of unestablished subgoals in the top-down construction of a demonstration tree. A refutation vine makes explicit the order in which clauses were used, while a demonstration tree shows which clauses were used to establish a particular proposition.

What have we gained from this chapter? Proplog programs now have a meaning apart from any particular interpreter. We understand the deductive methods behind the interpreter, and we know why what it does is the right thing. Also, the infinite behavior on some inputs is not inherent in Proplog but is a property of a particular search strategy. We now know that the top-down interpreter is correct relative to the formal semantics of Proplog given at the beginning of the chapter. Unfortunately, the depth-first search strategy in the interpreter is not complete. We traded completeness for implementation efficiency.

What about the bottom-up interpreter, *establishbu*? We can give a different restriction on resolution that gives rise to a refutation procedure matching that interpreter. In *unit resolution* one clause in each resolution step is a *unit clause*—that is, a clause with a single literal. Unit resolution is complete for Horn clauses, or any set of clauses for which input resolution is complete. For Horn clauses the unit clause can be restricted to be positive—that is, a Proplog fact. The function *establishbu* can be derived from positive unit resolution. (See Exercise 2.34.)

2.5. Negation and the Closed World Assumption

Proplog, being Horn clauses, is limited in its expressiveness compared to full propositional logic. It does not have the power to deduce goals that are negative literals. In this section we outline a means to adapt the top-down interpreter to establish negative goals by making an assumption that a Proplog database of rules and facts is exhaustive.

Recall the computer science requirements example of Section 1.2.1 that we used to determine whether Maria Marcatello had satisfied her computer science requirements. If we run the program consisting of the rules and facts there with the goal **csReq**, *establishtd* returns **true**, because it successfully derives the empty clause from the goal. Thus the answer to the question "Did Maria satisfy the computer science requirements?" is yes in every state of the world in which the program is true. If the rules and facts are valid in the current state of the real world, Maria has satisfied her requirements in that world.

Consider the situation where Hector Ng has completed Introduction to Computer Science I and wants to know if he has completed the basic computer science requirements. The clauses of interest are given by the Proplog program P =

```
basicCS :- introCS.
basicCS :- introI, introII.
introI.
```

If we give *establishtd* the goal **basicCS** with the program P, the answer will obviously be no, since the interpreter cannot derive the empty clause from that goal. Can the university argue from that answer that the real truth assignment makes the proposition "Hector satisfied the basic CS requirement" false? They cannot. (If we were in the *real* real world, they probably would. Suspend disbelief for a moment and assume college registrars are logical beasts.) Maria has an airtight case when *establishtd* returns **true** for the program with her facts, but the university does not have a case against Hector if the answer is **false** for his program. The truth assignment that assigns every proposition **true** makes every Proplog program true. Thus there is at least one model for program P in which **introI** is true. It is not hard to imagine many possible worlds in which the clauses of P, as well as the proposition "Hector Ng has satisfied the basic CS requirements," are all true. The basic CS requirement could be fulfilled by transfer credit or examination. There could be a third sequence of courses to satisfy the requirement. Perhaps the requirement is waived for anyone whose last name contains no vowels. The point is that if *establishtd* answers **false**, it has failed to prove that the desired proposition must be true in all models of P; it has *not* shown that the proposition must be false in all models.

In the real live world of students and universities, students are kept from graduating for not meeting requirements. Does it not seem reasonable that if the Proplog rules came from the university catalog correctly, and if the transcript was transcribed into facts correctly, and if the interpreter answered **false** on **basicCS**, then Hector has not met the basic CS requirement? The discrepancy arises from a hidden assumption—namely, that the rules given in the catalog and the facts on Hector's transcript are *all* the relevant rules and facts. If we believe that the **false** answer in Hector's case means that he has not satisfied the basic CS requirements in the real world, it is because we assume, not only that all the clauses in P are correct, but also that P is a complete statement of all rules and facts that pertain. We assume we have not left any relevant fact or rule out of the program. This assumption is called the *closed world assumption* (CWA).

How can this assumption be used by the university to argue that Hector has not met the basic CS requirement—that the *real* truth assignment makes **basicCS** false? The CWA is equivalent to assuming that the real truth assignment is the most conservative truth assignment that still makes the program true. By "conservative," we mean that it makes true as few propositions as possible. We can formalize the notion of "conservative" as follows. Let the *minimal* truth assignment for a clause set S, denoted MTA_S, be the truth assignment that assigns a proposition **p true** only if **p** is true in *all* models of S. That is, if **p** is false in some model of S, then $MTA_S(\mathbf{p}) = \mathbf{false}$.

EXAMPLE 2.36: In the case of program P for Hector, MTA_P(**basicCS**) = **false**, MTA_P(**introCS**) = **false**, MTA_P(**introI**) = **true**, and MTA_P(**introII**) = false. □

It is not immediately apparent that MTA_S is a model for S. For general clauses, it might not be, but it always is for a Proplog program. (See Exercises 2.35 and 2.36.) The CWA asserts that the real truth assignment for a Proplog program is the minimal truth assignment. If we all agree that the Proplog program P is correct with respect to the closed world assumption, the university has a case. Since *establishtd* returned **false**, there is a model TA for P where TA(**basicCS**) = **false.** Thus, MTA_P(**basicCS**) = **false**, and the CWA lets us conclude that Hector has not met the basic CS requirement in the real world.

It is also possible to express the CWA syntactically via adding formulas, rather than semantically through minimal truth assignments. One way is to take the program clauses and add to them some more formulas that state precisely the additional conditions we are assuming. If the program is P, the enlarged set of formulas is $CDB(P)$. (CDB stands for Completed Data Base.)

We construct CDB(P) by starting with the clauses of P. For each proposition symbol **p** in P, we add another formula. That formula is constructed by taking the bodies of all the rules in P that have **p** as head and disjoining them to get a formula g. We add g **:-** **p** to P. This formula is not usually a Horn clause, nor is it always equivalent to a set of Horn clauses. For any proposition symbol **q** that does not appear as the head of any clause (including a fact), add the formula ¬**q**. The resulting set of formulas is $CDB(P)$.

EXAMPLE 2.37: For the program P for Hector, the additional formulas in $CDB(P)$ are:

```
introCS; (introI, introII) :- basicCS.
¬introCS.
¬introII. □
```

Fairly often we we want tc ask questions about $CDB(P)$, not just P. For positive questions (the kind we ask in Proplog), the answers will be the same for P and $CDB(P)$. The problem is for negative queries, goals such as ¬**basicCS**. For a negative query, we could form $CDB(P)$ and drop back to a general theorem prover (that is, a deduction procedure for full propositional logic). A general theorem prover is necessary because $CDB(P)$ is not always a set of Horn clauses, and *establishtd* works only for Horn clauses.

We need not actually go through the bother of a full resolution theorem prover. We argued that if *establishtd* answers **false** for a goal **q** with a Proplog program P, then **q** is false under MTA_P. Conversely, if $MTA_P(\mathbf{g})$ = **false**, then *establishtd* cannot answer **true** on **q** because then P does not logically imply **q**. Thus, we could modify *establishtd* to handle a goal of the form **not(q)**, meaning **q** is false under the CWA on P, by reversing its output on **q**. This treatment of **not** goes by the name "negation-as-failure," since we assume a proposition is false if we fail to prove it is true. Note that **not** is different from '¬'. The meaning of **not**—not provable from P—is dependent on all of P, while the meaning of '¬' is more local.

Negation-as-failure allows *establishtd* to process negative literals as goals under the CWA. What about **not** in the body of a Proplog rule? Will the CWA give meaning to such a rule? For certain sets of rules, it will. Consider:

```
canGrad :- csReq, not(haveHold).
```

This rule might mean that a student can graduate if he or she has met the requirements and does not have a "hold" on his or her record. Other rules might say that a student has a hold if he or she has not returned a library book or has an unpaid tuition bill.

We can modify *establishtd* to handle a **not** in a clause body. Call the new interpreter *establishtdn*. We allow GOALLIST to contain items of the form **not(q)** along with regular propositions. When a **not(q)** item is first in CENTERCL, instead of matching it against a clause in the program, *establishtdn* invokes itself recursively on **q**. If the recursive invocation succeeds, the calling invocation fails. If the recursive invocation fails, the calling invocation continues with a recursive call on the rest of the items in CENTERCL. (See Exercise 2.37.) (Note this modification will not deal with **not** in the head of a clause.) If we pose the goal **canGrad** to *establishtdn*, it will happily compute away and (maybe) return an answer.

EXAMPLE 2.38: In the fabric identification program of Chapter 1.3.2, we used procedural means to assert a proposition **unknownA** when **knownA** could not be derived. With an interpreter that handles **not**, no procedural extension is needed. A rule such as:

```
unknownWeave :- not(knownWeave).
```

for each property suffices. □

Extending the interpreter to handle negative goals in the body of clauses is easy, but we must look more closely at what the answers given by *establishtdn* really mean. The minimal model approach to the CWA provides the handle.

We call a program that has negated goals in the bodies (but not in the heads) of rules a *generalized* Proplog program. The logical clauses for a generalized Proplog program are those obtained by treating the **not**'s in the bodies of rules as '¬'. For any generalized Proplog program, these clauses clearly have a model: The truth assignment that assigns **true** to every proposition symbol is such a model. A *minimal* model for a program P is a truth assignment that satisfies the clauses for P, but the change of the assignment for any proposition symbol from **true** to **false** results in its no longer satisfying the clauses. We saw earlier that for simple Proplog programs there is a unique minimal model. However, for generalized Proplog programs, there may be several minimal models.

EXAMPLE 2.39: Consider the program:

```
p :- not(q).
```

The corresponding clause:

```
{p; q}
```

has two minimal models, TA_1 and TA_2, as follows:

TA_1(**p**) = **true**
TA_1(**q**) = **false**

TA_2(**p**) = **false**
TA_2(**q**) = **true** □

If *establishtdn* answers yes for a query and a program, then the query is true in some minimal model for that program. And if *establishtdn* answers no, the query is false in some minimal model. For the program in the example, *establishtdn* computes answers relative to the minimal model TA_1.

The program

```
q :- not(p).
```

has the same clause and thus the same minimal models as the example. With this program, however, *establishtdn* computes answers relative to the minimal model TA_2.

These examples suggest the following conjecture: Given a generalized Proplog program, there is a single minimal model that characterizes the answers that *establishtdn* computes for queries to that program. It turns out that this conjecture is true for only a certain class of generalized Proplog programs.

EXAMPLE 2.40: Consider the following program:

```
p :- not(q).
q :- not(p).
```

The corresponding clause is:

```
{p; q}
```

and the minimal models are TA_1 and TA_2. However, *establishtdn* (and even a breadth-first *establishtdn*) does not give answers with respect to either TA_1 or TA_2; it goes into an infinite loop on both queries **p** and **q**. □

A class of programs for which a minimal model captures the behavior of *establishtdn* is the *stratifiable* programs. Loosely, a program is stratifiable if there can be no recursion that goes through a negative literal. This property can be checked by a simple analysis of the program.

Now consider *CDB*(*P*) for a generalized Proplog program *P*. If *P* is not stratifiable, *CDB*(*P*) may be inconsistent, that is, have no models at all. (Consider the program: **p :- not(p).**) If *P* is stratifiable, *CDB*(*P*) will have a model.

EXAMPLE 2.41: Again consider the program *P*:

```
p :- not(q).
```

CDB(*P*) is:

```
{p; q}
{¬q; ¬p}
```

Note that *CDB*(*P*) does not imply **p**, even though *establishtdn* gives a yes answer to this query. □

These facts mean that the syntactic operation of completing the program to form *CDB*(*P*) does not help much in characterizing what *establishtdn* will do on generalized Proplog programs, even on programs that are stratifiable.

2.6. EXERCISES

2.1. a. Complete the Proplog parser in Section 2.1.2.1.
b. Modify the completed parser to build the data structures used by *establishtd* for the program being parsed.

2.2. Let *P* be a Proplog program, and let **q** be a proposition not in B_P. Prove there exists a truth assignment *TA* that is a model for *P*, but *TA*(**q**) = **false**.

2.3. Show that a rule of the form:

```
p :- q, p, r.
```

can be removed from a Proplog program without changing the set of propositions the program implies.

2.4. Let P be a Proplog program, and let **q** be a proposition. Prove that P implies **q** if and only if there is a demonstration tree for **q** under P with root **q**.

2.5. Prove that *establishtd,* when it halts, always gives the same answer as *establishbu*. Exercise 2.4 may be helpful in the proof.

2.6. Let P be a set of Proplog rules. Say that set Q of Proplog rules *mimics* P if for any set $F \subseteq B_P$, $P \cup F$ and $Q \cup F$ imply the same propositions in B_P.
   a. Given a set P of rules, show there is a set Q that mimics P such that each rule in Q has at most two propositions in its body.
   b. Show that the result in (a) does not hold if rules in Q are restricted to have one proposition in their bodies.

2.7. Given a Proplog program P, consider the problem of determining whether a rule r in P is redundant. Rule r is redundant if its effect can be achieved by other rules and facts in P. That is, deleting r from P would not change the set of *clauses* implied by P. Consider the following procedure, which uses *establishbu*: Start with P, delete r, then add all the propositions in the body of r as facts. Call the result P'. Run *establishbu* with P', giving it the head of r as the goal. If *establishbu* returns **true**, r is redundant and can be eliminated from P.
   a. Prove that this procedure is sound: we will never delete a rule when deleting it would change the clauses that are implied.
   b. Prove that this procedure is complete: we will always delete a rule if it really is redundant.

2.8. Express the following sentences as propositional logic formulas using only the operators *and*, *or*, and *not*.
   a. Kale likes cool nights, or broccoli likes dry soil, but not both.
   b. If you water spinach and give it nitrogen fertilizer, it will thrive or it will bolt.
   c. It is not the case that if cucumbers turn purple, then they have a zinc deficiency.

2.9. Write a parser for full propositional logic that builds a tree corresponding to the formula that is input. You may want to change the grammar to make it easier to parse.

2.10. Show that the set of all Proplog clauses is regular, while the set of all propositional formulas is not.

2.11. Prove the following logical equivalences from Section 2.2.3.
   a. the associative law for *or*
   b. DeMorgan's laws
   c. the distributive law for *and* over *or*

2.12. Find a propositional formula involving six propositional symbols (with one occurrence each) that has the most symbols when converted to conjunctive form.

2.13. Consider the following propositional formulas:

i. `(p; ¬q), (¬p; q)`
ii. `(¬(p, q), ¬(¬p, ¬q)`
iii. `(p, q); ¬(p; q)`
iv. `(p; ¬q); (¬p; q)`
v. `¬((¬p; ¬q), ¬(¬p, ¬q))`
vi. `(p, ¬q), (¬p; q)`

a. Which formulas are tautologies?
b. Which formulas are satisfiable?
c. Which formulas logically imply which others?
d. Which formulas are logically equivalent?

2.14. Let S be a finite set of formulas, and f be a single formula. Prove that S logically implies f if and only if the function ¬ *conj*(S); f is valid.

2.15. Show, by using truth tables, that the formula:

```
(fritzWins; ronWins), ¬(fritzWins, ¬(pigsFly; grassIsBlue)),
¬pigsFly
```

implies the formula:

```
ronWins; grassIsBlue
```

2.16. Give a function *evalform* that traverses a formula represented as a tree and, using the truth assignment implemented as a Boolean function *ta*, returns the truth value of the formula for that truth assignment. Type *pform* gives the structure for formula trees.

```
type pform = ↑propnode;

    propnode = record
                  case TYP:(andnode, ornode, notnode, psymnode) of
                    andnode, ornode: (LEFTFORM, RIGHTFORM: pform);
                    notnode: (SUBFORM: pform);
                    psymnode: (PROPNUM: symtabindex)
               end;
```

2.17. Given a function *is_valid* that decides if a propositional formula is valid, show how to derive a function *is_satisfiable* that tests satisfiability, and another function *implies* that tests logical implication.

2.18. Suppose we used a truth table to prove Maria Marcatello satisfied the computer science requirements using the facts in Section 1.2.1. How many rows and columns would the truth table have?

2.19. Give a refutation proof that the formula:

(¬((inClass, asleep); ¬inClass); ¬listening),
(listening; ¬passing)

implies the formula

¬(passing, inClass); ¬asleep

2.20. Let S be a set of clauses, and let C be a clause that is the resolvent of two clauses in S. Show that $S \cup \{C\}$ is logically equivalent to S.

2.21. Let i be an inference node in a semantic tree T_S for a clause set S. Give an example to show that the resolvent of the indicated resolution step can fail at a node above i in T_S.

2.22. Use semantic trees to derive an upper bound on the minimum number of resolution steps needed to derive the empty clause for an unsatisfiable set of clauses S. Your bound should depend on $|B_S|$, but not $|S|$. (For a set A, $|A|$ is the *cardinality* of A: the number of elements in A.)

2.23. How many different refutation DAGs exist for the clause set in Example 2.19? Do not count two DAGs as different if one can be obtained from the other by reordering children of nodes.

2.24. Give refutation proofs using linear resolution for the implications in Exercises 2.15 and 2.18.

2.25. Let T be a linear resolution DAG, and let C be a center clause in T. Prove that the clauses for which C is a progenitor are consecutive center clauses in T. Are C's progenitors consecutive?

2.26. Show how the framed literal representation for model elimination can be used to avoid looping in *establishtd*.

2.27. a. Show that any Horn clause set with no facts is satisfiable.
b. Show that any Horn clause set with no headless clauses is satisfiable.

2.28. The set of clauses:

{p; q; ¬r}
{p; ¬s}
{s; t}

contains two non-Horn clauses. We can transform this set of clauses into all Horn clauses by "renaming" **p** to **¬p1** and **s** to **¬s1**. We then get:

{¬p1; q; ¬r}
{¬p1; s1}
{¬s1; t}

Renaming is a transformation that replaces a proposition with the negation of its opposite, such as "It is not the case that the light is off" for "The light is on."

a. Prove that renaming preserves satisfiability.

b. Give an algorithm to determine if a set of clauses can be transformed to Horn clauses through renaming.

2.29. Let H be a Horn clause set. Transform H to H' by adding # as the head of every headless clause. Prove that H has a refutation tree if and only if H' has a resolution tree for #.

2.30. a. Let T be a resolution tree for # for a Horn clause set H. Let U be a subtree of H with root **p** :- x, y, where x and y are sequences of propositions. Let U' be a resolution tree for H with root **p** :- x, where U' has no more nonleftwards nodes than U. Prove there exists a resolution tree T' for #, where T' has no more nonleftwards nodes than T.

b. Let T be a resolution tree for a set of Horn clauses H. Suppose the leftmost leaf of T is **q** :- z and the root is **q** :- x, where z and x are sequences of propositions. Prove there exists a resolution tree H' for $H \cup$ {**p**: - z, y} such that:

i. the leftmost leaf of T' is **p** :- z, y,
ii. the root of T' is **p** :- x, y', where y' is a subsequence of y, and
iii. T' has no more nonleftwards nodes than T.

2.31. Prove the Separability Lemma of Section 2.3.3. (Hint: Show that if there is a refutation vine with :- y at its leftmost leaf, then there is a refutation vine with :- y' at its leftmost leaf, for any y' that is a subsequence of y.

2.32. Let H be a set of Horn clauses. Let W_p and W_y be properly ordered refutation vines under H with leftmost leaves :- **p** and :- y, respectively. Here y may be a sequence of propositions, and the leftmost leaves might not be in H. Prove there is a properly ordered refutation vine W under H for :- **p**, y.

2.33. Use the result of Exercises 2.26 and 2.27 to show that if there is a refutation vine V for a Horn clause set H, then there is a properly ordered refutation vine W for H. The only sticky part of the proof is the case when V has :- **p** at its leftmost leaf, where **p** is a single proposition.

2.34. In *positive unit resolution* for Horn clauses, one clause in a resolution step is restricted to be a *positive unit clause* a clause with a single, positive literal (a fact). The positive unit clause need not be an input clause. Figure 2.29 shows a positive unit refutation tree for the clause set:

```
p :- q.
q :- r, s.
:- p, t.
r.
s.
t.
```

a. Show that positive unit resolution is a complete refutation procedure for Horn clauses.

b. Explain how *establishbu* implements positive unit resolution.

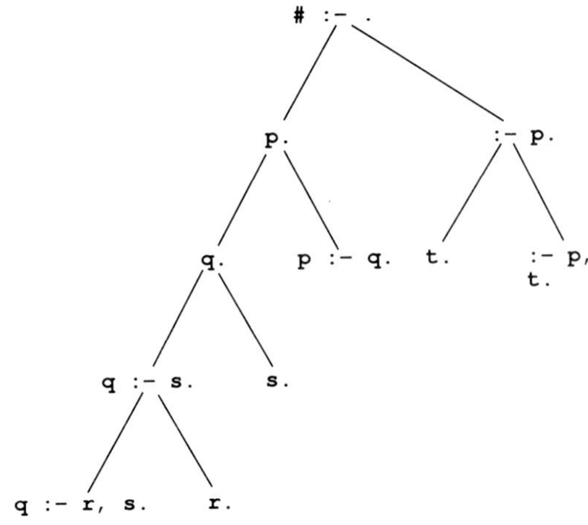

Figure 2.29

2.35. Let S be a set of clauses. A *minimal* model for S (as opposed to a minimal truth assignment) is a model for S where no true proposition can be made false and still be a model for S.

  a. Show that the minimal model for a Horn clause set H is unique, if it exists, and is the same as the minimal truth assignment for H.
  b. Exhibit a clause set with two minimal models.

2.36. Show that MTA_S is not necessarily a model for a clause set S.

2.37. Give a version of *establishtd* that handles goals of the form **not(q)**. Represent such a goal with an extra Boolean field in type *symlistrec*.

2.7. Comments and Bibliography

The theory of propositional logic is very old, the original ideas going back to the Greeks. Early modern contributers to the theory include Boole and Pierce near the end of the last century. A general introduction to propositional logic can be found in any modern mathematical logic book, such as Mendelson [2.1].

Mechanical theorem proving has been a very active field of research for the past 30 years or so, since computers have become available for implementations. Most of the work has involved the more general logics that we will see in later chapters, but we have used those results applied to the special case of propositional logic. Robinson's work [2.2] was instrumental in opening the area of resolution theorem proving and making it the most popular and most explored theorem-proving method. His contribution was to show how basic propositional resolution method could be extended to more general logics. We will see these extensions in later chapters.

Theorem proving in propositional logic is not currently an active area of research in its own right. Propositional Horn clause logic is known to be decidable in linear time. The method of truth tables gives an exponential decision algorithm for logical implication in general propositional logic, and no better algorithm is known. It is interesting to note, however, that satisfiability of general propositional clauses was the first problem shown to be NP-complete. It was used to define what has now become the most interesting outstanding problem in theoretical computer science: the question of whether P, the class of problems solvable in polynomial time by a deterministic machine, is the same as NP, the class of problems solvable in polynomial time by a nondeterministic machine [2.3].

A now old, but still very useful in-depth survey of the area of theorem proving can be found in Chang and Lee [2.4]. It introduces resolution in the propositional case and covers the various ways to restrict the set of resolution derivations that must be explored. The proof that a set of clauses has a refutation with unit resolution, if and only if it has one with input resolution is given there. A more recent text by Gallier [2.5] covers resolution and other sets of deduction rules for automatic theorem proving. The proof that positive unit resolution is complete for Horn clauses is given by Henschen and Wos [2.6] (again in the more general, and more difficult, case of functional logic). The method of model elimination was set forth by Loveland in a series of papers [2.7–2.9].

Wos et al. [2.10] provide a general introduction to theorem proving and its use in general problem solving. Nilsson [2.11, 2.12] gives a good introduction to logic and its application in the area of artificial intelligence, and is the source for our material on semantic trees. That treatment was in turn adapted from a paper by Kowalski and Hayes [2.13]. Manna [2.14] gives applications of theorem proving to computer science, in particular to proofs of program correctness. He covers resolution, clausal form, and also natural deduction, another approach to theorem proving.

The treatment of negation-as-failure and the definition of the completion of a pure Proplog program is due to Clark [2.15]. The characterization of stratified programs and their minimal models is due to Apt, Blair, and Walker in [2.16]. Their work was clarified and generalized by Przymusinski [2.17].

2.1. E. Mendelson, *Introduction to Mathematical Logic,* Van Nostrand, Princeton, 1964.

2.2. J. A. Robinson, A machine-oriented logic based on the resolution principle, *JACM 12*:1, January 1965, 23–41.

2.3. M. R. Garey and D. S. Johnson, *Computers and Intractability: A Guide to the Theory of NP-Completeness,* Freeman, San Francisco, 1979.

2.4. C.-L. Chang and R. C.-T. Lee, *Symbolic Logic and Mechanical Theorem Proving,* Academic Press, New York, 1973.

2.5. J. Gallier, *Logic for Computer Science: Foundations of Automatic Theorem Proving,* Harper & Row, New York, 1986.

2.6. L. Henschen and L. Wos, Unit refutations and Horn sets, *JACM 21*:4, October 1974, 590–605.

2.7. D. W. Loveland, Mechanical theorem-proving by model elimination, *JACM 15*:2, April 1968, 236–51.

2.8. D. W. Loveland, A simplified format for the model elimination theorem-proving procedure, *JACM 16*:3, July 1969, 349–63.

2.9. D. W. Loveland, A unifying view of some linear Herbrand procedures, *JACM 19*:2, April 1972, 366–84.

2.10. L. Wos, R. Overbeek, E. Lusk, and J. Boyle, *Automated Reasoning: Introduction and Applications,* Prentice-Hall, Englewood Cliffs, NJ, 1984.

2.11. N. J. Nilsson, *Problem Solving Methods in Artificial Intelligence,* McGraw-Hill, New York, 1971.

2.12. N. J. Nilsson, *Principles of Artificial Intelligence,* Tioga Publishing Company, Palo Alto, CA, 1980.

2.13. R. Kowalski and P. Hayes, Semantic trees in automatic theorem proving, in *Machine Intelligence 4,* B. Meltzer and D. Michie (eds.), American Elsevier, New York, 1969, 87–101.

2.14. Z. Manna, *Mathematical Theory of Computation,* McGraw-Hill, New York, 1974.

2.15. K. L. Clark, Negation as failure, in *Logic and Databases,* H. Gallaire and J. Minker (eds.) Plenum Press, New York, 1978, 293–322.

2.16. K. Apt, H. Blair, and A. Walker, Towards a theory of declarative knowledge, Preprints of Workshop on Foundations of Deductive Databases and Logic Programming, J. Minker (ed.), Washington, DC, August 1986, 547–623.

2.17. T. C. Przymusinski, On the semantics of stratified deductive databases, Preprints of Workshop on Foundations of Deductive Databases and Logic Programming, J. Minker (ed.), Washington, DC, August 1986, 433–43.

3

Improving the Proplog Interpreter

We return here to the top-down Proplog interpreter, *establishtd,* and look at two ways to make it more efficient. Because we deal with the top-down interpreter almost exclusively from here on, we shorten its name to *establish*. Recall the function as we left it:

```
type
        symbol = array [1..20] of char;

        symbollist = ↑symlistrec;

        symlistrec = record
                        SYM: symbol;
                        REST: symbollist
                     end;

        clauserec = record
                       HEAD: symbol;
                       BODY: symbollist
                    end;

        clausearray = array [1..MAXCLAUSES] of clauserec;

function establish(GOALLIST: symbollist): boolean;
    var I: integer;
    begin
      if isempty(GOALLIST) then return(true);
      for I := 1 to MAXCLAUSES do
        if CLAUSE[I].HEAD = first(GOALLIST) then
          if establish(copycat(CLAUSE[I].BODY, rest(GOALLIST))) then
            return(true);
      return(false)
    end;
```

We have modified the program slightly by introducing functions to manipulate the list of goals: *isempty*, *first*, and *rest*. Function *isempty* tests if the goal list is empty, *first* returns the first symbol on the goal list, and *rest* returns the goal list minus its first *symlistrec* record. These functions will make one of our optimizations clearer. Their implementation here should be obvious. Next we update the representation of clauses slightly. The parser for Proplog programs outlined in Section 2.1.2.1 used a symbol table to keep track of propositions. This data structure is useful for other reasons. Recall that a symbol table stores the character strings that are the symbols for the propositions. In any record representing a symbol in a clause, we use the index of the symbol in the symbol table, instead of the symbol itself.

3.1. Indexing Clauses

The most glaring inefficiency in *establish* is that the **for**-loop searches through *every* clause in the program. Only clauses that have heads the same as the first propositional symbol in GOALLIST need to be considered. Hence we use the first symbol in GOALLIST to index into the clauses that match. That is, given a symbol, we want to find quickly all and only those clauses with that symbol as head.

An easy way to support such indexing is to associate all the clauses that have the same head symbol with the symbol table entry for that symbol. We add another field, CLAUSES, to each symbol table entry and use it to anchor a list of the Proplog clauses having that symbol as HEAD. Now, given the index of a symbol, we have immediate access to the list of program clauses with that head.

```
type
    clauselist = ↑clauserec;

    clauserec = record
                    HEAD: symbol;
                    BODY: symbollist;
                    NXTCLAUSE: clauselist
                end;

    symbollist = ↑symlistrec;

    symlistrec = record
                     SYM: symtabindex;
                     REST: symbollist
                 end;

    symtabrec = record
                    NAME: symbol;
                    CLAUSES: clauselist
                end;

    symtabindex = 1..MAXSYMS;

var SYMTAB: array [symtabindex] of symtabrec;
```

EXAMPLE 3.1: Figure 3.1 shows how the clauses:

```
p :- q, r.
q :- s.
q :- t.
s.
```

are organized by a symbol table. Note that the numbers in HEAD and SYM fields are indices into the table. □

Here is the revised interpreter using clause indexing:

```
function establish(GOALLIST: symbollist): boolean;
    var NEXTCL: clauselist;
    begin
      if isempty(GOALLIST) then return(true);
      NEXTCL := SYMTAB[first(GOALLIST)].CLAUSES;
      while NEXTCL <> nil do
        begin
          if establish(copycat(NEXTCL↑.BODY, rest(GOALLIST))) then
          return(true);
          NEXTCL := NEXTCL↑.NXTCLAUSE
        end;
      return(false)
    end;
```

This program directly accesses the list of clauses that have the same head as the first goal on GOALLIST. It uses the variable NEXTCL to step through the list. Thus *first* must return a symbol table index, and we can eliminate the check for equality of the first goal and the clause head. In fact, the HEAD field of elements of type *clauserec* is never referenced and could be omitted.

3.2. Lazy Concatenation

The other improvement involves the concatenation of the BODY of a rule with GOALLIST. We wish to avoid copying the first list of symbols (the body of a rule) when constructing the new goal list. The idea is to represent GOALLIST as a list of lists of goals. It is then very easy to add a new sublist, but it is slightly more difficult to get the first goal or the rest of the list. We will call such a list a *lazy list*. The actual representation is slightly more complicated. In the current *establish* routine we compute the *rest* of GOALLIST before performing the concatentation.

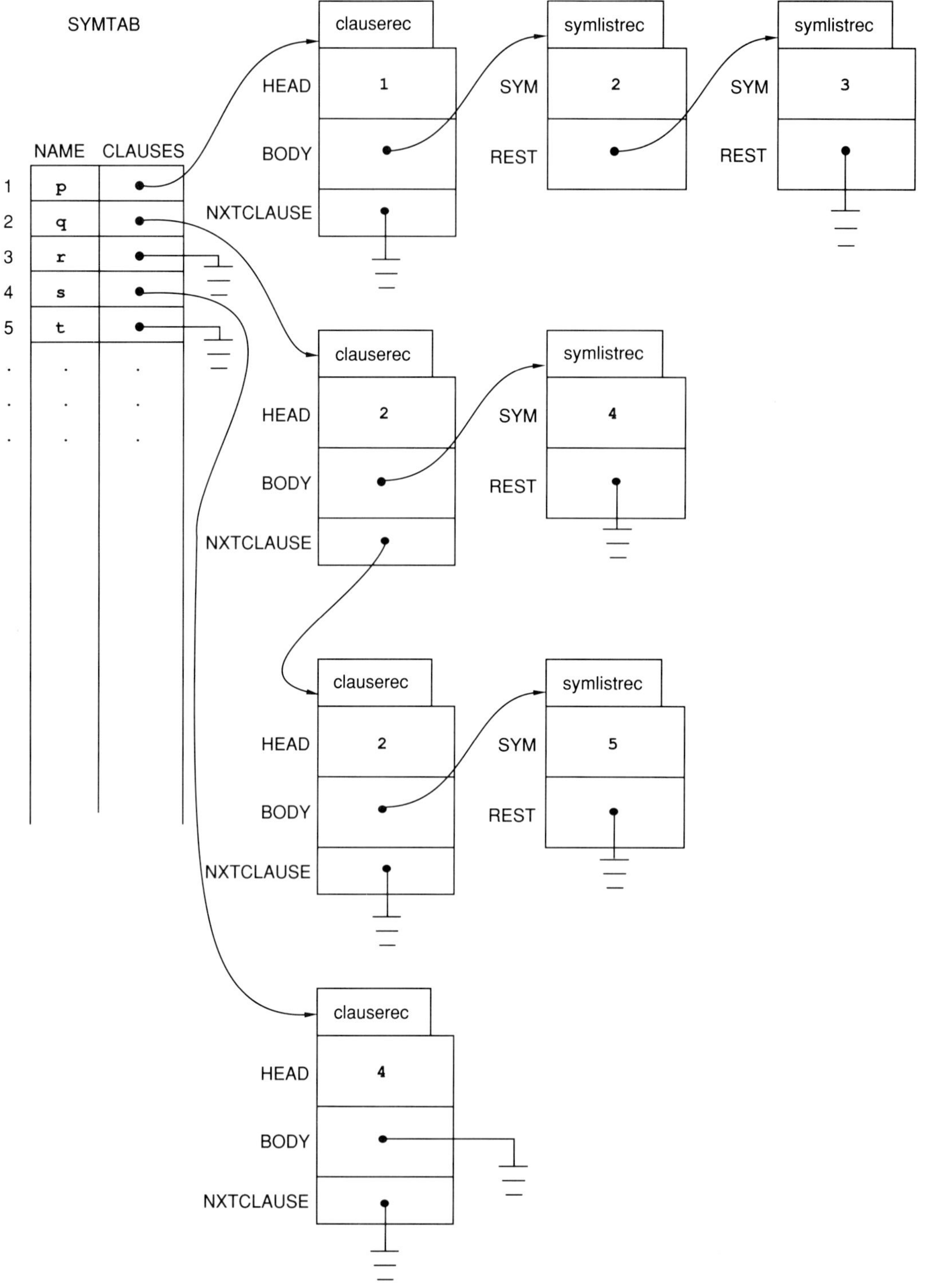
SYMTAB
NAME CLAUSES
1 p
2 q
3 r
4 s
5 t
clauserec
HEAD 1
BODY
NXTCLAUSE
symlistrec
SYM 2
REST
symlistrec
SYM 3
REST
clauserec
HEAD 2
BODY
NXTCLAUSE
symlistrec
SYM 4
REST
clauserec
HEAD 2
BODY
NXTCLAUSE
symlistrec
SYM 5
REST
clauserec
HEAD 4
BODY
NXTCLAUSE

Figure 3.1

With lazy lists we keep that entire list and ignore the first symbol on later access. The goal list that a lazy list represents is obtained by concatenating the first, or front, sublist with the *rest*'s of the remaining sublists.

EXAMPLE 3.2: The lazy list L in Figure 3.2 represents the goal list **h, i, e, f, b, c**. For clarity, it shows actual proposition symbols, rather than indices into the symbol table. □

The empty list is represented by a single empty sublist. We also stipulate that the first sublist in a lazy list is never empty unless the represented list is empty.

The types for lazy lists are:

```
type
      llist = ↑llnode;

      llnode = record
                  LLREM: llist;
                  LLFRONT: symbollist
               end;
```

The revised version of *establish,* using lazy lists for the goal list, is:

```
function establish(GOALLIST: llist): boolean;
    var NEXTCL: clauselist;
      NEWGL: llist;
    begin
      if isempty(GOALLIST) then return(true);
      NEXTCL := SYMTAB[first(GOALLIST)].CLAUSES;
      while NEXTCL <> nil do
        begin
          NEWGL := lconc_rest(NEXTCL↑.BODY, GOALLIST);
          if establish(NEWGL) then return(true);
          NEXTCL := NEXTCL↑.NXTCLAUSE
        end;
      return(false)
    end;
```

This version uses the following functions and procedure to manipulate lazy lists.

```
{Is the list empty?}
function isempty(GL: llist): boolean;
    begin
      return(GL↑.LLFRONT = nil)
    end;

{return the first symbol of the lazy list}
function first(GL: llist): symbol;
    begin
      return(GL↑.LLFRONT↑.SYM)
    end;
```

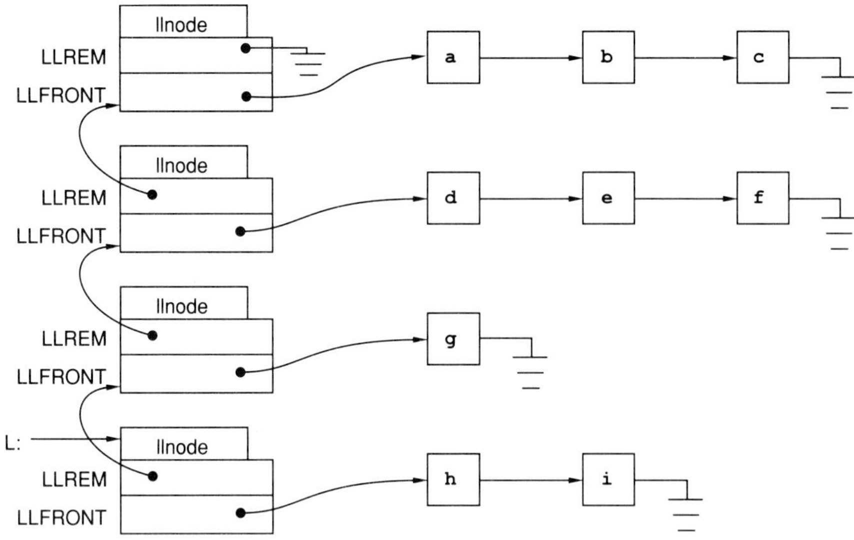

Figure 3.2

```
{lazily concatenate BODY with the rest of the lazy list GL, returning
 the result}
function lconcat_rest(BODY: symbollist; GL: llist): llist;
    var RESULT: llist;
    begin
      new(RESULT);
      if BODY = nil then lrest(GL, RESULT)
      else
        begin
          RESULT↑.LLFRONT := BODY;
          RESULT↑.LLREM := GL
        end;
      return(RESULT)
    end;

{set the llnode that RESULT references to represent the same list
 as LL with the first symbol removed}
procedure lrest(LL: llist; RESULT: llist);
    begin
      if LL = nil then RESULT↑.LLFRONT := nil
      else if LL↑.LLFRONT↑.REST = nil then lrest(LL↑.LLREM, RESULT)
      else
        begin
          RESULT↑.LLFRONT := LL↑.LLFRONT↑.REST;
          RESULT↑.LLREM := LL↑.LLREM
        end
    end;
```

EXAMPLE 3.3: Consider a Proplog program with clauses:

```
p :- r, s, t.
r :- u.
u.
s :- w, x.
```

and the goal list:

```
p, q.
```

Figure 3.3 shows the lazy list representing the initial value of GOALLIST, which we denote GOALLIST-1. The initial call to *establish* will recursively call itself on the body of:

```
p :- r, s, t.
```

lazily concatenated with the rest of GOALLIST-1 to give **r, s, t, q.** The new goal list, GOALLIST-2, is given in Figure 3.4. Figure 3.5 shows GOALLIST-3, which is **u** concatenated with the rest of GOALLIST-2. GOALLIST-3 is **u, s, t, q.** The head of this list is resolved away by the fact **u**, so the *llnode* that represents GOALLIST-4 (Figure 3.6) has its LLFRONT field pointing into the front of a previous lazy list. Figure 3.7 shows GOALLIST-5, the argument to the fifth invocation of *establish*, which represents the goal list **w, x, t, q.** □

Observe that *establish* never creates any new *symlistrec* records, as it used to do with *copycat*. All the LLFRONT fields of *llnode*s point into the representation of the program. There is an additional space optimization possible. We allocate space for the header of the new lazy list of goals, NEWGL, in *lconc_rest,* but we do not reclaim the space for that *llnode*. An *llnode* ceases to be referenced once the invocation of *establish* that created it returns. If we wanted, we could use an explicit stack of *llnode* records to manage this space.

Is the lazy version an improvement over the original implementation of concatenation? As is the case with most "optimizations," there are situations in which the "unoptimized" program is better; we just hope that these situations are not very likely. In this case it is cheaper to do the concatenation of two lists but more expensive to get the first element from the list and to get the tail of the list. All we are doing is postponing work. Why might this be a good idea? We make it cheaper now (putting new propositions on the goal list) at a cost of making it more expensive later (removing them). The point is, with the search strategy *establish* uses, postponed work might not have to be done. Because a particular search path can fail,

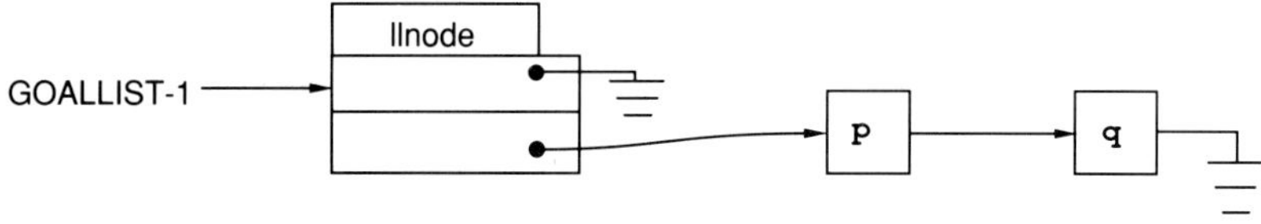

Figure 3.3

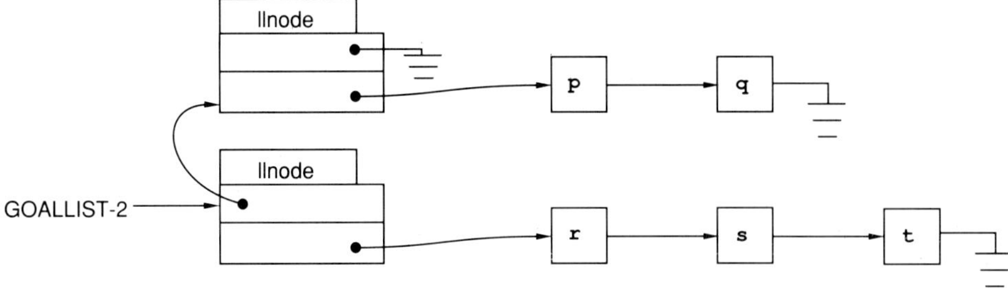

Figure 3.4

the program may never get to the point of removing some items on the list. If it spent a lot of time copying items to put them on the new goal list, that time is all wasted. Lazy concatenation is the first example of what we will call *The Procrastination Principle:* "Never do now what you can put off until later." The reason that procrastination is a good idea in the area of nondeterministic search is that "later" may never come.

[The Procrastination Principle reminds us of a story told by an old Iraqi: A man was charged by the king with treason and sentenced to death. Pleading with the king to spare his life, the man promised within a year to teach the king's horse to talk. If the horse could talk at the end of the year, the man would be freed; otherwise the man would be put to death. The king agreed, and the poor man went off to teach the horse to talk. A little later, in the king's stables, a stable hand came up to the man and asked why in the world he made such a deal. He knew that there was no way to make a horse really talk. "Of course," the man replied, "but who knows about next year? Maybe by then I'll be dead, or maybe the king will be dead, or maybe the horse will talk."

Is that "Maybe my path will fail, or maybe the user will do an interrupt before I get there, or maybe the machine will crash"?]

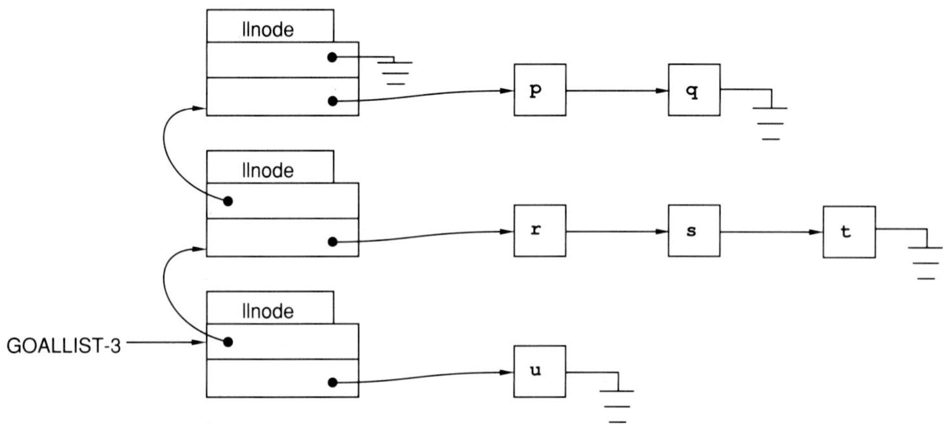

Figure 3.5

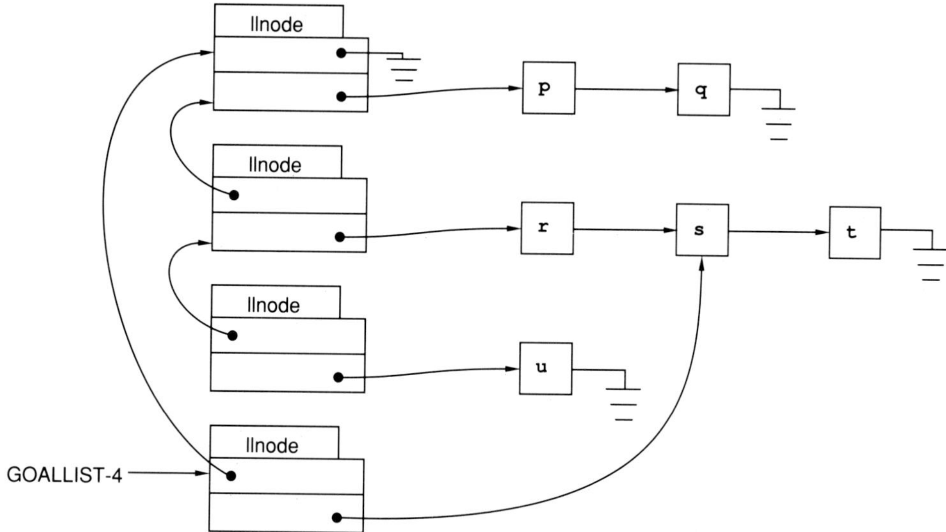

Figure 3.6

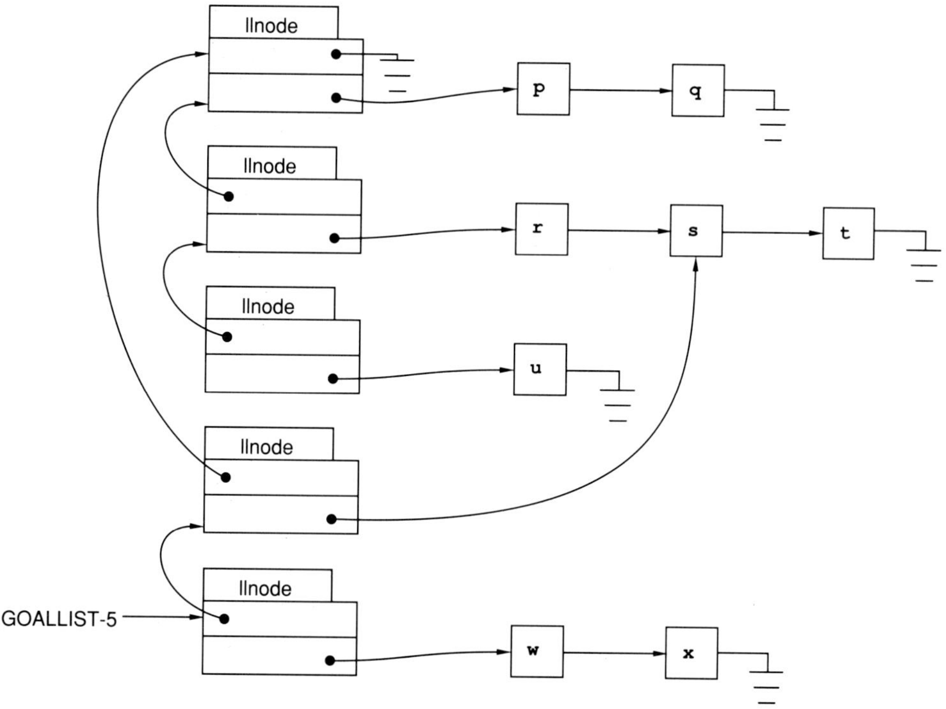

Figure 3.7

With respect to this particular implementation of lazy lists there is room for disagreement. There is a down side to the possibility in a nondeterministic situation that "tomorrow may never come": Tomorrow could come many times! By postponing work in a depth-first tree search to points lower in the tree, the program may have to do the postponed work many times, once for each of many descendents of the node at which it was postponed. We will continue to discuss these issues as we optimize the interpreters for Datalog and Prolog.

We encourage the reader to reread the introduction to Part I to see if it makes sense yet.

3.3. EXERCISES

3.1. As pointed out at the end of Section 3.1, clause indexing eliminates the need for clause heads. Thus, we can remove the HEAD field from type *clauserec*. Can we also remove the NAME field from type *symtabrec*?

3.2. Give a version of *establish* where facts are represented by tagging propositions in the symbol table.

3.3. Use clause indexing to produce a more efficient version of *establishbu*.

3.4. Using the interpreter with lazy lists, draw the successive values of GOALLIST, when *establish* is called with goal **p** and the program is:

```
p :- q.
p :- r, s.
r.
s :- t.
t.
```

3.5. What structure does *llrest* return as RESULT when called with GOALLIST-5 from Figure 3.6 as LL? What result is obtained if we call *llrest* again with that value for RESULT as LL?

3.6. Give versions of function *isempty* and procedure *lconcat_rest* when an *llnode* is interpeted as being LLFRONT concatenated with the list that LLREM represents, with no implicit *rest* assumed.

3.4. COMMENTS AND BIBLIOGRAPHY

The development in this chapter is preliminary to the more complex cases we will see later in the book. The purpose has been to introduce the "Procrastination Principle" and to introduce the kinds of optimizations that will show up later. Were the final goal a theorem prover for propositional Horn logic, an entirely different program structure would be appropriate.

The general structure of the top-down interpreter is that of a general search program. For example, a program to search a maze would have a similar structure.

Also related is recursive-descent parsing. The formulation of a simple Prolog interpreter given in [3.1] shows the simple recursive nature of its control. Campbell [3.2] is a collection of papers on aspects of Prolog implementation.

3.1. M. Nilsson, The world's shortest Prolog interpreter? in [3.2], 87–92.

3.2. J. A. Campbell, *Implementations of Prolog,* Ellis Horwood, Chichester, England, 1984.

PART II

Datalog and Predicate Logic

Proplog is clearly a very limited programming language. A traditional procedural programming language has two basic concepts: expressions involving variables and control flow. Proplog does not even contain a counterpart to variables. All it contains is control flow. In a language that supports only control flow, all that can be said about program behavior is whether control gets to a certain point. This is the information provided by the final "yes" or "no" answer of a Proplog program. To extend Proplog as a programming language, we must introduce some counterpart to the program variable.

Proplog is limited to expressing only control flow because the basic elements correspond to complete, concrete (English) statements; Proplog does not deal with the substructure of those statements. In Proplog we can state relationships only on an individual-by-individual basis—every statement is particular. It provides no way to make general statements about classes of individuals, because its semantics has no concept of such a class, only of a true or false sentence. Proplog can express, "If Maria has taken Introduction to Computer Science, then Maria has satisfied the introductory programming requirement" and "If Hector has taken Introduction to Computer Science, then Hector has satisfied the introductory programming requirement," but it cannot express, "Anyone who has taken Introduction to Computer Science has satisfied the introductory programming requirement." The last sentence captures the requirement more accurately than we can in Proplog. It is not possible to write down all the sentences expressing the relationship between the course and requirement for every student who might ever major in computer science. We seek a system in which we can make such general statements. To express the general statement in logic, we need to give a meaning to the word *anyone*. This requirement entails both a syntactic and a corresponding semantic extension to the logic.

If we had "templates" for propositions that could be filled in with particular words to yield various specific propositions, we could construct a single expression that stands for multiple propositional formulas. The syntax we develop can be understood as being based on patterns and templates. Templates, representing "parameterized" propositional statements, are called *predicates*, and the logic based on them is *predicate logic*. The parameters, called *logical variables*, serve to tie together several predicates in a single formula. The semantics that underlie this predicate logic is based on a set of individuals and relations among these individuals.

In Chapter 4, we develop this abstraction of Proplog into a more powerful language, Datalog. The interpreter for Datalog will be more complex because of the matching it has to do between predicates with logical variables. It must be able to match two templates to determine whether there is any way to fill in the parameters of both so that they become identical. The control structure for the interpreter will be the same as for the top-down interpreter for Proplog. Also, Datalog behaves more like a programming language than Proplog because it can return values as answers to queries, not just "yes" and "no." We chose the name Datalog because of its connection with database query languages, which we explore at the end of Chapter 4.

Chapter 5 follows the same line of development for Datalog and predicate logic as Chapter 2 did for Proplog and propositional logic. It begins with a logic that provides a formal semantics for Datalog. It extends that logic to full predicate logic, which includes predicates with logical variables and formulas with quantifiers. Those enhancements allow us to assert that a formula is true for all individuals or for some individuals. The next topic is *unification*, which allows the resolution rule to be extended to predicate logic. Unification is the formalization of the matching operation that the Datalog interpreter uses. The process of unification determines whether two different parameterized templates may, under some substitution for the parameters, actually become the same. The chapter concludes with a refutation procedure for predicate logic Horn clauses, which turns out to be the Datalog interpreter in disguise.

In Chapter 6, we optimize the Datalog interpreter from Chapter 4. The central data abstraction for the interpreter is the *substitution*, which tells how parameters are to be filled in templates. Considering Datalog as a programming language, the substitution associates program variables with their values. Substitutions are created by the matching procedure and applied to a goal list. Because applying a substitution changes the goal list, considerable copying is involved in the initial interpreter in order to preserve the state for backtracking. The first optimizations reduce the cost of copying the goal list in order to apply a substitution. Later optimizations concentrate on representing substitutions so they can be manipulated and searched more rapidly.

4

Computing with Predicate Logic

As you play with Proplog and try to solve problems with it, you will quickly find that it is quite a restricted language. In these chapters we explore some ways in which it is limited, and we develop a more powerful language, Datalog, that can represent complicated problems more easily. Datalog provides us with parameterized versions of Proplog clauses, and hence a greatly enhanced expressiveness. The first section develops Datalog clauses as "templates" for Proplog clauses. The first interpreter for Datalog is thus just the top-down Proplog interpreter: we fill in the Datalog templates to get Proplog clauses, then proceed to solve a goal as in Proplog. The second section shows how delaying the filling in produces an interpreter tailored for Datalog that backtracks less than the Proplog interpreter. The third section presents that interpreter in more detail. The key operation in it is matching one parameterized proposition, or *literal,* against another to determine the minimum amount of filling in needed for a clause to satisfy a subgoal. We then see how a Datalog interpreter can produce values as answers to a query; we also look at more examples and consider the semantics of Datalog informally. The chapter concludes with procedural extensions to Datalog and a digression into the connection between Datalog and relational database query languages.

4.1. Why Proplog Is Too Weak

As an example of some of the problems with Proplog, we return to the computer science requirements. Recall that the way we use the rules representing those requirements is to add someone's (such as Maria Marcatello's) transcript as facts. We can then ask a yes-no question concerning Maria's graduation status. What if we wanted to represent the status of several students in the same Proplog program? We might represent Maria's transcript as distinct from Hector's transcript by giving each a separate set of facts that encode who has taken which course. For example, Maria's transcript could be represented by the following facts:

```
introI_maria.
introII_maria.
compOrg_maria.
advProg_maria.
theory_maria.
opSys_maria.
arch_maria.
progLang_maria.
research_maria.
calcA_maria.
calcB_maria.
calcC_maria.
linAlg_maria.
absAlg_maria.
finStructI_maria.
stat_maria.
digSys_maria.
physicsI_maria.
physicsII_maria.
```

Then we would represent Hector's transcript as, say:

```
introCS_hector.
advProg_hector.
compOrg_hector.
calcI_hector.
calcII_hector.
```

We have distinguished the transcripts: a fact that says that a course was taken also says who took it. But what about the rules? We give some of those rules to recall their form:

```
csReq :- basicCS, mathReq, advancedCS, engReq, natSciReq.
basicCS :- introReq, compOrg, advProg, theory.
introReq :- introCS.
introReq :- introI, introII.
mathReq :- calcReq, algReq, finiteReq.
calcReq :- basicCalc, advCalc.
basicCalc :- calcI, calcII.
basicCalc :- calcA, calcB, calcC.
basicCalc :- honorsCalcI, honorsCalcII.
      .
      .
      .
```

But now the old rules will not work. To work, they also must be "personalized." In this case we need two sets of rules—one set personalized for Maria and one set for Hector, as follows:

```
csReq_maria :- basicCS_maria, mathReq_maria, advancedCS_maria,
   engReq_maria, natSciReq_maria.
basicCS_maria :- introReq_maria, compOrg_maria,
   advProg_maria, theory_maria.
introReq_maria :- introCS_maria.
introReq_maria :- introI_maria, introII_maria.
mathReq_maria :- calcReq_maria, algReq_maria, finiteReq_maria.
calcReq_maria :- basicCalc_maria, advCalc_maria.
basicCalc_maria :- calcI_maria, calcII_maria.
basicCalc_maria :- calcA_maria, calcB_maria, calcC_maria.
basicCalc_maria :- honorsCalcI_maria, honorsCalcII_maria.
      .
      .
      .
```

and:

```
csReq_hector :- basicCS_hector, mathReq_hector, advancedCS_hector,
   engReq_hector, natSciReq_hector.
basicCS_hector :- introReq_hector, compOrg_hector,
   advProg_hector, theory_hector.
introReq_hector :- introCS_hector.
introReq_hector :- introI_hector, introII_hector.
mathReq_hector :- calcReq_hector, algReq_hector, finiteReq_hector.
calcReq_hector :- basicCalc_hector, advCalc_hector.
basicCalc_hector :- calcI_hector, calcII_hector.
basicCalc_hector :- calcA_hector, calcB_hector, calcC_hector.
basicCalc_hector :- honorsCalcI_hector, honorsCalcII_hector.
      .
      .
      .
```

The modified rules do what we want. For example, we can ask the query:

```
csReq_maria, basicCS_hector.
```

These goals will be true if Maria has satisfied all her CS requirements and Hector has satisfied his basic CS requirements.

We can handle the requirements for all the CS majors. For each student, we add his or her transcript, with the name appended to the standard proposition symbol for each course taken. Then we have to add a personalized set of rules, taking our standard set of "generic" rules and suffixing the student's name to each proposition symbol. To produce a personalized set of rules easily, we could have a file of the rules in a special form, with, say, '_XX' appended to the end of each symbol. We could then use a text editor to replace all occurrences of the string '_XX' by say, '_**carlo**' to personalize a set of rules for a student Carlo. The editing makes it relatively painless to add a new set of personalized rules. Armed with a good text editor and patience, we can represent many more problems in Proplog.

To be a little more organized about the whole thing, we set some conventions. Rather than using the proposition symbol, **csReq_maria**, let's use **csReq(maria)**. The parentheses delimit both ends of the "personalizing" string and look better anyway. For the moment, the parentheses are considered just other characters in a proposition symbol. We use this notation to store Maria's transcript:

```
introI(maria).
introII(maria).
compOrg(maria).
advProg(maria).
        .
        .
        .
physicsII(maria).
```

The rule templates have similar syntax:

```
mathReq(XX) :- calcReq(XX), algReq(XX), finiteReq(XX).
```

If we use a text editor to personalize a set of rules for each new student's transcript, over time we collect many rules. Rather than using an editor to personalize a complete set of rules in advance, the Proplog interpreter can personalize rules on demand. It just creates special rules when they are needed to evaluate a goal list. When it finishes, the interpreter can discard the personalized rules. All we need to keep permanently is the rule templates. Say we are given the following goal:

```
basicCalc(hector), csReq(maria), natSciReq(carlo).
```

This query asks whether these three students have satisfied the three different requirements. How does the interpreter evaluate this query, given all the necessary transcripts but only the one set of rule templates? One simple solution is to generate three complete sets of personalized rules immediately, then proceed with solving the goals.

We can delay generating personalized rules even longer. We do not generate a personalized rule until it is actually needed to solve the first goal in the current goal list. What does it take to delay the rule personalization until then? Consider how the interpreter could evaluate **basicCS(hector)**: It begins with the goal list containing just **basicCS(hector)**. It needs a clause whose head is

basicCS(hector), but we have stored only rule templates. One of these templates is:

```
basicCS(XX) :- introReq(XX), compOrg(XX), advProg(XX), theory(XX).
```

If it replaces **XX** by **hector** in the head of this rule, the head matches the current goal. By making that replacement in the whole rule, the interpreter generates the personalized rule:

```
basicCS(hector) :- introReq(hector), compOrg(hector),
   advProg(hector), theory(hector).
```

The personalized rule is composed of propositions (albeit with funny syntax) and can be treated as a Proplog rule to solve the initial goal. Thus the new goal list, on which the interpreter continues processing, is:

```
introReq(hector), compOrg(hector), advProg(hector),
theory(hector).
```

The next goal is **introReq(hector)**. The interpreter can do the same thing—finding first the rule template:

```
introReq(XX) :- introCS(XX).
```

personalizing it to:

```
introReq(hector) :- introCS(hector).
```

and using that Proplog rule to generate a new goal list:

```
introCS(hector), compOrg(hector), advProg(hector), theory(hector).
```

The next goal, **introCS(hector)**, is a fact from Hector's transcript, so it is matched directly and removed. And computation continues. With this evaluation strategy, we have delayed the generation of the personalized rules until they are actually needed.

4.2. Pasta or Popovers

This section presents a more detailed problem along the same lines as the last example. We have some cooking ingredients—flour, eggs, salt, milk, and oil—and recipes for pasta and popovers. We want to know if we have enough ingredients to make, say, three batches of pasta and five of popovers.

Consider first how we might determine if we can make a certain number of batches of pasta. We have recipes for different numbers of batches of pasta, which we can express as Proplog rules.

```
onePasta :- oneCupFlour, oneEgg, twoTblspWater, oneTspSalt, oneTspOil.
twoPasta :- twoCupFlour, twoEgg, fourTblspWater, twoTspSalt, twoTspOil.
threePasta :- threeCupFlour, threeEgg, sixTblspWater,
   threeTspSalt, threeTspOil.
fourPasta :- fourCupFlour, fourEgg, eightTblspWater,
   fourTspSalt, fourTspOil.
```

We also need clauses to see if our stock of ingredients suffices for the amounts required by the recipe.

```
oneCupFlour :- haveOneCupFlour.
oneCupFlour :- haveTwoCupFlour.
oneCupFlour :- haveThreeCupFlour.
twoCupFlour :- haveTwoCupFlour.
twoCupFlour :- haveThreeCupFlour.
      .
      .
      .
```

and so on for other ingredients. For water, any amount is available:

```
oneTblspWater.
twoTblspWater.
threeTblspWater.
fourTblspWater.
      .
      .
      .
```

We add to these rules facts for the amounts of all ingredients on hand:

```
haveThreeCupFlour.
haveTwoEgg.
haveFourTspSalt.
haveThreeTspOil.
```

Now, how about the popovers? We can give a rule:

```
onePopover :- twoEgg, oneCupMilk, oneCupFlour, oneTspSalt, oneTblspOil.
```

for a single batch, and other rules for multiple batches. The "sufficiency" rules have to be augmented to handle teaspoon-tablespoon conversions on oil.

Some constraints on the problem are not captured in these rules and facts, however. If we pose the query:

```
twoPasta, onePopover.
```

we get a yes answer even though there are not enough ingredients, because the same ingredients are counted toward each recipe. Here, the rules:

```
oneEgg :- haveTwoEgg.
```

and:

```
twoEgg :- haveTwoEgg.
```

are both used to satisfy the two goals, consuming 150% of the eggs on hand. We might try to distinguish the ingredients as to what recipe they go toward, and then apportion the amount on hand between the two recipes. Say:

```
threeCupPasFlour :- threeCupFlour.

twoCupPasFlour :- threeCupFlour.
oneCupPopFlour :- threeCupFlour.

oneCupPasFlour :- threeCupFlour.
twoCupPopFlour :- threeCupFlour.

threeCupPopFlour :- threeCupFlour.
```

Even then we have not solved the problem, however, because we have no way to constrain the clauses to be invoked only in the groups just given.

Proplog has proved inadequate for this example in several ways:

1. There is a lot of tedious typing of clauses that are nearly the same.
2. All the clauses have a great deal of duplicated information, saying two of some measure is more than three of that measure.
3. We cannot keep our noodles apart from our muffins.

Take item 1. No reader familiar with computerized text editors really thinks we typed all the pasta recipe's clauses individually. We started with something like:

```
XXPasta :- XXCupFlour, XXEgg, YYTblspWater, XXTspSalt, XXTspOil.
```

duplicated it four times with the editor, and then replaced '**XX**' and '**YY**' with the appropriate amounts in each clause. As with the requirements example, we can make the interpreter do the editing. We write the rule template:

```
pasta(XX) :- cupFlour(XX), egg(XX), tblspWater(YY),
   tspSalt(XX), tspOil(XX).
```

and modify the interpreter to fill in values as needed. There is a little information that we held in our heads about what numbers can go in for **XX** and **YY** and that is needed to fill in values correctly. By changing the rule template slightly and adding more facts, we can represent that extra information explicitly.

```
pasta(XX) :-
   cupFlour(XX), egg(XX), tblspWater(YY), twice(XX, YY),
   tspSalt(XX), tspOil(XX).

twice(one, two).
twice(two, four).
twice(three, six).
twice(four, eight).
twice(five, ten).
      .
      .
      .
twice(ten, twenty).
```

This rule, along with the set of **twice** facts, stands for a large number of rules—any rule that can be obtained by substituting one of the numbers {**one**, **two**, . . ., **twenty**} consistently for the occurrences of **XX** and **YY**.

Until now we have assigned meaning not to clause templates but to their specialized versions. The templates are only syntactic conveniences. Now, however, we will start viewing clause templates as structured objects with their own meaning. We call such a clause template with placeholders in it a *Datalog clause*. The placeholder strings are called *logical variables*. The values, such as **one** and **two**, that replace the variables are *constants*. We distinguish variables from constants by beginning the former with uppercase letters. The result of replacing some or all the variables in a Datalog clause with values is a clause *instance*. The replacement process is called *instantiation*. A template for a single proposition, such as:

```
twice(XX, YY)
```

is a *literal*. Its *predicate name* or *predicate symbol* is **twice**. The variables **XX** and **YY** are the *arguments* of the literal. All the clauses with a given predicate name in their heads are collectively called the *predicate definition* for that predicate name. If all the variables in a Datalog clause have been replaced with constants, we call the instance a *ground* instance. The point we have been making through the last two examples is that a ground instance of a Datalog clause is essentially a Proplog clause. That identification is the basis for the formal semantics we give in Chapter 5.

The constants in the requirements example are {**one**, **two**, . . ., **twenty**}. Thus, one of the ground instances encoded in the last rule is:

```
pasta(two) :-
   cupFlour(two), egg(two), tblspWater(four), twice(two, four),
   tspSalt(two), tspOil(two).
```

Another is:

```
pasta(two) :-
   cupFlour(two), egg(two), tblspWater(one), twice(two, one),
   tspSalt(two), tspOil(two).
```

The second example might seem a trifle odd. Since twice two is not one, the rule here looks incorrect. But notice that the facts for **twice** do not include a fact **twice(two, one)**. This rule instance will never be used in a successful computation, because the subgoal **twice(two, one)** always fails. What happened is that we permitted extra rule instances over the Prolog case but then filtered them out using the **twice** facts. In this way we have encoded information that we had previously kept in our heads.

We also change the encoding of when the ingredients on hand suffice. But we still do not save much typing with:

```
cupFlour(one) :- haveCupFlour(one).
cupFlour(one) :- haveCupFlour(two).
cupFlour(one) :- haveCupFlour(three).
cupFlour(two) :- haveCupFlour(two).
cupFlour(two) :- haveCupFlour(three).
        .
        .
        .
```

In fact, we can do a little more. We use the same idea we used earlier, putting in a seemingly over-general Datalog rule, with appropriate facts to restrict which Proplog instances of it can succeed.

```
cupFlour(XX) :- haveCupFlour(XX).
cupFlour(XX) :- haveCupFlour(YY), less(XX, YY).

less(one, two).
less(one, three).
less(two, three).
less(one, four).
less(two, four).
less(three, four).
less(one, five).
less(two, five).
less(three, five).
less(four, five).
      .
      .
      .
less(nineteen, twenty).
```

The first rule says that we can satisfy a request for a certain amount of flour if we have exactly that amount of flour on hand. We can also satisfy a request if we have some amount on hand and the amount required is less than that amount. Now, having entered in all the **less** facts, we use them for all the ingredients:

```
cupMilk(XX) :- haveCupMilk(XX).
cupMilk(XX) :- haveCupMilk(YY), less(XX, YY).

egg(XX) :- haveEgg(XX).
egg(XX) :- haveEgg(YY), less(XX, YY).

tspSalt(XX) :- haveTspSalt(XX).
tspSalt(XX) :- haveTspSalt(YY), less(XX, YY).

tspOil(XX) :- haveTspOil(XX).
tspOil(XX) :- haveTspOil(YY), less(XX, YY).
```

We also add the facts about water and ingredients on hand, using the new format:

```
tblspWater(one).
tblspWater(two).
tblspWater(three).
tblspWater(four).
tblspWater(five).
      .
      .
      .
haveCupFlour(three).
haveEgg(two).
haveTspSalt(four).
haveTspOil(three).
```

Consider how a simple query just involving pasta is processed with this program in the new format:

```
pasta(two).
```

Again, we delay the creation of Proplog instances of Datalog rules until we need them. The first rule we need is one whose head matches **pasta(two)**. We can make an instance (but not a ground instance) of the **pasta(XX)** rule:

```
pasta(two) :-
   cupFlour(two), egg(two), tblspWater(YY), twice(two, YY),
   tspSalt(two), tspOil(two).
```

The variable **XX** has to be the constant **two**, so we substitute that constant into the rule. But what about **YY**? It can still be any constant at all. We could try each value for **YY** in turn, **one** through **twenty**. That strategy gives us as the next goal list:

```
cupFlour(two), egg(two), tblspWater(one), twice(two, one),
   tspSalt(two), tspOil(two).
```

We can go ahead and process the first goal, establishing it, then establishing **egg(two)**, then **tblspWater(one)**, which brings us to **twice(two, one)**. This goal clearly will fail, because the program has no such fact. The instance of the Datalog rule we chose will not serve to solve the original goal. We can try another instance of this rule—say with **XX** replaced by **two** and **YY** also replaced by **two**. The computation is the same up to the **twice** goal, which again fails. And so on, until we choose the right instance of the Datalog rule—the one with **XX** replaced by **two** and **YY** by **four**.

To avoid considering so many instances and doing all the backtracking, we can procrastinate on the choice of what to substitute for **YY** until we are forced to make that choice. We delay the choice for **YY** and just leave it as **YY** in the goal list; we will fill it in later. With this method, after we apply the instance of the rule with **XX** replaced by **two**, the goal list is:

```
cupFlour(two), egg(two), tblspWater(YY), twice(two, YY),
   tspSalt(two), tspOil(two).
```

We depart here from the Proplog interpreter to handle goal lists. The Proplog interpreter will not handle literals with variables, because they cannot be viewed as propositions. The next goal is **cupFlour(two)**. We have two rules for **cupFlour**, so we try the first:

```
cupFlour(XX) :- haveCupFlour(XX).
```

instantiate it to:

```
cupFlour(two) :- haveCupFlour(two).
```

and use it to get a new goal list:

```
haveCupFlour(two), egg(two), tblspWater(YY), twice(two, YY),
   tspSalt(two), tspOil(two).
```

Now we have to match **haveCupFlour(two)**, but we have no rule or fact that will provide the match. We go back to try the next **cupFlour** rule to match **cupFlour(two)**:

```
cupFlour(XX) :- haveCupFlour(YY), less(XX, YY).
```

We can instantiate this rule to:

```
cupFlour(two) :- haveCupFlour(YY), less(two, YY).
```

Applying this rule gives us the new goal list:

```
haveCupFlour(YY), less(two, YY), egg(two), tblspWater(YY),
   twice(two, YY), tspSalt(two), tspOil(two).
```

We have a slight problem here. We have used two instantiated rules to create this goal list—once when we first started processing the list and once just now. Looking at this goal list, we note that we have four occurrences of the variable **YY**, but they need not all be replaced by the same constant. Suppose we continued on, not worrying about the problem. We next use the fact **haveCupFlour(three)** to match the first goal. Thus the **YY** in the goal list must be replaced by **three**, so **three** replaces all occurrences of **YY** in the goal list. This replacement essentially gives us a ground instance of the **cupFlour** rule. We delayed the choice of what ground instance of the rule to use, until we knew what value to choose for **YY**. Now that we know that **three** is a good replacement for **YY**, we use it.

However, replacing all four occurrences of **YY** with **three** is clearly not correct. We should replace only the first two occurrences; they came from the same rule. The latter two came from another rule. We just happened to use the same variable name, **YY**, in two different rules. How can we handle this clash of variable names? One way is to say that no two rules can use the same variable names. This approach does not work in general, because the same rule might be used twice in constructing a goal list; each use should give rise to a separate instance of the rule.

Our solution is to change the variables uniformly to entirely new variables when we make a copy of a rule body to add to the goal list. In examples we will just add a sequential number to the end of the variable name. So, if we do this numbering consistently, we obtain the following goal list instead of the earlier one:

```
haveCupFlour(YY2), less(two, YY2), egg(two), tblspWater(YY1),
   twice(two, YY1), tspSalt(two), tspOil(two).
```

Now there is not the clash over the variable name **YY**; two different patterns keep the rule instances straight.

The evaluation continues. We need a rule or fact that matches **haveCup-Flour(YY2)**. The fact **haveCupFlour(three)** is the only candidate. So variable **YY2** should be replaced by **three**. We do so in the entire goal list and obtain the new goal list:

```
haveCupFlour(three), less(two, three), egg(two), tblspWater(YY1),
   twice(two, YY1), tspSalt(two), tspOil(two).
```

The same goal list would have resulted if we initially chose the instance of the rule for **cupFlour** with **XX** replaced by **two** and **YY** by **three**. The first goal matches a fact (we chose the replacement for **YY2** so that it would), leaving the goal list:

```
less(two, three), egg(two), tblspWater(YY1), twice(two, YY1),
   tspSalt(two), tspOil(two).
```

The next goal directly matches a fact, so it gets removed. The goal after that one, **egg(two)**, matches the first **egg** rule and the subgoal generated, **haveEgg(two)**, matches a fact. We proceed to **tblspWater(YY1)**. That goal matches all the **tblspWater** facts, so we consider them in order. First we match **tblspWater(YY1)** with the fact **tblspWater(one)** and replace **YY1** by **one**. We make that substitution in the entire goal list and obtain the new goal list:

```
twice(two, one), tspSalt(two), tspOil(two).
```

The goal **twice(two, one)** does not match any fact, so we go back and try the second **tblspWater** fact. That fact fails similarly, as does the third, so we eventually arrive at the fourth fact and replace **YY1** with **four**. The goal **twice(two, four)** then succeeds by directly matching a fact, and we can proceed to finish the computation.

Using Datalog to represent the information about the pasta recipe and availability of ingredients solves two of the problems cited at the beginning of the section. Most of the tedious typing is gone, and the information about one amount being less than another amount has been factored into one place. We still cannot split ingredients between pasta and popovers. We take up that problem shortly, but first we will present an interpreter for Datalog based on the processing strategy here.

4.3. A Simple Datalog Interpreter

What have we accomplished so far? We showed how to use a rule template with variables to represent many Proplog rules. These variables can be uniformly replaced by any constant to obtain an actual Proplog rule. These Proplog rule templates are Datalog rules, and a ground instance of a Datalog rule is a Proplog rule. We have also sketched an algorithm for evaluating queries in the presence of variables. The key in this algorithm is to use the control structure of the Proplog *establish* algorithm but to delay the actual choice of constants for variables in the Datalog rules as long as possible. If we start from the skeleton of the Proplog evaluation, the Datalog algorithm is as follows:

```
function establish(GOALLIST: litlist): boolean;
  var SUBS: subst;
    NEXTCL, CLAUSEINST: clauselist;
  begin
    if isempty(GOALLIST) then return(true);
    NEXTCL := SYMTAB[predsym(first(GOALLIST))].CLAUSES;
    while NEXTCL <> nil do
      begin
        CLAUSEINST := instance(NEXTCL);
        if match(CLAUSEINST↑.HEAD, first(GOALLIST), SUBS) then
          if establish(apply(SUBS, copycat2(CLAUSEINST↑.BODY,
                                            rest(GOALLIST)))) then
            return(true);
```

```
            NEXTCL := NEXTCL↑.NXTCLAUSE
        end;
      return(false)
    end;
```

This function uses a new data structure *(subst)*, four new functions *(predsym, instance, match*, and *apply)*, and a new version of the concatenation procedure. It also has literals, rather than proposition symbols, in the clauses and the goal list. A value of type *subst* represents a *substitution*, which is a set of pairs of variables and constants. Each pair is called a *replacement*. A substitution says which constants should be substituted for which variables. An example is:

```
{XX1 = two, YY2 = four}
```

Function *predsym* just extracts the predicate symbol (a symbol table index) from a literal. Function *instance* takes a rule and uniformly changes all the variables in it to new variables that have not been used before. It actually makes a copy of the rule, rather than modifying the program itself. Function *match* takes the head of a rule and a goal literal and does a comparison to determine what replacements are needed to make them match. If they cannot be made to match, the function returns **false**. If they can match, the function returns **true**, and it also returns (through its third argument) a substitution that contains replacements to make them match. Function *apply* takes a substitution and a goal list and makes all the appropriate replacements. It is like the "replace all" function of an editor.

The concatenation procedure, *copycat2*, makes a copy of its second argument, so that *apply* does not alter the current goal list when forming the next one. The unaltered goal list is needed for backtracking in case the recursive call with the new goal list fails. Since *instance* copies its argument, *copycat2* need not copy its first argument.

What exactly does *match* have to do? It takes two literals—one from the head of a clause and one that is the first goal in the goal list. Either can have variables. If it is called with the head **pasta(XX0)** and the goal **pasta(two)**, it must create the substitution {**XX0 = two**}, meaning that **XX0** should be replaced by **two**. If it compares clause head (actually fact) **haveCupFlour(three)** with goal **haveCupFlour(YY2)**, it must create the substitution {**YY2 = three**}. The question naturally arises as to whether it ever has to match two variables together, and, if so, what we would do then.

To see how variable-variable matching can occur, recall how we represented the information about water:

```
tblspWater(one).
tblspWater(two).
      .
      .
      .
```

There is a simpler way to represent this information. Just as we used patterns in rules, we can use them in facts. These **tblspWater** facts are a perfect opportunity to use a variable. Rather than having all the **tblspWater** facts explicitly, we have just one "fact template":

```
tblspWater(XX).
```

In a way completely analogous to rules, this template represents any propositional fact that can be obtained by substituting a constant for **XX**. Consider again the goal:

```
pasta(two).
```

but using this new definition of the water needs. Computation will be the same as in the last section up to the goal list:

```
tblspWater(YY1), twice(two, YY1), tspSalt(two), tspOil(two).
```

We match the fact **tblspWater(XX3)** (recall that we have to change all variables to new ones) with the next goal, **tblspWater(YY1)**. Now we have to match two variables. We want to indicate that we do not care what constant eventually replaces **XX3** and **YY1**, but the same constant must replace both. How can we represent this connection? By changing all occurrences of one variable to the other. Then, whatever happens later on, all those occurrences will get the same constant. So, at this point, we choose one variable to replace the other. We replace all occurrences of the variable **YY1** by the variable **XX3**, which is indicated by the substitution {**YY1 = XX3**}. Any later replacement of **XX3** will also change those positions that had **YY1**. The next goal list is:

```
twice(two, XX3), tspSalt(two), tspOil(two).
```

(It might seem as though we could just ignore this replacement, since **XX3** does not occur in the new goal list. However, the matching of two variables might occur between the head of a rule that contained a body with the same variable and a goal list with that variable. Since there could be several occurrences of each variable, the substitution is necessary in general.)

If we continue with the next goal, **twice(two, XX3)**, we quickly find that only **twice(two, four)** matches. Notice that in allowing variables to match variables, we delay the choice of what constant must be filled in. Delaying choices means less backing up and, in general, makes the algorithm faster. Delaying the instantiation of variables is another example of the Procrastination Principle.

With this discussion in mind, we must revise slightly our earlier description of a substitution. A substitution is a set of pairs, called replacements. The first component of each pair is a variable, and the second may be a constant or a variable. We give pseudocode for the match function:

```
function match(HEAD, GOAL: lit; var SUBS: subst): boolean;
    var I: integer;
    begin
      if predsym(HEAD) <> predsym(GOAL)
        then return(false); {wrong rule}
      SUBS := nil;
      for each argument I in HEAD do
        if argument(HEAD, I) is a variable then
          add replacement {argument(HEAD, I) = argument(GOAL, I)} to SUBS
        else if argument(GOAL, I) is a variable then
          add replacement {argument(GOAL, I) = argument(HEAD, I)} to SUBS
        else if argument(HEAD, I) <> argument(GOAL, I) then return(false);
      return(true)
    end;
```

This function steps through the corresponding arguments in the HEAD and GOAL literals, creating a replacement if at least one of them is a variable, but returning false if it encounters constants that do not agree. It assumes that two predicates with the same name but different numbers of arguments are represented as distinct entries in the symbol table. The function *argument* extracts the constant or variable at a given position in a literal. This *match* routine works for examples we have seen earlier, but it does not work in general. Consider the following example. We are matching head literal **e(XX, XX)** with goal literal **e(a, b)**. In this case *match* should return **false** because there is no choice for **XX** that makes the literals match. The version of the *match* routine here would return the substitution:

{**XX** = **a**, **XX** = **b**}

Once we have decided **XX** must be replaced by **a**, then other occurrences of **XX** in the head and goal should also be replaced by **a**. One way to ensure a uniform change is to apply every replacement to the rest of the goal and head literals. In this case *match* first constructs the replacement **XX** = **a**, then substitutes **a** for **XX** in the rest of the head, getting **e(a, a)**. When *match* moves to the second argument, it tries to match **a** against **b**, instead of **XX** against **b**. Since the two constants are not the same, matching fails. That change fixes this problem with repeated variables.

There is another minor problem. Consider matching **e(XX, XX)** with **e(YY, a)**. The improved algorithm would first create the substitution {**XX** = **YY**}, apply that substitution to both arguments, and move on to match **e(YY, YY)** and **e(YY, a)**. This match succeeds, and *match* returns the substitution {**XX** = **YY**, **YY** = **a**}. There is an order dependency here. When we apply this entire substitution to a goal list, we must consider the replacements in order. We must replace all **XX**'s by **YY**, and then replace all **YY**'s by **a**. Were we to apply the replacements in the other order, the goal list ends up containing **YY**'s, which should not be there. They should be **a**'s. When adding a new replacement to a substitution, *match* must apply the replacement to the right sides of the replacements already in the substitution.

In this example, it should construct the substitution {**XX** = **a**, **YY** = **a**} from {**XX** = **YY**} when adding the replacement **YY** = **a**. This substitution does not have an order dependency.

One final point. No substitution should include a replacement such as **XX** = **XX**. Clearly it is not necessary, and it could cause us problems later. (See Exercise 4.4.) An example where we might be tempted to construct such a replacement is in matching **e(XX, XX)** and **e(YY, YY)**. First *match* produces the replacement **XX** = **YY**, and the new head and goal **e(YY, YY)** and **e(YY, YY)**. Then it compares **YY** and **YY** and generates the replacement **YY** = **YY**.

The corrected *match* algorithm is:

```
function match(HEAD, GOAL: lit; var SUBS: subst): boolean;
    var I: integer;
    begin
      if predsym(HEAD) <> predsym(GOAL)
        then return(false); {wrong rule}
      SUBS := nil;
      for each argument I in HEAD do
        if argument(HEAD, I) is a variable then
          if argument(HEAD, I) and argument(GOAL, I) are the same variable then
            {do nothing, on to next arg}
          else
            add replacement {argument(HEAD, I) = argument(GOAL, I)} to SUBS
            and apply this replacement to all the arguments in HEAD and GOAL,
            and to the right sides of elements of SUBS
        else if argument(GOAL, I) is a variable then
          add replacement {argument(GOAL, I) = argument(HEAD, I)} to SUBS
          and apply this replacement to all the arguments in HEAD and GOAL,
          and to the right sides of elements of SUBS
        else if argument(HEAD, I) <> argument(GOAL, I) then return(false);
      return(true)
    end;
```

EXAMPLE 4.1: If we call *match* with literals:

e(a, XX, b, ZZ), e(a, YY, YY, WW)

the first arguments match, so no replacements are generated for them. Comparing second arguments, *match* generates the substitution:

{**XX** = **YY**}

and modifies the literals to:

e(a, YY, b, ZZ), e(a, YY, YY, WW)

Comparing **b** and **YY** makes the substitution:

{**XX** = **b**, **YY** = **b**}

and the literals:

e(a, b, b, ZZ), e(a, b, b, WW)

Matching the last arguments gives:

{**XX** = **b**, **YY** = **b**, **ZZ** = **WW**}

as the value returned for the substition. Both literals are now:

e(a, b, b, WW)

under this substitution. □

4.4. Separating Noodles from Muffins

Let's return to trying to automate (a small part of) our kitchen. The remaining problem is keeping separate the ingredients for our noodles and our muffins. As it now stands, with the program in Section 4.2, the same ingredients could go toward both recipes. The program does not capture the notion of consuming ingredients.

We can define a predicate **cannotMake** with two arguments: the first is the number of batches of pasta to make, and the second is the number of batches of popovers to make. It will be true if we cannot make the total number of batches. So, for example, **cannotMake(two, three)** is true if we do not have enough ingredients to make two batches of pasta and three of popovers. We also reformat the information on quantities needed for recipes and ingredients on hand:

```
cannotMake(NPasta, MPopovers) :-
        needs(pasta, Ingred, NPasta, NeedForPasta),
        needs(popovers, Ingred, MPopovers, NeedForPopovers),
        sum(NeedForPasta, NeedForPopovers, Needed),
        haveOnHand(Ingred, Amount),
        less(Amount, Needed).
```

Recall that a rule is true for every uniform substitution of constants for variables. To understand this rule, consider the case in which we do not have enough ingredients to make, say, two pasta and three popovers. There must be some ingredient for which the amount on hand is not enough. Therefore, the body of some instance of this rule is such that all the subgoals can be established. Perhaps the rule instance:

```
cannotMake(two, three) :-
        needs(pasta, cupFlour, two, two),
        needs(popovers, cupFlour, three, three),
        sum(two, three, five),
        haveOnHand(cupFlour, four),
        less(four, five).
```

obtained from the earlier instance by the substitution:

```
{NPasta = two,
 MPopovers = three,
 Ingred = cupFlour,
 NeedForPasta = two,
 NeedForPopovers = three,
 Needed = five,
 Amount = four}
```

can be used and each of the subgoals in the body can be established. Then, assuming that we define the predicates for the subgoals correctly, we will have shown that there is not enough flour to make our batches of pasta and popovers.

We now define the other predicates. The **needs** predicate is as follows:

```
needs(Food, Ingred, N, Needed) :-
        ingred(Food, M, Ingred),
        times(N, M, Needed).
```

This rule says that **N** batches of the food **Food** needs **Needed** amount of ingredient **Ingred**. That case holds if one batch of the food **Food** takes amount **M** of ingredient **Ingred** and **Needed** is **M** times **N**. The **ingred** predicate will store information on amounts for a single batch of a recipe, while **times** represents multiplication facts.

Now for the ingredients for one batch of each food. These amounts are defined by the facts:

```
ingred(pasta, one, cupFlour).
ingred(pasta, one, egg).
ingred(pasta, two, tblspWater).
ingred(pasta, one, tspSalt).
ingred(pasta, one, tspOil).

ingred(popover, two, egg).
ingred(popover, one, cupMilk).
ingred(popover, one, cupFlour).
ingred(popover, one, tspSalt).
ingred(popover, three, tspOil).
```

The same definition of **less** used in Section 4.2 works here. We still need to define **sum**:

```
sum(one, one, two).
sum(one, two, three).
sum(two, one, three).
sum(one, three, four).
     .
     .
     .
sum(twenty, twenty, forty).
```

and also **times**:

```
times(one, one, one).
times(one, two, two).
times(two, one, two).
times(one, three, three).
     .
     .
     .
times(twenty, twenty, fourHundred).
```

The reader might (or might not) want to put in some facts for **haveOnHand** and then trace the evaluation of the query **cannotMake(two, three)** using the *establish* algorithm. These definitions keep the ingredients separated. They do require, however, that we type in these arithmetic predicates, which is a pain. We will talk about this problem again in Section 4.8.2.

4.5. Answers

There are two basic limitations of Proplog. One is the limited type of problem we can represent. In Datalog, by allowing parameterized propositions, called *predicates,* we have greatly increased the variety of problems we can state. The other problem with Proplog is that we can ask only yes-no questions. Datalog gives us a way to solve that problem, too.

We can give the Datalog interpreter a goal list with a variable in it. What should the interpreter do with such a list? It could substitute each possible constant for the variable and try to establish each instance of the goal list so produced. Each time it succeeds in establishing such an instance, it could print out the constant it substituted for the variable. This approach allows us to get an answer (or many answers) from a Datalog program. As a very simple example, we can use the facts that we gave to define **less** in the pasta and popovers example. We start with the goal list:

```
less(two, X), less(X, four).
```

The interpreter first replaces **X** by **one**, obtaining:

```
less(two, one), less(one, four).
```

It then fails to to establish **less(two, one)**. Similarly, the substitution of **two** for **X** leads to failure. But replacing **X** by **three** yields:

```
less(two, three), less(three, four).
```

and this goal list can be established. The interpreter can then print out the substitution {**X** = **three**} that it used to create the winning goal list instance. It could then go back and try other substitutions to see if any allow the goal list to be established. In this case, of course, there are no more.

We now have a way of getting back an answer that is more than just yes or no. The goal list can be thought of as the command: "Give me the **X**'s that make this goal list true." Here that request asks for **X**'s such that **less(two, X)** and **less(x, four)** are both true. Used with an interpreter modified as just described, Datalog is much more like a traditional programming language in that we can ask it to compute a value as an answer and show it to us.

The interpreter need not try all substitutions exhaustively. In its current version it handles delayed variable instantiation in the goal list. Given a goal list with variables, the current version of *establish* will leave them as variables until a value for each is determined. The only problem is how to capture the replacements for those variables so that the interpreter can produce them when a goal list succeeds. One way is to add a "pseudoliteral," such as **$answer(XX, YY, ZZ)**, to the end of the initial goal list to capture replacements. The pseudoliteral includes each variable that appears in the rest of the goal list. Then *establish* will execute just as it does now, replacing **XX** in the **$answer** literal with whatever replaces it elsewhere. When (and if) *establish* reaches a goal list containing just an **$answer** literal, it prints out the values it finds there, rather than trying to solve the pseudoliteral as a goal. If no more answers are required, the invocation of *establish* that encountered the **$answer** literal returns **true** after printing. If more answers are sought, that invocation returns **false** after printing.

Let's trace such a computation for our earlier simple query, using **$answer** for answers. Starting with the initial goal list:

```
less(two, X), less(X, four).
```

we append an **$answer** pseudoliteral and obtain:

```
less(two, X), less(X, four), $answer(X).
```

upon which *establish* is called. The first invocation of *establish* matches the first goal, **less(two, X)**, against the program clauses (here just facts) and finds that **less(two, three)** is the first fact that matches. It substitutes the constant **three** for **X** in the goal list and gets:

```
less(three, four), $answer(three).
```

A recursive invocation of *establish* now takes the first goal, finds that it matches a fact, with no replacement of variables necessary, and produces a new goal list:

```
$answer(three).
```

The third invocation of *establish* intercepts this pseudogoal and prints out its arguments as bound under the accumulated substitutions. This response notifies the user that one answer is **X = three.**

Suppose we then have the third invocation of *establish* return **false** (to cause a search for more answers). Control passes back up to the second invocation, which looks for a new way to solve the first goal in the goal list:

```
less(three, four), $answer(three).
```

Finding none, control passes back to the initial invocation of *establish*, which seeks another match for:

```
less(two, X), less(X, four), $answer(X).
```

It finds that **less(two, four)** also matches the first goal. After replacing **X** by **four**, the initial invocation makes a recursive call with the goal list:

```
less(four, four), $answer(four).
```

Here the first goal cannot be established, so control passes back to the initial *establish* invocation to try the next value for **X**, **five**. This replacement, of course, leads to failure, just as the previous one did. The initial invocation of *establish* continues trying replacements for **X** up to **twenty**. None of those replacements succeeds, so the initial invocation halts. While only one answer was produced here, it is easy to see that the goal list:

```
less(three, Y), less(Y, six).
```

produces two different answers.

4.6. An Example of Recursion

Thus far we have presented a few simple examples of Datalog programs to introduce the ideas of parameterized propositions. It turns out, though, that we have developed quite a powerful interpreter. In this section we look at another example to see the kinds of problems that can be solved naturally in the Datalog framework.

As an interesting example, recall the predicate **less** from the last section and the recipe example. It was defined for pairs of names of numbers up to twenty. The way we defined it was to type in 190 facts—one fact for each pair of numbers, one to twenty, such that the first number is less than the second. Actually we did *not* type them in. We showed a few pairs and then used ellipses. Typing them all is a pain and it is easy to see what we meant. Is there another way we could define the same predicate **less** but not have to do so much typing? The answer, of course, is yes. First define a predicate **next**:

```
next(one, two).
next(two, three).
next(three, four).
next(four, five).
     .
     .
     .
next(nineteen, twenty).
```

(Much less typing, though still a lot.) Using this definition, we can define **less**:

```
less(Lo, Hi) :- next(Lo, Hi).
less(Lo, Hi) :- next(Lo, NextOne), less(NextOne, Hi).
```

We understand the first rule as saying that the number **Lo** is less than the number **Hi** if the next number after **Lo** is **Hi**. That statement is certainly true.

The second rule says that the number **Lo** is less than the number **Hi** if there is a number **NextOne** that is the next number after **Lo** and is less than **Hi**. This statement is also fairly evident. Our intuitive understanding of the semantics of Datalog programs tells us that these two rules constitute a perfectly good definition of the predicate **less**.

The appearance of the predicate **less** in the body of a rule that has **less** as the predicate symbol in the head is a little suspicious. In Proplog such a rule can be discarded without changing the meaning of a program. (See Exercise 2.3.) Is the situation similar here? No; such rules are reasonable for Datalog, since the arguments in the two occurrences of the **less** predicate can be different. Let's trace *establish* on the goal:

```
less(three, six).
```

with the definition of **less** given here. We give the sequence of goal lists constructed by successive invocations of *establish,* with an × denoting a goal list where the first goal fails and causes backtracking. (For readability, we use **N** instead of **NextOne** as the variable.):

```
less(three, six).

next(three, six). ×
```

```
next(three, N1), less(N1, six).

less(four, six).

next(four, six). ×

next(four, N2), less(N2, six).

less(five, six).

next(five, six).

yes.
```

So **less** works for that goal. We should also consider how the interpreter behaves on a query such as:

```
less(eighteen, three).
```

Again we give goal lists for successive invocations of *establish*:

```
less(eighteen, three).

next(eighteen, three). ×

next(eighteen, N1), less(N1, three).

less(nineteen, three).

next(nineteen, three). ×

next(nineteen, N2), less(N2, three).

less(twenty, three).

next(twenty, three). ×

next(twenty, N3), less(N3, three). ×

no.
```

When the interpreter encounters the goal **next(twenty, N3)**, it fails because **next** is not true (with our facts) of any pair of numbers, the first of which is twenty. So these rules define the **less** predicate correctly. (We still might be a little suspicious of how it works for pairs that are not in the correct relationship, because the computation seems to go off in the wrong direction. Here the computation does not run forever because of the limited range of numbers we are considering.)

4.7. Informal Semantics for Datalog

We have been depending on intuitions and experience with Proplog to understand what Datalog programs mean. Here we examine the connection between Datalog clauses and English statements.

We understood the proposition symbols in Proplog as standing for simple declarative English sentences. For example, **csReq** stood for "Maria Marcatello has satisfied the computer science requirements." How do we interpret a predicate symbol of Datalog? Say we have a two-place predicate symbol **p**, so occurrences look like **p**(_, _). Given a pair of constants, this pattern turns into a ground literal (a literal with no variables). A ground literal in Datalog is essentially a Proplog proposition symbol—that is, a declarative sentence. The constants represent objects in the world that can fill the blanks in the sentence. So **p** alone can be thought of as a declarative sentence with blanks in it. For example, the two-place predicate symbol **less** that we used in several previous sections can be understood as standing for the sentence "_____ is a number less than _____, and both are between one and twenty." Filling in the blanks with ordered pairs of words turns this partial sentence into a proposition that is true or false in each state of the world. Substituting the pair <*three, seven*> makes this sentence a true statement. Other substitutions can make it false.

Such a sentence with blanks is a *predicate*. We thus can think of a two-place predicate as determining a set of ordered pairs—the set of all pairs that, when substituted into the sentence for the predicate, give a true statement. When we defined **less** explicitly in Section 4.2, we listed all those pairs. Alternatively, a two-place predicate is a function that maps ordered pairs into {**true**, **false**}, depending on whether the sentence is true or not when the pair fills the blanks. The rule-based definition of **less** in Section 4.6 has more of the flavor of a Boolean function than the explicit listing of **less** facts. Of course, the actual function can depend on the state of the world, as the **introReq** predicate of Section 4.1 did.

EXAMPLE 4.2: The predicate **ingred** from the final formulation of the pasta and popover problem is a three-place predicate. It stands for the sentence "To make a batch of _____, you need ______ ______." For instance, **ingred(popover, two, egg)** corresponds to the complete sentence "For a batch of *popover* you need *two egg*." (Pardon the grammar; logicians are not all that concerned about syntax.) □

Given this intuition for the meaning of a predicate, consider how we understand a fact in a Datalog program. A fact says that for every substitution of constants for variables, the resulting sentence is true. For example, the fact **less(seven, twenty)** asserts that the sentence "*Seven* is a number less than *twenty*, and both are between one and twenty."

How should we understand a Datalog rule? Recall that a Proplog rule of the form:

```
p :- q, r.
```

was understood as asserting the statement "**p** if **q** and **r**." A Datalog rule should be understood as saying that all such statements obtained by substitutions are true.

EXAMPLE 4.3: Asserting the Datalog rule:

```
p(X, Y) :- q(X, Y), r(Y).
```

says that for every pair of values <*a*, *b*> for **X** and **Y**, this rule is true. In other words, for every pair <*a*, *b*>, **p**(*a*, *b*) is true if **q**(*a*, *b*) is true and **r**(*b*) is true. □

Consider a rule of the form:

```
p(X, Y) :- q(X, Z), r(Z, Y).
```

This rule says that for every triple <*a*, *b*, *c*> for **X**, **Y**, and **Z**, the rule instance is true. Equivalently, for every pair <*a*, *b*>, **p**(*a*, *b*) is true if there exists a *c* such that **q**(*a*, *c*) and **r**(*c*, *b*) are true. To see this equivalence, note that a given pair <*a*, *b*>, the proposition **p**(*a*, *b*) is either true or false, regardless of what *c* is. If **p**(*a*, *b*) is true, then the rule instance is true no matter what. If **p**(*a*, *b*) is false, then for no *c* can both **q**(*a*, *c*) and **r**(*c*, *b*) be true; otherwise the rule would be falsified for that *c*. So **p**(*a*, *b*) has to be true if some *c* makes both **q**(*a*, *c*) and **r**(*c*, *b*) true.

EXAMPLE 4.4: Consider the following rule from the pasta example:

```
needs(Food, Ingred, N, Needed) :-
    ingred(Food, M, Ingred),
    times(N, M, Needed).
```

This rule can be interpreted as:

> Quantity *Needed* of ingredient *Ingred* is needed to make *N* batches of *Food*, if there is a number *M* such that both one batch of *Food* needs quantity *M* of ingredient *Ingred*, and the number *Needed* is *N* times *M*. □

Thus a Datalog rule says that for every value of the variables appearing in the head, the sentence represented by the head is true if there exist values for the rest of the variables that make all the sentences of the body true.

This informal discussion of the meaning of Datalog facts, rules, and programs allows us to understand and thus develop programs without having to think about the way *establish* computes with the program. Datalog's power lies in this abstraction of meaning away from implementation. Chapter 5 presents the precise and formal underpinnings for the semantics of Datalog programs.

4.8. Procedural Extensions to Datalog

In this section we discuss two extensions to Datalog. These extensions bend the declarative semantics of Datalog slightly, since their proper use depends on knowing the order of evaluation that *establish* uses for Datalog programs, and knowing how it instantiates variables.

4.8.1. *Negation-as-Failure*

Recall the **not** operator from Proplog. To implement the **not** operator in Datalog, we could modify the Datalog interpreter in much the same way as for Proplog. When *establish* encounters a goal literal *g* as the argument to the **not** operator, it calls itself recursively on *g*. (The recursive call is on *g* alone, not on *g* plus the rest of the goal list.) If the recursive invocation succeeds, then the calling invocation fails. If the recursive invocation fails, the calling invocation invokes *establish* on the rest of the goal list. This change is easy to make to the interpreter. The question is whether this modification gives us what we want. What we want is the same behavior that we would get if we expanded out all the Datalog rules and facts by replacing variables with all combinations of constants and then applied the Proplog interpreter. We might think that this modification to *establish* has that effect. After all, the only difference between the Datalog interpreter and exhaustive instantiation is the late binding of variables. It turns out, however, that that optimization is not always correct in the presence of the **not** operator.

The problem is with variables in the goal list. If there are no variables in the scope of the **not** operator when the Datalog interpreter encounters it, everything works fine. But if there are variables, things can go wrong.

Consider the following example of a proposed definition of a bachelor as a person who is not married and is of the male persuasion:

```
bachelor(X) :- not(married(X)), male(X).
married(john).
male(john).
male(bill).
```

Now consider what happens when we pose the goal:

```
bachelor(X).
```

This query asks for **X** to be bound in turn to each bachelor. We would expect the interpreter to succeed, returning **X = bill**. But consider how the modified Datalog interpreter evaluates this query. It starts with the goal list:

```
bachelor(X).
```

This goal matches the **bachelor** rule, so the next goal list is:

```
not(married(X1)), male(X1).
```

Notice that the value for **X1** is still waiting to be determined. Now the interpreter tries to establish **married(X1)**. That goal succeeds (because of the fact **married(john)**), and so the goal **not(married(X1))** fails. Hence the whole query fails.

This behavior is not what we wanted! The problem is the free variable **X1** that appears both inside and outside the scope of the **not**. The meaning we have associated with a goal list containing variable **X1** is that it should succeed if there is *some* value, which if substituted for **X1** throughout the goal list, makes it true. That is what we want here: if we substitute **bill** for **X1** in this goal list, it can be established. But the modified Datalog interpreter does not succeed here. That interpreter returns **true** for **not(married(X))** if for *every* **X**, **X** is not married. (Here it returns **false** because John is married.) So if there is an uninstantiated variable in the argument of a **not** operator when it appears at the head of the goal list, we may not get the behavior we expected.

We can, however, change the **bachelor** rule slightly so that the interpreter will compute what we want. We simply change the order of the two literals in the rule:

```
bachelor(X) :- male(X), not(married(X)).
```

Now when we pose the same goal, the predicate **male(X)** will cause the variable **X** to be bound, and when the interpreter encounters the **not** goal at the head of the goal list, it will not contain an uninstantiated variable. The subsequent computation then gives us the desired behavior.

The modified Datalog interpreter is not completely correct in the presence of **not**'s; it is sometimes correct. If we wish to be able to use the **not** operator, we have three choices. One is to go back and try to correct the interpreter algorithm. That choice turns out to be rather difficult, and the fix will not generalize to later cases. An alternative is to modify *establish* so that it returns an "error" indication when it encounters a situation in which it may behave incorrectly. When it encounters a **not**, it first checks to see whether the argument contains a variable. If it does, *establish* gives a run-time error message to that effect and halts; otherwise, it proceeds as indicated earlier. The third choice (the one adopted by most Prolog interpreters) is to make no change in the interpreter. The programmer must ensure that **not** will never be called with variables in its arguments.

The run-time error message in the second option is the first we have proposed for the interpreter. Until now, any syntactically correct Datalog program could have no semantic errors; a syntactically correct program will execute without run-time errors. In some sense the first Datalog program using **not** is correct since it has a well-specified meaning, but in this situation the interpreter is too weak to find that meaning. The Datalog programmer now has an added burden. When writing a program that contains the **not** operator, he or she must know enough about the interpretation process to determine that there will be no free variables in the argument of a **not** when it is encountered. Here, for the first time, the programmer must know some details of the execution model for Datalog programs.

As an example of a Datalog program using **not**, let's consider the following map-coloring problem. We are given a two-dimensional map with the area divided into countries. Given some small number of colored crayons, how do we color the countries of the map so that no two adjacent countries have the same color? (We must also color neatly and stay within the lines.)

Consider the map in Figure 4.1, in which the regions are identified by number. How can we write a program to color this map with the four colors red, green, blue, and yellow? We want to determine the color of each region. We use variables, **CR1**, **CR2**, . . ., **CR6**, to represent the colors of the regions numbered 1, 2, . . ., 6. We can formulate this problem in two ways, each leading to a different, but logically equivalent, program. One uses **not** explicitly. In the other method the negation of a certain predicate has essentially been precomputed. The programs, however, differ greatly in their execution efficiency. In logic programming many problems have several different solutions. While they compute the same answers, such solutions have widely varying execution times. This example is our first consideration of execution efficiency.

Our first thought is each region must have a color from among those allowed. We define a one-place predicate, **color**, that is true of the names of the colors:

```
color(red).
color(green).
color(blue).
color(yellow).
```

A map-coloring query will then start with the goals:

```
color(CR1), color(CR2), color(CR3), color(CR4), color(CR5),
   color(CR6),...
```

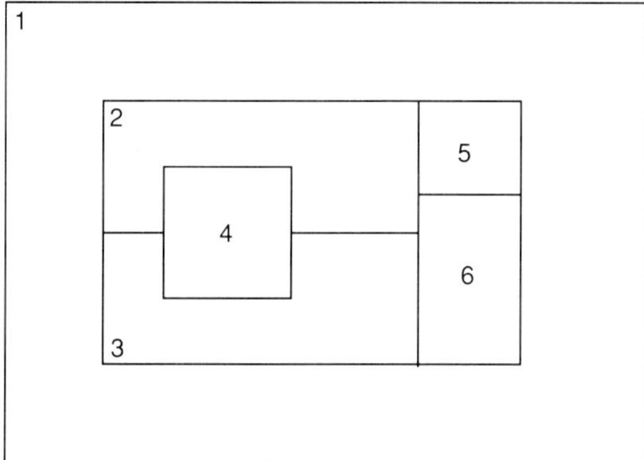

Figure 4.1

We must also specify that adjacent regions have different colors. To do so, we use a predicate to say that two colors are equal:

```
eq(X, X).
```

Now we can state that for every pair of adjacent regions, their colors are not equal. Thus the entire query is:

```
color(CR1), color(CR2), color(CR3), color(CR4), color(CR5),
color(CR6), not(eq(CR1, CR2)), not(eq(CR1, CR3)),
not(eq(CR1, CR5)), not(eq(CR1, CR6)), not(eq(CR2, CR3)),
not(eq(CR2, CR4)), not(eq(CR2, CR5)), not(eq(CR2, CR6)),
not(eq(CR3, CR4)), not(eq(CR3, CR6)), not(eq(CR5, CR6)).
```

The use of **not** here obeys the restriction that all variables in its argument be bound.

For the second formulation, we define a predicate, called **next**, that lists pairs of colors that can be adjacent:

```
next(yellow,blue).
next(yellow,green).
next(yellow,red).

next(blue,yellow).
next(blue,green).
next(blue,red).

next(green,blue).
next(green,yellow).
next(green,red).

next(red,blue).
next(red,yellow).
next(red,green).
```

With this predicate, the map-coloring query is:

```
next(CR1, CR2), next(CR1, CR3), next(CR1, CR5), next(CR1, CR6),
next(CR2, CR3), next(CR2, CR4), next(CR2, CR5), next(CR2, CR6),
next(CR3, CR4), next(CR3, CR6),
next(CR5, CR6).
```

The evaluation of this Datalog query will give the same answers. We can see how closely these two programs are related by noting that, rather than defining **next** by means of a set of facts, we could define it with the following rule:

```
next(C1, C2) :- color(C1), color(C2), not(eq(C1, C2)).
```

The use of the **color** predicate is necessary here to ensure that there are no free variables within the scope of the **not** when it is encountered.

The first program uses a programming paradigm called *generate and test*. It generates all colorings of the map in turn, then tests each to see if it is allowable. The second program is in essence doing generate and test but in a more subtle form. The second program delays the choice of a color for a region until it is needed to satisfy a **next** goal. Then the color is chosen to be different from at least one adjacent region. Thus many disallowed colorings are never generated. The change in the point of variable binding changes the shape of the search tree, and, in general, makes the second formulation execute faster. The choice of bindings in the second program is more constrained, so there is less branching in the search tree. Each region, except the first, is given a color different from at least one adjacent region.

This observation suggests that we can formulate a more efficient program by delaying the choice of colors as long as possible. Consider the following alternative query for the second program:

```
next(CR1, CR2), next(CR1, CR3), next(CR2, CR3),
next(CR1, CR6), next(CR2, CR6), next(CR3, CR6),
next(CR1, CR5), next(CR2, CR5), next(CR5, CR6),
next(CR2, CR4), next(CR3, CR4).
```

The only difference between this query and the last is the order of the goals. Reordering a goal list makes no difference in the set of answers obtained, since the logic is the same. However, this modified program will execute much faster than the earlier ones. For example, once colors **CR2** and **CR3** are chosen, the second query immediately checks if they can be adjacent, while the first query delays that choice. Simple reordering of goals, both in queries and bodies of rules, can have a large effect on the efficiency of a Datalog program.

4.8.2. *Numbers, Comparisons, and Arithmetic*

As the reader has no doubt noticed, the treatment of numbers in Datalog is unusual. Recall that one of the first predicates introduced in the recipe example was **less**, which we defined over pairs of numbers between one and twenty. When compared to more traditional programming systems, our treatment reveals two strange characteristics. First, we used the English words for the numbers, instead of the more usual Arabic notation. We called the numbers **one**, **two**, . . ., **twenty**, instead of **1**, **2**, . . ., **20**. Clearly our approach does not generalize well to large numbers. The second, and perhaps stranger, difference is that we had to define **less** explicitly. Most programming languages provide this relation as a primitive; there is no need for a Pascal programmer to define '<'. However, there is a method to our madness, which we explain in this section.

Consider the **less** predicate on integers. Our use of the English words for numbers was just pedagogical; it was intended to show how numbers are just like any other constants, and predicates on numbers are just like other predicates. But this naming scheme will not work as a serious approach to a general treatment of numbers. We will start using regular Arabic notation for representing constants that happen to be numbers.

Numeric predicates, such as **less**, are common in programming, so we might also wish to build them into the Datalog interpreter. The idea is to provide the definition of **less** as part of the system so that the user is not forced to define it explicitly. One approach is just to "pre-load" the set of facts that define this built-in predicate. Then the Datalog interpreter would be unchanged; it would access the **less** predicate just as it accesses any other predicate. The question immediately arises as to how much of the definition of **less** the interpreter should provide. In the recipe example we decided that we needed only integers from one up to twenty, so we defined **less** for only those numbers. But the integers up to twenty are not sufficient for most applications. Perhaps the integers up to 2^{32} or so will suffice. Most computer languages (and even some computer programmers) seem happy with such a constraint. Maybe we could provide the facts to define the **less** predicate for all the numbers in the range 1 to 2^{32}. Obviously, such a direct implementation is unreasonable; the storage space required is immense, and even if we had the space, the access time is too great.

A better approach is to alter the Datalog interpreter to recognize the **less** predicate and "fake" it. That is, the interpreter would not store the entire set of **less** facts but would behave as though it did. How can we achieve this end? First, we must settle on exactly what the **less** table contains. One might want it to be an infinite table. Since we are not going to store it, an infinite table is a possibility. For practical purposes, there is not much difference between a table that is infinite and a table that contains 2^{63} entries. For concreteness (and easier intuitions), let's assume that we just want the finite table for numbers up to the maximum wordsize of our favorite machine. The question now is how to make the interpreter behave as though it really has that table, without explicitly storing it.

With the problem stated this way, it is not hard to see the solution. Consider the situations that may obtain when the Datalog interpreter encounters a **less** predicate at the head of the goal list. The goal may have the form **less(12, 193)**—that is, with both arguments specified as numbers. In this case the interpreter simply compares the numbers, using an appropriate machine instruction, and succeeds if the first number is less than the second (as is here the case) or fails if not. The goal might instead have the form **less(a, 193)**, where one argument is a constant that is not a number. Here the interpreter should fail; there is no pair in the **less** relation that has a nonnumeric entry. The remaining case is a variable and a numeric constant, or two variables, such as **less(23, X4)**. Here matters are more problematic. To simulate the behavior of having a huge stored table, the interpreter ought in this case first to replace **X4** by **24** and succeed; then, if a subsequent goal fails, replace **X4** by **25**; then by **26**; . . .; then by $2^{32} - 1$. This behavior is not difficult to program and would simulate the table correctly. However, those three little dots stand for many numbers. In a real Datalog program the programmer would be unlikely to expect all these numbers to be enumerated. In this sense there is not much difference between simulating the 2^{63}-size table and an infinite table.

Rather than fully simulating the immense table, we will instead modify *establish* so that we report an error and stop if it encounters a **less** goal with a variable. This approach is similar to that for **not**. We could program the interpreter to generate replacements for the variable or variables. We do not, because it seems more likely that if a **less** goal is encountered without both arguments bound, the programmer has made a mistake and really does not want that program executed that way. A predicate that invokes an underlying function rather than being solved by program clauses is called *evaluable.* We will see more evaluable predicates in Chapter 8; most of them have some restriction on which variables can be uninstantiated on invocation.

We can now reconsider the **sum** predicate we used in Section 4.4. We treat it in a way similar to **less**. The idea again is to have the Datalog interpreter simulate a huge addition table but without actually storing it. For example, consider the situation in which the interpreter encounters a goal **sum(23, 35, 58)**. When all arguments are bound, *establish* checks to see if the first two do indeed sum to the third and succeeds or fails accordingly. If two of the three arguments are numbers and the other is a variable, the interpreter can determine what number should replace the variable (by adding or subtracting the other arguments appropriately). If two (or three) of the arguments are variables, we again have the situation encountered earlier. To simulate a table correctly, the interpreter must in turn bind the variables to all the pairs (or triples) of numbers that satisfy the sum relation. While this behavior can be programmed, it seems unlikely that it is what a programmer intended. We therefore adopt the convention that if the interpreter encounters a **sum** goal with two or more variables, it reports an error and stops.

4.9. Datalog and Databases

The "data" in the name Datalog comes from its connection to query languages for relational databases. In this section we introduce relational databases and relational algebra by example, and show that Datalog has all the power of relational algebra. Query languages based on relational calculus, which is basically Datalog with no recursive predicates, are among the purest examples of declarative languages. The evaluation problem has been solved for this subset of Datalog, which means the query processor can supply all the control information to evaluate a query. Contrast this situation with another class of declarative systems—parser generators (sometimes called compiler compilers). The input to a parser generator, an annotated context-free grammar, is not purely declarative. The grammar writer must take into account the parsing strategy in structuring the productions to ensure the resulting parser can handle all inputs. Relational query languages effectively eliminate the need for such knowledge about the execution model of the underlying evaluation process.

In relational databases all data are represented in tables called *relations*. Figure 4.2 shows two relations. The first, called *teaches,* gives the courses each instructor is teaching. The second, *takes,* gives the courses in which each student was enrolled and also the grade for each course. The column headings, such as INST and COURSE, are called *attributes*. The set of all attributes in a relation is its *scheme*: the scheme of *takes* is: {STUDENT, COURSE, GRADE}. A row of a relation, such as <Kim CS502>, is called a *tuple*.

teaches(INST	COURSE)	
Milton	CS507	
Milton	CS531	
Kim	CS502	
Barth	CS501	
Gupta	CS523	

takes(STUDENT	COURSE	GRADE)
Adams	CS507	A
Adams	CS502	B
Arnold	CS507	B
Arnold	CS531	C
Arnold	CS501	A
Alt	CS501	A

Figure 4.2

Evidently we can represent the data in a relation with a set of Datalog facts, one for each tuple in the relation. The predicate symbol for each fact is the name of the relation, and each fact contains one value for each attribute in the relation scheme. Thus the data in *teaches* and *takes* can be represented as:

```
teaches(milton, cs507).
teaches(milton, cs531).
teaches(kim, cs502).
teaches(barth, cs501).
teaches(gupta, cs523).

takes(adams, cs507, a).
takes(adams, cs502, b).
takes(arnold, cs507, b).
takes(arnold, cs531, c).
takes(arnold, cs501, a).
takes(alt, cs501, a).
```

Note that the Datalog representation loses the information on the attribute name connected with each position. We must remember the correspondence between positions and attributes. We also converted strings from the relations to lowercase to make them Datalog constants. Chapter 8 will show how to represent arbitrary strings.

Relational algebra is a system of operators that take one or two relations as arguments and return a relation as a result. Select, project, and join are the fundamental operators of relational algebra.

Select pulls out a subset of the tuples in a relation based on some selection condition. A *selection condition* is a comparison between an attribute and a constant or between two attributes. Selection is denoted by a sigma (σ) with the selection condition as a subscript.

EXAMPLE 4.5: To find out the courses that Milton teaches, we can use:

$$\sigma_{\text{INST}=\text{Milton}}(\textit{teaches}).$$

The result of this operation is shown in Figure 4.3. □

Project is similar to select, but it pulls out a subset of the columns of a relation, rather than a subset of the tuples. Project is denoted by a pi (π) with a subscript giving the attributes for the columns to be retained.

EXAMPLE 4.6: To get a list of grades in the various courses, we use:

$$\pi_{\text{COURSE,GRADE}}(\textit{takes}).$$

The result of this operation is given in Figure 4.4. Note that the tuple <CS501 A> appears only once. The tuples in a relation are treated as a set, so no duplicates are permitted. □

Join (sometimes called *natural join*) combines two relations on the common attributes in their schemes. A tuple *t* is in the join of relations *r* and *s* if *t* agrees with some tuple in *r* on the scheme of *r*, and with some tuple in *s* on the scheme of *s*. The result of a join, then, has a scheme that is the union of the schemes of the argument relations. We use a bow tie ($\bowtie$) to denote join.

EXAMPLE 4.7: To connect students with the instructors of their courses we can use:

$$\textit{teaches} \bowtie \textit{takes}.$$

INST	COURSE
Milton	CS507
Milton	CS531

Figure 4.3

COURSE	GRADE
CS507	A
CS502	B
CS507	B
CS531	C
CS501	A

Figure 4.4

INST	COURSE	STUDENT	GRADE
Milton	CS507	Adams	A
Milton	CS507	Arnold	B
Milton	CS531	Arnold	C
Kim	CS502	Adams	B
Barth	CS501	Arnold	A
Barth	CS501	Alt	A

Figure 4.5

The result of this join is shown in Figure 4.5. Note that the tuple <Gupta CS523> from the *teaches* relation does not participate in the join, because its COURSE-component does not match any tuple in *takes*. □

Many simple queries against a relational database can be expressed with just select, project, and join. Efficient evaluation of such queries has been widely studied.

EXAMPLE 4.8: The query "Which students have taken a course with Milton?" can be answered with the expression:

$$\pi_{\mathrm{STUDENT}}(\sigma_{\mathrm{INST=Milton}}(\mathit{teaches} \bowtie \mathit{takes})).$$

Figure 4.6 gives the result of this expression. □

Finally, there are three binary operators—union, intersect, and difference—that combine two relations over the same scheme with set operations on the sets of tuples in the arguments. *Union* (∪) yields all tuples in either relation. *Intersect* (∩) gives only tuples that are in both relations. *Difference* (−) produces all the tuples in its first argument that are not in the second.

EXAMPLE 4.9: Consider the relations *wants* and *avail* in Figure 4.7 that give all the courses each student wants and the courses that are available to him or her. The results of the operations:

$$\mathit{wants} \cup \mathit{avail}$$
$$\mathit{wants} \cap \mathit{avail}$$
$$\mathit{wants} - \mathit{avail}$$

are shown in Figures 4.8–4.10, respectively. □

STUDENT
Adams
Arnold

Figure 4.6

wants(STUDENT COURSE)

STUDENT	COURSE
Adams	CS509
Adams	CS511
Arnold	CS509
Arnold	CS511
Alt	CS513

avail(STUDENT COURSE)

STUDENT	COURSE
Adams	CS509
Arnold	CS511
Alt	CS509
Alt	CS511

Figure 4.7

STUDENT	COURSE
Adams	CS509
Adams	CS511
Arnold	CS509
Arnold	CS511
Alt	CS509
Alt	CS511
Alt	CS513

Figure 4.8

STUDENT	COURSE
Adams	CS509
Arnold	CS511

Figure 4.9

STUDENT	COURSE
Adams	CS511
Arnold	CS509
Alt	CS513

Figure 4.10

Any query language for relational databases that can perform select, project, join, union, intersect, and difference is called *relationally complete*. Relational completeness has been proposed as the yardstick for measuring relational query languages. In the rest of this section we demonstrate that Datalog is a relationally complete language by indicating how to represent each operator in relational algebra with Datalog rules. The representation is via a **result** predicate in Datalog with one argument for each attribute in the result of the algebraic expression. For example, we will define a predicate **result(S, C, G)** for an expression whose result is a relation on scheme {STUDENT, COURSE, GRADE}. The set of all answers to the goal:

```
result(S, C, G).
```

will be the tuples in the relation that is the value of the corresponding algebraic expression. The Datalog goal may return duplicate answers, where a relation should not have duplicate tuples. Chapter 8 introduces the evaluable predicate **setof**, which can eliminate such duplicates.

A select with an equality condition is handled by putting a constant in the position corresponding to the attribute involved. Equality between two attributes can be handled similarly. (See Exercise 4.16.)

EXAMPLE 4.10: The select:

$\sigma_{\text{INST}=\text{Milton}}(\textit{teaches})$.

is captured by the rule:

```
result(milton, C) :- teaches(milton, C). □
```

Select with an inequality condition relies on having an evaluable Datalog predicate on hand for the condition, as discussed in Section 4.8.2.

EXAMPLE 4.11: The select:

$\sigma_{\text{GRADE}\leq\text{C}}(\textit{takes})$

is represented by:

```
result(S, C, G) :- takes(S, C, G), lessEq(G, c). □
```

Project is handled by defining a result predicate containing only the columns of interest.

EXAMPLE 4.12: The project operation:

$\pi_{\text{COURSE,GRADE}}(\textit{takes})$.

is represented by the rule:

```
result(C, G) :- takes(C, S, G). □
```

A join can be captured with a literal for each of the arguments in the body of a rule, with the same variable in columns corresponding to the same attribute.

EXAMPLE 4.13: The operation:

teaches $\bowtie$ *takes.*

is represented with the rule:

```
result(I, C, S, G) :- teaches(I, C), takes(S, C, G). □
```

A relational algebra expression involving project, select, and join can often be represented with a single Datalog rule by combining the techniques for the individual operations.

EXAMPLE 4.14: The relational expression:

$\pi_{\text{STUDENT}}(\sigma_{\text{INST}=\text{Milton}}(\textit{teaches} \bowtie \textit{takes})).$

is captured by the rule:

```
result(S) :- teaches(milton, C), takes(S, C, G). □
```

Union requires two rules, one for each argument.

EXAMPLE 4.15: The operation:

wants $\cup$ *avail*

is represented by the rules:

```
result(S, C) :- wants(S, C).
result(S, C) :- avail(S, C). □
```

Intersection is really a degenerate case of join in which the schemes of the arguments overlap on all their attributes.

EXAMPLE 4.16: The operation:

wants $\cap$ *avail*

is captured with:

```
result(S, C) :- wants(S, C), avail(S, C). □
```

Difference relies on the use of **not**. The use of **not** here obeys the restriction that all variables in its argument are bound before it is evaluated.

EXAMPLE 4.17: The difference:

want $-$ *avail*

is represented by the rule:

```
result(S, C) :- wants(S, C), not(avail(S, C)).
```
□

We have exhibited a "proof by example" that Datalog is a relationally complete query language, provided we include **not** and the appropriate evaluable predicates as part of Datalog. Actually Datalog is strictly more powerful than relational algebra. In the relational algebra we cannot define recursive expressions, but in Datalog we can. Recall that the definition of **less** in Section 4.6 is recursive. That kind of definition is not possible in the relational algebra, even though there are times when a user wishes to ask exactly that kind of question of a database. Consider a relation *employee* that contains a tuple for each employee who works in a particular company. Each tuple contains two fields: the employee's name, and his or her direct supervisor. We might like to define the relation that contains all pairs of names such that the second is somewhere above the first in the company hierarchy. In Datalog this relation can be defined as follows:

```
below(Emp, Boss) :- employee(Emp, Boss).
below(Emp, Boss) :- employee(Emp, Super), below(Super, Boss).
```

These two rules define the desired relation. Notice that this predicate definition is identical in structure to the **less** definition in Section 4.6. The **below** relation cannot be defined in relational algebra. Hence Datalog can do some things that the relational algebra cannot.

This treatment of the connection between Datalog and relational algebra concludes our introduction to the language. The feature that sets Datalog apart from Proplog is the logical variable. Logical variables enable one Datalog clause to represent arbitrary numbers of Proplog clauses. The new topics in the next two chapters all derive from the introduction of logical variables. The formal semantics of Proplog have to be extended to deal with literals and their instantiations. The resolution rule must be revised to include a matching, or *unification,* process to make variables in the resolved literals agree. While the indexing and lazy lists optimizations are applicable to the Datalog interpreter, the more interesting ones have to do with delaying the instantiation of variables, and with representing the replacements for variables in substitutions.

4.10. EXERCISES

4.1. Write a Datalog program for a five-place predicate **twoPair** that is true if two different pairs of arguments are equal. Assume the arguments come from the list {**one**, **two**, . . ., **twenty**}.

4.2. Give a function *copyapply*(SUBS, LITS) that returns a copy of list of literals LITS with substitution SUBS applied.

4.3. For which of the following pairs of literals will the *match* function of Section 4.3 return **true**? For those pairs, give the value of SUBS upon return.

i. **p(a, X, X, b), p(Y, Y, Z, Z)**
ii. **q(a, X, b, X), q(Y, Y, Z, Z)**
iii. **r(X, V, X, V), r(Y, Y, Z, Z)**
iv. **s(X, V, V, a), s(Y, Y, Z, Z)**

4.4. It is possible to represent a substitution as a list of replacements that are to be applied repeatedly to a literal until no changes occur. For example:

{W = Z, X = Y, Y = b, V = W}

represents the substitution:

{W = Z, X = b, Y = b, V = Z}

We place the restriction on replacement lists that no variable occur more than once on the left of a replacement, and that there be no cycle of replacements such as **X1 = X2, X2 = X3, X3 = X4, X4 = X1.**

a. Give an algorithm to apply a replacement list to a literal.
b. Why are multiple occurrences of a variable on the left of replacements a problem?
c. Why are cycles of replacements a problem?
d. Give an algorithm to convert a replacement list to a substitution in the regular form.

4.5. Consider the following definitions of the transitive closure of a directed graph represented by predicate **g**. (The transitive closure of a directed graph has an edge wherever the graph has a path.)

```
I.   tc(X, Y) :- g(X, Y).
     tc(X, Y) :- g(X, Z), tc(Z, Y).
II.  tc(X, Y) :- g(X, Y).
     tc(X, Y) :- tc(X, Z), g(Z, Y).
III. tc(X, Y) :- tc(X, Z), g(Z, Y).
     tc(X, Y) :- g(X, Y).
```

Let the graph be defined as:

```
g(1, 2).
g(1, 3).
g(2, 4).
g(2, 5).
g(3, 4).
g(4, 7).
g(5, 6).
g(6, 7).
```

a. For each of the following goals, say what result the Datalog *establish* function will give for each of the preceding definitions I–III of **tc**, including the bindings for variables in the goals.

   i. **tc(3, 6).**
   ii. **tc(3, 7).**

iii. **tc(X, 5).**
iv. **tc(5, X).**
v. **tc(X, Y).**

b. For those cases in (a) where *establish* returns **true**, what would happen next if we forced backtracking?

c. For the following alternative definition of graph **g**, give the first ten answers that *establish* returns for the goal **tc(1, X)**, using definition I shown earlier.

```
g(1, 2).
g(1, 3).
g(2, 3).
g(3, 4).
g(4, 1).
```

4.6. Can the control structure of the *demo* function in Exercise 1.17 be adapted for Datalog? Show how, or explain why not.

4.7. Give an algorithm for bottom-up evaluation of Datalog programs. Your algorithm should start with all the unit clauses (clauses with no bodies), and use the rules to deduce more unit clauses. Note that to test implication of a goal, it is not sufficient simply to test if a goal is in the set of unit clauses so derived. Particular care is needed for a list of goals that share variables.

4.8. For the algorithm in the last exercise, can a rule be removed from further consideration once it is used to derive a unit clause?

4.9. For the recipe example, give a Datalog program for the predicate **canMake(N, M)** that is true if there are sufficient ingredients for **N** batches of pasta and **M** of popovers. Your program should not use **not**.

4.10. Give a version of *establish* that handles the **$answer** pseudoliteral described in Section 4.5.

4.11. Show how to simulate the correct behavior of **not** on a literal that contains a variable, given a one-place predicate **value**, where **value(c)** is a fact for every constant **c** mentioned in the current program.

4.12. If you have access to a Prolog interpreter with timing information, compare the times required to run the three versions of the map-coloring problem in Section 4.8.1.

4.13. Give a Datalog program for a ten-place predicate **sorted** that is true if its first five arguments are its second five arguments sorted according to a total ordering given by a two-place predicate **less**. The **less** predicate requires two bound arguments, while **sorted** should produce bindings for its first five arguments when the second five are bound.

4.14. Let **less** be a two-place predicate that defines a total order on the integers. Let **sum** be a three-place predicate that is true when the sum of its first two arguments is its third argument. Assume that **less** must have both arguments bound, and that **sum** must have at least its first two arguments bound. Write a Datalog program for a two-place predicate **allLess** that is equivalent to **less**, except it will work with only its first argument bound. For example, repeated backtracking to **allLess(3, X)** should return different values for **X** that are all greater than **3**.

4.15. Consider the following "database" about projects in a company, consisting of three relations:

> **suppliesTo(Supplier, Part, Project)**: tells that an external supplier supplies a part to a project.
> **produces(Project, Part)**: tells that a project of this company produces a part.
> **partof(Part, Subpart)**: tells what parts are immediate subparts of other parts.

Use Datalog to define the following predicates.

a. A one-place predicate that is true of all the parts supplied to any project by the supplier 'acme'.
b. A three-place predicate that is true of two projects and a part if the first project produces the part and the second project purchases that part from a supplier.
c. A two-place predicate over projects and parts such that the project either produces the part or obtains the part from a supplier.
d. A two-place predicate that is true of all pairs of parts such that the second is a component of the first—that is, goes into making the first part.
e. A one-place predicate true of all "lazy" projects—those that purchase, directly from an outside supplier, a part they themselves produce.

4.16. How can a relational select operator with an equality condition on two attributes be captured in Datalog? For example, suppose we have a relation *manages*(MGR EMP) that gives the manager of each employee. We could use the selection:

$$\sigma_{\text{MGR}=\text{EMP}}(\textit{manages})$$

to find employees who manage themselves.

4.17. Suppose the condition on a select operator is allowed to be an arbitrary number of comparisons, connected with **and**, **or**, and **not**, such as:

$$\sigma_{\text{STUDENT}=\text{Adams and (COURSE}=\text{CS501 or COURSE}=\text{CS502)}}(\textit{takes}).$$

How can a select operator with such a compound condition be represented in Datalog?

4.18. Consider **succ** (for *successor*) facts about roads in southwest Oregon in the following form. Each fact gives a pair of successive cities along various roads.

```
succ(or42, coquille, bridge).
succ(or42, bridge, remote).
succ(or42, remote, tenmile).
succ(or42, tenmile, winston).
```

```
succ(i5, eugene, creswell).
succ(i5, creswell, cottageGrove).
succ(i5, cottageGrove, anlauf).
succ(i5, anlauf, yoncalla).
succ(i5, yoncalla, sutherlin).
    .
    .
    .
```

Suppose we want to know if two cities are connected to each other by a given road. We can use the following clauses:

```
/* connect(Road, Start, Finish) is true if the Finish city is
   reachable from the Start city along Road. This predicate
   uses two other predicates, connectA and connectB, that indicate
   connection in the direction of succ and in the opposite
   direction to succ, respectively. */
connect(Road, Start, Finish) :- connectA(Road, Start, Finish).
connect(Road, Start, Finish) :- connectB(Road, Start, Finish).

connectA(Road, Start, Finish) :- succ(Road, Start, Finish).
connectA(Road, Start, Finish) :-
      succ(Road, Start, Middle), connectA(Road, Middle, Finish).

connectB(Road, Start, Finish) :- succ(Road, Finish, Start).
connectB(Road, Start, Finish) :-
      succ(Road, Middle, Start), connectB(Road, Middle, Finish).
```

We can use **connect** to define more complex connections. The predicate **connectIn2** here determines if two cities are connected by a route that uses exactly two roads.

```
/* Check that two cities are connected using two distinct
   roads. The notSame predicate holds all the information
   about which roads are different. */

connectIn2(Start, Finish) :-
      connect(Road1, Start, Middle),
      connect(Road2, Middle, Finish),
      notSame(Road1, Road2).

      notSame(or42, i5).
      notSame(or42, or38).
      notSame(or42, or126).
      notSame(or42, us101).
          .
          .
          .
```

Write Datalog programs to define the following predicates.

a. A predicate:

```
connectUsing(Start, Finish, Middle)
```

that indicates if there is a route of three or fewer roads going from **Start** to **Finish** and passing through **Middle**.

b. A predicate:

```
alternates(Start, Finish)
```

that indicates if there are two or more routes using three or fewer roads from **Start** to **Finish**.

c. A predicate:

```
connectAvoiding(Start, Finish, Road)
```

that determines if there is a route from **Start** to **Finish** avoiding a particular **Road**.

d. A predicate:

```
roundTrip(City)
```

that determines if there is a route using three, four, or five roads from a **City** back to itself, with no backtracking.

e. A predicate:

```
visitAll(City1, City2, City3, City4)
```

that determines if there is a route connecting four cities with no backtracking.

4.11. COMMENTS AND BIBLIOGRAPHY

A subset of the Datalog language, obtained by disallowing recursive rules, is equivalent to the relational algebra. The relational algebra was originally introduced by Codd [4.1] as a relational theory of databases. A comprehensive treatment of what is currently known in the area can be found in Maier [4.2]. The proof that transitive closure cannot be expressed in the relational algebra is given there; the original proof is by Aho and Ullman [4.3]. Recently there has been a developing interest in the database community in exploring more of the power of Datalog. This topic is becoming known in general as "deductive databases" [4.4, 4.5].

Gray [4.6] approaches the logic-database relationship more from a programming language point of view, while Li [4.7] shows how to program a database system using the full Prolog language.

4.1. E. F. Codd, A relational model of data for large shared data banks, *CACM 13*:6, June 1970, 377–87.

4.2. D. Maier, *The Theory of Relational Databases,* Computer Science Press, Potomac, MD, 1983.

4.3. A. V. Aho and J. D. Ullman, Universality of data retrieval languages, ACM Symposium on Principles of Programming Languages, 1979, 110–20.

4.4. H. Gallaire and J. Minker (eds.), *Logic and Databases,* Plenum Press, New York, 1978.

4.5. Workshop on Foundations of Deductive Databases and Logic Programming, Washington, DC, J. Minker (org.), August 1986.

4.6. P. Gray, *Logic, Algebra and Databases,* Ellis Horwood, Chichester, England, 1984.

4.7. D. Li, *A PROLOG Database System,* Research Studies Press Limited, Letchworth, England, 1984.

5

Predicate Logic

This chapter presents the formal underpinnings of the Datalog language. We want to give Datalog programs a declarative semantics and determine that the interpreter acts in accordance with that semantics. We will see that Datalog is a subset of predicate logic, as Proplog was a subset of propositional logic. The new wrinkle going from propositional logic to predicate logic is templates (literals) that represent sets of propositions. Informally, such a template represents the propositions obtained by all possible ways of replacing variables in the template. Predicate logic introduces *quantification* to formalize statements about "all possible" things (as well as "some possible"). To give meaning to such statements, we need to denote the range of possibilities explicitly. An abstraction of the world against which to interpret a predicate logic formula must include a *domain* of objects, which will be "all possible" things that can replace a variable. Truth assignments will now be relative to a particular domain.

Here complications arise. There are an infinite number of choices for a domain, the domains themselves possibly being infinite. If implication is still defined with respect to truth in all models, how do we effectively test implication in the presence of infinitely many models? We see that the problem is considerably simplified for a class of predicate logic expressions called *universal* formulas. (That class of formulas includes Datalog clauses and goals.) For universal formulas, we will be able to determine implication relative to models over one particular domain, called the *Herbrand universe*. For predicate logic, the Herbrand universe is finite, which means that a formula has only a finite set of *Herbrand models* (models whose domain is the Herbrand universe).

Even with this restriction, the prospect of checking all models of a predicate logic formula, as a means to test implication, is even more daunting than exhaustive enumeration of truth assignments for a propositional formula. Again we turn to clausal form and refutation proofs using resolution as a more directed approach to checking implication. In fact, by forming all possible propositional clauses from a predicate clause, via substituting values from the Herbrand universe, propositional resolution gives a sound and complete test for implication in predicate logic.

When developing the Datalog interpreter, we delayed constructing propositional clauses from predicate clauses by leaving some variables unbound. The *establish* routine uses the *match* function to determine exactly which variables to replace. In this chapter we develop the formal notion of *unification* to show why *match* does the right thing relative to the semantics of predicate clauses. Recall all the "fixes" the first attempt at a *match* routine required. The cautious reader might still be wondering if we missed some cases. The material here should be a strong argument that indeed we have covered all the bases.

At the end of the chapter we show that the same restrictions on the form of refutation DAGs can be made for predicate Horn clauses as for propositional Horn clauses. However, more work is required to show that the various graph transformations we made are still valid when variables are involved.

5.1. Predicate Logic for Datalog

Before embarking on full predicate logic, we consider a simpler logic for Datalog programs.

5.1.1. *Formal Syntax of Datalog*

We have been giving examples of Datalog programs. Let's be more precise and formally define their syntax. Figure 5.1 gives a context-free grammar that defines Datalog programs.

EXAMPLE 5.1: Figure 5.2 shows a derivation of the clause:

```
less(Lo, Hi) :- next(Lo, NextOne), less(NextOne, Hi).
```

from Section 4.6. □

Note that every Proplog program is also a Datalog program, since PARLIST (parameter list) can produce the empty string. Also note that the Datalog *establish* routine will compute the same result as the Proplog interpreter on a Proplog program.

5.1.2. *Semantics for Datalog*

For Proplog, we defined a logic that gave a precise meaning to programs. We do the same for Datalog. Recall that a logic consists of a syntactic component, a semantic component, and a deductive component. The syntax of Datalog was just described. The predicate logic for Datalog we develop here is a generalization of the propositional logic used for Proplog.

Let P be a Datalog program. The *domain* of P, denoted $\mathbf{D}_P$, is the set of all constants that appear in P. The *base* of P, denoted $\mathbf{B}_P$, is the set of all instantiations of literals in program P using constants in $\mathbf{D}_P$.

PGM → ε
PGM → CLAUSE PGM
CLAUSE → LITERAL TAIL .
LITERAL → predsym PARLIST
PARLIST → ε
PARLIST → (ARGLIST)
ARGLIST → TERM ARGTAIL
ARGTAIL → ε
ARGTAIL → , ARGLIST
TERM → csym
TERM → varsym
TAIL → ε
TAIL → : - LITLIST
LITLIST → LITERAL LITTAIL
LITTAIL → ε
LITTAIL → , LITLIST

where predsym = lc (lc + uc + digit)* | digit*
csym = lc (lc + uc + digit)* | digit*
varsym = uc (lc + uc + digit)*
lc = any lowercase letter
uc = any uppercase letter
digit = any digit

Figure 5.1

CLAUSE ⇒ LITERAL TAIL . ⇒ **less** PARLIST TAIL . ⇒
less (ARGLIST) TAIL . ⇒ **less** (TERM ARGTAIL) TAIL . ⇒
less (**Lo** ARGTAIL) TAIL . ⇒ **less** (**Lo** , ARGLIST) TAIL . ⇒
less (**Lo** , TERM ARGTAIL) TAIL . ⇒
less (**Lo** , **Hi** ARGTAIL) TAIL . ⇒ **less** (**Lo** , **Hi**) TAIL . ⇒
less (**Lo** , **Hi**) : - LITLIST . ⇒
less (**Lo** , **Hi**) : - LITERAL LITTAIL . $\stackrel{*}{\Rightarrow}$
less (**Lo** , **Hi**) : - **next** (**Lo** , **NextOne**) LITTAIL . ⇒
less (**Lo** , **Hi**) : - **next** (**Lo** , **NextOne**) , LITLIST . ⇒
less (**Lo** , **Hi**) : - **next** (**Lo** , **NextOne**) , LITERAL LITTAIL . $\stackrel{*}{\Rightarrow}$
less (**Lo** , **Hi**) : - **next** (**Lo** , **NextOne**) ,
less (**NextOne** , **Hi**) LITTAIL . ⇒
less (**Lo** , **Hi**) : - **next** (**Lo** , **NextOne**) , **less** (**NextOne** , **Hi**) .

Figure 5.2

EXAMPLE 5.2: For the program P:

```
p(X, Z) :- q(X, Z), r(Z).
q(a, b).
q(a, d).
r(X) :- s(a, X).
s(a, d).
s(a, a).
```

$\mathbf{D}_P = \{\mathbf{a}, \mathbf{b}, \mathbf{d}\}$.

and:

$B_P =$
{p(a, a), p(a, b), p(a, d), p(b, a), p(b, b), p(b, d), p(d, a), p(d, b), p(d, d), q(a, a), q(a, b), q(a, d), q(b, a), q(b, b), q(b, d), q(d, a), q(d, b), q(d, d), r(a), r(b), r(d), s(a, a), s(a, b), s(a, d)}.

Note that certain literals with predicate symbol **s**, such as **s(b, a)**, are not in B_P, since they are not instances of any literal in P. □

Let V be the set of all possible Datalog variables. Recall that variables are represented by sequences of characters, the first of which is an uppercase character. So V is a countable set of variables; we may think of them listed in lexicographic order, if we wish.

By an *instantiation* for P, we mean any function I that maps V to $\mathbf{D}_P$. An instantiation assigns a constant from the program P to each variable in V. We extend I to map a clause C of P to a ground clause made up of ground literals from B_P. (Ground clauses and ground literals are those with no variables.) We simply replace each variable in the clause by its image under I. Note that we need only know the value of I on the variables in P to apply I to a clause in P. Defining instantiations over all possible variables simplifies the definition of meaning function for full predicate logic.

EXAMPLE 5.3: Let I be an instantiation such that $I(\mathbf{X}) = \mathbf{b}$. Then:

$I($**r(X) :- s(a,X).**$) =$ **r(b) :- s(a, b).** □

Consider what a truth assignment should be in this context. In the Proplog case it mapped the proposition symbols of the program into the set {**true**, **false**}. For Datalog, a truth assignment is any function that maps B_P into {**true**, **false**}. We use a truth assignment TA to define a meaning function M_{TA} that assigns **true** or **false** to any Datalog ground clause. We use the same definition of M_{TA} we used in Proplog: M_{TA} maps a ground fact directly to **true** or **false** according to the value of TA; it assigns a ground rule **true** if TA makes the head true or if it makes one of the literals in the body false; otherwise it assigns the rule **false**.

We extend M_{TA} to a Datalog clause C (perhaps with variables) as follows:

$M_{TA}(C)$ = **true** if and only if, for every instantiation I, $M_{TA}(I(C))$ = **true**.

This definition says that a Datalog clause is true under a truth assignment *TA* if for every instantiation, the ground instance of the rule obtained by using that instantiation is true under *TA*. This definition is just a careful statement of our earlier informal description of how we should understand a Datalog rule: No matter what constants we substitute uniformly for the variables, we obtain a true Proplog rule.

EXAMPLE 5.4: Consider the clause:

```
r(X) :- s(a, X).
```

from Example 5.2. Let *TA* be the truth assignment that assigns every literal in B_P **true** unless it contains a **d**, in which case it assigns **false**. We want to know the value of:

M_{TA}(**r(X) :- s(a, X).**).

While there are an infinite number of instantiations for *P*, they can be partitioned into three classes, depending on where they map **X**. Thus we need find the values only of:

M_{TA}(**r(a) :- s(a, a).**)
M_{TA}(**r(b) :- s(a, b).**)
M_{TA}(**r(d) :- s(a, d).**)

M_{TA} assigns **true** to the heads and bodies of the first two rules, and **false** to the head and body of the last rule. Thus it assigns **true** to all the rules, and hence **true** to **r(X) :- s(a, X).**

Consider another truth assignment *TA′* that assigns **true** to every literal in B_P containing **a**, and **false** to all the rest.

$M_{TA'}$(**r(b) :- s(a, b).**) = **false**

since $M_{TA'}$ makes the head false and the body true. Hence $M_{TA'}$ assigns **false** to **r(X) :- s(a, X).** □

For a Datalog program P, $M_{TA}(P)$ = **true** if $M_{TA}(C)$ is true for every clause C of P. A truth assignment *TA* that makes a program *P* true is a *model* for *P*. We see now why B_P need contain only ground literals that can arise by substitution from literals in *P*. Any other ground literal never appears when instantiating a clause in *P*. Therefore, whether such a literal is true or false in the current state of the world is irrelevant to the meaning of *P*. Since we want truth assignments to abstract the minimum information from the world to decide the meaning of a program, B_P need contain only ground instances of literals from *P*.

An *atom* is a positive literal. Let *A* be a ground atom. We say that *P logically implies A* if every truth assignment that is a model for *P* makes *A* true. A set of ground literals is logically implied by a program if each one is logically implied. When deciding implication, we must include any constants from A and A itself in constructing B_P. Unlike Proplog, if A contains symbols not in P, P might still imply A. (See Exercise 5.1.)

EXAMPLE 5.5: The ground atom **p(a, d)** is logically implied by the program P given in Example 5.2. Any truth assignment TA that makes P true must make the following instances of clauses in P true:

```
p(a, d) :- q(a, d), r(d).
q(a, d).
r(d) :- s(a, d).
s(a, d).
```

TA must make **s(a, d)** true, hence **r(d)** true. Since **q(a, d)** is true, so must **p(a, d)** be true under TA. □

Just as for Proplog, the *establish* function is intended to determine logical implication. That is, given a list of ground atoms as a goal list, *establish* will return **true** if that set of facts is logically implied by the program. Recall that the *establish* routine we developed for Datalog is an optimization of the algorithm that "fills in" rules and nonground facts and then simply applies the Proplog *establish* algorithm. That algorithm is clearly consistent with the formal definitions we have made here. Instantiations are simply a formal device to fill in the nonground clauses in all possible ways to make them ground. Once we have done that, we simply fall back on the Proplog definitions applied to all the ground instances of the clauses in the program.

We can go a little further. We can give a meaning to a goal list that has variables in it. For a goal list g, $M_{TA}(g)$ = **true** if there is *some* instantiation I such that $M_{TA}(I(g))$ = **true**. This definition coincides with the intuition we developed for a goal list with variables in Section 4.7: Any substitution is acceptable to use in trying to establish a goal list; we need succeed only for a single one. If we invoke *establish* on a goal list containing a variable, we are asking for any (or perhaps all) instantiations of the variables in g that result in ground instances that are logically implied by the program.

5.2. Full Predicate Logic

Just as Proplog programs are a subset of full propositional logic, Datalog is a particular subset of a more natural, and well-studied, logic that includes a more general treatment of quantification and connectives. Quantification captures the English phrases "for all" and "for some." This full logic is known as *predicate logic*. Again, we develop the syntax, semantics, and deduction for this logic.

Predicate logic is a refinement of propositional logic. Propositional logic describes how basic declarative sentences combine by means of certain conjunctions: *and*, *or*, and *not*. In that logic the basic sentences were left unanalyzed. Since the meaning of a basic sentence is taken to be true or false in a world, the complexity and expressive power of the semantics are rather low. Predicate logic attempts to capture *quantification* in natural language. Just as propositional logic gave meaning to the logical connective words *and*, *or*, and *not*, predicate logic gives meaning to the quantifying words *some* and *every*. Again the emphasis is on the semantics, not the syntax.

To begin in the (almost) traditional way, consider Hector, the student, and his mortality. Consider the three sentences: "Every student is mortal," "Hector is a student," and "Hector is mortal." If we model these sentences in propositional logic, we must use three different, unrelated, proposition symbols, one for each basic sentence. But these sentences are related. Because of the meanings of the words, the truth of the third sentence follows from the truth of the first two. Propositional logic cannot capture this relationship. Predicate logic can.

What is the essence here? These sentences talk of objects or entities—in this case students. Objects are what the quantifiers, such as "every," quantify over. When we say "every," we mean every object. So our logic has to be able to speak of objects. It also must talk of sets and relationships. We can capture (at least part of) the meaning of the word *student* by giving the set of objects that are students. So in predicate logic we can refine further the meanings of simple declarative sentences by looking at what objects they talk about and what relationships hold among the objects.

Consider again the simple sentence "Hector is a student." We can model that sentence by saying that *Hector* is the name of an object, and *student* is a set of objects. This sentence means that the object named *Hector* is in the set of objects denoted by *student*. Since to capture the essence of this sentence we use only *student* and *Hector*, we can use a simpler, sparser formal language to express it. We write simply **`student(hector)`**. For a sentence such as "Hector likes Maria," we say that *Hector* and *Maria* are names of objects and that *likes* is a set of pairs of objects: those pairs such that the first object likes the second object. We write this sentence in abbreviated form as **`likes(hector, maria)`**.

Now that we have "looked inside" simple declarative sentences, how do we model quantifiers? First, we introduce variables. They are placeholders for objects. We use them together with quantifiers to express the meaning of quantified sentences. For example, to formalize the sentence "There exists a student," we use the expression:

```
∃ X student(X)
```

Here *student* is the same set as the earlier one containing Hector. The quantifying prefix **∃ X** can be read "There is some object **X** such that. . . ." We are saying some object (we do not necessarily know which object) is in the set of students. Similarly, we formalize the sentence "All students are mortal" as:

```
∀ X (mortal(X) :- student(X))
```

We read ∀ **X** as "For every object **X**. . . ." This example shows how we can use the logical connectives of propositional logic to put together our new "analyzed" sentences. This formalization says that for every object **X**, **X** is among the set of objects that are mortal if **X** is among the objects that are students.

To give an idea of what we expect of the deduction component of this logic, consider the first three sentences concerning Hector, mortality, and students. We have seen the formal expressions for the first two. The formal expression for the third, "Hector is mortal," is simply:

```
mortal(hector).
```

Clearly, if the first two sentences are true in our world, then the third statement, sadly, is also true. The deductive component should be able to capture this semantic relationship among the three sentences.

As another example of capturing an English sentence in predicate logic, consider the statement "All student papers not graded by their authors are graded by an instructor." When rendering this sentence in predicate logic, we first must express the condition that an object is a "student paper." Using predicates **paper**, **student**, and **wrote**, we can describe a student paper as an object **X** that is a paper such that there is some student **Y** who wrote **X**:

```
paper(X), ∃ Y (student(Y), wrote(Y, X))
```

This formula is true of any **X** that is a student paper. With predicates **instructor** and **graded**, we can express the situation that an instructor graded some object **X**:

```
∃ Z (instructor(Z), graded(Z, X))
```

To express that every object that is a student paper was graded by an instructor, we use *not* and *or* to express the implication, and quantify over all objects. We arrive at:

```
∀ X ¬(paper(X), ∃ Y (student(Y), wrote(Y, X), ¬graded(Y, X)));
   ∃ Z (instructor(Z), graded(Z, X))
```

To paraphrase this expression: "For every object **X**, it is not the case that **X** is a student paper and **X** was not graded by its author, or some instructor graded **X**."

These paragraphs have been a brief introduction to predicate logic. The following sections give its syntax, semantics, and deductive theory in more detail than we really care to consider.

5.2.1. *Syntax of Predicate Logic*

The grammar in Figure 5.3 defines the language of predicate logic. The grammar is meant to elucidate the structure of predicate logic expressions rather than to be easy to parse. *Predicate formulas* are similar in structure to propositional formulas, since a predicate formula can be a disjunction of one or more *predicate terms*, each of which is a conjunction of one or more *predicate factors*. A predicate factor is a negated or unnegated *predicate unit*, which is either an *atom* (sometimes called an *atomic formula*), or a parenthesized predicate expression. We now have *quantifiers*, so a predicate formula can have a quantifier, with an associated variable, in front of it. The quantifier is either the *universal quantifier* (∀) or the *existential quantifier* (∃). The notation ∀ **X** is read "for all **X**," and the notation ∃ **X** is read "there exists **X** such that." Also, atoms are structured, being either a solitary predicate symbol, or a predicate symbol followed by a list of one or more *terms* enclosed in parentheses. Each term is either a variable or a constant.

Do not confuse "predicate term" with just "term." The first "term" is an algebraic notion indicating an expression that is the conjunction (product) of factors, and that is disjoined (added) with similar expressions. The second "term" means an entity that can be an argument in an atom. When we use "term" with no further qualification, we will always mean the second kind of "term." As before, we will use "expression" and "formula" more or less interchangeably.

```
PREDEXP → PREDFORM
PREDEXP → QUANT PREDEXP
QUANT → ∀ varsym
QUANT → ∃ varsym
PREDFORM → PREDTERM
PREDFORM → PREDTERM ; PREDFORM
PREDTERM → PREDFACT
PREDTERM → PREDFACT , PREDTERM
PREDFACT → PREDUNIT
PREDFACT → ¬ PREDUNIT
PREDUNIT → PREDATOM
PREDUNIT → ( PREDEXP )
PREDATOM → predsym
PREDATOM → predsym ( ARGLIST )
ARGLIST → TERM
ARGLIST → TERM , ARGLIST
TERM → csym
TERM → varsym

where predsym = lc (lc + uc + digit)*
      csym = lc (lc + uc + digit)*
      varsym = uc (lc + us + digit)*
      lc = any lowercase letter
      uc = any uppercase letter
      digit = any digit
```

Figure 5.3

EXAMPLE 5.6: Figure 5.4 shows a derivation tree for the predicate formula

∀ X r(X, Y), p(Y); ¬(∃ Z s(Z, X, b)); q □

In this grammar we distinguish symbols that denote predicates from symbols that denote constants. A symbol generated by 'predsym' is called a *predicate symbol.* The *arity* of a predicate symbol is the number of terms in the list following the predicate symbol. The arity of a predicate symbol is part of its identification. That is, two predicate symbols are considered different if they have the same name but different arities. To include arity information with a predicate symbol, we use the form 'predsym/arity'.

EXAMPLE 5.7: The atoms:

r(X, Y), p(Y), s(Z, X, b), q

have predicate symbols with arities two, one, three, and zero, respectively. Their predicate symbols are denoted **r/2**, **p/1**, **s/3**, and **q/0**. The atoms:

r(X, Y) and **r(X, Y, Z)**

have different predicate symbols, **r/2** and **r/3**. □

Here we define various syntactic properties of predicate formulas that will come in handy later.

As we can see from the grammar and the example derivation, the precedence of ',', ';', and '¬' is the same as for propositional logic. Quantifiers have the lowest precedence. Thus, the subformula associated with a quantifier, called its *scope,* extends to the end of the enclosing formula, or to the next unmatched right parenthesis, if the latter comes first. In a derivation the scope of a quantifer is the formula generated by the second PREDEXP in the application of:

PREDEXP → QUANT PREDEXP

that generated the quantifier.

EXAMPLE 5.8: In:

∀ X r(X, Y), p(Y); ¬(∃ Z s(Z, X, b)); q

the scope of **∀ X** is the subformula:

r(X, Y), p(Y); ¬(∃ Z s(Z, X, b)); q

and the scope of **∃ Z** is:

s(Z, X, b) □

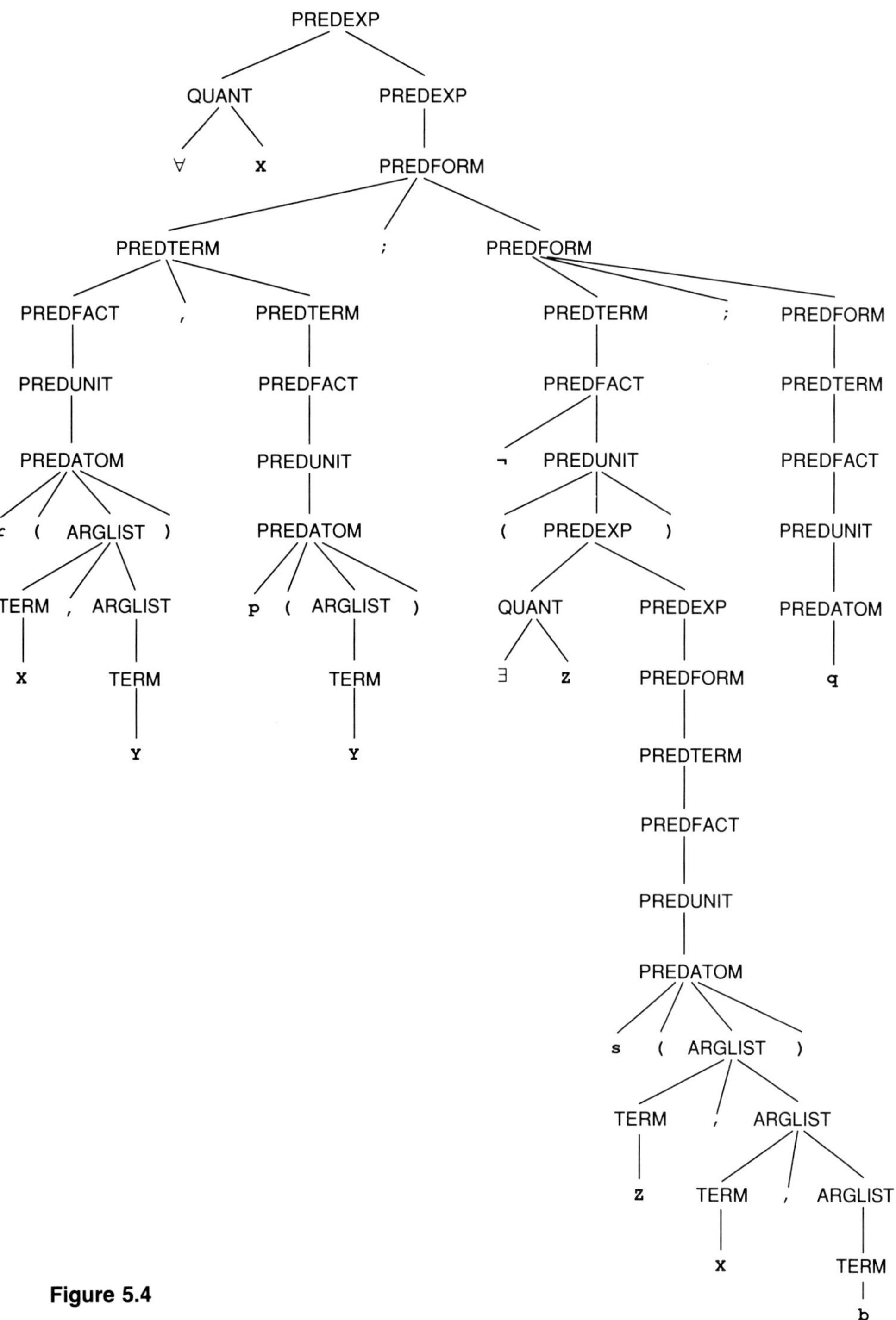
PREDEXP
QUANT PREDEXP
∀ x PREDFORM
PREDTERM ; PREDFORM
PREDFACT , PREDTERM PREDTERM ; PREDFORM
PREDUNIT PREDFACT PREDFACT PREDTERM
PREDATOM PREDUNIT ¬ PREDUNIT PREDFACT
r (ARGLIST) PREDATOM (PREDEXP) PREDUNIT
TERM , ARGLIST p (ARGLIST) QUANT PREDEXP PREDATOM
x TERM TERM ∃ z PREDFORM q
y y PREDTERM
PREDFACT
PREDUNIT
PREDATOM
s (ARGLIST)
TERM , ARGLIST
z TERM , ARGLIST
x TERM
b

Figure 5.4

A quantifier *binds* all occurrences of its associated variable in its scope that are not bound in subformulas. A variable that is not bound by any quantifier is called a *free* variable. Notice that a single variable may have both free and bound occurrences in the same formula. A formula that contains at least one free variable is called an *open* formula. A formula that contains no free variables—that is, in which all occurrences of all variables are bound—is called a *closed* formula. A closed formula is sometimes called a *sentence*.

EXAMPLE 5.9: In:

```
∀ X r(X, Y), p(Y); ¬(∃ Z s(Z, X, b)); q
```

the ∀ **X** binds the occurrences of **X** in **r(X, Y)** and **s(Z, X, b)**. The ∃ **Z** binds the occurrence of **Z** in **s(Z, X, b)**. Both occurrences of **Y** are free in this formula, hence the formula is open. Adding ∃ **Y** to the beginning gives a closed formula:

```
∃ Y ∀ X r(X, Y), p(Y); ¬(∃ Z s(Z, X, b)); q
```
□

A special case of variable binding arises when two quantifiers have the same associated variable and one occurs within the scope of the other. In that case the inner quantifier takes precedence over the outer for variable occurrences within the scope of the inner quantifier. The situation is analogous to a programming language with nested procedures: Within the body of a subprocedure, variable declarations in the subprocedure always override declarations in outer procedures. As with programming languages, we can uniformly change the name of a bound variable to a name not appearing elsewhere to avoid confusion.

EXAMPLE 5.10: In the formula:

```
∀ X ∃ Y p(X, Y); ∀ X q(X, Y)
```

the occurrence of **X** in **p(X, Y)** is bound by the first ∀ **X**, whereas the **X** in **q(X, Y)** is bound by the second ∀ **X**. Both occurrences of **Y** are bound by ∃ **Y**. This binding situation is analogous to that in the fragment of code shown in Figure 5.5. The X in 'X := Y + 1' is the one declared in *main*, whereas the X in 'Y := X + 2' is the one declared in *sub2*. The Y in both expressions is the one declared in *sub1*.

We can change the second **X** to **Z** in the formula to get:

```
∀ X ∃ Y p(X, Y); ∀ Z q(Z, Y)
```

which avoids the clash of variable names. □

5.2.2. *Semantics for Predicate Logic*

For propositional logic we simply use a truth assignment to give meaning to propositional formulas. There we only have to abstract truth values of simple sentences

```
procedure main;
    var X;
      .
      .
      .
    procedure sub1
      var Y;
        .
        .
        .
      procedure sub2
        var X
        begin
          .
          .
          .
          Y := X + 2;
          .
          .
          .
        end;
      begin
        .
        .
        .
        X := Y + 1;
        .
        .
        .
      end;
      .
      .
      .
    end;
```

Figure 5.5

from the world. Here in predicate logic we have to deal also with the objects in our world, as outlined in the discussion in Section 5.2. The world for interpretation of predicate formulas provides a set of objects, **D**, called the *domain* or *universe*. **D** may be finite or infinite (even uncountably infinite for those who wish to think about such things). **D** allows us to give meaning to the constants and variables in predicate formulas.

Given a predicate formula f, we need to know what objects are referenced by constants that appear in f. Let Con_f be the set of constants in f. We need a *constant mapping*, C_D, that takes Con_f into **D**. Thus, for constant **a**, C_D(**a**) is the object in the world to which **a** refers.

EXAMPLE 5.11: Let f be the formula:

```
∀ M ¬(movie(M), hasChar(M, butler), hasChar(M, villain));
   (∃ Y detective(Y), suspects(Y, butler), hasChar(M, Y)),
   (∃ Z person(Z), kills(villain, Z), hasChar(M, Z)).
```

This formula says that every movie that has **butler** and **villain** as characters also has a detective who suspects **butler** and a person whom **villain** kills. Assume the domain **D** we consider consists of all movies $\{m_1, m_2, m_3, \ldots\}$ and all characters of those movies $\{c_1, c_2, c_3, \ldots\}$. Here, Con_f = {**butler**, **villain**}. One constant mapping for Con_f is C_D where:

C_D(**butler**) $= c_1$
C_D(**villain**) $= c_3$

which makes the butler and the villain the same character. □

We still must give truth values to basic sentences as expressed in predicate logic. To assign those values, we have to form the set of all possible basic sentences that could go into the meaning of a formula. Given a formula f, a domain **D**, and a constant function C_D, we define the *base* of f with respect to **D** and C_D, denoted B_{f,D,C_D}, as follows. Take any atom A from f. Form a new atom by replacing each constant **a** in the argument list of A by C_D(**a**), and replacing each variable in the argument list by any member of the domain **D**.

EXAMPLE 5.12: Consider formula f from the last example, with the domain **D** and the constant mapping C_D' given there. Starting with the atom **hasChar (M, butler)**, we replace **butler** by C_D'(**butler**) $= c_2$ to get **hasChar** (**M**, c_2). We then know that any replacement of **M** by an element of **D** will yield an element of $B_{f,D,C_D'}$. Some elements so obtained are:

hasChar (c_1, c_2)
hasChar (c_2, c_2)
hasChar (c_3, c_2)

and:

hasChar (m_1, c_2)
hasChar (m_2, c_2)
hasChar (m_3, c_2) □

We now can describe formally how the world determines the truth values for basic sentences of a formula f. It provides a truth assignment TA_{D,C_D} that maps B_{f,D,C_D} into {**true**, **false**}. The truth assignment gives a meaning to each ground atom that can be obtained from an atom in f through replacement of constants using C_D and replacement of variables with elements from **D**. This situation is exactly analogous to the truth assignments we used in the propositional case; it tells us whether our basic sentences are true or false in this world.

Aside: The elements in the base for a formula f are odd birds. We cannot really write down **p** $(d_1, d_2, \ldots, d_n)$, where **p** is a predicate symbol and each d_i is a domain element. The d_i's are the actual objects of interest (integers, movies, people in the world), not names for those objects. It is as if we spoke a sentence, but whenever we got to the place for a noun, we pointed at some object rather than using a word for it. We could get around having to construct such hybrids if we let a truth assignment *TA* map an n-ary predicate symbol **p** to a function from $\mathbf{D}^n$ to {**true**, **false**}. We would then have to deal only with $TA[\mathbf{p}](d_1, d_2, \ldots, d_n)$, rather than $TA(\mathbf{p}(d_1, d_2, \ldots, d_n))$.

Why do we choose the former course over the latter? First, it conforms better to the semantics we give to Datalog programs. With them, the domains are sets of names (the constant symbols in the program). An atom made up of a predicate symbol and elements from such a domain is not an unwieldy beast. Second, the former course allows us to make our structures more parsimonious. A truth assignment must give meaning to **p** only for combinations of domain elements that can actually arise in interpreting a formula, while $TA[\mathbf{p}]$ must be defined for all n-tuples of domain elements. □

To collect these pieces that characterize a world in which we give meanings to formulas, we form a *structure*. A structure *ST* is a triple $<\mathbf{D}, C_\mathbf{D}, TA_{\mathbf{D},C_\mathbf{D}}>$. Note the dependency, indicated by the subscripts, of the second component on the first, and of the third on the first two. The base over which the truth assignment is defined is implicit in the structure. We also let the particular formula f be understood; otherwise, the clutter of subscripts would be totally unmanageable.

EXAMPLE 5.13: Consider again the formula f from the last two examples. A structure for f is:

$$ST = <\mathbf{D}, C_\mathbf{D}', TA_{\mathbf{D},C_\mathbf{D}'}>$$

where **D** and $C_\mathbf{D}'$ are the same as in Example 5.11, and $TA_{\mathbf{D},C_\mathbf{D}'}$ is the truth assignment that makes the following elements of $B_{f,\mathbf{D},C_\mathbf{D}'}$ true (and no others).

movie (m_1)
movie (m_2)

hasChar (m_1, c_1)
hasChar (m_1, c_2)
hasChar (m_1, c_3)
hasChar (m_2, c_1)
hasChar (m_2, c_2)

detective (c_1)

person (c_3)

suspects (c_1, c_2)

kills (c_2, c_3) □

Henceforth we usually will omit the subscripts on the constant mapping and truth assignment in a structure, keeping in mind the dependencies among the components. Some treatments of predicate logic define a structure for a formula relative to some fixed set of constants. (See Exercise 5.7.) That approach has the advantage that a structure for a formula f is also a structure for any subformula of f. For the definition here, a structure has to be restricted to be a structure for a subformula. Our stinginess with information about the real world in structures guided the decision to make a structure particular to a formula.

Having said what a structure is, we define the meaning of a formula in a structure ST for that formula. That definition will be recursive over the definition of a formula. Free variables are a problem for a recursive definition, because if the same free variable occurs in two subformulas, there is no immediate mechanism to ensure that those occurrences get replaced by the same domain elements. Even if we care only about the meaning of closed formulas, we still must give a meaning to subformulas that contain free variables. In propositional logic we give meaning to a formula with respect to just a truth assignment. Here we give meaning to a formula f with respect to a structure $ST = \langle \mathbf{D}, C, TA \rangle$ and an *instantiation* for that structure. An instantiation I for structure ST is a function from variables to **D**. An instantiation tells us how to interpret the free variables in a formula. As with Datalog logic, we assume that every instantiation is defined over all possible variables. However, in any particular case, we will be interested only in the value of the instantiation on a finite subset of those variables.

EXAMPLE 5.14: Consider again the formula f from Example 5.11. For the domain **D** given there, an instantiation I might map variables **M**, **Y**, and **Z** as follows:

$I(\mathbf{M}) = m_2$
$I(\mathbf{Y}) = c_2$
$I(\mathbf{Z}) = c_1$ □

We define a *meaning function*, $M_{ST,I}$ for ST and an instantiation I. The meaning function will map predicate formulas into {**true**, **false**}. For an atom $\mathbf{p}(\alpha_1, \alpha_2, \ldots, \alpha_n)$:

$$M_{ST,I}(\mathbf{p}(\alpha_1, \alpha_2, \ldots, \alpha_n)) = TA\ (\mathbf{p}(d_1, d_2, \ldots, d_n))$$

where $d_i = I(\alpha_i)$ if α_i is a variable, and $d_i = C(\alpha_i)$ if α_i is a constant. Note that $\mathbf{p}(d_1, d_2, \ldots, d_n)$ will be in the base of formula f. For the logical connectives, the definition of the meaning function follows that for propositional logic.

$M_{ST,I}$(g, h) = **true** if $M_{ST,I}(g)$ = **true and** $M_{ST,I}(h)$ = **true.**
$M_{ST,i}$(g; h) = **true** if $M_{ST,I}(g)$ = **true or** $M_{ST,I}(h)$ = **true.**
$M_{ST,I}(\neg g)$ = **true** if $M_{ST,I}(g)$ = **false.**

The following two definitions give meaning to the quantifiers:

$M_{ST,I}(\forall$ **X** $g)$ = **true** if for every I' that agrees with I on all variables except **X** (and possibly on **X** as well), $M_{ST,I'}(g)$ = **true.**

$M_{ST,I}(\exists$ **X** $g)$ = **true** if there is some I' that agrees with I on all variables except **X** (and possibly on **X** as well), such that $M_{ST,I'}(g)$ = **true.**

Notice that $M_{ST,I}(\forall$ **X** $g)$ is independent of the value of I(**X**). For $M_{ST,I}(\forall$ **X** $g)$ to be true, the formula g must be true for every value that **X** may assume. Similarly, $M_{ST,I}(\exists$ **X** $g)$ is independent of I(**X**). There need only be some value for **X** in **D** that makes g true for ∃ **X** g to be true. This independence means that $M_{ST,I}(f)$ only depends on I if f has free variables. For a closed formula f, $M_{ST,I}(f)$ is not affected by the choice of I. In such cases we may write simply $M_{ST}(f)$.

EXAMPLE 5.15: Consider the following formula f, which is the one in Example 5.11 with predicate symbols and constants abbreviated to single letters:

```
∀ M ¬(m(M), h(M, b), h(M, v));
      (∃ Y d(Y), s(Y, b), h(M, Y)),
      (∃ Z p(Z), k(v, Z), h(M, Z))
```

We want to deduce the meaning of this formula under the structure ST = <D, C_D', TA>, where D and C_D' are given in Example 5.11 and TA is from Example 5.13. Since f is a closed formula, its meaning will be independent of whichever instantiation I we choose.

Let us write f as:

∀ **M** g[**M**].

The notation g[**M**] means g is a formula with one or more free occurrences of **M**. For $M_{ST,I}(f)$ to be true, we must have $M_{ST,I'}(g[\mathbf{M}])$ = **true** for any instantiation I' that agrees with I except possibly on **M**. At the moment the only thing that interests us about I' is its value on M. Consider I_1 such that $I_1(\mathbf{M}) = m_1$. We can expand $M_{ST,I_1}(g[\mathbf{M}])$ into:

M_{ST,I_1}(¬(**m(M), h(M, b), h(M, v)**)) or
  M_{ST,I_1}((∃ **Y** i[**M, Y**]), (∃ **Z** j[**M, Z**]))

where i[**M, Y**] is short for:

```
d(Y), s(Y, b), h(M, Y)
```

and j[**M, Z**] is short for:

p(Z), k(v, Z), h(M, Z)

Since the first disjunct contains no quantifiers, we expand it and apply C_D' and I_1 to get:

not(TA(**m**(m_1)) **and** TA(**h**(m_1, c_2)) **and** TA(**h**(m_1, c_2)))

Here C_D' mapped both **b** and **v** to c_2, whereas I_1 mapped **M** to m_1. We determine that this formula is false by consulting TA. All the atoms here are true, so the negation of their conjunctions is false. Thus the value of $M_{ST,I_1}(g[\mathbf{M}])$ depends on:

$M_{ST,I1}$(($\exists$ **Y** i[**M**, **Y**]), ($\exists$ **Z** j[**M**, **Z**]))

which is:

M_{ST,I_1}($\exists$ **Y** i[**M**, **Y**]) and $M_{ST,I1}$($\exists$ **Z** j[**M**, **Z**]).

To make the first conjunct true, we must find an instantiation that agrees that I_1 except on **Y** and that makes i[**M**, **Y**] true. Peeking ahead, we choose I_{11}, where I_{11}(**M** $= m_1$ (to agree with I_1 on **M**) and I_{11}(**Y**) $= c_1$. Now we need the value of:

$M_{ST,I_{11}}$(**d**(**Y**), **s**(**Y**, **b**), **h**(**M**, **Y**))

which we determine is **true** by applying the instantiation I_{11} and the constant mapping to get:

TA(**d**(c_1)) **and** TA(**s**(c_1, c_2)) **and** TA(**h**(m_1, c_1))

and noting that TA makes all these atoms true. For the second conjunct, we need an instantiation that agrees with I_1 except on **Z** and that makes j[**M**, **Z**] true. Serendipitously, we pick I_{12}, where I_{12}(**M**) $= m_1$ and I_{12}(**Z**) $= c_3$. We see:

$M_{ST,\ I_{12}}$(**p**(**Z**), **k**(**v**, **Z**), **h**(**M**, **Z**))

is **true** by applying I_{12} and the constant mapping to get:

TA(**p**(c_3)) **and** TA(**k**(c_2, c_3)) **and** TA(**h**(m_1, c_3))

and consulting TA to see that each of the atoms is true.

Working our way back to the top, we see that we have shown g[**M**] is true for one instantiation. What about all the other choices? For any instantiation that maps **M** to anything other than m_1 or m_2, g[**M**] will be true. Such an instantiation makes **m(M)** false under TA, hence makes the disjunct:

$\neg$(**m**(**M**), **h**(**M**, **b**), **h**(**M**, **v**))

true. We have considered the m_1 case already. Thus the only instantiation that could make g[**M**] false is the one that maps **M** to m_2, call it I_2. Now:

M_{ST,I_2}($\neg$(**m**(**M**), **h**(**m**, **b**), **h**(**M**, **v**))) = **false**,

as I_2 makes all three atoms in the conjunct true. Skipping ahead, we see for g[**M**] to be true, we must have:

$M_{ST,I_2}(\exists$ **Z** j[**M**, **Z**]) = **true.**

Since there is an existential quantifier at the outermost level, to make this subformula true we need an instantiation I_{21} such that I_{21}(**M**) = I_2(**M**) and:

$M_{ST,I_{21}}$(**p(Z), k(v, Z), h(M, Z)**) = **true.**

After all this work, unfortunately, no such instantiation exists. I_2(**Z**) must be c_3 to make **p(Z)** true, but then the meaning of **h(M, Z)** is TA(**h**(m_2, c_3)) = **false.**

Thus I_2 makes g[**M**] false, so $M_{ST,I}(f)$ = **false** for any instantiation I. Note that if TA also made **h**(m_2, c_3) true, then f would be true under ST. □

A structure for a formula is sometimes called an *interpretation* for the formula. For a closed formula, any structure that makes the formula true is a *model* for the formula. A closed formula where all structures are models is said to be *valid,* whereas if no structure is a model, the formula is *unsatisfiable.*

Aside: There is an alternative way to assign meaning to quantified formulas. We can deal with free variables in subformulas by replacing them with domain objects at the correct moment and omitting instantiations. The notation f[**X**] represents a predicate formula f in which **X** occurs free. For an object d in D, f[**X**/d] represents the formula derived from f by replacing all *free* occurrences of **X** by d. Thus, if f is:

∃ Y r(X, Y); ∀ X s(X, Y)

then f[**X**/d] is:

∃ Y r(d, Y); ∀ X s(X, Y)

We would then give meaning to, say, the universal quantifier by a definition:

$M_{ST}(\forall$ **X** g[**X**]) = **true** if for every $d \in$ D, $M_{ST}(g$[**X**/d]) = **true.**

We did not choose this development for two reasons. First, the construction g[**X**/d] is not really a predicate formula, since it contains domain objects. Second, instantiations allow us to apply the meaning function to open formulas if we want to, whereas this alternative does not give meaning to such formulas. □

5.3. Deduction in Predicate Logic

Logical implication for predicate logic has much the same flavor as for propositional logic. It is an assertion that one formula is true in all worlds where another formula is true. We give particular examples of logical implications and equivalences here. Later we present a more general deduction procedure for determining logical implication, but it will apply only to the subset of predicate logic formulas that can be converted to conjunctive form. There are deduction procedures for the entire predicate logic, but we choose not to develop one here, because we will see one for functional logic in Chapter 9. Formula f *logically implies* formula g if for every structure ST for f, g and every instantiation I, if $M_{ST,I}(f)$ = **true** then $M_{ST,I}(g)$ = **true**. Note that ST must map constants from both f and g.

The definition does not say: For every structure ST if for every instantiation I $M_{ST,I}(f)$ = **true,** then for every instantiation J $M_{ST,J}(g)$ = **true**. That is, the requirement is that given any structure ST, if f is true for a particular instantiation I, then g is true for that instantiation. Contrast that requirement to the weaker condition that g has to be true under all instantiations only if f is true under all instantiations. The following example demonstrates that the second definition embodies a weaker notion.

EXAMPLE 5.16: Let f be the formula **p(Y)** and g the formula **p(a)**. Consider the structure ST = <{1, 2}, C, TA> where C(**a**) = 1 and TA makes only **p(2)** true. With the instantiation I that maps **Y** to 2, we have:

$M_{ST,I}$(**p(Y)**) = **true,**

but:

$M_{ST,I}$(**p(a)**) = **false,**

so **p(Y)** does not logically imply **p(a)**. Consider the second definition. For any ST where $M_{ST,I}$(**p(Y)**) = **true** for all choices of I, we must have M_{ST}(**p(a)**) = **true,** since when I(**Y**) = 1, TA(**p(*I*(Y))**) = TA(**p(1)**) = TA(**p(**C(**a**)**)**). We see the definitions are not equivalent. □

Formulas f and g are *logically equivalent*, denoted $f \equiv g$, if for every structure ST for f, g and every instantiation I:

$M_{ST,I}(f) = M_{ST,I}(g)$.

Equivalently, $f \equiv g$ if f logically implies g and g logically implies f.

EXAMPLE 5.17: The following predicate formulas f and g are equivalent.

f = ¬∀ **X p(X); q(X)**
g = ∃ **X ¬p(X), ¬q(X)**

Since both formulas are closed, their meaning is dependent only on the structure used, not on any instantiation. If $M_{ST}(f)$ = **true** for some structure ST, then:

M_{ST}(∀ **X p(X); q(X)**) = **false.**

Thus it is not the case that for every instantiation I:

$M_{ST,I}$(**p(X); q(X)**) = **true.**

Hence there is some instantiation J where:

$M_{ST,J}$(**p(X); q(X)**) = **false.**

It must be that:

$M_{ST,J}$(**p (X)**) = **false** and $M_{ST,J}$(**q (X)**) = **false.**

Now consider $M_{ST}(g)$. $M_{ST}(g)$ = **true** if there is some instantiation I such that:

$M_{ST,I}$(**¬p (X) , ¬q (X)**) = **true.**

Instantiation J fits this requirement. Thus, for any structure ST, $M_{ST}(f)$ = **true** means $M_{ST}(g)$ = **true,** so f logically implies g. A similar argument shows that g logically implies f, so $f \equiv g$. □

EXAMPLE 5.18: Consider the formula h =

∃ X ¬p (X) ; r (X)

along with formula g from the last example. Formula g logically implies h, since if there is a structure ST and an instantiation I such that:

$M_{ST,I}$(**¬p (X) , ¬q (X)**) = **true,**

then:

$M_{ST,I}$(**¬p (X)**) = **true**

and so:

$M_{ST,I}$(**¬p (X) ; r (X)**) = **true.**

However, h does not logically imply g. Consider the structure ST =

$<\{d\}$, C, {**p** (d), **q** (d), **r** (d)}$>$.

(Here we represent a truth assignment by the set of base elements it maps to **true.**) $M_{ST}(h)$ = **true,** since any instantiation I where I(**X**) = d makes **¬p (X) ; r (X)** true. However, for no instantiation I is:

$M_{ST,I}$(**¬p (X) , ¬q (X)**) = **true.**

(Note there is only one possible instantiation consistent with ST, since ST has but one domain element.) Hence h does not logically imply g, so the two formulas are not equivalent. □

The equivalences involving commutativity, associativity, distributivity, and DeMorgan's laws given in Section 2.2.3 all hold here. The following are some useful equivalences involving quantifiers.

¬∀ X $f \equiv$ **∃ X ¬**f
¬∃ X $f \equiv$ **∀ X ¬**f
∀ X ∀ Y $f \equiv$ **∀ Y ∀ X** f

The validity of these equivalences is evident upon examination. For example, if **¬∃ X** f is true, then there can be no value for **X** that makes f true, which is to say that all values of **X** make f false, or ∀ **X** ¬f. Note that ∃ **X** ∀ **Y** f is *not* equivalent to ∀ **Y** ∃ **X** f, as the next example demonstrates.

EXAMPLE 5.19: Consider the two formulas:

```
∀ X ∃ Y less(X, Y)
∃ Y ∀ X less(X, Y)
```

Consider a structure with the integers as its domain and giving the obvious truth assignment for **less**. The first formula says that for each integer, there is some larger integer, whereas the second says that some integer is larger than all integers (including itself). □

Two equivalences allow quantifiers to be distributed over connectives.

∀ **X**(f, g) ≡ (∀ **X** f), (∀ **X** g)
∃ **X** (f; g) ≡ (∃ **X** f); (∃ **X** g)

However, the universal quantifier does not distribute over *or* and the existential quantifier does not distribute over *and*. Note that we do have logical implications that relate the formulas involved in those two cases.

(∀ **X** f); (∀ **X** g)

logically implies:

∀ **X** (f; g)

and:

∃ **X** (f, g)

logically implies:

(∃ **X** f), (∃ **X** g)

but we do not have equivalence.

EXAMPLE 5.20: The formula:

```
∃ X student(X); mortal(X)
```

can be read as "Some **X** is a student or is a mortal." That formula is equivalent to:

```
(∃ X student(X)); (∃ X mortal(X))
```

We can change one of the quantified variables to get:

$(\exists$ **X student(X)); $(\exists$ Y mortal(Y))**

which we can read as "Some **X** is a student or some **Y** is mortal." The formula:

$\exists$ **X student(X), mortal(X)**

states, "Some **X** is a student and is mortal," which certainly implies, "Some **X** is a student and some **Y** is mortal," or:

$(\exists$ **X student(X)), $(\exists$ Y mortal(Y))**

However, the last statement does not imply the previous one. In a world with just two people, A and B, if A is an immortal student and B is a mortal dropout, then the second statement, but not the first, is true. □

In the next subsection, on special forms, we will want to move quantifiers to give them the largest possible scope. The following equivalences hold if **X** does not occur free in g.

$(\forall \ \mathbf{X} f),\ g \equiv \forall\ \mathbf{X}\ (f,\ g)$
$(\forall \ \mathbf{X} f);\ g \equiv \forall\ \mathbf{X}\ (f;\ g)$
$(\exists \ \mathbf{X} f),\ g \equiv \exists\ \mathbf{X}\ (f,\ g)$
$(\exists \ \mathbf{X} f);\ g \equiv \exists\ \mathbf{X}\ (f;\ g)$

The commutativity of "and" and "or" yield similar equivalences, such as:

$f,\ \forall\ \mathbf{X} g \equiv \forall\ \mathbf{X}\ (f,\ g)$

when **X** is not free in f. (See Exercise 5.13.)

5.3.1. *Special Forms*

The deduction procedures in later sections require special forms for predicate formulas. A closed formula f is in *prenex form* if all the quantifiers appear at the left of the formula, and the scope of each is the rest of the formula. The formula:

$\exists$ **X** $\forall$ **Y** $\forall$ **Z p(X, Y, Z), q(X); ¬r(Y)**

is in prenex form. The string of quantifiers $\exists$ **X** $\forall$ **Y** $\forall$ **Z** is called the *prefix,* whereas the remainder of the formula is the *matrix*. Any closed formula has a logically equivalent formula in prenex form. We can transform a formula to prenex form by applying the following steps.

1. Rename variables so that no variable is associated with more than one quantifier.
2. Move all '¬'s inward, using DeMorgan's laws and the equivalences:

   $\neg\forall\ \mathbf{X} f \equiv \exists\ \mathbf{X}\ \neg f$
   $\neg\exists\ \mathbf{X} f \equiv \forall\ \mathbf{X}\ \neg f$

3. Move all quantifiers outward to give them maximum scope, using the equivalences:

$$(\forall\ \mathbf{X}\, f),\ g \equiv \forall\ \mathbf{X}\ (f,\ g)$$
$$(\forall\ \mathbf{X}\, f);\ g \equiv \forall\ \mathbf{X}\ (f;\ g)$$
$$(\exists\ \mathbf{X}\, f),\ g \equiv \exists\ \mathbf{X}\ (f,\ g)$$
$$(\exists\ \mathbf{X}\, f);\ g \equiv \exists\ \mathbf{X}\ (f;\ g)$$

and commutativity of ',' and ';'.

EXAMPLE 5.21: If we start with the formula:

s(a); ∀ X ¬(p(X); ∃ Y q(X, Y))

we can use one of DeMorgan's laws to get:

s(a); ∀ X ¬p(X), ¬∃ Y q(X, Y)

We then move the ¬ in past the existential quantifier:

s(a); ∀ X ¬p(X), ∀ Y ¬q(X, Y)

We finally move both quantifiers to the left:

∀ X ∀ Y s(a); ¬p(X), ¬q(X, Y)

to get a formula in prenex form. □

A formula is *universal* if it has a prenex form that contains only universal quantifiers in the prefix. If f is a universal formula, we can represent f schematically as $\forall\ \hat{X}\ g[\hat{X}]$, where $\hat{X}$ is a sequence of all the variables in g. Thus $\forall\ \hat{X}\ g[\hat{X}]$ might be:

∀ X ∀ Y ∀ Z p(X, Z); ¬p(Y, Z)

For a structure ST for f, note that $M_{ST}(f)$ = **true** exactly if for every instantiation I, $M_{ST,I}(g)$ = **true.** (See Exercise 5.9.) A universal formula is in *conjunctive form* if its matrix is a conjunction of disjunctions of literals. Each disjunction in the conjunction is called a *clause*. Any universal formula can be transformed to an equivalent conjunctive form formula, using the same strategy as for propositional formulas.

EXAMPLE 5.22: The last formula from the last example is equivalent to the formula:

∀ X ∀ Y (s(a); ¬p(X)), (s(a); ¬q(X, Y))

which is in conjunctive form. Its clauses are **s(a); ¬p(X)** and **s(a); ¬q(X, Y)**. □

Unlike propositional formulas, not every predicate formula can be converted to clausal form. The problem is existential quantifiers, which prevent us from obtaining a universal formula.

EXAMPLE 5.23: The formula f =

∃ X ∀ Y p(X, Y)

cannot be put into clausal form, because it is not equivalent to any universal formula. However, if we are considering only unsatisfiability, the formula g =

∀ Y p(a, Y)

which is f with **X** replaced with **a**, is unsatisfiable if and only if the first formula is unsatisfiable. In f, an instantiation provides a domain value for the first argument of the **p**-literal; in the second formula, a constant mapping provides a value for that argument. However, if an existential quantifier occurs within the scope of a universal quantifier, this technique will not work. (See Exercise 5.15.) □

As with propositional formulas, a formula in clausal form can be represented as a set of sets of literals, each set of literals representing a clause.

EXAMPLE 5.24: The formula from the Example 5.21 is represented as the clause set S =

{{s(a); ¬p(X)},
{s(a); ¬q(X, Y)}} □

Because the universal quantifier distributes over ',', we can view each clause as being separately quantified, and change a variable within a single clause without changing the meaning of the formula.

5.3.2. *If*

In connection with Datalog, the "if" operator, ':-', is defined by f :- $g \equiv f$; ¬g. A Datalog program P can be viewed as a conjunctive form predicate formula, since Datalog clauses are assumed to be universally quantified. The task in Datalog is to decide if P logically implies a goal list g_1, g_2, ..., g_k, where each g_i is an atom, and the list is assumed to be existentially quantified. We want to know if:

∀ $\hat{X}$ P logically implies ∃ $\hat{Y}$ g_1, g_2, ..., g_k

Where $\hat{X}$ and $\hat{Y}$ represent all the variables in P and the g's, respectively. This implication holds if the formula:

¬(∀ $\hat{X}$ P); ∃ $\hat{Y}$ g_1, g_2, ..., g_k

is valid, or the formula:

$$\neg(\neg(\forall \hat{X}\ P)\ ;\ \exists \hat{Y}\ g_1,\ g_2,\ \ldots,\ g_k)$$

is unsatisfiable. (See Exercise 5.10.) Doing a little manipulation, we get:

$$\forall \hat{X}\ P,\ \neg(\exists \hat{Y}\ g_1,\ g_2,\ \ldots,\ g_k)$$

and then:

$$\forall \hat{X}\ P,\ \forall \hat{Y} \neg(g_1,\ g_2,\ \ldots,\ g_k)$$

and finally:

$$\forall \hat{X}\ P,\ \forall \hat{Y}(\neg g_1;\ \neg g_2;\ \ldots;\ \neg g_k)$$

This last formula is easily converted to conjunctive form. As a clause set, it looks like the clause set for P plus the clause $\{\neg g_1;\ \neg g_2;\ \ldots;\ \neg g_k\}$ Thus implication of a goal list by a Datalog program can be reduced to unsatisfiability of a predicate formula in conjunctive form.

5.4. Herbrand Interpretations

Again we are interested in logical implication of formulas, which, as we just saw, can be reduced to testing unsatisfiability of a formula in conjunctive form in some cases. In propositional logic we could just enumerate all truth assignments to test unsatisfiability. For predicate logic we would have to enumerate all structures to use that approach. There are clearly too many structures (particularly infinite ones) to make this approach feasible. Is there some way to decide unsatisfiability by examining only some structures? Yes. For each universal formula, there is a special domain and a special constant mapping, such that we need look only at structures using that domain and mapping.

Through the rest of this section, formulas will always be universal, unless otherwise stated. For a formula f, the *Herbrand universe* of f is just Con_f, the constants appearing in f. (If there are no constants in f, let $Con_f = \{\mathbf{a}\}$.) A *Herbrand interpretation* for f is any structure $<Con_f, Id, TA>$ over the Herbrand universe for f, where Id is the identity mapping on Con_f and TA is a truth assignment for $B_{f,Con_f,Id}$. $B_{f,Con_f,Id}$ is called the *Herbrand base* for f. A Herbrand intepretation just uses the constants of f as the domain of discourse and lets every constant name itself. Thus, for a formula f, the only way Herbrand interpretations vary is in their truth assignments.

EXAMPLE 5.25: Consider the formula f =

$$\forall X\ \forall Y\ \forall Z\ \neg(\mathbf{plus}(X,\ a,\ Y),\ \mathbf{plus}(b,\ X,\ Z));\ \mathbf{greater}(Y,\ Z)$$

The intuitive semantics of this formula is that $\mathbf{X} + \mathbf{a} = \mathbf{Y}$ and $\mathbf{b} + \mathbf{X} = \mathbf{Z}$ imply $\mathbf{Y} > \mathbf{Z}$. The Herbrand universe for f is $\{\mathbf{a},\ \mathbf{b}\}$. The Herbrand base of f is:

```
plus(a, a, a)    greater(a, a)
plus(a, a, b)    greater(a, b)
plus(b, a, a)    greater(b, a)
plus(b, a, b)    greater(b, b)
plus(b, b, a)
plus(b, b, b)
```

One Herbrand interpretation for f is $H = <\{\mathbf{a}, \mathbf{b}\}, Id, TA>$ where TA makes:

```
plus(b, a, a)
plus(b, b, b)
greater(b, a)
```

true. (Is H a model for f?) □

The key property of Herbrand interpretations is given in the following theorem. Observe that instantiations do not figure in the theorem statement because the formula involved is closed.

THEOREM 5.1: For a universal formula f, if there exists a structure $ST = <\mathbf{D}, C, TA_{ST}>$ that is a model for f, then there is a Herbrand interpretation $H = <Con_f, Id, TA_H>$ that is a model for f.

Proof: We must show that if $M_{ST}(f) = \mathbf{true}$, then there is a choice for TA_H such that $M_H(f) = \mathbf{true}$. Let $\mathbf{p}(c_1, c_2, \ldots, c_n)$ be any atom in the Herbrand base of f, where each c_i is a constant. Let:

$$TA_H(\mathbf{p}(c_1, c_2, \ldots, c_n)) = TA_{ST}(\mathbf{p}(C(c_1), C(c_2), \ldots, C(c_n))).$$

The formula f can be written as $\forall \hat{X}\, g$, where $\forall \hat{X}$ signifies a universal quantifier for each variable in g. Thus, $M_{ST}(f) = \mathbf{true}$ if and only if $M_{ST,I}(g) = \mathbf{true}$ for every instantiation I. Similarly, to show $M_H(f) = \mathbf{true}$, we must show that for every instantiation I, $M_{H,I}(g) = \mathbf{true}$.

Consider any instantiation I that maps variables to the Herbrand universe, Con_f. Consider the function $I' = C \circ I$. (The $\circ$ denotes functional composition, so $I'(\mathbf{X}) = C(I(\mathbf{X}))$ for each variable $\mathbf{X}$.) I' maps variables to values in $\mathbf{D}$, so I' is an instantiation relative to ST. Thus, $M_{ST,I'}(g) = \mathbf{true}$. Consider any atom:

$$\mathbf{p}(\alpha_1, \alpha_2, \ldots, \alpha_n)$$

in g. We have:

$$M_{H,I}(\mathbf{p}(\alpha_1, \alpha_2, \ldots, \alpha_n)) = TA_H(\mathbf{p}(c_1, c_2, \ldots, c_n)),$$

where $c_i = Id(\alpha_i) = \alpha_i$ if α_i is a constant, and $c_i = I(\alpha_i)$ if α_i is a variable. Also:

$$M_{ST,I'}(\mathbf{p}(\alpha_1, \alpha_2, \ldots, \alpha_n)) = TA_{ST}(\mathbf{p}(d_1, d_2, \ldots, d_n)),$$

where $d_i = C(\alpha_i) = C(c_i)$ if α_i is a constant, and $d_i = I'(\alpha_i) = C(I(\alpha_i)) = C(c_i)$ if α_i is a variable, since $I' = C \circ I$. We have that $d_i = C(c_i)$ for every i. Therefore:

$$M_{ST,I'}(\mathbf{p}(\alpha_1, \alpha_2, \ldots, \alpha_n)) = TA_{ST}(\mathbf{p}(C(c_1), C(c_2), \ldots, C(c_n))) =$$
$$TA_H(\mathbf{p}(c_1, c_2, \ldots, c_n)) = M_{H,I}(\mathbf{p}(\alpha_1, \alpha_2, \ldots, \alpha_n)).$$

Since $M_{ST,I'}$ and $M_{H,I}$ assign the same truth values to every atom in g, they assign the same value to g itself. Thus $M_{H,I}(g)$ = **true**, and hence, since I was arbitrary, $M_H(f)$ = **true**. □

The importance of the theorem is that if f has *no* Herbrand model (that is, a Herbrand interpretation that is a model), then f is unsatisfiable. (Why?) Note that structures used for defining logical implication in Datalog were Herbrand interpretations, and this theorem links that definition to the definition for implication in full predicate logic. (See Exercise 5.20.)

EXAMPLE 5.26: Consider the formula:

∀ X ∀ Y ∀ Z ¬(**plus**(X, a, Y), **plus**(b, X, Z)); **greater**(Y, Z)

from the last example. The structure *ST* = <*Int*, C, TA_{Int}> makes this formula true, where *Int* is the integers; C(**a**) = 1 and C(**b**) = 0; and TA_{Int} maps **plus**(i, j, k) to **true** exactly when $i + j = k$ and maps **greater**(i, j) to **true** exactly when $i > j$. Theorem 5.1 guarantees that a Herbrand model must exist. One such Herbrand model is H = <{**a**, **b**}, *Id*, TA_H> where *TA* is defined as:

TA_H(**plus**(a, a, a)) =
  TA_{Int}(**plus**(C(**a**), C(**a**), C(**a**))) =
  TA_{Int}(**plus**(1, 1, 1)) = **false**

TA_H(**plus**(a, a, b)) =
  TA_{Int}(**plus**(C(**a**), C(**a**), C(**b**))) =
  TA_{Int}(**plus**(1, 1, 0)) = **false**

TA_H(**plus**(b, a, a)) =
  TA_{Int}(**plus**(C(**b**), C(**a**), C(**a**))) =
  TA_{Int}(**plus**(0, 1, 1)) = **true**

and similarly letting TA_H map **plus**(b, b, b) and **greater**(a, b) to **true**, and the rest of the Herbrand base to **false**. □

5.4.1. *Herbrand's Theorem*

With Herbrand interpretations, we now have a method to detect unsatisfiability of a universal formula f. Since the Herbrand universe for f is finite, so is the base of f and hence the number of possible truth assignments. Thus we could enumerate all Herbrand interpretations and test if any is a model. Testing if a Herbrand interpretation is a model for f is decidable. (See Exercise 5.17.) The efficiency of this method is not at all attractive. The next theorem shows that we can use propositional resolution to show unsatisfiability. In its statement, ground instances of clauses are those that can be constructed by replacements from the Herbrand universe. For the proof of the theorem, we extend an instantiation to apply to an entire clause C, by applying it to every literal in C.

THEOREM 5.2 (HERBRAND'S THEOREM): A clause set S is unsatisfiable if and only if some finite set of ground instances of clauses in S is unsatisfiable.

Herbrand's Theorem was actually formulated for functional logic and is not that profound in the predicate logic setting. Here the Herbrand base of S will be finite, so the set of all ground instances of clauses in S is finite, and the proof of the theorem is simple. In the functional case the Herbrand base is not guaranteed to be finite, and hence neither is the set of ground instances.

Proof: Let G be the set of all ground instances of clauses in S. As we remarked, G is finite. We shall show S is unsatisfiable exactly when G is unsatisfiable. This result suffices to establish the theorem, because if any subset of G is unsatisfiable, so is G.

We actually prove that any Herbrand model for S is a model for G, and vice versa. By Theorem 5.1, we need consider only Herbrand models, for if either clause set has a model, it has a Herbrand model. First note that S and G have the same set of Herbrand interpretations. They have the same set of constants and the same Herbrand bases. (Why?) Let H be a Herbrand model for S. Let C_G be a clause in G. There must be a clause C_S in S such that C_G is a ground instance of C_S. Let I be an instantiation such that $I(C_S) = C_G$. We know that $M_H(S) =$ **true**, hence $M_H(\forall\ \hat{X}\ C_S) =$ **true**, where $\hat{X}$ represents all the variables in C_S. Since we have $M_H(\forall\ \hat{X}\ C_S) =$ **true**, $M_{H,I}(C_S) =$ **true**. But:

$$M_{H,I}(C_S) = M_H(I(C_S)) = M_H(C_G),$$

so $M_H(C_G) =$ **true**. Since C_G was arbitrary, $M_H(G) =$ **true**, hence H is a model for G.

Similarly, suppose H is a Herbrand model for G. Let C_S be any clause in S. We want to show that $M_H(\forall\ \hat{X}\ C_S) =$ **true**, where $\hat{X}$ is the set of all variables in C_S. For any instantiation I, $I(C_S)$ is some clause C_G in G. So:

$$M_{H,I}(C_S) = M_H(I(C_S)) = M_H(C_G) = \textbf{true}.$$

Hence H makes every clause in S true, and thus is a model for S. □

Since a set of ground instances of predicate logic clauses is essentially a set of propositional clauses, Herbrand's Theorem says propositional resolution on the set of ground instances will yield a refutation if the original clause set is unsatisfiable.

EXAMPLE 5.27: Let S be the set of clauses:

```
{¬p(X); q(a, X)}
{p(Y)}
{¬q(Z, b)}
```

The following set G consists of all ground instances from S:

```
{¬p(a); q(a, a)}
{¬p(b); q(a, b)}
{p(a)}
{p(b)}
{¬q(a, b)}
{¬q(b, b)}
```

We can treat each ground atom as a distinct proposition symbol. We replace each atomic formula by a proposition symbol derived by concatenating the predicate symbol with the arguments. The result is:

```
{¬pa; qaa}
{¬pb; qab}
{pa}
{pb}
{¬qab}
{¬qbb}
```

Using propositional resolution, we resolve the second and fourth clauses to get {**qab**}, which we then resolve with {¬**qab**} to get the empty clause. We have a refutation, hence G is unsatisfiable, as is S. □

EXAMPLE 5.28: Let us modify the clause set from the last example to get:

```
{¬p(X); q(a, X)}
{p(Y)}
{¬q(b, Z)}
```

The set G of all ground instances from S is:

```
{¬p(a); q(a, a)}
{¬p(b); q(a, b)}
{p(a)}
{p(b)}
{¬q(b, b)}
{¬q(b, a)}
```

Resolution on G does not yield the empty clause. G has a model, namely:

H = <{**a**, **b**}, *Id*, {**q(a, a)**, **q(a, b)**, **p(a)**, **p(b)**}>,

so both G and S are satisfiable. □

5.5. Resolution in Predicate Logic

Herbrand's Theorem gives us a more efficient means to test unsatisfiability than enumerating all Herbrand interpretations. Given a set S of predicate logic clauses, we can form G, the set of all ground instances of clauses in S (using the Herbrand universe). We then treat G as a set of propositional clauses, and apply resolution to seek a refutation. G can be much larger than S, though (see Exercise 5.22.), and many clauses in G may be irrelevant to finding a refutation. We can avoid generating G. In this section we show how to extend resolution to clauses with variables. For this extension we need a mapping, called a *substitution*. A substitution is similar to an instantiation, except it may map a variable to a constant *or* to another variable.

We will use a special kind of substitution, called a *unifier,* to formalize the ideas of delayed instantiation of variables in the last chapter. A unifier lets us match up two literals in clauses we want to resolve. The key result is that there is a unifier (the *most general unifier*) that does the maximum procrastination on variable binding. This most general unifier is unique since any other unifier is a specialization of it. Thus we need not consider multiple substitutions for resolving the same pair of literals in two clauses, unlike the approach that maps a clause to a ground instance upon use. The most general unifier collapses many matching pairs of ground instances of two clauses into one pair of matching nonground instances.

A substitution is a set of replacements of the form **X** = α, where **X** is a variable and α is a variable or constant. The replacement **X** = α means that **X** should be replaced by α throughout a formula. For instance, applying the replacement **Y** = **b** to the atom **q(Y, Z, b)** yields **q(b, Z, b)**. Applying a substitution θ to an atom A, denoted $A\theta$, means simultaneously applying each replacement in θ to A. (Algebraists and logicians, being conservative individuals, write their functions on the right.) A substitution is applied to an entire formula f, denoted $f\theta$, by applying it to every atom in f. We read the expression f{**W** = **U**, **Y** = **b**} as "f with **W** replaced by **U** and **Y** replaced by **b**." We read $f\theta$ as "f under θ."

EXAMPLE 5.29: Let θ be the substitution:

{**W = U, Y = b**}

and let f be the formula:

p(X, Y), ¬(q(Y, Z, b); r(W, U, a))

To compute $f\theta$, we apply the replacements **W** = **U** and **Y** = **b** throughout f to get:

p(X, b), ¬(q(b, Z, b); r(U, U, a)) □

We place two restrictions on a substitution. First, it must define a function. Therefore, no two replacements in a substitution may have the same variable on the left side. Thus {**X = b, X = Y**} is not a legal substitution. While we imagine all of the replacements in a substitution being applied at once (so, for example, **r(X, Y)**{**X = Y, Y = X**} = **r(Y, X)**), for computational purposes it is best to have substitutions where replacements can be applied one at a time. The second restriction is that a substitution be *idempotent*: for any formula f, $(f\theta)\theta = f\theta$. That is, applying the substitution twice has the same effect as applying it once. Idempotence requires that a variable appearing on the left of a replacement in a substitution θ may not appear on the right of any replacement in θ. Thus both {**X = b, Y = X**} and {**X = X**} are illegal substitutions.

We will have need shortly to apply several substitutions to a formula in sequence. If θ and σ are substitutions, then the *composition* of θ with σ, denoted $\theta \circ \sigma$, is a mapping defined by:

$$(f)\theta \circ \sigma = (f\theta)\sigma.$$

That is, first apply θ, then apply σ. Note that this order is opposite what is used for functions written on the left. The composition $\theta \circ \sigma$ might not be a substitution. For instance, the mapping defined by:

$\{$**X** = **U**, **Y** = **V**$\}\circ\{$**U** = **Y**, **V** = **X**$\}$

is not idempotent. If we want to ensure that $\theta \circ \sigma$ is a substitution, we can restrict composition so that no variable on the left of a replacement in θ is on the right of a replacement in σ. (This condition is not necessary, though.) To have a theory of substitutions closed under composition, the idempotence requirement must be removed. (See Exercise 5.23.) However, idempotence makes certain concepts simpler, and all compositions that arise in our algorithms will obey the preceding restriction anyway.

If the restriction on composition is satisfied, there is a straightforward algorithm to produce a substitution $\rho = \theta \circ \sigma$, which works as follows. Let ρ initially be θ. Apply σ to the right side of every replacement in ρ. Finally, add each replacement **Y** = α in σ to ρ, as long as no replacement in ρ already has **Y** on the left side. The set of replacements ρ is now a legal substitution such that $(f)\theta \circ \sigma = f\rho$ for any predicate formula f. (See Exercise 5.24.) Composition of substitutions is associative. That is $(\theta \circ \sigma) \circ \rho$ is the same mapping as $\theta \circ (\sigma \circ \rho)$. We can therefore write a sequence of compositions without parentheses: $\theta \circ \sigma \circ \rho$. One order of composition may, however, satisfy the restriction on composition, whereas another would not. (See Exercise 5.25.)

EXAMPLE 5.30: If θ =

$\{$**U** = **W**, **X** = **Y**, **Z** = **a**$\}$

and σ =

$\{$**W** = **V**, **Y** = **b**, **Z** = **d**$\}$

we form $\rho = \theta \circ \sigma$ as follows. Initially, $\rho = \theta$ =

$\{$**U** = **W**, **X** = **Y**, **Z** = **a**$\}$

We then apply σ to the right side of each replacement in ρ to get:

$\{$**U** = **V**, **X** = **b**, **Z** = **a**$\}$

Finally, we add in **W** = **V** and **Y** = **b** (but not **Z** = **d**) to arrive at:

$\{$**U** = **V**, **W** = **V**, **X** = **b**, **Y** = **b**, **Z** = **a**$\}$

Just as a check on the method, consider the atom:

A = **p(U, V, W, X, Y, Z).**

We have:

$A\theta =$ **p(W, V, W, Y, Y, a)**

so:

$A(\theta \circ \sigma) = (A\theta)\sigma =$ **p(V, V, V, b, b, a),**

which is the same as $A\rho$. □

We will use substitution during predicate resolution to make literals "match up." Substitution is a partial instantiation of sorts. Since we are trying to keep above the ground level, we will want to use substitutions that map the fewest variables to constants, while still making the match. The following definitions formalize this requirement. Let $A_1, A_2, \ldots, A_n$ be a list of atoms. A substitution θ is a *unifier* for the A_i's if $A_1\theta = A_2\theta = \cdots = A_n\theta$. That is, applying θ to the A_i's makes them match up. A unifier for a list of atoms need not exist. If a unifier does exist, we say the atoms are *unifiable.*

EXAMPLE 5.31: A unifier for the atoms:

p(X, b, Z), p(Y, W, a), p(Y, b, Z)

is θ =

{**W = b, X = c, Y = c, Z = a**}

which maps all three atoms to **p(c, b, a).** □

A unifier σ for a set of atoms is a *most general unifier* (mgu) if for any other unifier θ for the atoms, $\theta = \sigma \circ \theta$. In essence any other unifier does at least as much replacement as σ. The composition $\sigma \circ \theta$ might not satisfy the restriction that allows the preceeding composition algorithm to work, but the mapping defined by the composition is always a substitution. For example, {**X = Y**} and {**Y = X**} are both unifiers of **g(X)** and **g(Y)**, and {**X = Y**} ∘ {**Y = X**} = {**Y = X**}.

An mgu need not be unique nor need it even exist. However, if a unifier exists for a set of atoms, an mgu exists. Among all the unifiers for a list of atoms, an mgu has the fewest replacements mapping variables to constants, although this condition is not a sufficient characterization for an mgu. (See Exercise 5.27.) Given the set of all unifiers of a list of atoms, any unifier with the minimum number of replacements is an mgu, and no mgu has more than the minimum number. (See Exercise 5.28.) Also, an mgu for a set of atoms will mention only variables that appear in at least one of the atoms. (See Exercise 5.29.) Finally, notice that even if we dropped the idempotence requirement on substitutions, an mgu would be idempotent. Letting σ be θ in the definition, we must have $\sigma = \sigma \circ \sigma$.

EXAMPLE 5.32: The unifier θ from the last example is not an mgu. For the atoms given, the substitution σ =

{W = b, X = Y, Z = a}

is an mgu for those atoms. Note that $\theta = \sigma \circ \theta$, but $\sigma \neq \theta \circ \sigma$ $(= \theta)$. □

EXAMPLE 5.33: The list of atoms:

p(X, b, Z), p(Y, Y, a), p(Y, b, X)

has no unifiers, hence no mgu. For **p(X, b, Z)** to match **p(Y, Y, a)**, **Y** must be replaced by **b**, for the atoms to match in the second argument. It follows that **X** must be replaced by **b**, so those two atoms match in the first argument. However, for **p(Y, Y, a)** to match **p(Y, b, X)**, **X** must be replaced by **a**. We cannot replace **X** by different constants, so the list of atoms is not unifiable. □

Many texts define an mgu as a unifier σ such that for any unifier θ, there is a substitution ρ such that $\theta = \sigma \circ \rho$. In Example 5.32, ρ would be **{Y = c}**. Clearly our definition implies this one, taking θ for ρ. Also, if $\theta = \sigma \circ \rho$, then $\theta = \sigma \circ \sigma \circ \rho$ by idempotence, so $\theta = \sigma \circ \theta$. However, if substitutions are not required to be idempotent, there are mgus that satisfy this definition but not the original definition. In fact, such an mgu may have more replacements than one that conforms to the original definition. (See Exercise 5.30.) The original definition has handy theoretical properties, and all mgus produced by the algorithms we use will satisfy the original definition already.

The *match* function of the Datalog *establish* function finds the mgu of two atoms.

THEOREM 5.3: If HEAD and GOAL are unifiable atoms, then the *match* function of Section 4.3 succeeds and returns an mgu of HEAD and GOAL via SUBS. If HEAD and GOAL are not unifiable, *match* will fail.

Proof: We sketch the proof of the first part of the theorem, leaving the second part as Exercise 5.31. Let σ_i be the value of SUBS after the ith iteration of the **for**-loop, and let σ_0 be the empty substitution. If **X** = α is the replacement constructed during the ith iteration, then $\sigma_i = \sigma_{i-1} \circ$ {**X** = α}. From the way the replacement arises, neither **X** nor α appear on the left of a replacement in σ_{i-1}. Also, σ_i will have no variable appearing on both right and left sides of replacements, guaranteeing idempotence. If no replacement is added, $\sigma_i = \sigma_{i-1}$. Let $HEAD_0$ and $GOAL_0$ be the initial values of HEAD and GOAL. Let $HEAD_i$ and $GOAL_i$ be the values of HEAD and GOAL after the ith iteration, so $HEAD_i = (\mathrm{HEAD}_0)\sigma_i$ and $GOAL_i = (\mathrm{GOAL}_0)\sigma_i$.

Let σ_k be the final value for SUBS on a successful return. Then $(HEAD_0)\ \sigma_k = (GOAL_0)\sigma_k$, so σ_k is a unifier. To show that it is an mgu, we will show that for any unifier θ of $HEAD_0$ and $GOAL_0$, $\theta = \sigma_i \circ \theta$, for $0 \leqslant i \leqslant k$. Clearly, $\theta =$

$\sigma_0 \circ \theta$, since σ_0 is empty. Assume $\theta = \sigma_{i-1} \circ \theta$. If the ith arguments of $HEAD_i$ and $GOAL_i$ match at the ith iteration, then $\sigma_i = \sigma_{i-1}$ and $\theta = \sigma_i \circ \theta$. Otherwise, assume the ith argument of $HEAD_i$ is variable **X** and the ith argument of $GOAL_i$ is α. (The case where $GOAL_i$ has a variable and $HEAD_i$ a constant is treated similarly.) We have $\sigma_i = \sigma_{i-1} \circ \{\mathbf{X} = \alpha\}$. Since θ maps the ith arguments of $HEAD_0$ and $GOAL_0$ to the same argument, but σ_{i-1} does not, θ must map **X** and α to the same value, call it β. (We may have $\beta = \mathbf{X}$ or $\beta = \alpha$). Now $\sigma_i \circ \theta = \sigma_{i-1} \circ \{\mathbf{X} = \alpha\} \circ \theta$. Consider the value of this substitution on an arbitrary variable **Y**. If $\mathbf{Y}\sigma_{i-1} = \mathbf{Z}, \mathbf{Z} \neq \mathbf{X}$, then $\mathbf{X} = \alpha$ has no effect, and $\mathbf{Y}(\sigma_{i-1} \circ \{\mathbf{X} = \alpha\} \circ \theta) = \mathbf{Y}(\sigma_{i-1} \circ \theta) = \mathbf{Y}\theta$. If $\mathbf{Y}\sigma_{i-1} = \mathbf{X}$, then $\mathbf{Y}(\sigma_{i-1} \circ \{\mathbf{X} = \alpha\} \circ \theta) = \alpha\theta = \beta = \mathbf{X}\theta = \mathbf{Y}(\sigma_{i-1} \circ \theta)$. Hence, for any **Y**, $\mathbf{Y}(\sigma_{i-1} \circ \theta) = \mathbf{Y}(\sigma_i \circ \theta)$, so $\sigma_i \circ \theta = \sigma_{i-1} \circ \theta = \theta$. It follows that σ_k is an mgu. □

The *match* function is a *unification procedure*—a procedure that produces the mgu of a set of atoms. Whereas *match* deals with just a pair of atoms, pairwise unification can be used to obtain a unification procedure for an arbitrary number of atoms. (See Exercise 5.32.) A unifiable set of atoms may have several mgus, but the *match* function produces a specific one. When we refer to *the* mgu for a set of atoms, we mean the one that *match* produces.

We now use unifiers to define resolution on predicate logic clauses. If A and B are unifiable atoms, then the literals $\neg A$ and B are said to *match*. If C is a clause $\{L_1;\ L_2;\ \ldots;\ L_k\}$, then $C\theta$ denotes the clause $\{L_1\theta;\ L_2\theta;\ \ldots;\ L_k\theta\}$, where $(\neg A)\theta = \neg(A\theta)$. $C\theta$ is called an *instance* of C. $C\theta$ can have fewer literals than C, if $L_i\theta = L_j\theta$ for some i and j.

EXAMPLE 5.34: If C =

```
{p(a, W); q(W, Z); ¬r(b, Z)}
```

and θ =

```
{W = a, Y = a}
```

then $C\theta$ =

```
{p(a, a); q(a, Z); ¬r(b, Z)}
```
□

Let:

$C = \{L_1;\ L_2;\ \ldots;\ L_k\}$
$D = \{M_1;\ M_2;\ \ldots;\ M_n\}$

be two clauses, with no variable in common between C and D. Let L_i and M_j be literals from C and D that match, and let θ be the mgu of their atoms. The *binary resolvent* of C and D on L_i and M_j is the clause:

$$E = (C - \{L_i\})\theta \cup (D - \{M_j\})\theta.$$

That is, form E by removing L_i and M_j, and then applying θ to the remaining literals.

EXAMPLE 5.35: Let:

C = {**p(a, W)**; **q(W, Z)**; **¬r(b, Z)**}
D = {**¬p(Y, Y)**; **t(Y, X)**}

C and D will resolve on **p(a, W)** and **¬p(Y, Y)**. The mgu of **p(a, W)** and **p(Y, Y)** is θ =

{**W = a, Y = a**}

which maps both atoms to **p(a, a)**. Thus the binary resolvent of C and D is:

E = {**q(W, Z)**; **¬r(b, Z)**}$\theta \cup$ {**t(Y, X)**}θ =
{**q(a, Z)**, **¬r(b, Z)**} ∪ {**t(a, X)**} =
{**q(a, Z)**, **¬r(b, Z)**, **t(a, X)**}. □

In propositional logic, resolution could take place only on a single literal from each clause. In predicate logic we can have multiple literals in one clause with the same "sign" and predicate symbol. In *full resolution* we form a resolvent of clauses C and D by taking one or more literals from C, all with the same sign, and one or more literals from D, all with sign opposite from those chosen from C. Rename variables, if necessary, so no variable is shared between C and D. Let C' be the literals from C, and let D' be the literals from D. All the chosen literals must have the same predicate symbol. Furthermore, the literals in C' must have an mgu σ, and C' must include *all* the literals from C that unify under σ. Likewise for D'. We form the *resolvent* E of C and D by finding the mgu θ of the atoms for the literals in C' and D'. We then let:

$$E = (C - C')\theta \cup (D - D')\theta.$$

Note that here $(C - C')\theta = C\theta - C'\theta = C\theta - \{L\theta\}$ for any literal L in C'. (See Exercise 5.33.)

EXAMPLE 5.36: Let:

C = {**p(X, Y, Z)**; **q(X, c)**}
D = {**¬p(a, W, U)**; **¬p(V, T, b)**; **r(U, V)**}

The substitution θ =

{**T = W, U = b, V = a, X = a, Y = W, Z = b**}

is an mgu of **p(X, Y, Z)**, **p(a, W, U)**, and **p(V, T, b)**, mapping them all to **p(a, W, b)**. Hence a resolvent of C and D is:

E = {**q(X, c)**}$\theta \cup$ {**r(U, V)**}θ = {**q(a, c)**, **r(b, a)**}. □

A refutation proof using resolution on predicate clauses proceeds the same way as for propositional clauses. Starting with a clause set S, form resolvents of clauses in S until the empty clause is generated, or no new clause can be formed. Since the resolution procedure requires the two clauses involved to have distinct variables, rename variables in each resolvent before adding it to S.

EXAMPLE 5.37: Consider the following statements. If X is the brother of Z, and Y is the brother of Z, then X is the brother of Y, or X and Y are the same person. If X is male and X and Y have the same mother, then X is the brother of Y, or X and Y are the same. Elizabeth is the mother of Charles and Margaret, Charles is male, Andrew is Margaret's brother, Charles and Andrew are not the same person, nor are Charles and Margaret the same. We want to cast these statements into logic and use them to prove that Charles is the brother of Andrew. Using **a**, **c**, **e**, and **m** to stand for Andrew, Charles, Elizabeth, and Margaret, we get a clause set S =

1. {**brotherOf(X1, Y1); same(X1, Y1); ¬brotherOf(X1, Z1); ¬brotherOf(Y1, Z1)**}
2. {**brotherOf(X2, Y2); same(X2, Y2); ¬male(X2); ¬motherOf(M2, X2); ¬motherOf(M2, Y2)**}
3. {**motherOf(e, c)**}
4. {**motherOf(e, m)**}
5. {**male(c)**}
6. {**brotherOf(a, m)**}
7. {**¬same(c, a)**}
8. (**¬same(c, m)**}

along with the negation of the goal:

9. {**¬brotherOf(c, a)**}

Resolving clauses 1 and 9 gives:

10. {**same(c, a); ¬brotherOf(c, Z3); ¬brotherOf(a, Z3)**}

which resolves with clause 7 to give:

11. {**¬brotherOf(c, Z4); ¬brotherOf(a, Z4)**}

Resolving clauses 2 and 5 gives:

12. {**brotherOf(c, Y5); same(c, Y5); ¬motherOf(M5, c); ¬motherOf(M5, Y5)**}

which we can resolve with clause 3 to obtain:

13. {**brotherOf(c, Y6); same(c, Y6); ¬motherOf(e, Y6)**}

Combining clauses 11 and 13 yields:

14. {**¬brotherOf(a, Z7); same(c, Z7); ¬motherOf(e, Z7)**}

Which resolves with clause 4 to give:

15. **¬brotherOf(a, m); same(c, m)**}

and then with clauses 6 and 8 finally to produce the empty clause. Thus we have proved the desired implication via binary resolution. □

Full resolution is strictly more powerful than binary resolution. There are clause sets that yield the empty clause under full resolution but not under binary resolution.

EXAMPLE 5.38: Let S be the clause set:

```
{p(X); p(Y)}
{¬p(U); ¬p(V)}
```

Any binary resolvent of these two clauses, or of their binary resolvents, has two literals. Therefore, the empty clause will never be obtained. The clauses are unsatisfiable, because one application of full resolution with the unifier:

```
{U = Y, V = Y, X = Y}
```

yields the empty clause. □

There is an operation on clauses, called *factoring*, that gives binary resolution the power of full resolution. That is, if full resolution yields the empty clause from a clause set, so will binary resolution and factoring. To form a *factor* of a clause C, we choose a set of literals in C that are all of the same sign and have the same predicate symbol. Let θ be the mgu of the chosen literals. Then $C\theta$ is a factor of C. When using factoring in attempting a refutation from a clause set S, we may at any point add a factor of a clause in S to S.

EXAMPLE 5.39: Consider the clause D =

```
{¬p(a, W, U); ¬p(V, T, b); r(U, V)}
```

from Example 5.36. The substitution θ =

```
{U = b, V = a, W = T}
```

is an mgu for the first two literals in D. Hence $D\theta$ =

```
{¬p(a, T, b); r(b, a)}
```

is a factor of D. Note that a binary resolution of $D\ \theta$ with clause C of Example 5.36 yields the same resolvent obtained there. □

Any resolvent obtainable from clauses C and D by full resolution can be obtained from factors of C and D with binary resolution. (See Exercise 5.36.)

5.5.1. *Correctness of Resolution*

To see that predicate resolution is correct, we must show that the resolvent of two clauses is logically implied by the two clauses.

LEMMA 5.4: If C and D are predicate logic clauses with resolvent E, then C and D logically imply E.

Proof: We use the fact that a clause logically implies all of its instances—in particular, its factors—but we leave the proof for Exercise 5.37. Since any resolvent generated by full resolution can be obtained from factors of C and D by binary resolution, we assume E was generated by binary resolution. Let L and M be the literals from C and D, respectively, that were resolved upon, and let θ be the unifier used for L and M. We know C and D imply instances $C\theta$ and $D\theta$. Let ST be a model for $C\theta$ and $D\theta$. For any instantiation I, $M_{ST,I}(C\theta) = \textbf{true}$ and $M_{ST,I}(D\theta) = \textbf{true}$. Now $M_{ST,I}(L\theta) = M_{ST,I}(\neg M\theta)$. Thus either $C\theta - \{L\theta\}$ or $D\theta - \{M\theta\}$ must contain a literal that $M_{ST,I}$ maps to true. Thus:

$$M_{ST,I}(E) = M_{ST,I}((C - \{L\})\theta \cup (D - \{M\})\theta) =$$
$$M_{ST,I}((C\theta - \{L\theta\}) \cup (D\theta - \{M\theta\})) = \textbf{true}$$

(although it is not true that $C\theta - \{L\theta\}$ always equals $(C - \{L\})\theta$). (See Exercise 5.33.) So ST is a model for E, since I was arbitrary. Thus C and D logically imply E. □

5.5.2. *Completeness of Resolution*

We want to know that a complete deduction procedure for predicate logic clauses can be built with resolution. We must show that if a set of clauses is unsatisfiable, they will yield a refutation via resolution. Without completeness, taking resolution as the basis for the Datalog interpreter would a priori prevent it from producing all correct answers. By Herbrand's Theorem, we know that if a clause set S is unsatisfiable, we can obtain the empty clause by resolution on ground instances of clauses in S. The next result, the *Lifting Lemma*, says that we can "lift" those ground resolutions into resolutions on predicate clauses and avoid generating ground instances.

LEMMA 5.5 (LIFTING LEMMA): If predicate clauses C and D have instances C' and D', and E' is a resolvent of C' and D', then C and D have a resolvent E such that E' is an instance of E.

The situation described by the lemma is depicted in Figure 5.6. The solid arrows denote a clause-instance connection, while the dashed arrows connect clauses to their resolvents.

Proof: We show how to find E, given the substitutions that produced C' and D', and the unifier used to produce resolvent E'. Let θ_C and θ_D be substitutions such that $C\theta_C = C'$ and $D\theta_D = D'$. (See Figure 5.7.) We may assume C and D have disjoint sets of variables. Thus there is a single substitution $\theta = \theta_C \cup \theta_D$ such that $C\theta = C'$ and $D\theta = D'$. Let σ be the mgu used with C' and D' to produce resolvent E'. Then:

$$E' = (C'\sigma - \{L'\sigma\}) \cup (D'\sigma - \{M'\sigma\})$$

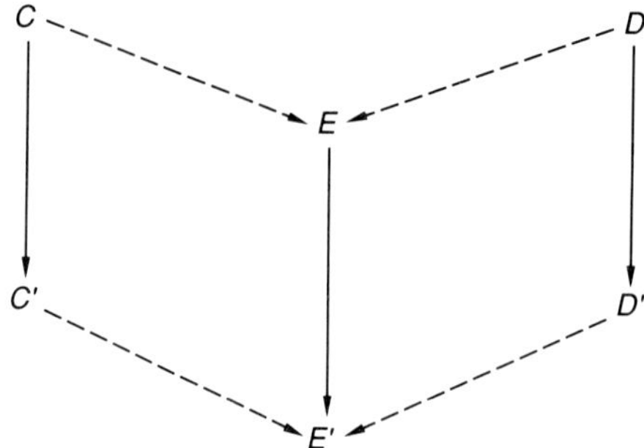

Figure 5.6

for some literals L' in C' and M' in D'. (Note that σ may have unified multiple literals from C' and D', but we need just one representative from each clause to represent E'.) Assume L' is positive and M' is negative; $\neg M'$ will mean M' without the negation. Let literal $N' = L'\sigma = \neg M'\sigma$.

There must be literals in C and D that θ maps onto L' and M'. Let L be a literal in C such that $L\theta = L'$, and let M be a literal in D such that $M\theta = M'$. Thus, $L\theta \circ \sigma = \neg M\theta \circ \sigma = N'$. Let $L_1, L_2, \ldots, L_k$ be *all* the literals in C that $\theta \circ \sigma$ maps to N'. Likewise, let $M_1, M_2, \ldots, M_n$ be all the literals in D that $\theta \circ \sigma$ maps to $\neg N'$. We show the situation in Figure 5.8.

We see that the atoms of $L_1, L_2, \ldots, L_k$ and $M_1, M_2, \ldots, M_n$ are unifiable with unifier $\theta \circ \sigma$. Let ρ be an mgu of the L_i's and $\neg M_j$'s. Since $\theta \circ \sigma$ is a unifier, and ρ is an mgu, $\theta \circ \sigma = \rho \circ \theta \circ \sigma$. This situation is depicted in Figure 5.9, where $N = L_1\rho$ (or, equivalently, ρ applied to any of the L_i's).

We use ρ to form a resolvent of C and D:

$$E = (C - \{L_1, L_2, \ldots, L_k\})\rho \cup (D - \{M_1, M_2, \ldots, M_n\})\rho = (C\rho - \{L_1\rho\}) \cup (D\rho - \{M_1\rho\}).$$

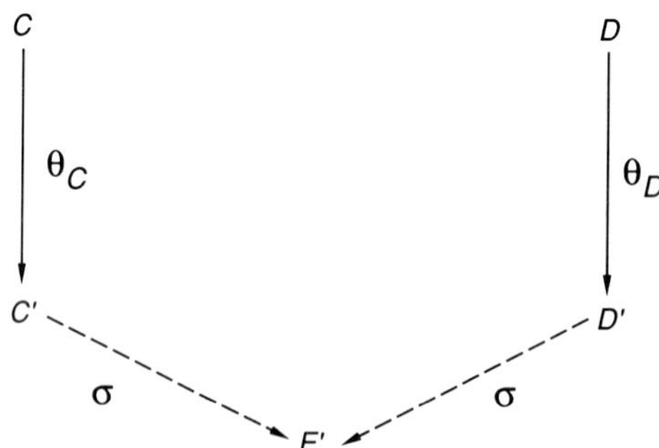

Figure 5.7

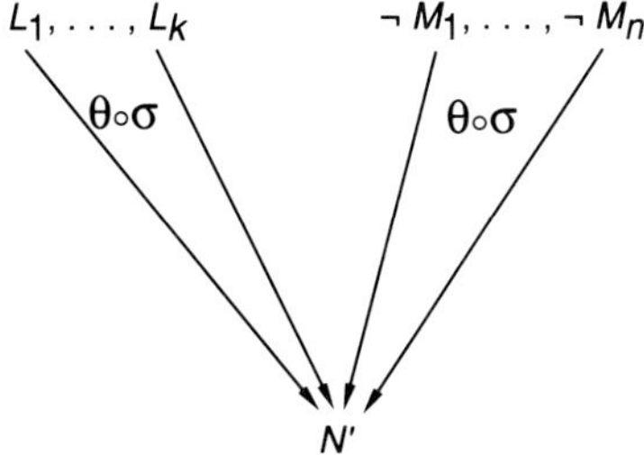

Figure 5.8

All that remains is to show that clause E' is an instance of E. We apply $\theta \circ \sigma$ to E:

$$\begin{aligned}
&E\theta \circ \sigma = ((C\rho - \{L_1\rho\}) \cup (D\rho - \{M_1\rho\}))\theta \circ \sigma = \\
&\quad (C\rho - \{L_1\rho\})\theta \circ \sigma \cup (D\rho - \{M_1\rho\})\theta \circ \sigma = \\
&\quad (C\rho \circ \theta \circ \sigma - \{L_1\rho \circ \theta \circ \sigma\}) \cup (D\rho \circ \theta \circ \sigma - \{M_1\rho \circ \theta \circ \sigma\}) = \\
&\quad (C\theta \circ \sigma - \{L_1\theta \circ \sigma\}) \cup (D\theta \circ \sigma - \{M_1\theta \circ \sigma\}) = \\
&\quad (C'\sigma - \{L_1'\sigma\}) \cup (D'\sigma - \{M_1'\sigma\}) = E'.
\end{aligned}$$

There is only one shady step here. How do we know:

$$(C\rho - \{L_1\rho\})\theta \circ \sigma = (C\rho \circ \theta \circ \sigma - \{L_1\rho \circ \theta \circ \sigma\})?$$

In general, substitutions do not distribute over difference. (See Exercise 5.33.) Suppose there is a literal $\hat{L}$ in C such that $\hat{L} \in C\rho - \{L_1\rho\}$, but $\hat{L}\rho \circ \theta \circ \sigma = L_1\rho \circ \theta \circ \sigma$. Then the left difference in the preceding equation could contain a literal not in the right difference. Not to worry. Since $\hat{L}\rho \circ \theta \circ \sigma = L_1\rho \circ \theta \circ \sigma$, we have $\hat{L}\theta \circ \sigma = L_1\theta \circ \sigma = N'$. Thus, $\hat{L}$ is one of the L_i's, so $\hat{L}\rho = L_1\rho$, and $\hat{L}\rho$ is not in $C\rho - \{L_1\rho\}$. □

EXAMPLE 5.40: Let:

C = {**q(a, X, Y); r(Y)**}
D = {**¬q(W, Z, b); s(Z, U); ¬t(W)**}

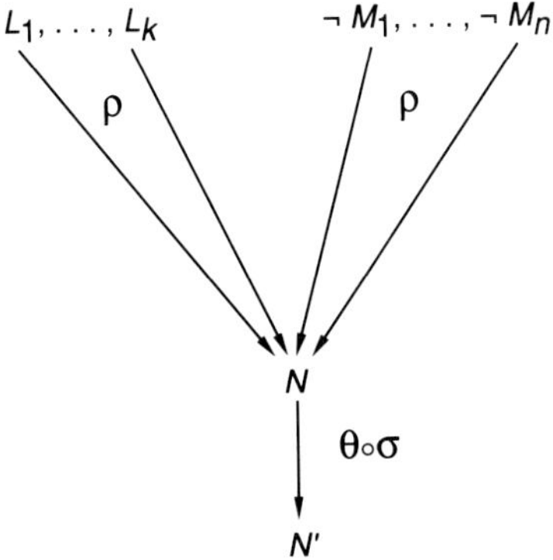

Figure 5.9

The clauses:

$C' = \{$**q(a, X, b), r(b)**$\}$
$D' = \{\neg$**q(a, Z, b); s(Z, e);** $\neg$**t(a)**$\}$

are instances of C and D with resolvent:

$E' = \{$**r(b); s(X, e);** $\neg$**t(a)**$\}$

Using the mgu:

$\rho = \{$**W = a, X = Z, Y = b**$\}$

for the **q**-literals in C and D, we get the resolvent:

$E = \{$**r(b); s(Z, U);** $\neg$**t(a)**$\}$

of which E' can be seen to be an instance via the substitution:

$\theta \circ \sigma = \{$**U = e, Z = X**$\}$ □

The Lifting Lemma tells us that if we can generate the empty clause from a clause set S by resolving on the ground instances of S, we can also generate the empty clause from S directly by predicate resolution. (A trivial "Lowering Lemma" establishes the converse. See Exercise 5.38.) The proof of this statement is an easy induction on the derivation of the empty clause by ground resolution. For every clause E' we generate by ground resolution, we can generate a clause E by predicate resolution, such that E' is an instance of E. If E' is the empty clause, then E must be the empty clause.

EXAMPLE 5.41: Consider the clause set S =

1. $\{$**p(U, V); p(U, W);** $\neg$**q(V, a, W)**$\}$
2. $\{\neg$**p(X, Y);** $\neg$**q(b, X, Y)**$\}$
3. $\{$**q(b, T, Z)**$\}$

We consider three ground instances of clauses in S:

4. $\{$**p(a, b);** $\neg$**q(b, a, b)**$\}$
5. $\{\neg$**p(a, b);** $\neg$**q(b, a, b)**$\}$
6. $\{$**q(b, a, b)**$\}$

We can obtain the empty clause by resolving clauses 4 and 5 to get:

7. $\{\neg$**q(b, a, b)**$\}$

and then resolving with clause 6. To "lift" this derivation into predicate resolution, we note that clause 4 is an instance of clause 1 and that clause 5 is an instance of clause 2. We can resolve clauses 1 and 2 on all the **p**-literals to get:

8. $\{\neg$**q(V1, a, V1);** $\neg$**q(b, U1, V1)**$\}$

of which clause 7 is an instance. We can resolve clause 8 with clause 3, of which clause 6 is an instance, to derive the empty clause. □

5.6. **Horn Clauses**

In this section we look at a subset of predicate logic for which the search space for a refutation does not grow so explosively. This limitation is important to get an efficient programming language from the resolution method. The particular refutation procedure for Horn clauses described here also is important to understand how the Datalog interpreter goes about searching for a proof of a goal. This understanding allows a programmer to arrange clauses within a program and literals within a clause so as to guide the search and avoid pathologically inefficient (infinite) searches.

As with propositional logic, we can write clauses in *implication form* using the "if" connective '`:-`'. Recall that implication form means a formula with a single '`:-`', a disjunction of atoms to the left (the positive literals), and a conjunction of atoms to the right (the negative literals), such as:

```
q(X); s(X) :- p(X, Z), p(X, W), r(Z, W).
```

A *Horn clause* is a clause with at most one positive literal. We see that Datalog clauses and goals are Horn clauses in implication form.

For refutation proofs with a set *H* of Horn clauses, we can make four restrictions on the kind of resolution trees we need consider.

1. We use input resolution: One clause in the next resolution step is always the previous resolvent (the *center clause*) and the other (the *side clause*) comes from *H*.
2. The initial center clause is a headless clause from *H*. Thus the center clause will always contain only negative literals, and clauses from *H* will resolve on their positive literals.
3. We use a certain kind of selected literal resolution: The first literal in the current center clause is the one chosen to resolve upon, and the body of the side clause goes at the beginning of the new center clause.
4. We use only binary resolution.

The first three conditions are the same ones we imposed on propositional Horn clause resolution. Thus, when seeking a refutation, we can restrict the search for a resolution DAG to one that is a vine with a headless clause on the leftmost leaf. In the case of Datalog programs this leaf will always be the clause derived by negating the initial goal list. Condition 4 held only trivially for the propositional case, since there was no opportunity for resolving upon multiple literals from a clause.

We can show that Horn clause resolution under the first three conditions is complete by appealing to the results for propositional Horn clauses. The strategy is to lower resolution DAGs to the ground level, rearrange them into the appropriate form by treating them as propositional resolution DAGs, and then lift them back up to the predicate level. Suppose *H* is a set of Horn clauses, and *T* is a refutation tree under *H*. (If *T* were a DAG, we could transform it to a tree by duplicating nodes.) Let *G* be the set of all (Herbrand) ground instances of clauses in *H*. We can lower T to become a refutation tree under G. First we apply the unifier used in each resolution step to the clauses in T. We start at the last resolution step, which corresponds to the root of T, and propagate the substitution downward through the subtrees. Then we consider the rest of the resolution steps of the subtrees, proceeding in turn down from their roots. After all those substitutions have been propagated, any variables that still remain in T are replaced by an arbitrary constant **a** from the Herbrand universe of H. Call the resulting tree T'. T' is a refutation tree under G. (See Exercise 5.39.)

EXAMPLE 5.42: Consider the clause set H =

```
q(X1) :- p(X1, Z1), p(X1, W1), r(Z1, W1).
p(X2, Y2) :- s(X2, X2, Y2).
r(a, X3).
r(X4, a).
s(b, b, b).
s(b, b, a).
```

with goal clause:

```
:- q(b).
```

and the refutation tree T in Figure 5.10. We will transform T into a refutation tree T' under G, the set of ground instances of S. Since no clause appears twice as a leaf in T, we have not renamed variables in resolvents in T.

The last resolution in T needed no unifier. The next-to-last resolution used the unifier:

{**X1** = **b**}

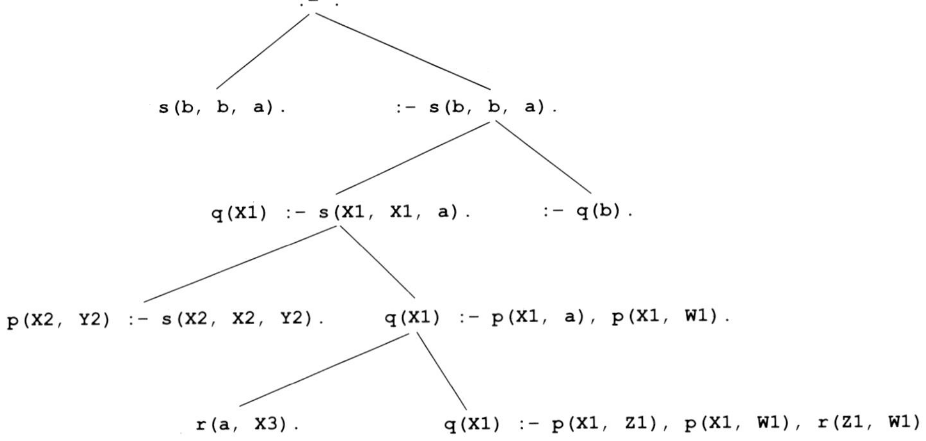

Figure 5.10

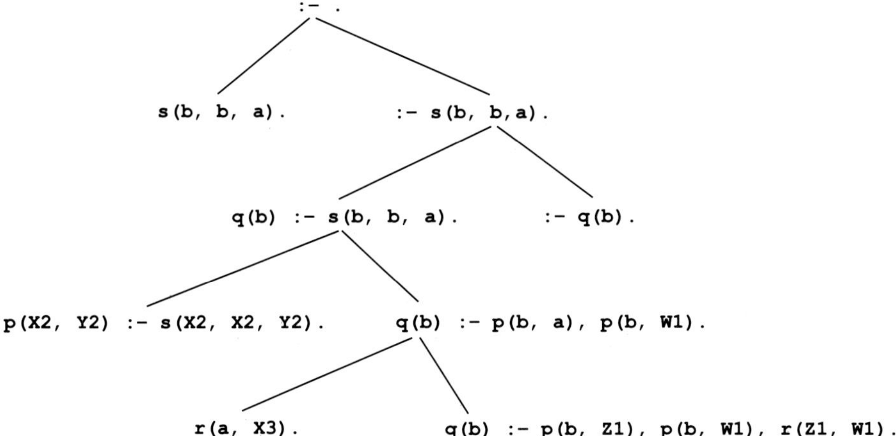

Figure 5.11

We replace **X1** by **b** throughout the tree. (If we had been renaming variables in resolvents, we would have to propagate the replacement down to renamed variables as well.) The result is shown in Figure 5.11.

The unifier used at the third-from-last resolution step was:

{**W1** = **a**, **X2** = **X1**, **Y2** = **a**}.

X1 has already been replaced by **b**, so we must replace **X2** by **b**, as well as replace **W1** and **Y2** by **a**. We obtain the tree shown in Figure 5.12. Note that we lose a literal at one of the nodes.

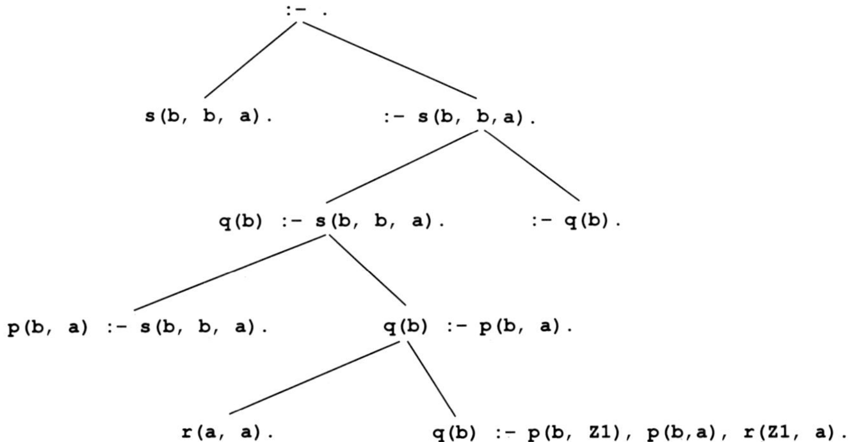

Figure 5.12

The unifier for the first resolution step was:

{**X3** = **W1**, **Z1** = **a**}

Since **W1** was already replaced by **a**, we replace **X3** by **a**, and also **Z1** by **a**, to get the tree shown in Figure 5.13. Since this tree contains no more variables, it is the desired refutation T' under G. □

Once we have transformed T to tree T' under G, the results for propositional Horn clauses in Section 2.3.3 prove that there is a refutation vine V' under G. Ground predicate clauses behave no differently from propositional clauses. Furthermore, we can require that in V' each resolution must take place on the first literal in the current center clause, and that the body of the side clause must appear at the beginning of the new center clause.

EXAMPLE 5.43: Figure 5.14 shows a refutation vine V' under the clause set G from the last example. Note that V' has the same leaves as tree T' in Figure 5.13, and that all resolutions in V' take place on the first literal in the center clause. □

Using the Lifting Lemma, we can now lift up the refutation vine V' under G to a refutation vine V under H. We begin by generalizing the leaves back to the original clauses in H and then work up from the leaves to the empty clause at the root. We do lose a little in the lifting. The resulting vine V may contain a node with more literals than the corresponding node in V'. Whereas in V' we always matched the head of the side clause with the first literal of the center clause, in V we may match the head with the first literal in the center clause and *other* literals in the center clause.

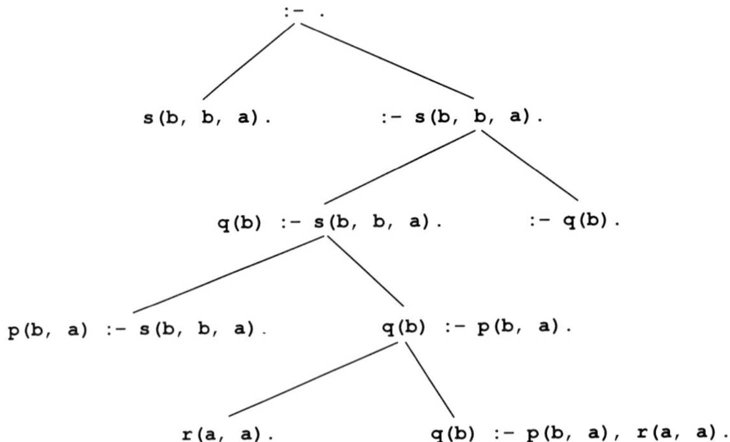

Figure 5.13

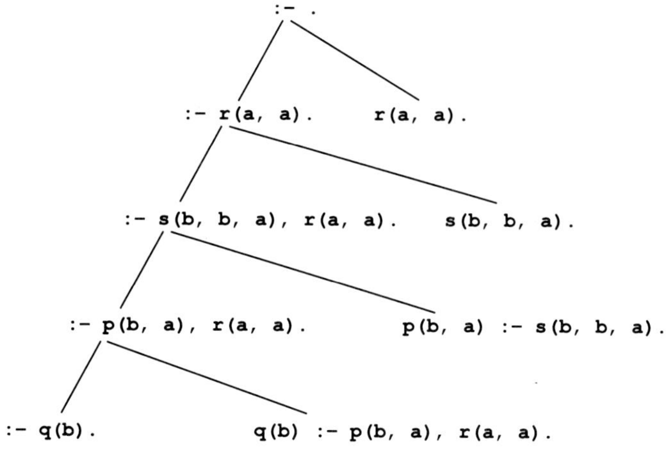

Figure 5.14

EXAMPLE 5.44: Figure 5.15 gives the result of lifting up the refutation vine V' in Figure 5.14 to a refutation vine V under the clause set H from Example 5.42. Note that the second resolution step involves two literals from the center clause. □

Our strategy of normalizing predicate refutation trees by lowering them to the ground level, finding an equivalent vine there, and then lifting the vine back up to the predicate level leaves us short on two accounts. First, the predicate vines we obtain do not completely satisfy Condition 3, because resolution may involve other center clause literals in addition to the selected literal. Second, we do not satisfy

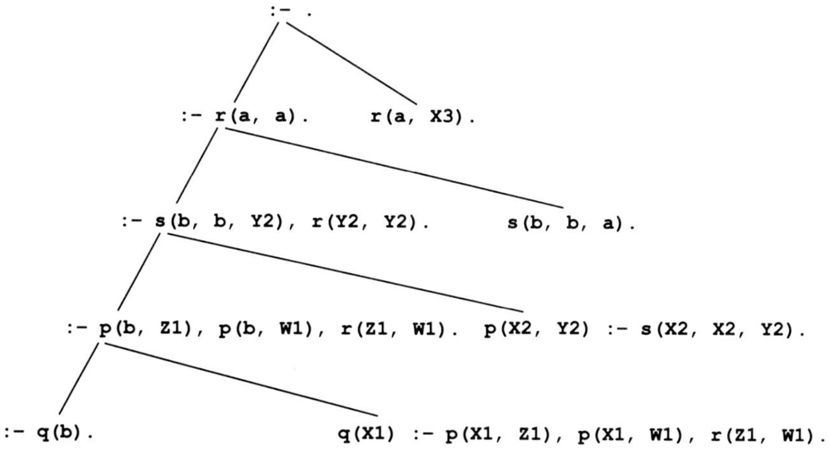

Figure 5.15

Condition 4, because the vines can have nonbinary resolutions. Clearly both conditions will be satisfied if we can reduce full resolution steps to binary resolution steps on the first literals of center clauses.

When a resolution step involves more than one literal from a center clause, we can instead take each literal in turn, using binary resolution.

EXAMPLE 5.45: The vine V in Figure 5.15 has a nonbinary resolution at the second step, where both **p(b, Z1)** and **p(b, W1)** from the center clause are resolved upon. We can resolve upon one literal at a time to get the vine shown in Figure 5.16. Here we rename variables in some of the side clauses to avoid duplication. □

A simple way to see that the full resolutions can be replaced by multiple binary resolutions is to make the transformation in the refutation vine V' under G. We allow clauses there to contain duplicate literals—one for each literal in the corresponding clause of H. We have already seen that, for propositional resolution, having a duplicated literal poses no problem. If a refutation vine exists without the duplicate occurrence, one exists with the duplicate but with more resolution steps. The vine with duplicates—call it V''—can be lifted directly to a refutation vine under H that uses only binary resolution steps.

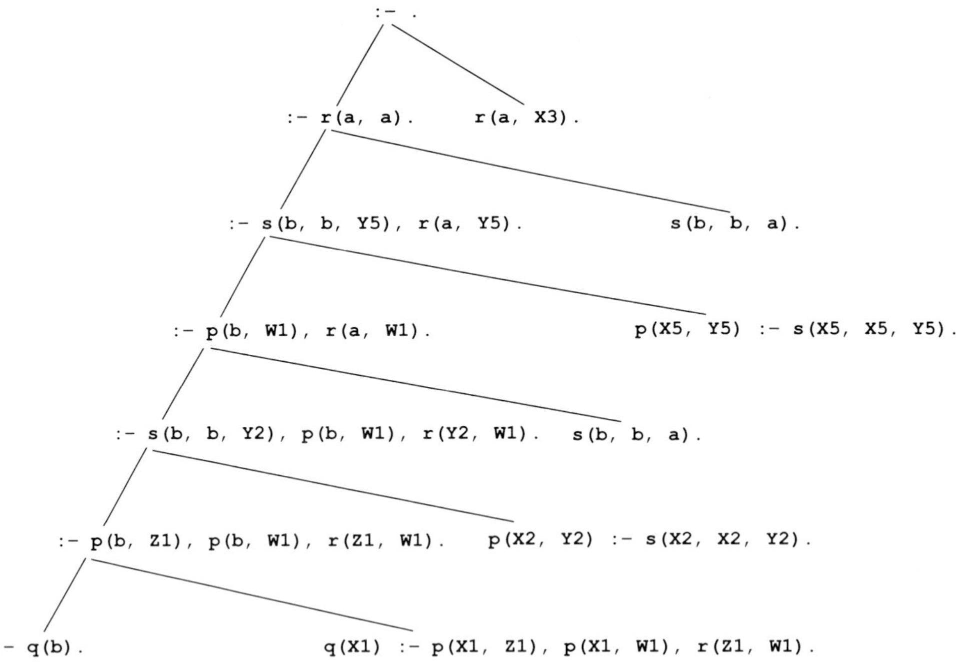

Figure 5.16

EXAMPLE 5.46: For the vine V' in Figure 5.14, we can take:

```
q(b) :- p(b, a), p(b, a), r(a, a).
```

as the instance of:

```
q(X1) :- p(X1, Z1), p(X1, W1), r(Z1, W1).
```

rather than:

```
q(b) :- p(b, a), r(a, a).
```

With this change, we get a new refutation vine V'', shown in Figure 5.17, that lifts directly to the vine in Figure 5.16. □

Finally we look back at the *establish* interpreter for Datalog from Section 4.3. We consider it now as a Horn clause refutation procedure. We duplicate *establish* here with only slight modification.

```
var MGU: subst;
    FIRSTCLAUSE: clauselist;

function establish(CENTERCL: litlist): boolean;
    var NEXTCL, SIDECL, NEWCENTER: clauselist;
    begin
      if isempty(CENTERCL) then return(true);
      NEXTCL := FIRSTCLAUSE
      while NEXTCL <> nil do
        begin
          SIDECL := instance(NEXTCL);
          if unify(SIDECL↑.HEAD, first(CENTERCL), MGU) then
            begin
              NEWCENTER := apply(MGU, copycat(SIDECL↑.BODY,
                                                rest(CENTERCL)));
              if establish(NEWCENTER) then return(true)
            end;
          NEXTCL := NEXTCL↑.NXTCLAUSE
        end;
      return(false)
    end;
```

Here we assume that the set of clauses we wish to consider is stored as a linked list starting at FIRSTCLAUSE. This list need not contain headless clauses. Those clauses can be segregated and tried one at a time as the initial center clause. Also, to make their roles clear, we have renamed GOALLIST to CENTERCL, CLAUSEINST to SIDECL, SUBS to MGU, and *match* to *unify*. As in the propositional case, covered

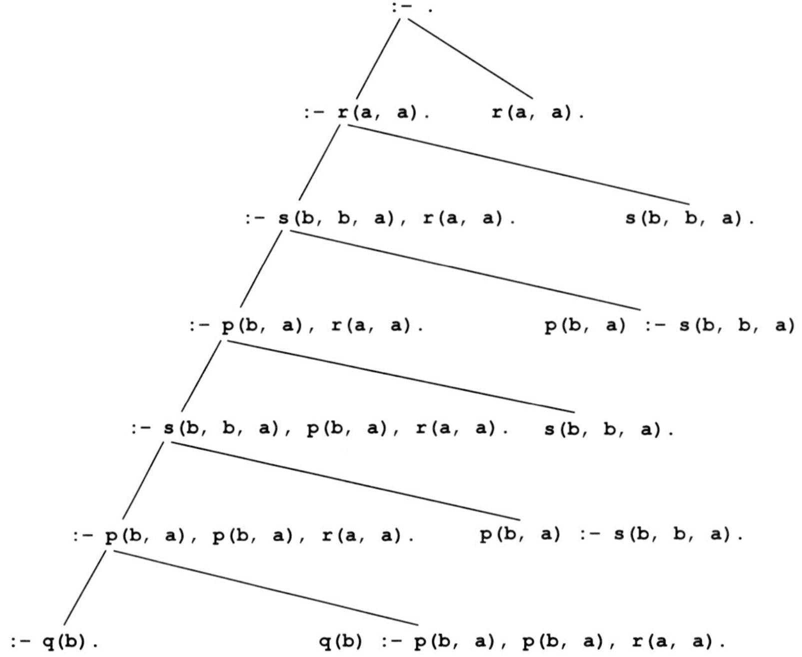

Figure 5.17

at the end of Section 2.3.4, *establish* is searching depth first through the space of resolution vines for a refutation. The root of the current vine is passed in through CENTERCL, which holds a list of literals assumed to be negative. Note that the center clause and the original clause set are all that *establish* needs in order to determine if it can proceed further with a vine. If CENTERCL is empty, it has produced a refutation vine, and hence returns **true**. If CENTERCL is not empty, *establish* searches through the list of input clauses, for a side clause, SIDECL, whose head unifies with the first literal in CENTERCL. Here, to avoid clash of variables, we rename variables in an input clause before considering it for SIDECL. If unification succeeds, MGU holds the mgu of the two literals. Function *establish* extends the vine by a level, forming the resolvent NEWCENTER of SIDECL and CENTERCL by concatenating the body of SIDECL with the rest of CENTERCL, and applying MGU to the resulting list. NEWCENTER is then used in a recursive call to *establish*.

A few observations here. First, we are treating the center clause as a list of literals, rather than as a set. Hence CENTERCL may contain duplicate literals. As in the propositonal case, leaving in the duplicates affects only the efficiency, not the completeness, of the method. Second, we have to make only two kinds of choices regarding the type of resolution vines. The first choice is which headless clause to use for the initial center clause. (For a Datalog program and goal, there is no choice.) The second kind of choice is which input clause to use as a side clause at each step.

We have eliminated the choice of the other clause in the resolution step, as well as which literals from each clause to use. Finally, although the restrictions we have placed on Horn clause resolution can still yield a complete refutation procedure, *establish* is not complete, because of its search strategy. The search space of resolution vines can have infinite paths. If *establish* encounters such a path, it will run forever without considering all possible resolution vines.

Note that a decision procedure for satisfiability of a predicate clause set S exists, because there are only a finite number of Herbrand interpretations for S, and because checking if a Herbrand interpretation is a model is decidable. (See Exercise 5.17.) In functional logic, satisfiability of clause sets is only *semidecidable*—that is, we can always find a refutation if the clauses are unsatisfiable, but we cannot always find a model if the clauses are satisfiable. Although the notion of Herbrand interpretation carries over to functional logic, Herbrand universes will generally be infinite there. Further, there are clause sets that have infinite models but do not have finite models.

5.7. EXERCISES

5.1. Give an example of a Datalog program P and a ground atom A that contains a constant not appearing in P, such that P logically implies A.

5.2. What is the meaning of the following Datalog program under the truth assignment TA_1 that makes just the ground literals:

```
p(a, b), p(b, b), q(a), q(c), r(a, a),
r(a, b), r(b, b), r(c, c)
```

true? Under the truth assignment TA_2 that makes just the literals:

```
p(a, a), q(a), q(c), r(a, a),
r(a, b), r(b, b), r(c, c)
```

true? Give the meaning of each clause in the program with your answers.

```
p(X, Y) :- q(X), r(X, Y).
p(X, X) :- r(X, b).
q(a).
q(c).
r(X, X).
```

5.3. Express the following English sentences in predicate logic. Which can be expressed as Datalog programs?
   a. No instructor grades his own paper.
   b. Every instructor is a student.
   c. Every instructor grades some of his own papers or has all of his papers graded by a student who is not an instructor.
   d. Nobody grades Smith's papers and Smith grades everybody's papers.

5.4. Write a program to parse atoms, as defined by the nonterminal symbol PREDATOM in the grammar of Figure 5.3.

5.5. For each occurrence of a variable in the following predicate expression, determine whether it is free or bound. For the bound occurrences, indicate the binding quantifier.

    ∃ X p(X, Y), ∀ Y q(Y); ¬(∃ X r(X, Y)); ∀ X r(Y, X)

5.6. Give a structure that is a model for the following predicate logic formula:

    ∀ X (∃ Y p(Y, b), ¬p(a, Y)); ¬(¬p(X, a); p(a, X))

5.7. a. Give an alternative definition of a structure relative to a given set of predicates and constants. Give a condition for such a structure to apply to a formula *f*, and show that if such a structure applies to *f*, it applies to any subformula *g* of *f*.
b. Using the original definition of a structure, explain how to modify a structure *ST* for *f* to a structure *ST'* for a subformula *g* of *f*.

5.8. Prove that if a predicate logic formula is true under some structure with a finite domain, then it is true under some structure with an infinite domain. Does there exist a formula that is true for some structure with an infinite domain but is false for every structure with a finite domain?

5.9. Let *f* be a closed predicate logic formula of the form:

    ∀ X1 ∀ X2 ... ∀ Xk *g*.

For any structure *ST* for *f*, prove that $M_{ST}(f)$ = **true** if and only if $M_{ST,I}(g)$ = **true** for every instantiation *I*.

5.10. Let *f* and *g* be closed predicate logic formulas.
a. Show that *f* logically implies *g* exactly when the formula ¬*f*; *g* is valid.
b. Show that *f* is logically equivalent to *g* exactly when the formula *f*, *g*; ¬*f*, ¬*g* is valid.
c. How should the constructions in (a) and (b) be modified when *f* and *g* can contain free occurrences of variables?

5.11. Determine all the logical equivalences and implications between the following formulas:

i. ∀ X ∀ Y ¬g(X, Y)
ii. ∀ X ∃ Y ¬g(X, Y)
iii. ∃ X ∀ Y ¬g(X, Y)
iv. ∃ Y ∃ X ¬g(X, Y)
v. ¬(∀ X ∀ Y g(X, Y))
vi. ¬(∀ X ∃ Y g(X, Y))
vii. ¬(∃ X ∀ Y g(X, Y))
viii. ¬(∃ X ∃ Y g(X, Y))

5.12. Use the equivalences given in Section 5.3 to deduce:

$\exists$ **X** $\exists$ **Y** *f* ≡ $\exists$ **Y** $\exists$ **X** *f*.

5.13. Show that:

$\forall$ **X** (*f*, *g*) ≡ *f*, $\forall$ **X** *g*

when **X** does not occur free in *f*.

5.14. Put the following formulas into prenex form. Put the ones that end up as universal formulas into clausal form.

i. ¬($\exists$ **X p(X)**; $\forall$ **Y** ¬**q(X, Y)**)
ii. $\forall$ **X** $\exists$ **Y q(X, Y)**, $\forall$ **Y r(X, Y)**
iii. ¬($\exists$ **X** $\forall$ **Y q(X, Y)**); ¬($\forall$ **Y** $\exists$ **X q(Y, X)**)

5.15. Consider a formula *f* in which exactly **X** and **Y** occur free.
a. Prove that no universal formula is logically equivalent to $\exists$ **X** $\forall$ **Y** *f*.
b. For the two closed formulas:

$\forall$ **X** $\exists$ **Y** *f*
$\forall$ **X** *f*[**Y/a**]

show that one could be unsatisfiable and the other satisfiable.

5.16. Must a satisfiable predicate logic formula necessarily have a Herbrand model?

5.17. Let *f* be a predicate logic formula, and let H = <Con_f, *Id*, *TA*> be a Herbrand interpretation in which *TA* is represented as the set of all ground atoms that map to **true**. Describe an algorithm for deciding whether *H* is a model for *f*.

5.18. Since predicate logic structures can be infinite, we cannot write out every structure explicitly. However, we can represent some countably infinite structures with computer programs for the various components. We represent such a structure *ST* for formula *f* by:

A universe function *univ* that maps the positive integers to successive elements of the universe.
A function *const* that gives the element of the universe for each constant in Con_f.
A truth assignment function *ta* that returns **true** or **false** for any atom in the base of *f*.

For a Herbrand interpretation, we need to give only the *ta* function.
a. Given a structure *ST* in the form of programs, is it decidable if *ST* is a model for *f*? Why or why not?
b. What if *f* is a universal formula and *ST* is a Herbrand interpretation (represented with programs)?
c. What if *f* is a universal formula but *ST* is any structure (represented with programs)?

5.19. Demonstrate that a given predicate logic formula f has only a finite number of Herbrand interpretations.

5.20. Prove that the definition of logical implication for Datalog programs as defined in Section 5.1.3 agrees with the definition in Section 5.3, if Datalog clauses are assumed to be universally quantified.

5.21. Let G be a set of ground clauses. The following is the *Davis and Putnam method* for determining if G is satisfiable. The method consists of repeating the following tests and modifications of G until its satisfiability or unsatisfiability is determined.

1. If G contains the empty clause, then G is unsatisfiable.
2. If G contains no clauses, then G is satisfiable.
3. If G contains a clause C consisting of the single literal L, remove C from G, remove all other clauses containing L from G, and remove $\neg L$ from every clause of G in which it appears. (By $\neg L$ we intend the complement of L. Thus, if L is **¬p(a)**, then $\neg L$ is **p(a)**.)
4. If L occurs in some clause C in G, and $\neg L$ does not occur in G, remove C from G.
5. If G contains a clause C with literals L and $\neg L$, remove C from G.
6. If G contains both occurrences of L and $\neg L$, then create clause sets G_1 and G_2, where:

   G_1 = all clauses in G that contain L, plus all clauses containing neither L nor $\neg L$,
   G_2 = all clauses in G that contain $\neg L$, plus all clauses containing neither L nor $\neg L$.

Run the method on G_1 and G_2. G is unsatisfiable if and only if both G_1 and G_2 are unsatisfiable.

a. Use the Davis and Putnam method on the ground clause set in Examples 2.27 and 2.28.
b. Prove that the method always terminates and produces the correct answer.

5.22. Let C be a predicate clause, with at most k distinct predicates, k distinct constants, and k distinct variables. If C has m literals, how many ground instances can C have?

5.23. Prove that if the idempotence requirement is removed, substitutions are closed under composition. Give an algorithm to compute the substitution that is equal to the composition of two others.

5.24. Let ρ be the substitution constructed from substitutions θ and σ as described in Section 5.5. Prove that for every variable **X**, $\mathbf{X}\rho = (\mathbf{X}\theta)\sigma$.

5.25. a. Prove that composition of substitutions is associative.
b. Prove that composition of substitutions is not commutative.
c. Give an example where $\theta \circ (\sigma \circ \rho)$ satisfies the restriction on composition (the second substitution not having a variable on the right of any replacement that is on the left of a replacement in the first substitution) but $(\theta \circ \sigma) \circ \rho$ does not.

5.26. Which of the following pairs of atoms has a unifier that is not an mgu?

```
i.   p(U, U, V, V), p(X, Y, Y, Z)
ii.  p(U, U, V, V), p(X, a, b, X)
iii. p(U, U, V, V), p(X, a, a, Z)
```

5.27. Let θ be an mgu of atoms A and B. Prove that θ has as few replacements mapping variables to constants as any unifier A and B. Show that a unifier with the minimum number of variable-to-constant replacements need not be an mgu.

5.28. Let θ be a unifier for atoms A and B. Prove θ has as few replacements as any unifier for A and B if and only if θ is an mgu.

5.29. Prove that an mgu of atoms A and B may not mention variables not present in A or B.

5.30. Using the alternative definition that σ is an mgu if for any other unifier θ there exists a ρ such that $\theta = \sigma \circ \rho$, and removing the idempotence condition on substitutions:

a. exhibit an mgu σ that does not satisfy $\theta = \sigma \circ \theta$ for some unifier θ, and
b. exhibit two mgus for the same set of atoms with different numbers of replacements.

5.31. For the *match* function of Section 4.3, prove that if HEAD and SUBS contain nonunifiable atoms, then *match* returns **false**.

5.32. Give an algorithm that computes the mgu of a list of two or more atoms. Demonstrate your algorithm on the following first three atoms and then on all four atoms.

```
p(X1, X1, Y1, b)
p(X2, Y2, Z2, X2)
p(X3, Y3, a, Y3)
p(b, X4, X4, b)
```

5.33. Let C be a clause and let C′ be a subset of the literals in C. Prove that in general, for a substitution θ:

$$(C - C')\theta = C\theta - C'\theta$$

is false. Prove that the equality holds if C′ is a maximal subset of literals unified by θ.

5.34. For clauses C and D and substitution θ, is:

$$C\theta \cap D\theta = (C \cap D)\theta$$

true in general? What about:

$$C\theta \cup D\theta = (C \cup D)\theta?$$

5.35. Either Cookie Monster can eat anything, or anything can eat any kind of cookie. A macaroon is a kind of cookie. Anything Cookie Monster likes tastes yucky. Cookie Monster likes macaroons.

Express these sentences as clauses in predicate logic, and use them in a resolution proof of: There is something Cookie Monster can eat that tastes yucky.

5.36. Prove that any resolvent of clauses C and D generated by full resolution can be generated from factors of C and D by binary resolution. (If you have not used the condition that the set C' of literals resolved upon in C is maximal, there is a flaw in your proof.)

5.37. Let C be a predicate logic clause, and let θ be a substitution. Prove that C logically implies $C\theta$, hence C implies all its factors.

5.38. Prove:

LOWERING LEMMA: If E is a resolvent of predicate logic clauses C and D, and E' is a ground instance of E, then there exist ground instances C' and D' of C and D that have resolvent E'.

5.39. Give a precise algorithm for lowering a refutation tree T over a clause set S to a refutation tree T' over the set G of ground instances of S. You may assume that each interior node in T holds the mgu used to generate the resolvent at that node.

5.40. In *unit resolution* one clause for each resolution step must be a unit (single-literal) clause.
   a. Prove that unit resolution is a complete refutation procedure for Horn clauses.
   b. Give an example to show that unit resolution is not complete for general clauses.

5.8. COMMENTS AND BIBLIOGRAPHY

Predicate logic is a well-studied area. The references to logic in the bibliography for Chapter 2 are relevant here. A collection of papers edited by van Heijenoort [5.1] gives an excellent history of modern mathematical logic. A very early computerized theorem-proving method similar to resolution is described by Davis and Putnam [5.2]. That method used Herbrand's theorem but not unification; it essentially exploded all rules, not employing any delaying tactics, and as a result was extremely inefficient. The idea of using unification as a "delaying" method in resolution theorem proving is due to Robinson [2.2]. This generalization was the seminal idea that opened the entire field of resolution theorem proving and led to the idea of logic programming. Chang and Lee [2.4] provide a good reference book for much of what is known about resolution theorem proving. Many of the proofs we have given here (and many we have not) can be found there. The proof that positive unit resolution is complete for Horn clauses, with binary resolutions and no factoring (Exercise 5.40), is given by Henschen and Wos [2.6].

The original ideas of how to extract answers from resolution proofs were due to Green [5.3]. The theory of answers is also presented by Chang and Lee [2.4] and Nilsson [2.12].

The precise definitions of substitution and most general unifier are rather delicate, and there have been several slightly different (and inequivalent) ones used in the literature. Lassez et al. [5.4] point out the differences in the definitions and do much to clarify the issues.

5.1. J. van Heijnoort, *From Frege to Goedel—A Source Book in Mathematical Logic,* Harvard University Press, Cambridge, MA, 1967.

5.2. M. Davis and H. Putnam, A computing procedure for quantification theory, *JACM* 7:2, March 1960, 201–15.

5.3. C.C. Green, Theorem proving by resolution as a basis for question-answering systems, in *Machine Intelligence 4,* B. Meltzer and D. Michie (eds.), American Elsevier, 1969, 183–205.

5.4. J.-L. Lassez, M. J. Maher, and K. G. Marriott, Unification revisited, IBM Report RC 12395 (#55630), Yorktown Heights, NY, December 1986.

6

Improving the Datalog Interpreter

Why study the implementation of Datalog? Direct implementation of the refutation principle, even in the Horn clause case, is not by itself sufficient for an efficient programming language. A body of technology is necessary to convert the naive interpreter into a respectable implementation. This technology is important because it is applicable to other declarative languages, pattern matching and symbolic manipulation, and dynamic storage management.

We convert the naive interpreter, via a sequence of small changes, into a sophisticated interpreter that bears little resemblance to a resolution theorem prover. We think the intermediate steps make it clearer that the naive and sophisticated versions are equivalent. All the techniques in this chapter are reused in Chapter 10, where we develop an efficient Prolog interpreter. Seeing them here in a simpler setting should provide a foundation for understanding them in the more complex setting later.

We begin by making the naive interpreter more concrete, giving representations for the different data types involved. The next few sections are all "delaying tactics": delaying the copying of the goal list, the application of substitutions to the goal list, the composition of a new mgu with the accumulate substitution, as well as the lazy list technique for delaying concatenation and computing the rest of the goal list. Eventually we get to the point where the interpreter does no copying at all. Rather, different invocations of the interpreter *structure share* the program code: an instance of a clause is represented by a pair consisting of a reference to the clause and a *local substitution* for the variables in the clause. These improvements, which are all applications of the Procrastination Principle, deal chiefly with time complexity. The final improvement is a space-efficient representation of substitutions, using an array of bindings indexed by variables. These binding arrays give a handle on storage management, enabling the interpreter to reclaim space used for substitutions on search paths that fail. (This last improvement is why we are not too concerned with reclaiming space in intermediate versions of the algorithm.) The chapter concludes with a few words on implementing evaluable predicates.

6.1. Representations

First, we look in more detail at how Datalog terms and programs are represented. We maintain a symbol table. The symbol table contains three kinds of entries—one for each kind of basic symbol in a Datalog program: predicate, constant, and variable. The following variant record type describes a symbol table entry:

```
type
    stentry = record
        NAME: string;
        case STYPE: (pred, cnst, vble) of
          pred: (ARITY: integer;
                 CLAUSES: clauselist);
          cnst: ();
          vble: ()
        end;
```

For each type of entry, the symbol table contains the name of the symbol. For predicate symbols, the symbol table contains the arity of the symbol and a reference to a list of clauses that have that symbol as the predicate symbol in their heads. The symbol table, SYMTAB, is an array of such records, indexed by a variable of type *symtabindex*.

A literal for an n-place predicate is represented as a record with $n + 1$ fields: the first field contains the index in the symbol table for the predicate symbol; the $i + 1^{st}$ field contains the index in the symbol table for the ith argument. We use *litrec* for the type of such a record (which lies outside the variant record structure of Pascal), and we let type *lit* be a pointer to a *litrec*.

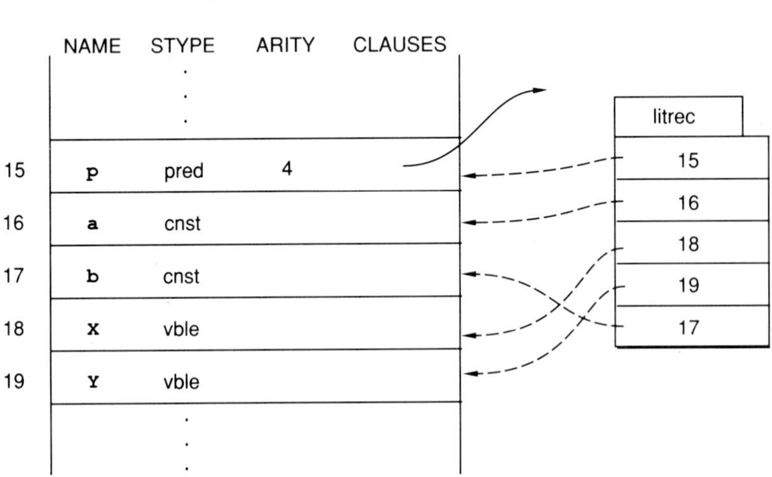

Figure 6.1

EXAMPLE 6.1: The literal **p(a, X, Y, b)** is represented as shown in Figure 6.1. The dashed arrows indicate indexed references—that is, logical pointers. □

The body of a program clause is represented by a list of the literals that make it up. We use *lits* for the type of list of literals, and *litlist* for a pointer to *lits*.

EXAMPLE 6.2: The literal list:

q(X, a), r(X, Y)

is represented by the data structure shown in Figure 6.2. In that figure we have used symbols themselves to represent the indexes of their symbol table entries. □

A clause is represented by a record with three fields:

```
type
      clauselist  =  ↑clauserec;
      clauserec  =  record
            HEAD: lit;
            BODY: litlist;
            NXTCLAUSE: clauselist
         end;
```

The first field references the literal that is the head of the clause. The second refers to the list of literals that is the body of the clause. The third references the next clause with the same predicate symbol in its head.

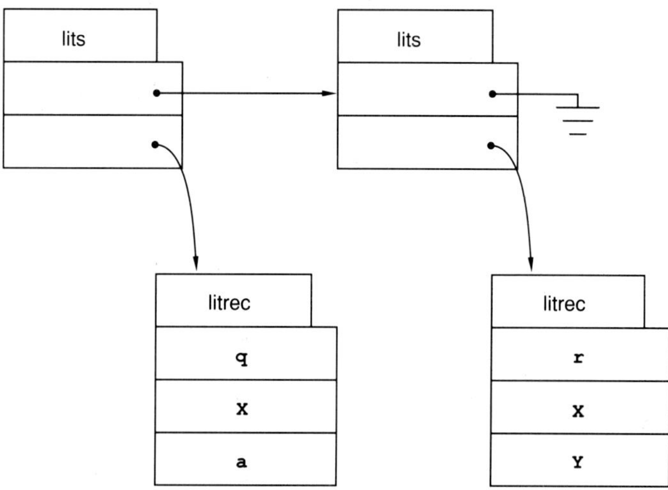

Figure 6.2

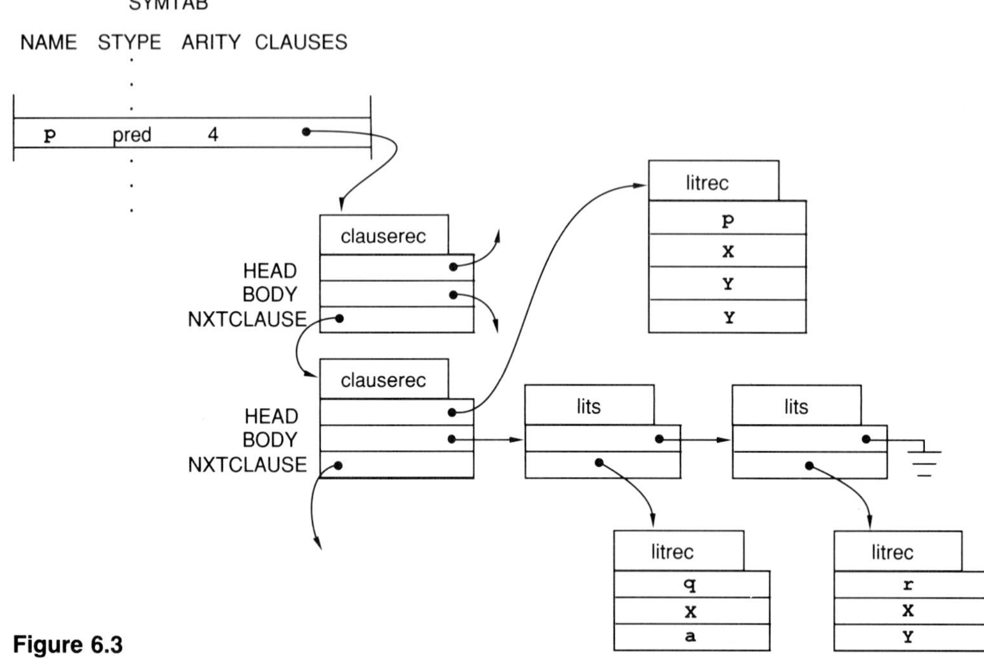

Figure 6.3

EXAMPLE 6.3: The clause:

```
p(X, Y, Y) :- q(X, a), r(X, Y).
```

is represented by the data structure shown in Figure 6.3. □

Note that we have already stored a Datalog program in such a way that access to all the clauses for a single predicate is direct; all clauses in a program need not be scanned. Thus the "indexing" optimization of Proplog is incorporated into the Datalog interpreter. The "lazy list" optimization of the goal list in Proplog is not included in the initial Datalog interpeter. We have already noted that the variables in Datalog complicate matters. It will take some work to get to the point where lazy lists can be used for Datalog. One of the advantages of lazy lists was to structure share clause bodies. At this point we cannot have a lazy list point directly into a clause, because the interpreter must make an instance of a clause with new variables each time it uses the clause.

6.2. Naive Datalog Interpreter

Given these representations, we can write the Datalog interpreter as we left it but now with slightly more precision. We make a few cosmetic changes, such as introducing an explicit variable, NEWGL, for the newly constructed goal list, that will make later refinements easier. Also, CLAUSEINST, SUBS, and NEWGL can all be global variables, since their values are never examined after the recursive call. However, NEXTCL must be local to the procedure, because it keeps track of which clauses have been tried so far.

```
var CLAUSEINST: clauselist;
    SUBS: subst;
    NEWGL: litlist;

function establish1(GOALLIST: litlist): boolean;
    var NEXTCL: clauselist;
    begin
      if isempty(GOALLIST) then return(true);
      NEXTCL := SYMTAB[predsym(first(GOALLIST))].CLAUSES;
      while NEXTCL <> nil do
        begin
          CLAUSEINST := instance(NEXTCL);
          NEWGL := copy(GOALLIST);
          if match(CLAUSEINST↑.HEAD, first(NEWGL), SUBS) then
            begin
              NEWGL := concat(CLAUSEINST↑.BODY, rest(NEWGL));
              apply(SUBS, NEWGL);
              if establish1(NEWGL) then return(true)
            end;
          NEXTCL := NEXTCL↑.NXTCLAUSE
        end;
      return(false)
    end;
```

The functions *isempty, first,* and *rest* are used to test and access the goal list. Function *isempty* tests if there are no literals in the goal list. Function *first* retrieves a reference to the first literal in the list, and *rest* returns a reference to the remainder of the list. The function *predsym* picks off the predicate symbol of a literal. (Actually, it returns the symbol table index for the predicate symbol.) The function *instance* takes a clause and makes a copy of it, replacing all variables with new variables. Thus *instance* adds new variables to the symbol table.

We have moved the copying out of the concatenation function. Function *copy* just makes a copy of a list of literals. We must take care that neither the program nor the goal list that is passed into *establish1* is modified within the **while**-loop. If unification fails or the recursive call to *establish1* returns **false**, we may come around the loop again and try to apply another clause. In that case the goal list and program must be exactly the same as when the routine was first entered. For this reason we must pay strict attention to what data structures get changed.

For simplicity, we first take a copy of the entire goal list. Hence we can allow *match, concat,* and *apply* all to be destructive. That is, they may modify their arguments. The *match* routine takes two literals and tries to unify them. If they are unifiable, it returns **true** and passes back, through its third argument, the substitution that is their most general unifier. If they are not unifiable, it returns **false**. Function *concat* performs concatenation, possibly modifying its first argument. It runs down the list that is its first argument and changes the NXTCLAUSE field of the last record to reference the beginning of the list that is its second argument. Procedure *apply* applies a substitution to a list of literals. It directly modifies the goal list NEWGL. Had a copy of the goal list not been made before the statement 'apply(SUBS, NEWGL)', *apply* would have to do so.

EXAMPLE 6.4: Consider the computation of *establish1* given the goal list:

```
:- p(a, X5, X5), s(X5, b).
```

and using the following program:

```
p(X, Y, Z) :- q(Z, a), r(X, Y).
q(b, a).
r(a, b).
s(b, b).
```

The following lists show the initial values of variables and the new value after a change, tracing *establish1* through two cycles. We show the value of NEWGL three times for each invocation: once after it is initially assigned a copy of GOALLIST, then immediately after the *concat* operation, and finally after SUBS is applied. In the case of pointer variables we indicate the structure referenced.

INITIAL INVOCATION:

GOALLIST:	p(a, X5, X5), s(X5, b)
NEXTCL:	p(X, Y, Z) :- q(Z, a), r(X, Y).
CLAUSEINST:	p(X6, Y6, Z6) :- q(Z6, a), r(X6, Y6).
NEWGL:	p(a, X5, X5), s(X5, b)
SUBS:	{X6 = a, Y6 = X5, Z6 = X5}
NEWGL:	q(Z6, a), r(X6, Y6), s(X5, b)
NEWGL:	q(X5, a), r(a, X5), s(X5, b)

RECURSIVE INVOCATION:

GOALLIST:	q(X5, a), r(a, X5), s(X5, b)
NEXTCL:	q(b, a).
CLAUSEINST:	q(b, a).
NEWGL:	q(X5, a), r(a, X5), s(X5, b)
SUBS:	{X5 = b}
NEWGL:	r(a, X5), s(X5, b)
NEWGL:	r(a, b), s(b, b) □

Consider now the details of the *match* routine. A substitution is simply a list of pairs that indicate the replacements to be done:

```
type
    subst = ↑repl;
    repl = record
        V: symtabindex; {symbol table entry of the left-side variable}
        VC: symtabindex; {symbol table entry of right-side variable or constant}
        NXTR: subst {reference to next repl record}
      end;
```

Given a reference, LT, to a literal, the selector function *predsym* returns the predicate symbol (first field in the representation of LT) and the selector function *arg*(LT, I) returns the Ith argument (the $I+1^{st}$ field in the representation of LT). Both functions return symbol table indexes. As a consequence, two predicate symbols with the same name but different arities are judged distinct. The function *variable* returns **true** if its argument is a variable. The code for *match* follows:

```
function match(T1, T2: lit; var MGU: subst): boolean;
    var REPL: subst;
    begin
      if predsym(T1) <> predsym(T2) then return(false);
      MGU := nil;
      for I := 1 to SYMTAB[predsym(T1)].ARITY do
        begin
          if variable(arg(T1, I)) then
            if arg(T1, I) = arg(T2, I) then {same variable, do nothing}
            else
              begin
                new(REPL); REPL↑.V := arg(T1, I);
                REPL↑.VC := arg(T2, I); REPL↑.NXTR := nil;
                MGU := compose(MGU, REPL);
                apply1(REPL, T1);
                apply1(REPL, T2)
              end
          else if variable(arg(T2, I)) then
            begin
              new(REPL); REPL↑.V := arg(T2, I);
              REPL↑.VC := arg(T1, I); REPL↑.NXTR := nil;
              MGU := compose(MGU, REPL);
              apply1(REPL, T1);
              apply1(REPL, T2)
            end
          else if arg(T1, I) <> arg(T2, I) then return(false)
        end;
      return(true)
    end;
```

Here *compose* is a routine that composes two substitutions; it uses the second substitution to replace variables in the second component of replacements in the first substitution, and then adds the second substitution to the first. It is destructive in that it makes the changes in place in the first substitution. Procedure *apply1* is similar to *apply* in *establish1,* except that it applies a substitution to a single literal instead of a list of literals. It, too, is destructive. It can safely modify its parameters, because the actual values with which it is called, CLAUSEINST↑.HEAD and first(NEWGL), are copies.

EXAMPLE 6.5: To see how *match* works, consider the following trace in which **s (X, X, a, a)** is unified with **s (Y, b, Z, Z)**:

match(**s (X, X, a, a)**, **s (Y, b, Z, Z)**)

I = 1 REPL: **X = Y**
MGU: {**X = Y**}
T1: **s (Y, Y, a, a)**
T2: **s (Y, b, Z, Z)**

I = 2 REPL: **Y = b**
MGU: {**X = b, Y = b**}
T1: **s (b, b, a, a)**
T2: **s (b, b, Z, Z)**

I = 3 REPL: **Z = a**
MGU: {**X = b, Y = b, Z = a**}
T1: **s (b, b, a, a)**
T2: **s (b, b, a, a)**

I = 4 **a = a** so succeed and return MGU: {**X = b, Y = b, Z = a**}
□

A note about how *establish1* uses space: The invocation of *copy* allocates a significant amount of space. The question arises as to whether the space can be reclaimed. Also, *match* allocates space for new replacements to be added to the substitution it is constructing as the mgu. All this space could be reclaimed when we move to the next clause and start around the **while**-loop again. That is, if *match* fails, or the recursive call to *establish1* returns **false**, nothing allocated during that iteration through the **while**-loop is needed anymore. So, if all space is allocated from a stack (as is the case in many implementations of Pascal), and we could save the current top of the stack just before entering the **while**-loop (as is allowed in some Pascal systems, UCSD Pascal, in particular), we could reset the top of the stack as the last thing in the body of the **while**-loop. This change would allow us to reclaim efficiently the space consumed by all the copying.

Even though we could reclaim the *space* taken by the copies, it is still *time*-inefficient to do so much copying. In the next section we look at ways to modify the interpreter to do less copying.

6.3. Delayed Copying and Application

The most glaring inefficiency of the *establish1* algorithm is the amount of copying it must do. The entire goal list, which may become very long, is copied in its entirety before each match is attempted. If *match* fails, *establish* has needlessly copied the entire list, when only the first goal on the list has been examined or modified. Thus one obvious and simple improvement is to copy only the first goal before the call to *match* and then to copy the rest of the goal list only after *match* succeeds.

Even with that improvement, a lot of copying still must be done. Perhaps after copying a long list of goals, the next unification fails, and so *establish* never sees the whole list just constructed. Even if the entire goal list ultimately succeeds, consider how many times the last goal on that goal list gets copied—once for every subgoal that gets added to the list along the way.

The Procrastination Principle suggests that *establish* delay the copying until absolutely necessary. Notice that the only reason to copy the whole goal list is in order to apply the current substitution to it. To avoid the copying, *establish* must delay applying the substitution. It need not apply each substitution returned by *match* to the entire goal list immediately. Instead it can simply accumulate the substitutions and apply them all at once to a literal on the goal list when it has to process that literal. Thus the next version of the interpreter, *establish2*, has two parameters: a list of goals and an accumulated substitution. The actual goal list (the one that *establish1* would use) is the result of applying the substitution to the list of goals. By delaying the application of the substitution to the goal list until it is needed, *establish2* need not copy the entire goal list every time.

```
var CLAUSEINST: clauselist;
    SUBS, NEWACCSUBS: subst;
    THISGOAL: lit;
    NEWGL: litlist;


function establish2(GOALLIST: litlist; ACCSUBS: subst): boolean;
    var NEXTCL: clauselist;
    begin
      if isempty(GOALLIST) then return(true);
      NEXTCL := SYMTAB[predsym(first(GOALLIST))].CLAUSES;
      while NEXTCL <> nil do
        begin
          CLAUSEINST := instance(NEXTCL);
          THISGOAL := copyapply2(ACCSUBS, first(GOALLIST));
          if match(CLAUSEINST↑.HEAD, THISGOAL, SUBS) then
            begin
              NEWGL := concat(CLAUSEINST↑.BODY, rest(GOALLIST));
              NEWACCSUBS := copycompose(ACCSUBS, SUBS);
              if establish2(NEWGL, NEWACCSUBS) then return(true)
            end;
```

```
            NEXTCL := NEXTCL↑.NXTCLAUSE
        end;
    return(false)
end;
```

We need to explain several subprocedures used here. First, *copyapply2* makes a new copy of a literal and applies a substitution to the result; thus it is nondestructive. Second, as before, *concat* is a destructive concatenation routine. Third, *copycompose* is a routine that composes two substitutions; it applies the second substitution to the right sides of replacements in the first substitution and adds the new replacements of the second substitution. It is nondestructive; that is, the new substitution is constructed by copying the old one and modifying the copy. The code for *copycompose* is:

```
function copycompose(SUBS1, SUBS2: subst): subst;
    var NEXTREPL: subst;
    begin
      if SUBS1 = nil then return(SUBS2)
      else
        begin
          new(NEXTREPL);
          NEXTREPL↑.V := SUBS1↑.V;
          NEXTREPL↑.VC := apply(SUBS2, SUBS1↑.VC);
          NEXTREPL↑.NXTR := copycompose(SUBS1↑.NXTR, SUBS2)
        end
    end;
```

Function *copycompose* is not a general-purpose routine for composing substitutions. We have omitted a step from the method for composing substitutions described in Section 5.5. We apply SUBS2 to the right sides of replacements in SUBS1, but we do not remove replacements from SUBS2 that have the same left sides as replacements in SUBS1. It turns out that for the call from *establish2* to *copycompose*, SUBS2 will never contain replacements with left sides the same as for replacements in SUBS1. (See Exercise 6.6.) Also, *copycompose* does not copy SUBS2, because the substitution returned by *copycompose* will be copied before it is next modified.

EXAMPLE 6.6: Let's trace the execution of *establish2* through two invocations on the same Datalog query and program we used earlier:

```
:- p(a, X5, X5), s(X5, b).

p(X, Y, Z) :- q(Z, a), r(X, Y).
q(b, a).
r(a, b).
s(b, b).
```

Again we give the values of the main variables when they are set:

INITIAL INVOCATION:

```
GOALLIST:      p(a, X5, X5), s(X5, b)
ACCSUBS:       {}
NEXTCL:        p(X, Y, Z) :- q(Z, a), r(X, Y).
CLAUSEINST:    p(X6, Y6, Z6) :- q(Z6, a), r(X6, Y6).
THISGOAL:      p(a, X5, X5)
SUBS:          {X6 = a, Y6 = X5, Z6 = X5}
NEWGL:         q(Z6, a), r(X6, Y6), s(X5, b)
NEWACCSUBS:    {X6 = a, Y6 = X5, Z6 = X5}
```

RECURSIVE INVOCATION:

```
GOALLIST:      q(Z6, a), r(X6, Y6), s(X5, b)
ACCSUBS:       {X6 = a, Y6 = X5, Z6 = X5}
NEXTCL:        q(b, a).
THISGOAL:      q(X5, a).
SUBS:          {X5 = b}
NEWGL:         r(X6, Y6), s(X5, b)
NEWACCSUBS:    {X6 = a, Y6 = b, Z6 = b, X5 = b}
```

Comparing this trace with the one for *establish1* in Example 6.4, we can see that on entry to the routines, GOALLIST of *establish1* is obtained by applying ACCSUBS to GOALLIST of *establish2*. □

We have reduced the amount of copying of goals. The application of substitutions is localized to a single goal and to a single place in *establish2*—just before the goal is passed to *match* for matching with the head of CLAUSEINST.

Concatenation of a clause body with the rest of the goal list is quite simple in *establish2*. Concatenation involves no copying and changes only a single pointer. It does require traversing the list of literals in the clause body to find the last literal, so that this *lit* record can be changed to reference the first record of the remaining goal list. This traversal is not really necessary. Notice that *instance* already must traverse the body of CLAUSEINST when constructing it from NEXTCL. If we wished, we could pass '*rest*(GOALLIST)' to *instance* and have *instance* make the last literal of the new clause's body point to the rest of GOALLIST. Then CLAUSEINST↑.BODY would really be the new goal list, and we would not have to use *concat* at all. (See Exercise 6.8.) However, further modifications to the algorithm will remove the copying of NEXTCL altogether, so we do not pursue this optimization further.

Now what is expensive in *establish2*? Instead of copying the goal list, *establish2* constructs a large substitution. Every time it adds more to the accumulated substitution (by composing it with the most recent mgu), it must copy that substitution in case *match* or the recursive call fails. Apparently we have traded copying the goal list for copying the substitutions. Let's look more closely at how we might optimize the handling of the substitutions.

6.4. Delayed Composition of Substitutions

The Procrastination Principle suggests that we avoid composing substitutions until we need the result. Notice that the only place *establish2* uses the accumulated substitution is to apply it to the first goal on the goal list in preparation for passing that literal to *match*.

To obtain the third version of the interpreter, *establish3*, we apply the Procrastination Principle to the composition of the mgu with the current substitution. Rather than compose them, we simply concatenate the mgu with the current substitution. The type *subst* works to represent lists of replacements, even if they do not constitute a proper substitution. Then we modify the function performed by *copyapply2* so that it composes substitutions "on the fly."

```
var CLAUSEINST: clauselist;
    SUBS, NEWREPLS: subst;
    THISGOAL: lit;
    NEWGL: litlist;

function establish3(GOALLIST: litlist; REPLS: subst): boolean;
    var NEXTCL: clauselist;
    begin
      if isempty(GOALLIST) then return(true);
      NEXTCL := SYMTAB[predsym(first(GOALLIST))].CLAUSES;
      while NEXTCL <> nil do
        begin
          CLAUSEINST := instance(NEXTCL);
          THISGOAL := copyapplyrepls(REPLS, first(GOALLIST));
          if match(CLAUSEINST↑.HEAD, THISGOAL, SUBS) then
            begin
              NEWGL := concat(CLAUSEINST↑.BODY, rest(GOALLIST));
              NEWREPLS := rconcat(SUBS, REPLS);
              if establish3(NEWGL, NEWREPLS) then return(true)
            end;
          NEXTCL := NEXTCL↑.NXTCLAUSE
        end;
      return(false)
    end;
```

We have changed the name of the second parameter from ACCSUBS to REPLS to emphasize that this parameter is just a list of replacements, not a substitution. That is, a variable now may appear on the right side of one replacement and on the left side of another that was added later. Thus, to apply REPLS to a literal, we may have to pass each variable through the list of replacements several times. For example, if REPLS is:

```
[Z = a, Y = Z, X = Y]
```

we have to make three passes to find to what symbol **X** is mapped ultimately. (We use brackets instead of braces to emphasize that REPLS is just a list of replacements, not necessarily a proper substitution.) As we remarked in the last section, SUBS and REPLS (ACCSUBS there) do not have replacements with common left sides. Thus no ambiguity exists as to which replacement to apply to a variable each time we pass through REPLS. There can be only one replacement with that variable on the left.

Note that SUBS is concatenated to the front of REPLS in *establish3*, whereas in *establish2*, SUBS was added to the end of ACCSUBS. There are two reasons for this change. First, *rconcat* (concatenation for lists of replacements) is destructive in its first argument but not in its second. The value of SUBS is particular to a single iteration of the **while**-loop, while the value of REPLS must be kept intact for subsequent iterations. Second, SUBS generally will be a shorter list than REPLS, and the time the *rconcat* requires is proportional to the length of its first argument and independent of the length of its second argument.

The complicated part of this version of the interpreter is buried in the function *copyapplyrepls*. This function must create a new literal that is the result of applying the substitution represented by a list of replacements to a goal. We give the code for *copyapplyrepls*:

```
function copyapplyrepls(REPLS: subst; GOAL: lit): lit;
    var NEWGOAL: lit;
      I: integer;
    begin
      NEWGOAL := newcopy(GOAL);
      for I := 1 to SYMTAB[predsym(GOAL)].ARITY do
        arg(NEWGOAL, I) := deref(arg(GOAL, I), REPLS);
      return(NEWGOAL)
    end;

function deref(TERM: symtabindex; REPLS: subst): symtabindex;
    var NEXTREPL: subst;
    begin
      if variable(TERM) then
        begin
          NEXTREPL := REPLS;
          while NEXTREPL <> nil do
            if NEXTREPL↑.V = TERM then return(deref(NEXTREPL↑.VC, REPLS))
            else NEXTREPL := NEXTREPL↑.NXTR
        end;
      return(TERM)
    end;
```

The function *copyapplyrepls* first creates a copy of the literal record using the function *newcopy* to allocate the necessary new space. Function *newcopy* returns a new literal record of the same size and with the same predicate symbol as its argument. Function *copyapplyrepls* then uses *deref* to apply the substitution represented by REPLS to each argument of GOAL in turn and puts the result in the corresponding field of the newly allocated record.

The function *deref* is where the substitution is applied. It *dereferences* a term (a variable or a constant) relative to a list of replacements. If *deref* is given a constant, it simply returns the constant. If it is given a variable, it must scan through the list of replacements and see if that variable has been replaced in the accumulated substitution. If it finds a replacement for the variable, it then takes the new value and returns the result of applying *deref* to that. This recursive call must be made because REPLS is just a list of replacements, not a substitution. This call to *deref* is where the composition of the separate mgu's is actually done. If the variable does not have a replacement for it in REPLS, then *deref* returns the (index of the) variable itself.

EXAMPLE 6.7: Let REPLS be:

```
[Z = a, Y = Z, X = Y]
```

A call to *deref* with **X** and REPLS recursively invokes *deref* on **Y**, then on **Z**, and then on **a**. The invocation on **a** returns simply **a**, and that value is passed up through all the calls as the value of the original invocation. A call to *deref* with **W** and REPLS returns **W** as the value immediately, without any recursive calls. □

EXAMPLE 6.8: Let's trace the execution of *establish3* through three invocations on our Datalog query and program:

```
:- p(a, X5, X5), s(X5, b).

p(X, Y, Z) :- q(Z, a), r(X, Y).
q(b, a).
r(a, b).
s(b, b).
```

Once again we give the values of the main variables when they are set in each invocation:

INITIAL INVOCATION:

GOALLIST:	**p(a, X5, X5), s(X5, b)**
REPLS:	**[]**
NEXTCL:	**p(X, Y, Z) :- q(Z, a), r(X, Y).**
CLAUSEINST:	**p(X6, Y6, Z6) :- q(Z6, a), r(X6, Y6).**
THISGOAL:	**p(a, X5, X5)**
SUBS:	**{X6 = a, Y6 = X5, Z6 = X5}**
NEWGL:	**q(Z6, a), r(X6, Y6), s(X5, b)**
NEWREPLS:	**[X6 = a, Y6 = X5, Z6 = X5]**

FIRST RECURSIVE INVOCATION

```
GOALLIST:    q(Z6, a), r(X6, Y6), s(X5, b)
REPLS:       [X6 = a, Y6 = X5, Z6 = X5]
NEXTCL:      q(b, a).
CLAUSEINST:  q(b, a).
THISGOAL:    q(X5, a).
SUBS:        {X5 = b}
NEWGL:       r(X6, Y6), s(X5, b)
NEWREPLS:    [X5 = b, X6 = a, Y6 = X5, Z6 = X5]
```

SECOND RECURSIVE INVOCATION:

```
GOALLIST:    r(X6, Y6), s(X5, b)
REPLS:       [X5 = b, X6 = a, Y6 = X5, Z6 = X]
NEXTCL:      r(a, b).
CLAUSEINST:  r(a, b).
THISGOAL:    r(a, b).
SUBS:        {}
NEWGL:       s(X5, b)
NEWREPLS:    [X5 = b, X6 = a, Y6 = X5, Z6 = X]
```

Notice how *deref* works on **Y6** in **r(X6, Y6)**. It scans REPLS and finds **Y6** = **X5**, so it applies *deref* recursively to **X5**. That invocation scans the list again and finds **X5** = **b**. Thus **Y6** is mapped to **b** by the accumulated substitution that REPLS represents. As with *establish2,* the "real" goal list on entry to *establish3* is the result of applying REPLS to the value of GOALLIST. □

What are the trade-offs in delaying compostion of the accumulated substitutions? With delayed composition, we compute only the value of the composed substitution for variables in the first goal of the goal list. When the explicit composition of the accumulated substitutions is computed immediately, the value of the composed substitution is computed for all variables—even ones that do not appear in the rest of the goal list. We also get the two counterbalancing effects of the Procrastination Principle that we have seen before—never having to do delayed work versus perhaps having to do it many times. Not computing the explicit composed substitution saves time if a subsequent goal fails and the composed substitution is no longer needed. However, the work of computing the value of a variable under the accumulated substitution must be redone if that variable appears multiple times in the rest of the goal list.

There is one advantage to delaying composition that is not apparent yet. In a later version of the interpreter, delayed composition will allow us more flexibility in choosing an efficient data structure to represent substitutions.

We could modify *deref* to reduce somewhat the amount of searching through REPLS. If *deref* obtains a variable **Y** from a replacement **X** = **Y** in REPLS, and the recursive call does not find a replacement for the **Y** by the time it comes to **X** = **Y** in the list, it need not search further. No replacement past **X** = **Y** in REPLS can have **Y** on the left side. If a variable appears on the right side of a replacement, it cannot appear on the left side of a replacement later in the list. (See Exercise 6.10.) Thus, as the following routine shows, we could add to *deref* another argument—a pointer to the place in REPLS at which to stop searching.

```
function derefopt(TERM: symtabindex; REPLS, STOPAT: subst): symtabindex;
  var NEXTREPL: subst;
  begin
    if variable(TERM) then
      begin
        NEXTREPL := REPLS;
        while NEXTREPL <> STOPAT do
          if NEXTREPL↑.V = TERM then
            return(derefopt(NEXTREPL↑.VC, REPLS, NEXTREPL))
          else NEXTREPL := NEXTREPL↑.NXTR
      end;
    return(TERM)
  end;
```

The new *derefopt* is called initially with **nil** as the third argument to indicate that the entire list must be searched the first time.

6.5. Avoiding Copies Altogether

Copying literals is an operation expensive both in time and space. It invokes the overhead of dynamic storage allocation and can fill up memory with copies of nearly identical clauses. In this section we see how to avoid copying any literals. First we address copying the first literal in GOALLIST, and then we consider the copy of NEXTCL by *instance*. Along the way we bring in lazy lists.

6.5.1. *Applying Substitutions in the Matching Routine*

The matching routine and the routines for applying substitutions are the only ones in the interpreter that care about anything in a literal other than its predicate symbol. If we put *match* in charge of applying substitutions, *establish* can avoid copying the first literal in GOALLIST. Rather than applying REPLS to that literal in *establish*, we pass REPLS to *match* and let it do the application of REPLS as needed on individual variables.

If *match* has access to REPLS, it can avoid applying each newly generated replacement to its literal arguments. Further, it can avoid composing each replacement with the mgu it generates. We simply continue to procrastinate and have *match* append each new replacement to the front of REPLS. Each time *match* examines a variable, it first dereferences the variable through the most recent version of REPLS. The effect of the dereferencing is to compose and apply all the replacements, including the ones added earlier in the same invocation of *match*.

Function *match* should put new replacements at the front of the list of replacements, so that it does not change the replacement list that is passed to it. Since *establish* needs to retain the state of REPLS before the call to *match* in case of failure, it does not pass REPLS itself to *match*. Instead *establish* lets NEWREPLS point to the same list of replacements as REPLS and passes NEWREPLS to *match*.

We incorporate these changes to get a new version of the interpreter, *establish4*, and a modified unification procedure, *match4*.

```
var CLAUSEINST: clauselist;
    NEWREPLS: subst;
    NEWGL: litlist;

function establish4(GOALLIST: litlist; REPLS: subst): boolean;
    var NEXTCL: clauselist;
    begin
      if isempty(GOALLIST) then return(true);
      NEXTCL := SYMTAB[predsym(first(GOALLIST))].CLAUSES;
      while NEXTCL <> nil do
        begin
          CLAUSEINST := instance(NEXTCL);
          NEWREPLS := REPLS;
          if match4(CLAUSEINST↑.HEAD, first(GOALLIST), NEWREPLS) then
            begin
              NEWGL := concat(CLAUSEINST↑.BODY, rest(GOALLIST));
              if establish4(NEWGL, NEWREPLS) then return(true)
            end;
          NEXTCL := NEXTCL↑.NXTCLAUSE
        end;
      return(false)
    end;

function match4(T1, T2: lit; var NEWREPLS: subst): boolean;
    var REPL: subst;
      ARG1, ARG2: symtabindex;
    begin
      if predsym(T1) <> predsym(T2) then return(false);
      for I := 1 to SYMTAB[predsym(T1)].ARITY do
        begin
          ARG1 := deref(arg(T1, I), NEWREPLS);
          ARG2 := deref(arg(T2, I), NEWREPLS);
          if variable(ARG1) then
            if ARG1 = ARG2 then {same variable, do nothing}
            else
              begin
                new(REPL); REPL↑.V := ARG1;
                REPL↑.VC := ARG2; REPL↑.NXTR := NEWREPLS;
                NEWREPLS := REPL
```

```
            end
          else if variable(ARG2) then
            begin
              new(REPL); REPL↑.V := ARG2;
              REPL↑.VC := ARG1; REPL↑.NXTR := NEWREPLS;
              NEWREPLS := REPL
            end
          else if ARG1 <> ARG2 then return(false)
        end;
    return(true)
  end;
```

EXAMPLE 6.9: Consider a sample execution of *match4*, similar to the example for the previous version of *match*. The term **s(X5, X5, a, a)** is unified with **s(Y2, W2, Z2, Z2)** under initial replacement list **[W2 = b]**:

match(**s(X5, X5, a, a), s(Y2, W2, Z2, Z2), [W2 = b]**)

```
I = 1   arg(T1, 1):   X5
        arg(T2, 1):   Y2
        ARG1:         X5
        ARG2:         Y2
        REPL:         X5 = Y2
        NEWREPLS:     [X5 = Y2, W2 = b]

I = 2   arg(T1, 2):   X5
        arg(T2, 2):   W2
        ARG1:         Y2
        ARG2:         b
        REPL:         Y2 = b
        NEWREPLS:     [Y2 = b, X5 = Y2, W2 = b]

I = 3   arg(T1, 3):   a
        arg(T2, 3):   Z2
        ARG1:         a
        ARG2:         Z2
        REPL:         Z2 = a
        NEWREPLS:     [Z2 = a, Y2 = b, X5 = Y2, W2 = b]

I = 4   arg(T1, 4):   a
        arg(T2, 4):   Z2
        ARG1:         a
        ARG2:         a
```

so succeed and return the last value of NEWREPLS. □

6.5.2. *Structure Sharing for Code*

Function *establish4* never applies a substitution to the entire goal list being passed around. (That change was first incorporated back in *establish2*.) Thus *establish* could use lazy lists and lazy concatenation, as in Section 3.2 for Proplog. However, these lazy list records would not point to the actual program clauses, because *establish* needs a new instance of each clause used. That copy is created by the routine *instance*. In this section we find out how to avoid the copying done to create the clause instance and how to make lazy lists refer to the actual program code.

All that *instance* does is uniformly replace all the variables of a clause with variables not used previously (or, more accurately, not currently in use). In doing so, it makes a copy of the clause so as not to modify the program. This method of isolating the current clause from the program code is called *copy on use* for code; a program clause gets copied whenever it is used. There is a way to avoid making the copy. We represent a clause instance by a pair consisting of the original clause and a substitution that gives the new variable that replaces each original variable. We call this substitution the *local substitution*. This method of isolation is known as *structure sharing* for code. It is termed structure sharing because it allows the representation of several different uses of the same clause body to share the same "skeleton" or "template" representation; only the variables are changed to protect the innocent.

EXAMPLE 6.10: If *establish* has the program clause:

```
p(X, Y) :- q(a, X), r(Y, Z).
```

and wants to form the instance:

```
p(X11, Y11) :- q(a, X11), r(Y11, Z11).
```

it can simply point to the original clause and refer to the local substitution:

```
{X = X11, Y = Y11, Z = Z11}
```
□

With this change, to construct the correct instance of a goal, *establish* must keep the local substitution associated with the original clause. Within a single invocation, there is no problem making this association. The problem comes when passing the body of a clause instance away as part of a new goal list. In a later invocation, when a goal from that body comes to the front of the goal list, *establish* will need the local substitution for the clause that contains that body. It must apply the local substitution to that goal first in order to get the correct instance of that goal. Thus, when concatenating the body of the current clause with the rest of the previous goal list to form the new goal list, *establish* must arrange to keep the local substitution associated with the goals of the body. Every goal in the body of the clause has the same local substitution. Since we want to use lazy lists to represent the goal list, consider how we might store the local substitution in this representation. Recall that a lazy list is a list of sublists. The goals on any sublist come from the body of the same clause instance. The lazy list record turns out to be a good place to keep the local substitution for all the goals in its sublist.

```
type
        llist  =  ↑llnode;
        llnode =  record
                    LLREM: llist;
                    LLFRONT: litlist;
                    LSUB: subst
                  end;
```

EXAMPLE 6.11: Recall the lazy list convention that an *llnode* represents LLFRONT concatenated with the rest of LLREM. Thus the lazy list L depicted in Figure 6.4 represents the goal list:

t(U12, X12), r(U12, U12), r(X12, X12), r(Y11, Z11) □

When *establish* has to represent a literal, such as the first one in GOALLIST or the head of NEXTCL, it must refer to a program literal and a local substitution. We call such a pair a *molecule*.

```
type
        molecule = record
                     ATOM: lit;
                     LSUB: subst
                   end;
```

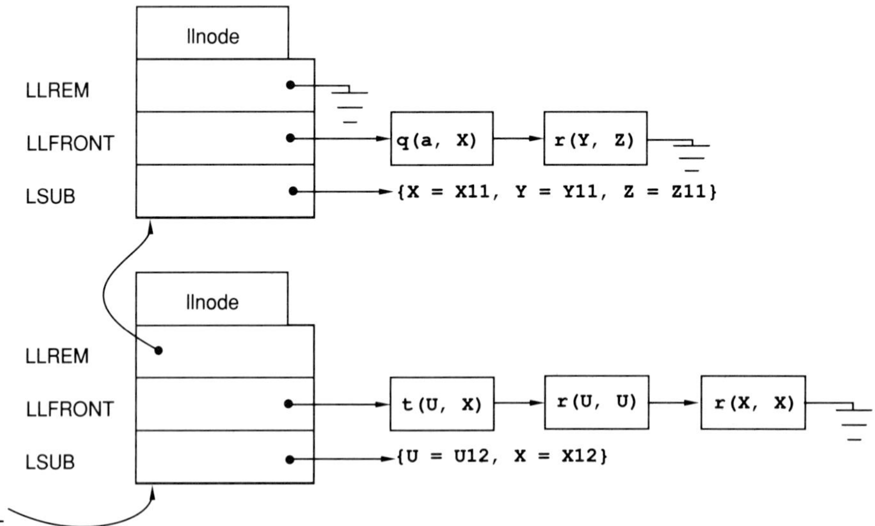

Figure 6.4

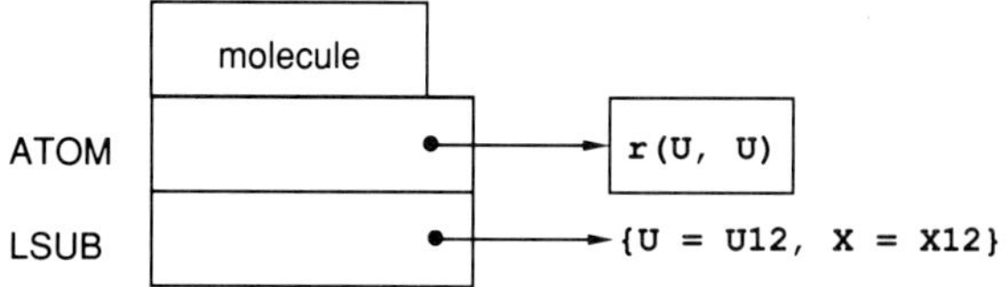

Figure 6.5

EXAMPLE 6.12: To denote the implicit literal **r(U12, U12)** in the last example, we use the molecule shown in Figure 6.5. Note that this molecule can refer to the same copy of the local substitution used in the lazy list. □

Here is the new version of the interpreter, *establish5*, which incorporates local substitutions and lazy lists.

```
var NEWREPLS: subst;
    HEADMOL: molecule;
    NEWGL: llist;

function establish5(GOALLIST: llist; REPLS: subst): boolean;
    var NEXTCL: clauselist;
      GOALMOL: molecule;
    begin
      if isempty5(GOALLIST) then return(true);
      GOALMOL := first5(GOALLIST);
      NEXTCL := SYMTAB[predsym(GOALMOL.ATOM)].CLAUSES;
      while NEXTCL <> nil do
        begin
          HEADMOL.ATOM := NEXTCL↑.HEAD;
          HEADMOL.LSUB := newvars(NEXTCL);
          NEWREPLS := REPLS;
          if match5(HEADMOL, GOALMOL, NEWREPLS) then
            begin
              NEWGL := lconcat_rest(NEXTCL↑.BODY, HEADMOL.LSUB,
                                                   GOALLIST);
              if establish5(NEWGL, NEWREPLS) then return(true)
            end;
          NEXTCL := NEXTCL↑.NXTCLAUSE
        end;
      return(false)
    end;
```

GOALLIST is now a lazy list. Thus *establish5* needs new list manipulation functions *isempty5, first5, lrest5,* and *lconcat_rest,* which deal with lazy lists. They are similar to their counterparts in Section 3.2 except for two slight changes: *first5* returns a molecule rather than a literal. (Again, we are taking liberties with Pascal, having a function return a structure.) Also, the concatenation function, *lconcat_* *rest,* now needs a local substitution in order to build a lazy list from a clause body and the current goal list.

```
{return molecule for first of lazy list}
function first5(GL: llist): molecule;
    var FRST: molecule;
    begin
      FRST.ATOM := GL↑.LLFRONT;
      FRST.LSUB := GL↑.LSUB;
      return(FRST)
    end;

{lazily concatenate BODY with the rest of the lazy list GL, returning
 the result}
function lconcat_rest(BODY: litlist; LOCSUBS: subst; GL: llist): llist;
    var RESULT: llist;
    begin
      new(RESULT);
      if BODY = nil then lrest(GL, RESULT)
      else
        begin
          RESULT↑.LLREM := GL;
          RESULT↑.LLFRONT := BODY;
          RESULT↑.LSUB := LOCSUBS
        end;
      return(RESULT)
    end;

{set the llnode that RESULT references to represent the
 same list as LL with the first literal removed}
procedure lrest(LL: llist; RESULT: llist);
    begin
      if LL = nil then RESULT↑.LLFRONT := nil
      else if LL↑.LLFRONT↑.REST = nil then lrest(LL↑.LLREM, RESULT)
      else
        begin
          RESULT↑.LLREM := LL↑.LLREM;
          RESULT↑.LLFRONT := LL↑.LLFRONT↑.REST;
          RESULT↑.LSUB := LL↑.LSUB
        end
    end;
```

The function *newvars* in *establish5* creates a local substitution for its argument, which will be a program clause. The function must enter the new variables it uses into the symbol table. The matching function, *match5,* takes two molecules as arguments now. It could simply apply the local substitution in each molecule to the corresponding literal and pass the resulting literals to *match4*. However, this approach would subvert the point of this section, since it would involve copying the literals.

Thus, we also avoid applying local substitutions as long as possible, dereferencing a variable first through the correct local substitution, and then through REPLS.

```
function match5(MOL1, MOL2: molecule; var NEWREPLS: subst): boolean;
    var REPL: subst;
      ARG1, ARG2: symtabindex;
    begin
      if predsym(MOL1.ATOM) <> predsym(MOL2.ATOM) then return(false);
      for I := 1 to SYMTAB[predsym(MOL1.ATOM)].ARITY do
        begin
          ARG1 := deref(arg(MOL1.ATOM, I), MOL1.LSUB);
          ARG1 := deref(ARG1, NEWREPLS);
          ARG2 := deref(arg(MOL2.ATOM, I), MOL2.LSUB);
          ARG2 := deref(ARG2, NEWREPLS);
          if variable(ARG1) then
            if ARG1 = ARG2 then {same variable, do nothing}
            else
              begin
                new(REPL); REPL↑.V := ARG1;
                REPL↑.VC := ARG2; REPL↑.NXTR := NEWREPLS;
                NEWREPLS := REPL
              end
          else if variable(ARG2) then
            begin
              new(REPL); REPL↑.V := ARG2;
              REPL↑.VC := ARG1; REPL↑.NXTR := NEWREPLS;
              NEWREPLS := REPL
            end
          else if ARG1 <> ARG2 then return(false)
        end;
      return(true)
    end;
```

Note that the local substitution and the accumulated replacement list are managed differently and are kept entirely separate; no replacement on a local substitution list ever appears on any accumulated replacement list. Local substitutions are used only to get the right instance of a goal. The accumulated replacement list is used to keep track of the effects of the unification procedure.

EXAMPLE 6.13: We trace the execution of *establish5* through three invocations on the following Datalog query and program:

```
:- p(a, W, W), s(W, b).

p(X, Y, Z) :- q(Z, a), r(X, Y).
q(b, a).
r(a, b).
s(b, b).
```

This time we give a picture of the data structures for GOALLIST and REPLS at each entry to *establish5*. We are assuming here that the initial goal is passed in as a molecule by some initial driving program.

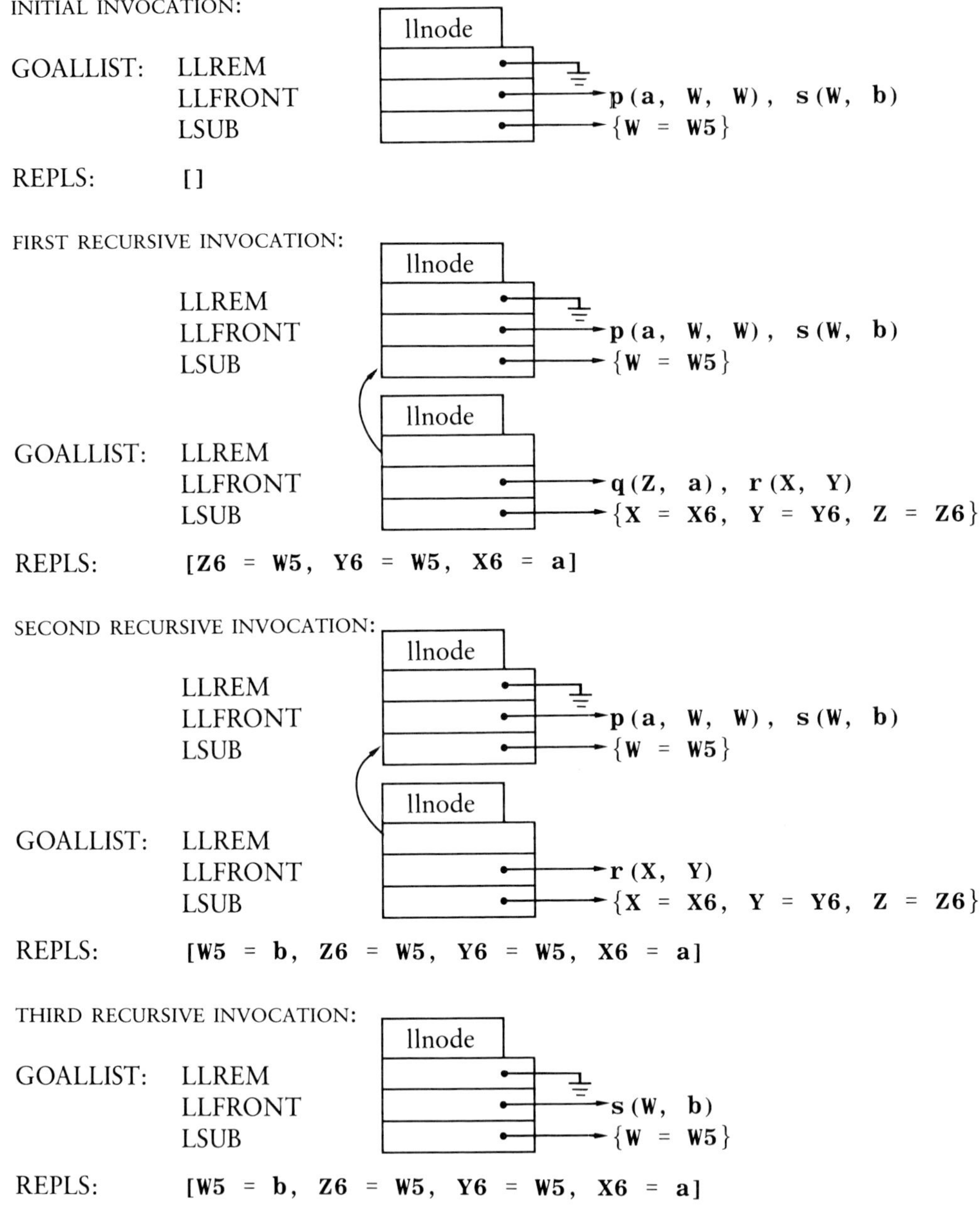

We have duplicated all the information at each step in the trace. Actually there is much sharing of data structures between steps. For instance, while the *llnode*'s labeled GOALLIST in the first and second recursive invocation are different records, the LSUB field of each can reference the same copy of the local substitution. Similarly, the LLFRONT fields in each record point into the same program clause, just at different places in its body. □

6.6. **Simplifying Local Substitutions**

A local substitution has a very rigid and regular form. Its regular structure and limited use allow a very simple representation, which we detail in this section. We need to distinguish two kinds of variables: *program variables* are ones encountered in parsing a Datalog program and in the initial goal, while *new variables* are those generated by the function *newvars*. Recall that the function *newvars* creates the local substitutions. For each distinct variable in a clause, *newvars* creates a new variable at the current end of the symbol table. What does it put in the NAME field in the symbol table entry for this new variable? Inspection of the interpreter code shows that *newvars* need not put anything there; all references to this new variable use only its symbol table index. Thus records in the symbol table for new variables need only one field, the STYPE field, which indicates they are variables. Only the function *variable* uses that field, and even that use can be eliminated. After the program clauses and the goal have been parsed, we can save the end of the symbol table in a global variable, LASTPROGINDEX. The function *variable* will then test to see if a symbol table index is greater than LASTPROGINDEX. If so, the index represents a (new) variable. (Life will be simpler later if LASTPROGINDEX points one location past the last program symbol in the symbol table.) Since new variables need no fields in their symbol table entries, *newvars* need not really add them to the symbol table at all; it just generates new indices. It maintains a global variable, NEWVARINDEX, that points to the place where the next symbol table entry would go if it were really adding new variables to the symbol table. Each time *newvars* needs a new variable, it uses the current value of NEWVARINDEX and then increments it by one.

Consider now what the replacements in a local substitution actually are. Take, for example, the clause:

```
p(X, a, Y) :- q(X, b, Z), r(Y, Z).
```

If we assume that NEWVARINDEX is 215, the local substitution, LOCAL, created by *newvars* is:

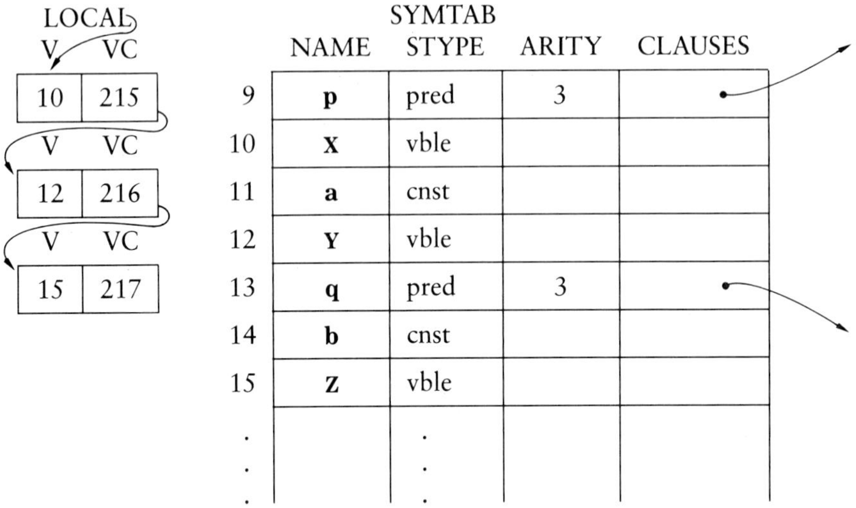

LOCAL

V	VC
10	215

V	VC
12	216

V	VC
15	217

SYMTAB

	NAME	STYPE	ARITY	CLAUSES
9	**p**	pred	3	•
10	**X**	vble		
11	**a**	cnst		
12	**Y**	vble		
13	**q**	pred	3	•
14	**b**	cnst		
15	**Z**	vble		
. . .		. . .		

The first replacement of this local substitution says to replace the variable in the 10th location in the symbol table, **X**, by the new variable at location 215, which does not have, or need, a name. The other replacements are similar—one for each variable in the clause.

Notice that the indices of new variables are consecutive locations: If we know the index of the first new variable, we can compute the rest. Thus we can represent the entire local substitution by a single index. Now suppose we number the program variables in the clause consecutively (in order of their first appearance), starting from 0. For the preceding clause, **X** is number 0, **Y** is number 1, and **Z** is number 2. LOCAL need hold only a single symbol table index: the current value of NEWVARINDEX. Any procedure can now compute the replacement under LOCAL for the Ith variable in a clause as simply LOCAL + I.

For this scheme to work, the symbol table must associate a position number with each variable. We add a NUM field to the symbol table entry for a program variable to store its position number. Variables occurring in two different clauses will need separate symbol table entries, even if they have the same name, since they may have different position numbers in their respective clauses.

EXAMPLE 6.14: With this new representation, the preceding example now looks as follows:

LOCAL		SYMTAB NAME	STYPE	ARITY	NUM	CLAUSES
215	9	**p**	pred	3		• →
	10	**X**	vble		0	
	11	**a**	cnst			
	12	**Y**	vble		1	
	13	**q**	pred	3		
	14	**b**	cnst			
	15	**Z**	vble		2	• →
	⋮			⋮		

The local substitution is now represented simply by the single symbol table index, 215, which is of type *symtabindex*. Given the index of a program variable V, we compute the result of applying the local substitution with the formula LOCAL + SYMTAB[V].NUM. For example, given 15, the index for variable **Z**, we compute new variable index 215 + 2 = 217, which is the same result as obtained by scanning the list of replacements used before. □

We can now represent a local substitution simply by an index—the index of the first new variable for the clause. All the function *newvars* has to do is return the current value of NEWVARINDEX and then add the number of variables in the clause to it. We assume a function *numvars,* with an argument of type *clauselist,* that returns the number of distinct variables in a clause. (See Exercise 6.13.) Also, the types *llnode* and *molecule* must be changed so that the LSUB field of each has type *symtabindex.*

6.7. Binding Arrays

Another major improvement can still be made to *establish5*. The way we represent replacement lists makes dereferencing inefficient. Even with the improvement suggested at the end of Section 6.4, we continue to do much running through the replacement list. The technique we use to solve this problem uses *binding arrays.* We noted before that no variable appears more than once as the left side of a replacement in a list that represents an accumulated substitution. Instead of representing replacements in REPLS as a list of pairs, we use an array with one entry per variable, where each entry stores the right-side constant or variable that replaces the left-side variable. The replacement constant or variable is called the *binding* of the replaced variable.

This change will allow a dramatic improvement in speed and space utilization. We can dereference quickly, and we need store only the right-side terms of replacements. Furthermore, it gives us a way to manage the space for substitutions in a stack discipline. With the previous representation of a replacement list, reclaiming space would mean maintaining a free list. With the binding array, a group of replacements can be freed with a single assignment statement. Also, activity in variable binding exhibits locality in the most recently instantiated clauses, which fits well with virtual memory schemes. The downside is that the binding array will contain space for unbound variables.

Only new variables can appear in any replacement of REPLS. (See Exercise 6.15.) New variables are just symbol table indices in the subrange LASTPROGINDEX to MAXSYMS of *symtabindex*. (Recall that MAXSYMS is the upper bound on values from *symtabindex*.) We give this subrange type the name *baindex*, which stands for "binding array index." The array we need, which we will call the *binding array* (BA), is indexed by *baindex*.

EXAMPLE 6.15: Consider the REPLS list:

```
[W113 = Y111, Z112 = a, X110 = Z112]
```

These variables are all new variables, so they are really represented just by indices. We have used a name starting with a letter just for readability. Let's assume now that LASTPROGINDEX is 110, and that the number part of the variable name is its symbol table index. The binding array to represent REPLS is:

i	BA[i]
110	112
111	0
112	↑**a**
113	111

The notation '↑**a**' represents the index of the constant **a** in the symbol table. Notice there is a variable 111 that does not appear on the left side of any replacement in REPLS, so it does not have a binding. We will use a 0 to indicate that the variable has no binding. □

Consider how *deref* can use BA to dereference a variable. To determine whether a variable appears on the left side of a replacement, *deref* simply indexes, using the variable's symbol table index, into BA; no searching is necessary. If the variable appears on the left of a replacement, *deref* finds its binding at the variable's index in BA. To find the binding for **Z112** in the last example, *deref* looks at BA[112] and sees it is **a**. If the binding for a variable is another variable, *deref* must look up that other variable in BA to find its binding. If that binding is a variable, *deref* probes BA again and continues probing in this manner until it encounters a constant or an unbound variable. To find the ultimate value for **W113**, *deref* looks at BA[113]. That entry contains another variable, **Y111**, so *deref* next looks at BA[111]. Since that entry is 0, it knows no further replacement should be done, and the ultimate value for **W113** is **Y111**.

With this representation, we can rewrite the *deref* function. The function no longer has a second argument REPLS. Rather, it assumes BA is a global variable holding a representation of the current accumulated substitution.

```
function deref6(TERM: symtabindex): symtabindex;
  begin
    while variable(TERM) do
      if BA[TERM] <> 0 then { has a binding }
        TERM := BA[TERM]
      else return(TERM);
    return(TERM)
  end;
```

The use of the binding array BA eliminates the sequential search of the REPLS list in *deref*, significantly improving the efficiency of our interpreter. However, if we want to use the binding array instead of the list of replacements, we must be able to retain an old state of BA while letting *match* modify BA. We could copy the BA and pass the copy to *match*, but such copying is anathema to our laziness. Rather, we let *match* modify BA directly but insist it keep track of any changes it makes so that *establish* can undo the changes later, if necessary.

Just how much information is needed to undo a change to BA? Certainly, if *match* saves an index and previous value every time it updates an entry in BA, *establish* will have enough information to restore BA to the state before *match* modified it. But we recall that REPLS, now represented by BA, can have only one replacement with a given left side. Thus updates to BA always change a zero value to a nonzero value. We see that *match* need only keep track of the index of a changed entry; the previous value must always be zero.

We use another array, TRAIL, called the *trail stack*, to record changes to BA made by invocations of *match*. Procedures share a global pointer to the top of TRAIL, called TRAILTOP, which *match* updates each time it records a change. Each invocation of the interpreter then records the top of TRAIL on entry to *match* in a local variable, TRAILSAVE. On return from *match*, its changes can be undone by scanning TRAIL from TRAILTOP back to TRAILSAVE, resetting the appropriate entries in BA to zero.

The astute reader will have noticed one glaring inefficiency with the binding array representation of substitutions, as described so far. The binding array must have slots for all new variables generated during execution, even if those new variables belong to clause instances that did not match, or whose bodies could not be satisfied. For any Datalog program with an appreciable number of multiclause predicates, much of the binding array will be unused storage! Obviously we would like to reclaim the space in the binding array for new variables of failed clauses. The way we reclaim this space is to reclaim new variables. If a recursive call to *establish* fails, all new variables allocated during that recursive call belong to clause instances no longer of interest. Thus we add a local variable, LOCALSUBS, to the interpreter to save the value of NEWVARINDEX upon invocation. On a failure of *match* or a recursive call of the interpreter, NEWVARINDEX is reset to LOCALSUBS to reclaim new variables. As should be apparent from its name, LOCALSUBS is also the index used to represent the local substitution associated with an invocation of *establish*.

The following declarations of global variables are for manipulating the new variable index, the binding array, and the trail stack:

```
var BA: array [baindex] of symtabindex;
    NEWVARINDEX: baindex;
    TRAIL: array [trailindex] of baindex;
    TRAILTOP: trailindex;
```

We next modify *establish5* to keep track of the new variable index and the top of the trail stack upon entry, and to undo changes to the binding array using the trail stack upon failure of a recursive call.

```
var HEADMOL, GOALMOL: molecule;
    NEWGL: llist;

function establish6(GOALLIST: llist): boolean;
    var NEXTCL: clauselist;
      LOCALSUBS: baindex;
      TRAILSAVE: trailindex;
    begin
      if isempty5(GOALLIST) then return(true);
      GOALMOL := first5(GOALLIST);
      NEXTCL := SYMTAB[predsym(GOALMOL.ATOM)].CLAUSES;
      LOCALSUBS := NEWVARINDEX;
      TRAILSAVE := TRAILTOP;
      while NEXTCL <> nil do
        begin
          newvars6(NEXTCL);
          HEADMOL.ATOM := NEXTCL↑.HEAD;
          HEADMOL.LSUB := LOCALSUBS;
          if match6(HEADMOL, GOALMOL) then
            begin
              NEWGL := lconcat_rest(NEXTCL↑.BODY, LOCALSUBS, GOALLIST);
              if establish6(NEWGL) then return(true)
            end;
          restore(TRAILSAVE, LOCALSUBS);
          NEXTCL := NEXTCL↑.NXTCLAUSE
        end;
      return(false)
    end;
```

The unification procedure, *match6*, now takes care of dereferencing through the local substitution by computing an offset into BA.

```
function match6(MOL1, MOL2: molecule): boolean;
    var ARG1, ARG2: symtabindex;
    begin
      if predsym(MOL1.ATOM) <> predsym(MOL2.ATOM) then return(false);
      for I := 1 to SYMTAB[predsym(MOL1.ATOM)].ARITY do
        begin
          ARG1 := arg(MOL1.ATOM, I);
          if variable(ARG1) then
            ARG1 := deref6(MOL1.LSUB + SYMTAB[ARG1].NUM);
          ARG2 := arg(MOL2.ATOM, I);
          if variable(ARG2) then
            ARG2 := deref6(MOL2.LSUB + SYMTAB[ARG2].NUM);
          if variable(ARG1) then
            if ARG1 = ARG2 then {same variable, do nothing}
            else
              begin
                BA[ARG1] := ARG2;
                TRAILTOP := TRAILTOP + 1;
                TRAIL[TRAILTOP] := ARG1
              end
          else if variable(ARG2) then
            begin
              BA[ARG2] := ARG1;
              TRAILTOP := TRAILTOP + 1;
              TRAIL[TRAILTOP] := ARG2
            end
          else if ARG1 <> ARG2 then return(false)
        end;
      return(true)
    end;
```

The *newvars* function just bumps up the end of the binding array by the number of variables in the current clause and sets the entry of each new variable to zero. Actually, each entry of BA needs to be set to zero just once; the following *restore* function ensures that all entries are reset to zero before reuse. (See Exercise 6.16.)

```
procedure newvars6(CLAUSE: clauselist);
    var I, LAST: baindex;
    begin
      LAST := NEWVARINDEX + numvars(CLAUSE) - 1;
      for I = NEWVARINDEX to LAST do
        BA[I] := 0;
      NEWVARINDEX := LAST + 1
    end;
```

Finally, the procedure *restore* restores the new variable index and the binding array to their conditions before the call to *match6*, using LOCALSUBS and the information in TRAIL.

```
procedure restore(TRAILPT: trailindex; SAVEDVARINDEX: baindex);
   var T: trailindex;
   begin
     for T := TRAILTOP downto TRAILPT+1 do
       BA[TRAIL[T]] := 0;
     TRAILTOP := TRAILPT;
     NEWVARINDEX := SAVEDVARINDEX
   end
```

EXAMPLE 6.16: We trace *establish6* through four invocations on our familiar Datalog query and program:

```
:- p(a, W0, W0), s(W0, b).

p(X0, Y1, Z2) :- q(Z2, a), r(X0, Y1).
q(b, a).
r(a, b).
s(b, b).
```

A program variable is now indicated by a letter and a number; the number is its position number within its clause. This time we give the value of GOALLIST and the current states of BA and TRAIL on each entry to *establish6*. When displaying the BA here, we add a letter to the index just as a mnemonic to indicate which variable its entry represents.

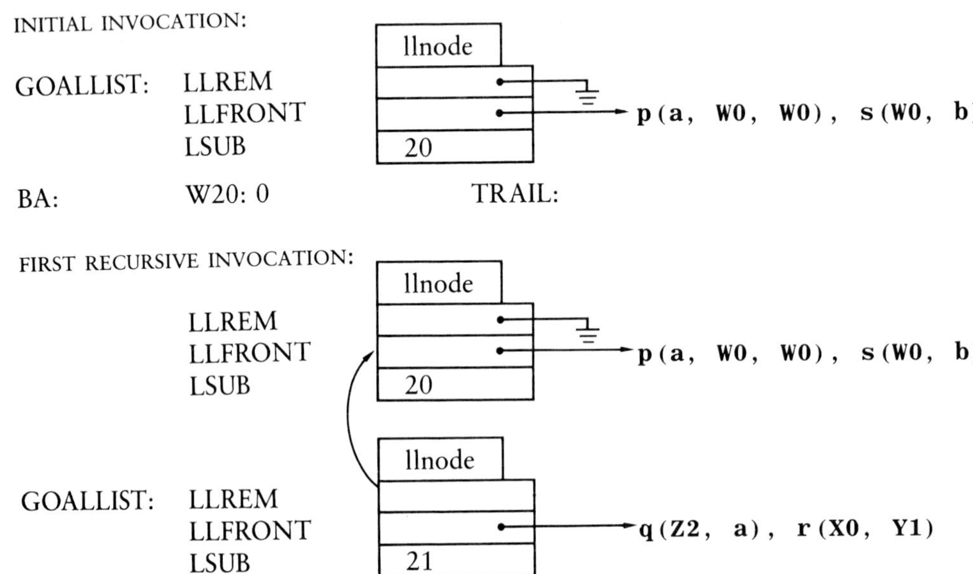

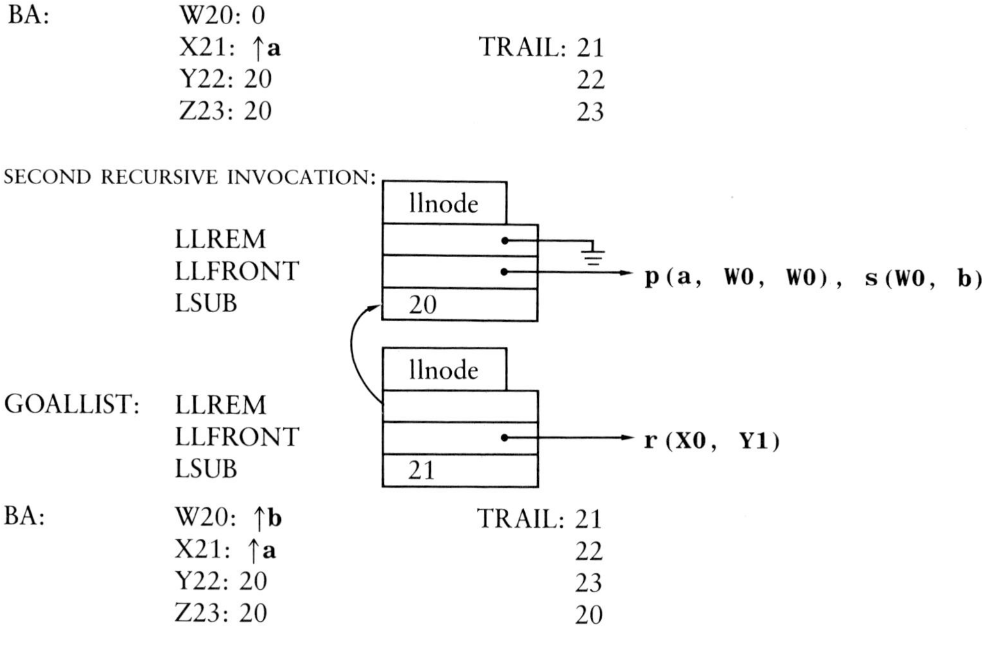

THIRD RECURSIVE INVOCATION:

		llnode	
GOALLIST:	LLREM	• → (nil)	
	LLFRONT	• →	s(W0, b)
	LSUB	20	

BA:		TRAIL:
	W20: ↑**b**	21
	X21: ↑**a**	22
	Y22: 20	23
	Z23: 20	20 □

The current version of the interpreter replaces the REPLS list of earlier versions by BA and TRAIL. Notice the relationship between the REPLS list of *establish5* and BA and TRAIL in *establish6* at corresponding points in their executions. (See Example 6.13.) Consider a replacement **X** = **Y** in REPLS in *establish5*. At the corresponding point in *establish6*, BA[**X**] contains **Y**, and **X** is in TRAIL. The combination of BA and TRAIL captures the information in REPLS exactly.

6.7.1. *Looking Back*

Let's see if we can still pick out the elements of the Horn clause refutation procedure in *establish6*. It is searching the space of resolution vines depth first, having only one vine (or partial vine) constructed at a time. It uses selected literal resolution, where the selected literal is always the first one in GOALLIST. Each active invocation of *establish6* represents one resolution step made in the vine under construction. GOALLIST contains the current center clause, represented as a lazy list composed of pieces of bodies of program clauses along with an accumulated substitution.

Alternative choices for the side clause are captured by the local variable NEXTCL in each recursive invocation. The accumulated substitution is represented in uncomposed form as BA, which is a sequence of variable bindings. BA grows in segments—one for each side clause used in constructing the current vine. Notice this segmentation is different from the way REPLS is built up in earlier versions of *establish*. In those versions the segments correspond to mgu's returned by *match*. Segmenting the accumulated substitution as in BA means that prefixes of the list of replacements no longer encode the state of the accumulated substitution at previous choice points. Thus *establish6* needs to keep a little extra information in TRAIL to restore a previous state. Note that the length of TRAIL is equal to the number of replacements in the accumulated substitution at corresponding points in earlier versions of the interpreter.

The depth-first search strategy for vines lets the interpreter manage the accumulated substitution in this way. With depth-first search, there is one set of bindings in effect at a time, and the interpreter can play update-in-place tricks with the binding array. For breadth-first search, the interpreter would need a set of bindings for partial vine under consideration, which is a reason to prefer depth-first to breadth-first search. Those sets of bindings cannot share prefixes unless we revert to representing the accumulated substitution as a list of replacements. However, that representation makes dereferencing quite expensive.

Unification is handled by the *match6* routine, which actually applies the accumulated substitution at the minimum possible granularity, dereferencing a single variable as needed to compute the current replacement for the variable.

We could construct a bottom-up interpreter for Datalog, and it would be complete. (It would be based on unit resolution. See Exercise 5.40.) This approach is advocated by the deductive database community. The bottom-up approach trades the space to store intermediate results for the time required to recompute those results. That trade-off is most often worthwhile when looking for all answers to a query, rather than just one. The top-down approach ends up finding all refutations for a query, but many of those may generate the same answer. A bottom-up interpreter does not need to manage an accumulated substitution, because as it goes it applies mgus to generate intermediate results.

6.8. Implementing Evaluable Predicates

In Section 4.8.2, we briefly discussed handling comparison and arithmetic predicates with underlying functions. In this section we consider in a bit more detail how to implement a predicate whose definition is a function rather than a set of clauses.

We first need a representation for numbers in literals. For simplicity, we consider only integers. An integer could be a character string of its decimal digits. However, if a Datalog program does a lot of computation, such a representation consumes an enormous amount of symbol table space. A better approach is to use a tag bit in the representation of a term to distinguish between references to constants in the symbol table and constants that are integers. In the case of integers the reference is not a pointer but the binary representation of the number. We will use three functions for manipulating number references: *isnumber*, which tests if its parameter is a number, *asnumber,* which removes the tag bit from a reference and returns an integer, and *asref,* which adds the tag bit to an integer and returns a reference.

To see how to implement an evaluable predicate, consider the *sum* function from Section 4.8.2 and the last version of the Datalog interpreter, *establish6*. The function for an evaluable predicate steps in when a literal with **sum** as predicate symbol is first on the goal list. Since *establish* needs to dereference the arguments of the goal through the binding array before the function does any computation, we might as well let *match6* do the dereferencing. Hence we add a clause:

```
sum(X, Y, Z) :- special8.
```

to all Datalog programs. We assume a set of special 0-ary predicate symbols **special1**, **special2**, **special3**, . . . that occupy contiguous entries in the symbol table—say between SPECIALMIN and SPECIALMAX. (In fact, the names of the special predicates are not important, so their entries in the symbol table need not actually exist.) The head of this clause always unifies with any **sum** goal, causing **X**, **Y**, and **Z** to be bound to the dereferenced arguments of the goal. If **sum(N, 2, M)** is the goal, where **N** is bound to integer 3 and **M** is bound to variable **Q122**, then *match6* will bind **X**, **Y**, and **Z** to **3**, **2**, and **Q122**, respectively. That unification leaves **3**, **2**, and **Q122** as the last three entries in BA before NEWVARINDEX. For those values to end up in the right place, it is essential that in variable-to-variable matching the reference always goes from the variable in the head molecule to the variable in the goal molecule. Fortunately, *match* behaves this way. Thus none of **X**, **Y**, and **Z** will be bound to 0. The function that computes **sum** can easily find the data upon which to operate. Note that we know **special8** will always be the next goal considered after a **sum** goal, so no intervening unifications will modify BA. Also, since the preceding clause is the only one with **sum** in the head, **sum** succeeds if and only if **special8** succeeds.

We need to include a test for special predicates in *establish6*. We modify the segment of code:

```
if isempty5(GOALLIST) then return(true);
GOALMOL := first(GOALLIST);
NEXTCL := SYMTAB[predsym(GOALMOL.ATOM)].CLAUSES;
LOCALSUBS := NEWVARINDEX;
```

to:

```
if isempty5(GOALLIST) then return(true);
GOALMOL := first(GOALLIST);
HEADSYM := predsym(GOALMOL.ATOM);
if (SPECIALMIN <= HEADSYM) and (HEADSYM <= SPECIALMAX)
  then case HEADSYM of
    SPECIAL1: if spec1 then return(establish6(rest(GOALLIST))
      else return(false);
    SPECIAL2: if spec2 then return(establish6(rest(GOALLIST))
      else return(false);
```

```
    SPECIAL3: if spec3 then return(establish6(rest(GOALLIST))
      else return(false);
        .
        .
        .
    SPECIAL20: if spec20 then return(establish6(rest(GOALLIST))
      else return(false)
  end {case}
else begin
  NEXTCL := SYMTAB[HEADSYM].CLAUSES;
  LOCALSUBS := NEWVARINDEX;
```

Here, SPECIAL1, SPECIAL2, . . ., SPECIAL20 are program constants containing the symbol table locations for **special1**, **special2**, . . ., **special20** (assuming 20 evaluable predicates). The routines *spec1, spec2, . . ., spec20* are Boolean-valued *implementing functions* for the evaluable predicates. The new code for *establish6* inserts a **case** statement to check if the current goal is a special predicate. If so, it calls the corresponding implementing function. If that function succeeds, interpretation proceeds with the rest of the goal list.

We look at the implementing function *spec8* for **sum**. Function *spec8* gets its parameters implicitly from the last three full entries of BA. It can return an error condition if any of the arguments to **sum** are nonnumeric or if either of the first two is unbound.

```
function spec8: boolean;
    var ADD1REF, ADD2REF, SUMREF: symtabindex;
      ADDEND1, ADDEND2, SUM: integer;
    begin
      ADDREF1 := BA[NEWVARINDEX - 3]; {get arguments from binding array}
      ADDREF2 := BA[NEWVARINDEX - 2];
      SUMREF := BA[NEWVARINDEX - 1];
      if isnumber(ADD1REF) then ADDEND1 := asnumber(ADD1REF)
        else error('first argument not a number');
      if isnumber(ADD2REF) then ADDEND2 := asnumber(ADD2REF)
        else error('second argument not a number');
      SUM := ADDEND1 + ADDEND2;
      if isnumber(SUMREF) then
        if SUM = asnumber(SUMREF) then return(true) else return(false)
      else if variable(SUMREF) then
        begin
          BA[SUMREF] := asref(SUM);
          TRAILTOP := TRAILTOP + 1;
          TRAIL[TRAILTOP] := SUMREF;
          return(true)
        end
      else error ('third argument not a number or variable')
    end;
```

When the third argument to **sum** is a variable, *spec8* binds this variable to a number and must record this binding on the trail stack. We do not include any call to restore BA if we backtrack through the predicate **special8**. Rather, backtracking through **special8** means backtracking through:

```
sum(X, Y, Z) :- special8.
```

and that clause will do the restoring for **special8**.

The function *spec8* does a lot of work just to add two numbers (or check a sum). In practice we can code it in assembly language. The number-checking and conversion functions are all done with single bit-manipulation instructions, and registers can hold the references and numbers involved. In Chapter 8, we will see an evaluable Prolog predicate **is** for evaluating arbitrary arithmetic expressions. That predicate does not require a unification for each arithmetic operation.

6.9. EXERCISES

6.1. Variable-length records for literals in Datalog can be implemented in Pascal using an array. A record with n fields occupies n contiguous locations in the array. A reference to the record contains the index of its first location in the array. The last location for the record can be deduced from the arity of the predicate symbol. Give routines for *predsym, arg,* and *copy,* using this implementation of variable-length records.

6.2. Give a representation for Datalog literals that does not depend on having variable-length records.

6.3. In Section 3.1, we noted that indexing obviated storing clause heads in Proplog. Can clause heads be omitted in Datalog if we index clauses?

6.4. Complete the execution trace of *establish1* in Example 6.4.

6.5. Give an implementation for the *compose* routine as used in Section 6.2.

6.6. Consider the *establish2* Datalog interpreter.
   a. Prove that ACCSUBS and SUBS never contain replacements with the same left sides.
   b. Give a general-purpose version of *copycompose* that does not assume the replacements in its arguments have disjoint left sides, and that copies its second argument as well as its first.

6.7. Complete the execution trace of *establish2* in Example 6.6.

6.8. Give a version of the function *instance* from *establish2* that takes a *litlist* as a second argument and concatenates it to the end of the newly created instance.

6.9. The *copyapplyrepls* function in *establish3* might call *deref* on the same variable many times. Modify *copyapplyrepls* to cache the result of dereferencing a variable for possible later use. Comment on whether this change is likely to improve the efficiency of *copyapplyrepls*.

6.10. For *establish3*, prove that no replacement **Y** = α could appear after the replacement **X** = **Y** in REPLS.

6.11. Suppose that REPLS in *establish3* also has pointers from each replacement to the previous replacement. Give a version of *deref* that traverses REPLS only once. (Hint: See the previous exercise.)

6.12. Write the initial calling programs for the Datalog interpreter with and without lazy lists (versions *establish4* and *establish5,* for example). You may assume a parser to convert an input goal into a *litlist,* but your programs must build all other necessary structures themselves.

6.13. Give an implementation for the function *numvars* that appears at the end of Section 6.6.

6.14. In the binding-array implementation of the Datalog interpreter, what information about a clause, apart from its literals, would be useful to store with the clause?

6.15. For *establish5,* prove that replacements in REPLS contain only new variables.

6.16. In *establish6,* variables from NEXTCL do not need to be entered on the trail stack. Why? Modify *match6* and *restore* to avoid trailing variables from the current clause. With this modification, does *newvars6* have to initialize BA to zeros?

6.17. Consider a variable in a Datalog clause that appears only in the head of the clause, such as **X** in:

```
p(X, a, Y, X) :- q(Y, Y).
```

What kind of space optimization can be made for such a "head-only" variable?

6.18. Redo the code in Section 6.8 that implements the computed predicate **sum** to work if any two arguments are bound to numbers.

6.10. COMMENTS AND BIBLIOGRAPHY

Efficient evaluation of Datalog programs has only recently begun to be studied in its own right. The approach we have taken in this chapter is to use Prolog's evaluation strategy specialized to the Datalog case. Prolog implementation strategies have been described in various papers, such as those of Bruynooghe [6.1] and van Emden [6.2], but these simply give a final algorithm. They do not derive the algorithm through a series of program transformation steps as we have done in this chapter. The first complete, in-depth, detailed description of a Prolog implementation is by D. H. D. Warren [6.3], but that focuses more on compilation issues, which we will see in Chapter 11. The concept of the binding array as expressed in this chapter is discussed in a paper by D. S. Warren [6.4], but it is used there for full Prolog.

Recently in the database community there has been research into the efficient evaluation of recursive queries—that is, Datalog programs. In that context the completeness of the algorithm is critical, so the incomplete evaluator that we have developed here is not considered an acceptable solution to the problem. Most of the proposed algorithms [6.5–6.8] are bottom up in nature, but some [6.9–6.11] are top down. The top-down strategies cache results and have a breadth-first search component. Bancilhon [6.12] surveys Datalog evaluation strategies in the database context and compares their performance, while Ullman [6.13] provides a common framework for expressing many of the Datalog compilation techniques.

6.1. M. Bruynooghe, The memory management of Prolog implementations, in *Logic Programming,* K. L. Clark and S.-A. Tarnlund (eds.), Academic Press, New York, 1982, 83–98.

6.2. M. H. van Emden, An interpreting algorithm for Prolog programs, 1st Int. Logic Programming Conference, University of Marseille, 1982, reprinted in [3.2].

6.3. D. H. D. Warren, Implementing Prolog—Compiling predicate logic programs, Dept. of Artificial Intellignece, D.A.I. Research Report No. 39, University of Edinburgh, Scotland, 1977.

6.4. D. S. Warren, Efficient Prolog memory management for flexible control strategies, *Proc. 1984 Int. IEEE Conference on Logic Programming,* Atlantic City, NJ, February 1984, 198–202. Reprinted in *New Generation Computing* 2:4 1984, 361–70.

6.5. F. Bancilhon, D. Maier, Y. Sagiv, and J. D. Ullman, Magic sets and other strange ways to implement logic programs, *Proc. 5th ACM SIGACT-SIGMOD Symposium on Principles of Database Systems,* Boston, MA, March 1986, 1–15.

6.6. L. Henschen and S. Naqvi, On compiling queries in recursive first-order data bases, *JACM 31*:1 January 1984, 47–85.

6.7. D. McKay and S. Shapiro, Using active connection graphs for reasoning with recursive rules, *Proc. 7th Int. Joint Conference on Artificial Intelligence,* Vancouver, B.C., 1981, 368–74.

6.8. D. Saccà and C. Zaniolo, On the implementation of a simple class of logic queries for databases, *Proc. 5th ACM SIGACT-SIGMOD Symposium on Principles of Database Systems,* Boston, MA, March 1986, 16–23.

6.9. S. Dietrich and D. S. Warren, Dynamic programming strategies for the evaluation of recursive queries, Department of Computer Science TR 85/31, State University of New York at Stony Brook, Stony Brook, NY, September 1985.

6.10. M. Kifer and E. L. Lozinskii, Query optimization in logical databases, Department of Computer Science 85/16, State University of New York at Stony Brook, Stony Brook, NY, 1985.

6.11. L. Vieille, Recursive axioms in deductive databases: The query/subquery approach, *Proc. 1st Int. Conference on Expert Database Systems,* Charleston, SC, April 1986, 179–93.

6.12. F. Bancilhon and R. Ramakrishnan, An amateur's introduction to recursive query processing strategies, *Proc. ACM-SIGMOD Int. Conference on Management of Data,* Washington, DC, May 1986, 16–52.

6.13. J. D. Ullman, Implementation of logical query languages for databases, *ACM Trans. on Database Systems 10*:3 September 1985, 289–321.

PART III

Prolog and Functional Logic

In Datalog we have the capability of making general statements about classes of individuals, but we have no way to say anything about the internal structure of individuals. Also, there is no way to create new individuals; we start with a finite set of individuals, about which all we know is a simple name, and then we can produce no others. Thus Datalog can be compared to the subset of Pascal programs in which only variables of enumeration types appear. (An enumeration type is one in which the programmer lists the finite set of values that a variable of that type can take on.) To extend Datalog beyond this straitjacket of a predetermined finite set of objects it can manipulate, we must add a general data structure facility.

In the analogy of predicate logic to English, variables and constants stand for noun phrases. So the data objects of Datalog programs are noun phrases—that is, the names of things. To have complex data structures, we must add the concept of a compound noun phrase, or complex name, to the logic. Along with complex names must come the ability to construct new names from simpler ones and the ability to see the structure inside of names. These compound noun phrases will turn out to be the only new data structures we need.

Consider an example. Suppose we have an inventory of various kinds of cables to connect audio equipment with their different kinds of plugs and jacks, such as an RCA plug, a phono jack, and a 3-prong plug. Consider expressing the following statement in logic:

> If there is a cable of type 163 with a phono jack on one end and an RCA plug on the other, and a cable of type 174 with an RCA jack on one end and a 3-prong plug on the other, then we can construct a compound cable with a phono jack on one end and a 3-prong plug on the other.

It does not matter for the resulting cable what the inner connection is (in this case RCA); all that matters is that the connection can be made. We would like to use that compound cable as a component of another compound cable of even more pieces. How can we abstract a general rule that does not care whether it is working with a single cable or a compound cable previously constructed? A stock number is the name that identifies each single cable, but how do we talk about a compound cable when using it as a piece of a larger cable? We could make up a name for it, based on the names of its components. For example, we might call the cable just described **(163/174)**.

And if we combined that cable with an **(85/110)**, we would call it a **((85/110)/(163/174))**. With this naming scheme, we can abstract the preceding rule and say:

> If we have a cable **X** with a **Y** jack on one end and a **Z** plug on the other, and a cable **W** with a **Z** jack and a **U** plug, we can construct a cable **(X/W)** with a **Y** jack and a **U** plug.

Variables **X** and **W** can stand for basic or compound cables.

In Prolog we can construct and pick apart such compound names for individuals. Consider the kind of programming improvement over Datalog this ability gives us. There we had complex control structures but no data structures. Prolog adds data structures, including recursive data structures, such as lists and trees, that fit in well with the recursive predicates that Datalog supports. This addition allows Prolog to construct and manipulate arbitrarily complex structures (names) to represent objects about which it must reason. Complex structures bring logic programming up to the level of a general-purpose programming language. However, the addition is not without cost. Implication in Datalog (excluding arithmetic predicates) is decidable, while Prolog has general computational power, and so implication is undecidable.

Chapter 7 starts by showing that we can parse an input string from an expression language in Datalog, but that we need Prolog to build a parse tree for the input. Then we adapt the simple Datalog interpreter of Chapter 4 to Prolog. It may seem surprising at first, but *establish* needs no modification; only *match* and the other subroutines that manipulate literals do need such modification. They are the only routines that make a distinction between simple constants and compound data structures. The rest of the chapter provides examples involving tree, list, and graph structures.

Chapter 8 presents predicates for procedural and metalogical extensions to Prolog. Some of these extensions are for expressibility purposes, while others are for efficiency. In the expressibility category, there are not only mundane features such as I/O but also more powerful extensions making the language reflexive—that is, they treat programs as data structures. We exploit the syntactic similarity between literals and terms (data structures) to do such things as construct literals to call, or to add new clauses to a program. In the efficiency category we have the arithmetic and comparison operators and added control constructs.

Chapter 9 extends predicate logic to functional logic by adding function symbols. It follows the same course as the last two logic chapters, 2 and 5. The new twist is that the semantics must handle an infinite base and the mapping of compound names to individuals in the domain. Unification is extended from simple constants and variables to handle these compound structures, but the algebra of substitutions remains essentially unchanged. Hence the results on resolution carry over largely unchanged from Chapter 5. We revisit model elimination as a complete deduction method for full functional logic.

We have two chapters on implementation here. Chapter 10 parallels Chapter 6, with the optimizations centered around delaying application of substitutions and efficient representation of substitutions. There is a bit of added complexity in representing data structures that appear in terms. A replacement cannot point simply to structures in the Prolog program. The two alternatives are: (1) to copy program structures or (2) to point to a structure in the program, which acts as a template, and to a local substitution for variables in that structure. The latter approach is similar to the structuring sharing on code used in Chapter 6 but applied to structures instead of lists of literals. A final section adapts Prolog evaluation techniques to implement model elimination.

The optimizations in Chapter 10 concentrate on manipulation of the interpreter's data structures. Opportunities for optimization based on control structures are limited because much of that control is buried in Pascal's management of its run-time stack. To permit control-based optimizations, Chapter 11 introduces a nonrecursive version of the interpreter that manages activation records explicitly. This change permits optimizations such as collapsing sequences of returns and reclaiming activation records early. We then turn to compilation, in which the basic strategy is partial evaluation of interpreter routines at compile time. In addition we split activation records into deterministic and nondeterministic parts, so that we may use deterministic implementation techniques when backtracking is not necessary. The compiled code takes advantage of registers and also, in one instance, reverses the Procrastination Principle. It performs certain work early once (dereferencing variables) that would have to be done many times if performed later.

Chapter 12 is an extended example to show the strengths of Prolog. It concerns areas where Prolog seems particularly well suited: databases, parsing, and code translation. It tries to demonstrate the many uses of the logical variable and illustrates the power of the evaluable predicates introduced in Chapter 8.

7

Computing with Functional Logic

Datalog was an improvement over Proplog because it introduced variables and allowed programs to calculate answers. Datalog, however, remains limited in what it can do. To make the final step to a complete programming language, it must have just one new facility: a way of constructing and manipulating complex data structures.

The running example of this chapter will concern the evaluation of arithmetic expressions. We start by showing that Datalog has sufficient power to support the control structures needed to parse such an expression. The Datalog code will compute a numeric value for an expression, but Datalog cannot capture what is discovered about the structure of the expression. We redo the example with the addition of record structures (which turns Datalog into Prolog) to show that we can build a parse tree for an arithmetic expression while using exactly the same control structure that the Datalog program used. Later in the chapter we give a Prolog program to evaluate the expression trees that the Prolog-based parser produces.

Constructing a parse tree shows how Prolog can build new structures; evaluating a tree shows how Prolog can pull structures apart. The surprising thing about our Prolog interpreter is that a straightforward extension to the *match* routine allows it to handle both operations. One advantage of this duality is that the Prolog language does not need separate syntax for record construction and record field selection. As a consequence Prolog predicates will have little bias as to which arguments are "input" and which are "output." The same clauses that concatenate two lists will split a single list into two parts.

7.1. Evaluating Arithmetic Expressions Using Datalog

We develop a Datalog program that takes a sequence of symbols representing an arithmetic expression and returns the value of the expression. For simplicity, the arithmetic expressions will include only the operators '+' and '*'. So, for example, our program should take an arithmetic expression such as '(5 + 3) * 4' and produce the value 32.

How do we represent the input string while staying in the realm of Datalog? One representation is to encode the input as a set of facts that describe which symbol is at which position in the string, as follows:

string: 7 + 9 * 8

encoded as:
```
input(0, 7, 1).
input(1, '+', 2).
input(2, 9, 3).
input(3, '*', 4).
input(4, 8, 5).
```

Imagine a number between each consecutive pair of symbols in the input string. The fact **input**($i-1$, C, i) is true if the ith input symbol is C. (The quote marks are a lexical device that enables the scanner to pick up the operator symbols as simple constants.) Why do we associate numbers with positions between symbols rather than with the symbols themselves? Why do we not represent the input as:

```
input(1, 7).
input(2, '+').
input(3, 9).
input(4, '*').
input(5, 8).
```

Numbers between the positions make it a little easier to talk about breaking the input into substrings, since the same number that marks the end of one substring also marks the beginning of the next. Also, notice later that we do not make any special use of the order of the position numbers—any set of distinct symbols would work as well.

A grammar for the arithmetic expressions we wish to evaluate is given in Figure 7.1.

We can construct a Datalog program to evaluate simple expressions directly from the grammar for the language. The Datalog program will have one clause for each production in the grammar. One Datalog clause handles the first production:

production:
EXP → TERM + EXP

Datalog clause:
```
exp(Beg, R, End) :-
        term(Beg, T, Mida),
        input(Mida, '+', Midb),
        exp(Midb, E, End),
        sum(T, E, R).
```

The production says that from an EXP, one can derive TERM + EXP. In the Datalog program the three-place predicate **exp** corresponds to the symbol EXP in the grammar, where **exp(P1, Val, P2)** is true if there is an expression spanning

EXP → TERM + EXP
EXP → TERM
TERM → FACTOR ∗ TERM
TERM → FACTOR
FACTOR → constant
FACTOR → (EXP)

Figure 7.1

from position **P1** to **P2** in the input and **Val** is the value of that expression. The Datalog rule says that **exp** is true of a certain portion of the input (from **Beg** to **End**) if **term** is true of an initial segment (from **Beg** to **Mida**), a '+' symbol follows, and **exp** is true of the final segment (from **Midb** to **End**). The value of the whole expression is obtained by adding the values for the component term and expression. The **sum** predicate is the evaluable predicate from Section 4.8.2, which (in this case) adds together its first two arguments to set the value of its third.

In a similar way we can write a clause for each production and obtain a Datalog program. The entire Datalog expression evaluator is as follows:

```
exp(Beg, R, End) :-
            term(Beg, T, Mida),
            input(Mida, '+', Midb),
            exp(Midb, E, End),
            sum(T, E, R).
exp(Beg, T, End) :- term(Beg, T, End).

term(Beg, R, End) :-
            factor(Beg, F, Mida),
            input(Mida, '*', Midb),
            term(Midb, T, End),
            product(F, T, R).
term(Beg, F, End) :- factor(Beg, F, End).

factor(Beg, C, End) :- input(Beg, C, End), number(C).
factor(Beg, E, End) :-
            input(Beg, '(', Mida),
            exp(Mida, E, Midb),
            input(Midb, ')', End).
```

The **product** predicate, which is used in the first clause for **term**, is true of triples of numbers, such that the first two multiply together to produce the third. This predicate would also be implemented as an evaluable predicate in the Datalog interpreter. The **number** predicate succeeds only if its argument is a number.

This Datalog program exhibits complex behavior. To invoke the program, we add the appropriate facts for the **input** predicate, and then for an input string of length—say, 7—we enter the query **exp(0, V, 7)**. The Datalog interpreter responds by binding **V** to the result obtained by evaluating the expression.

EXAMPLE 7.1: Consider the trace of program on the input '(5 + 3) * 4'. The input facts are:

```
input(0, '(', 1).
input(1, 5, 2).
input(2, '+', 3).
input(3, 3, 4).
input(4, ')', 5).
input(5, '*', 6).
input(6, 4, 7).
```

We start with the goal:

```
exp(0, V, 7).
```

looking for the value of an expression that spans from position 0 to position 7. Using in sequence the first **exp** rule, the first **term** rule, and the first **factor** rule, we get the following goal lists:

```
(1) term(0, T, Mida), input(Mida, '+', Midb), exp(Midb, E, 7),
      sum(T, E, V).
(2) factor(0, F1, Mida1), input(Mida1, '*', Midb1),
      term(Midb1, T1, Mida), product(F1, T1, T),
      input(Mida, '+', Midb), ...
(3) input(0, F1, Mida1), number(F1), input(Mida1, '*', Midb1), ...
```

The first goal of (3) matches an **input** fact with the replacement **F1 = '('**, leaving:

```
(4) number('('), input(Mida1, '*', Midb1), ...
```

which fails. We backtrack to (2) and try the second rule for **factor**. We follow with a match to an **input** fact, which succeeds, replacing **Mida2** by **1**, and then use the first **exp** rule and the first **term** rule.

```
(5) input(0, '(', Mida2), exp(Mida2, F1, Midb2),
      input(Midb2, ')', Mida1), input(Mida1, '*' Midb1), ...
(6) exp(1, F1, Midb2), input(Midb2, ')', Mida1), ...
(7) term(1, T3, Mida3), input(Mida3, '+', Midb3),
      exp(Midb3, E3, Midb2), sum(T3, E3, F1), input(Midb2, ')', Mida1), ...
(8) factor(1, F4, Mida4), input(Mida4, '*', Midb4),
      term(Midb4, T4, Mida3), product(F4, T4, T3),
      input(Mida3, '+', Midb3), ...
```

When we next apply the first **factor** rule, we get an **input** goal that we can satisfy by binding **F4** to **5** and **Mida4** to **2**. The **number** goal that follows then succeeds.

```
(9) input(1, F4, Mida4), number(F4), input(Mida4, '*', Midb4), ...
(10) number(5), input(2, '*', Midb4), ..., product(5, T4, T3), ...
(11) input(2, '*', Midb4), term(Midb4, T4, Mida3), ...
```

Goal list (11) fails, because the next input symbol is a '+', not a '*'. Backtracking to (8), we try the second **factor** rule, which requires a '(' as the next input symbol. We will then fail back to (7), and try the second **term** rule, followed by the first **factor** rule.

```
(12) factor(1, T3, Mida3), input(Mida3, '+', Midb3), ...
(13) input(1, T3, Mida3), number(T3), input(Mida3, '+', Midb3), ...
```

The first two goals in (13) can be satisfied if **T3** is replaced by **5** and **Mida3** by **2**, leaving an **input** goal that is satisfied with **Midb3** replaced by **3**.

```
(14) number(5), input(2, '+', Midb3), ...
(15) input(2, '+', Midb3), exp(Midb3, E3, Midb2), ...
(16) exp(3, E3, Midb2), sum(5, E3, F1), ...
```

Applying the first **exp** here will lead to failure, because it requires another '+' in the input to succeed. We skip ahead to the second **exp** rule and follow with an application of the first **term** rule.

```
(17) term(3, E3, Midb2), sum(5, E3, F1), ...
(18) factor(3, F5, Mida5), input(Mida5, '*', Midb5),
        term(Midb5, T5, Midb2), product(F5, T5, E3),
        sum(5, E3, F1), input(Midb2, ')', Mida1), ...
```

This goal list is doomed to fail eventually, because it expects a '*' before the next ')' in the input. Rather than working through to the point of failure, we backtrack here to (17) and apply the second **term** rule and then the first **factor** rule.

```
(19) factor(3, E3, Midb2), sum(5, E3, F1), ...
(20) input(3, E3, Midb2), number(E3), sum(5, E3, F1),...
```

The first two goals are solved with **E3 = 3** and **Midb2 = 4**, leaving:

```
(21) number(3), sum(5, 3, F1), ...
(22) sum(5, 3, F1), input(4, ')',
        Mida1), input(Mida1, '*', Midb1), ...
```

The **sum** predicate will return a value of **8** for **F1**. We can satisfy the next **input** goal for **Mida1 = 5**.

```
(23) input(5, '*', Midb1), term(Midb1, T1, Mida),
        product(8, T1, T), ...
```

The **input** goal succeeds with **Midb1** bound to **6**, to get:

(24) `term(6, T1, Mida), product(8, T1, T), ...`

We exercise our omniscience again to see that using the first **term** rule here leads to failure. Applying the second one instead, followed by the first **factor** rule, gives:

(25) `factor(6, T1, Mida), product(8, T1, T), ...`
(26) `input(6, T1, Mida), number(T1), product(8, T1, T), ...`

The **input** goal is solved with **T1** = **4** and **Mida** = **7**, which means the **number** goal will succeed. The resulting goal list is:

(27) `product(8, 4, T), input(7, '+', Midb), ...`

The **product** predicate will return **32** for **T**, but we have reached the end of the input with an **input** goal still on the goal list. Backtracking and further computation eventually reveal that we went astray in applying the first **exp** rule in step (1). Trying the second **exp** rule against the original goal, we get:

(28) `term(0, V, 7).`

That goal will succeed with a binding of **32** for **V**, following essentially the same steps as we used for removing:

```
term(0, T, Mida)
```

from goal list (1) to get to goal list (27). □

This example program shows that Datalog can begin to express programs that implement complex algorithms. What is keeping us from writing an arbitrary algorithm in Datalog? Say we want to write a compiler; the ideas presented in the preceding program seem to suggest a way to proceed. But the program actually implements more of an interpreter than a compiler. It produces the value of the expression. It does not produce another representation of the expression, such as intermediate code or machine code to evaluate the expression. Furthermore, a compiler for a real programming language, or even an interpreter, must deal with assignment of results to program variables and use of variable values in expressions. To write a compiler, we will want first to construct a parse tree (or abstract syntax tree) for the program, while maintaining a symbol table, and then manipulate that tree. The problem in Datalog is that we have no way to construct and manipulate such a complex data object as a tree. We could represent a complex data object by numbering edges in the tree, as we represented the input string earlier. However, we would be hard pressed in Datalog to produce a single value that represents an entire string or tree. In Datalog, data values are constrained to be simple constants.

7.2. Adding Structures to Datalog

What does it take to extend Datalog so that we can write the beginnings of a compiler? Rather than directly evaluating the arithmetic expression that is the input, we want to construct an expression tree that represents it. For example, for the arithmetic expression '(5 + 3) * 4', we want to construct the tree:

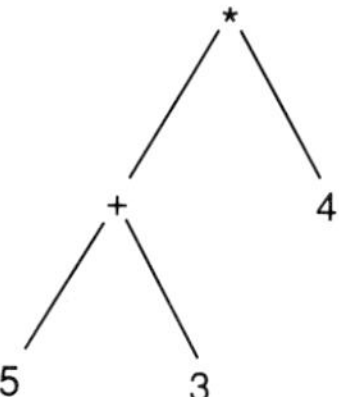

The problem is how to represent the expression tree we want to build. In Datalog we have no way of constructing a compound structure and assigning it to a variable. Representing an expression tree requires a structured data value. To extend Datalog to Prolog, we introduce one simple data-structuring facility: the *record* (also called a *record structure*). In Prolog a variable may have as its value a record, instead of a constant or another variable. A record consists of the record name, followed by a parenthesized list of values, one for each field of the record:

recordName(v_1, v_2, . . ., v_n)

The type of a record is denoted by its name and the number of fields. We use *term* to mean any value: record, variable, or constant.

We now can represent simple expressions with two-field records whose names correspond to the operators.

7 + 5
    add(7, 5)

9 * 8
    mult(9, 8)

Here a record with name **add** represents an addition expression. Another record type, with name **mult**, represents a multiplication expression. The preceding expressions are records, not literals, even though records and literals are structurally the same.

To represent complex expressions, we can nest records. The field of any record can have as a value any constant or record. So far, just (numeric) constants have appeared as the values of fields, but we can use record structures, too. The expression '(5 + 3) * 4' is represented by the record structure **mult(add(5, 3), 4)**, and the expression '5 + 3 * 4' by **add(5, mult(3, 4))**. Nested records can represent all expression trees (and many other things besides).

Record structures can include variables: **mult(add(5, X), 4)**. Such a record structure will match any structure obtained by replacing **X** with a variable, constant, or record structure, such as:

```
mult(add(5, 3), 4)
mult(add(5, mult(3, 2)), 4)
mult(add(5, mult(Y, Z)), 4)
```

If the same variable occurs more than once in a structure, it must be replaced uniformly throughout for matching. Thus **mult(add(5, X), X)** matches:

```
mult(add(5, 3), 3)
mult(add(5, mult(3, 2)), mult(3, 2))
```

but not:

```
mult(add(5, 3), 4)
```

In the next section we will see a general procedure for matching that handles variables in both records.

Now we can write a Prolog (Datalog + record structures) program to construct an expression tree for an arithmetic expression. The expression tree is much easier to manipulate than the original input, because the structure of the expression is made explicit. Subexpressions can be picked out readily, and any scheme that processes an expression by first processing its subexpressions is supported. We use the same representation for input.

```
expTree(Beg, add(T, E), End) :-
            termTree(Beg, T, Mida),
            input(Mida, '+', Midb),
            expTree(Midb, E, End).
expTree(Beg, T, End) :- termTree(Beg, T, End).

termTree(Beg, mult(F, T), End) :-
            factorTree(Beg, F, Mida),
            input(Mida, '*', Midb),
            termTree(Midb, T, End).
termTree(Beg, F, End) :- factorTree(Beg, F, End).

factorTree(Beg, const(C), End) :- input(Beg, C, End), number(C).
factorTree(Beg, E, End) :-
            input(Beg, '(', Mida),
            expTree(Mida, E, Midb),
            input(Midb, ')', End).
```

Note the similarity in structure to the Datalog program of the last section. The added **-Tree** on each predicate points out that this program constructs an expression tree. The predicate **expTree** is true of triples where the first and third arguments indicate a portion of the input string that is spanned by an expression (as before for **exp**) and the second argument is the expression tree for the spanned expression. The first clause for **expTree** expresses this relationship. It says that the second argument of an instance of **expTree** that spans an expression with principal operator '+' is a record of type **add**. That record's first field contains the tree **T** spanned by the subterm that is the first operand of '+'. Its second field contains the tree **E** spanned by the subexpression that is the second operand of '+'. Notice that **T**, **F**, and **E** represent expression trees, not numeric values, so we no longer need the arithmetic predicates **sum** and **product**. We use a record named **const** with a single field to hold constants. This change will help us distinguish cases when we later write an evaluator for expression trees. Thus the expression tree for '(5 + 3) * 4' is now:

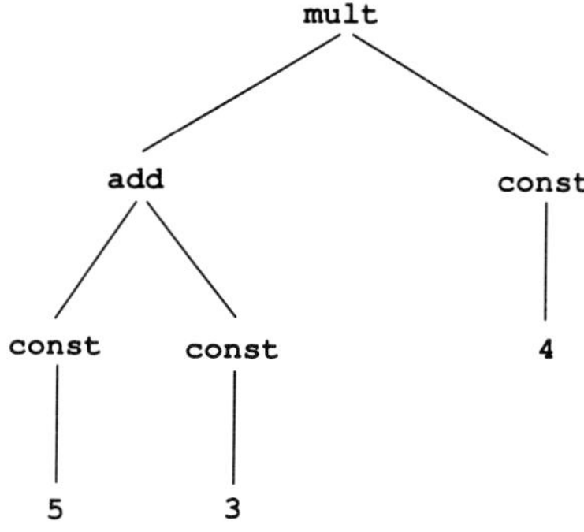

which corresponds to the record structure:

```
mult(add(const(5), const(3)), const(4))
```

We could have written the first rule even more similarly to the corresponding Datalog rule, as:

```
expTree(Beg, R, End) :-
        termTree(Beg, T, Mida),
        input(Mida, '+', Midb),
        expTree(Midb, E, End),
        sum(T, E, R).
```

but with a new definition of **sum**:

```
sum(T, E, add(T, E)).
```

Rather than performing the computation, **sum** constructs a record to represent the operation that is to be done later. This construction is the difference between an interpreter doing the operation and a compiler generating instructions to perform it.

EXAMPLE 7.2: We show the trace for the new program on '(5 + 3) * 4' using the same evaluation sequence as for the Datalog-based interpreter. Rules and goals are considered in the same order; matching is slightly more complicated. The **input** facts are the same as for Example 7.1, and the goal is the similar: **expTree(0, V, 7)**. Here we expect **V** to be bound to a record structure rather than a numeric value, however. The rules here are still based on the grammar in Figure 7.1, so we will get a trace that parallels that of Example 7.1. We omit the deadends in the search for a solution and use the numbers of the corresponding steps of the last trace to show the connection. We start with the second **expTree** rule.

```
(1) termTree(0, T, 7).
```

The first **termTree** rule applies by letting **V** = **mult(F1, T1)**. The second **factorTree** rule then applies.

```
(2) factorTree(0, F1, Mida1), input(Mida1, '*', Midb1),
       termTree(Midb1, T1, Mida).
(5) input(0, '(', Mida2), expTree(Mida2, F1, Midb2),
       input(Midb2, ')', Mida1), input(Mida1, '*' Midb1), ...
```

We follow with a match to an **input** fact, letting **Mida2** be bound to **1**, then use the first **expTree** rule, with **F1** = **add(T3, E3)**.

```
(6) expTree(1, F1, Midb2), input(Midb2, ')', Mida1), ...
(7) termTree(1, T3, Mida3), input(Mida3, '+', Midb3),
       expTree(Midb3, E3, Midb2), input(Midb2, ')', Mida1), ...
```

We now try the second **termTree** rule, followed by the first **factorTree** rule, using **T3** = **const(C3)**.

```
(12) factorTree(1, T3, Mida3), input(Mida3, '+', Midb3), ...
(13) input(1, C3, Mida3), number(C3), input(Mida3, '+', Midb3), ...
```

The first two goals in (13) can be satisfied if **C3** = **5** and **Mida3** = **2**. The next **input** goal is then satisfied with **Midb3** = **3**.

```
(14) number(5), input(2, '+', Midb3), ...
(15) input(2, '+', Midb3), expTree(Midb3, E3, Midb2), ...
(16) expTree(3, E3, Midb2), input(Midb2, ')', Mida1), ...
```

We use the second **expTree** rule, followed by the second **termTree** rule and the first **factorTree** rule, with **E3** = **const(C4)**.

```
(17) termTree(3, E3, Midb2), input(Midb2, ')', Mida1), ...
(19) factorTree(3, E3, Midb2), input(Midb2, ')' Mida1), ...
(20) input(3, C4, Midb2), number(C4), input(Midb2, ')', Mida1), ...
```

The first two goals are solved with **C4 = 3** and **Midb2 = 4**, leaving:

```
(21) number(3), input(4, ')', Mida1), ...
(22) input(4, ')', Mida1), input(Mida1, '*', Midb1), ...
```

We can satisfy the next two **input** goals with **Mida1 = 5** and **Midb1 = 6**.

```
(23) input(5, '*', Midb1), termTree(Midb1, T1, 7).
(24) termTree(6, T1, 7).
```

We apply the second **termTree** rule, followed by the first **factorTree** rule with **T1 = const(C5)**.

```
(25) factorTree(6, T1, 7).
(26) input(6, C5, 7), number(C5).
```

These last two goals are solved with **C5 = 4**.

We now go back and apply the successive substitutions to **V** to see what answer is finally generated.

```
V
mult(F1, T1)
mult(add(T3, E3), T1)
mult(add(const(C3), E3), T1)
mult(add(const(5), E3), T1)

mult(add(const(5), const(C4)), T1)

mult(add(const(5), const(3)), T1)

mult(add(const(5), const(3)), const(C5))

mult(add(const(5), const(3)), const(4))
```

which is what we expected. □

7.3. A Simple Prolog Interpreter

The previous section traced an execution of a Prolog program and showed briefly how an interpreter for Prolog should perform. In this section we modify the Datalog interpreter to turn it into a Prolog interpreter. The changes will concern mainly the *match* routine, extending it to handle record structures. Although our simple implementation for *match* here may seem quite different from the Datalog version, similarities will reappear in Chapter 10 when we are able to delay the application of substitutions. The changes there will permit *match* to call itself recursively to unify subterms.

We return to the very simple (and inefficient) Datalog interpreter of Section 4.3. We go back to that version, rather than the final optimized version, because it is easier to see what is going on.

```
function establish(GOALLIST: litlist): boolean;
    var SUBS: subst;
      NEXTCL, CLAUSEINST: clauselist;
    begin
      if isempty(GOALLIST) then return(true);
      NEXTCL := SYMTAB[predsym(first(GOALLIST))].CLAUSES;
      while NEXTCL <> nil do
        begin
          CLAUSEINST := instance(NEXTCL);
          if match(CLAUSEINST↑.HEAD, first(GOALLIST), SUBS) then
            if establish(apply(SUBS, copycat2(CLAUSEINST↑.BODY,
                                                    rest(GOALLIST)))) then
              return(true);
          NEXTCL := NEXTCL↑.NXTCLAUSE
        end;
      return(false)
    end;
```

Observe that nothing in *establish* looks at values of arguments to a literal; *establish* delves no further into a literal than its predicate symbol. All manipulation of terms is done in the *match, instance, apply,* and *copycat2* routines. Thus we need modify only those routines to get a Prolog interpreter. The main changes are in the *match* function. Recall the version of *match* that went with this simple *establish* function.

```
function match(HEAD, GOAL: lit; var SUBS: subst): boolean;
    var I: integer;
    begin
      if predsym(HEAD) <> predsym(GOAL)
        then return(false); {wrong rule}
      SUBS := nil;
      for each argument I in HEAD do
        if argument(HEAD, I) is a variable then
          if argument(HEAD, I) and argument(GOAL, I) are the same variable then
            {do nothing, on to next arg}
          else
            add replacement {argument(HEAD, I) = argument(GOAL, I)} to
            SUBS and apply this replacement to all the arguments in HEAD and
            GOAL, and to the right sides of elements of SUBS
        else if argument(GOAL, I) is a variable then
          add replacement {argument(GOAL, I) = argument(HEAD, I)} to
          SUBS and apply this replacement to all the arguments in HEAD and
```

```
            GOAL, and to the right sides of elements of SUBS
          else if argument(HEAD, I) <> argument(GOAL, I) then return(false);
      return(true)
    end;
```

The *match* function scans its two literals from left to right, looking for disagreements, which it attempts to fix via replacements. We want a new matching routine for record structures. This routine is more complicated than *match* for Datalog. That routine can keep a single integer index and step through the arguments of the two literals in order. In the new routine it is more difficult to keep track of where we are, since we could be examining, say, a field of a record structure that is a field of another record structure. Instead of trying to maintain a pointer, we use a procedure *findfirst* to scan the two literals left to right. It descends into fields and subfields, if necessary, finding the first point of mismatch. If the mismatch can be corrected with a replacement, *findfirst* returns that replacement. The new matching routine, *match1,* applies the replacement to both literals, adds it to the substitution being accumulated, and continues to call *findfirst* until no mismatches remain or a mismatch is found that cannot be fixed with a replacement.

```
function match1(T1, T2: struct; var SUBS: subst): boolean
    var OC: (none, clash, match);
      REPL: replacement;
    begin
      SUBS := nil;
      OC := none;
      findfirst(T1, T2, REPL, OC);
      while (OC <> none) and (OC <> clash) do
        begin
          if violates(REPL) then OC := clash
          else
            begin
              SUBS := compose(SUBS, REPL);
              apply(REPL, T1);
              apply(REPL, T2);
              OC := none;
              findfirst(T1, T2, REPL, OC)
            end
        end;
      if OC = clash then return(false) else return(true)
    end;
```

Procedure *findfirst* finds the first mismatch in two literals. It exploits the syntactic similarity between literals and record structures. We lump predicate symbols and record types together, call them all *structure symbols*, and represent them with one type, *struct*. The selector function *structsym* applied to a literal returns the predicate symbol. When applied to a term that is a record structure, *structsym* returns the record name. For example, *structsym*(**add(4, 5)**) is **add**. (Actually, *structsym* will return a symbol table reference, from which we can get both the record name and the number of fields.) For a term that is a constant, *structsym* returns the constant. We extend the function *arity* to return the number of fields for a record structure, as well as the number of arguments for a literal. Likewise, the *arg* function picks out field values or arguments, depending on whether its first parameter is a literal or a structure.

Procedure *findfirst* first deals with the case that one of its arguments is a variable (which case never arises on the initial call from *match1*). If neither is a variable, it then checks for agreement of structure symbols and recursively looks for a mismatch in the arguments or fields of its parameters. In Chapter 10, we will see how to avoid having *findfirst* search from the beginning of its parameters each time. For these purposes (and many others) a constant can be thought of as a 0-ary structure symbol—that is, a record type with zero fields. Thus the arity of a constant is zero. If the mismatch can be fixed through the replacement of a variable by a term, *findfirst* returns that replacement and sets OUTCOME to 'match'; if the mismatch cannot be fixed, it sets OUTCOME to 'clash'; if everything matches already, it sets OUTCOME to 'none'. The procedure *findfirst* is as follows:

```
procedure findfirst(T1, T2: struct; var REPL: subst;
                         var OUTCOME: (none, clash, match));
  begin
    if variable(T1) then
      if variable(T2) and (T1=T2) then OUTCOME := none
      else
        begin
          REPL := {T1 = T2};
          OUTCOME := match
        end
    else if variable(T2) then
      begin
        REPL := {T2 = T1};
        OUTCOME := match
      end
    else if structsym(T1) = structsym(T2) then
      begin
        I := 1;
        while (I <= arity(structsym(T1))) and (OUTCOME = none) do
          begin
            findfirst(arg(T1, I), arg(T2, I), REPL, OUTCOME);
            I := I + 1
          end
      end
    else OUTCOME := clash
  end;
```

EXAMPLE 7.3: Consider the behavior of *match1* on the pair of literals:

```
p(add(X, 4), X)
p(add(mult(Y, Z), Z), mult(W, W))
```

Initially SUBS is empty. For the first call to *findfirst,* neither parameter is a variable, but the predicate symbols match, so *findfirst* calls itself recursively on the first arguments:

```
add(X, 4)
add(mult(Y, Z), Z)
```

Neither of these records is a variable, but their record types match, so there is a second recursive call on:

```
X
mult(Y, Z)
```

Here *findfirst* sets OUTCOME to 'match' and returns the replacement **X** = **mult(Y, Z)**. Function *match1* applies this replacement to both literals and calls *findfirst* with the result:

```
p(add(mult(Y, Z), 4), mult(Y, Z))
p(add(mult(Y, Z), Z), mult(W, W))
```

This time *findfirst* detects the first mismatch in the second field of **add** and returns the replacement **Z** = **4**. SUBS is updated to:

```
{X = mult(Y, 4), Z = 4}
```

and the two literals become:

```
p(add(mult(Y, 4), 4), mult(Y, 4))
p(add(mult(Y, 4), 4), mult(W, W))
```

The next call to *findfirst* returns the replacement **Y** = **W**. The literals become:

```
p(add(mult(W, 4), 4), mult(W, 4))
p(add(mult(W, 4), 4), mult(W, W))
```

and SUBS is:

```
{X = mult(W, 4), Z = 4, Y = W}
```

The next call to *findfirst* finds the final mismatch and returns **W** = **4**. When *match1* applies this replacement, the literals become identical:

```
p(add(mult(4, 4), 4), mult(4, 4))
```

and SUBS becomes:

```
{X = mult(4, 4), Z = 4, Y = 4, W = 4}
```

A subsequent call to *findfirst* returns OUTCOME = 'none', so *match1* terminates. □

There is one nuance of *match1* we have not yet mentioned. Function *violates* checks whether a particular kind of failure has occurred. It looks for replacements in which the variable being replaced is mentioned in the term replacing it, such as **X = add(X, 3)**. Such a replacement means the substitution will not be idempotent. Repeated applications of such a replacement build larger and larger terms. The next example shows how such a replacement can arise.

EXAMPLE 7.4: Assume the initial input to *match1* is the following pair of literals:

```
p(Y, add(Y, 3))
p(X, X)
```

The first call to *findfirst* gives the replacement **Y = X**, making the two literals:

```
p(X, add(X, 3))
p(X, X)
```

A call to *findfirst* on these two literals yields the replacement **X = add(X, 3)**. □

It is possible to give meaning to such replacements if we allow infinite record structures, and Prolog systems using that approach have been proposed. (See the Comments and Bibliography section at the end of the chapter.)

7.4. Evaluating Expression Trees

As another example of a Prolog program, consider how given an expression tree, we can evaluate the expression. This example shows how easy it is to traverse a record structure in Prolog, and that the same syntax that worked for constructing records also works for selecting their components.

The predicate **evalTree** evaluates expression trees such as those constructed by the predicate **expTree** in Section 7.2. It takes an expression tree as its first argument and binds its second argument to the value of that tree. These two predicates together evaluate an arithmetic expression just as the first predicate **exp** did alone. The definition of **evalTree** is as follows:

```
evalTree(add(T1, T2), Value) :-
     evalTree(T1, V1),
```

```
      evalTree(T2, V2),
      sum(V1, V2, Value).

evalTree(mult(T1, T2), Value) :-
      evalTree(T1, V1),
      evalTree(T2, V2),
      product(V1, V2, Value).

evalTree(const(C), C).
```

Observe that **evalTree** has one clause for each possible root of an arithmetic expression tree. Consider the second clause for **evalTree**. It says that to evaluate a tree with **mult** at the root, first evaluate the left subtree to get value **V1**, then evaluate the right subtree to get value **V2**, and finally compute the value of the whole tree as the product of **V1** and **V2**.

EXAMPLE 7.5: The behavior of **evalTree** on a given expression tree is deterministic, since only one of the three rules can match a given subtree. Let the initial goal be:

```
evalTree(mult(add(const(5), const(3)), const(4)), V).
```

Applying the second rule, we match **T1** to **add(const(5), const(3))** and **T2** to **const(4)** to get:

```
evalTree(add(const(5), const(3)), V1), evalTree(const(4), V2),
      product(V1, V2, V).
```

We apply the first rule to get:

```
evalTree(const(5), V3), evalTree(const(3), V4), sum(V3, V4, V1),
      evalTree(const(4), V2), ...
```

We can use the third **evalTree** rule on the next two goals, binding **V3** to **5** and **V4** to **3**, leaving:

```
sum(5, 3, V1), evalTree(const(4), V2), ...
```

The **sum** predicate returns a value of 8 for **V1**, yielding:

```
evalTree(const(4), V2), product(8, V2, V).
```

Applying the third rule again gives:

```
product(8, 4, V).
```

which returns a final value of **32** for **V**. □

7.5. Informal Semantics for Prolog

Now that we have some experience with using records in Prolog, we want to explore the logic that includes them. We develop here an informal understanding of the logic of record types by showing how they correspond to certain constructs in English.

We understand a Datalog predicate as a "sentence with blanks in it." For example, a two-place predicate **couple(_, _)** might stand for the sentence "There is a married couple with ______ as the husband and ______ as the wife." We fill in the blanks in this English sentence with proper noun phrases—in this case proper names. So the literal **couple(ralph, alice)** stands for the sentence "There is a married couple with Ralph as the husband and Alice as the wife." Here we filled in the blanks with the proper nouns "Ralph" and "Alice." To continue the example, we might extend this predicate to include the date the couple were married. Thus we would have the three-place predicate **coupleMarried(_, _, _)** standing for "There is a couple with ______ as the husband and ______ as the wife who were married on ______." How do we fill in the final blank? We need to add a proper noun phrase indicating the date. In English we would simply say something like "13 January 1940." This proper noun phrase fits nicely in the third blank. But notice that there is structure to this noun phrase. Record structures allow us to include analogs of structured noun phrases in our formal language. In predicate logic we were constrained to atomic representations of the English noun phrases; in Datalog we would have to represent the noun phrase "13 January 1940" with a single constant such as **13jan1940**. That representation makes it difficult to find all couples married in a certain month or in a certain year. Whereas in English there is structure in the noun phrase "13 January 1940," that structure is lost in Datalog.

In Prolog we can give structure to the noun phrase. We have noun phrases with blanks in them. For example, we can use the record name **date(_, _, _)** for the noun phrase template "the ______ day of ______ in the year ______," and we can get a real noun phrase by filling in the template blanks. Thus the record structure **date(13, january, 1940)** represents the noun phrase "the 13th day of January in the year 1940." In Prolog, unlike Datalog, we can easily refer to subparts of this noun phrase. For example, if we are interested in couples married in June 1940, we can use the literal:

```
coupleMarried(Person1, Person2, date(Day, june, 1940)).
```

Just as we abbreviated sentence templates with shorter predicate names, we abbreviate a noun phrase template by a record name. The record name has as its arity the number of blanks in the noun phrase template it represents. Just as noun phrases in English can contain embedded noun phrases, we allow record structures as values in other record structures. We've been using the record name **add(_, _)** to represent the noun phrase template "the result of adding ______ to ______" and **mult(_, _)** for "the result of multiplying ______ by ______." Thus:

```
add(7, mult(9, 8))
```

represents the nested noun phrase "the result of adding 7 to the result of multiplying 9 by 8."

7.6. Lists

Adding the simple record structure to Datalog to obtain Prolog has far-reaching consequences. It actually makes Prolog a language that can express any computable function. In fact a single record type with two fields would suffice to make the language that expressive. In this section we look at computing under this model, using a single record type **cons** to represent lists of constants. We are using Prolog to manipulate the same kind of data structures that exist in the programming language LISP. Lists *are* a powerful data type, particularly in conjunction with the logical variable. In this section we begin to show the variety of ways that records can be used.

The expression-parsing example shows how records can be used to construct trees. Other data structures can be encoded as records. Notice that a list can be represented as a linear tree—what we called a vine in Chapter 5. We have seen how to represent trees with nested records. Composing these two representations gives an encoding of lists into record structures. A **cons** record will represent an internal node of the tree, and the constant **nil** denotes the end of the list. A **cons** record has two subfields. The first is a term representing the first element of the list; the second is another **cons** record structure representing the rest of the list, or it is **nil**. (Note that a list is, therefore, represented as a *right* vine.) The particular record name **cons** is borrowed from the programming language LISP, where it is used for historical reasons. The empty list is represented by the constant **nil**. The list consisting of the single element **a** is represented by the record: **cons(a, nil)**. Similarly, the list consisting of four elements—**a**, **b**, **c**, and **d**, in that order—is represented by the record structure:

```
cons(a, cons(b, cons(c, cons(d, nil)))).
```

One common list-processing operation is that of concatenating two lists. For example, given lists:

```
cons(a, cons(b, cons(c, nil)))
cons(m, cons(n, nil))
```

the result of concatenating them is:

```
cons(a, cons(b, cons(c, cons(m, cons(n, nil))))).
```

The following predicate, called **append**, takes two lists as its first two arguments and returns the result of concatenating them in its third argument.

```
append(nil, List, List).
append(cons(First, Rest1), List2, cons(First, Rest3)) :-
      append(Rest1, List2, Rest3).
```

The first clause says that concatenating the empty list with any list gives that list back. The second clause says that the result of concatenating a list whose first element is **First** and whose tail is list **Rest1** with any list **List2** is the list with first element **First** and tail **Rest3**, if the lists **Rest1** and **List2** concatenate together to form **Rest3**.

A little thought, and a rereading of that rather complicated last sentence, shows that these two statements are clearly true statements about lists and the concatenate (or append) operation. Furthermore, they cover all the possibilities for the first two arguments of **append**. What might be somewhat surprising is that we can actually use this program, as it is, with the Prolog interpreter and actually carry out the process of appending two lists.

EXAMPLE 7.6: Consider the trace of the Prolog interpreter given the query:

```
append(cons(a, cons(b, cons(c, nil))), cons(m, cons(n, nil)), Result).
```

The first rule does not match this goal. To use the second rule, we need to match the first arguments of the goal and the clause head:

```
cons(a, cons(b, cons(c, nil)))
cons(First, Rest1)
```

The matching succeeds with the replacements:

```
First = a
Rest1 = cons(b, cons(c, nil))
```

Matching the second and third arguments gives the replacements:

```
List2 = cons(m, cons(n, nil))
Result = cons(a, Rest3)
```

The new goal list is:

```
append(cons(b, cons(c, nil)), cons(m, cons(n, nil)), Rest3).
```

The second **append** rule solves this goal. Renaming variables in the head of that rule gives:

```
append(cons(First1, Rest4), List5, cons(First1, Rest6)).
```

Matching the goal and the rule head succeeds with the replacements:

```
First1 = b
Rest4 = cons(c, nil)
List5 = cons(m, cons(n, nil))
Rest3 = cons(b, Rest6)
```

leaving the goal list:

```
append(cons(c, nil), cons(m, cons(n, nil)), Rest6).
```

Again we use the second rule, letting the head be:

```
append(cons(First2, Rest7), List8, cons(First2, Rest9)).
```

and getting replacements:

```
First2 = c
Rest7 = nil
List8 = cons(m, cons(n, nil))
Rest6 = cons(c, Rest9)
```

The goal list is now:

```
append(nil, cons(m, cons(n, nil)), Rest9).
```

which is solved by the first rule, letting:

```
Rest9 = cons(m, cons(n, nil))
```

We can now apply the accumulated replacements to **Result** to get the answer.

```
Result
cons(a, Rest3)
cons(a, cons(b, Rest6))
cons(a, cons(b, cons(c, Rest9)))
cons(a, cons(b, cons(c, cons(m, cons(n, nil))))) □
```

The last example shows how the matching process serves as both a selector function to decompose record structures and a constructor to build up new structures. When we matched:

```
cons(a, cons(b, cons(c, nil)))
cons(First, Rest1)
```

we were selecting the first and second fields of the first record and holding them in **First** and **Rest1**. When we matched:

```
Result
cons(a, Rest3)
```

we were constructing a new record from **a** and **Rest3**. At the point the match took place, **Rest3** was unbound. However, it later held a structure.

7.6.1. *List Syntax*

Since it is clumsy to type all those **cons** records when writing out the representation of a list, most Prolog interpreters provide some syntactic sugar for lists. For the five-member list constructed at the end of the last example, we will write **[a, b, c, m, n]**. This notation is just an abbreviation used in discussion and for system I/O; a list still is "really" a record structure with a bunch of **cons** and a **nil** at the end. (Some Prolog interpreters use '**.**' for the list constructor and '**[]**' for the empty list.)

The notation **[First|Rest]** represents the record structure **cons(First, Rest)**. Note that this notation represents something quite different from **[First, Rest]**. In the latter expression **Rest** is a single list element in a two-element list:

```
cons(First, cons(Rest, nil))
```

In **[First|Rest]**, we expect **Rest** to be a list. With this new syntax, **append** becomes:

```
append(nil, List, List).
append([First|Rest1], List2, [First|Rest3]) :-
      append(Rest1, List2, Rest3).
```

which is a bit more readable.

EXAMPLE 7.7: The duality of the matching process as both a selector and constructor of lists means that there is no presupposed bias about what is an input argument and what is an output argument in a predicate. We can call **append** with lists for its first and third arguments, and a variable for its second. Such a goal, with the new list syntax, is:

```
append([a, b], Result, [a, b, c, d]).
```

This goal matches the head of the second **append** rule using the replacements:

```
First = a
Rest1 = [b]
Result = List2
Rest3 = [b, c, d]
```

to get a new goal:

```
append([b], List2, [b, c, d]).
```

Note that the second replacement is not **Rest1 = b** but **Rest = [b]**, where **[b]** is the same as **[b|nil]**. We match again to an instance of the second rule. Let the head be:

```
append([First1|Rest4], List5, [First1|Rest6]).
```

The replacements needed for matching are:

```
First1 = b
Rest4 = nil
List2 = List5
Rest6 = [c, d]
```

The new goal is:

```
append(nil, List5, [c, d]).
```

Solving this goal with the first **append** rule gives the replacement:

```
List5 = [c, d]
```

Composing replacements yields:

```
Result = [c, d] □
```

Now that we know about lists, let's go back to the expression-parsing program and reconsider how we represent the input to that program with lists. Recall that we represented the input expression as a set of facts: **input**($i-1$, C, i), where C is the ith symbol in the input expression. Note that an expression can more naturally be represented as a list of the symbols that make it up. The expression '(5 + 3) * 4' can be represented by the list:

```
['(', 5, '+', 3, ')', '*', 4]
```

which is shorthand for the structure:

```
cons('(', cons(5, cons('+', cons(3, cons(')',
    cons('*', cons(4, nil)))))))
```

We now can rewrite the **expTree** predicate from the Section 7.2 so that it is a two-place predicate whose first argument is a list that represents the input expression, and whose second argument is the parse tree of that expression. We no longer need pointers into the input string.

```
expTree(EList, add(T, E)) :-
        append(TList, ['+'|SubEList], EList),
        termTree(TList, T),
        expTree(SubEList, E).
```

```
expTree(EList, T) :- termTree(EList, T).

termTree(TList, mult(F, T)) :-
            append(FList, ['*'|SubTList], TList),
            factorTree(FList, F),
            termTree(SubTList, T).
termTree(TList, F) :- factorTree(TList, F).

factorTree([C], const(C)) :- number(C).
factorTree(FList, E) :-
            append(['('], EList, List),
            append(List, [')'], FList),
            expTree(EList, E).
```

The first **expTree** rule states that the list **EList** represents an expression with expression tree **add(T, E)**, if **EList** can be broken into a list **TList** followed by a '+' followed by a list **SubEList**. Further, **TList** represents an expression with expression tree **T**, and **SubEList** represents an expression with expression tree **E**.

EXAMPLE 7.8: We trace a few steps of the Prolog interpreter on the goal:

(1) **expTree(['(', 5, '+', 3, ')', '*', 4], V).**

under the new parsing program. Knowing from previous examples how this expression parses, let's skip ahead and apply the second **expTree** rule to get the goal:

(2) **termTree(['(', 5, '+', 3, ')', '*', 4], T).**

and the replacement **V = T**. This goal matches the head of the first **termTree** rule using the replacements:

```
TList1 = ['(', 5, '+', 3, ')', '*', 4]
T = mult(F1, T1)
```

giving the new goal list:

(3) **append(FList1, ['*'|SubTList1], ['(', 5, '+', 3, ')', '*', 4]),**
factorTree(Flist1, F1), termTree(SubTList1, T1).

The **append** goal will eventually succeed and return the replacements:

```
FList1 = ['(', 5, '+', 3, ')']
SubTList1 = [4]
```

leaving the goal list:

(4) **factorTree(['(', 5, '+', 3' ')'], F1), termTree([4], T1).**

Again jumping ahead, we can satisfy the first goal with the second **factorTree** rule by using the replacements:

```
FList2 = ['(', 5, '+', 3, ')']
F1 = E2
```

obtaining:

```
(5) append(['('], EList2, List2), append(List2, [')'],
                                     ['(', 5, '+', 3, ')']),
    expTree(EList2, E2), termTree([4], T1).
```

as the next goal list. The two **append** goals succeed with the net effect of:

```
EList2 = [5, '+', 3]
List2 = ['(', 5, '+', 3]
```

leaving the goal list:

```
(6) expTree([5, '+', 3], E2), termTree([4], T1).
```

Notice that we can backtrack forever on the first **append** goal. We leave the rest of the trace as Exercise 7.8. □

7.6.2. *Difference Lists*

The calls to append in the last example make it quite expensive to use. (However, for the second **factorTree** goal, one use of **append** will suffice. See Exercise 7.9.) There is a technique, somewhat like lazy lists, for manipulating lists without incurring the overhead of **append**. The technique is called *difference lists*. By using a logical variable to represent the end of a list, we can compose and decompose lists without the use of **append** and without having to traverse or copy them. In essence the variable stands for an indeterminate place in the list. It allows us to procrastinate on the choice on where to break in two until we have information on what should appear in the first part. Contrast delaying the choice to the use of **append**, which backtracks and tries all choices. The problem is that we want to take some prefix of the input list, pull it off, and parse it as a term or factor or whatever. We can represent a list prefix by the entire list plus the remainder of the list past the prefix. We combine these two pieces into a single record of type **dlist**: **dlist(Whole, Rem)**. Thus, the prefix:

```
['(', 5, '+', 3, ')']
```

of:

```
['(', 5, '+', 3, ')', '*', 4]
```

is represented as:

```
dlist(['(', 5, '+', 3, ')', '*', 4], ['*', 4])
```

The efficiency of this representation may not be immediately evident. It combines the best of the indexed representation and the list representations for input. Treating the input as a list is useful when dealing with individual symbols. On the other hand, in **dlist(Whole, Rem)**, **Whole** and **Rem** can be references into the same longer list, so we avoid copying.

EXAMPLE 7.9: To see how the delayed splitting of a list occurs, consider the following program fragment for breaking a difference list into a first part and a second part, and for solving the first part.

```
all(dlist(W, R)) :-
      firstPart(dlist(W, M)), secondPart(dlist(M, R)).

firstPart(dlist([a, b|End], End)).
```

(The term **[a, b|End]** is alternative syntax for **cons(a, cons(b, End))**.) Starting with the goal:

```
all(dlist([a, b, c, d, e], nil).
```

and applying the first rule gives the new goal list:

```
firstPart(dlist([a, b, c, d, e], M)), secondPart(dlist(M, nil)).
```

Notice that **M**, which represents where the original list is broken, is unbound in this goal list. Choosing the dividing point between the first list and the second list waits until the **firstPart** goal is solved, using **End = [c, d, e]**:

```
secondPart(dlist([c, d, e], nil))
```

With the proper interpreter, **W** and **M** will be bound to parts of the same existing structure, as pictured in Figure 7.2. □

EXAMPLE 7.10: Suppose we are building a parser for English and some of our productions are as shown in Figure 7.3.

We can render these productions as the following Prolog rules:

```
sentence(dlist(L1, L2)) :-
            nounPhrase(dlist(L1, L3)), verbPhrase(dlist(L3, L2)).
```

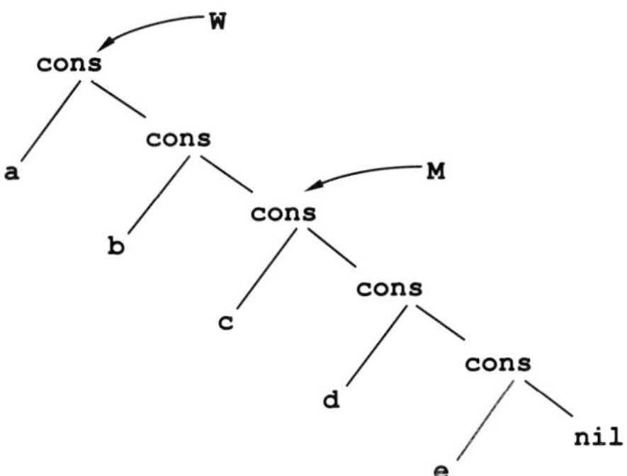

Figure 7.2

```
nounPhrase(dlist(L1, L2)) :-
            adjective(dlist(L1, L3)), nounPhrase(dlist(L3, L2)).
nounPhrase(D) :- noun(D).

verbPhrase(dlist(L1, L2)) :-
            verb(dlist(L1, L3)), adverb(dlist(L3, L2)).

adjective(dlist([small|Rem], Rem)).
adverb(dlist([quickly|Rem], Rem)).
noun(dlist([programs|Rem], Rem)).
verb(dlist([run|Rem], Rem)).
```

Of course, a real English parser would have to incorporate checks for linguistic features such as tense and number. Most such checks are expressed readily in Prolog. (See the Comments and Bibliography section.)

Let us take:

(1) **sentence(dlist([small, programs, run, quickly], nil)).**

as the initial goal. We solve this goal with the only **sentence** rule and then apply the first **nounPhrase** rule to get the goal lists on page 296.

<sentence> → <noun-phrase> <verb-phrase>
<noun-phrase> → <adjective> <noun-phrase>
<noun-phrase> → <noun>
<verb-phrase> → <verb> <adverb>
<adjective> → small
<adverb> → quickly
<noun> → programs
<verb> → run

Figure 7.3

```
(2) nounPhrase(dlist([small, programs, run, quickly], L3)),
        verbPhrase(dlist(L3, nil)).
(3) adjective(dlist([small, programs, run, quickly], L5)),
        nounPhrase(dlist(L5, L3)), verbPhrase(dlist(L3, nil)).
```

The **adjective** rule matches with the bindings:

```
Rem = [programs, run, quickly]
L5 = [programs, run, quickly]
```

to give the new goal list:

```
(4) nounPhrase(dlist([programs, run, quickly], L3)),
        verbPhrase(dlist(L3, nil)).
```

If we apply the first **nounPhrase** rule to the first goal, we get the goal list:

```
(5) adjective(dlist([programs, run, quickly], L8)),
        nounPhrase(dlist(L8, L3)), verbPhrase(dlist(L3, nil)).
```

which fails for lack of a match for the **adjective** goal. We need the second **nounPhrase** rule at (4) instead, followed by the **noun** rule, which binds **L3** to **[run, quickly]**.

```
(6) noun(dlist([programs, run, quickly], L3)),
        verbPhrase(dlist(L3, nil)).
(7) verbPhrase(dlist([run, quickly], nil)).
```

We apply the rules for **verbPhrase**, **verb**, and **adverb** in order to solve this goal:

```
(8) verb(dlist([run, quickly], L11)), adverb(dlist(L11, nil)).
(9) adverb(dlist([quickly], nil)).
```

Note that we delay picking the point to break the input into two sublists until we are sure the first sublist is something we can parse. If we used **append**, we would first generate a pair of sublists and then check if the first sublist can be parsed. □

7.6.3. *Transitive Closure with Cycles*

We have already seen the problem of computing transitive closure. The **below(Emp, Boss)** predicate of Section 4.9 computes the transitive closure of the **employee** predicate. Exercise 4.5 had the program:

```
tc(X, Y) :- g(X, Y).
tc(X, Y) :- g(X, Z), tc(Z, Y).
```

which expresses the transitive closure of a graph whose edges are expressed as **g(A, B)** facts. We saw in that exercise that the graph:

```
g(1, 2).
g(1, 3).
g(2, 3).
g(3, 4).
g(4, 1).
```

pictured in Figure 7.4 caused the Datalog interpreter to produce answers forever on the goal **tc(1, X)** because of the cycle 1-2-3-4-1. However, the interpreter generates only a finite number of different answers for the goal. Repeated applications of the second **tc** rule are analogous to tracing a path through the graph, with successive bindings of **Z** being the nodes along that path. The looping behavior arises from following paths that contain the same node more than once.

Here we extend the transitive closure program to handle graphs with cycles. The Datalog version gets caught in a cycle because it has no means to remember what nodes the search has been through. That set of nodes can grow arbitrarily large (depending on the graph), but any Datalog predicate has a fixed number of arguments. In Prolog we can construct a list of any size to hold all nodes visited thus far and make sure the search visits no node twice.

To construct the transitive closure predicate with checking for repeated nodes, we need a predicate that tests if two nodes are different. Assume a predicate **notEqual(X, Y)** that is true of all pairs of distinct nodes. From **notEqual**, we can define a predicate **notIn(N, L)** that is true if node **N** is not in list **L**:

```
notIn(N, nil).
notIn(N, [M|Rest]) :- notEqual(N, M), notIn(N, Rest).
```

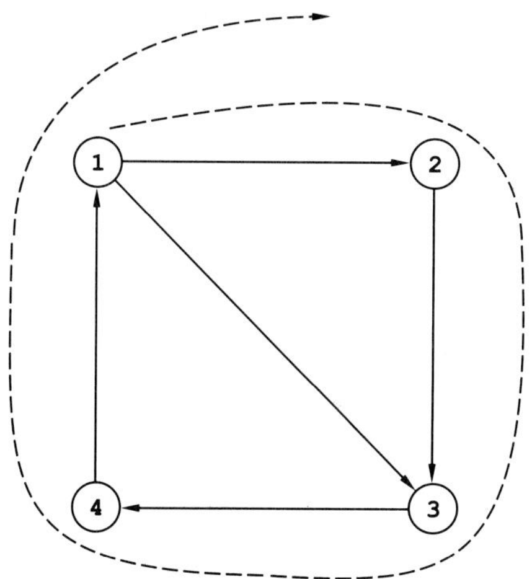

Figure 7.4

The first rule states that no node is in the empty list. The second rule states that node **N** is not in a list if it is not equal to the first node in the list, and if it is not in the rest of the list.

We now define the transitive closure predicate with path checking, called **tcp**. The first two arguments in **tcp** are the pair of nodes we are checking for membership in the transitive closure, and the third argument is the list of nodes visited so far. That list does not include the start and end nodes. (Why?)

```
tcp(X, Y, Path) :- g(X, Y), notIn(Y, Path).
tcp(X, Y, Path) :- g(X, Z), notIn(Z, Path), tcp(Z, Y, [Z|Path]).
```

We trace the Prolog interpreter on the goal **tcp(1, Y, nil)** using the graph given at the beginning of this section. Applying the first rule gives the new goal list:

(1) **g(1, Y), notIn(Y, nil).**

which is satisfied for the two bindings **Y** = **2** and **Y** = **3**. There are no other ways to satisfy (1), so we backtrack to the original goal and use the second rule.

(2) **g(1, Z1), notIn(Z1, nil), tcp(Z1, Y, [Z1]).**

The binding **Z1** = **2** satisfies the first two goals. The first rule then matches the third goal.

(3) **notIn(2, nil), tcp(2, Y, [2]).**
(4) **tcp(2, Y, [2]).**
(5) **g(2, Y), notIn(Y, [2]).**

The two goals in (5) are satisfied with the binding **Y** = **3**. Note that we have generated an answer twice. The duplication is due to multiple paths in the graph (1-3 and 1-2-3), not looping. The search backtracks to (4), where we try the second rule.

(6) **g(2, Z2), notIn(Z2, [2]), tcp(Z2, Y, [Z2, 2]).**

The binding **Z2** = **3** solves the first two goals, after which we can apply the first rule.

(7) **tcp(3, Y, [3, 2]).**
(8) **g(3, Y), notIn(Y, [3, 2]).**

The last goal list yields the answer **Y** = **4**, after which we backtrack to (7) and try the second rule.

(9) **g(3, Z3), notIn(Z3, [3, 2]), tcp(Z3, Y, [Z3, 3, 2]).**

We solve the first two goals with **Z3 = 4** and apply the first rule.

```
(10) tcp(4, Y, [4, 3, 2]).
(11) g(4, Y), notIn(Y, [4, 3, 2]).
```

The replacement **Y = 1** satisfies (11), after which we backtrack to (10) and use the second rule.

```
(12) g(4, Z4), notIn(Z4, [4, 3, 2]), tcp(Z4, Y, [Z4, 4, 3, 2]).
```

The binding **Z4 = 1** satisfies the first two goals, leaving:

```
(13) tcp(1, Y, [1, 4, 3, 2]).
(14) g(1, Y), notIn(Y, [1, 4, 3, 2]).
```

While **Y = 2** and **Y = 3** both solve the first goal in (14), both cause the second goal to fail. We go back and try the second rule on (13), getting:

```
(15) g(1, Z5), notIn(Z5, [1, 4, 3, 2]),
       tcp(Z5, Y, [Z5, 1, 4, 3, 2]).
```

No binding that solves the first goal solves the second, so this goal list also fails. Backtracking at this point takes us all the way back to (2), where we can go forward again with the binding **Z1 = 3**. Some answers seen before are generated again, but the computation eventually terminates.

7.6.4. *An Extended Example: Poker*

In this section we follow an extended example on evaluating poker hands. We will see how a predicate written to check a condition can also be used to generate structures that satisfy that condition. If the condition does not constrain the structure fully, the program will generate partially specified structures (record structures with variables). The first thing we need to represent is playing cards. A record structure **card(R, S)** represents a playing card of rank **R** and suit **S**. The following rule defines the legal cards in the deck.

```
legal(card(R, S)) :- rank(R), suit(S).
```

This rule needs the allowable ranks and suits:

```
rank(two).
rank(three).
rank(four).
   .
   .
   .
```

```
rank(queen).
rank(king).
rank(ace).

suit(clubs).
suit(dmnds).
suit(hearts).
suit(spades).
```

Next we give some "utility" predicates for describing relationships between cards and between hands. The first such predicate gives the order of the ranks.

```
nextRank(two, three).
nextRank(three, four).
nextRank(four, five).
   .
   .
   .
nextRank(queen, king).
nextRank(king, ace).
```

The predicate **lowerRank** represents the transitive closure of **nextRank**.

```
lowerRank(R1, R2) :- nextRank(R1, R2).
lowerRank(R1, R2) :- nextRank(R1, R3), lowerRank(R3, R2).
```

The next three predicates are used to determine that two cards differ, either in rank or in suit, or in both.

```
diffSuits(clubs, dmnds).
diffSuits(clubs, hearts).
diffSuits(clubs, spades).
   .
   .
   .
diffSuits(spades, clubs).
diffSuits(spades, dmnds).
diffSuits(spades, hearts).

different(card(R1, S1), card(R2, S2)) :- diffSuits(S1, S2).
different(card(R1, S), card(R2, S)) :- lowerRank(R1, R2).
different(card(R1, S), card(R2, S)) :- lowerRank(R2, R1).
```

Note that the suits are the same in the second and third rules for **different**. We could have used different variables for the suits and still have been correct. However, with that change, there would be two ways to show that certain pairs of cards are different, such as **card(two, clubs)** and **card(three, spades)**. Less overlap among the rules, however, means fewer chances to backtrack and come up with the same result, making the program more efficient.

Hands are represented as lists of cards. A legal hand consists of five different legal cards. The predicates to check that a list of cards is a legal hand are written so that they can be easily modified for other card games with other hand sizes, such as cribbage and bridge.

```
hand(CardList) :- length(CardList, 5), diffCards(CardList).
```

The **length** predicate, which makes use of an evaluable predicate **sum**, computes the number of elements in list. (We switch to using `[ ]` for **nil**.)

```
length([], 0).
length([C|Rest], M) :- length(Rest, N), sum(N, 1, M).
```

In many Prolog systems **length** is a system-supplied predicate. The predicate **diffCards** tests that a list of cards has no duplicates. It checks that the first card in the list does not appear in the rest of the list and that the rest of the list contains distinct cards. It also ensures that all cards are legal.

```
diffCards([]).
diffCards([C|Rest]) :- legal(C), notIn(C, Rest), diffCards(Rest).

notIn(C, []).
notIn(C1, [C2|Rest]) :- different(C1, C2), notIn(C1, Rest).
```

The order of hands in poker is:

one pair
two pairs
three of a kind
straight (cards in consecutive rank order)
flush (cards of the same suit)
full house (a pair and three of a kind)
four of a kind
straight flush

For two hands of the same kind, order is determined by comparing ranks. For example, three jacks beats three sevens. (Unless this is the first time you've played, kiddo—in which case three sevens is a Smazola, and you pay twice the pot to me.)

The predicate **onePair** takes a hand and checks for two cards of the same rank, with the second argument being the rank of the two cards.

```
onePair(CardList, Rank) :- hand(CardList), hasTwo(CardList, Rank).

hasTwo([card(Rank, S)|Rest], Rank) :- hasOne(Rest, Rank).
hasTwo([C|Rest], Rank) :- hasTwo(Rest, Rank).

hasOne([card(Rank, S)|Rest], Rank).
hasOne([C|Rest], Rank) :- hasOne(Rest, Rank).
```

EXAMPLE 7.11: Consider the following goal:

```
onePair([card(eight, dmnds), card(six, clubs), card(two, clubs),
      card(six, hearts), card(four, clubs)], Rank1).
```

Applying the only rule for **onePair**, we get the new goals:

```
hand([card(eight, dmnds), card(six, clubs), card(two, clubs),
            card(six, hearts), card(four, clubs)]),
     hasTwo([card(eight, dmnds), card(six, clubs),
            card(two, clubs), card(six, hearts),
            card(four, clubs)], Rank1).
```

The **hand** goal succeeds, but we do not trace its execution here. Applying the first **hasTwo** rule to the second goal gives:

```
hasOne([card(six, clubs), card(two, clubs), card(six, hearts),
      card(four, clubs)], eight).
```

which ultimately fails. The second **hasTwo** rule gives:

```
hasTwo([card(six, clubs), card(two, clubs), card(six, hearts),
      card(four, clubs)], Rank1).
```

to which the first **hasTwo** rule applies with **Rank1 = six**, leaving:

```
hasOne([card(two, clubs), card(six, hearts),
      card(four, clubs)], six).
```

The head of the first **hasOne** rule will not unify with this goal, but the second **hasOne** rule yields:

```
hasOne([card(six, hearts), card(four, clubs)], six).
```

The first **hasOne** rule solves that goal. Thus the original goal succeeds with **Rank1 = six**. □

The **onePair** predicate is not quite complete. Its clauses do not check that the hand is no better than one pair. As given earlier, **onePair** succeeds on other hands, such as three of a kind. (See Exercise 7.18.)

We can reuse the predicates from **onePair** to define a predicate for two pairs.

```
twoPair(CardList, Rank1, Rank2) :-
      hand(CardList),
      hasTwo(CardList, Rank1),
      hasTwo(CardList, Rank2),
      lowerRank(Rank1, Rank2).
```

We must make sure the ranks of the pairs are different, so that **hasTwo** does not succeed on the same pair twice.

EXAMPLE 7.12: Although the **hand** predicate was originally written to check that a list of cards is a legal hand, it can also be used to generate legal hands, when called with a variable. Consider how we might generate a hand containing two pairs. Starting with the goal:

```
twoPair(CardList, Rank1, Rank2).
```

we get as the next goal list:

```
hand(CardList), hasTwo(CardList, Rank1),
      hasTwo(CardList, Rank2), lowerRank(Rank1, Rank2).
```

These goals function as a "generate and test" routine. The **hand** goal produces legal hands as bindings for **CardList**, while the rest of the goals check whether that legal hand is two pair. We trace the evaluation of the **hand** goal to see which is the first hand generated to pass the check. Applying the only **hand** rule to the **hand** goal gives the new goal list:

```
length(CardList, 5), diffCards(CardList).
```

The **length** goal succeeds by binding **CardList** to a list of five distinct variables, leaving:

```
diffCards([C1, C2, C3, C4, C5]).
```

This goal matches only the second **diffCards** rule, giving the new goal list:

```
legal(C1), notIn(C1, [C2, C3, C4, C5]),
      diffCards([C2, C3, C4, C5]).
```

legal succeeds by binding **C1** to **card(two, clubs)**, leaving the new goal list:

```
notIn(card(two, clubs), [C2, C3, C4, C5]),
      diffCards([C2, C3, C4, C5]).
```

Only the second **notIn** rule succeeds here, giving:

```
different(card(two, clubs), C2),
      notIn(card(two, clubs), [C3, C4, C5]),
      diffCards([C2, C3, C4, C5]).
```

Next, the first **different** rule binds **C2** to **card(R2, S2)**, leaving:

```
diffSuits(clubs, S2), notIn(card(two, clubs), [C3, C4, C5]),
      diffCards([card(R2, S2), C3, C4, C5).
```

The **diffSuits** goal succeeds with **S2 = dmnds**, which yields:

```
notIn(card(two, clubs), [C3, C4, C5]),
      diffCards([card(R2, dmnds), C3, C4, C5).
```

We jump over some details at this point. The net effect of satisfying the remaining **notIn** goal is to produce the bindings:

```
C3 = card(R3, dmnds)
C4 = card(R4, dmnds)
C5 = card(R5, dmnds)
```

and leave the goal:

```
diffCards([card(R2, dmnds), card(R3, dmnds), card(R4, dmnds),
            card(R5, dmnds)]).
```

Again, only the second **diffCards** rule matches the goal, giving the new goal list:

```
legal(card(R2, dmnds)),
      notIn(card(R2, dmnds), [card(R3, dmnds), card(R4, dmnds),
            card(R5, dmnds)]),
      diffCards([card(R3, dmnds), card(R4, dmnds),
            card(R5, dmnds)]).
```

The **legal** goal succeeds by binding **R2** to **two**, leaving:

```
notIn(card(two, dmnds), [card(R3, dmnds), card(R4, dmnds),
            card(R5, dmnds)]),
      diffCards([card(R3, dmnds), card(R4, dmnds),
            card(R5, dmnds)]).
```

Only the second **notIn** rule matches the first goal. Applying that rule gives:

```
different(card(two, dmnds), card(R3, dmnds)),
            notIn(card(two, dmnds),
            [card(R4, dmnds), card(R5, dmnds)]),
      diffCards([card(R3, dmnds), card(R4, dmnds),
            card(R5, dmnds)]).
```

Using the first **different** goal produces the new goal:

```
diffSuits(dmnds, dmnds)
```

which fails. The second **different** rule produces the new goal list:

```
lowerRank(two, R3), notIn(card(two, dmnds), [card(R4, dmnds),
            card(R5, dmnds)]), ...
```

The first rule for **lowerRank** gives:

```
nextRank(two, R3), notIn(card(two, dmnds), [card(R4, dmnds),
            card(R5, dmnds)]), ...
```

The first goal succeeds with **R3 = three**, leaving:

```
notIn(card(two, dmnds), [card(R4, dmnds), card(R5, dmnds)]),
      diffCards([card(three, dmnds),
            card(R4, dmnds), card(R5, dmnds)]).
```

The trace for solving the current **notIn** goal will be quite similar to that for the last **notIn** goal. It eventually spawns a:

```
lowerRank(two, R4)
```

goal that binds **R4** to **three**, giving the goal:

```
notIn(card(two, dmnds), [card(R5, dmnds)]),
      diffCards([card(three, dmnds), card(three, dmnds),
            card(R5, dmnds)]).
```

Looking ahead, we see that the **diffCards** goal will ultimately fail and keep failing until we backtrack to:

```
lowerRank(two, R4), notIn(card(two, dmnds), [card(R5, dmnds)]),
      diffCards([card(three, dmnds), card(R4, dmnds),
            card(R5, dmnds)]).
```

and get a binding of **R4 = four**, leaving:

```
notIn(card(two, dmnds), [card(R5, dmnds)]),
      diffcards([card(three, dmnds), card(four, dmnds),
            card(R5, dmnds)]).
```

We must backtrack to the current **notIn** goal twice before we get a binding for **R5** such that the remaining goal succeeds:

```
diffCards([card(three, dmnds), card(four, dmnds),
            card(five, dmnds)]).
```

We finally have a value for **CardList**, namely:

```
[card(two, clubs), card(two, dmnds), card(three, dmnds),
      card(four, dmnds), card(five, dmnds)]
```

If this binding is produced by a call to **hand** from the **twoPair** predicate, a subsequent goal will fail, because the hand has only one pair. What bindings will

hand(CardList) produce on backtracking, and which will be the first to contain two pairs? Recall that from the goal:

```
notIn(card(two, clubs), [C3, C4, C5]),
      diffCards([card(R2, dmnds), C3, C4, C5).
```

we eventually produced the goal:

```
diffCards([card(R2, dmnds), card(R3, dmnds), card(R4, dmnds),
            card(R5, dmnds)]).
```

Until we backtrack from that goal, we keep producing hands with a two of clubs and four diamonds (a Grand Smazola!), which cannot contain two pairs. The fifth (partial) card in this goal is the result of a previous goal:

```
different(card(two, clubs), C5)
```

that yielded the goal:

```
diffSuits(clubs, S5)
```

with the binding **C5 = card(R5, S5)**. The first time through this last goal gave **S5 = dmnds**. When we backtrack to it, we get the binding **S5 = hearts**, which leaves the goal:

```
diffCards([card(R2, dmnds), card(R3, dmnds), card(R4, dmnds),
            card(R5, hearts)]).
```

to solve. This goal first succeeds with the bindings:

```
R2 = two
R3 = three
R4 = four
R5 = two
```

giving:

```
CardList = [card(two, clubs), card(two, dmnds),
      card(three, dmnds), card(four, dmnds), card(two, hearts)]
```

which does not have two pairs, either. However, the next binding we get for **R5** on backtracking is **three**, which does give us a hand with two pairs:

```
CardList = [card(two, clubs), card(two, dmnds),
      card(three, dmnds), card(four, dmnds), card(three, hearts)]
```

□

For a straight, we must check if the cards are in rank sequence. That check is easier if the cards are arranged in descending order. We leave the check for consecutive ranks in a sorted hand as an exercise. (See Exercise 7.20.)

```
straight(CardList, Rank) :-
      hand(CardList),
      sorted(CardList, SortedCards),
      sequential(SortedCards, Rank).
```

The sort routine we give is a selection sort. It repeatedly pulls out the largest element of the remainder of the initial list as the next element in the sorted list.

```
sorted([], []).
sorted(List, [C|SortedRest]) :-
      largest(C, List),
      remove(C, List, Rest),
      sorted(Rest, SortedRest).
```

The **largest** predicate takes the first element if it is the largest; otherwise, it selects the largest element in the rest of the list.

```
largest(C, [C]).
largest(C1, [C1|Rest]) :- largest(C2, Rest), lowerOrEqual(C2, C1).
largest(C2, [C1|Rest]) :- largest(C2, Rest), lowerOrEqual(C1, C2).

lowerOrEqual(card(R, S1), card(R, S2)).
lowerOrEqual(card(R1, S1), card(R2, S2)) :- lowerRank(R1, R2).
```

The **sorted** predicate works on lists of other types of elements by changing the definition of the **lowerOrEqual** predicate. The **remove** predicate takes a list and a card, and returns the list without the card. This predicate fails if the card is not in the list.

```
remove(C, [C|Rest], Rest).
remove(C1, [C2|Rest1], [C2|Rest2]) :-
       different(C1, C2), remove(C1, Rest1, Rest2).
```

We partially define a predicate to tell when one hand beats another. Pairs are compared by rank. Two-pair hands are compared by the higher-ranking pair; if there is a tie, the lower-ranking pair is compared. The correctness of the **beats** predicate given here depends on **onePair** being modified so as not to succeed on any hand better than one pair.

```
beats(Hand1, Hand2) :-
      onePair(Hand1, Rank1), onePair(Hand2, Rank2),
      lowerRank(Rank2, Rank1).
```

```
beats(Hand1, Hand2) :-
      twoPair(Hand1, Rank1, Rank2), onePair(Hand2, Rank3).

beats(Hand1, Hand2) :-
      twoPair(Hand1, Rank1, Rank2),
      twoPair(Hand2, Rank3, Rank4),
      lowerRank(Rank4, Rank2).

beats(Hand1, Hand2) :-
      twoPair(Hand1, Rank1, Rank2),
      twoPair(Hand2, Rank3, Rank2),
      lowerRank(Rank3, Rank1).
```

It is possible that the ranks match for two one-pair hands or two two-pair hands. In that case the ranks of the remaining cards are considered. (See Exercise 7.26.)

This last example demonstrates some of the power of logical variables, record structures, and unification as a basis for manipulating compound data objects. The flexibility in using the same program for both testing a condition and generating structures that satisfy the condition is unequaled in other languages. Yet there is much that is outside the scope of "pure Prolog," or that cannot be implemented efficiently in it. For that reason pure Prolog is augmented by evaluable predicates. We saw evaluable predicates for arithmetic and comparisons in Chapter 4. Other evaluable predicates cover I/O, program update, and set manipulation. Two particularly useful extensions are control predicates and metalogical predicates. The control predicates give the programmer the ability to control the search space of the Prolog interpreter, using information about the problem domain. The metalogical predicates allow new terms to be synthesized from pieces (arguments and structure symbols), and for a term to be called as a literal. Thus a Prolog program can create, modify, and execute other Prolog code.

The next chapter takes up these extensions.

7.7. EXERCISES

7.1. Using the grammar in Figure 7.1, give the derivation that corresponds to the computation in Example 7.1.

7.2. Consider including subtraction and division in terms for arithmetic expressions, and using constants to represent arithmetic variables:

```
mult(add(3, div(x, 6)), sub(y, add(3, div(x, 6))))
```

a. Give a Prolog program for a predicate **comSubexp(Exp, Common)** that takes an arithmetic expression and returns a common subexpression. A common subexpression is an expression that occurs twice or more in the original expression, such as **add(3, div(x, 6))** here.

b. Define a predicate **same(Exp1, Exp2)** whose arguments are arithmetic expressions. The predicate should succeed if the two expressions are equivalent, taking the commutativity of **add** and **mult** into account. For example:

```
same(plus(3, div(x, 6)), plus(div(x, 6), 3))
```

should succeed. Be sure your program avoids infinite loops.

7.3. For the literal **eq(union(rev(X), Y), rev (Y))** as the first parameter, say what result *match1* gives when called with each of the following literals as the second parameter:

i. **eq(union(W, W), V)**
ii. **eq(W, rev(W))**
iii. **eq(union(W, rev(W)), rev(union(V, V)))**

7.4. What are all the bindings for **L1** and **L2** that the goal:

```
append(L1, L2, [a, b, c])
```

will produce if backtracking is forced after each success?

7.5. Give a grammar for the bracket notation for lists introduced in Section 7.6.1.

7.6. Give a Proplog interpreter written in Prolog. Assume that Proplog clauses are represented as **pClause(Head, Body)** facts in Prolog, where **Body** is a list. Thus:

```
p :- q, r, t.
r.
```

are represented as:

```
pClause(p, [q, r, t]).
pClause(r, []).
```

Your interpreter predicate should take a list of goals as an argument.

7.7. Redo the map-coloring example of Section 4.6 to work on arbitrary undirected graphs. Let such graphs be represented by facts giving pairs of adjacent nodes: **adj(I, J)**. For example, if we take the regions of Figure 4.1 as nodes and include an edge whenever two regions touch, we get the graph:

```
adj(1, 2)    adj(1, 3)    adj(1, 5)    adj(1, 6)
adj(2, 3)    adj(2, 4)    adj(2, 5)    adj(2, 6)
adj(3, 4)    adj(3, 6)
adj(5, 6)
```

Let the palette of possible colors be given by **color** facts, for example:

```
color(yellow)
color(blue)
```

```
color(green)
color(red)
color(white)
```

Let a coloring of the graph be denoted by a list of node-color pairs:

```
[c(1, red), c(2, blue), c(3, green), c(4, red), c(5, blue),
    c(6, white)]
```

Give a predicate **goodColoring(ColorList)** that succeeds if **ColorList** is a coloring of the graph nodes such that no two adjacent nodes have the same color. Your predicate may use **not**, but it must handle a list with the colors unspecified:

```
[c(1, C1), c(2, C2), c(3, C3), c(4, C4), c(5, C5), c(6, C6)]
```

7.8. Finish the trace of the computation in Example 7.8. What happens if backtracking is forced after the computation first succeeds?

7.9. Rewrite the second **factorTree** rule to use only one **append** subgoal.

7.10. Write a routine that converts a context-free grammar to a Prolog program with difference lists for parsing sentences in the grammar.

7.11. If we translate a grammar rule of the form:

<sentence> → <sentence> <prep-phrase>

to a Prolog rule using difference lists, we get:

```
sentence(dlist(L1, L2)) :-
    sentence(dlist(L1, L3)), prepPhrase(dlist(L3, L2)).
```

Such productions and rules are called *left recursive*. This rule will cause an infinite loop with the Prolog interpreter given in Section 7.3.

a. What is wrong with the strategy of stopping loops on left recursion by keeping a list of leftmost nonterminals generated from a given nonterminal and truncating the search when the same nonterminal is generated twice?
b. Give an alternative interpreter for Prolog that can solve goals in the presence of left-recursive rules.

7.12. Rewrite the expression tree parser of Section 7.4 using difference lists instead of **append**.

7.13. Write a version of **append** that runs in constant time, using difference list representation with a variable for the end of a list:

```
dlist([a, b|X], X)
```

7.14. For the transitive closure predicate of Section 7.6.2, what will the predicate compute on a goal:

```
tcp(X, Y, List)
```

when **List** is a nonempty list of nodes?

7.15. Give a definition of the **diffSuits** predicate in terms of **not** and a predicate **sameSuit**. Your predicate should work correctly when invoked with unbound variables as arguments.

7.16. Will the goal **hand(CardList)** ever produce the same cards in the same order twice if backtracking is forced?

7.17. What is the first "hand" that the goal **hand(CardList)** would generate if the **legal** subgoal were removed from **diffCards**?

7.18. Give a predicate for **onePair** that fails if the hand is better than one pair. Your predicate should not use **not**.

7.19. Rewrite the **twoPair** predicate as a "test and generate" routine: check for a legal hand after checking for the other conditions. Compare the performance of your version to the original "generate and test" version for producing a hand with two pair from an initially unbound card list.

7.20. Write a program for the **sequential** predicate used in **straight**. The predicate should determine if the cards in a sorted hand have consecutive ranks.

7.21. Trace the **straight** predicate on a goal representing a draw to an inside straight:

```
straight([card(four, clubs), card(three, spades), C3,
        card(seven, clubs), card(six, dmnds)])
```

7.22. Write a Prolog program to do insertion sort on a list. In insertion sort, at the ith step, the first i elements of a list are sorted, and the $i+1^{st}$ element is inserted in order.

7.23. Write a predicate **quickSort(In, Out)** that sorts a list using the Quicksort method: pick an element s from the input, divide the remaining elements into a sublist of smaller elements and a sublist of larger elements, sort the sublists, and then construct the output as the smaller elements followed by s followed by the larger elements.

7.24. In Mergesort the intermediate data structure is a list of lists, where the sublists are sorted:

```
[[1, 3, 9, 18], [2, 4, 5], [2, 7, 13], [6, 7], [8, 11, 17]]
```

In one pass of the algorithm pairs of sublists are merged. For an odd number of sublists, the last sublist is passed through unchanged:

```
[[1, 2, 3, 4, 5, 9, 18], [2, 6, 7, 7, 13], [8, 11, 17]]
```

Write a Prolog predicate **onePass(In, Out)** that performs one pass of the Mergesort algorithm. You may assume predicates **lessEq(X, Y)** and

greater (X, Y) for comparing elements in the sublists, but you may not assume any other predicates.

7.25. Give predicates to recognize the rest of the poker hands: three of a kind, flush, full house, four of a kind, and straight flush.

7.26. When two poker hands have the same features, such as a pair of jacks versus a pair of jacks, the winning hand is decided by comparing the remaining cards in descending order of rank. Thus, remaining cards of a ten, eight, and two will beat a ten, five, and three. Add clauses to **beats** to decide the winner in one-pair and two-pair hands with the same features. Note that comparing ranks on all the cards is equivalent to comparing ranks of the remaining cards.

7.8. COMMENTS AND BIBLIOGRAPHY

In this chapter we finally see the full power of Horn clause programming. Horn clauses with the SLD proof procedure have been championed as an excellent programming language by Kowalski [1.1]. Hogger [7.1] also shows how logic programming, and general Horn clause programs in particular, can be used to solve many problems. Clark and Tarnland [7.2] have edited a collection of papers dealing with various aspects of logic programming. In that collection, one paper by Colmerauer [7.3] proposes to extend logic programming to handle certain classes of infinite terms—namely, those resulting from a replacement such as **X = f (Y, g (X))**, which would normally be disallowed by the occurs check.

Planner, an AI programming language developed by Hewitt at MIT in the late 1960s [7.4], can be seen a precurser to Prolog. The first actual implementation of Prolog was done by Colmerauer and his group [7.5] in Marseille, France. They developed it in the early 1970s as an engine for natural language processing.

7.1. C. J. Hogger, *Introduction to Logic Programming,* Academic Press, London, 1984.

7.2. K. L. Clark and S. A. Tarnlund (eds.), *Logic Programming,* Academic Press, New York, 1982.

7.3. A. Colmerauer, PROLOG and infinite trees, in [7.2], 231–52.

7.4. C. Hewitt, Description and theoretical analysis (using schemata) of PLANNER: A language for proving theorems and manipulating models in a robot, Ph.D. Thesis, MIT, AI Lab report AI-TR-258, 1971.

7.5. A. Colmerauer, H. Kanoui, R. Pasero, and P. Roussel, Un Systeme de Communication Homme-machine en Francais, Research report, Groupe Intelligence Artivicielle, University of Marseille, 1973.

8

Prolog Evaluable Predicates

8.1. Prolog Pragmatics

To make a pure logic programming language into a usable programming system, we must add a number of features. These features involve the programmer's convenience, efficient implementation of arithmetic, ways of doing input and output, primitives to support metaprogramming, and ways to change the global database of clauses. In addition, the programmer must have more control over how the refutation procedure tries to solve goals. The programmer controls the order in which subgoals are tried by ordering the literals in the body of a clause and by ordering the clauses for a predicate. These orderings mainly control forward execution. Prolog has an operation, called "cut," that allows the programmer more control over backtracking.

The mechanism for adding facilities to a logic programming language is to add *evaluable* predicates, which look like predicates but are treated specially by the system. They are processed by executing a procedure written in a lower-level procedural programming language, not by proving further subgoals. (Actually, not every evaluable predicate has its own procedure. Some are defined in terms of other evaluable predicates.) The ability to add arbitrary code makes the logic programming system very open-ended and flexible but also can make it non-logical. Almost no evaluable predicate is completely reversible; for example, almost none will take variables for all arguments at once. Further, while most evaluable predicates will have a declarative definition, cut has none, because it works through side effects on the evaluation order. The evaluable predicates we introduce in subsequent sections are predicates found in CProlog and other derivatives of DEC-10 Prolog.

8.1.1. *Documentation Conventions*

While all pure logic programs are in principle reversible—that is, they can be called with arguments in any state of instantiation—almost all evaluable predicates are not. To use an evaluable predicate, we need to know not only its declarative semantics—the set of tuples for which it is true—but also the allowable instantiation patterns of its arguments. Imagine a two-place predicate **sign** that is true of pairs, such that if the first is a negative number, the second is the constant **minus**, and if the first is a nonnegative number, the second is the constant **plus**. When **sign** is called, its first argument must be bound. It will not create a new number of a given sign if called with only the second argument bound. To indicate this limitation, we use the following notation in a comment:

```
sign(+Number, ?Sign)
```

This notation looks somewhat like a goal for the predicate. The '+' in front of the first argument indicates that it must not be an unbound variable when it is called. The '**?**' before the second argument indicates that it can be any term (including a variable) when **sign** is called. (Of course, the predicate can succeed when the second argument is nonvariable only if it is one of the constants **plus** or **minus**.) If an evaluable predicate requires that a particular argument be a variable on call, we annotate that argument with a '–'. The sequence of '+', '–', and '**?**' tags associated with a particular predicate is called its *mode*. We will give mode declarations as part of the declarative description of the evaluable predicates.

The mode notation has some limitations. For example, consider how we would describe the mode of the predicate **sum**. Recall that **sum(X, Y, Z)** is true if **X** plus **Y** is **Z**. For a call to be legitimate, two of the three arguments must be bound to a nonvariable, but any one of the arguments might be a variable on a particular call. The only mode we could use is:

```
sum(?X, ?Y, ?Z)
```

which indicates any pattern of values and variables in a call is legal. The problem is that our notation is not rich enough to express all possibly interesting calling patterns. This problem is not serious for us here. We will always use English to describe the declarative semantics of predicates. We include those aspects of the instantiation requirements of an evaluable predicate that are not captured by the mode notation as part of the description.

8.2. Input/Output

Every programming language must have a way to communicate with the environment provided by the operating system. This environment normally consists of files (and pseudofiles such as printers and the user's terminal), so a programming language must allow a program to read and write them. To make reading and writing as logical as possible, we would have to make them backtrackable. That is, on failure they would have to "unread" and "unwrite," which are somewhat problematical operations. Unreading is definable (see Exercise 8.2), but unwriting requires remembering a preimage of a file (or erasing characters off a terminal screen?). For this reason (and others) the read and write operations are not backtrackable but are implemented as side effects. That is, they are both deterministic, and their effects are global and not undone on backtracking.

In a logic programming system, terms are the data objects that programs manipulate, so it is appropriate that they be the objects that are read from and written to files. Internally terms are represented as rather convoluted data structures involving pointers and a symbol table. To put terms in a file, we need some external representation for them. We have been using such a representation throughout this book: constants and function symbols are written by name (starting with a lower case letter) and arguments (when any exist) are written immediately following the function symbol enclosed in parentheses and separated by commas. A variable is represented by a character string that begins with an uppercase letter or an underscore. Single quotes override the convention; any input string in single quotes is treated as the name of a constant. These same conventions are used as the basic external representation of terms in CProlog and other Prologs based on DEC-10 Prolog. (Throughout this chapter we will introduce groups of evaluable predicates with a comment section set off, as follows, giving the modes and brief statements of the declarative semantics.)

```
/* read(?Term) reads the next term from the input stream and
   unifies it with Term. */

/* read(?Term, -Vars) reads the next term from the input and
   unifies Vars with a list of pairs, each consisting of a
   variable name and a variable. */

/* write(?Term) writes an external representation of Term to the
   output stream. */

/* nl forces a new line on the output stream. */
```

The Prolog system maintains a *current input stream* and a *current output stream*. Both streams are set initially to the user's terminal but can be changed to access other files by using other evaluable predicates. The **read** predicate reads a term from the current input stream. The term must be in external format, as described earlier, and terminated by a '.' followed by white space (blank, tab, or return). Variables are converted to internal form, and their external names are lost. Some Prologs provide another **read** predicate with two arguments that return the term and also a list that associates the external variable names with the internal variables. We will see the usefulness of this operation later.

The **write** predicate writes its argument to the current output stream. That is, it produces on the current output device the sequence of characters that represents the term in external format. For variables, it uses some convenient name, usually the integer (or address) that is used internally, prefixed with an underscore.

The **write** predicate does not terminate the term with a '**.**' and writes the entire term on a single line. To force a new line, the evaluable predicate **nl** is provided. When invoked, it forces a new line in the current output stream, so that the next write will start on a new line.

These predicates provide the basics of term reading and writing, but there is a complication: *operators*. Some binary function symbols are conventionally written as infix operators. For example, rather than writing **+(5, 7)**, we are more accustomed to writing **5 + 7**. CProlog supports this alternative representation for a number of infix operators. All the arithmetic operators and comparators are infix operators. CProlog also allows unary functor symbols to be declared as prefix operators, such as unary minus '-', so we can write **-X** instead of **-(X)**. Also, postfix operators are supported but are less commonly used. Operators can be used for other than just arithmetic operators. For example, '**:-**' and '**,**' are both infix operators, so the notation:

```
p(X) :- q(X), X < 7
```

actually represents the term (written in the standard term notation):

```
:-(p(X), ','(q(X), <(X, 7)))
```

(More on literals and clauses as terms later in Section 8.7.2.) Note that we have to quote the '**,**' when it is used as a binary function symbol.

With infix operators, the possibility of ambiguity arises. That is, **1 + 2 * 3** could represent either of two terms: **+(1, *(2, 3))** or ***(+(1, 2), 3)**. To disambiguate such expressions, each operator has a priority, and operators with a lower-numbered priority bind tighter than those with higher-numbered priority. In this case '*' has a lower priority than '+', so the first of the two terms is the one the expression represents. Parentheses can override the priorities.

Some operators are predefined, and the user can declare others. When declaring an operator, the user must say whether it is prefix, infix, or postfix and give its priority. The same operator can be declared to be of multiple kinds—for example, '-' is both prefix and infix.

In addition to supporting operators, Prolog has various conventions for representing certain special terms. Lists have a special representation. The list notation:

```
[a, b, c]
```

is just a shorthand for the term:

```
.(a, .(b, .(c, [])))
```

(We used **cons** previously, instead of '**.**', because it is easier to read in prefix notation.) Also, rather than writing:

```
.(H, R)
```

we can write:

```
[H|R]
```

The **read** and **write** evaluable predicates support square-bracket notation for lists; **read** will accept both forms as equivalent, **write** always uses the square-bracket notation.

Another special external representation involves character strings. One way to represent a character string in CProlog is as a list of small integers, where each integer is the ASCII code for a character. For example, the string 'abc' would be represented internally as **[97, 98, 99]**, since these are the ASCII codes for those letters. The **read** predicate supports a special notation for such lists: a sequence of characters enclosed in double quotes ('"') is read as a list of ASCII codes.

Since a character is often represented as the integer that is its ASCII code, there is also a special way of representing such an integer. The input token **0'a** is read as the integer **97**, since **97** is the ASCII code for **a**. The token **0'(** is read as **40** since **40** is the ASCII code for the left parenthesis. These representations (while somewhat unusual) allow us to specify characters and strings to a Prolog system without memorizing the ASCII codes. We use them in Chapter 12.

In summary then, **read(X)** reads the next term, which must be terminated by a '.', from the current input stream, and unifies it with **X**. If the current stream is at the end of the file, **X** is unified with the constant **end_of_file**. If the next characters in the file do not make up a syntactically correct term, an error message is printed, and another term is automatically read. The goal **write(X)** produces the external representation of the term currently bound to **X** on the current output stream. All I/O predicates, including **read** and **write**, are nonbacktrackable. They immediately fail on retry.

```
/* get0(?Int) reads a character from the input stream and binds
   its ascii code to Int. */

/* put(+Int) writes the character whose ascii code is Int to the
   output stream. */
```

The **read** and **write** evaluable predicates allow a Prolog programmer to read and write terms to and from files. But sometimes a program must read data from a file that is not represented as a term. Prolog provides lower-level evaluable predicates to allow single-byte input and output. The predicate **get0** reads a single character from the current input stream and binds its argument to the integer that is the ASCII code of that character. If there are no more characters in the file, the argument is unified with **-1**. If its argument is bound on call, **get0** checks to ensure that the next character matches the argument. Successive **get0** calls will read through an entire file one character at a time. There is a corresponding evaluable predicate for character output: **put**. When given an integer that represents the ASCII code of a character, **put** writes that single character to the current output stream.

8.3. Call

One aspect of Prolog that we have noted before is that a term and a literal are represented in exactly the same way. This similarity is a very powerful feature: we can construct a term as a data object and then use it as a goal. Consider the following simple example. We are writing a command processor for a simple interactive graphics system. (Shall we call it Prologo?) The user types a command along with its arguments, and the program, depending on the command, invokes the appropriate code to carry out the indicated action. We will represent a command as a term, the main functor name is the command name, and the field values of the term will be parameters to the command. For example, to move the cursor forward 5 centimeters, the user enters:

```
forward(5).
```

To turn the cursor left 50 degrees, the user enters:

```
turn(left, 50).
```

There will be many more commands. Since the command is a term (terminated by a period), we can use the **read** evaluable predicate to get it from the user. For each n-argument command, we would define an n-ary predicate to carry out the necessary actions, plus one predicate to dispatch commands.

```
/* Predicates to carry out the commands. There may be many. */

forward(Distance) :- ....

turn(Direction, Degrees) :- ....


/* Command processor. */

prologo :- read(X), callCommand(X), prologo.


/* Command dispatcher. One clause for each command. */

callCommand(forward(X)) :- forward(X).
callCommand(turn(X, Y)) :- turn(X, Y).
```

Notice that all **callCommand** does is solve the goal that is structurally identical to its argument.

```
/* call(+Goal) treats the term Goal as a literal and calls it.
   Goal may be a structured term with unbound variables in it. */
```

```
/* fail always fails. */

/* halt stops processing and exits the session. */
```

Prolog provides an evaluable predicate, named **call**, that is a general version of **callCommand**. Given a term, **call** treats it as a goal and invokes it. With **call**, we can write the command processor just shown as follows:

```
/* Command processor, using call. */

prologo :- read(X), call(X), prologo.
```

We do not need the **callCommand** predicate at all. Notice that **call** implicitly converts a function symbol into a predicate symbol. We can see this "conversion" being done explicitly in the definition of **callCommand** shown earlier: the symbol **forward** in the head of the first clause of **callCommand** is a function symbol; the symbol **forward** in the body is a predicate name. In **callCommand** we could easily change the name of the predicate that carries out a particular command, while leaving the command name the same. When **call** is used, this change is not possible.

Notice that if the argument to **call** is a variable, there is no predicate to call. In this case **call** gives an error. The argument to call can be a term that contains unbound variables, however.

EXAMPLE 8.1: Consider the top level of the Prolog processor: it prompts the user for a query, reads in the query, evaluates it, and prints out the answers. Consider a simple version of such a processor written in Prolog:

```
/* callLoop is the top-level read-eval-print-fail loop */

callLoop :- write('?:- '), read(Query, Vars), call(Query),
        printList(Vars), fail.
callLoop :- callLoop.
```

The predicate **callLoop** first prints out a prompt to indicate that it is waiting for input. Then it uses **read/2** to read in the query. Here **read/2** is the read predicate that reads a term and returns the term in the first argument and a list of **VariableName = Variable** pairs indicating the names of the variables in the term. For example, when given the input:

```
p(X, a, Y), q(Y).
```

the goal **read(Query, Vars)** would return the bindings of:

```
Query = ','(p(_1, a, _2), q(_2))
Vars = ['X'=_1, 'Y'=_2]
```

Notice that the variable names are constants (which is why we indicate them as quoted) and the actual variables have internally generated names. After reading the query, **callLoop** uses **call** to evaluate that term as a goal. When the goal succeeds, a predicate **printList** prints out the answers. At the point **printList** is invoked, **Vars** will be bound to a list of **VariableName = VariableValue** pairs. It recurses down the list and uses **write** (and **nl**) to write each pair on a new line. (See Exercise 8.4.) The **fail** predicate is an evaluable predicate that always fails. Here it causes the system to backtrack to find another answer for the called query. Each answer is found and printed out until there are no more answers, at which time the first clause for **callLoop** fails and the second clause is tried. The second clause simply calls **callLoop** again to process the next query. Note how backtracking over I/O predicates does not undo the side effects.

Giving **callLoop** as a goal puts Prolog into an infinite loop (as Prologo did earlier), but we intend the top level of the processor to be an infinite loop anyway. Prolog also provides an evaluable predicate, **halt**, which, when executed, terminates the entire session and returns to the operating system. We can use **halt** to break the loop.

Notice that the top-level loop in this simple processor always prints out all the answers. The user is not given any option of seeing only some of the answers. (See Exercise 8.5.) □

8.4. Controlling Backtracking: The Cut

We may think of Prolog as a nondeterministic procedural language. For various reasons, therefore, the programmer might like to say that, if some particular goal succeeds, the program should not try some other alternative. For example, suppose we want to make the **callLoop** predicate work more like the standard Prolog top-level processor. Thus, after printing an answer, the program must prompt the user to determine if any more answers are to be calculated and printed. If the user types a ‘;’, the processor can simply fail back to compute the next answer. But if the user enters a return, we want to “throw away” any remaining alternatives and then fail back to read another query.

```
/* ! (cut) remove all alternatives set up since the call was made
   that the clause containing the cut is trying to solve. */
```

The ‘!’ evaluable predicate (pronounced “cut”) allows a programmer to cause such behavior. The cut is actually quite different in nature from the other evaluable predicates because it has a nonlocal effect on what other goals are solved.

When executed, the cut removes some alternatives that are waiting to be tried when the system backtracks. As a result, when the system does backtrack, those removed alternatives will *not* be tried. The alternatives removed are all those that have been set up since the call to the predicate in whose body the cut appears. The cut itself always succeeds on its first call and always fails on backtracking.

EXAMPLE 8.2: In the **callLoop** example we could use the cut to remove all alternatives set up in the **call** to evaluate **Query**. In this way we could allow the user to determine interactively whether another answer should be computed and printed. When the user has seen enough, we will use a cut to throw away the alternatives not yet tried:

```
/* callLoop is the top-level read-eval-print-fail loop */

callLoop :- write('?:- '), read(Query, Vars),
      callAndPrint(Query, Vars).
callLoop :- callLoop.


/* callAndPrint(+Query, +Vars) evaluates Query, prints an answer,
   and asks the user whether another answer is desired. It
   continues until the user says no more answers are desired, or
   until there are no more answers, in which case it prints 'no'.
   As a predicate, callAndPrint always fails. */

callAndPrint(Query, Vars) :-
      call(Query),
      printList(Vars),
      wantNoMore,
      !,
      fail.
callAndPrint(_, _) :- write(no), nl, fail.


/* wantNoMore prompts user.  If user types return, succeed.  If
   the user types anything else then fail. */

wantNoMore :- get0(10).  /* typed a return (ascii 10), so no more */
wantNoMore :- get0(10), fail.  /* anything followed by a return
                                  means more */
```

Consider the definition of **callAndPrint**. The query is called, an answer is printed, and then **wantNoMore** is called. That goal succeeds if the user does not want to see any more answers. If **wantNoMore** returns successfully, the cut is executed. The cut removes all alternatives set up since this invocation of **callAndPrint** was made, including any alternatives remaining for **callAndPrint** itself. So if the user types a return, the '**!**' is executed, removing all alternatives set up in the **call(Query)** and also removing the alternative represented by the second clause of **callAndPrint** (the one that prints '**no**'.) Then the **fail** is executed, and control goes back to the next remaining alternative—in this case the second clause of **callLoop**, which loops to read in another query. If the user enters a '**;**' (or anything other than a return) followed by a return, then **wantNoMore** will fail, and the next alternative answer to **call(Query)** is found and printed, and the user prompted again. (Note that each call to **get0** consumes a character, whether or not it succeeds.) If there are no more alternatives in the **call(Query)**, the second clause of **callAndPrint** is executed, which prints '**no**' and then fails back to read another query. □

With the definition of **callLoop** given here, once it is called, it can never return. But now that we have the cut, we have a way of removing an alternative after it has been set up. So with appropriate coding, we could use a cut to eliminate the alternative set up by the second clause of **callLoop** if, say, the user typed in an end-of-file in response to the request for a query. (See Exercise 8.5.)

There is another common use for cut. Consider the if-then-else construct of a procedural language. A Boolean condition—say, **p(X)**—is evaluated. If it is true, one statement—say, **q(X, Y)**—is executed. If not, another statement—say, **r(X, Y)**—is executed. This effect can be achieved with Horn clauses and negation-as-failure as follows:

```
t(X, Y) :- p(X), q(X, Y).
t(X, Y) :- not(p(X)), r(X, Y).
```

(We will assume that **t** will always be called with **X** bound to a ground term, so that this use of negation is safe.) One problem with this implementation is that it is inefficient. The Boolean test **p(X)** is evaluated twice—once in the first clause and then again on backtracking in the second clause. Since **p(X)** will evaluate the same each time, this redundant computation is unnecessary. We would really like the system to evaluate **p(X)** once and then either call **q(X, Y)** or call **r(X, Y)**. We can achieve this effect with cut:

```
/* t(+X, ?Y) is if p(X) then q(X, Y) else r(X, Y) */

t(X, Y) :- p(X), !, q(X, Y).
t(X, Y) :- r(X, Y).
```

As long as **X** is fully bound on entry and **p** has no side effects, this construction has the same semantics as the pair of clauses. When **t** is called, **p** is executed. If it succeeds, the cut eliminates the second clause as an alternative for **t**, and **q(X, Y)** is called. Whether **q** succeeds or fails, the second clause will not be executed. If, instead, the call to **p** fails, then the second clause is used and **r(X, Y)** is evaluated. Note that if the Boolean condition **p** succeeds, the cut also eliminates all backtrack alternatives set up during its evaluation. But since the call to **p** should be ground, this behavior is no problem; the call to **p** cannot bind any variables, so we care only whether it succeeds or fails.

All cut does is eliminate some answers; it never adds more of its own. So we might say that the declarative semantics of cut is "true." This interpretation might seem reasonable since cut always succeeds and it has no effect until a later failure occurs. The set of tuples satisfying a predicate defined using cut is always a subset of the tuples we would obtain by eliminating all the cuts in the definition—that is, treating them as true. While this declarative definition of cut is tempting and in some cases helpful, it can also be somewhat misleading. Simply saying that the "cut semantics" is a subset of the "declarative semantics" is a very weak statement. Notice that every set is a subset of the universal set. As an example, consider the following definition of a predicate '\+':

```
/* \+(+Goal) unsafe negation-as-failure on Goal. */

\+(Goal) :- call(Goal), !, fail.
\+(Goal).
```

Assume that **Goal** is a ground term when '\+' is invoked. The **call** treats it as a goal and invokes it as a subgoal, trying to establish it. If the **call(Goal)** succeeds, the cut is executed, eliminating the second '\+' clause as an alternative, and the **fail** is executed, so the entire invocation of '\+' fails. If, however, the **call(Goal)** fails, then the second '\+' clause is used, and it succeeds, no matter what **Goal** is. So notice that \+**(Goal)** fails if **call(Goal)** succeeds and succeeds if **call(Goal)** fails. It is essentially the **not** operator, differing only in that it will not give an error if **Goal** is not ground at the time of invocation. A few interpreters do check if the argument to **not** is ground, but most Prolog compilers and interpreters define negation-as-failure in the unsafe way.

If we compute the "declarative semantics" of '\+' (interpreting '**!**' as true) and then say the "cut semantics" is a subset of that, do we get any useful information? The first clause will *always* fail, since it has **fail** in its body, so "declaratively" we could simply ignore this clause. The second clause always succeeds—that is, is always true. So the "declarative semantics" of '\+' is that it is true of all terms. Indeed the actual semantics of '\+' is a subset of the universal set. The problem is that this description is not very helpful. The interesting property of '\+' has to do with precisely which subset it is true of. So the subset semantics of clauses with cut, while correct, is often not tight enough to be useful.

Cut is a powerful operator that can be used to implement many "nonlogical" predicates. (See Exercise 8.8 for another example.) Its use should be carefully controlled so that a program using cuts retains a declarative reading. Where its use cannot be given a declarative reading, it is best packaged within another predicate, such as '\+', where the enclosing predicate can be understood more or less logically. It is most often used for efficiency, as in the case of the earlier "if-then-else" example. Notice that because a cut eliminates alternatives, it can be used to make programs more deterministic. We will see in Chapter 11 how determinism can make Prolog programs much more space and time efficient.

8.5. Arithmetic

Arithmetic in logic programming was first covered in Chapter 4. Here we reiterate some of that discussion and describe how arithmetic is implemented in CProlog.

Logic programming languages are mainly symbolic, but they do have to deal with arithmetic. Actually arithmetic is just a special case of symbolic computation. A logic programming language can (in theory) represent numbers as standard terms, such as **zero**, **succ(zero)**, and **succ(succ(zero))**, and incorporate the axioms for addition, multiplication, and so forth. However, this implementation of arithmetic would be horribly inefficient when compared to the way most languages (and computers) represent and manipulate numbers. The **succ** representation is essentially monadic (or tally) notation and requires space proportional to i to represent integer i. Computers have special representations for numbers and special algorithms for performing symbolic operations on them very efficiently. Those representations are binary, not monadic, and so n bits can represent integers up to 2^n. Also, many of the algorithms to operate on numbers in this format can be performed by a single instruction cycle of a machine. These representations and algorithms are supported by hardware to make arithmetic operations fast. Prolog must be able to use this hardware support when appropriate to perform acceptably on arithmetic.

As an aside, we point out that while a large (and necessary) amount of efficiency is gained by using the hardware's numeric representations and operations, something is also lost. The machine representation does not allow partially specified numbers. Were we to use the successor representation for unsigned integers, we could represent some (as yet unknown) number greater than or equal to 2 as **succ(succ(X))**. The machine's hardware cannot capture such an animal. Its numbers must be "ground," which is what forces the evaluable predicates for arithmetic to require that certain arguments be bound and to give an error when they are not.

Prolog uses a special representation for numbers, which distinguishes them from any of the terms we have seen so far. The representation is essentially that of the underlying hardware but normally with a few bits taken away for tagging. The Prolog system can then recognize these special "terms" and apply special operations to them. As terms, numbers must be able to participate in the unification process. But this participation requires a definition of equality (and thus inequality). The machine provides an operation for equality of numbers, and the interpreter ensures that no numeric object is equal to any nonnumeric term. Some systems support distinct floating point and integer representations, and perform various kinds of conversion between them before checking equality.

```
/* is(?Result, +Exp) evaluates the arithmetic expression
   represented by the term Exp and unifies the answer with
   Result. */
```

In CProlog all arithmetic computation can be done in a single evaluable predicate: **is**. A sequence of arithmetic operations is naturally expressed as an expression tree. Since trees are so easily represented in Prolog, we use a term to represent an arithmetic expression. For example, the terms **+(4, 5)** and **+(-(7, 2), *(4, 19))** represent the numeric expressions $4 + 5$ and $(7 - 2) + 4 * 19$, respectively, and can be written in the second way, since these operators are infix operators. The predicate **is(?X, +Exp)** evaluates the term tree that is the value of **Exp** (which must be ground and have only appropriate operators or else an error is reported), and unifies the numeric result of that computation with **X**. The symbol **is** is also an infix operator but has lower priority than any of the arithmetic operators.

EXAMPLE 8.3: A simple application of **is** is to find the average of a list of numbers:

```
/* avg(+List, ?Avg) if List is a nonempty list of numbers and Avg
   is the average of those numbers. */

avg(List, Avg) :- sumCount(List, Sum, Cnt), Avg is Sum/Cnt.


/* sumCount(+List, ?Sum, ?Cnt) if List is a list of numbers of
   length Cnt and Sum is their sum. */

sumCount([], 0, 0).
sumCount([N|L], Sum, Cnt) :-
      sumCount(L, Subsum, Subcnt),
      Sum is Subsum + N,
      Cnt is Subcnt + 1.
```

Notice that we could have written the final subgoal of the clause for **avg** as **is(Avg, /(Sum, Cnt))**, but the use of the infix notation makes the subgoal much more readable. □

```
/* =:=(+Exp1, +Exp2) if Exp1 evaluates to a number equal to the
   evaluation of Exp2. */

/* =\=(+Exp1, +Exp2) if Exp1 evaluates to a number not equal to
   the evaluation of Exp2. */

/* =<(+Exp1, +Exp2) if Exp1 evaluates to a number less than or
   equal to the evaluation of Exp2. */

/* >=(+Exp1, +Exp2) if Exp1 evaluates to a number greater than or
   equal to the evaluation of Exp2. */

/* <(+Exp1, +Exp2) if Exp1 evaluates to a number less than the
   evaluation of Exp2. */

/* >(+Exp1, +Exp2) if Exp1 evaluates to a number greater than the
   evaluation of Exp2. */
```

Prolog supports comparison of numbers through the use of evaluable predicates for comparisons. These predicates evaluate both of their operands, which must be ground numeric expressions, and succeed if the named relationship holds. The comparison predicates are =:=, =\=, =<, >=, <, and >, which mean, respectively, equal, not equal, less than or equal, greater than or equal, less than, and greater than. (The trick to remembering the >= and =< symbols is that they do *not* look like arrows.) The comparison predicates are all infix operators.

8.6. Control Convenience

Prolog provides several predicates that allow a programmer to specify more complex control within a single clause. Anything a programmer can do using these predicates can be done with other constructs in the language, so they are really only for the programmer's convenience.

```
/* true always succeeds. */

/* ;(+Goal1, +Goal2) succeeds if either Goal1 or Goal2 succeeds. */

/* ->(+Cond, +ThenGoal) performs if Cond then Goal.  If cond fails
   the entire goal fails. */
```

We have seen the evaluable predicates **fail**, which always fails, and **halt**, which terminates the entire Prolog session and returns to the operating system. The **true** predicate is the opposite of **fail**; it always succeeds. We used **fail** before to force backtracking to retrieve all answers. The predicate **true** is useful as a placeholder in the other control constructs described in this chapter.

Disjunction arises in Horn clause programming through multiple clauses in the definition of a predicate. In the definition of a predicate, however, it might be inconvenient to write several clauses when the disjunction needed is of a particularly simple kind. For example, consider defining a predicate for sad employees. Employees are sad if they make less than $10,000 or if they have taxes greater than 40% of their salary, no matter how much they make. Prolog provides a disjunction operator ';', and with this operator the predicate can be defined as follows:

```
sadSack(Name) :-
      employee(Name, Sal, Tax), (Sal < 10000 ; Tax > 0.40 * Sal).
```

This clause first retrieves a tuple from **employee**. It then checks if **Sal** is less than **10000** and succeeds if so. On backtracking it checks to see if **Tax** is greater than 40% of **Sal** and succeeds if so. Clearly this view could be written by defining another predicate with two clauses (how?), but the ';' seems simpler here. The ',' that links goals in a clause body can also be viewed as an infix operator on the subgoals. (See Exercise 8.9.) The priorities of the infix operators ',' and ';' are such that commas bind tighter than semicolons, so the extra parentheses are needed in **sadSack**.

The ';' predicate could be defined with the following clauses:

```
;(G1,G2) :- call(G1).
;(G1,G2) :- call(G2).
```

(By convention, we use the standard term notation when infix operators are being defined in the head of a clause. It is easier to see what the predicate name is.) If a cut is used within a ';' expression in a clause body, the cut eliminates the alternative set up by the operator and also any other alternatives set up since entry to the predicate, including later clauses.

The final control construct we discuss is '->', which functions as an "if-then" construct. Recall the example concerning "if-then-else" when we discussed **not**. Since "if-then-else" is so useful, Prolog supplies a special syntax for it. To evaluate the goal **p(X) -> q(X, Y)**, we first evaluate the goal **p(X)**. If it fails, the entire '->' goal fails; if it succeeds, then all alternatives set up in the evaluation of **p(X)** are cut away, and **q(X, Y)** is evaluated. The definition of '->' could be given as follows:

```
->(Cond, ThenGoal) :- call(Cond), !, call(ThenGoal).
```

When '->' is combined with a disjunction, ';', these predicates act like an "if-then-else" operation. Consider the definition:

```
t(X, Y) :-
        p(X)
        -> q(X, Y)
        ;  r(X, Y).
```

This definition is read as "**t(X, Y)** is if **p(X)** then **q(X, Y)** else **r(X, Y)**." The '->' has higher priority than the ';'. We prefer to format these operators as shown when using them to implement "if-then-else." This definition of **t(X, Y)** is exactly equivalent to the following one using multiple clauses and cut:

```
t(X, Y) :- p(X), !, q(X, Y).
t(X, Y) :- r(X, Y).
```

The clauses are exactly the ones given in the "if-then-else" Section 8.4 when introducing the cut. Notice that Prolog performs no check to ensure that **p(X)** is a ground term when called, so its evaluation could bind variables. The cut would still eliminate the alternatives set up during the evaluation of **p(X)**, and they are never tried. When unbound variables occur in the Boolean condition, the preceding definition is not equivalent to the definition using **not**, which should report an error.

8.7. Metaprogramming Features

The term *metaprogramming* refers to the use of programs as data (and data as programs). We saw an instance of metaprogramming in the evaluable predicate **call**, which takes a term and treats it as a literal to be evaluated. In all the programs we have written so far, we can understand a variable as standing for an as yet unknown object in the semantic domain. We need not think about whether a variable is bound or free at a particular time to understand a program. (If there is some problem with unbound variables—for example, with arithmetic predicates—the system gives an error message and the program aborts.) Another property of all the predicates we have written so far is the following: If we call a predicate with any pattern of variables and terms that gives an answer, then reinvoke it with the variables replaced by the answers from that call, the second call is guaranteed to succeed.

These properties follow from the inability of any predicates seen so far to test whether a program variable is currently instantiated. (But we could write such a predicate using cut. See Exercise 8.8.) Variables exist only in the language (not in the semantic domain), so if a program can determine whether a variable is unbound, it is determining something in the language itself, not something about the semantic domain. To write a program to manipulate other programs, a programmer must manipulate language constructs as the objects of interest without reference to what they might denote semantically. Prolog therefore provides evaluable predicates for manipulating terms, possibily containing unbound variables, as if they were domain objects. Those predicates treat variables as objects themselves, rather than as placeholders for other values. One particular predicate tests whether a variable has a binding. In this section we look at several evaluable predicates associated with metaprogramming.

8.7.1. *Term Testing and Comparison*

```
/* var(?Term) if Term dereferences to an unbound variable at the
   point of call. */

/* nonvar(?Term) if Term dereferences to something other than a
   variable. */

/* atom(?Term) if Term dereferences to a nonnumeric constant. */

/* number(?Term) if Term dereferences to a numeric constant. */
```

The evaluable predicate **var(Term)** succeeds if the argument, **Term**, is currently bound to a variable; otherwise, it fails. There is a complementary evaluable predicate **nonvar(Term)** that succeeds if **Term** is currently bound to a nonvariable term and fails if **Term** is instantiated to a variable.

EXAMPLE 8.4: The goal list:

```
var(X), X = a, nonvar(X).
```

succeeds. (The '=' goal succeeds if its arguments unify. It can be defined by the single fact **=(X, X)**.) As part of a top-level goal, **X** starts as a variable, so the **var(X)** succeeds; then **X** is bound to the atom **a** by the equality; then **nonvar(X)** succeeds, because now **X** is bound to the nonvariable term **a**. Notice that any reordering of the subgoals does not succeed. We have now moved beyond our logical semantics in which ',' means logical "and." In the presence of nonlogical predicates the order of the literals connected by ',' matters very much. □

EXAMPLE 8.5: Given the **is** evaluable predicate, we can write a version of the **sum** predicate that works if any two of its three arguments are bound:

```
sum(Op1, Op2, Sum) :- nonvar(Op1), nonvar(Op2), Sum is Op1 + Op2.
sum(Op1, Op2, Sum) :- nonvar(Op1), var(Op2), nonvar(Sum), Op2 is Sum - Op1.
sum(Op1, Op2, Sum) :- var(Op1), nonvar(Op2), nonvar(Sum), Op1 is Sum - Op2.
sum(Op1, Op2, Op3) :-
       ( var(Op1), var(Op2)
       ; var(Op1), var(Sum)
       ; var(Op2), var(Sum)
       ),
       write('Instantiation Error in sum'), nl,
       fail.
```

Since this particular definition uses explicit conditions on each clause to force determinacy, it does some redundant testing. We could use cuts instead as follows:

```
sum(Op1, Op2, Sum) :- nonvar(Op1), nonvar(Op2), !, Sum is Op1 + Op2.
sum(Op1, Op2, Sum) :- nonvar(Op1), nonvar(Sum), !, Op2 is Sum - Op1.
sum(Op1, Op2, Sum) :- nonvar(Op2), nonvar(Sum), !, Op1 is Sum - Op2.
sum(Op1, Op2, Sum) :-
       write('Instantiation Error in sum'), nl,
       fail.
```

Now, if any test succeeds, the cut is executed, and the later clauses are not tried. There is a third way to write this predicate, using a nested if-then-else:

```
sum(Op1, Op2, Sum) :-
       nonvar(Op1)
       -> (nonvar(Op2)
            -> Sum is Op1 + Op2
            ; nonvar(Sum)
              -> Op2 is Sum - Op1
              ; printerror)
       ; nonvar(Op2)
         -> (nonvar(Sum)
              -> Op1 is Sum - Op2
              ; printerror)
         ; printerror.
```

Here the cuts are implicit in the '->' operators. □

There are also other evaluable predicates to determine the current instantiation state of a program variable. The predicate **atom(Term)** succeeds if **Term** is instantiated to a nonnumeric constant. (Do not confuse this use of "atom" with its use for an unsigned literal.) The predicate **number (Term)** succeeds if **Term** is instantiated to a number.

EXAMPLE 8.6: We could use **number** instead of **nonvar** in the definition of **sum** in the previous example to weed out cases in which terms of the incorrect type are given. □

```
/* ==(?Term1, ?Term2) if Term1 is the same as Term2, without
   unification. */

/* \==(?Term1, ?Term2) if Term1 is not the same as Term2. */

/* @<(?Term1, ?Term2) if Term1 comes before Term2 in the term
   ordering. */

/* @>(?Term1, ?Term2) if Term1 comes after Term2 in the term
   ordering. */

/* @=<(?Term1, ?Term2) if Term1 comes before Term2 in the term
   ordering, or is the same as Term2. */

/* @>=(?Term1, ?Term2) if Term1 comes after Term2 in the term
   ordering, or is the same as Term2. */
```

Prolog defines an ordering on all terms and provides evaluable predicates for testing the order relationship of two terms. Variables, which are the "smallest" terms, are put in a standard order (by internal representation). Next are numbers, ordered in numeric order. Next are other constants, ordered alphabetically by name. Complex terms are the largest, ordered first by arity of the main function symbol, then alphabetically on the name of the main function symbol, and finally by the arguments in left-to-right order. The term comparison predicates are ==, \==, @<, @>, @=<, and @>=, which, respectively, mean equal, not equal, less than, greater than, less than or equal, and greater than or equal in the term ordering just described.

EXAMPLE 8.7: The goal list:

```
X = z, X @> a, Y = f(b), X @< Y.
```

succeeds. □

EXAMPLE 8.8: The top-level goal:

```
X == Y.
```

fails because **X** and **Y** are distinct variables, but the goal list:

```
X = Y, X == Y, g(X) == g(Y).
```

succeeds because **X** = **Y** makes **X** and **Y** the same variable, so now in **X == Y**, **X** and **Y** are both instantiated to the same variable. □

The == predicate is used to test whether two terms are identical, variables and all. This ability is necessary when manipulating programs as terms.

The term-comparison predicates are most often used for sorting constants into alphabetic order.

8.7.2. *Structure Manipulation*

To manipulate programs as data values, one must be able to construct terms from pieces and break complex terms into their subcomponents. Prolog provides predicates to perform these operations.

```
/* name(?Const, ?String) if String is the list of ascii codes of
   characters in the name of Const.  May not be called as
   name(-Const, -String). */

/* functor(?Term, ?Func, ?Arity) if the function symbol of Term
   has the same name as the constant Func and Arity arguments.
   May not be called as functor(-Term, ?Func, -Arity) or
   functor(-Term, -Func, ?Arity). */

/* arg(+N, +Term, ?Subterm) if Subterm unifies with the Nth
   argument of Term.  Term may contain variables. */

/* =..(?Term, ?SymbolList) if SymbolList is a list of symbols,
   consisting of the name of the function symbol of Term followed
   by its subterms in order.  May not be called as
   =..(-Term, -SymbolList). */
```

An important operation is constructing a constant from a character string. As discussed earlier, a character string in Prolog is represented as a list of ASCII integers. The predicate **name** converts between constants and strings. So **name(Const, String)** is true if the name of **Const** is the string **String**. This predicate will convert either way, but at least one of the arguments must be bound.

EXAMPLE 8.9: The goal:

```
name(abc, "abc").
```

succeeds, as does:

```
name(abc, [97, 98, 99]).
```

The goal list:

```
name(himom, String), String = [First|Rest], put(First), nl.
```

prints the first letter of the constant **himom**: **h**. □

EXAMPLE 8.10: The following definition allows the creation of a new constant name as the concatenation of the names of two other constants.

```
/* concatConsts(+Const1, +Const2, ?NewConst) if the name of NewConst
   is the result of concatenating the names of Const1 and Const2. */

concatConsts(A1, A2, A3) :-
      name(A1, L1),
      name(A2, L2),
      append(L1, L2, L3),          /* the usual append for lists */
      name(A3, L3).
```

For example, **concatConsts(hi, mom, X)** succeeds with **X = himom**. □

Occasionally, we need to break down and build up arbitrary structure records from their components. With the predicates so far, we can construct a record only if we know the structure symbol and can write it explicitly in the program. If the structure symbol is not known until the Prolog program is running, we have no way as yet to build a new term using that structure symbol. Prolog provides two evaluable predicates for manipulating arbitrary structured terms: **functor** and **arg**.

The evaluable predicate **functor** allows a programmer to determine the main function symbol of an arbitrary structure term and to construct such a term. To determine the function symbol of an arbitrary term, the programmer uses **functor(+Term, ?Func, ?Arity)**, which succeeds if **Func** is a constant with the same name as the function symbol of **Term** and if **Arity** is the arity of the function symbol. To construct an arbitrary term, the programmer uses **functor(-Term, +Func, +Arity)**, which succeeds, binding **Term** to a term with main function symbol **Func** and arity **Arity**. The **functor** predicate also works when **Term** is a constant or a number, in which case **Arity** is **0**. All the fields of the constructed term are distinct new variables.

EXAMPLE 8.11: The goal list:

```
Term = f(a, b, c), functor(Term, F, A).
```

succeeds with **F = f** and **A = 3**. The goal list:

```
F = str, A = 4, functor(Term, F, A).
```

succeeds with **Term = str(_1, _2, _3, _4)**. □

The evaluable predicate **arg** provides access to the subfields of an arbitrary term. A goal **arg(+N, +Term, ?Subterm)** succeeds by unifying **Subterm** with the Nth field of the complex structure **Term**. Using **arg**, a programmer can both retrieve and set a field of an arbitrary term.

EXAMPLE 8.12: The goal:

```
arg(3, f(a, b, c), Subterm).
```

succeeds with **Subterm = c**. The goal list:

```
Term = f(a, X, c), arg(2, Term, g(b)).
```

succeeds with **Term = f(a, g(b), c)**. □

EXAMPLE 8.13: With **functor** and **arg**, we can write a Prolog predicate that tests whether an arbitrary term is ground—that is, has no unbound variables.

```
/* ground(?Term) if Term is variable-free. */

ground(Term) :-
        nonvar(Term),
        functor(Term, Func, Arity),
        groundSubterms(Arity, Term).

groundSubterms(0, _).
groundSubterms(ArgNo, Term) :-
        ArgNo > 0,
        arg(ArgNo, Term, Subterm),
        ground(Subterm),
        NextArgNo is ArgNo - 1,
        groundSubterms(NextArgNo, Term).
```

The predicate **groundSubterms** processes the subterms "backward," from right-to-left, so that another argument is not necessary. The predicate **functor** handles constants as 0-ary functor symbols, so for constants, **groundSubterms** returns immediately. Note that if **Term** is an unbound variable, the **functor** goal is never called. □

Another metaprogramming predicate for manipulating terms is '=..', pronounced "univ." Univ converts a term into a list (and vice versa) such that the first element of the list is a constant representing the function symbol of the term and the remaining elements of the list are the fields of the term. The predicate '=..' is an infix operator.

EXAMPLE 8.14: The goal:

```
f(a, b, c) =.. [f, a, b, c].
```

succeeds. The goal list:

```
Term = g(1, h(a), c, d), Term =.. List.
```

succeeds with **List = [g, 1, h(a), c, d]**. The goal list:

```
List = [p, X, a], Term =.. List.
```

succeeds with something like **X = _17** and **Term = p(_17, a)**. □

The '=..' predicate is simply a convenience since it can be defined using **functor** and **arg**. (See Exercise 8.11.)

8.8. Lists of All Answers

Sometimes we need to collect all answers to a particular subgoal and have them all available to another goal. For example, say we have a predicate that returns answers and for each answer a number that represents a rating for that answer. (Recall Exercise 1.18 on Proplog with probabilities.) If we had a list of all pairs of answers and ratings, we could easily find the answer with the highest rating. But with only a goal that succeeds for such pairs, all a program can do is print out the sequence of pairs; there is no way for the program to compare one answer with another, choose the best answer, and continue computing, knowing it is computing with the best answer.

```
/* setof(?Template, +Goal, ?List) unifies List with the list of
   all instances of Template, where the bindings of variables in
   Template are answers to Goal.  Eliminates duplicates and sorts
   the list. */

/* bagof(?Template, +Goal, ?List) unifies List with the list of
   all instances of Template, where the bindings of variables in
   Template are answers to Goal.  Retains duplicates and does no
   sorting. */
```

Prolog has an evaluable metapredicate, **setof**, which collects all the answers to a subgoal into a list. When the goal **setof(Template, Goal, List)** succeeds, it binds **List** to a list of instances of **Template** whose variable bindings represent the set of answers obtained by invoking **Goal**. This metapredicate **setof** can exhibit rather complicated behavior, so we will explain its details through a series of graduated examples.

Assume the following simple database of facts:

```
p(a, 1).
p(a, 2).
```

```
p(b, 3).
p(b, 2).
p(b, 4).
```

The goal:

```
setof(X, p(b, X), L).
```

succeeds with **L** = **[2, 3, 4]**. The list **[2, 3, 4]** represents the *set of* answers to the call **p(b, X)**. They are in sorted order and all duplicates are eliminated. The template **X** determines how the answers will be represented in the resulting list. In this case each answer is a simple term—the term bound to **X** when the subgoal has succeeded.

The declarative semantics of **setof(T, Goal, L)** is that **L** is the *set of* **T**'s such that **Goal** is true.

We can also collect pairs of answers. If we use the same definition for **p**, the goal:

```
setof(pair(X, Y), p(X, Y), L).
```

succeeds with:

```
L = [pair(a, 1), pair(a, 2), pair(b, 2), pair(b, 3), pair(b, 4)]
```

Each element of the resulting list is an instance of the template, and they are sorted in the term order described in Section 8.7.1.

In these two examples all variables in the subgoal appear in the template. In this case the **setof** goal is determinate: it succeeds at most once. Consider the following goal:

```
setof(X, p(c, X), L).
```

This goal fails since the subgoal **p(c, X)** fails. Again, using the same definition for **p**, consider the following more complicated query:

```
setof(X, p(Y, X), L).
```

Notice that there is a variable (**Y**) in the goal that does not appear in the template. In this case **setof** is in general nondeterministic and may succeed in multiple ways—one for each binding of **Y**. In this case **setof** succeeds once with **Y** = **a** and **L** = **[1, 2]**, and then on backtracking succeeds a second time with **Y** = **b** and **L** = **[2, 3, 4]**. (**X** is not bound by this goal, nor by any of the earlier goals, and remains a variable.) This behavior of **setof** causes the two goals:

```
Y = a, setof(X, P(Y, X), L).
```

and:

```
setof(X, P(Y, X), L), Y = a.
```

to be the same. This desirable property is the reason that **setof** is made to fail when its subgoal fails, rather than return an empty list of answers.

EXAMPLE 8.15: We might want to collect all the answers on the second argument for **p** regardless of what the answer on the first argument is. One way to gather those answers is to define a subsidiary predicate, **psub**:

```
psub(X) :- p(Y, X).
```

and then use that predicate as the subgoal:

```
setof(X, psub(X), L).
```

which succeeds once with **L = [1, 2, 3, 4]**. Notice that duplicates are generated, but they are subsequently eliminated. □

There is another way to get the same result as in the last example by using the "exists" operator: '^'. This infix operator is useful only in the body of a **setof** (or **bagof**, described in the next example).

```
setof(X, Y^p(Y, X), L).
```

gives the same result as the previous example: **L = [1, 2, 3, 4]**. The infix operator '^' masks a variable in the subgoal, so that any binding for that variable is accepted when building the result list. The declarative reading of this goal is that **L** is the *set of* all **X**'s such that there *exists* a **Y** such that **p(Y, X)**.

Another more elementary predicate is also provided for collecting answers into a list: **bagof**. It is very similar to **setof** except that it does not sort its answers and does not eliminate duplicates.

EXAMPLE 8.16: Given the definition of **p**, the following **bagof** goals give the indicated results:

```
bagof(X, p(b, X), L).

X = _37
L = [3, 2, 4] ;
no

bagof(X, p(Y, X), L).

X = _37
Y = a
L = [1, 2] ;
```

```
X = _37
Y = b
L = [3, 2, 4] ;
no

bagof(X, Y^p(Y, X), L).

X = _37
Y = _52
L = [1, 2, 3, 2, 4] ;
no □
```

EXAMPLE 8.17: As an example of the use of **bagof**, we will use it to define a predicate to find the maximum number for which an arbitrary goal succeeds.

```
/* max(-X, ?Goal, -Max) if Max is the maximum X such that Goal
   is true. */

max(X, Goal, Max) :- bagof(X, Goal, [F|R]), maxNum(R, F, Max).


/* maxNum(+List, +CMax, ?Max) if Max is the maximum number in
   [CMax|List]. */

maxNum([], M, M).
maxNum([N|R], C, M) :- N =< C, maxNum(R, C, M).
maxNum([N|R], C, M) :- N > C, maxNum(R, N, M). □
```

8.9. Modifying the Program

One property of Prolog immediately evident to traditional programmers is the lack of global variables. In Prolog only the program database itself is global and so must contain whatever global state information a program requires.

For example, consider again the "Prologo" graphics system we sketched in Section 8.3, when discussing **call**. It would be appropriate to store the shape of the cursor globally in the program database. Then any command would simply call a predicate—say, **shape**—to determine the shape of the cursor when we need to draw it. We would like to support a command that allows the user of "Prologo" to change the cursor's shape whenever desired. To implement this command, Prolog must allow the program itself to change the Prolog database.

```
/* assert(+Clause) adds Clause to the program database. */

/* asserta(+Clause) adds Clause to the program database at the
   beginning of the appropriate predicate definition. */
```

```
/* assertz(+Clause) adds Clause to the program database at the
   end of the appropriate predicate definition. */

/* retract(+Clause) removes the clauses matching Clause from
   the program database. */
```

The predicate **assert(Clause)** adds the clause **Clause** to the database. It is deterministic and always succeeds. The change to the database is permanent, since it is *not* undone on backtracking. That is, a clause asserted into the database remains there throughout the entire Prolog session (or until it is explicitly removed). The clause is added to the sequence of clauses already present for this predicate. It is added at an undetermined point in that sequence, so the programmer cannot count on it being at the beginning or at the end. Two other closely related predicates are provided for when the ordering of the clauses is critical: **asserta** asserts the new clause as the first one; **assertz** asserts the new clause as the last one.

Another example of where **assert** could be used effectively is implementing a relational database in Prolog. The **assert** predicate would be used for inserting a new tuple into a relation. In this case **assert** would be applied only to ground facts, which is its most common use.

But **assert** can also be used to add facts (and even clauses) with variables in them. For example, consider the following query, executed in a database that does not contain any clauses for the predicate **p**:

```
Fact = p(a, X), assert(Fact), p(Y, b).
```

First, the variable **Fact** is bound to the term **p(a, X)**. Then **assert** uses this term to add a fact to the database: the fact **p(a, _X)**. Notice that here again, the function symbol **p** in the term represents the predicate symbol **p** in the fact. Also, the existential variable **X** in the term is used to represent a universal variable in the fact, here denoted by **_X** to stress that these are different, and unconnected, variables. The next goal in the query **P(Y, b)** now uses that just-added fact and succeeds binding **Y** = **a**, with **b** matching **_X**. The entire goal list succeeds with **Y** = **a** and **X** still unbound. Subsequent goals submitted by the user would execute in the database that includes the fact **p(a, _X)**, since that fact remains even if the **assert** is backtracked over.

In the preceding query notice that, after the **assert** goal, we could bind **X** to some arbitrary term. Doing so would not change the asserted fact. However, binding **X** to the term before calling **assert** would clearly change the fact that gets added to the database. The way to understand this behavior is to imagine that a copy of the current instantiation of the argument to **assert** is made and the copy is added to the database as a new clause.

The dual evaluable predicate in Prolog is **retract**, which removes clauses from the Prolog database. The goal **retract(Clause)** removes from the database the first clause that matches the argument **Clause**. If such a clause exists, the goal succeeds. If there is no matching clause in the database, **retract** fails. It is non-deterministic: on backtracking, if there is another matching clause in the database,

retract removes it and succeeds; and so on until there are no more matching clauses, at which point it fails.

These predicates, **assert** and **retract**, are normally used to insert and delete facts from the database, but they do apply to rules as well. The semantics of such programs, however, can be very complicated, since through this facility, a program can modify itself while it is running. The most appropriate use of these predicates is to maintain rarely changing "environment" information—information that provides an environment for the other predicates to run in, or that several "unrelated" predicates must share.

EXAMPLE 8.18: The predicates **assert** and **retract** together can be used to simulate global variables and assignment. Say we want to maintain a global counter, perhaps to count certain kinds of events that may occur anywhere in the program, such as the number of lines printed to a file. Another use of such a global counter is to be able to generate a unique number that is guaranteed to be distinct from other such generated numbers: a "gensym" facility. The current value of the counter will be kept in a predicate **counter**, which will always have at most one fact. We will have two predicates to manipulate the counter: **initCntr**, which will initialize the counter to **0**, and **bumpCntr**, which will retrieve the current value of the counter and add 1 to it.

```
/* initCntr sets the global counter, counter, to 0. */

initCntr :-
      (counter(X)
       -> retract(counter(X))
       ;  true),
      assert(counter(0)).

/* bumpCntr(?Cnt) if Cnt is the current value of the global counter.
   As a side effect, it increments the counter. */

bumpCntr(Cnt) :-
      retract(counter(Cnt)),
      NewCnt is Cnt + 1,
      assert(counter(NewCnt)). □
```

From this last example we can easily see how **assert** and **retract** can simulate global variables and traditional destructive assignment. Although there are cases in which such a simulation is called for, we have good reasons to try to find ways to avoid such a use. First, **assert** and **retract** are procedural extensions to Prolog. They operate as permanent side effects of the proof procedure used by the Prolog interpreter, and as such, they have no logical declarative semantics. Programs that use these operators indiscriminately can be extremely hard to understand; the only way to understand them is as procedural programs. Second, because **assert** and **retract** are very general and in effect allow arbitrary modification of a program, they are quite inefficient. Programs written in pure Horn clause logic are almost always more efficient than "equivalent" ones written using **assert** and **retract**.

EXAMPLE 8.19: A well-known evaluable predicate for collecting all answers to a goal is called **findall**. Here we will use **assert** and **retract** to implement **findall**. It is similar in function to **bagof** but slightly more primitive. Recall that **bagof(Template, Goal, List)** succeeds if **List** is the list of answers (formatted as in **Template**) to the query **Goal**. The **findall** predicate differs from **bagof** only in that it treats all variables in **Goal** that are not in the template as existentially quantified. As a result it is deterministic. It also differs in that if there are no answers to the subgoal, it succeeds with the empty answer list. Therefore, it always succeeds exactly once.

The program calls the subgoal; each time it succeeds, it asserts an answer in the database. After all the answers have been collected, the program builds a list of the answers while removing them from the database.

```
/* findall(?Template, +Goal, ?List) if List is the list of instances
   of Template for which Goal succeeds.  Goal may not use findall
   itself. */

findall(Template, Goal, List) :-
      assertAnswers(Template, Goal),
      collectAnswers(ComputedAnswers),
      List = ComputedAnswers.


/* assertAnswers(?Template, +Goal) calls Goal and asserts Template
   into the database for success. It always succeeds. */

assertAnswers(Template, Goal) :-
      call(Goal),
      assertz(answerFact(Template)),
      fail.
assertAnswers(_, _).


/* collectAnswers(-List) collects answers from the database,
   deleting them as it goes. List must be a variable to insure that
   all answers are indeed deleted. */

collectAnswers([AnAnswer|List]) :-
      retract(answerFact(AnAnswer)),
      !,
      collectAnswers(List).
collectAnswers([]).
```

The predicate **assertAnswers** uses **assertz** to ensure that the order of answers is correctly maintained. The effects of **assert** (and friends) must be retained over backtracking. The second clause of **assertAnswers** is just to force it to succeed after it has finished asserting all answers. In **collectAnswers**, the cut is necessary since we want to remove just one answer; subsequent (recursive) invocations of **collectAnswers** will remove the rest. With this implementation a subgoal in a **findall** cannot itself use **findall**. If it did, the two would interfere with each other's use of the global predicate **answerFact**. (See Exercise 8.15). □

This example shows a common "local" use of **assert** and **retract**. In Prolog there are two ways to do iteration: recursion and nondeterminism. For example, to print out a list of terms, we could use recursion:

```
/* printList(?L): print list L recursively */

printList([]).
printList([T|L]) :- write(T), nl, printList(L).
```

or we could use nondeterminism:

```
/* printList(?L): print list L using nondeterminism */

printList(L) :- member(X, L), write(X), nl, fail.
printList(L).


/* member(?E, ?L) if E is a member of list L, used here to
   generate all members nondeterministically.  */

member(X, [X|L]).
member(X, [Y|L]) :- member(X, L).
```

When it is possible to use the nondeterminism for iteration, that approach is usually more space efficient, since the failure reclaims space. So all the stack space used in the "body" of the loop, here just **write** and **nl**, is automatically reclaimed for each new iteration. In the recursive case that space is not reclaimed but accumulates. But notice that nondeterminism can be used only when the effect of "body" of the iteration is entirely a side effect; no information can be passed out of a particular iteration on to the next one. Anything done in the body is "forgotten" when failing back for the next iteration.

There are cases in which the body of the loop is very complex but requires only some small amount of information to be passed from one iteration to the next. In this case a recursive loop could be written and the information returned from one iteration can be passed directly on to the next. Alternatively a nondeterministic loop (sometimes called a *repeat-fail* loop) could be used, and **assert** could be used to pass the information from one iteration to the next.

Other evaluable predicates are also commonly found in Prolog. We have given here a representative selection of the kinds of evaluable predicates found, and it should provide an adequate basis for understanding the workings of the others.

8.10. EXERCISES

8.1. Use the evaluable predicate **read** in your Prolog system to read in the input **.(a, .(b, []))** and then use **write** to write it. What is written? Find other examples in which the characters that are read are different from the ones written.

8.2. Use the evaluable predicates of this section to define a backtrackable read operation. A backtrackable read is one that can be thought of as resetting the current position in the file when it is backtracked over.

8.3. Discuss pros and cons of using **call** in the implementation of a command processor, such as "Prologo," versus an explicit predicate such as **callCommand**.

8.4. Give clauses to define the predicate **printList**.

8.5 a. Modify the definition of **callLoop** of Example 8.1 so that if there are no variables in a query, and the query succeeds, then '**yes**' is printed once, and if the query fails, '**no**' is printed.

b. Extend that definition to ask the user after each answer whether more answers are wanted. Interpret a return as a request to quit and a ';' followed by a return as a request for another answer.

c. Using cut, further modify **callLoop** so that if **read** returns **end_of_file** instead of a query, **callLoop** is exited.

8.6. In the refined definition of **callLoop** of Example 8.2, when the user enters a return, the program could simply invoke **callLoop** again, recursively. Why is this approach not a good idea?

8.7. Give a pure Horn clause definition of the evaluable predicate **fail**.

8.8. Define **var(X)** using only cut and pure Horn clauses. (Hint: Only a variable can be bound to two distinct constants.)

8.9. An interpreter for Prolog goals written in Prolog might include the following definition of ',':

```
call(','(A, B)) :- call(A), call(B).
```

This clause defines the comma operator as conjunction. Consider using this clause, such as in the goal **call(','(p(X), q(X)))**. The infix comma operator is written as prefix to emphasize that it will match the head of the given clause. Normally this term would be written as **(p(X), q(X))**. This goal matches the given clause, so first **p(X)** would be called, and if that succeeds, then **q(X)** would be called. Backtracking would proceed normally. What would be the problem if we gave the goal: **call(','(p(X), !))**? Could we give a clause (or several) to define **call** to handle this case correctly?

8.10. Define a metaprogramming predicate **freeVariables(?Term, -VarList)** where **VarList** is the list of unbound variables in **Term**.

8.11. Define the evaluable predicate '=..' using **arg** and **functor**.

8.12. Write a definition for the predicate **max** that does not take space proportional to the number of elements, by using **assert** and **retract** directly.

8.13. Consider a general aggregate predicate:

```
aggregate(+Template, +Goal, ?List)
```

where **List** is a copy of **Template** except that where **Template** has a subterm **max(X)** (**min(X)**, **sum(X)**, **count(X)**), **List** has the maximum (respectively, minimum, sum, number) of the values of **X** for which **Goal** succeeds. The **aggregate** predicate is similar to **setof** in that it succeeds once for each set of values for the variables appearing in **Goal** and not in **Template**. For example, given the facts:

```
p(1, 2, 3).
p(5, 6, 7).
p(1, 2, 7).
p(2, 6, 7).
```

the goal:

```
aggregate(ans(max(X), sum(Y), count(X)), p(X, Y, Z), List).
```

succeeds once with **List = ans(1, 2, 1)** and **Z = 3**, and a second time with **List = ans(5, 14, 3)** and **Z = 7**.
Use **bagof** to implement **aggregate**.

8.14. Consider the two goals:

```
X = a, setof(Y, p(X, Y), L).
```

and

```
setof(Y, p(X, Y), L), X = a.
```

Assuming **p** is defined just by facts, do these two goal lists always produce the identical results? How about the two goals:

```
Y = 2, setof(Y, p(X, Y), L).
```

and:

```
setof(Y, p(X, Y), L), Y = 2.
```

Do these goal lists always produce the same answers, given the same facts for **p**? (Hint: Consider the database of just the two facts **p(U, 2).** and **p(V, 2).**)

8.15. Fix the definition of **findall** to allow for embedded calls. (Hint: Change the definition given in the text to use **asserta** and then use the predicate **findallAnswers** as a "stack.)"

8.16. Can you define **findall** without using **assert** or **retract**? Why or why not?

8.17. Write a Prolog program to simulate the entire traffic light example of Section 1.3.1. Use **assert** and **retract** to modify the program database when the value of a sensor or the state of a light changes. Use a repeat-fail loop as the main driver.

8.18. Consider a program database of facts of the form:

```
sched(Course, Section, Days, StartTime, EndTime)
```

that gives the schedule of all sections of courses at a college. **Days** is a list of days the section meets, and **StartTime** and **EndTime** give the starting and ending times using terms of the form **time(Hour, Minutes, AMorPM)**. A section of a course meets at the same time on all days it meets. Section numbers are unique throughout the database (not just within a course).

a. Give the definition for a predicate:

```
noConflict(Section1, Section2)
```

that is true if the scheduled times for **Section1** and **Section2** do not overlap.

b. Write a predicate:

```
makeSched(CourseList, SectionList)
```

that selects a list of nonconflicting sections given the list of courses a student wants. Use metaprogramming predicates in your definition, so that it constructs a list of **sched** and **noConflict** goals, then calls the goals in that list. Make sure that two sections are checked for conflict as soon as they are bound. That is, after the two goals **sched(C1, S1, _, _, _)** and **sched(C2, S2, _, _, _)**, a **noConflict(S1, S2)** goal should immediately follow.

c. Modify the definition of **makeSched** so that the next **sched** goal to solve is chosen dynamically (at run time). The choice should be made on the basis of which course has the fewest sections remaining that do not conflict with sections picked so far.

8.19. The "Four Fours" problem is to see how many integers can be represented by an arithmetic expression involving four occurrences of the numeral 4, and arbitrary numbers of the operators '+', '−' (unary and binary), '*', '/', '^' (exponentiation), '.' (decimal point), and juxtaposition (such as '44'). Parentheses are also allowed. Write a Prolog predicate **fourFours(Exp, Value)** that is true if **Exp** is an expression as just described and **Value** is its value.

Your predicate definition should have a generate and test structure, so that it can be called with **Exp** unbound. One possible approach is to use a regular expression to generate sequences of symbols with four 4's and all possibilities of intervening operators, then to parse the sequences and accept the ones representing legally formed expressions.

8.11. COMMENTS AND BIBLIOGRAPHY

We have now seen almost the entire Prolog programming language. The standard introduction to the full Prolog programming language is Clocksin and Mellish [8.1]. Other texts on the Prolog language and its use are fast becoming available [8.2, 8.3].

This chapter developed various extensions to pure Horn clause programming that have been deemed necessary for solving practical problems. Each particular Prolog implementation has its own set of evaluable predicates, which are described in the language manuals (for example [8.4–8.7]).

Research effort has gone into trying to understand various sets of evaluable predicates in a more logical framework. Bowen and Kowalski [8.8] begin to develop a framework in which the metalogical evaluable predicates could be given a logical semantics. The **setof** operator has also been the object of study [8.9, 8.10]. Warren [8.11] explores a more logical alternative to **assert**.

8.1. W. F. Clocksin and C. S. Mellish, *Programming in Prolog,* Springer Verlag, Berlin, 1981.

8.2. W. D. Burnham and A. R. Hall, *Prolog Programming and Applications,* John Wiley and Sons, New York, 1985.

8.3. L. Sterling and E. Shapiro, *The Art of Prolog,* MIT Press, Cambridge, MA, 1986.

8.4. *DECsystem-10 Prolog User's Manual,* Department of Artificial Intelligence, University of Edinburgh, Scotland, 1983.

8.5. *CProlog User's Manual,* version 1.5, F. Pereira (ed.), EdCAAD, Department of Architecture, University of Edinburgh, Scotland, 1984.

8.6. *Quintus Prolog Reference Manual,* Quintus Computer Systems, Inc., Mountain View, CA, 1986.

8.7. *The Arity/Prolog Programming Language,* Arity Corporation, Concord, MA, 1986.

8.8. K. A. Bowen and R. A. Kowalski, Amalgamating language and metalanguage in logic programming, in [7.2], 153–72.

8.9. D. H. D. Warren, Higher-order extensions to Prolog: Are they needed?, in *Machine Intelligence 10,* D. Michie, J. Hayes, and Y.H. Pao (eds.), Ellis Horwood Limited, Chichester, England, 1981, 441–54.

8.10. L. Naish, All solutions predicates in Prolog, *Proc. Symposium on Logic Programming,* Boston, 1985, 73–77.

8.11. D. S. Warren, Database updates in pure Prolog, *Proc. Int. Conference on Fifth Generation Computing Systems,* Tokyo, 1984, 244–53.

9

Functional Logic

The structure of this chapter follows that of the previous chapters on logic. After presenting a logic for Prolog, we consider its generalization to *functional logic*—predicate logic with function symbols. Interpretations will now have to assign meanings to structured terms, not just constants. From a programming language point of view, terms are rather special data structures. They are unlike records in other languages, since they contain unbound variables. Other languages require data structures to be completely defined, but they allow programs to update them arbitrarily. Logic languages allow partially defined structures, but the only modification that they allow is instantiation of unbound variables. The benefit of their limited modifiability is that we can reason about terms more easily than unrestricted record structures. In most languages with records and pointers, a statement can change the value of a variable in arbitrary ways without actually mentioning the variable. In logic languages we know that any structure bound to a variable will change only in a limited way. Hence such structures have a simpler formal semantics than arbitrary records.

The meaning of a term will derive from the interpretation of its function symbol. That interpretation will be a function that maps a list of field values into another value. For example, the **enrollment** function symbol in **enrollment(Student, Course)** can be interpreted as a function that maps a student and a course to an enrollment object. Two functions can have the same domain in general. For example, the interpretations of **cartesian** in **cartesian(Num1, Num2)** and **polar** in **polar(Radius, Angle)** might both be functions whose range is points in the plane.

The interpretation of a ground term will thus be the domain element obtained by applying the interpretation of the function symbol to the interpretation of the arguments. How do we reconcile this view of a term as a function application in the formal semantics with the treatment of a term as a data structure by the interpreter? The key is the use of Herbrand interpretations again, which will be sufficient for examining satisfiability. In predicate logic a Herbrand interpretation assumed all constants are mapped to distinct domain elements. For functional logic, a Herbrand interpretation will assume that all function applications give rise to distinct domain values. That is, different terms cannot have identical meanings. With this restriction we can just let the term itself name its value, which is what justifies the treatment of terms as data structures rather than as expressions that the interpreter must evaluate. An advantage of the restriction to Herbrand interpretations is that a single logical operation—unification—provides a formal basis for both building data structures and selecting their components.

Why is this restriction on the meaning of terms permissible in connection with implication? The reason is that our logic cannot express the equality of two different function applications, such as **cartesian(0, 1)** and **polar(1, 90)**. Thus there is always some model where the equality does not hold, so it cannot be used in a deduction. (There are logics with equality, which give rise to more complicated deduction systems. Functional programming languages can be cast as logic languages with equality and no other predicates.) For purposes of reasoning, applications of two different function symbols always yield different results, and the application of the same function symbol to different arguments yields different results. Thus the application expression itself can represent the result.

Since general terms may contain variables, they are templates, and can be viewed as a type description for a set of ground terms. Since function symbols can be nested arbitrarily, a term can represent an infinite number of ground terms. While domains could be infinite in predicate logic, we could only talk about a finite number of elements by name, so the Herbrand universe could be finite. Now we will be forced to have an infinite Herbrand universe—all ground terms that can be built from the function symbols and constants.

Since the universe is infinite, the Herbrand base is infinite. We need to reconsider our basis for resolution theorem proving to see how it depended on finiteness. We must re-prove Herbrand's Theorem, allowing for infinite semantic trees. A refutation proof will always exist for an unsatisfiable set of clauses, but there is no general procedure to determine if a set of clauses is satisfiable. Previously, the number of possible resolvents for a clause set was finite, so if no refutation existed, we would eventually detect that fact. In functional logic there may be an infinite number of resolvents. There is no way to know when to stop looking for a derivation of the empty clause. Hence implication is semidecidable: there is a procedure that will correctly answer yes when one formula implies another, but that procedure may never halt when the implication does not hold.

Substitutions are fancier in functional logic and unification is more complicated, because we have to match complex record structures instead of just constants and variables. However, full logic does allow conversion of an arbitrary formula to an equivalent formula in clausal form. (Here "equivalent" will be something slightly weaker than "logically equivalent.") We can use a function symbol to construct unique names for existential variables and let the logical structure "choose" the right domain element instead of the quantifier.

The chapter concludes with a reexamination of model elimination in the presence of terms and variables.

9.1. Functional Logic for Prolog

9.1.1. *Formal Syntax of Prolog*

We do not give a complete grammar for the Prolog syntax here, since it is so close to that for Datalog. Rather, we will simply add one production to the Datalog grammar in Figure 5.1:

TERM → csym (ARGLIST)

where *csym* is the syntactic category for constant symbols. (This usage is reasonable, because we have viewed constants as 0-ary function symbols before.) Figure 9.1 shows a derivation of a literal in the extended grammar.

Note that in this new grammar a literal is syntactically indistinguishable from a term. If we choose an identical internal representation for them in the interpreter, built-in predicates that convert between code and data, such as **call**, are easier to implement. Clauses can even be represented as terms with the head and body as arguments. (See Exercise 9.1.)

9.1.2. *Semantics for Prolog*

The semantics for Prolog is the same as for Datalog with the exception of how we form the base for a program. Rather than the domain being a finite set of constants from a program, we use all terms formed from the function symbols and constants.

Let P be a Prolog program. Let F_P be all the constant and function symbols appearing in P (but not predicate symbols). The *domain* of P, $\mathbf{D}_P$, is the set of all terms we can form from symbols in F_P. We respect the arity of function symbols in forming $\mathbf{D}_P$. For example, if **k** appears in P as a two-place function symbol, then **k(c, a)**, but not **k(c)** or **k(c, a, b)**, might be a term $\mathbf{D}_P$. If F_P contains any function symbols that are not constants, then $\mathbf{D}_P$ is infinite. The *base* of P, B_P, is, as before, the set of all instantiations of literals in P using terms in $\mathbf{D}_P$.

EXAMPLE 9.1: For the Prolog program P =

```
p(d(X, Y), e(Y)) :- q(X, Y), r(e(X)).
q(a, d(a, b)).
q(d(b, a), b).
r(e(d(Z, W))) :- s(Z, e(W)).
s(b, e(X)).
s(e(X), b).
```

LITERAL ⇒ **p** (ARGLIST) ⇒ **p** (TERM ARGTAIL) ⇒
p (TERM , ARGLIST) ⇒ **p** (TERM , TERM ARGTAIL) $\overset{*}{\Rightarrow}$
p (TERM , TERM) ⇒ **p** (**add** (ARGLIST) , TERM) $\overset{*}{\Rightarrow}$
p (**add** (TERM , TERM) , TERM) $\overset{*}{\Rightarrow}$ **p** (**add** (**Y** , **four**) , **X**)

Figure 9.1

the set of symbols (with arities) is F_P =

{a/0, b/0, d/2, e/1}

and some of the terms of $\mathbf{D}_P$ are:

```
a, b, e(a), e(b),
d(a, a), d(a, b), d(b, a), d(b, b),
e(e(a)), e(e(b)),
e(d(a, a)), e(d(a, b)), e(d(b, a)), e(d(b, b),
d(e(a), a), d(e(b), a), d(d(a, a), a),...
```

Some of the literals in B_P are:

```
p(d(a, a), e(a)), q(a, a), r(e(a)),
p(d(e(e(a)), e(b)), q(e(a), e(b)), r(e(d(e(a), d(b, b)))),...
```

but **p(e(a), d(a, a))** is not in B_P, and neither are infinitely many other literals. □

The remainder of the semantics of Prolog is identical to that of Datalog: V is the set of all possible Prolog variables. An *instantiation* I for P is a function from V to $\mathbf{D}_P$. I is extended to entire clauses in the obvious way. Thus an instantiation maps program clauses to ground instances of those clauses.

EXAMPLE 9.2: Let I be an instantiation for program P in the last example, with I(**Z**) = **e(a)** and I(**W**) = **b**. Then:

I(**r(e(d(Z, W))) :- s(Z, e(W)).**) =
  r(e(d(e(a), b))) :- s(e(a), e(b)). □

A *truth assignment* for program P maps B_P to {**true, false**}. Ground literals formed from P are sentence templates containing noun-phrase templates in which all the slots are filled. A ground literal is hence just a proposition and can be classified as true or false in a particular world. We get a meaning function M_{TA} from truth assignment TA for P just as with Datalog: M_{TA} maps ground facts and ground instances of rules to {**true, false**}. Recall that a ground instance of a rule is mapped to false only if the head literal is mapped to false and all the literals of the body are mapped to true. M_{TA} is extended to arbitrary clauses including variables as before, with:

$M_{TA}(C)$ = **true** if and only if, for every instantiation I, $M_{TA}(I(C))$ = **true**.

Thus a Prolog clause is true if all its ground instances are true.

EXAMPLE 9.3: Evaluating a meaning function in Prolog is a grander undertaking than evaluating such a function in Datalog. Instantiations cannot be divided into a finite number of equivalence classes on the basis of where they map program variables, since the range of instantiations, $\mathbf{D}_P$, may now be infinite.

Consider the clause C =

```
p(d(X, Y), e(Y)) :- q(X, Y), r(e(X)).
```

from program P in Example 9.1. Let TA be a truth assignment for B_P that assigns **false** to exactly those literals that contain **e(b)** as a subterm. Then $M_{TA}(C)$ = **false**: The instantiation I where $I(\mathbf{X})$ = **a** and $I(\mathbf{Y})$ = **b** yields the ground clause $I(C)$ =

```
p(d(a, b), e(b)) :- q(a, b), r(e(a)).
```

and $M_{TA}(I(C))$ = **false**, since the head literal contains **e(b)** as a subterm and so is mapped to **false**, while the two body literals do not and so are both mapped to **true**.

As another example, let TA' be the truth assignment for B_P that assigns **true** to exactly those literals that contain **e(a)** as a subterm. Then $M_{TA'}(C)$ = **true**, as the following reasoning shows. For $M_{TA'}(I(C))$ to be **false**, we must have:

$M_{TA'}(I($**p(d(X, Y), e(Y))**$)$ = **false**.

Thus a falsifying I cannot map **X** or **Y** to any term containing **e(a)**, nor can it map **Y** to **a**. But for any such I:

$M_{TA'}(I($**q(X, Y)**$)$ = **false**,

so I makes the rule as a whole true. □

The definitions of *model* and *logically implies* are essentially the same as before. M_{TA} makes a Prolog program P true if it makes every clause in P true. A truth assignment TA for which $M_{TA}(P)$ = **true** is a *model* for P. Let g be a goal list of literals. P *logically implies* g if in every model TA for P plus g, $M_{TA}(g)$ = **true**. As in Datalog, for a goal list g, $M_{TA}(g)$ = **true** if for some instantiation I, $M_{TA}(I(g))$ = **true**.

EXAMPLE 9.4: The program P in Example 9.1 logically implies the literal **p(d(d(b, a), b), e(b))**, since any model TA for P must make the following ground clauses true

```
p(d(d(b, a), b), e(b)) :- q(d(b, a), b), r(e(d(b, a))).
q(d(b, a), b).
r(e(d(b, a)) :- s(b, e(a)).
s(b, e(a)).
```

Simple propositional resolution shows that:

$M_{TA}($**p(d(d(b, a), b), e(b))**$)$ = **true**,

which is sufficient, since I(**p(d(d(b, a), b), e(b))**) = **p(d(d(b, a), b), e(b))** for any instantiation I. □

9.2. Full Functional Logic

In this section we develop functional logic, which subsumes Prolog, just as predicate logic subsumed Datalog. We examine the full logic for the same reasons as in Chapters 2 and 5: It is a natural superset of the logic for Prolog and allows arbitrary combination of the logical connectives. In particular we see quantification in its full generality. In Prolog the quantification on clauses is implicit. The novel concept going from predicate logic to functional logic is function symbols. The semantics we will develop shortly for this logic will thus have to extend predicate logic semantics by providing a meaning for complex terms. In predicate logic the meaning of a simple term (a constant) is some element in the domain of the structure. Similarly, the meaning of a complex term is some element in the domain of the structure. The meaning of a function symbol must tell us how to obtain some domain element given the domain elements that are its arguments. Such an animal is simply (and not surprisingly) a function. So the meaning of an n-ary function symbol in a structure is an n-ary function of domain elements to a single domain element. Thus, given the meaning of each function symbol in a complex (possibly nested) ground term, we can use those functions to evaluate the term to a single domain element.

This interpretation of function symbols and terms fits in with some of our previous examples. Consider the term:

```
mult(add(5, 3), 4)
```

Let's take the domain of interpretation to be the integers, with the constants **3**, **4**, and **5** representing the obvious elements of that domain. Then a possible interpretation of the symbol **mult** is the multiplication function—that function we all spent so much time memorizing when we were young. The symbol **add** can be interpreted as the addition function. The domain element that is the meaning of this complex term, under this interpretation, is the integer 32.

There are other interpretations we could choose; we could let the symbol **mult** be the function that returns its first argument, ignoring its second, and let **add** be integer subtraction. The value of the term under this interpretation is 2.

We can also change the underlying domain of the structure. For example, we can interpret the term over the domain of integers modulo 6, with **3**, **4**, and **5** representing the appropriate residue classes. Then we might let the symbol **mult** stand for multiplication modulo 6 and let the symbol **add** be addition modulo 6. With this interpretation the preceding term evaluates to the residue class of 2.

There are other examples in which interpreting function symbols as functions may seem a bit odd, as in:

```
cons(a, cons(b, cons(c, nil)))
```

We have regarded this term as just a record structure over constants **a**, **b**, **c**, and **nil**. Perhaps the most natural way to interpret such terms is to choose as the domain some set of elements plus all finite lists over those elements. Then the binary function symbol **cons** is interpreted as a function that maps an element and a list to another list—the list obtained by prefixing the given element to the given list. The constant symbol **nil** would be mapped to the empty list in this domain. Of course, other choices of interpretation are possible; nothing prevents choosing the integers as the domain of interpretation and letting **cons** be addition.

9.2.1. *Syntax of Functional Logic*

We consider the formal syntax of functional logic expressions no more than to note that we obtain a grammar for functional logic by augmenting the grammar for predicate logic in Figure 5.3 with the production:

TERM → csym (ARGLIST)

This production is the same one we added to form the Prolog grammar. All other aspects of scoping and precedence carry over unchanged from predicate logic.

9.2.2. *Semantics for Functional Logic*

Structures for functional logic formulas will be similar to those for predicate logic, except we extend the constant mapping component to give meaning to function symbols as well. Thus, to interpret a functional logic formula f, we must first choose a domain **D**. Let Fun_f be the set of all function symbols in f, treating constants as 0-ary function symbols. A *function mapping* for f under **D**, denoted $F_\mathbf{D}$, maps symbols in Fun_f to functions over **D** of the appropriate arity. Thus, if **k** is an n-ary function symbol in Fun_f, then $F_\mathbf{D}[\mathbf{k}]$ is a function from $\mathbf{D}^n$ to **D**. (We use brackets when applying $F_\mathbf{D}$ for readability.) That is, $F_\mathbf{D}[\mathbf{k}]$ is a function that maps n-tuples of domain elements to a single domain element. If **k** is a 0-ary symbol, then $F_\mathbf{D}[\mathbf{k}]$ is a 0-ary function, which we treat as simply an element in **D**.

EXAMPLE 9.5: Here is a formula f that intuitively means the sum of two squares can be factored.

```
∀X ¬(∃Y ∃Z
      equal(add(mult(Y, Y), mult(Z, Z)), X), ¬equal(X, zero),
            ¬equal(add(Y,Z), one));
      ∃U ∃V
            equal(mult(U, V), X), ¬equal(U, one), ¬equal(V, one)
```

"Intuitively" means here "under the intended interpretation." This intended interpretation is the structure in which the domain is the nonnegative integers, and $F_\mathbf{D}$ is as follows:

$F_\mathbf{D}[\mathbf{zero}] = 0$
$F_\mathbf{D}[\mathbf{one}] = 1$

F_D[**mult**] = integer multiplication
F_D[**add**] = integer addition

Also, as expected, **equal** is true of a pair of integers if they are the same integer. With this interpretation the formula says that if **X** is nonzero and is the sum of the squares of two integers that do not sum to one, then **X** is the product of two integers, neither of which is one. Note that f is not a true statement about integers under this interpretation.

However, we can also consider other structures in which to interpret the formula. Let the domain and the interpretation of **equal** be as before. Consider F'_D where:

F'_D[**zero**] = 0
F'_D[**one**] = 1
F'_D[**mult**] = integer multiplication
F'_D[**add**] = monus

For integers i and j, i monus j is i minus j if $i > j$ and 0 otherwise. That is, monus is subtraction where would-be negative results are zero instead. Under this interpretation our formula has a different meaning. It says that for any integer **X**, if **X** is nonzero and the difference of the squares of two numbers that differ by other than one, then **X** is the product of two integers, neither of which is one. (Is f true with this interpretation?) □

With the foregoing example as intuition, we now proceed to a more formal development of the notions of structure, truth, and model. The *base* of a formula f, relative to a domain **D** and a function mapping F_D, denoted B_{f,D,F_D}, is defined as follows. Take any atom A appearing in f. We must reduce the terms that are arguments of A to elements of **D**. We first choose an instantiation I that maps variables to domain elements in **D**. We want to evaluate terms from A using F_D and I to get elements from **D**. We introduce an *evaluation function* $E_{F_D,I}$ that maps terms to domain elements. Whenever we encounter a variable, we will apply I to it to get a domain element. Whenever we have a constant, we use F_D to map it to a domain element. Thus:

$E_{F_D,I}(\mathbf{X}) = I(\mathbf{X})$ for a variable **X**, and
$E_{F_D,I}(\mathbf{c}) = F_D(\mathbf{c})$ for a constant **c**.

Note that we had an implicit evaluation function for predicate logic terms. We did not introduce one explicitly, as we had only the preceding two cases. For functional logic, we have another case, where the term is a complex one. Let t be the term $\mathbf{k}(t_1, t_2, \ldots, t_n)$. That is, t is a term with n-ary function symbol **k** and whose arguments are terms $t_1, t_2, \ldots, t_n$. Then:

$$E_{F_D,I}(t) = F_D[\mathbf{k}](E_{F_D,I}(t_1), E_{F_D,I}(t_2), \ldots, E_{F_D,I}(t_n)).$$

Thus we apply the interpretation of function symbol **k** to the evaluation of its arguments under F_D and I. We form an atom in the base by evaluating each argument in A with the extended version of F_D. Again, the elements of the base are "hybrids," which we discussed in Section 5.2.2.

EXAMPLE 9.6: Consider the atom A =

equal(add(mult(Y, Y), mult(Z, Z)), X)

from the last example. To get an element of the base of f from A, we choose an instantiation I for the variables, say:

$I(\mathbf{X}) = 12$, $I(\mathbf{Y}) = 3$ and $I(\mathbf{Z}) = 2$.

Consider the value of the first argument using $E_{F_D,I}$, which we denote as simply E in this example.

E(**add(mult(Y, Y), mult(Z, Z))**) =
F_D[**add**](E(**mult(Y, Y)**), E(**mult(Z, Z)**)) =
F_D[**add**](F_D[**mult**](E(**Y**), E(**Y**)), F_D[**mult**](E(**Z**), E(**Z**))) =
F_D[**add**](F_D[**mult**](3, 3), F_D[**mult**](2, 2)) =
F_D[**add**](9, 4) = 13.

Since E[**X**] = 12, the base atom we get from atom A' in this case is:

equal(13, 12)

Had we used F'_D we would have obtained **equal**(5, 12). Other base atoms we can get using F_D are: **equal**(22, 0), **equal**(13, 13), **equal**(22, 1), and **equal**(17000, 741). There are many, many more. (See Exercise 9.3.) □

A *truth assignment* TA_{D,F_D} for g under **D** and F_D is similar to that in predicate logic; it tells what basic atoms are true statements. Thus, it is a mapping from B_{f,D,F_D} to {**true**, **false**}.

EXAMPLE 9.7: For example, the intuitive definition of TA_{D,F_D} for the formula f from Example 9.5 would have the following values:

TA_{D,F_D}(**equal**(13, 12)) = **false**
TA_{D,F_D}(**equal**(22, 0)) = **false**
TA_{D,F_D}(**equal**(13, 13)) = **true**
TA_{D,F_D}(**equal**(22, 1)) = **false**

In general, TA_{D,F_D} maps all **equal**-atoms that have different arguments to **false** and those with the same number as each argument to **true**. Using the base B_{f,D,F'_D}, we might define TA_{D,F'_D} in a similar manner. We could, however, define an alternative truth assignment TA'_{D,F_D} for B_{f,D,F_D} to assign another meaning—perhaps one that maps atoms in which the second number is larger than the first to **false**, and all others to **true**. Such a truth assignment is a perfectly acceptable for these base atoms. □

A *structure* ST for f is a triple <**D**, F_D, TA_{D,F_D}>. From here on, we omit subscripts on the function mapping and the truth assignment. We next define the meaning of a formula f under a structure ST = <**D**, F, TA>. Again, we make use of instantiations, which are mappings from variables to D. A *meaning function* $M_{ST,I}$ for structure ST and instantiation I is defined as follows. For an atom $\mathbf{p}(t_1, t_2, \ldots, t_n)$ in f:

$$M_{ST,I}(\mathbf{p}(t_1, t_2, \ldots, t_n)) = TA(\mathbf{p}(d_1, d_2, \ldots, d_n))$$

where $d_i = E_{F,I}(t_i)$. That is, convert the terms in the atom to domain elements by evaluating them with respect to F and I.

Note that the meaning function is defined relative to a structure, which is defined relative to a base, which is defined relative to a formula. Thus it might seem that we need a different structure for every formula. But note that the only requirement for a meaning function to be defined for some arbitrary formula is that the base of that formula be a subset of the base used to define the structure. Thus a structure for a formula will work as a structure for a subformula. It is also possible to construct a single base that will work for all formulas over some set of predicate and function symbols. (Exercise 5.7).

The rest of the definition of $M_{ST,I}$ is the same as for predicate logic. We repeat it here just for completeness.

$M_{ST,I}(g, h) =$ **true** if $M_{ST,I}(g) =$ **true** and $M_{ST,I}(h) =$ **true**.
$M_{ST,I}(g; h) =$ **true** if $M_{ST,I}(g) =$ **true** or $M_{ST,I}(h) =$ **true**.
$M_{ST,I}(\neg g) =$ **true** if $M_{ST,I}(g) =$ **false**.

The following two definitions give meaning to the quantifiers.

$M_{ST,I}(\forall \mathbf{X}\ g) =$ **true** if for every I' that agrees with I on all variables except **X** (and possibly on **X** as well), $M_{ST,I'}(g) =$ **true**.

$M_{ST,I}(\exists \mathbf{X}\ g) =$ **true** if there is some I' that agrees with I on all variables except **X** (and possibly on **X** as well), such that $M_{ST,I'}(g) =$ **true**.

For closed formulas, the terms *satisfiable, unsatisfiable,* and *valid* are defined as for predicate logic. A *model* is again a structure that satisfies a closed formula.

EXAMPLE 9.8: Consider the following two structures for formula f =

```
∀X ¬(∃Y ∃Z
      equal(add(mult(Y, Y), mult(Z, Z)), X), ¬equal(X, zero),
            ¬equal(add(Y,Z), one));
      ∃U ∃V
            equal(mult(U, V), X), ¬equal(U, one), ¬equal(V, one)
```

from Example 9.5:

$ST = \langle \mathrm{D}, F_{\mathrm{D}}, TA\rangle$
$ST' = \langle \mathrm{D}, F'_{\mathrm{D}}, TA'\rangle$

where the first two components come from Example 9.5 and both truth assignments define **equal** in the obvious way. We show that the formula is false in the first structure and true in the second. Consider the instantiation I where:

$I(\mathbf{X}) = 2$
$I(\mathbf{Y}) = 1$
$I(\mathbf{Z}) = 1$

Using this instantiation, we find that:

```
M_ST,I(equal(add(mult(Y, Y), mult(Z, Z)), X),
              ¬equal(X, zero), ¬equal(add(Y,Z), one))
    = true
```

so:

```
M_ST,I(¬(∃Y ∃Z
    equal(add(mult(Y, Y), mult(Z, Z)), X),
              ¬equal(X, zero), ¬equal(add(Y,Z), one))
    = false
```

and since the only two nonnegative integers that multiply together to give 2 (= **X**) are 1 and 2:

```
M_ST,I(∃U ∃V equal(mult(U, V), X), ¬equal(U, one), ¬equal(V, one))
  = false
```

so the disjunction is **false**, and so we have an instantiation I with $I(\mathbf{X}) = 2$ that shows that the entire formula is **false**.

To see that the formula is **true** under ST', recall that **add** is interpreted as monus in ST'. Note that if $i = j^2 - k^2$ then $i = (j + k) * (j - k)$. This simple identity shows how to choose values for **U** and **V** for any instantiation that falsifies the first disjunct of formula f. □

9.3. Deduction in Functional Logic

Having a formal notion of equivalent expressions is the first step toward computing in a logic. Logical implication for functional logic formulas is the same as for predicate logic formulas: Formula f *logically implies* formula g if for every structure ST for (f, g) and all instantiations I, if $M_{ST,I}(f) =$ **true**, then $M_{ST,I}(g) =$ **true.** They are *logically equivalent* if each logically implies the other.

EXAMPLE 9.9: Consider the formulas $f =$

```
∀X ∀Y ∀N (height(X, N); height(Y, N) :- height(tree(X, Y), inc(N))),
      height(leaf, zero)
```

and $g =$

```
∀Z ∀M height(Z, inc(M)) :-
      height(tree(tree(Z, leaf), leaf), inc(inc(inc(M))))
```

The intuitive semantics for f is that if a tree has height **N** + 1 (function symbol **inc** is for "increment"), then one of its subtrees has height **N**. Also, a tree consisting of just a leaf has height **zero**. The intuition for g is if a tree of the form:

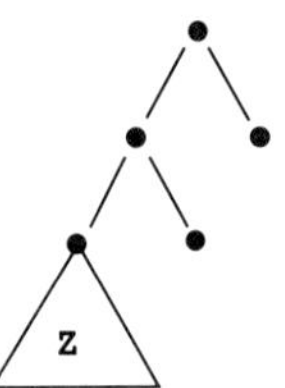

has height **M** + 3, then **Z** must have height **M** + 1. Under these intuitive semantics, f would seem to imply g. However, the implication does not hold. The problem is that f does not abstract all the relevant parts of the intuitive semantics—in particular, that a tree has a unique height. Consider a structure ST = <**D**, F, TA>, where D is the set of nonnegative integers and binary trees. Let F[**tree**] be the function that takes a pair of trees and returns a new tree with the input trees as right and left subtrees. We do not care much what F[**tree**] does to a pair of integers, or an integer and a tree. Let it map such pairs to 0. Let F[**inc**] be the "increment by 1" function on integers, and let it map trees to the tree with a single leaf, call it sl. Finally, let F[**leaf**] = sl and F[**zero**] = 0. So far, ST agrees with our intuitive semantics. However, consider TA. It must assign meaning to atoms of the form **height**(d_1, d_2). Let TA(**height**(d_1, d_2)) = **false** if d_1 is not a tree or d_2 is not an integer. Let TA(**height**(d_1, d_2)) = **true** if d_2 is the length (in edges) of the rightmost path in tree d_1, or that length plus 50. Thus, TA(**height**(sl, 0)) = TA(**height**(sl, 50)) = **true**. TA makes every other base atom false.

We have $M_{ST}(f)$ = **true**. For any instantiation I such that:

$M_{ST,I}$(**height(tree(X, Y), inc(N))**) = **true**

we must have:

$M_{ST,I}$(**height(Y, N)**) = **true,**

since height is computed from the right. Also:

$M_{ST,I}$(**height(leaf, zero)**) = TA(**height**(sl, 0)) = **true.**

However, consider g. Look at:

$M_{ST,I}$(**height(tree(tree(Z, leaf), leaf), inc(inc(inc(M)))))**

when I(**Z**) = sl and I(**M**) = 48. Now $E_{F,I}$(**tree(tree(Z, leaf), leaf)**) is the tree d =

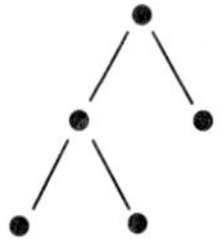

and $E_{F,I}$(**inc(inc(inc(M)))**) = 51 and *TA*(**height**(*d*, 51)) = **true**. But:

$M_{ST,I}$(**height(Z, inc(M))**) = *TA*(**height**(*sl*, 49)) = **false**,

so $M_{ST}(g)$ = **false**.

The problem is that *f* does not capture everything we intend for the **height** predicate, such as trees having only one height. How do we express this restriction? We want to say that if **height(X, M)** and **height(X, N)** are both true, then **M** = **N**. However, we do not have an implicit way to express equality. We must introduce an **equal** predicate and add subformulas to *f* to capture its properties. We can also use **equal** to constrain the behavior of the function that is the interpretation for **inc**. Some properties of **equal** are:

```
∀M equal(M, M)
∀M ∀N equal(M, N) :- equal(N, M)
∀M ∀N equal(inc(M), inc(N)) :- equal(M, N)
¬∃M equal(inc(M), zero)
```

The first formula says everything is equal to itself. The second says **equal** is a symmetric relationship. The third says increments of equal numbers are equal, while the last asserts there is no object whose increment is **zero**. We leave other formulas describing **equal** for an exercise. (See Exercise 9.7.) The last formula for **equal** is the property of interest to us. We modify *f* to *f′* =

```
∀X ∀Y ∀M ∀N (height(X, N); height(Y, N) :- height(tree(X, Y), inc(N))),
      height(leaf, zero),
      (equal(M, N) :- height (X, M), height(Y, N)),
      ¬equal(inc(M), zero)
```

We have incorporated enough of our intuitive semantics into this formula to constrain the possible models to be ones where *g* is also true. Suppose:

$M_{ST,I1}$(**height(tree(tree(Z, leaf), leaf)), inc(inc(inc(M))))**) = **true**

for some model *ST* = <D, *F*, *TA*> of *f′* and some instantiation *I*1. Let:

$E_{F,I1}$(**tree(Z, leaf)**) = d_{left},
$E_{F,I1}$(**leaf**) = d_{leaf}, and
$E_{F,I1}$(**inc(inc(M))**) = d_{num}.

If we take *I*2 with *I*2(**X**) = d_{left}, *I*2(**Y**) = d_{leaf} and *I*2(**N**) = d_{num}, then:

$M_{ST,I2}$(**height(tree(X, Y), inc(N))**) =
$M_{ST,I1}$(**height(tree(tree(Z, leaf), leaf)), inc(inc(inc(M))))**) = **true**.

So either:

$M_{ST,I2}$(**height(X, N)**) = **true**

or:

$M_{ST,I2}$(**height(Y, N)**) = **true**.

The latter expression has value $TA($**height**$(d_{leaf}, d_{num}))$. However, from f' we can conclude $TA($**height**$(d_{leaf}, d_0)) =$ **true**, where $d_0 = E_{F,I2}($**zero**$)$, and $TA($**equal**$(d_{num}, d_0)) =$ **false.** By the third line of f', we see that $TA($**height**$(d_{leaf}, d_{num})) =$ **false**, forcing $M_{ST,I2}($**height(X, N)**$) =$ **true.** We leave as an exercise to show that:

$M_{ST,I}1($**height(Z, inc(M))**$) =$ **true,**

and hence that $M_{ST}(g) =$ **true.** (See Exercise 9.8.) □

All the equivalences from Section 5.2 having to do with implications hold. We make one observation here about closed formulas with universal quantifiers. If we take such a formula g and substitute ground terms for the variables, we get a formula that is logically implied by g.

EXAMPLE 9.10: The formula f =

∀X ∀Y p(k(X), h(Y))

logically implies:

p(k(a), h(j(a))

We can also replace the bound variable with a subterm that includes variables that are universally quantified, under the condition that all the variables in the subterm do not appear elsewhere in the formula. The formula f above implies:

∀U ∀V p(k(m(U, V)), h(j(m(V, a))))

This property of substitution follows from the definition of ∀: **∀ X p(X)** is true if **p**(d) is true for every domain element d. Therefore, for any particular term t, **p**(t) is true, because the value of t is some domain element d. If the requirement of using new variables is not met, we can produce new formulas that are not logically implied by the original. (See Exercise 9.10.) □

9.3.1. *Special Forms and Skolem Functions*

A new twist on deduction in functional logic comes from the interplay of function symbols and quantification. We will see that although we cannot always remove existential quantifiers from prenex formulas, we can derive a formula without such quantifiers that is satisfiable if and only if the original formula is satisfiable. We will replace the "choice" of **X** in **∃X** by a choice in a structure of an interpretation for a function symbol. We will always be able to find a "satisfaction equivalent" formula in clausal form for any initial formula.

We define *prenex form* for closed functional logic formulas as before: all quantifiers appear to the left of the formula, and the scope of each quantifier is all of the formula to its right. The stages of moving ¬'s inward and then moving all quantifiers outward will produce an equivalent formula in prenex form. This process is identical to that for predicate logic. Recall that the list of quantifiers is called the *prefix* and the rest of the formula is the *matrix*. As before, a formula *f* is in *clausal form* if it is *universal* (its prefix contains only universal quantifiers) and its matrix is a conjunction of disjunctions of literals. With predicate logic we could not always find an equivalent formula in clausal form for a formula *f* in prenex form, if *f* was not universal. We still have that problem for functional logic. However, our interest in clausal form is for showing unsatisfiability of clausal formulas by refutation using resolution. And for the functional logic, we *can* say the following: For any closed formula *f*, there is a formula *g* in clausal form such that *f* is satisfiable if and only if *g* is satisfiable. Formulas *f* and *g* will not be logically equivalent, but will exhibit only this weaker "satisfiability equivalence." Obviously, we can show *f* is unsatisfiable by showing *g* unsatisfiable, so for the purposes of logical deduction, we can use *g* in place of *f*.

The mechanism for constructing *g* from *f* relies on a type of term called a *Skolem function*. Recall the example from Chapter 5 that argued that:

$f = \exists \mathbf{X}\ \forall \mathbf{Y}\ \mathbf{p(X,\ Y)}$

is unsatisfiable if and only if:

$g = \forall \mathbf{Y}\ \mathbf{p(a,\ Y)}$

is unsatisfiable. What is happening in this example is that in computing the meaning of *f* under a structure $ST = \langle \mathbf{D}, F, TA \rangle$, we need to determine if there is an instantiation *I* such that:

$M_{ST,I}(\forall \mathbf{Y}\ \mathbf{p(X,\ Y)}) = \mathbf{true}.$

Suppose there is such an *I*, and that $I(\mathbf{X}) = d$, *d* an element of **D**. *TA* must make $\mathbf{p}(d,\ e)$ true for every *e* in **D**. Consider the structure $ST' = \langle \mathbf{D}, F', TA \rangle$, where $F'[\mathbf{a}] = d$. Then:

$M_{ST',I}(\mathbf{p(a,\ Y)}) = TA(\mathbf{p}(F'[\mathbf{a}], I(\mathbf{Y}))) = TA(\mathbf{p}(d,\ e)) = \mathbf{true}$

for any value of $I(\mathbf{Y})$. Conversely, if we know:

$M_{ST'}(\forall \mathbf{Y}\ \mathbf{p(a,\ Y)}) = \mathbf{true}$

we then know that:

$M_{ST,I}(\forall \mathbf{Y}\ \mathbf{p(X,\ Y)}) = \mathbf{true}$

if we let *F* be the empty function mapping and choose instantiation *I* such that $I(\mathbf{X}) = F'[\mathbf{a}]$. This argument shows why, for this simple case, *f* is satisfiable if and only if *g* is satisfiable: We must choose a value for the first argument of the **p**-literal. For *f* under *ST*, this value is chosen by an instantiation; for *g* under *ST'*, it is chosen by the function mapping.

Suppose instead that *f* is:

$\forall \mathbf{Y}\ \exists \mathbf{X}\ \mathbf{p(X,\ Y)}$

We cannot conclude that g =

```
∀Y p(a, Y)
```

is satisfiable exactly when f is. The problem is that since the **∃X** is within the scope of **∀Y**, there may be a different value of **X** for each **Y** for which the predicate **p** holds. However, a function mapping picks out just a single value for **a**. To be concrete, consider the domain of all integers, and let the **p** in the formula represent the "less than" relation; for every integer **Y**, we can find an **X** less than **Y**, but we cannot find a single integer less than every integer, since there is no smallest integer.

In the predicate logic we were stuck at this point. Functional logic gives us an out. We want the choice of **X** to depend on the value for **Y**. If we can set things up so that the structure picks a possibly different **X** for each **Y**, we can remove the existential quantifier. We can do exactly that with a term that has **Y** as an argument. Consider:

```
∀Y p(h(Y), Y).
```

Here the structure specifies some interpretation for the function symbol **h**. If for every value e in **D**, there is a value d such that **p**(d, e) is true, then we can choose F[**h**] so that F[**h**](e) = d. That is, we choose the meaning of the function symbol **h** to be a function that picks out the right values for the first argument of **p**. For example, when **p** is the "less than" predicate, we can choose F[**h**] to be the "subtract one" function. Conversely, given some truth assignment for **p**, if some interpretation for **h** exists such that **p**(F[**h**](e), e) is true for all $e \in D$, then:

```
∀Y ∃X p(X, Y)
```

is true with the same truth assignment for **p**, because F[**h**] tells us for each **Y**-value what **X**-value we can choose to make **p(X, Y)** true.

The function **h** in the preceding discussion is an example of a *Skolem function*. Skolem functions can be used to convert any functional logic formula f in prenex form to a universal functional logic formula g, such that f is satisfiable if and only if g is satisfiable. Formulas f and g will *not* be logically equivalent, since g will have function symbols not present in f. However, whenever we can find a model for g, we can use it to construct a model for f, and vice versa. Function g will be called the *Skolemized* version of f. What are the particulars of converting f to g? Assume that f is already in prenex form. We remove the existential quantifiers from f, working left to right. Let **∃X** be the first existentially quantified variable in the prefix of f. Remove **∃X** from the prefix. Throughout the matrix of f, replace **X** by **h**(α_1, α_2, ..., α_k) where:

1. $\alpha_1, \alpha_2, \ldots, \alpha_k$ are all the universally quantified variables to the left of **∃X**, and
2. **h** is a new k-ary function symbol not already appearing in f.

If $k = 0$, then **h** will be just a new constant symbol. The process is repeated until all existential quantifiers are removed.

EXAMPLE 9.11: Consider the Skolemization of the formula:

∃U ∀V ∃X ∀Y ∃Z (¬p(U, k(V), X, b); r(j(X, Y), U), s(Y, j(a, Z)))

It is already in prenex form. The first existentially quantified variable in the prefix is **U**. There are no preceding universal quantifiers, so we introduce a new 0-ary function symbol, the constant **h1**, and substitute it for **U** in the matrix obtaining:

∀V ∃X ∀Y ∃Z (¬p(h1, k(V), X, b); r(j(X, Y), h1), s(Y, j(a, Z)))

The next existentially quantified variable in the prefix is **X**. It has one universally quantified variable preceding it in the prefix, **V**, so we introduce a new unary function symbol, **h2**, and substitute **h2V** for each occurrence of **X** in the matrix, obtaining:

∀V ∀Y ∃Z (¬p(h1, k(V), h2(V), b); r(j(h2(V), Y), h1), s(Y, j(a, Z)))

Z is the last existential variable, and we introduce a new binary function symbol, **h3**, and substitute **h3(V, Y)** for occurrences of **Z** in the matrix:

∀V ∀Y (¬p(h1, k(V), h2(V), b); r(j(h2(V), Y), h1),
s(Y, j(a, h3(V, Y)))) □

With Skolemization, we can now take any functional logic formula *f* and convert it to a formula *g* that is satisfiable if and only if *f* is satisfiable. Since we will be testing implication via unsatisfiability, *g* will serve for *f* in such tests. As with Datalog, we can represent a formula in clausal form as a set of clauses, or in implication form with ':-'.

EXAMPLE 9.12: Consider the formula we just Skolemized. We drop the prefix, since we know that all variables are universally quantified.

¬p(h1, k(V), h2(V), b); r(j(h2(V), Y), h1), s(Y, j(a, h3(V, Y)))

We can convert it to clausal form by distributing the first literal over the conjunction:

(¬p(h1, k(V), h2(V), b); r(j(h2(V), Y), h1)),
(¬p(h1, k(V), h2(V), b); s(Y, j(a, h3(V, Y)))))

Then we can standardize the variables apart (rename variables in different conjuncts):

(¬p(h1, k(V), h2(V), b); r(j(h2(V), Y), h1)),
(¬p(h1, k(R), h2(R), b); s(S, j(a, h3(R, S)))))

and form the set of (two) clauses:

{¬p(h1, k(V), h2(V), b); r(j(h2(V), Y), h1)}
{¬p(h1, k(R), h2(R), b); s(S, j(a, h3(R, S)))}

We can also put them in implication form:

```
r(j(h2(V), Y), h1) :- p(h1, k(V), h2(V), b).
s(S, j(a, h3(R, S)) :- p(h1, k(R), h2(R), b).
```
□

9.4. Herbrand Interpretations

In the last section we saw that we can reduce testing of satisfiability (and hence implication) to testing satisfiability of universal formulas. Here the main result is that satisfiability of universal formulas can be limited to searching for a model of a certain type, a *Herbrand model.* Such a model is characterized by all function values being distinct, and so terms can be identified with data structures. Whereas the *Herbrand universe* was earlier just the set of constants in a formula f, here we form the Herbrand universe from all combinations of constants and function symbols in f. Intuitively, we are trying to construct all possible noun phrases relevant to the statement f; we use these "names" themselves as the domain elements. We form the Herbrand universe for formula f in much the same way as we formed the domain $\mathbf{D}_P$ for a Prolog program P. Let Fun_f be the set of all constant and function symbols in f. We let the Herbrand universe for f, denoted $\mathbf{D}_f$, be the set of strings that represent terms formed using symbols in Fun_f. That is, $\mathbf{D}_f$ will be all strings that can be derived from the nonterminal TERM in the grammar for functional logic, where 'csym' ranges over symbols in Fun_f (and arities of symbols are respected). To reinforce the distinction between strings in $\mathbf{D}_f$ and actual terms (which are more like record structures), we will write elements of $\mathbf{D}_f$ in bold for the moment: **h(k(a), b)**. However, note that each string in $\mathbf{D}_f$ can be parsed as a distinct term, and every term has a corresponding string. If Fun_f contains no constants, we add one. Observe that if Fun_f contains any proper function symbols, then $\mathbf{D}_f$ is an infinite set of strings.

EXAMPLE 9.13: For the previous example:

Fun_f = {j/2, k/1, b/0, h1/0, h2/1, h3/2}
$\mathbf{D}_f$ = {**b, h1, j(b, b), j(h1, b), j(b, h1), j(h1, h1), k(b), k(h1), h2(b), h2(h1), h3(b, b), h3(h1, b), h3(b, h1), h3(h1, h1), j(j(b, b), b), j(j(h1, b), b), j(j(b, h1), b), j(j(h1, h1), b)**, . . .} □

The next part of a Herbrand interpretation is the function mapping. For each function symbol in our language, this mapping gives an actual function on domain objects—in this case, strings. As with predicate logic, we call this mapping *Id*, although it behaves a little differently from the equivalent mapping there. We define *Id* as follows. For an n-ary function symbol **k**, if $s_1, s_2, \ldots, s_n$ are strings of $\mathbf{D}_f$, then:

$$Id[\mathbf{k}](s_1, s_2, \ldots, s_n) = \mathbf{k}(s_1, s_2, \ldots, s_n)$$

Here we use juxtaposition to represent concatenation of strings. So, for example:

Id[**k**](**b, j (h1, h1)**) = **k(b, j(h1, h1))**.

Thus the evaluation function E will just give a textual representation when applied to a term.

EXAMPLE 9.14: Let I be an instantiation where I(**X**) = **a** and I(**Y**) = **b**. (Recall that I maps variables to elements of D_f.) Then, letting E stand for $E_{Id,I}$, we have:

E(**j (k (X), j (Y, b))**) =
Id[**j**](E(**k (a)**), E(**j (b, b)**)) =
Id[**j**](Id[**k**](E(**a**)), Id[**j**](E(**b**), E(**b**))) =
Id[**j**](Id[**k**](**a**), Id[**j**](**b, b**)) =
Id[**j**](**k (a), j (b, b)**) =
j (k (a), j (b,b)) □

While it is important to recognize the distinction between elements of D_f and actual terms, it is typographically awkward to continue to mix fonts, so we will write elements in D_f the same as terms and let context determine which we mean. We will abuse the distinction between atoms in the Herbrand base and ground literals at times—for example, by viewing instantiations as mapping arbitrary terms to base elements.

The *Herbrand base* for f is $B_{f,D_f,Id}$: all the ground atoms formed by applying $E_{Id,I}$ to atoms in g under all instantiations I. A *Herbrand interpretation* is a structure H = <D_f, Id, TA>, where TA is a truth assignment on the Herbrand base for f.

EXAMPLE 9.15: Part of the Herbrand base for the formula at the end of Example 9.12 is:

```
r(j(h2(b), b), h1)
r(j(h2(b), h1), h1)
r(j(h2(h2(b)), k(b)), h1)
r(j(h2(h2(h2(h1))), k(b)), h1)
    .
    .
    .
p(h1, k(b), h2(k(b)), b)
p(h1, k(h3(b, k(b))) , h2(k(k(k(b)))), b)
p(h1, k(j(b, b)), h2(j(j(b, b), b)), b)
    .
    .
    .
s(b, j(a, h3(b, b)))
s(k(b), j(a, h3(h1, h1)))
s(j(b, b), j(a, h3(b, h2(h1))))
    .
    .
    .
```

interpretation. C is universally quantified, so for C *not* to be satisfied, there must be some instantiation I such that $I(C)$ is not satisfied, by the meaning of universal quantification. Let $C' = I(C)$. All the literals in C' must be mapped to **false** by *TA*. Consider the path for *TA* in the semantic tree T_S. The complements of all the literals in C' will appear along that path, and the last one will appear at some node i at finite level. At that point, without knowing the rest of *TA*, we know C' (hence C, hence S) will not be satisfied. Call i a *failure node* for C if there is no other such node for any ground instance of C on the path between i and the root. (A clause may have many failure nodes in the tree. See Exercise 9.15.) Call i a *failure node* for S if it is a failure node for some clause of S and there is no other failure node for any other clause of S on the path between i and the root.

EXAMPLE 9.17: Consider the clause set S from the last example. In the tree of Figure 9.2, node 7 is a failure node for clause {**p(X); q(a)**}, using instance {**p(a); q(a)**}, as is node 11, using instance {**p(f(a)); q(a)**}. The failure nodes for S are:

4: {¬**q(a)**}
20: {¬**q(f(a))**}
21: {¬**p(a); q(f(a))**}
11: {**p(f(a)); q(a)**}
6: {¬**q(a)**}
7: {**p(a); q(a)**} □

Proof continued:

6. If S is unsatisfiable, it has a failure node at finite depth along every path in T_S. In that case, call T_S a *failure tree* for S. View T_S as cut off below the failure nodes for S.
7. T_S, after clipping, has a finite number of nodes, by König's Lemma: Any finitely branching tree with an infinite number of nodes has an infinite path. Since T_S has no infinite path, it has a finite number of nodes.
8. Now, for each failure node, take the corresponding clause instance C'. This finite set of instances of clauses of S is unsatisfiable. □

EXAMPLE 9.18: Using the clause instances from the preceding example, and propositional resolution, we have:

1. {¬**q(a)**} instance
2. {¬**q(f(a))**} instance
3. {¬**p(a); q(f(a))**} instance
4. {**p(f(a)); q(a)**} instance
5. {**p(a); q(a)**} instance
6. {¬**p(a)**} 2, 3
7. {**q(a)**} 5, 6
8. {} 1, 7 □

9.5. Resolution in Functional Logic

Herbrand's Theorem provides an algorithm, albeit inefficient, for proving a set of clauses unsatisfiable. Enumerate the semantic tree a level at a time. After each level, check to see if there is a failure node on every path. If so, the clause set is unsatisfiable. If not, enumerate another level. Resolution has the effect in general of moving failure nodes higher in the tree, ultimately making the root a failure node if the clause set is unsatisfiable. Thus none of the semantic tree need then be generated to check unsatisfiability. As with predicate logic, we could do resolution on ground instances of clauses. The set of ground clauses for a clause set is generally infinite in functional logic. Hence a refutation procedure based on ground resolution would have to operate by generating some ground clauses, looking for a ground refutation, generating some more clauses, attempting a refutation again, and so on. (Early theorem-proving algorithms used this strategy.) Unifiers give a means to lift the resolution to nonground clauses—one general resolution captures the effect of an infinite number of ground resolutions. General resolution means a refutation procedure can begin with a fixed, finite set of initial clauses and need not enumerate ground instances.

For functional logic, a substitution is a set of replacements, where a replacement is **X** = α, α a term (not necessarily ground). We have the same restrictions as before:

1. No two replacements can have the same left side.
2. The substitution is idempotent, so no variable that appears on the left of any replacement may appear on the right of any replacement.

Observe that restriction 2 forbids **X = f(a, g(X))**, a variable on the right side of its replacement. Substitutions are composed as before, $\theta \circ \sigma$ meaning first apply substitution θ and then apply σ. Again, under certain constraints on variable occurrences, substitutions are closed under composition. A sufficient condition is that no variable appearing on the left of a replacement in θ may appear on the right of a replacement in σ. As before, we can form a single substitution ρ representing $\theta \circ \sigma$: Let ρ initially be θ. Apply σ to right sides in ρ. Add replacements from σ to ρ if their left sides do not clash with replacements already in ρ.

EXAMPLE 9.19: Let θ be:

{**X = a, Y = f(Z), U = h(f(Z), W)**}

For atom A = **p(U, g(Y, X), V)**, $A\theta$ is **p(h(f(Z), W), g(f(Z), a), V)**. Let σ be:

{**V = b, U = f(T), Z = f(S)**}

Then $\theta \circ \sigma$ is:

{**X = a, Y = f(f(S)), U = h(f(f(S)), W), V = b, Z = f(S)**} and $(A\theta)\sigma$ is:

```
p(h(f(f(S))), W), g(f(f(S)), a), b)
```

which is the same as $A(\theta \circ \sigma)$. □

For a set of atoms $A_1, A_2, \ldots, A_n$, a substitution θ is a *unifier* if $A_1\theta = A_2\theta = \cdots = A_n\theta$. So a unifier is a substitution that makes a set of atoms the same. Substitution σ is a *most general unifier* (mgu) for the atoms if for any other unifier θ, $\theta = \sigma \circ \theta$. A set of atoms is *unifiable* if the atoms have a unifier.

EXAMPLE 9.20: Consider the set of atoms:

```
p(X, f(W, a))
p(Y, U)
p(X, f(X, V))
```

The substitution θ =

```
{X = c, W = c, Y = c, U = f(c, a), V = a}
```

is a unifier for this set since applying θ to each atom yields **p(c, f(c, a))**. The substitution σ =

```
{W = X, Y = X, U = f(X, a), V = a}
```

is also a unifier, since applied to each element in the set, it yields **p(X, f(X, a))**. Substitution σ is a more general unifier than θ, since $\theta = \sigma \circ \theta$. Substitution σ turns out to be an mgu. □

The *match* function of Section 7.3 performs unification of two literals.

THEOREM 9.3: If HEAD and GOAL are unifiable atoms, the *match* function of Section 7.3 succeeds and returns an mgu of HEAD and GOAL via SUBS. If HEAD and GOAL are not unifiable, *match* will fail.

Proof: The proof of the first statement follows the proof of Theorem 5.3. For the second statement we note that *match* always halts; there are only finitely many distinct variables in $HEAD_0$ and $GOAL_0$ to begin with, and each time around the **while**-loop removes one variable. Thus *match* always returns failure or success. We must show that if *match* succeeds, the final value of SUBS is a unifier. Let $HEAD_0$ and $GOAL_0$ be the state of arguments T1 and T2 before the first call to *findfirst*, and let $HEAD_i$ and $GOAL_i$ be the state of T1 and T2 at the end of the ith pass through the **while**-loop after the *apply*'s (thus after the ith call to *findfirst*). Let σ_i be the value of SUBS after the ith pass through the **while**-loop. Function *match* succeeds when $HEAD_i = GOAL_i$ for some i. Since at the beginning of each iteration of the **while**-loop, $(HEAD_0)\sigma_i = HEAD_i$ and $(GOAL_0)\sigma_i = GOAL_i$, the final value of SUBS unifies HEAD and GOAL. The only thing that remains to check is that at each point σ_i is a legal substitution. The *match* function cannot generate two replacements with the same left side **X**, because all occurrences of **X** disappear from both atoms after the first such replacement is applied. We also cannot have a variable **X** on both the left and right sides of replacements. Suppose SUBS contains both **X** = α and **Y** = β, where **X** is in β. Note that replacements, once added to SUBS, never change their left sides. Suppose **X** = α was added to SUBS first. Then β cannot contain **X**, because neither HEAD nor GOAL have **X** at that point. Suppose **X** = α was added after **Y** = β. Then **X** = α would be applied to β to replace **X** in composing substitutions. There is one more case—the two replacements are actually the same one. The *violates* check in *match* prevents that possibility. □

Substitutions and unifiers for functional logic have the same properties as were listed for predicate logic in Section 5.5. Hence the definitions for resolution in that section all carry over. *Binary resolution, full resolution,* and *factoring* have all the same form for functional logic as for predicate logic. Since every set of predicate logic clauses is a set of functional logic clauses, we also know that full resolution is necessary in general for refutation proofs with functional logic clauses. As before, we will need only binary resolution with Horn clauses.

EXAMPLE 9.21: Returning to Example 9.9, we can represent formula f' in clausal form as:

1. {**height(X, N); height(Y, N);**
   ¬height(tree(X, Y), inc(N))}
2. {**height(leaf, zero)**}
3. {**equal(M, N); ¬height(X, M); ¬height(X, N)**}
4. {**¬equal(inc(M), zero)**}

The negation of *g* is:

```
¬∀Z ∀M height(Z, inc(M)) :-
      height(tree(tree(Z, leaf), leaf), inc(inc(inc(M))))
```

Moving the negation in gives

```
∃Z ∃M ¬(height(Z, inc(M)) :-
      height(tree(tree(Z, leaf), leaf), inc(inc(inc(M)))))
```

Skolemizing to remove the two existential quantifiers leaves:

```
¬(height(t, inc(h)) :-
      height(tree(tree(t, leaf), leaf), inc(inc(inc(h)))))
```

This formula can be expressed as the clauses:

5. {**¬height(t, inc(h))**}
6. {**height(tree(tree(t, leaf), leaf), inc(inc(inc(h))))**}

Resolving 1 and 6 gives:

7. {**height(tree(t, leaf), inc(inc(h)));**
height(leaf, inc(inc(h)))}

One resolvent of 2 and 3 is:

8. {**equal(M, zero); ¬height(leaf, M)**}

which can be resolved with 4 (with **M** renamed to **M1**) to yield:

9. {**¬height(leaf, inc(M1))**}

Resolving 7 and 9 leaves:

10. {**height(tree(t, leaf)), inc(inc(h)))**}

Resolving this clause with 1 gives:

11. {**height(t, inc(h)); height(leaf, inc(h))**}

which can be resolved with 8 to get:

12. {**height(t, inc(h)); equal(inc(h), zero)**}

This last clause can be reduced to the empty clause by resolving with clauses 4 and 5. □

Similarly, the arguments for correctness and completeness of resolution carry over from the predicate logic case, since Lemma 5.4 (correctness) and Lemma 5.5 (Lifting Lemma) are expressed in terms of clauses and substitutions. A few remarks on completeness are in order. Herbrand's Theorem tells us that if a set *S* of clauses is unsatisfiable, then a finite set of ground instances is unsatisfiable. We know from propositional logic that those ground instances have a refutation DAG. We might anticipate a problem in trying to select that particular finite set of ground instances of *S* from the potentially infinite set of such clauses. However, with the Lifting Lemma, we need not worry about actually finding that set of ground instances. Whatever the ground clauses happen to be that yield the refutation DAG, we can lift that DAG to a refutation over the finite set of clauses in *S*.

9.6. Answers

Throughout this book we have seen how deduction can be used to extract information from a set of logical statements. We consider this question again now in the very general context of full functional logic. In predicate logic, for a formula $\exists$**X** *f*, if we wanted to know which values for **X** made *f* true, we could iterate through a fixed set of constants, trying each for **X** to see if it makes the formula true. In functional logic there are an infinite number of values that **X** can range over, so we must view answers as being constructed, rather than selected.

Given a set of formulas, we can easily see how to extract yes-no answers from this information by simply posing the question as a closed formula. Then we add the negation of the question-formula to the clause set and use a resolution theorem prover to try to generate the empty clause. If it succeeds, the answer is yes. If it fails to derive the empty clause, we might pose the negative of the question to see if that can be answered.

We can also extract answers to other kinds of questions, such as wh-questions that ask "Who" or "What." Instead of formulating a closed formula that corresponds to our question, we make up an open formula—one that contains a free variable. The "who" or "what" that our question seeks is any object (or description of some object) that, when substituted for the variable, makes the sentence true.

EXAMPLE 9.22: Consider, for example, the simple wh-question:

"Who is John's father?"

This question can be seen as asking how to fill in the blank in the open sentence:

"The father of John is ______."

to get a true statement. This question corresponds to the (simple) open formula:

father(**john**, **X**). □

We can also have question sentences that have more than one blank and are expressed by formulas with several free variables. The question now is, how do we get a general resolution theorem prover to fill in those blanks? Let us denote the question formula by q and assume it has free variables: **X**, **Y** and **Z**. We make up a new predicate symbol, call it **answer**, and add the formula:

∀X ∀Y ∀Z **answer**(X, Y, Z) :- q[X, Y, Z]

(after converting it to clausal form) to our set of axioms. This formula says that every triple <a, b, c> that makes q true is an answer. Now we use resolution on this modified set of clauses, but, instead of deriving the empty clause, we try to derive a clause consisting solely of some instance of the atom **answer**(**X**, **Y**, **Z**). The terms in the arguments of that derived atom provide an answer to our original question. This atom is an answer because every clause derivable by resolution from a set of clauses is a logical consequence of that set.

EXAMPLE 9.23: Consider the formulas:

```
∀N ∃M succ(N, M)
∀N ∀M ge(N, M) :- succ(M, N)
```

These formulas say that every number has a successor, and a successor of a number is greater than or equal to the number. Our question is, what number is greater than or equal to **0**?

```
ge(X, 0)
```

We add the answer formula and then convert all the formulas to clausal form:

1. {**succ (N, s (N))**}
2. {**ge (N, M) ; ¬succ (M, N)**}
3. {**answer (X) ; ¬ge (X, 0)**}

Notice that we had to introduce a unary Skolem function, called **s (X)**, in the process of converting the first formula to clausal form. Now we use resolution as follows to derive a clause consisting of a single atom for the predicate **answer**. Resolving 2 and 3, then the result with 1, gives:

4. {**answer (X1) ; ¬succ (0, X1)**}
5. {**answer (s (0))**}

This last clause is an answer clause: it says that **s (0)** is an answer to our original question. □

This very simple example shows how an answer might contain a Skolem function. In such a case, to understand the answer, one has to understand what the Skolem function means. Here the Skolem function is clearly the successor function, which has a natural intuitive meaning. We could make a minor change in the (intended interpretation of the) preceding axioms by using a predicate **lessThan** instead of **succ**. We will get the identical syntactic answer, but how do we interpret the Skolem function, **s**, in this case? Now the Skolem function, **s**, picks out some number such that its argument is less than it, and we must use that interpretation to understand the answer.

9.7. Model Elimination

In this section we again consider model elimination, which we first saw with propositional logic in Section 2.3.2. Model elimination is a complete resolution strategy for functional logic. Further, it is amenable to implementation using the same data structures and techniques used for Prolog, as we will see in Chapter 10. The applicability of Prolog implementation technology is the main reason we treat model elimination in this text.

Let S be a clause set. Recall that model elimination is a form of SL-resolution (hence a form of linear resolution) in which the choice of side clause is limited. If C is the current center clause, the side clause must be an input clause from S or a previous center clause D that is a *progenitor* of C. Clause D is a progenitor of C if solving the selected literal of D directly or indirectly introduces the selected literal of C. Also only the selected literal of D may be used to resolve with the selected literal of C.

These restrictions on the choice of side clause allow progenitors of the current side clause to be represented by simply retaining their selected literal after a resolution step. Recall that a resolution step with an input clause as side clause is called an *extension* step in model elimination, and that the selected literal is *framed* and kept in place in the new center clause. For example, if the current center clause is:

```
{q; ¬r; [s]; t}
```

and a clause in *S* is:

```
{¬s; ¬q; t; v}
```

we get the resolvent:

```
{¬s; v; [q]; ¬r; [s]; t}
```

Remember that:

1. Order of literals in a clause is important. The first literal of the center clause is assumed to be the selected one, and when the resolvent is formed, the literals of the side clause go at the beginning.
2. If there are duplicate literals in the resolvent, the copy from the side clause is removed.

Another possibility in model elimination is a *reduction* step, in which the selected literal is matched to a framed literal, and removed. A reduction step corresponds to using a progenitor center clause as a side clause. The preceding clause can be reduced to:

```
{v; [q]; ¬r; [s]; t}
```

The final possibility is a *contraction* step, in which a framed literal is removed if it becomes first in the clause, because the center clause that the framed literal represents is no longer a progenitor of the current center clause. For example, from {[q]; ¬r; [s]; t}, we must go to {¬r; [s]; t}.

The main change to model elimination for functional logic is in the reduction step. In propositional logic it was always advantageous to perform a reduction step if possible. In functional logic, when the first literal is matched to a framed literal, the two literals are unified, and the resulting substitution applied to the next center clause (including framed literals). Thus a reduction step can specialize other literals in the clause, and so is not always to be favored over an extension step.

EXAMPLE 9.24: In:

```
{¬p(X, Y); ¬q(X, W); [p(W, h(a, X))]; r(Y)}
```

to reduce the first literal by the framed literal, we must apply the substitution:

```
{X = W, Y = h(a, W)}
```

The next center clause is:

```
{¬q(W, W); [p(W, h(a, W))]; r(h(a, W))}
```

If the only **q**-clause is **q(a, b)**, we can operate no further on this clause. However, an extension step could allow further progress. Assume there is a **p**-clause **p(a, Z)**. Then we can perform an extension step on the first clause to get:

{¬**q(a, W); [p(W, h(a, a))]; r(Z)**}

in which we can solve the **q**-literal with **q(a, b)**. □

Model elimination for functional logic has more choice points than the propositional logic version. For a regular literal as the first in the center clause, there may be a choice between extension and reduction. When a framed literal reaches the front of the center clause, a contraction step must always be taken, as with propositional logic. For extension, there is the usual choice of which input clause and which literal in that clause. (However, binary resolution suffices for extension steps; see Exercise 9.21.) For reduction, there may also be a choice of framed literals for matching.

When used for proving implication through refutation, model elimination as described is complete only for goals with no variables. A slight modification is needed for goals with variables. (See Exercise 9.22.)

9.8. Horn Clauses

It should come as no surprise by now that Prolog is Horn clauses in functional logic with Herbrand interpretations. A Prolog rule is just a definite Horn clause in another form; a Prolog goal is a headless Horn clause. The arguments we made in Chapter 5 for predicate logic work here as well; we can restrict resolution trees to the following: use input resolution, use a headless clause as the initial center clause, use selected literal resolution, and use only binary resolution steps. We can use the same routine as for predicate logic (with a new *match* function) to search for Horn clause refutations. Again, it is equivalent to our naive interpreter, except for duplicate literal elimination.

The novelty in functional Horn logic is unifying terms. A single operation works for both construction and selection on terms. In fact both operations can arise in a single variable binding. Binding a variable to a subterm of a term can simultaneously provide a handle on the subterm while elaborating any other term containing an instance of the variable.

9.9. EXERCISES

9.1. Give a structure for representing a Prolog clause as a term. (Hint: Think of ':-' and ',' as infix operators.)

9.2. For a Prolog program P, show that $\mathbf{D}_P$ can be enumerated. That is, there is a program that will output members of $\mathbf{D}_P$, such that any particular term is eventually listed.

9.3. Give a general description of the atoms in the base for formula *f* from Example 9.5 using the function mapping F_D given there.

9.4. We can define a "universal" base *B* for all formulas that have the same set of predicate and function symbols—just let *B* be all atoms formed using the predicate and function symbols. Show that for a particular formula *f*, and a truth assignment *TA* over *B*, part of *TA* can be irrelevant to *f*. That is, the value of *TA* on certain atoms of *B* is not used in computing the meaning of *f*.

9.5. For the formula *f* =

```
∀X ∃Y ∀Z ¬equal(concat(X, Y), Z); equal(rev(Z), Z)
```

compute its meanings under the following two interpretations.

STRUCTURE 1: D is sets of strings over {a, b}, *F*[**concat**] = elementwise concatenation, *F*[**rev**] = elementwise reversal, and *TA* is true only for **equal**(*d*, *d*) where *d* is an element of D.

STRUCTURE 2: D is strings over {a, b}, *F*[**concat**] = string concatenation, *F*[**rev**] = string reversal, and *TA* is true only for **equal**(*d*, *d*) where *d* is an element of D.

9.6. Let *f* be a predicate logic formula, and *ST* = <D, *F*, *TA*> be a functional logic structure for *f*. *ST* can be viewed as a predicate logic structure as well, since the function mapping, *F*, maps only constant symbols. Show that $M_{ST,I}(f)$ gives the same value for a given instantiation *I* when $M_{ST,I}$ is considered as the predicate logic meaning function or as the functional logic meaning function.

9.7. Suppose we are given an arbitrary set of universally quantified **equal** facts, involving terms constructed from a set of function symbols, for example:

```
∀X equal(f(X), g(X, a))
equal(h(a, b), f(c))
∀Y equal(k(Y), k(k(Y)))
```

What formulas involving **equal** are needed to be able to imply any formula of the form **equal**(t_1, t_2), where t_2 is obtained from t_1 by substitution of terms for equal terms? For example, from the preceding **equal** facts, we want to be able to prove:

```
equal(k(f(f(c))), k(k(g(h(a, b), a)))).
```

9.8. a. Finish the argument in Example 9.9 that formula *f*′ implies *g*.
b. Consider the formula *g*′ =

```
∀Z ∀M height(Z, M) :- height(tree(tree(Z, leaf), leaf),
    inc(inc(M))).
```

Does formula *f*′ in Example 9.9 imply *g*′? Prove your answer.

9.9. a. Augment formula f' in Example 9.9 to capture that the **inc** function is one-to-one.
b. Augment formula f' to require that the height of a tree be the **inc** of the height of the tallest of its subtrees. You may want to introduce a **greater** predicate.

9.10. If we ignore the restriction on the replacement formula for a universal variable given in Example 9.10, we can replace **X** in:

```
∀X ∃Y p(X, Y)
```

with **f(Y)** to get:

```
∀Y ∃Y p(f(Y), Y).
```

Show that the first formula does not imply the second.

9.11. Give a Skolemized version g' of formula g:

```
∀X ∃Y ∀Z ¬equal(concat(X, Y), Z); equal(rev(Z), Z).
```

Show how to derive a model of g from a model for g', and prove that your derivation produces a model.

9.12. Consider the formula f =

```
∃U ∀X ¬p(X);
        (¬∀Y (¬q(X, Y); p(f(a))), ∀Y (¬q(X, Y); p(X))).
```

a. Find a formula f' in clausal form that is satisfiable if and only if f is satisfiable. Simplify f' where possible.
b. Give a model for f' from part (a).

9.13. a. Show that the truth assignment *TA* described in Example 9.15 makes the last formula in Example 9.11 false.
b. Give a Herbrand model for that formula.

9.14. Use Herbrand interpretations to show why, in the definition of implication of a goal list g in Prolog, we interpret $M_{ST}(g)$ = **true** if for *some* I, $M_{ST}(I(g))$ = **true**, rather than for *all* I.

9.15. Given a semantic tree T_S for a clause set S, and a clause C in S, must all failure nodes for C in T_S be at the same depth?

9.16. Draw a failure tree for the first six clauses in Example 9.18, and also for the first seven.

9.17. Give a refutation proof, using linear resolution, for the clauses in Example 9.20.

9.18. Consider the following set of clauses S =

```
{equal(rev(rev(X)), X)}
```

```
{equal(concat(rev(X), rev(Y)); rev(concat(Y, X)))}
{¬equal(rev(X), X); palin(X)}

{¬equal(U, V); equal(V, U)}
{equal(X, X)}
{equal(X, Z); ¬equal(X, Y); ¬equal(Y, Z)}
{¬equal(U, V); equal(rev(U); rev(V))}
{¬equal(U1, U2); ¬equal(V1, V2); equal(concat(U1, V1);
    concat(U2, V2))}
```

Some intuition for these clauses can be gained from Exercise 9.5. The **palin** predicate is intended to assert that its argument is a palindrome (reads the same forward as backward). Use these clauses in a refuation proof of the formula:

∀X ∃Y **palin(concat(X, Y))**.

That is, for any **X**, there is something you can concatenate with **X** to get a palindrome.

9.19. In model elimination, a framed literal is only one literal out of possibly many in a previous center clause. Why can the other literals in that center clause be omitted from the resolvent formed by a reduction step with the framed literal?

9.20. In model elimination, if duplicate literals appear after an extension step, what is the advantage of eliminating the first one rather than the second?

9.21. For an extension step in model elimination, binary resolution is adequate. Consider an extension step using full resolution to unify two literals in a side clause. Show that if the resolvent can eventually be solved, then the two literals can be eliminated via a binary resolution followed by a later reduction step.

9.22. Suppose we have clause {¬**p(X, Y)**} that we wish to show inconsistent with a clause set S using model elimination.
   a. Give a satisfiable clause set S such that $S \cup \{\{$¬**p(X, Y)**$\}\}$ is unsatisfiable, but S alone does not yield the empty clause with model elimination using {¬**p(X, Y)**} as the initial center clause.
   b. For S in part (a), show that $S' = S \cup \{\{$¬**p(X, Y)**$\}\}$ *will* yield the empty clause with {¬**p(X, Y)**} as the initial center clause.

9.10. COMMENTS AND BIBLIOGRAPHY

The syntax and model theory of full first-order logic with function symbols is developed in many textbooks, for example [2.1, 9.1]. For the resolution strategies, the references of Chapters 2 and 5 are relevant here. In fact, most of the works referenced there are actually in the more general context of full functional logic that we have come to only now.

The unification algorithm we use throughout this book, in the worst case, takes time exponential in the size of the terms being unified. There are algorithms for unification (with occur-check) that take only linear time [9.2].

Lloyd [9.3] is an excellent book that covers in detail fundamental results in logic that underlie logic programming. That book is appropriate as a follow-on to this chapter to expand and solidify what we have presented here.

9.1. J. Shoenfield, *Mathematical Logic,* Addison-Wesley, Reading, MA, 1967.

9.2. A. Martelli and U. Montanari, An efficient unification algorithm, *ACM Trans. on Programming Languages and Systems,* 4(2), April 1982, 258–82.

9.3. J. Lloyd, *Foundations of Logic Programming,* Springer-Verlag, New York, 1984.

10

Improving the Prolog Interpreter

In this chapter we explore ways to make the Prolog interpreter more efficient than the naive implementation. Much of this development will parallel that of Chapter 6. Why do we start from the beginning again, rather than where we left off at the end of Chapter 6? We must redo our steps to consider the effect of structured terms upon each. We also have a new issue to consider: how to represent a term that occurs on the right side of a replacement. The choices duplicate the ways of representing an instance of a program clause—copy on use or structure sharing. For terms, copy on use creates a copy of a term with program variables replaced by new variables, while structure sharing references the term in the program, along with a local substitution. Thus the techniques are familiar from Datalog implementation, but their use for terms is novel with Prolog.

10.1. Representations

The representation chosen for atoms (unsigned literals) and terms that the Prolog interpreter manipulates greatly affects efficiency. Because atoms and terms are syntactically identical, the same data structures can represent both. One possible representation is to use a record for every atom or term, even if it is only a variable or a constant. A record for an *n*-ary atom or term consists of $n + 1$ fields. The first field contains a reference to the symbol table entry of the structure symbol (the predicate name or the function symbol); the remaining fields contain pointers to other records representing the subterms. A constant is a 0-ary structure symbol and therefore is represented by a record with a single field referencing a symbol table entry. A variable is represented similarly with a one-field record. Figure 10.1 shows the representation of the literal **p(f(X), a, g(b, Y))** as a set of records and a symbol table. A heavy bar in each record sets off the structure-symbol field from the rest.

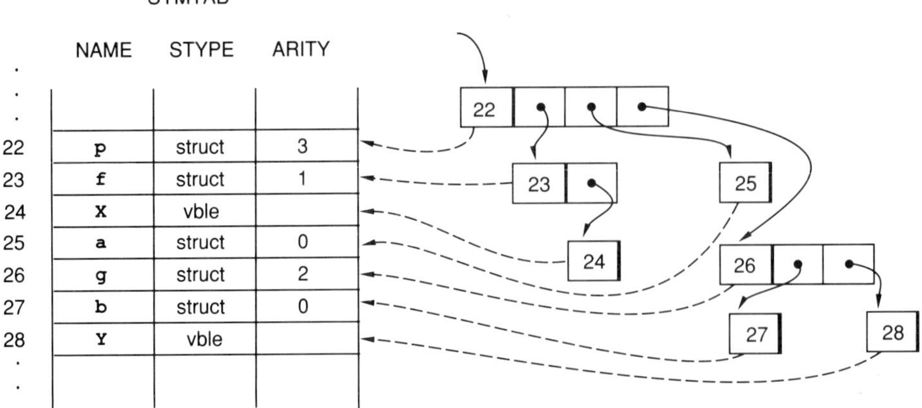

Figure 10.1

Using one-field records to reference constants and variables in the symbol table is wasteful of space. For example, why not let the third field of the top record directly reference the **a** entry in the symbol table? If it did so, we would not know if the field references a symbol table entry or another record, and so could not interpret the reference correctly. With the representation in Figure 10.1, the first field of any record always points to the symbol table; the remaining fields all point to other records.

This representation does have a certain simplicity and elegance to it, but it wastes space and adds a level of indirection for accessing constants and variables. One-field records can be eliminated by allowing any field to reference the symbol table directly and by using a tag to indicate whether a reference is to the symbol table or another record. Figure 10.2 shows the same term in this more space-efficient representation. Each field now has a one-bit tag, which is marked '×' if the field references the symbol table. The first field of a record does not need a tag, since it always references the symbol table. We will assume this second representation for our development. (Note that if the address spaces for the symbol table and structure records are disjoint, the tag bit is unnecessary. In that situation the tag bit is implicit in an address.)

We use the following types in the development: *symtabindex,* for symbol table references; *structref,* for references to structure records; and *structure,* which is the union of *symtabindex* and *structref.*

Pascal does not support variable-length records directly, but they can be implemented with an array and various access functions. (See Exercise 6.1.) We use the following functions to access such records. First, three Boolean functions determine the form of a value, all taking an argument of type *structure*:

variable(S) is true if *S* is a variable in the symbol table,
constant(S) is true if *S* is a constant, and
struct(S) is true if *S* is a record structure.

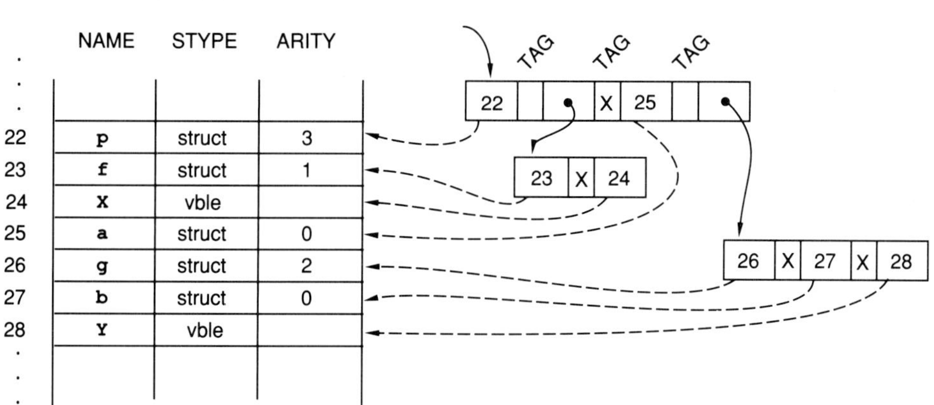

Figure 10.2

As with Datalog, we also have three functions for decomposing structured terms. They all take a parameter of type *structref*; the second also takes an integer:

> *structsym(S)* returns the *symtabindex* to the structure symbol of record *S*,
> *arg(S, I)* returns the *structure* that is the Ith field of record *S*, and
> *arity(S)* returns the number of fields in record *S*.

The functions *structsym* and *arg* can appear on the left side of assignments to modify a field in a record.

Some of the old types we used to implement Datalog must now be updated, because literals and right sides of replacements have more complex structure. A *litlist* is now a list of arbitrary structures, not just literals, and *subst* may contain structured terms as right sides of replacements.

```
type
      litlist  =  ↑lits; {for lists of literals}

      lits = record
                LITERAL: structure;
                REST: litlist
           end;

      subst  =  ↑repl;

      repl  =  record {for replacements}
                V: symtabindex;
                VCS: structure;
                NXTR: subst;
           end;
```

The *clauserec* type must also change accordingly.

10.2. Naive Prolog Interpreter

With these modifications we can now give the code for the Prolog interpreter described in Chapter 7. This naive *establish* routine for Prolog is almost identical to the one for Datalog in Section 6.2. (What is the difference?)

```
var CLAUSEINST: clauselist;
    SUBS: subst;
    NEWGL: litlist;

function establish1(GOALLIST: litlist): boolean;
    var NEXTCL: clauselist;
    begin
      if isempty(GOALLIST) then return(true);
      NEXTCL := SYMTAB[structsym(first(GOALLIST))].CLAUSES;
      while NEXTCL <> nil do
        begin
          CLAUSEINST := instance(NEXTCL);
          NEWGL := copy(GOALLIST);
          if match1(CLAUSEINST↑.HEAD, first(NEWGL), SUBS) then
            begin
              NEWGL := concat(CLAUSEINST↑.BODY, rest(NEWGL));
              apply(SUBS, NEWGL);
              if establish1(NEWGL) then return(true)
            end;
          NEXTCL := NEXTCL↑.NXTCLAUSE
        end;
      return(false)
    end;
```

The functions used in *establish1* must be extended from the Datalog definitions, because they must deal with a more general data structure. They must handle structured terms, not just constants and variables. The function *copy* copies a list of literals, making a copy of all subterms. We give the code only for its subfunction *copystruct*, which is used to copy each literal on the list:

```
function copystruct(STR: structure): structure;
    var TS: structure;
      I: integer;
    begin
      if variable(STR) then return(STR)
      else if constant(STR) then return(STR)
      else
        begin
          TS := newcopy(STR);
```

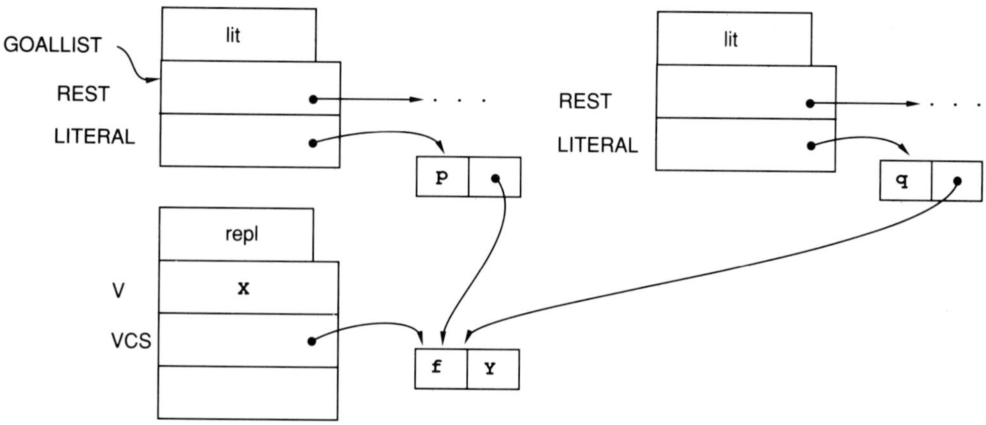

Figure 10.3

```
        for I = 1 to arity(structsym(STR)) do
            arg(TS, I) := copystruct(arg(STR, I));
        return(TS)
    end
end;
```

The function *newcopy* takes a structure record as a template, allocates a new record with the same size and structure symbol, and returns the new record. Here we use *arg* as a pseudofunction to modify the fields of a structure record.

The function *apply* need not copy the goal list, but it does have to make a copy, using *copystruct,* of the right side of a replacement each time it replaces a variable. Consider what can go wrong if it does not copy the replacement term. Assume **p (X)** and **q (X)** are two literals in the goal list, and *apply* must perform the replacement **X = f (Y)** to apply. Suppose it modifies the structures representing **p (X)** and **q (X)** to point directly to the structure in the VCS field of the replacement, as shown in Figure 10.3. (The figure shows structure symbols instead of symbol table references.) Suppose we solve the **p**-goal and later apply the replacement **Y = g (a)**, again by modifying existing structures. (See Figure 10.4.) Should we backtrack to the **p**-goal, we find the later application has permanently altered the first replacement. The goal **p (f (g (a)))** is not restored to **p (f (Y))**.

We next give the matching function that finds the mgu of two atoms. Recall that it calls a function *findfirst* to find the first mismatch between two subterms. If *findfirst* returns a replacement that resolves the mismatch, then *match1* applies it to both terms, composes it with the current substitution, and iterates until no mismatch is found. We have *match1* create and pass in a replacement record that *findfirst* fills in. If its arguments are unifiable, *match1* returns **true** and MGU contains their mgu.

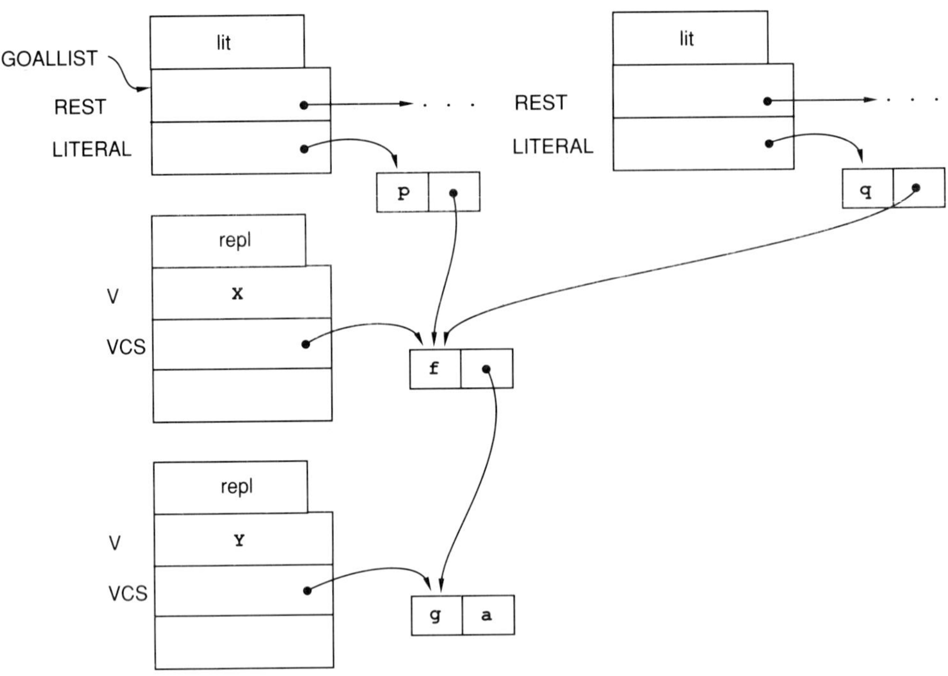

Figure 10.4

```
type matchtest = (none, clash, match);

function match1(T1, T2: structure; var MGU: subst): boolean;
    var OC: matchtest;
      REPL: subst;
    begin
      MGU := nil;
      begin
        new(REPL);
        findfirst(T1, T2, REPL, OC);
        if OC = none then return(true);
        if OC = clash then return(false);
        if violates(REPL) then return(false);
        MGU := compose(MGU, REPL);
        apply(REPL, T1);
        apply(REPL, T2)
      end
    end;
```

The *findfirst* procedure treats its first two arguments as trees and traverses them in preorder, looking for a mismatch of subterms. If one of the subterms is a variable, REPL is filled in with a replacement that fixes the mismatch, unless the *violates* check in *match1* subsequently rejects the replacement. Note that neither structure will be a variable on the initial invocation from *match1*, since *findfirst* is called first with two literals.

```
procedure findfirst(T1, T2: structure; var REPL: subst; var OUTCOME: matchtest);
    var I: integer;
    begin
      if variable(T1) then
        if variable(T2) and (T1=T2) then OUTCOME := none
        else
          begin
            REPL↑.V := T1; REPL↑.VCS := T2;
            OUTCOME := match
          end
      else if variable(T2) then
        begin
          REPL↑.V := T2; REPL↑.VCS := T1;
          OUTCOME := match
        end
      else if structsym(T1) = structsym(T2) then
        begin
          I := 1;
          OUTCOME := none;
          while (I <= arity(structsym(T1))) and (OUTCOME = none) do
            begin
              findfirst(arg(T1, I), arg(T2, I), REPL, OUTCOME);
              I := I + 1
            end
          end
        else OUTCOME := clash
    end;
```

The function *compose* copies the substitution. It adds REPL to the end of the modified substitution and returns the result. The function *violates* checks whether the replacement is legal—that is, whether the variable being replaced occurs in the term replacing it. If so, T1 and T2 cannot be made to match; no matter what term replaces the variable in one term, the other will contain a larger term at the corresponding position. Allowing such a replacement can lead to infinite loops in *match1*, since it will build larger and larger structures trying to get T1 and T2 to match. Later versions of the *match* routine that dereference variables rather than applying replacements immediately do not run the danger of infinite behavior. In practice, *violates* is usually omitted for efficiency, because it has to walk an entire right-side term to see that the left-side variable is not used.

This section presented a direct formalization of the naive Prolog interpreter we saw in Chapter 7. The resulting interpreter is extremely inefficient because of the amount of copying of structures that it does, and the amount of retracing of terms *findfirst* does to find new mismatches. Once a mismatch is fixed with a replacement, any remaining mismatches must occur after the point of the last mismatch. The improvements we can make to this algorithm initially mirror those made in the development of our efficient Datalog interpreter. As much as possible, we follow the same development as in Chapter 6. We will be able to discard *findfirst* once substitution application is moved into *match*. A new problem arises in representing terms in replacements once we delay application of the local substitution.

10.3. Delayed Copying and Application

Just as in Datalog, repetitive copying of the entire goal list can be avoided by accumulating the substitution and applying it only as goals come to the front of the goal list. The modified interpreter, *establish2,* is now passed a goal list *and* the accumulated substitution. It applies the substitution to only the first goal in the list, immediately before calling *match1*. If *match1* succeeds, the resulting mgu is composed with the accumulated substitution before the recursive call to solve the rest of the goal list.

```
var SUBS, NEWACCSUBS: subst;
    THISGOAL: lit;
    NEWGL: litlist;

function establish2(GOALLIST: litlist; ACCSUBS: subst): boolean;
    var NEXTCL: clauselist;
    begin
      if isempty(GOALLIST) then return(true);
      NEXTCL := SYMTAB[structsym(first(GOALLIST))].CLAUSES;
      while NEXTCL <> nil do
        begin
          CLAUSEINST := instance(NEXTCL);
          THISGOAL := copyapply2(ACCSUBS, first(GOALLIST));
          if match1(CLAUSEINST↑.HEAD, THISGOAL, SUBS) then
            begin
              NEWGL := concat(CLAUSEINST↑.BODY, rest(GOALLIST));
              NEWACCSUBS := copycompose(ACCSUBS, SUBS);
              if establish2(NEWGL, NEWACCSUBS) then return(true)
            end;
          NEXTCL := NEXTCL↑.NXTCLAUSE
        end;
      return(false)
    end;
```

The function *copyapply2* creates a new copy of the goal literal and applies the accumulated substitution to the copy. Neither argument is altered. In Chapter 6, right sides of replacements were not complex structures, so they needed no copying. Here *copyapply2* must use *copystruct* to duplicate right sides. The function *copy-compose* (given in Section 6.3) composes a copy of its first argument with its second.

Actually *copycompose* need not copy all right sides of replacements in its first argument. (See Exercise 10.1.)

10.4. Delayed Composition of Substitutions

The next step in refining the interpreter is to postpone the composition of substitutions. In *establish3* we simply collect a list of replacements and dereference variables through that list during application of the substitution to a goal literal. Notice we have changed the name of the second argument from ACCSUBS to REPLS to emphasize that it is simply a list of replacements, not necessarily a substitution.

```
var CLAUSEINST: clauselist;
    SUBS, NEWREPLS: subst;
    THISGOAL: structure;
    NEWGL: litlist;

function establish3(GOALLIST: litlist; REPLS: subst): boolean;
    var NEXTCL: clauselist;
    begin
      if isempty(GOALLIST) then return(true);
      NEXTCL := SYMTAB[structsym(first(GOALLIST))].CLAUSES;
      while NEXTCL <> nil do
        begin
          CLAUSEINST := instance(NEXTCL);
          THISGOAL := copyapplyrepls(REPLS, first(GOALLIST));
          if match1(CLAUSEINST↑.HEAD, THISGOAL, SUBS) then
            begin
              NEWGL := concat(CLAUSEINST↑.BODY, rest(GOALLIST));
              NEWREPLS := rconcat(SUBS, REPLS);
              if establish3(NEWGL, NEWREPLS) then return(true)
            end;
          NEXTCL := NEXTCL↑.NXTCLAUSE
        end;
      return(false)
    end;
```

We now use *copyapplyrepls* to copy the head of the goal list and apply the replacements in REPLS. It is similar to *copyapply2,* except that variables are dereferenced through REPLS before they are copied. The code of the *deref* function is identical to the corresponding function in Section 6.4 but for a subtle difference. Given variable **V**, the Datalog version of *deref* always returned the image of **V** under the substitution represented by REPLS. Not so with the Prolog version. The term that *deref* returns may have variables embedded in it that can be dereferenced further. For example, if REPLS =

```
[X = h(a), Y = Z, Z = k(X)]
```

deref returns **k(X)** when called with **Y**, whereas the replacement for **Y** in the substitution represented by REPLS is **k(h(a))**. Thus the new *copyapplyrepls* must descend into STRUCT.

```
function copyapplyrepls(REPLS: subst; STRUCT: structure): structure;
    var NEWSTR: structure;
      I: integer;
    begin
      STRUCT := deref(STRUCT, REPLS);
      if struct(STRUCT) then
        begin
          NEWSTR := newcopy(STRUCT);
          for I := 1 to arity(structsym(STRUCT)) do
            arg(NEWSTR, I) := copyapplyrepls(REPLS, arg(STRUCT, I));
          return(NEWSTR)
        end
      else return(STRUCT)
    end;

function deref(ST: structure; REPLS: subst): structure;
    var NEXTREPL: subst;
    begin
      if variable(ST) then
        begin
          NEXTREPL := REPLS;
          while NEXTREPL <> nil do
            if NEXTREPL↑.V = ST then return(deref(NEXTREPL↑.VCS, REPLS))
            else NEXTREPL := NEXTREPL↑.NXTR
        end;
      return(ST)
    end;
```

10.5. Avoiding Copies Altogether

The next two steps will eliminate all copying of literals, both from GOALLIST and in taking an instance of NEXTCL. By doing so, we will simplify the form of the *match* function.

10.5.1. *Applying Substitutions in the Matching Routine*

Following the optimizations applied to the Datalog interpreter, we move the application of a replacement list to a goal into the *match* routine. Our initial matching function, *match1*, was based on the subfunction *findfirst*, which terminates its search and returns to *match1* when it finds a mismatch. Why must control pass back up to *match1* and the search be restarted after a mismatch is patched? The reason is that *match1* has to apply the replacement globally throughout both literals. When *findfirst* has descended within a literal, there is no ready means to find all occurrences of a variable. For example, in matching **p(h(a), Y)** to **p(h(X), X)**, the invocation of *findfirst* that actually constructs the replacement **X** = **a** does not have access to the other occurrence of **X** in **p(h(X), X)**. Instead we let *match* itself apply substitutions and simply forge onward after creating a new replacement. Once a replacement is added to the list of replacements, it is as though it has been applied globally in the literal, since the entire list will be applied before looking at any variable. We substitute access to the replacement list for access to the entire literals. At any point the replacement list and any subterm of the input literals implicitly provide the image term under the accumulated substitution.

In *establish4* the first goal on the goal list need not be copied, since it is only examined, not changed. The only data structure that is updated is the list of replacements, which grows only by having a new replacement added to the front. The original list is always present and unchanged in the modified list. Thus to restore that data on backtracking, we need only maintain a pointer to the original list.

```
var CLAUSEINST: clauselist;
    NEWREPLS: subst;
    NEWGL: litlist;

function establish4(GOALLIST: litlist; REPLS: subst): boolean;
    var NEXTCL: clauselist;
    begin
      if isempty(GOALLIST) then return(true);
      NEXTCL := SYMTAB[structsym(first(GOALLIST))].CLAUSES;
      while NEXTCL <> nil do
        begin
          CLAUSEINST := instance(NEXTCL);
          NEWREPLS := REPLS;
          if match4(CLAUSEINST↑.HEAD, first(GOALLIST), NEWREPLS) then
            begin
              NEWGL := concat(CLAUSEINST↑.BODY, rest(GOALLIST));
              if establish4(NEWGL, NEWREPLS) then return(true)
            end;
          NEXTCL := NEXTCL↑.NXTCLAUSE
        end;
      return(false)
    end;
```

Function *match4* first dereferences its arguments through the replacement list. If one is a variable, it builds a replacement and adds it to the front of the list. If the arguments are similar structured terms, it descends into them recursively. Comparing *match4* to its namesake in Section 6.5.1, we see that the **for**-loop has been moved to the end and surrounds a recursive call to the matching routine. The version in Chapter 6 is a special case of the version here in which the recursive call is unwound one level, and the initial call is optimized with the knowledge that T1 and T2 will not be variables.

```
function match4(T1, T2: structure; var NEWREPLS: subst): boolean;
    var REPL: subst;
      ARG1, ARG2: structure;
      I: integer;
    begin
      ARG1 := deref(T1, NEWREPLS);
      ARG2 := deref(T2, NEWREPLS);
      if variable(ARG1) then
        if ARG1 = ARG2 then {same variable, do nothing}
        else
          begin
            if violates4(ARG1, ARG2, NEWREPLS) then return(false);
            new(REPL); REPL↑.V := ARG1;
            REPL↑.VCS := ARG2; REPL↑.NXTR := NEWREPLS;
            NEWREPLS := REPL
          end
      else if variable(ARG2) then
        begin
          if violates4(ARG2, ARG1, NEWREPLS) then return(false);
          new(REPL); REPL↑.V := ARG2;
          REPL↑.VCS := ARG1; REPL↑.NXTR := NEWREPLS;
          NEWREPLS := REPL
        end
      else if structsym(ARG1) = structsym(ARG2) then
        for I = 1 to arity(structsym(ARG1)) do
          if not match4(arg(ARG1, I), arg(ARG2, I), NEWREPLS) then return(false)
      else return(false);
      return(true)
    end;
```

Recall that the *violates* function checks to see whether a variable occurs in the term that is replacing it. The function *violates4* takes the replacement term as two separate parameters. It must fully dereference the variables in the term it is searching. For this reason we must pass it the current list of replacements, NEWREPLS. This check is expensive, since *violates4* must traverse the entire term, dereferencing any variables it encounters. Many Prolog interpreters omit *violates,* leaving it up to the programmer to avoid binding a variable to a term containing it. The reasoning is that adding a replacement to the list corresponds to the basic assignment operation of procedural programming languages, and such a basic and frequent operation should be done in constant time.

10.5.2. *Structure Sharing for Code*

Next we introduce local substitutions to avoid copying clauses. This change permits the use of lazy lists and lets the goal list incorporate original code literals rather than copies. The type *molecule* contains a reference to a structure, which is a part of a program clause, and a reference to a substitution, which is constructed when an instance of the clause is needed. We call the first field STRUCT instead of ATOM because we will also use a *molecule* for a term in the *match* routine.

```
type
      molecule = record
                     STRUCT: structure;
                     LSUB: subst
                 end;
```

The functions for manipulating lazy lists, *isempty5, first5,* and *lconcat_rest,* are the same as given in Section 6.5.2. Recall that *first5* returns a molecule.

```
var NEWREPLS: subst;
    HEADMOL: molecule;
    NEWGL: llist;

function establish5(GOALLIST: llist; REPLS: subst): boolean;
    var NEXTCL: clauselist;
      GOALMOL: molecule;
    begin
      if isempty5(GOALLIST) then return(true);
      GOALMOL := first5(GOALLIST);
      NEXTCL := SYMTAB[structsym(GOALMOL.STRUCT)].CLAUSES;
      while NEXTCL <> nil do
        begin
          HEADMOL.STRUCT:= NEXTCL↑.HEAD;
          HEADMOL.LSUB := newvars(NEXTCL);
          NEWREPLS := REPLS;
          if match5(HEADMOL, GOALMOL, NEWREPLS) then
            begin
              NEWGL := lconcat_rest(NEXTCL↑.BODY, HEADMOL.LSUB,
                                                  GOALLIST);
              if establish5(NEWGL, NEWREPLS) then return(true)
            end;
          NEXTCL := NEXTCL↑.NXTCLAUSE
        end;
      return(false)
    end;
```

The first major deviation from the development of the interpreter as done in Chapter 6 comes now—in that the *match* function must be changed substantially to handle local substitutions. Consider what *match5* must do. It is called with two molecules and the replacement list, NEWREPLS. Our first thought might be simply to use *match4*. We would have to change the types of its first two arguments to be molecules and apply the local substitution when dereferencing variables. Also, when *match4* recurs on subterms, it must pass along the appropriate local substitution with the subterm. A molecule can package that subterm with a local substitution.

To see that this approach does not work, we trace the execution of (such a modified) *match4* on a call. For simplicity, assume that NEWREPLS is initially empty. Let the two molecules be as follows:

```
MOL1: STRUCT:   g(X, f(Y))
      LSUB:     {X = X1, Y = Y1}

MOL2: STRUCT:   g(f(Y), X)
      LSUB:     {Y = Y2, X = X2}
```

Since the structure symbols of the two arguments are equal, these inputs cause a recursive call to *match4* with the following two molecules:

```
MOL1: STRUCT:   X
      LSUB:     {X = X1, Y = Y1}

MOL2: STRUCT:   f(Y)
      LSUB:     {Y = Y2, X = X2}
```

Next *deref* takes **X** to **X1** and **f(Y)** to **f(Y)** (since **f(Y)** is not a variable and so no substitution is performed). Because ARG1 is now a variable, *match4* creates the replacement **X1 = f(Y)**. Similarly, matching the second arguments of the original structures results in another replacement, **X2 = f(Y)**. The new replacement list is now **[X2 = f(Y), X1 = f(Y)]**. The problem emerges that the occurrences of the variable **Y** in the replacement are out of place. No program variables should appear in this replacement list. To see that this replacement list is incorrect, consider applying the local substitution and then this replacement list to the original structure of the first molecule. The result is **g(f(Y), f(Y))**. It should really be **g(f(Y2), f(Y1))**; the two occurrences of **Y** are actually different variables. The problem is that the replacement **X1 = f(Y)** ignores the LSUB of MOL2. The program variable **Y** on the right of the replacement should be replaced by **Y2**, not left intact.

There are two solutions to this problem, and both are used in practice. One solution is to carry the local substitution along with the right side of the replacement, making the replacing structure a molecule instead of a term. This solution is called *structure sharing for terms*. The other solution is to go ahead and apply the local substitution to the replacing term when the replacement is constructed. This method is called *copy on use for terms*, because the replacing term must be copied out of the program code before the local substitution is applied. Notice the similarities to the structure-sharing and copy-on-use methods for dealing with program clauses. The next two subsections describe the two methods, giving a *deref* and *match* procedure for each.

10.5.2.1. Structure Sharing for Terms

Consider the structure-sharing solution. Here the replacing term is a molecule, so we need a new type for replacements.

```
type
    subst = ↑molrepl;
```

```
molrepl = record {for replacements}
            V: symtabindex;
            VCS: molecule;
            NXTR: subst;
        end;
```

The structure in any molecule must be dereferenced twice, once through the local substitution in LSUB of the molecule, and then through the replacement list in REPLS. Rather than invoking *deref* twice from *match,* we pass it a molecule as input and let it perform both dereferences. A special case arises when *match* recurses down to a molecule whose STRUCT field is a new variable. In that case only REPLS should be applied. Where can a molecule representing a new variable arise? It can be created only in *newvars*. When *newvars* creates a local substitution for a clause, it creates a list of *molrepls*. The V field of each *molrepl* is a program variable. The VCS field is a molecule containing a new variable in its STRUCT field. We set the LSUB field to **nil** so that *deref* can detect that no local substitution is needed.

The procedure *deref5ss* given here returns a molecule, because it must associate a local substitution with any structured term it returns. If it returns a variable, it will never be a program variable, since such a variable would have been dereferenced through a local substitution. Thus *match5ss* can never construct a replacement where the V or VCS.STRUCT field is a program variable, avoiding the problem with **g(X, f(Y))** and **g(f(Y), X)** we saw earlier. Previously, *deref* was passed a structure and a replacement list, and returned a structure. We make *deref5ss* a procedure that changes its first argument, rather than a function, since the molecule it gets is newly created and can be modified without danger.

```
{If MOL.STRUCT is a variable, apply MOL.LSUB, then REPLS}
procedure deref5ss(var MOL: molecule; REPLS: subst);
  var NEXTREPL: subst;
  begin
    if variable(MOL.STRUCT) then
      begin
        if MOL.LSUB <> nil then
          begin {apply local substitution}
            NEXTREPL := MOL.LSUB;
            while MOL.STRUCT <> NEXTREPL↑.V do
              NEXTREPL := NEXTREPL↑.NXTR;
            MOL := NEXTREPL↑.VCS
          end;
        NEXTREPL := REPLS; {apply replacement list}
        while NEXTREPL <> nil do
          if NEXTREPL↑.V = MOL.STRUCT then
            begin
              MOL := NEXTREPL↑.VCS;
              deref5ss(MOL, REPLS)
            end
```

```
            else NEXTREPL := NEXTREPL↑.NXTR
        end;
    end;
```

The test that MOL.LSUB is not **nil** screens out the case that MOL represents a new variable. The first **while**-loop does the variable-for-variable replacement defined by the local substitution. Applying a local substitution to a variable is special, since we know there is a replacement for the variable. Further, once a replacement is applied to the variable, no other replacement from the local substitution can change the result, since replacements in a local substitution always have a program variable on the left (and a new variable on the right). The second loop searches the accumulated list of replacements for one to apply to the variable. It uses a recursive call in case the result is a variable that can be dereferenced further. We now use *deref5ss* to define the *match5ss* function.

```
function match5ss(MOL1, MOL2: molecule; var NEWREPLS: subst): boolean;
    var REPL: subst;
      NMOL1, NMOL2: molecule;
      I: integer;
    begin
      deref5ss(MOL1, NEWREPLS);
      deref5ss(MOL2, NEWREPLS);
      if variable(MOL1.STRUCT) then
        if MOL1.STRUCT = MOL2.STRUCT then {same variable, do nothing}
        else
          begin
            if violates5(MOL1, MOL2, NEWREPLS) then return(false);
            new(REPL); REPL↑.V := MOL1.STRUCT;
            REPL↑.VCS := MOL2; REPL↑.NXTR := NEWREPLS;
            NEWREPLS := REPL
          end
      else if variable(MOL2.STRUCT) then
        begin
          if violates5(MOL2, MOL1, NEWREPLS) then return(false);
          new(REPL); REPL↑.V := MOL2.STRUCT;
          REPL↑.VCS := MOL1; REPL↑.NXTR := NEWREPLS;
          NEWREPLS := REPL
        end
      else if structsym(MOL1.STRUCT) = structsym(MOL2.STRUCT) then
        for I = 1 to arity(structsym(MOL1.STRUCT)) do
          begin
            NMOL1.STRUCT := arg(MOL1.STRUCT, I);
            NMOL1.LSUB := MOL1.LSUB;
            NMOL2.STRUCT := arg(MOL2.STRUCT, I);
            NMOL2.LSUB := MOL2.LSUB;
            if not match5ss(NMOL1, NMOL2, NEWREPLS) then return(false)
          end
```

```
    else return(false);
    return(true)
end;
```

The main difference between *match4* and *match5ss* is that when *match5ss* descends into the substructure of MOL1 and MOL2, it must create new molecules NMOL1 and NMOL2 to represent those substructures. The molecules are required because these substructures may contain program variables that must be dereferenced through a local substitution. Also, the VCS field for each replacement is now a molecule rather than simply a structure. A further change is the *violates5* function, which checks for an occurrence violation, now takes two molecules as parameters.

EXAMPLE 10.1: We trace *match5ss* with arguments:

```
m1:   STRUCT:    p(f(Y), X)
      LSUB:      {X = X1, Y = Y1}

m2:   STRUCT:    p(X, g(X, Y))
      LSUB:      {X = X2, Y = Y2}
```

and the initial replacement list:

```
r1:   V:      X1
      VCS:    STRUCT:     g(Z, Z)
              LSUB:       {W = W3, Z = Z3}
      NXTR: nil
```

On the first call to *match5ss*, no change is made on dereferencing. It discovers that the outermost structure symbols match, so it calls itself recursively on:

```
m3:   STRUCT:    f(Y)
      LSUB:      {X = X1, Y = Y1}

m4:   STRUCT:    X
      LSUB:      {X = X2, Y = Y2}
```

Here *m4* is changed by dereferencing, yielding:

```
m4:   STRUCT:    X2
      LSUB:      nil
```

The next replacement *match5ss* generates is:

```
r2:   V:      X2
      VCS:    STRUCT:     f(Y)
              LSUB:       {X = X1, Y = Y1}
      NXTR: r1
```

Note that the VCS field of *r2* holds a molecule different from *m3* but that the VCS.STRUCT field for *r2* and the STRUCT field of *m3* both point to the same term in the program, which is an example of structure sharing. Likewise, VCS.LSUB and the LSUB field of *r2* reference the same substitution object. Control returns to the initial invocation of *match5ss*. That invocation now makes a recursive call on the second arguments:

```
m5:   STRUCT:   X
      LSUB:     {X = X1, Y = Y1}

m6:   STRUCT:   g(X, Y)
      LSUB:     {X = X2, Y = Y2}
```

Here molecule *m5* is changed by *deref5ss*. First **X** is dereferenced to **X1** using the local substitution; then the molecule is updated using the first replacement in the accumulated replacement list. The new state of molecule *m5* is then:

```
m5:   STRUCT:   g(Z, Z)
      LSUB:     {W = W3, Z = Z3}
```

Again the structure symbols agree, so *match5ss* makes a recursive call, using molecules:

```
m7:   STRUCT:   Z
      LSUB:     {W = W3, Z = Z3}

m8:   STRUCT:   X
      LSUB:     {X = X2, Y = Y2}
```

Here **Z** gets dereferenced to **Z3**, which is not mapped anywhere by the replacement list. **X** is dereferenced to **X2**, for which *r2* is a replacement. Hence *deref5ss* changes molecule *m8* to:

```
m8:   STRUCT:   f(Y)
      LSUB:     {X = X1, Y = Y1}
```

and *match5ss* generates another replacement:

```
r3:   V:      Z3
      VCS:    STRUCT:   f(Y)
              LSUB:     {X = X1, Y = Y1}
      NXTR:   r2
```

The next call to *match5ss* is on the second arguments of *m5* and *m6*:

```
m9:   STRUCT:   Z
      LSUB:     {W = W3, Z = Z3}

m10:  STRUCT:   Y
      LSUB:     {X = X2, Y = Y2}
```

Here **Z** is dereferenced to **Z3** by the local substitution, and then *r3* is used to change *m9* to:

```
m9:   STRUCT:   f(Y)
      LSUB:     {X = X1, Y = Y1}
```

The **Y** in *m10* is dereferenced to **Y2** by the local substitution but is unaffected by the replacement list, so *match5ss* generates the replacement:

```
r4:   V:      Y2
      VCS:    STRUCT:   f(Y)
              LSUB:     {X = X1, Y = Y1}
      NXTR: r3
```

At this point all active invocations of *match5ss* succeed.

To recapitulate, the original input to *match5ss* was:

```
p(f(Y1), g(Z3, Z3))
p(X2, g(X2, Y2))
```

taking the local substitutions and the initial replacement list into account. The entire list of replacements after *match5ss* suceeds is:

```
[Y2 = f(Y1), Z3 = f(Y1), X2 = f(Y1), X1 = g(Z3, Z3)]
```

again taking note of local substitutions. (Recall the convention of square brackets for replacement lists that are not necessarily substitutions.) Applying this replacement list to either input yields:

```
p(f(Y1), g(f(Y1), f(Y1))) □
```

10.5.2.2. Copy on Use for Terms Consider the copy-on-use solution. We copy a term when using it in a replacement, substituting new variables for program variables. In this method we no longer need the type *molrepl*, since replacements will not (in general) share replacement terms.

```
{If MOL.STRUCT is a variable, apply MOL.LSUB, then REPLS}
procedure deref5cu(var MOL: molecule; REPLS: subst);
   var NEXTREPL: subst;
   begin
     if variable(MOL.STRUCT) then
       begin
         if MOL.LSUB <> nil then
           begin {apply local substitution}
             NEXTREPL := MOL.LSUB;
             while MOL.STRUCT <> NEXTREPL↑.V do
               NEXTREPL := NEXTREPL↑.NXTR;
             MOL.STRUCT := NEXTREPL↑.VCS;
             MOL.LSUB := nil
           end;
         NEXTREPL := REPLS; {apply replacement list}
         while NEXTREPL <> nil do
           if NEXTREPL↑.V = MOL.STRUCT then
```

```
            begin
               MOL.STRUCT := NEXTREPL↑.VCS;
               deref5cu(MOL, REPLS)
            end
          else NEXTREPL := NEXTREPL↑.NXTR
      end
  end;
```

Again the first loop in the dereferencing function does the variable-for-variable replacement defined by the local substitution; the second loop searches the accumulated list of replacements to apply them to the variable. Once *deref5cu* applies the local substitution, it sets MOL.LSUB to **nil**. This explicit assignment was unnecessary in *deref5ss,* since a molecule with **nil** for LSUB was copied.

To understand the behavior of *match5cu,* we distinguish *program terms* from *copy terms*. Program terms are those that are subparts of the Prolog program. Copy terms are those created by *match5cu* when it generates a replacement from a program term, or a subterm of another copy term. The V field in a replacement in REPLS will always be a new variable, avoiding the problem of program variables appearing in replacements. The VCS field will always be a copy term. The matching function must be able to detect copy terms, since a copy term does not need to be copied for use in a replacement. A copy term contains no program variables and so requires no local substitution. We set the LSUB field associated with a copy term to **nil**, and so a **nil** LSUB will indicate that a term need not be copied.

```
function match5cu(MOL1, MOL2: molecule; var NEWREPLS: subst): boolean;
    var REPL: subst;
      NMOL1, NMOL2: molecule;
      I: integer;
    begin
      deref5cu(MOL1, NEWREPLS);
      deref5cu(MOL2, NEWREPLS);
      if variable(MOL1.STRUCT) then
        if MOL1.STRUCT = MOL2.STRUCT then {same variable, do nothing}
        else
          begin
            if violates5(MOL1, MOL2, NEWREPLS) then return(false);
            new(REPL); REPL↑.V := MOL1.STRUCT;
            if MOL2.LSUBS = nil then REPL↑.VCS := MOL2.STRUCT
            else REPL↑.VCS := copyapplyrepls(MOL2.LSUBS, MOL2.STRUCT);
            REPL↑.NXTR := NEWREPLS; NEWREPLS := REPL
          end
      else if variable5(MOL2.STRUCT) then
        begin
          if violates5(MOL2, MOL1, NEWREPLS) then return(false);
          new(REPL); REPL↑.V := MOL2.STRUCT;
          if MOL1.LSUBS = nil then REPL↑.VCS := MOL1.STRUCT
          else REPL↑.VCS := copyapplyrepls(MOL1.LSUBS, MOL1.STRUCT);
```

```
        REPL↑.NXTR := NEWREPLS; NEWREPLS := REPL
      end
    else if structsym(MOL1.STRUCT) = structsym(MOL2.STRUCT) then
      for I = 1 to arity(structsym(MOL1.STRUCT)) do
        begin
          NMOL1.STRUCT := arg(MOL1.STRUCT, I);
          NMOL1.LSUB := MOL1.LSUB;
          NMOL2.STRUCT := arg(MOL2.STRUCT, I);
          NMOL2.LSUB := MOL2.LSUB;
          if not match5cu(NMOL1, NMOL2, NEWREPLS) then return(false)
        end
    else return(false);
    return(true)
  end;
```

An added advantage of the test for LSUB equal to **nil** before copying a term is that if the term comes from a variable-free program clause, no copying is done either, because *newvars* returns a **nil** local substitution in that case. Other opportunities for avoiding copy exist as well. (See Exercise 10.5b.)

EXAMPLE 10.2: Consider invocation of *match5cu* on the same molecules used in the last example.

```
m1:   STRUCT:   p(f(Y), X)
      LSUB:     {X = X1, Y = Y1}

m2:   STRUCT:   p(X, g(X, Y))
      LSUB:     {X = X2, Y = Y2}
```

We assume the same initial replacement, now represented without a molecule.

NEWREPLS = **[X1 = g(Z3, Z3)]**

The structure symbols agree, so *match5cu* calls itself on the first arguments:

```
m3:   STRUCT:   f(Y)
      LSUB:     {X = X1, Y = Y1}

m4:   STRUCT:   X
      LSUB:     {X = X2, Y = Y2}
```

The first molecule is not changed by *deref5cu,* but the second has **X** mapped to **X2**. Thus the variable **X2** is matched to the term **f(Y)**, which is copied with the local substitution applied to yield another replacement.

NEWREPLS = **[X2 = f(Y1), X1 = g(Z3, Z3)]**

Next the initial invocation of *match5cu* considers the second arguments:

```
m5:   STRUCT:   X
      LSUB:     {X = X1, Y = Y1}
```

m6: STRUCT: **g(X, Y)**
LSUB: **{X = X2, Y = Y2}**

The first molecule dereferences to **X1** and then to **g(Z3, Z3)**, so *match5cu* calls itself on:

m7: STRUCT: **Z3**
LSUB: **nil**

m8: STRUCT: **X**
LSUB: **{X = X2, Y = Y2}**

Here **X** in molecule *m8* is dereferenced to **X2** and thence to **f(Y1)**. When *deref5cu* dereferences **X2**, it returns **f(Y1)** in a molecule with LSUB set to **nil**. Therefore **f(Y1)** is recognized as a copy term and no additional copying is done.

NEWREPLS = **[Z3 = f(Y1), X2 = f(Y1), X1 = g(Z3, Z3)]**

The next call to *match5cu* is with:

m9: STRUCT: **Z3**
LSUB: **nil**

m10: STRUCT: **Y**
LSUB: **{X = X2, Y = Y2}**

Molecule *m9* is dereferenced to **f(Y1)**, while in *m10*, **Y** is dereferenced to **Y2**. Again since **f(Y1)** is a copy term, no further copying is needed for the replacement, and we get:

NEWREPLS = **[Y2 = f(Y1), Z3 = f(Y1), X2 = f(Y1), X1 = g(Z3, Z3)]**

which, fortunately, is the same answer we obtained with structure sharing. □

10.5.2.3. Comparison of Methods Earlier Prolog systems, such as DEC-10 Prolog and CProlog, tended to use the structure-sharing representation of terms. More recent systems, such as Quintus Prolog, use a copy-on-use representation. As with any design decision, there are trade-offs.

Space: One might assume that copy on use takes more space, since it may require copying large terms. First, note that any copy term is isomorphic to some term in the original program, so there is a bound on the maximum size for a copy term. Second, note that for structure sharing, the VCS field of a replacement requires two words of memory, whereas for copy on use, it requires only one. So the space trade-off depends on the average replacement: is it a constant, variable, or structure? It turns out that for many Prolog programs, copy on use takes less space. The space used for the copied terms can be allocated on a stack, so that its management is quite simple.

Time: The copy-on-use representation of terms is simpler, which allows the code that traverses them to be simpler. The structure-sharing approach has to apply the local substitution on every access to a program variable in a term. For the copy-on-use approach, once the term is copied, subsequent accesses to variables in that term need not apply the local substitution. Also, consider the pattern of access to memory. Hardware is often designed with caching systems that provide more efficient access to clustered accesses to memory. The copy-on-use method seems to result in a more clustered pattern of memory access, because many accesses are to portions of recently copied terms, which are close together.

Optimizations: Copy on use is more amenable to certain optimizations and lends itself better to compilation. We will see why in Chapter 11.

10.6. Binding Arrays

Just as for Datalog, we will compute the variable-for-variable replacement for the local substitution from a single index into the symbol table. We simply number each variable that appears in a clause, and we put that number in the symbol table entry for that program variable (in a field called NUM). New variables use entry indices past the end of the symbol table. A local substitution LSUB is just the index of the first new variable for this instance of a clause. Adding LSUB to the NUM field of a program variable yields the replacement variable for that program variable under the local substitution.

With new variables as simple indices, we can convert the replacement list to a binding array BA. Each entry in BA tells whether the new variable with that index is bound to a replacement term, and if so, which one. We therefore modify the *structure* type to be either *symtabindex, structref,* or *baindex*—an index into the symbol table, a reference to a structure, or an index into the binding array, respectively. The type of the entry in BA depends on whether we are using structure sharing or copy on use for terms. With structure sharing, a replacement uses a molecule, so BA is an array of *molecule.* With copy on use, BA is simply an array of *structure.* Note that if a BA entry references the symbol table, either via a molecule or directly, it will point only to a constant. Replacements never reference program variables in either scheme.

The following dereferencing routine for structure sharing uses a binding array. Unlike Section 6.7, where the argument to the similar routine was just a term, we pass the structure plus a local substitution and let *deref* apply that substitution. We could combine those two arguments into a single *molecule,* but that would be inefficient, because *deref* would immediately pull the *molecule* apart. (We make a similar change in the *match* function.) Another change is that *deref* returns its result through its arguments. We use LSUB = 0 to signify no local substitution and let BA[**V**].STRUCT = 0 mean that new variable **V** is as yet unbound.

```
procedure deref6ss(var STR: structure; var LSUB: baindex);
  begin
    if variable(STR) then
      if LSUB <> 0 then
```

```
        begin {apply local substitution}
          STR := LSUB + SYMTAB[STR].NUM;
          LSUB := 0
        end
      else if BA[STR].STRUCT <> 0 then
        begin {apply replacement bindings}
          STR := BA[STR].STRUCT;
          LSUB := BA[STR].LSUB;
          deref6ss(STR, LSUB)
        end
  end;
```

There is another way, instead of the test LSUB <> 0, to determine if LSUB must be applied. We can distinguish a program variable from a local variable by the range of its index. New variables do not need the local substitution. (See Exercise 10.9.)

Producing a copy-on-use version of the dereferencing procedure requires little change: BA[STR] contains the replacement rather than BA[STR].STRUCT, and LSUB need not be changed for the recursive call.

```
procedure deref6cu(var STR: structure; var LSUB: baindex);
  begin
    if variable(STR) then
      if LSUB <> 0 then
        begin {apply local substitution}
          STR := LSUB + SYMTAB[STR].NUM;
          LSUB := 0
        end
      else if BA[STR].STRUCT <> 0 then
        begin {apply replacement bindings}
          STR := BA[STR];
          deref6cu(STR, LSUB)
        end
  end;
```

We will not develop the structure-sharing interpreter with binding arrays further; instead we leave it as an exercise. (See Exercise 10.10.) We next look at the binding-array version of the matching routine for the copy-on-use interpreter.

```
function match6(STR1, STR2: structure; LSUB1, LSUB2: baindex): boolean;
  var NSUB1, NSUB2: baindex;
    I: integer;
  begin
    deref6cu(STR1, LSUB1);
    deref6cu(STR2, LSUB2);
    if variable(STR1) then
      if STR1 = STR2 then {same variable, do nothing}
```

```
      else
         begin
            if violates6(STR1, STR2, LSUB2) then return(false);
            if LSUB2 = 0 then BA[STR1] := STR2
            else BA[STR1] := copyapplyrepls6(STR2, LSUB2);
            TRAILTOP := TRAILTOP + 1;
            TRAIL[TRAILTOP] := STR1
         end
   else if variable(STR2) then
      begin
         if violates5(STR2, STR1, LSUB1) then return(false);
         if LSUB1 = 0 then BA[STR2] := STR1
         else BA[STR2] := copyapplyrepls6(STR1, LSUB1);
         TRAILTOP := TRAILTOP + 1;
         TRAIL[TRAILTOP] := STR2
      end
   else if structsym(STR1) = structsym(STR2) then
      for I = 1 to arity(structsym(STR1)) do
         begin
            NSUB1 := LSUB1; NSUB2 := LSUB2;
            if not match6(arg(STR1, I), NSUB1, arg(STR2, I), NSUB2) then
               return(false)
         end
   else return(false);
   return(true)
end;
```

Recall that when a goal fails, the interpreter must undo any changes made to BA in attempting to solve that goal. Recall also that we can reuse new variables when the clause instance containing them fails. The first eventuality is dealt with by the TRAIL stack, implemented as an array of *baindex*. Since BA entries change only from 0 to some *structure*, TRAIL need save only the index of an entry in BA to reset it upon backtracking. A global variable TRAILTOP keeps track of the top of TRAIL, and it is the duty of *match6* to record all changes to BA there. The main interpreter routine, *establish6*, keeps track of the new variables used by each clause.

EXAMPLE 10.3: We trace a call to *match6* from the same initial configuration as in the last two examples. We change some of the variable names to emphasize the connection between a program variable and corresponding new variable. The molecules are:

```
m1:   STRUCT:   p(f(U0), V1)
      LSUB:     22

m2:   STRUCT:   p(X0, g(X0, Y1))
      LSUB:     24
```

Where the initial states of the binding array and trail stack are:

BA:	TRAIL:
W20: 0	23
Z21: 0	
U22: 0	
V23: ↑**g(Z1, Z1)**	
X24: 0	
Y25: 0	

The numbers in program variables indicate their order of occurrence in a clause (**U0** first, **V1** second). The binding array starts at index 20, and we use the letter of the program variable along with the binding array index to identify entries. Of course, only the indices are actually used in the implementation. We see that in satisfying a previous goal, one binding has already been made: **V23** to a copy term **g(Z21, Z21)**. The arrow denotes a reference to a structure.

The initial call to *match6* gives rise to a recursive call on:

m3:	STRUCT:	**f(U0)**
	LSUB:	22
m4:	STRUCT:	**X0**
	LSUB:	24

X0 is a program variable, so it is dereferenced by adding the local substitution to get **X24**. The matching function creates a binding for **X24** by copying **f(U0)** under the local substitution. The new situation is:

BA:	TRAIL:
W20: 0	23
Z21: 0	24
U22: 0	
V23: ↑**g(Z1, Z1)**	
X24: ↑**f(U22)**	
Y25: 0	

The next call to *match6* is on:

m5:	STRUCT:	**V1**
	LSUB:	22
m6:	STRUCT:	**g(X0, Y1)**
	LSUB:	24

Here **V1** is dereferenced to **V23** by the local substitution and then to **g(Z21, Z21)** through the binding array. Note that the call to *deref6cu* sets *m5*.LSUB to zero. Since the structure symbols of **g(Z21, Z21)** and **g(X0, Y1)** agree, *match6* calls itself with:

m7:	STRUCT:	**Z21**
	LSUB:	0

m8:	STRUCT:	**X0**
	LSUB:	24

Now **X0** is dereferenced to **X24** and thence to **f(U22)**. A new binding is entered in BA:

BA:	TRAIL:
W20: 0	23
Z21: ↑**f(U22)**	24
U22: 0	21
V23: ↑**g(Z1, Z1)**	
X24: ↑**f(U22)**	
Y25: 0	

Finally, *match6* calls itself with:

m9:	STRUCT:	**Z21**
	LSUB:	0
m10:	STRUCT:	**Y1**
	LSUB:	24

Z21 dereferences to **f(U22)**, and **Y1** dereferences to **Y25**. The final version of BA is:

BA:	TRAIL:
W20: 0	23
Z21: ↑**f(U22)**	24
U22: 0	21
V23: ↑**g(Z1, Z1)**	25
X24: ↑**f(U22)**	
Y25: ↑**f(U22)**	

Compare the accumulated replacements represented in BA to the replacement list at the end of Example 10.2. □

The main interpreter procedure, *establish6*, is little changed from the version in Chapter 6. A global variable NEWVARINDEX serves to keep track of the end of the binding array. Each invocation remembers the initial value of NEWVARINDEX in LOCALSUBS. Calls to *newvars6* advance NEWVARINDEX by the number of variables in the clause under consideration. When a clause fails, a call to *restore* resets NEWVARINDEX to its initial value. TRAILSAVE remembers the top of the TRAIL stack before a call to *match6*, so *restore* knows which entries in TRAIL are a result of the call.

The only substantive change is the introduction of structure space for copy terms, which we represent by a global variable HEAP. HEAP is an array of variable length records indexed by *heapref*. (Chapter 11 covers its representation in more detail.) The *structure* type is now the union of *symtabindex, baindex,* and *heapref.* All structures referenced by BA entries will be in HEAP; none will be in program clauses. We manage HEAP as a stack, so that space used to hold copy terms may be reclaimed on backtracking. HEAPEND is a global variable marking how much of HEAP is used. The function *copyapplyrepls6* in *match6* is responsible for advancing HEAPEND whenever it consumes storage to create copy terms. Each invocation of *establish6* saves the initial value of HEAPEND on entry, using HEAPSAVE, and *restore* resets HEAPEND upon failure of a clause.

```
var GOALMOL: molecule;
    NEWGL: llist;

function establish6(GOALLIST: llist): boolean;
    var NEXTCL: clauselist;
      LOCALSUBS: baindex;
      TRAILSAVE: trailindex;
      HEAPSAVE: heapref;
    begin
        if isempty5(GOALLIST) then return(true);
        GOALMOL := first5(GOALLIST);
        NEXTCL := SYMTAB[structsym(GOALMOL.STRUCT)].CLAUSES;
        LOCALSUBS := NEWVARINDEX;
        TRAILSAVE := TRAILTOP;
        HEAPSAVE := HEAPEND;
        while NEXTCL <> nil do
          begin
            newvars6(NEXTCL);
            if match6(NEXTCL↑.HEAD, GOALMOL.STRUCT,
                    LOCALSUBS, GOALMOL.LSUB) then
              begin
                NEWGL := lconcat_rest(NEXTCL↑.BODY, LOCALSUBS,
                                                        GOALLIST);
                if establish6(NEWGL) then return(true)
              end;
            restore(TRAILSAVE, LOCALSUBS, HEAPSAVE);
            NEXTCL := NEXTCL↑.NXTCLAUSE
          end;
        return(false)
      end;
```

We look back at this point to see how the changes in the logic from Datalog to Prolog affected the implementation. The difference in the logics was the introduction of terms. The Herbrand base for a functional logic formula in usually infinite and contains terms of arbitrary size. The implementation must be prepared to represent terms with no a priori limit on size. One implementation advantage of terms over arbitrary record structures is that the logic for Prolog has no notion of "locations." A logical variable is an abstraction of a location, but it need not be implemented as a single storage location. Also, terms change only by having variables filled in, never by having a new value replace an existing value. These properties leave us free to do a lot of sharing among the representations of terms. An implementation need not make a complete copy of every term it uses.

Even though the binding of a variable can be an arbitrarily large term in Prolog, constructing a representation of the term requires little additional space. The structure-sharing representation of that binding requires just two words of storage, and the copy-on-use representation requires no more space than is used for any term in the program. The modest space requirements for a binding have ramifications for Prolog programming. Pure code (without **assert** and **retract**) is often more efficient than impure code. Passing state from a goal to a subgoal is almost always faster than asserting that information into the program database. The **assert** may seem like less work, but it ultimately manipulates many more data structures than does copying a state value, which can often be accomplished by binding a single variable. In the next chapter we will see optimizations that can further improve the performance of passing state information down recursive calls. Some recursive predicates can be made to execute in time and space comparable to that of an iterative loop in an imperative programming language.

One other point we touch on here is the choice of overall control strategy for the interpreter: depth-first search of a space of refutation vines being built top-down. First, why do we choose a depth-first over a breadth-first search to explore the space of refutation vines? Depth-first search needs only one (partial) vine to exist at a time. That vine can be represented efficiently with techniques we have seen in this chapter. It requires a single binding array, and the space in that array is easily reclaimed on backtracking using a trail stack. Breadth-first search requires multiple sets of bindings and does not release much space during execution. Of course, depth-first search does not give rise to a complete refutation procedure, whereas breadth-first search does. A middle ground, *staged* depth-first search, is described in the next section. That strategy manages space as for a depth-first search but has the completeness of depth-first search. It can often consume more time than either, however, as it repeats work.

What about a bottom-up approach against the top-down one used? With a recursive program involving terms, there may be an infinite number of different facts derivable from the initial facts under the rules of a program. The generation of information is so undirected as to be almost hopeless as a general interpretation strategy for a programming language.

10.7. Implementing Model Elimination with Prolog Techniques

This section sketches an implementation of model elimination as described in Section 9.7, using techniques developed in this chapter for Prolog. Mark Stickel (see [10.4]) first suggested this approach. The key observation is that the information describing framed literals is available in the lazy-list representation of a goal list. In this discussion we will use "goal list" for "center clause" and "first goal" for "selected literal." When we refer to a clause, we will mean a side clause from the input set of clauses.

There are some simple changes we must make to the representation of clauses and the goal list so they can represent clauses with arbitrary numbers of negative literals. The type *litrec* requires a SIGN field to indicate whether the literal is positive or negative. Also, since the first goal in the goal list may be positive or negative, and clauses may have multiple negative literals, we cannot simply distinguish a single literal in a program clause as the head. Instead, a clause with n literals is represented as n versions of the clause in Prolog form, with each literal taking a turn at head. So, the clause:

```
{p; ¬q; ¬r; s}
```

is represented by the following Prolog-style clauses:

```
p :- q, r, ¬s.
¬q :- ¬p, r, ¬s.
¬r :- ¬p, q, ¬s.
s :- ¬p, q, r.
```

We next show how the framed literals are available in the lazy-list representation of the goal list. We shall illustrate with Proplog, but it should be clear the information on framed literals is available in Prolog with structure sharing on code. Let the initial goal list be:

```
:- p, ¬t.
```

The clause:

```
p :- q, r, ¬s.
```

extends the goal list to yield:

```
:- q, r, ¬s, [p], ¬t.
```

which the fact:

```
q.
```

extends to:

```
:- [q], r, ¬s, [p], ¬t.
```

This goal list contracts to:

```
:- r, ¬s, [p], ¬t.
```

We next extend with the clause:

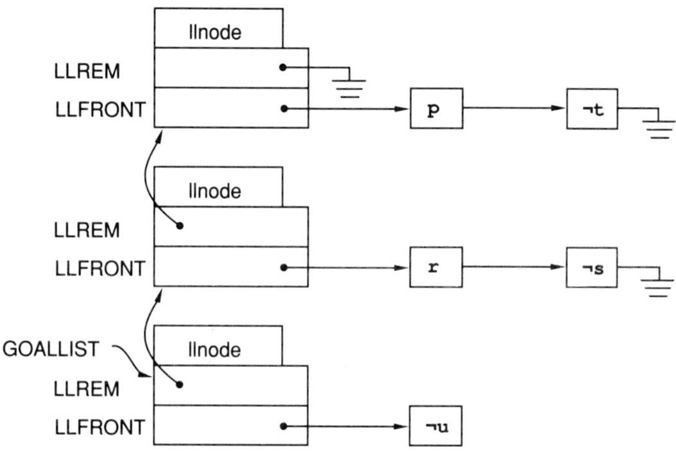

Figure 10.5

```
r :- ¬u.
```

to yield:

```
:- ¬u, [r], ¬s, [p], ¬t.
```

The corresponding Prolog-style goal list is:

```
:- ¬u, ¬s, ¬t.
```

Figure 10.5 shows its representation with lazy lists.

Recall in a lazy list that we ignore the first literal in the LLFRONT field of a remainder list. But those "ignored" literals are exactly the framed literals we need! Thus, for any goal list, the framed literals are available by following LLREM fields and looking at the first literal in the LLFRONT field of every *llnode* encountered. A reduction must then search the LLFRONT fields for a literal that matches the first goal. The contraction operation is automatic. If the **¬u** goal in Figure 10.5 is solved by a **u** fact, the resulting goal list will be as shown in Figure 10.6. The framed literals for **¬u** and **r** are gone.

The remaining issue is the choice between extension and reduction steps. The decision could be built into the interpreter: always try reduction before extension, for example. Alternatively, the programmer could be given a mechanism to mark certain clauses to try for extension before attempting reduction; unmarked clauses would be tried if reduction fails. There must also be a decision about which order to try the formal literals for reduction.

While model elimination is a complete refutation procedure, the particular implementation of it outlined here is not complete, because of Prolog's depth-first

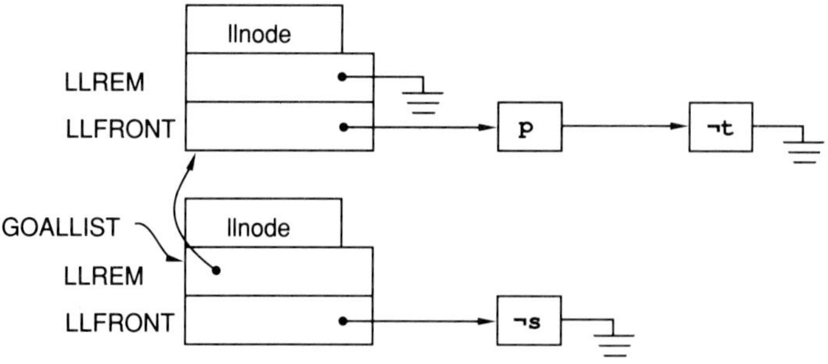

Figure 10.6

search strategy. Much of the parsimony of the Prolog representation of goal lists and substitutions depends on using that search strategy. Stickel suggests a variant on depth-first search: *staged depth-first search*, which is refutation complete. In staged depth-first search, there is a bound b to the depth of recursive calls to the interpreter. Any attempt for a call at depth b to call the interpreter recursively will fail and cause backtracking. Such a bound guarantees the interpreter will always halt. If a computation halts without success, using a bound b, the computation is restarted with a bound of $b + 1$, then $b + 2$, and so forth. If there is a refutation proof, the interpreter will succeed with some finite value for the bound. Of course, if no refutation exists, the interpreter may continue forever, trying deeper and deeper bounds. (If an invocation of the interpreter fails without encountering the bound, we may conclude there is no refutation.)

Note that staged depth-first search gives a complete refutation procedure when used with Prolog programs.

10.8. EXERCISES

10.1. The representation for Prolog literals given in Section 10.1 makes use of variable-length records. Describe a representation for Prolog literals that uses fixed-length records. Show how to express **p(f(X), a, g(b, Y))** in your representation.

10.2. When can *copycompose* avoid copying right sides of replacements in its first argument? In its second argument?

10.3. When can *repl* records be reclaimed in *establish4*?

10.4. Consider the simple Prolog definition for **append**:

```
append([],L,L).
append([X|L1],L2,[X|L3]) :- append(L1,L2,L3).
```

and the query **append([a, U, c], [V, d], Ans)**. Assuming the structure-sharing representation of terms, show the replacement list constructed by *establish5* during evaluation of this query. Do the same for the copy-on-use implementation. Assume a local substitution is supplied initially for the goal.

10.5. a. When the matching routine for structure sharing, *match5ss,* constructs a replacement in which VCS.STRUCT is a ground term, then VCS.LSUB has no effect. Is there any advantage in having *match5ss* detect this situation and set LSUB to **nil**?

b. In *match5cu* for copy on use, we could have *deref5ss* set LSUB to **nil** when it returns a molecule whose structure is a ground term. Then *match5cu* would not copy that term when creating a replacement from it. Alternatively, *copyapplyrepls* could detect that the structure passed to it is ground and not copy in that case. What are the advantages of each approach?

10.6. Give two Prolog programs: One that is much more efficient when run with the structure-shared representation, and one that is much more efficient when run with the copy-on-use representation. Discuss.

10.7. Consider copy on use for terms in *establish5* before the introduction of binding arrays. If we wanted to bind **X1** to the term **f(Y, Z)** with the local substitution:

```
[Y = Y2, Z = Z2]
```

we would copy **f(Y, Z)** with code variables replaced by new variables to get **X1 = f(Y2, Z2)**. Suppose, at the point of replacement, **Y2** has been bound to **g(a, Z2)**, but **Z2** is unbound. We can imagine a variant strategy, call it *deep-copy on use*, that would insert the bindings for all bound variables during copying. Deep-copy on use would give the replacement **X1 = f(g(a, Z2), Z2)**. Compare deep-copy on use to normal copy on use. Describe how deep-copy on use is implemented with binding arrays.

10.8. Another variant of copy on use is similar to deep-copy on use but is not quite so radical. During copying, variable-for-variable and constant-for-variable replacements, but not structure-for-variable replacements, are made. Compare the space and time costs of this strategy to copy on use and deep-copy on use.

10.9. For *deref6cu,* add functions to test for different kinds of variables, so that LSUB is not used to distinguish program variables from copy variables. Show that this change removes the need for NSUB1 and NSUB2 in *match6* and makes *deref* look more like the binding-array version in Chapter 6.

10.10. Give the *match* and *establish* routines for structure sharing with binding arrays. Note that each entry in the binding array will be a *molecule.*

10.11. Consider some state of the binding array. Each unbound variable is the root of a tree of variables, whose child-to-parent edges are the pointers created by binding one variable to another. Each dereference of a variable in the tree requires running a path from the node for that variable to the root.

One might consider an optimization in which every time we run such a path we modify all entries on that path to point directly to the root, thus making subsequent accesses of the variables on that path faster. Is this a good optimization?

10.12. The early versions of the interpreter copy program clauses via the *instance* function. The later versions structure share the clauses. Give an interpreter that does copy on use for code but in a procrastinated manner: a literal is copied, with its variables replaced by new variables, only when it reaches the front of goal list. How can the right side of a replacement be represented in such an interpreter?

10.13. Look at what representation for binding arrays might be used for a Prolog interpreter that uses breadth-first rather than depth-first search.

10.14. Consider the following clauses that implement a Prolog interpreter.

```
interp(true).
interp((A, B)) :-
        interp(A), interp(B). /* infix comma for literal lists */
interp(A) :- db(A, B), interp(B).
```

The database of clauses for the program to be interpreted are stored as **db** facts. A rule:

H :- *B*.

is stored as:

db(*H*, *B*)

where *H* is the head literal and *B* is a comma-list of the body literals. For a fact, *B* is the constant **true**. For example, the **append** predicate is:

```
db(append([], L, L), true).
db(append([X|L1], L2, [X|L3]), append(L1, L2, L3)).
```

a. Trace the evaluation of **interp(append([a, b], [C], Ans))**, showing the bindings created in a structure-sharing (for terms) environment and in a copy-on-use environment.
b. For each evaluation environment, is **interp** itself doing structure sharing or copy on use for code?

10.15. Consider the staged depth-first search algorithm we used in the implementation of model elimination. In that algorithm the search fails when it reaches a recursion depth of *b*. How might we modify the algorithm to fail earlier in some cases?

10.16. Modify *establish* for Proplog with lazy lists (Section 3.2) to do model elimination.

10.9. COMMENTS AND BIBLIOGRAPHY

The issue of whether to use the structure-sharing or copy-on-use representation for terms has attracted some interest. Early Prolog implementations tended to use structure-sharing representations. That representation was developed and used in the theorem-proving community [10.1]. More recent Prolog implementations have all seemed to use copy on use. This representation is more consistent with how programming languages, such as LISP, represent their data. Mellish [10.2] analyzes and compares the two representations.

The "occur-check problem" has always been the subject of much controversy. At the risk of overgeneralizing, logicians and those in theorem proving generally feel that the lack of the occur-check in Prolog systems is a very serious defect and really means that Prolog does *not* implement logic. Logic programmers, in general, accept the lack of occur-check with the attitude of "Let the programmer beware." The occur-check cannot simply be added to Prolog, because that would severely affect Prolog's efficiency. The most promising approach to having your occur-check (but not eating it, too) is developed by Plaisted [10.3]. His idea is to analyze Prolog programs statically to determine where an occurs violation might arise and then do the occur-check in those places only.

The idea to augment the Prolog evaluation strategy to implement the model-elimination refutation strategy is due to Stickel [10.4].

10.1. R. S. Boyer and J. Moore, The sharing of structure in theorem proving programs, in *Machine Intelligence 2,* B. Meltzer and D. Michie (eds.), Edinburgh University Press, Scotland, 1972, 101–16.

10.2. C. S. Mellish, An alternative to structure sharing in the implementation of a PROLOG interpreter, in [7.2], 99–106.

10.3. D. A. Plaisted, The occur-check problem in Prolog, *Proc. 1984 Int. Symposium on Logic Programming,* Atlantic City, NJ, 1984, 272–80.

10.4. M. E. Stickel, A Prolog technology theorem prover, *Proc. 1984 Int. Symposium on Logic Programming,* Atlantic City, NJ, 1984, 212–19.

11

Interpreter Optimizations and Prolog Compilation

In this chapter we continue optimizing the Prolog interpreter and then turn to compiling Prolog. Up to this point we have expressed our algorithms using the features of a high-level language—in particular, recursion. The next steps require that we look "inside" the high-level language implementation and see exactly what it stores in its run-time stack of activation records. To explain the upcoming optimizations and compilation, we need to develop a nonrecursive interpreter that does its own space management. Going to explicit storage management uncovers some redundant variables and provides opportunities to reclaim storage for a call before the recursive implementation does. We will also be able to split activation records in half, allocating the portion for the calling literal and variable bindings, the *binding frame*, separately from the portion containing information on alternative clauses for the calling literal, the *choice point*. Not all calls will require choice points, and a choice point can be reclaimed before the corresponding binding frame. Managing the stack explicitly also paves the way for more subtle optimizations when we turn to compilation. Certain bindings and Pascal variables formerly kept in the stack may reside in registers instead, and the space in a binding frame can be incrementally reclaimed as a clause body progresses toward solution.

Throughout this chapter we assume a copy-on-use implementation for terms unless otherwise stated.

11.1. Activation Records

Consider how Pascal storage management code works when the *establish6* routine executes. On entry to any procedure it allocates an activation record, which contains space for all the local variables declared in that procedure. In addition, the activation record contains space for each parameter passed in, a pointer to the activation record of the calling procedure, and the program address to return to when the procedure completes.

For the *establish6* routine, the activation record that Pascal allocates has fields for the local variables NEXTCL, LOCALSUBS, TRAILSAVE, and HEAPSAVE; the parameter GOALLIST; a pointer to the activation record of the calling procedure, call it BACK; and a pointer to the return address, call it RETURN_PT. Recall that two of the variables used by *establish6,* GOALMOL and NEWGL, while having values particular to a single invocation, are not "live" after the recursive call, so all invocations can share space for them in global variables. Actually, GOALMOL is not needed; its value is always available as the first entry on GOALLIST. If we are willing to access GOALLIST whenever we need the first goal, we can dispense with GOALMOL.

Thus the activation record for *establish6* contains the following fields:

BACK:	pointer to caller's activation record
RETURN_PT:	return address
GOALLIST:	reference to a (lazy) list of goals
NEXTCL:	reference to the program clause being tried for the first goal
LOCALSUBS:	index to the top of the binding array before matching
TRAILSAVE:	index to the top of the trail stack before matching
HEAPSAVE:	index in the heap of copy terms before matching

The global variables have their space allocated statically, apart from the stack of activation records:

BA:	the binding array
NEWVARINDEX:	index of the first free location in the binding array
TRAIL:	the list of BA locations to reset on backtracking
TRAILTOP:	index of the last entry used in TRAIL
HEAP:	storage space for copy terms
HEAPEND:	index of the first free location in HEAP
NEWGL:	temporary pointer to the new (lazy) list of goals

Also, the Pascal object code must maintain a global pointer to the current activation record.

Consider the interpretation of a simple Prolog program with the following skeleton. The form **p()** means we are not concerned with the actual arguments here. Figure 11.1 shows a (partial) picture of the run-time data structures for *establish6* at the point at which the first clause for **r** has been tried in solving **p**. The double lines delimit activation records.

```
a :- ..., p(), ...
p() :- q(), r(), s().
p() :- ...
r() :- ...
r() :- ...
r() :- ...
```

To gain more control over flow of control and storage management, we can represent activation records for calls to *establish* explicitly with a data structure

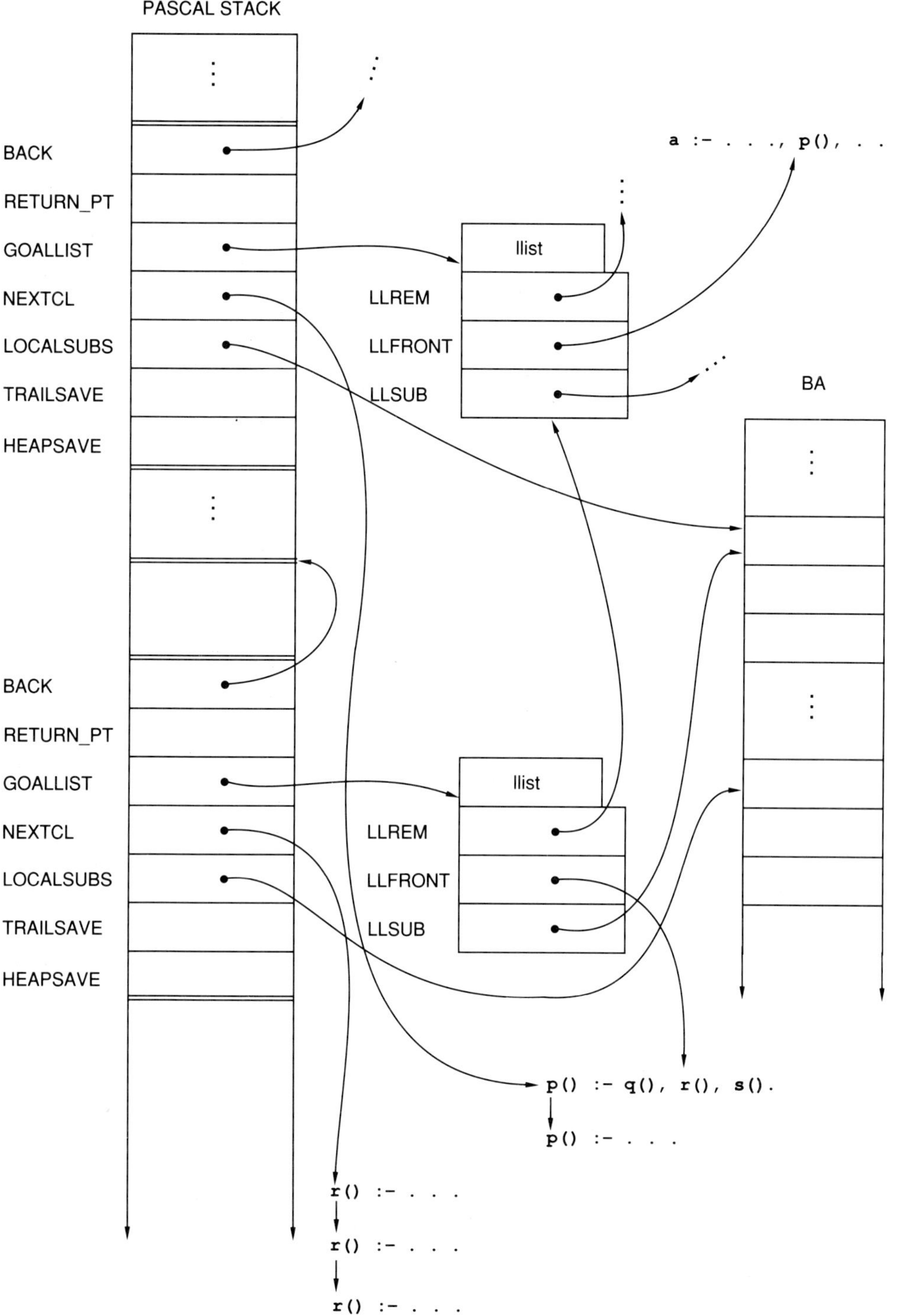
PASCAL STACK
BACK
RETURN_PT
GOALLIST
NEXTCL
LOCALSUBS
TRAILSAVE
HEAPSAVE
BACK
RETURN_PT
GOALLIST
NEXTCL
LOCALSUBS
TRAILSAVE
HEAPSAVE
a :- . . ., p(), . . .
llist
LLREM
LLFRONT
LLSUB
BA
llist
LLREM
LLFRONT
LLSUB
p() :- q(), r(), s().
p() :- . . .
r() :- . . .
r() :- . . .
r() :- . . .

Figure 11.1

manipulated directly by the interpreter. For the time being, other subprocedures of the interpreter, such as *match,* will use the standard Pascal storage management. The explicit run-time stack, RS, will be an array of *frame* records. A global variable CF references the current (top) frame on RS. What simplifications can we make to the Pascal storage structures? Since RS is an array of records, we do not need the BACK pointer, since decrementing an index serves to get from one frame in RS to the calling frame. The RETURN_PT field is also unnecessary, because *establish6* has a unique return point on recursive calls. Rather than worrying about the interpreter allocating *llist* nodes, we dispense with the GOALLIST record and pull its three fields directly into the frame. To make this change work, we must modify the LLREM pointer of the lazy-list record so that it points to the entire frame containing the fields for the remainder of the list. With these changes we can define the supporting types for RS as follows:

```
type
      stackindex = [0..MAXFRAMES];

      frame = record
                  LLREM: stackindex
                  LLFRONT: litlist;
                  LLSUB: baindex;
                  NEXTCL: clauselist;
                  LOCALSUBS: baindex;
                  TRAILSAVE: trailindex;
                  HEAPSAVE: heapref
              end;
```

If we use this definition of *frame,* the situation of Figure 11.1 would be represented as shown in Figure 11.2. The dotted lines indicate the fields that originally made up the value of the *llist* record for GOALLIST.

We can simplify this structure further and also rename some of the fields to make their purposes in later optimizations more transparent. If the LLREM field of the frame at index k in the stack refers to the frame at index j, the body of the NEXTCL clause of the jth frame contains the subgoal that the kth frame is trying to solve. In Figure 11.2, frame k is solving the **r ()** subgoal in the NEXTCL clause of frame j. We rename the LLREM field to PARENT to indicate the parent-child relationship between the clauses for j and k in a demonstration tree. We rename LLFRONT to CALL to indicate that the field points to the goal that the field's frame is trying to solve. The LLSUB field is redundant: it is always the same as the value in the LOCALSUBS field of the PARENT frame. Therefore we eliminate LLSUB and rename LOCALSUBS to BINDINGS to indicate the dual use. With these changes the type for a frame is:

```
type
      frame = record
                  PARENT: stackindex;
                  CALL: litlist;
                  NEXTCL: clauselist;
```

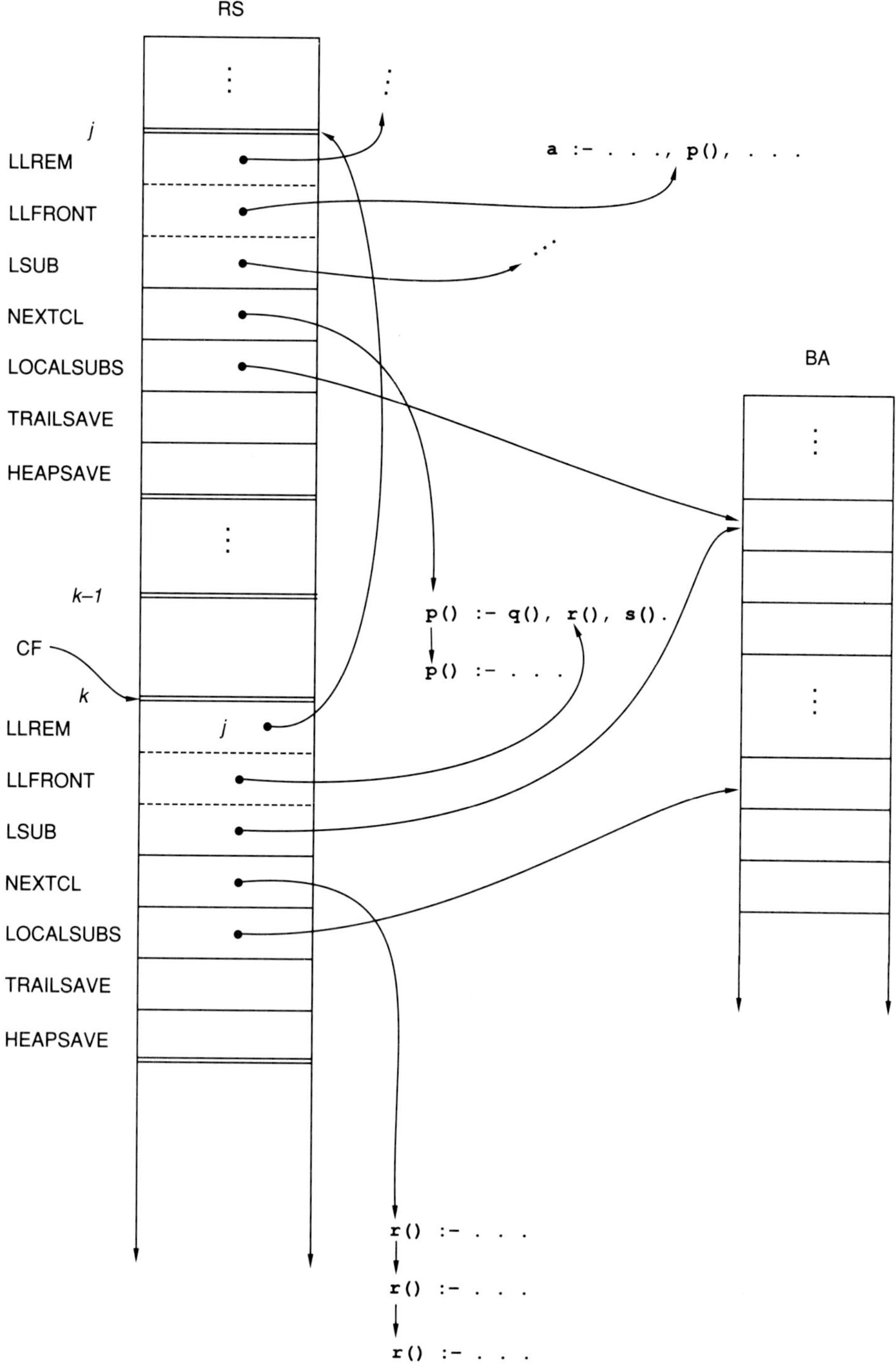
RS
j
LLREM
LLFRONT
LSUB
NEXTCL
LOCALSUBS
TRAILSAVE
HEAPSAVE
k–1
CF
k
LLREM
j
LLFRONT
LSUB
NEXTCL
LOCALSUBS
TRAILSAVE
HEAPSAVE
a :- . . ., p(), . . .
p() :- q(), r(), s().
p() :- . . .
r() :- . . .
r() :- . . .
r() :- . . .
BA

Figure 11.2

```
            BINDINGS: baindex;
            TRAILSAVE: trailindex;
            HEAPSAVE: heapref
          end;
```

Figure 11.3 shows the storage state that corresponds to the same execution point as Figure 11.2 but with the modified *frame* records. The nonrecursive version of *establish* will use this definition of the *frame* record. The *clauserec* type also is changed slightly to include the number of variables in the clause. That addition makes allocating new variables on the binding array easier:

```
type
    CLAUSEREC = record
                  HEAD: structtype;
                  BODY: litlist;
                  NUMVARS: integer;
                  NXTCLAUSE: clauselist
                end;
```

The global variables for the nonrecursive interpreter are:

```
var BA: array [baindex] of structure;
    NEWVARINDEX: baindex;
    RS: array [stackindex] of frame;
    CF, NCF: stackindex;
    TRAIL: array [trailindex] of baindex;
    TRAILTOP: trailindex;
    HEAP: array [heapref] of heapcell;
    HEAPEND: heapref;
```

CF and NCF stand for "current frame" and "next current frame." Note that NEWGL is not necessary. The new goal list produced in solving the goal for CF can be constructed directly in NCF, rather than being assembled in NEWGL and then copied into the PARENT and CALL fields of NCF.

Given a query, these data structures must be initialized before the first call to *establish*. We create a *clauserec* with the query as BODY. The frame in RS[0] represents the query, so its NEXTCL field references the *clauserec* for the query, and RS[1].CALL references the first goal in BODY of that *clauserec*. RS[0].BINDINGS points to the beginning of BA, and NEWVARINDEX is set past the beginning of BA by the number of variables in the query. TRAILTOP and HEAPEND are both initialized to 0. We set RS[1].PARENT to 0 and begin interpretation with CF = 1.

In the following code for the nonrecursive interpreter we use **goto** statements so as to mimic the control flow of recursive calls in *establish6* as closely as possible.

```
function establish7: boolean;
    begin
    estabenter: {solve the first goal in RS[CF].CALL}
      if RS[CF].CALL = nil then return(true);
```

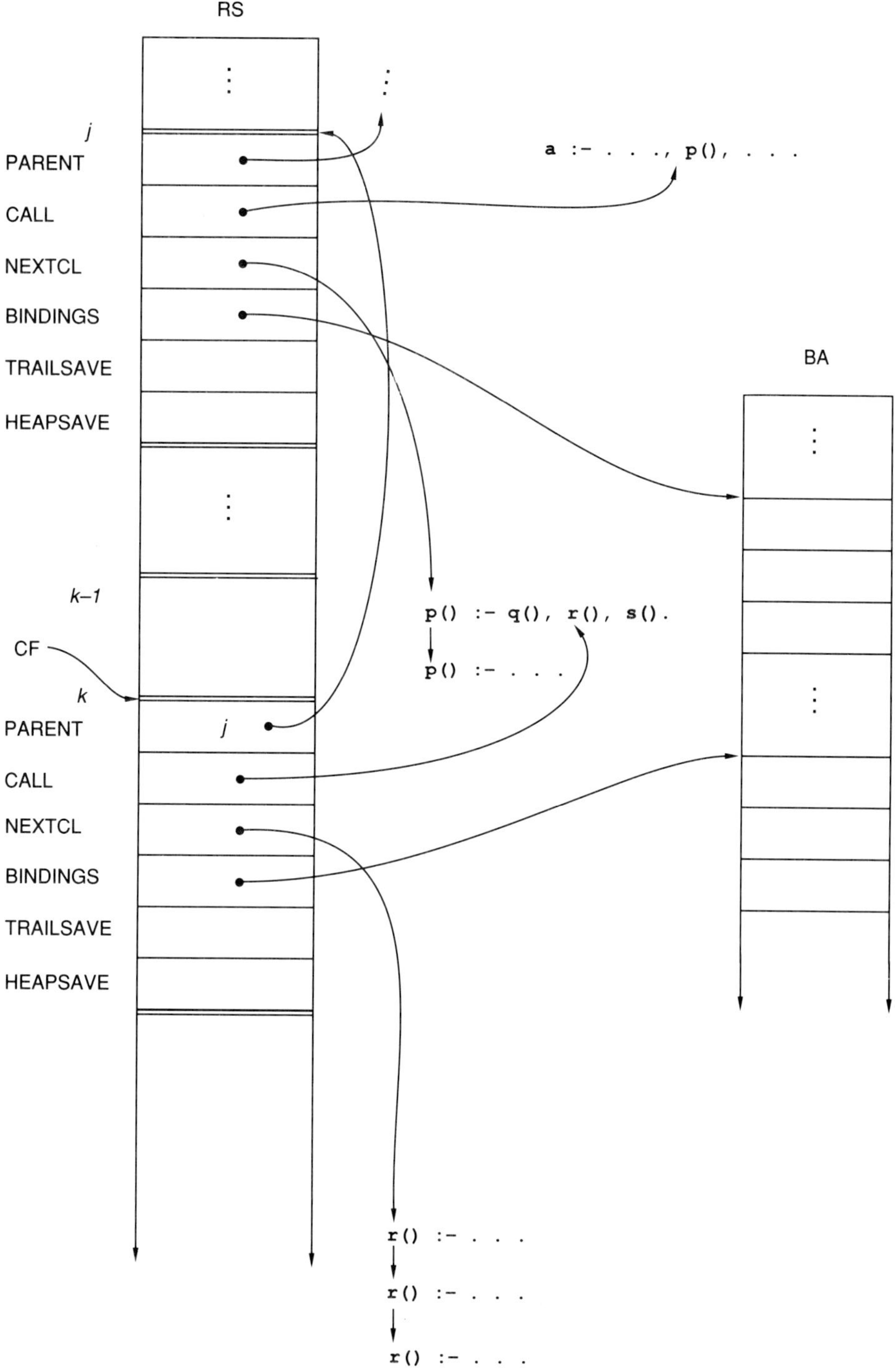
RS
j
PARENT
CALL
NEXTCL
BINDINGS
TRAILSAVE
HEAPSAVE
a :- . . ., p(), . . .
BA
k–1
CF
k
PARENT
j
CALL
NEXTCL
BINDINGS
TRAILSAVE
HEAPSAVE
p() :- q(), r(), s().
p() :- . . .
r() :- . . .
r() :- . . .
r() :- . . .

Figure 11.3

```
      RS[CF].NEXTCL := SYMTAB[structsym(RS[CF].CALL)].CLAUSES;
      RS[CF].BINDINGS := NEWVARINDEX;
      RS[CF].TRAILSAVE := TRAILTOP;
      RS[CF].HEAPSAVE := HEAPEND;
    trynext: {try the next clause to solve the goal}
      if RS[CF].NEXTCL <> nil then
        begin
          newvars(RS[CF].NEXTCL);
          if match6(RS[CF].NEXTCL↑.HEAD, RS[CF].CALL↑.LITERAL,
                    RS[CF].BINDINGS, RS[RS[CF].PARENT].BINDINGS) then
            begin
              NCF := CF + 1;
              {set new call and parent}
              nextgoal(CF, NCF);
              CF := NCF;
              goto estabenter
            end;
        estabreturn: {undo bindings from last unification on backtracking}
          if CF = 0 then return(false); {last frame, query fails}
          restore(RS[CF].TRAILSAVE, RS[CF].BINDINGS, RS[CF].HEAPSAVE);
          RS[CF].NEXTCL := RS[CF].NEXTCL↑.NXTCLAUSE;
          goto trynext
        end;
      CF := CF - 1; {no more clauses to try, so backtrack}
      goto estabreturn
    end;
```

The procedure *nextgoal* constructs a lazy list for the new goal list of CF in the fields RS[NCF].PARENT and RS[NCF].CALL (which were LLREM and LLFRONT in an *llist* record). It uses RS[CF].PARENT, RS[CF].CALL, and RS[CF].NEXTCL to do so. Procedure *nextgoal*, which operates much as *lconcat_rest* in *establish6*, is left as an exercise. (See Exercise 11.1.)

In subsequent sections we describe optimizations to this nonrecursive code. Most of these optimizations require manipulation of the run-time stack by the interpreter and hence were not readily expressible using the recursive version.

11.2. Including Variable Bindings in the Stack Frame

Consider BINDINGS; it is an index to a chunk of the binding array BA. There is no particular reason why the entire BA must be stored in contiguous storage locations in memory, nor why variable indexes must be consecutive between each group of new variables. Thus, rather than having BINDINGS point to the binding array, we just let it *be* a piece of the binding array and store it directly in the frame. This change means that the allocation and deallocation of space for new variables are handled by the same instructions that add and remove stack frames, rather than by a separate set of instructions. Also, it means mapping one fewer dynamic structure into memory. We call the segment of the frame that stores this piece of the binding array BINDENV, for "binding environment." PARENT then gives access to the BINDENV segment in the parent frame and thus leads to the binding environment for variables in the CALL literal.

However, by folding chunks of the binding array into a frame, we make the size of a frame variable. In fact, when the CALL goal is being resatisfied, the size of BINDENV may change to accommodate a different number of variables in NEXTCL. We can accommodate this variation by putting BINDENV at the end of the frame. The offset to each frame variable from the beginning of the stack frame is still fixed; only the number of slots for the BINDENV segment can change. Here we must abandon looking at RS as an array of *frame* records in which a new frame can be added simply by incrementing an index. Instead we treat it as an array of words, where multiple words must be allocated for each stack frame. Since frames have a varying number of words, we must reintroduce the BACK field to find the beginning of the previous frame on RS. We must be able to return to that frame if the current frame is backtracked. Also, the PARENT field must point to the beginning word of a frame. It is important to notice that BACK is not necessarily the frame that holds CALL. That is, BACK and PARENT need not be the same.

To summarize, we eliminate BA by folding it into the frame stack. Since this interpolation makes frame lengths variable, we add a field BACK to point to the first word of the previous frame on the stack. Why not bring chunks of TRAIL and HEAP into the stack as well? We want to leave TRAIL as a separate data structure because of the optimization of the next section. Adding pieces of HEAP to the stack would mean that each frame would have two variable-length segments, and we would need to store an offset to the the first slot in the second segment. Also, while the amount of space for BINDENV can be determined from NEXTCL, the amount of space in a frame for TRAIL and HEAP is not known until after the call to *match6*. Thus, if chunks of both were included, it would be problematic to determine how much space is needed for each chunk before *match6* starts.

To summarize, the slots in a frame are:

BACK:	index of the previous frame on the stack
PARENT:	index of the frame for the CALL literal
CALL:	the literal that is first on the goal list
NEXTCL:	reference to the program clause being tried for CALL
TRAILSAVE:	index to the the top of the trail stack before matching
HEAPSAVE:	index in the heap of copy terms before matching
BINDENV:	the bindings for variables in NEXTCL

11.3. Backtrack Points

This section introduces an optimization that allows the interpreter to remove multiple frames at once during backtracking. By inspecting NEXTCL before branching to *estabenter,* the interpreter can tell if there is an alternative clause that must be tried if the body of NEXTCL fails to be satisfied. In fact, we can advance NEXTCL before matching by keeping a variable CURCL that references the current clause. The value of CURCL is dead after the branch to *estabenter*, and so it can be a shared global variable rather than a part of a frame. If there is no alternative (NEXTCL is **nil**), there is no reason to return to the frame on backtracking. The interpreter might as well backtrack straight to the previous frame on the frame stack. If that frame has no alternatives left for NEXTCL, the interpreter can go to the frame before that, and so forth. We can maintain a global variable LASTBACK that points to the last frame on the stack that has an alternative. In the BACK slot of frames we will store not a pointer to the previous frame but rather the current value of LASTBACK, which will be the frame the interpreter should uncover upon backtracking from the current frame.

When the top frame on the stack fails, we head back to the frame—call it *f*—referenced by its BACK field of the top frame. Frame *f* will hold (in its CALL field) the last goal satisfied that has a chance of being resatisfied. The interpreter can undo all the bindings made by frames above *f* in the frame stack by calling *restore* using the values of TRAILSAVE and HEAPSAVE in *f*. Note that TRAILTOP and HEAPEND have the values given them by the failed frame.

We give the pseudo-Pascal code for this version of the interpreter. We will continue to use dot notation for accessing fields in a frame, even though Pascal does not support it. For example, an expression such as RS[CF].TRAILSAVE would properly be RS[CF + TRAILSAVE_OFFSET]. Again, for initialization, we must create a frame on RS for the query being processed, including its binding environment, and set up the second frame on the stack to reference this query as its goal list, via the PARENT and CALL fields. We let CF point to the second frame and initialize TRAILTOP, HEAPEND, and LASTBACK to 0.

```
function establish8: boolean;
  begin
  estabenter: {solve the first goal in RS[CF].CALL
    if RS[CF].CALL = nil then return(true);
    CURCL := SYMTAB[structsym(RS[CF].CALL)].CLAUSES;
    RS[CF].TRAILSAVE := TRAILTOP;
    RS[CF].HEAPSAVE := HEAPEND;
  trynext: {try the next clause to solve the goal}
    if CURCL <> nil then
      begin
        newvars8(CURCL);
        RS[CF].NEXTCL := CURCL↑.NXTCLAUSE;
        if match8(CURCL↑.HEAD, RS[CF].CALL↑.LITERAL,
                RS[CF].BINDENV, RS[RS[CF].PARENT].BINDENV) then
          begin
            if RS[CF].NEXTCL <> nil then LASTBACK := CF;
            NCF := CF + framelength(CURCL);
            RS[NCF].BACK := LASTBACK;
            {set new call and parent}
```

```
            nextgoal8(CF, NCF);
            CF := NCF;
            goto estabenter
          end;
      estabreturn: {undo bindings from last unification on backtracking}
        if CF = 0 then return(false);
        restore8(RS[CF].TRAILSAVE, RS[CF].HEAPSAVE);
        CURCL := RS[CF].NEXTCL;
        goto trynext
      end;
    CF := LASTBACK; {not more clauses to try, so backtrack}
    LASTBACK := RS[CF].BACK;
    goto estabreturn
  end;
```

In *establish8* the *match* routine is modified so the local substitution is an index into RS. Also, the *restore* routine deals no longer with BA but rather with the BINDENV fields of individual frames. The new *restore8* procedure resets bindings and global variables using the values in the TRAILSAVE and HEAPSAVE fields of the BACK frame, which is the highest frame in the stack at that point with any chance of resatisfying a goal. One reason we kept TRAIL as a separate data structure rather than folding it into RS was so that *restore8* would not have to traipse through individual frames in backtracking the stack. The *newvars* procedure no longer allocates any space; it just zeros all the slots in the BINDENV segment in the current frame. If we assume that RS is initially "clean," and that *restore8* cleans released stack space, the call to *newvars8* could be eliminated. (See Exercise 6.16.) The *match* function does not need to trail bindings for new variables in the head of the current clause, since all bindings for those variables can be cleared on backtracking. With the optimization of this section, *match8* need not trail bindings for variables in frames after the one referenced by LASTBACK. The *framelength* function determines the size of the frame to allocate for a clause, using the NUMVARS field of the current clause.

11.4. Implementing Evaluable Predicates

We provide a few words here about implementing the evaluable predicates described in Chapter 8. We consider these predicates grouped by the internal data structures they manipulate.

Most evaluable predicates can be explained in the context of the recursive interpreter, as in Section 6.8. The predicates for arithmetic comparisons function much as shown there, while `is` needs the ability to pick apart terms. An exception is cut, which had to wait for the explicit representation of return points on the stack and the introduction of LASTBACK. Now that we have access to the workings of the run-time stack, the implementation of cut is quite simple. When the interpreter encounters a stack frame whose CALL literal is '**!**', LASTBACK should be set to the BACK value of the PARENT of the current frame. Upon failure back to the '**!**', control should pass back to the call before the call that the clause containing the '**!**' is solving. For instance, for a cut arising from the clause **p :- q, !, r.**, control should pass to the last nondeterministic frame before the one containing the **p**-goal that the clause is solving. The change to *establish8* is to perform the statement:

LASTBACK := RS[RS[CF].PARENT].BACK

instead of the call to *match8,* when the call literal is a cut. Other control predicates, such as '\+' and '->', are expressible in terms of cut and other predicates, as we saw in Chapter 8. Some interpreters implement them directly for efficiency.

The implementation of **call** is easy in the interpreter, because the same data structures represent literals and terms. A goal **call(X)** just needs to replace itself by what term **X** is abound to. Depending on the exact details of the data structures, this replacement could take place during parsing. For example:

```
p(X) :- q(X, Y, Z), call(Y), call(r(Z)).
```

is modified to:

```
p(X) :- q(X, Y, Z), Y, r(Z).
```

The functions for **assert** and **retract** must know about the representation of clauses (which are just terms of a certain form in some systems) and how to modify the list in the CLAUSES field of a symbol table entry. The aggregation predicates **setof** and **bagof** can be implemented with **assert** and **retract**, similarly to the **findall** predicate in Section 8.9.

Predicates for classifying terms such as **var**, **atom**, and **number** must be privy to the internal representation of bindings, terms, and numbers. Most of the remaining evaluable predicates need access to the symbol table. Term comparisons have to examine the NAME field in symbol table entries. Obviously, the **name** predicate looks at that field as well and must be able to add an entry to the symbol table. The **functor** and '**=..**' predicates need access to the symbol table and the ability to produce a predicate symbol, such as **p/3**, from a constant, such as **p/0**. Those two predicates also must know how to build records on the heap. The **arg** predicate must know the format of record structures.

The I/O predicates (**get**, **put**, **read**, **write**) must make the appropriate system calls in order to interface to the file system and user terminal. Additionally, **read** and **write** need to access the symbol table to add or look up names, and **read** requires a parser. (That parser can be written in Prolog using **get**.)

We do not go into more detail here, because the exact implementation of evaluable predicates is highly dependent on the internal data structures of a particular system.

11.5. Reclaiming Deterministic Frames

The optimization of introducing LASTBACK does not save space on RS, just in TRAIL. Can we also save space by popping entire frames if they hold no alternatives for backtracking? When we examine that question in this section, we see that we can indeed discard a *portion* of such frames. Compare Prolog to a procedural language such as Pascal. A clause is analogous to a procedure with the head of the clause as the procedure declaration, and the goals in the body as a list of calls to other procedures. For example:

```
r(X) :- p(X), q(X, f(a)).
```

has the procedural reading "To perform procedure **r**, call procedure **p**, then call procedure **q**." The analogy is inexact, of course. In Prolog we can have several definitions for each procedure—multiple clauses with the same predicate symbol in the head. These are the aspects of Prolog that make it *nondeterministic*. Calls in procedural languages are *deterministic*: there is only one procedure definition associated with a given procedure name. In procedural languages the object code pops the activation record from the run-time stack on return from a subprocedure call. In Prolog, however, a later procedure call may fail, causing control to return to a previously called procedure in order to try another procedure definition (clause). Thus Prolog activation records (frames) remain on the run-time stack in order to undo the effects of the procedure invocation and to keep track of what procedure definition to try next. When there are no more alternative definitions to try for a procedure call, we have something close to a completed call in a deterministic program. How can we remove frames from the frame stack on successful return from a deterministic call (a call for which no alternatives remain)?

To examine the relationship between Prolog and a procedural language more closely, consider the following procedural program skeleton and a corresponding Prolog program sketch:

```
program
    proc p(. . .);
        .
        .
        .
      return;

    proc q(. . .);
        .
        .
        .
      return;

    proc r(. . .);
      call p(. . .);
```

```
        call q(. . .);
        return;

    call r(. . .);
end.
```

```
p().
q().
r() :- p(), q().

:- r().
```

In the execution of the procedural code, when *r* is invoked, an activation record for *r* is created on the run-time stack. Then *r* invokes *p*, and an activation record for *p* is pushed on the stack. When *p* returns, its activation record is removed from the stack. In the corresponding Prolog program, when a call to a **p**-literal successfully completes, we do not pop the frame that solved it from the stack. In either case a frame for *q* or **q** goes on the stack next. Why not pop **p**'s frame on completion, as we did *p*'s activation record in the procedural case? There are two reasons:

1. **Possible backtracking:** We may have to return to the frame for **p** to find an alternative way to satisfy it. Suppose the **p**-clause is not just a fact, but **p :- s**, and that there are two ways to satisfy **s**. If **q** fails, we have to return to the frame for the call to **s** and try an alternative. If we pop frames as their goals are satisfied, we lose the information needed for backtracking. (However, by keeping TRAIL separate from RS, we have not lost the information to undo the effect of the call to **p**.)
2. **Forward references:** Removing the frame for the call to **p** removes the BINDENV for the clause that solved **p**. Other frames might point to variables in that BINDENV. Recall that with copy on use for terms, we represent a variable's value by a pointer to that value.

EXAMPLE 11.1: Suppose a variable **Y27** in one frame references variable **X32** in the BINDENV of the frame for **p**. If the frame for **Y27** is above the frame for **p** on the run-time stack, the frame for **Y27** will be popped first, so there is no problem with pointers. If, however, the frame for **Y27** is deeper in the stack than **p**'s frame and the frame for **p** is popped early, the binding for **Y27** becomes a "dangling reference." The following example shows how a forward reference may arise. Consider the following program segment:

```
m :- p(X).
p(V) :- q(V, W).
q(Z, Z).
```

The frame for a call to **m** has a slot for variable **X**. Unifying the **p**-goal with the head of the **p**-clause points **V** in the frame of that clause (actually, the new variable for **V**) to **X**. Unifying the **q**-goal with the **q**-fact points **Z** to **X** (the variable that **V** dereferences to) and thus points **X** (what **Z** then dereferences to) to **W**, which is a forward reference. □

A structure in HEAP may contain references to new variables in a frame. Early deallocation of the frame could cause a dangling reference from the heap structure, if that structure is referenced from a frame deeper in the stack.

Both these problems can be overcome with a little care. A frame is said to be *nondeterministic* if it has other alternative clauses to try—that is, if its NEXTCL field is not **nil**. If NEXTCL is **nil**, the frame is *deterministic*. A frame is *completed* if it is deterministic and all frames for its subgoals are completed. Thus a deterministic frame where CURCL was a fact is always completed because it has no subgoal frames. So a frame is completed if CURCL was on the last alternative, and all the frames solving subgoals of CURCL (transitively) also have no alternatives. We do not remove any frame from the frame stack unless it is completed. This restriction solves some of the preceding problems. At the point a frame becomes completed, only completed frames are on the stack above it. (See Exercise 11.3.) Thus if we remove frames immediately as they complete, we need not worry about having to extract a frame from the middle of the stack.

How do we detect when a frame is completed? A frame is deterministic if it is above LASTBACK. A deterministic frame where CURCL is a fact is completed. The parent of a completed clause is completed if it is above LASTBACK and its CALL literal is the last in its body. So the *nextgoal* routine can determine what frames to reclaim early as it is traversing the lazy list of goals.

The problem of dangling pointers can be avoided by some care in the *match* routine and a little pointer twiddling on the heap. We must modify the *match* routine to pay special attention to the direction that references from a BINDENV point. References must point deeper into the frame stack or from the frame stack to the HEAP stack. When unifying two variables, **match** can direct the pointer in the proper direction. What about the case in the previous discussion, where we have a term in the heap, such as **f(X32, g(Z33))**, that refers to variables in the run-time stack, **X32** and **Z33**? The situation is depicted in Figure 11.4. There we are using the same representation for terms as in Figure 10.2; we just show the record structures laid out as blocks of consecutive words in the heap. The references from HEAP to RS are the only impediment to popping completed frames before backtracking. How can we reverse those pointers?

Consider the creation of a copy term in HEAP as a two-step process. First, we create the copy term with its own new variables: **f(X155, g(Z158))**. Second, we match the new variables with the variables in BINDENV: **X155** = **X32**, **Z158** = **Z33**. Since we are unifying two variables, we again have a choice of which variable to point to the other. Here we choose to point from the frame stack to the HEAP. The new arrangement is shown in Figure 11.5.

When it is necessary to copy a term that would contain a stack variable, we "shift" that variable to the heap. Whereas a variable might have been dereferenced to **X32** before, the dereferencing now goes one more step to **X155**. Reversing these references requires careful re-examination of the interpreter routines. Previously, when *copyapplyrepls* copied a program term relative to a local substitution LSUB,

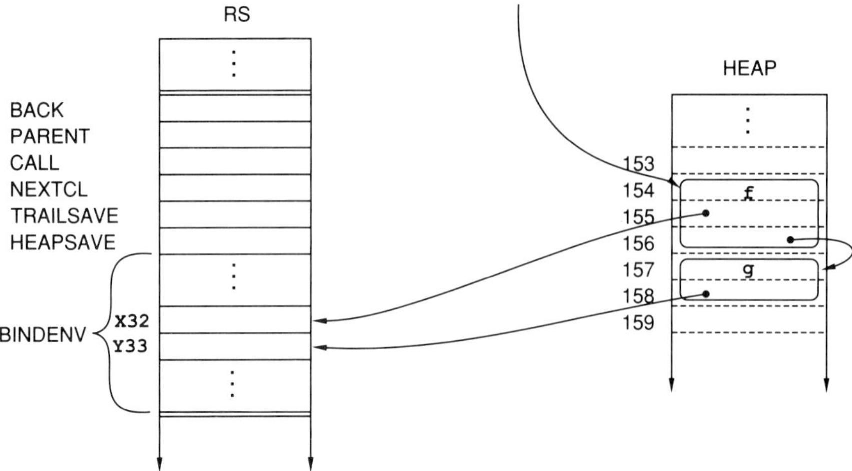

Figure 11.4

it needed only to add LSUB to the position number of each program variable to get the proper new variable. Now that a new variable can be "globalized," *copyapply-repls* must check for that possibility. After adding LSUB to a program variable, it must dereference the result at least one step. (See Exercise 11.4.) As always, in matching, any new binding must be recorded in TRAIL to be undone on backtracking.

11.5.1. *Deterministic Frames with Structure Sharing*

For an interpreter based on structure sharing for terms, we cannot always orient references the correct way. Instead we can determine by a syntactic analysis of a clause those variables that can avoid being the target of forward references and those that cannot. The former we call *private* variables; the latter, *common* variables. We then split BINDENV into PRIVENV and COMENV. The PRIVENV part remains on the run-time stack, so it may be reclaimed when its frame is completed. The COMENV part must go on a stack of bindings for common variables, COMBA, where it remains until the frame is backtracked. In effect the COMBA stack in a structure-shared implementation replaces the HEAP in a copy-on-use system.

How can we classify a variable as private or common by looking at the contexts in which it appears in a clause? A variable is common if some occurrence of the variable in the clause is as an argument of a term, in either the head or the body of the clause. (See Exercise 11.6.) If no occurrence is as an argument, the variable is private. Most authors call these classes of variables *local* and *global,* but we do not wish to create confusion with local and global Pascal variables used in the interpreter.

EXAMPLE 11.2: In the clause:

```
p(X, Y, f(Z), W) :- r(Y, Z), s(g(X), W, U), t(U).
```

the private variables are **U**, **W**, and **Y**, and the common variables are **X** and **Z**. □

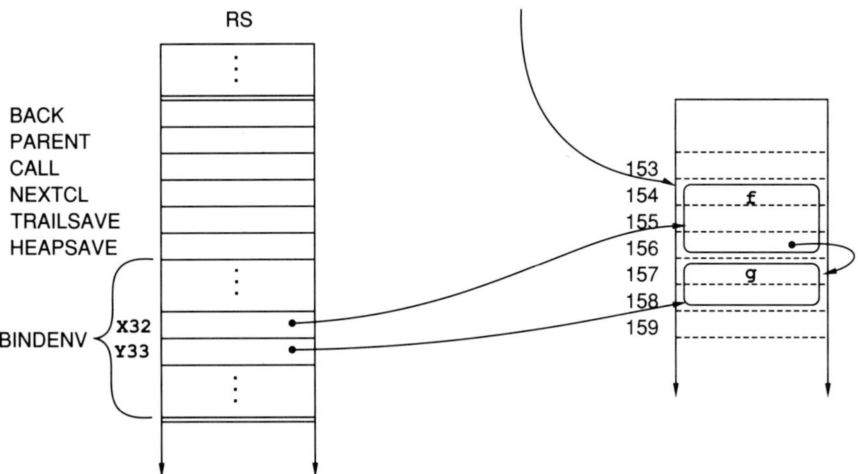

Figure 11.5

Turning to the manipulation of the two binding environments, observe that any binding in PRIVENV can be made to point to other PRIVENVs deeper in the stack, or into COMBA. We do not care which way references go between two common variables, since we will not pop COMENVs except on backtracking. It is also useful to keep separate numbering schemes for private and common variables in a clause. (See Exercise 11.7.)

We need a new field, COMBASAVE, in each frame to keep track of the corresponding COMENV. We also need a global variable in the interpreter, COMBAEND, to keep track of the top of the common bindings array. We must modify the *restore* routine so that on backtracking it reclaims space on COMBA by popping COMENVs down to and including the one corresponding to new current frame. Actually, we may only need to reset COMBAEND to the COMBASAVE value of that frame if we retain the *newvars* function and charge it with initializing slots in both PRIVENV and COMENV.

Finally, it might seem that we have to expand a *molecule* to three fields—one for the variable or code term, one for a PRIVENV, and one for the COMENV. It turns out, however, that any given molecule need only access one binding environment or the other in a frame. (See Exercise 11.8.)

11.6. Indexing

The deterministic optimization of the last section allows us to reclaim space on the run-time stack on successful completion of a deterministic clause. If all our programs were deterministic, this improvement would be very effective and could make our programs approach the space efficiency of more traditional programming languages. But deterministic Prolog is extremely limited; any conditional operation requires nondeterminism. There are things we can do, however, that increase the effective determinism of a program. With our current interpreter, only when a frame is on the last clause for a predicate can it be deterministic. Note, however, that the frame *could* be deterministic on an earlier clause; we just need to determine that no other untried clause could possibly succeed.

EXAMPLE 11.3: Consider the following simple Prolog program and query:

```
:- p(c), r(Y),..

p(X) :- q(X).
q(a).
q(b).
q(c).
q(d).
q(e).
```

Consider the execution of the interpreter on this program. It will first call **p**, binding **X** to **c**. Then it will try to match the goal **q(c)** with **q(a)**, which will fail, as will the match with **q(b)**. Then the match of **q(c)** will succeed and **q** will return, leaving NEXTCL of the frame for **q** pointing to the clause **q(d)**. The frame for the **p**-rule succeeds. It is deterministic, but not completed, because the frame for **q** is above it on the run-time stack and is nondeterministic. Thus **r(Y)** will execute with these two frames still on the stack. Of course, when execution does backtrack to the frame for **q**, neither of the remaining two clauses **q(d)** or **q(e)** will match. By discovering that the frame for **q** can be considered to be deterministic at the point **q(c)** is used, we can remove the frame when we return, which allows the **p** frame to be removed. It is easy to extend this example to show arbitrary savings of space are possible. □

One straightforward implementation of this strategy would be to add a routine that, instead of simply setting NEXTCL to the next clause after the one matched, does some checks to see if the head of that next clause could possibly match the CALL literal successfully. If not, the routine moves on to check the following clause, continuing until it finds one that might match, or until there are no more clauses. It may conclude that there are no more clauses that can match and thus discover the frame is deterministic before it would be noted normally. The idea is to bring some of the searching for matching clauses earlier and, therefore, increase the determinism by filtering out clauses that are not real alternatives.

This change goes counter to the "Procrastination Principle"; it performs work eagerly, rather than lazily. In fact, the change will never decrease the total amount of work that must be done. The work done to filter clauses that might match is work that the current interpreter does not necessarily perform. The current interpreter might succeed on a goal without ever considering further choices for NEXTCL. The entire idea of this modification is to use some extra *time* for "look-ahead," so that *space* can be reclaimed earlier.

If we want to implement this modification, the question arises as to what filtering tests we should use. The most complete test, of course, is to check whether the head of the next clause actually will unify with the CALL literal. This test guarantees that we will achieve the maximum determinism possible. However, complete unification may be rather expensive, and it requires that we be willing to construct binding environments and build structures on the heap. Bruynooghe [6.1] suggested a simpler matching test. This matching can be understood as unification after all variables in both operands are made distinct. This kind of matching is a safe approximation to unification, since if two literals unify, they will necessarily pass this test. It also can be implemented efficiently without recording bindings or building new structures. (See Exercise 11.10.)

There is another approach to filtering clauses. Consider again the situation in the earlier motivating example: We have a goal **q(c)** that we must match against the heads of all clauses for **q**. By preorganizing those clauses with an index, we can quickly find the ones that match. (Recall that the interpreter already uses a limited form of indexing by organizing clauses on the predicate symbol of the head literal.) There are various ways to support an index—for example, hash tables or search trees—and various possibilities of what to use as a key for the index. We will discuss the use of hash tables here with the function symbol of the first argument of the head literal as key. We could key on more arguments, but in practice, indexing on more than one gives diminishing returns. Also, keying on just the first argument means the same routines work for predicates of any arity greater than 0.

A hash table is a way to simulate a direct-look-up array for a large range of values. If **M** is the set of values that we might want to look up, we use a *hash function* $h:\mathbf{M} \rightarrow \mathbf{K}$ to map **M** down to a smaller range of *hash keys*, **K**. The keys in **K** index an array, called the *hash table*, in which the values are actually stored. To store a value $m \in \mathbf{M}$ in the hash table, we compute $k = h(m)$ and store m at the kth location in the hash table. Since $|\mathbf{M}| > |\mathbf{K}|$, there are values m_1 and m_2 for which $h(m_1) = h(m_2)$. If we try to store both m_1 and m_2 in the hash table, a *collision* results: We have two values that should be stored at the same location in the table. Various techniques exist for resolving collisions, such as *probing* to the next free space in the table, or maintaining an *overflow* area. We will handle the problem by assuming that each location in the hash table actually contains a *bucket* that can hold multiple entries, and that if the bucket fills up, we can link more buckets to it.

Given a goal literal that has **q** as predicate symbol and term t for the first argument, we must quickly find all clauses that might match that goal. So we build a hash table, hashing on the function symbol of t. The range of possible values **M** is function symbols. There are many possibilities for a hash function h. (See Exercise 11.11.) For our examples we will assume $\mathbf{K} = \{0, 1, 2, 3\}$, although in practice the best size would depend on the number of clauses for the predicate. Each bucket in the hash table contains the list of clauses that have principal functors that hash to that bucket. Within each bucket the order of the original clauses is maintained. (For a declarative reading of a Prolog program, the order would not matter. The order is important only to preserve the ordering of clauses in a predicate for the procedural reading.) In *establish,* rather than using the list of all clauses as alternatives for a goal, we use only the list in the bucket obtained by hashing on the first argument of the goal.

There are two complications to this simple scenario. First, the goal may have a variable for the first argument. In this case there is no information in the goal that can be used to reduce the set of alternative clauses, and so all the clauses must be tried. For this reason we must have a special bucket that contains all the clauses for a predicate. The other complication is a clause head that has a variable for the first argument. Such a clause must be tried regardless of the value of the first argument in the goal. That clause must appear in every bucket.

To implement this indexing scheme, we replace the CLAUSES field of a *symtabrec* entry with the fields ALL, H0, H1, H2, and H3—each of which points to a linked list of buckets. Each bucket holds a list of pointers to *clauserec*. A *clauserec* record no longer needs a NEXTCLAUSE field, because the order of clauses is maintained by the buckets.

EXAMPLE 11.4: Consider the following predicate definition (we choose unit clauses to make the example simpler to illustrate):

```
p(c, X).
p(f(X), d).
p(X, b).
p(a, []).
p(c, d).
p(g(a), e).
```

Assume a hash function h where:

$$h(\mathbf{c}) = 0$$
$$h(\mathbf{f}) = 1$$
$$h(\mathbf{a}) = 1$$
$$h(\mathbf{g}) = 2$$

The symbol table entry for predicate **p** is shown in Figure 11.6. Note that the clause **p(X, b)** is on every bucket list, since it will match any goal (with respect to the first argument). Also, one of the hash table locations has no value mapped to it, but it still needs a bucket containing the clause **p(X, b)**, which would match any goal with a first argument that hashed there. □

With this kind of indexing, NEXTCL contains a position within a bucket. Its initial value is determined from the first argument of the CALL literal. If that argument is a variable, then NEXTCL starts at the first position in the ALL bucket. If the argument has principal functor m, then NEXTCL starts at the beginning of the bucket corresponding to $h(m)$. Since we are using hash tables, the selected bucket may contain clauses with first arguments that do not match CALL's first argument, as bucket H1 did in the last example. Other indexing schemes can avoid such clauses but at a greater cost in finding the right bucket initially. (See Exercise 11.13.)

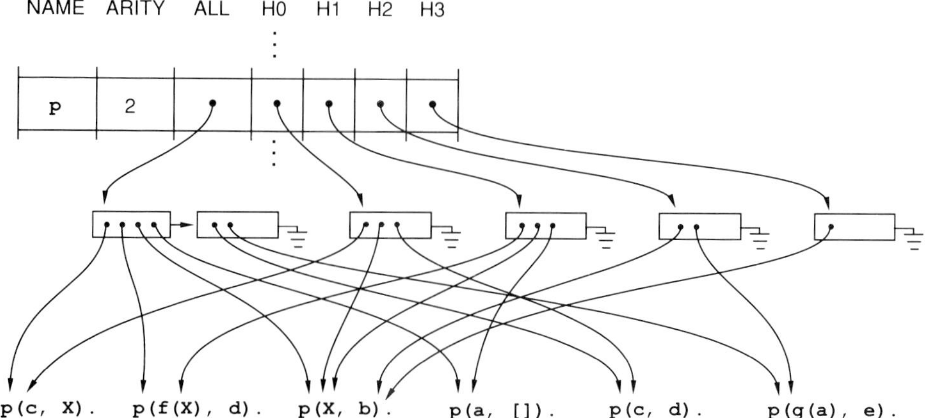

Figure 11.6

11.7. Last Call and Tail Recursion Optimizations

Recall the optimization of Section 11.5, which allows us to remove completed frames from the frame stack on successful return from a clause. This optimization allows Prolog to approach the space efficiency of procedural languages on deterministic calls. However, there is another aspect of Prolog, as well as any purely recursive language, that would seem to keep any implementation from being as efficient as the more conventional procedural languages. This aspect is that iteration is done via recursion. Any looping or list traversal requires procedure calls and the corresponding space for the frame of each call. Thus the amount of space used by any looping program is proportional to the number of times the loop is executed. Conventional programming languages have loop constructs that allow the body of a loop to be executed any number of times using only constant space. The optimization that allows Prolog to execute some loops in constant space is known as the *tail recursion optimization* (TRO). The deterministic frame optimization allowed us to free a frame on successful return from a completed call, rather than having to wait until backtracking. TRO allows us to free the frame *before* making the last (deterministic) call in a deterministic frame. We first discuss the last call optimization and then look at its specialization to TRO.

Consider the following simple program:

```
p(X, Z) :- q(X, Y), r(Y, Z).

q(a, b).
r(b, c).
r(b, d).

:- p(X, Z).
```

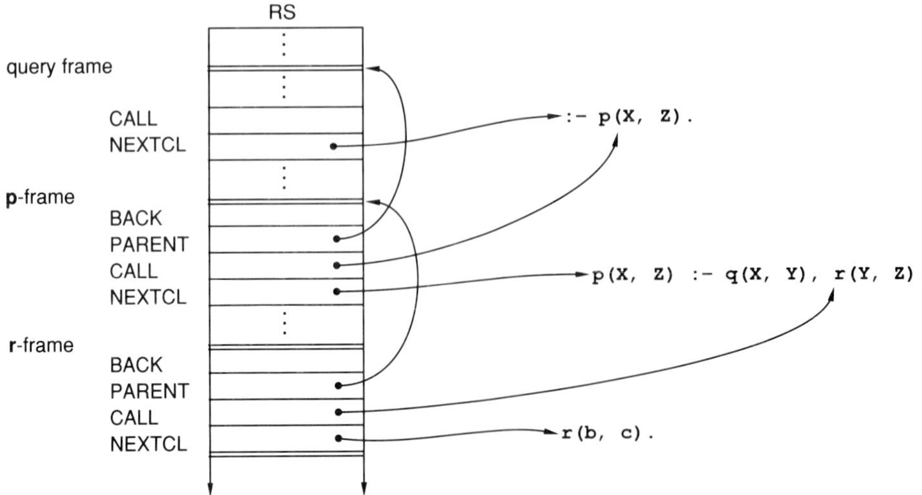

Figure 11.7

Figure 11.7 sketches the state of the frame stack when the first answer <**a**, **c**> is returned. The **q**-frame was removed when **q** successfully returned using the deterministic frame optimization. On forced failure the system backtracks to the **r**-frame and tries the second, and final, alternative clause. The situation is now that the **p**-frame is calling the last **r**-clause. When that call to **r** returns, all **p** will do is return. So, as far as control is concerned, we can let the **r**-frame return directly to **p**'s caller, by giving it **p**'s PARENT and CALL values.

This branching around and release of **p**'s deterministic frame *before* the call to the final literal in the **p**-clause is known as the *last call optimization*. Note carefully the conditions that must hold for early release:

1. The **p**-frame must be deterministic. In this case it is because there is only one clause for **p**.
2. The **p**-frame must be completed except for satisfying its last literal. In this case there are no more alternatives for the **q**-literal in the **p**-clause.
3. That final literal of the **p**-clause must be on its *last call*: the literal must be about to be matched to the last alternative clause. Here the last **r**-clause is about to match the **r**-literal in the **p**-clause.

What all these conditions guarantee is that control will either continue forward from the **r**-frame to some literal for a frame that is before the **p**-frame in the stack, or that control will backtrack from the **r**-frame to a frame before the **p**-frame. Under any eventuality, control need not return to the **p**-frame.

Before looking in detail at how to handle bindings to allow the last call optimization, consider why it is worthwhile. The conditions just described seem so restrictive that the effort to detect the opportunity to avoid returning to a frame and exploit it may exceed the payoff. The real advantage to this optimization is not in situations such as the preceding example but in the case of a tail-recursive predicate—that is, a predicate in which the final literal in the definition of the predicate is the predicate itself. In that case we will be able to reuse the space of the skipped frame at the time of the last call.

Consider our old friend, the **append** predicate:

```
append([], L, L).
append([X|L1], L2, [X|L3]) :- append(L1, L2, L3).
```

Here the final literal in the definition of **append** is the **append** predicate itself. The last call will always be to the second **append** clause, except when the recursive call has an empty list. Consider how the state of the frame stack changes when we execute the goal:

```
append([a, b, c, d, e], [f], A).
```

First on the stack is the frame for the query. Then comes an **append**-frame for the **[a, b, c, d, e]** call. The first clause fails, leaving the first **append**-frame deterministic, and we get a second **append**-frame for the **[b, c, d, e]** call. The first clause for that call fails, and we are ready to try the last alternative for the final literal in the first **append**-frame. The last call optimization is applicable: the first **append**-frame is deterministic; it is completed except for the final literal, and that literal is on its last call. With this optimization the first **append**-frame is no longer accessible, so its space can be reclaimed. However, it lies beneath the second **append**-frame in the stack. We will show shortly how the second **append**-frame can be shifted to use the space occupied by the first. This overlay is the essence of TRO. Continuing, we see that the same situation arises with regard to the second and third **append**-frames. We can again do the last call optimization, overlaying the third **append**-frame on the second. The stack never gets more than three frames deep. This example illustrates how Prolog programs can do looping with only a constant amount of space using TRO.

We blithely skipped over some difficulties: How do we set the fields in the overlaid frame, and how do we handle variable bindings correctly so that this optimization can be made? Consider the situation with the first and second **append**-frames. It turns out that we want the second frame to acquire almost all the field values from the first frame. Thus when overlaying the second frame on the first, we leave those fields alone. BACK remains the same, since the backtrack points for the first and second frame are the same. PARENT and CALL are left alone because successful completion of the second frame means successful completion of the first, and control will advance to the same point (in this case, to successful completion of the query). NEXTCL is the same for the two frames (**nil**), because they are both on the last clause for **append**. We want the second frame to get the values for TRAILSAVE and HEAPSAVE from the first frame, so that if the second frame fails, it undoes the effects of the first frame. Only BINDENV will be different between the two frames. Thus "overlaying" the second frame on the first merely means replacing the BINDENV of the first frame by the second.

Before we can overwrite the first frame's BINDENV, we must use its variable bindings to set the variables in the second BINDENV. The first thought is to allocate the new (second) BINDENV on the top of the frame stack, do the unification by calling *match,* and then copy the second BINDENV over the first. The problem here is that *match* may set up pointers in the second BINDENV that point into the first, and then simply writing over the first can be disastrous. But if we move the first BINDENV out above the second *before* calling *match,* our earlier care with which direction pointers go (for the deterministic frame optimization) will guarantee no pointers into the first BINDENV. So the strategy is actually to move the second frame into place before matching the head of its clause with the final literal of the first frame. We use the following steps:

1. Discard the second frame.
2. Copy the BINDENV of the first frame far enough out in the stack to leave room for the second frame. Call it BINDENV-1. This shift moves BINDENV-1 by the length of BINDENV of the second frame. With the deterministic frame optimization, there are no frames between the first and the second at this point. (The length of BINDENV-1 may differ from that of the other BINDENV, because, with indexing, those frames can go deterministic on different clauses.)
3. Clear the BINDENV segment of the first frame. Call it BINDENV-2.
4. The first frame now becomes the second frame. Note that we need to remember only BINDENV-1 from the first frame and CALL from the second to call *match,* because the other arguments to *match* are available in the NEXTCL and BINDENV fields of the second frame.
5. Call *match.* If it fails, pop the remaining frame. If it succeeds, discard BINDENV-1.

Because of our care always to point variables deeper in the frame stack, there are no pointers into the variables of BINDENV-1 (and so we can shift them). Also, no pointers into BINDENV-1 will be created by the unification, since those variables look as though they are on the top of the frame stack. One complication is that, while there are no pointers from outside into BINDENV-1, there may be a pointer from one variable within it to another. This possibility just means that we must be careful in moving BINDENV-1, readjusting such pointers by the distance we move BINDENV-1.

A few figures will clarify the frame-shifting process. Figure 11.8 shows the situation for the **append** example when the second frame is about to match the second **append**-clause to its CALL of **append(L1-38, L2-37, L3-40)**. In each case the NEXTCL field is **nil** because the last (second) clause in the definition of **append** is being considered. We assume the interpreter copies all code terms to the heap, even if they have no variables. We do not show all the individual words in the heap, but pointers from RS and HEAP itself do reference subterms there. Variable **X-187** in the heap is bound to the constant **a** in the symbol table. Figure 11.9 shows the situation after the BINDENV of the first **append**-frame has been copied to create BINDENV-1. Since BINDENV-1 contains no internal references in this example, no adjustment of pointers was necessary during the copy. The CALL literal for the second **append**-frame must be held in a global variable until

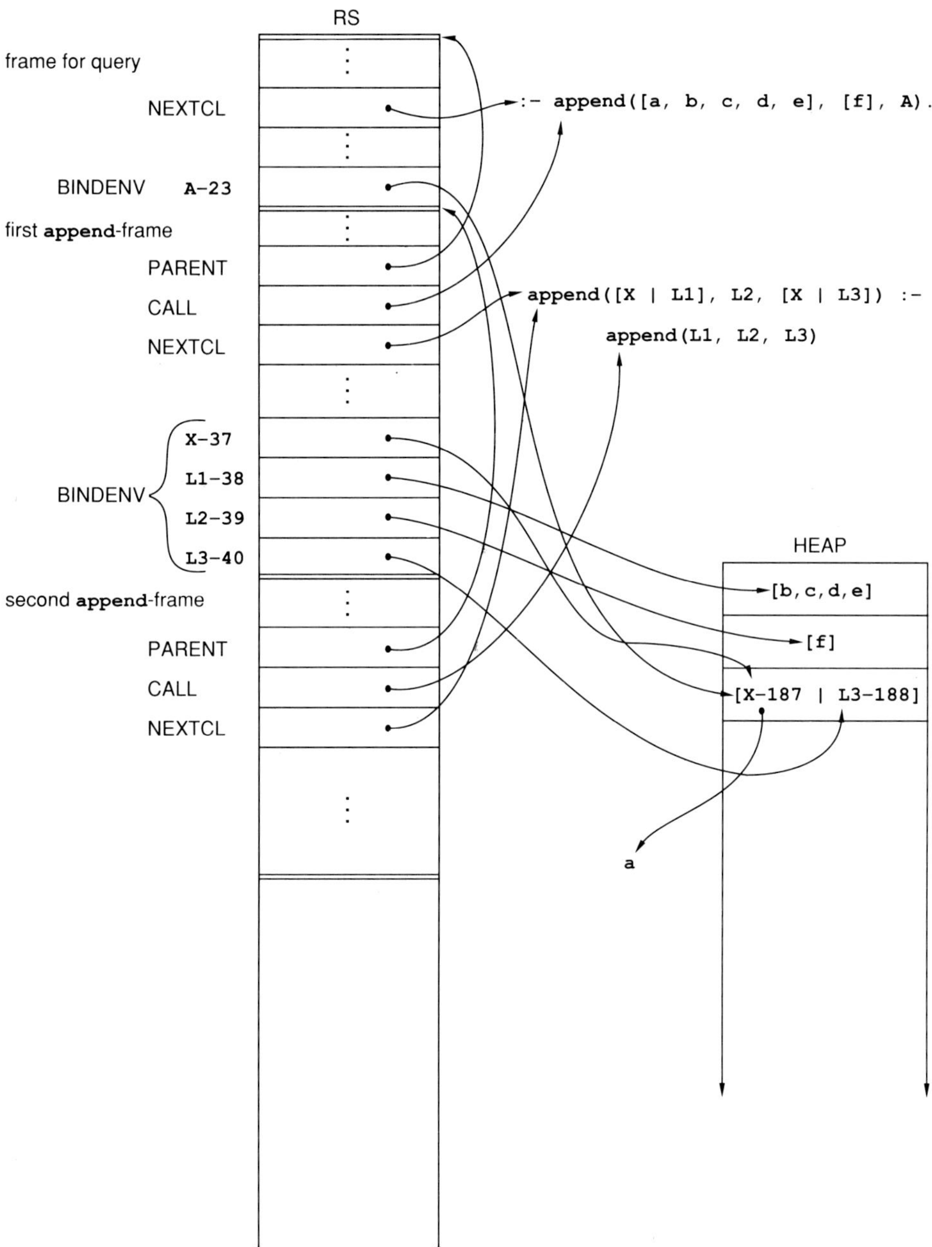

Figure 11.8

after the call to *match*. The value it inherits from the first frame is for continuing the computation on success, not for unification. Figure 11.10 shows a successful match for the second frame, and BINDENV-1 has been discarded. We have rewritten **[b, c, d, e]** as **[b|[c, d, e]]** (although no changes are really made in

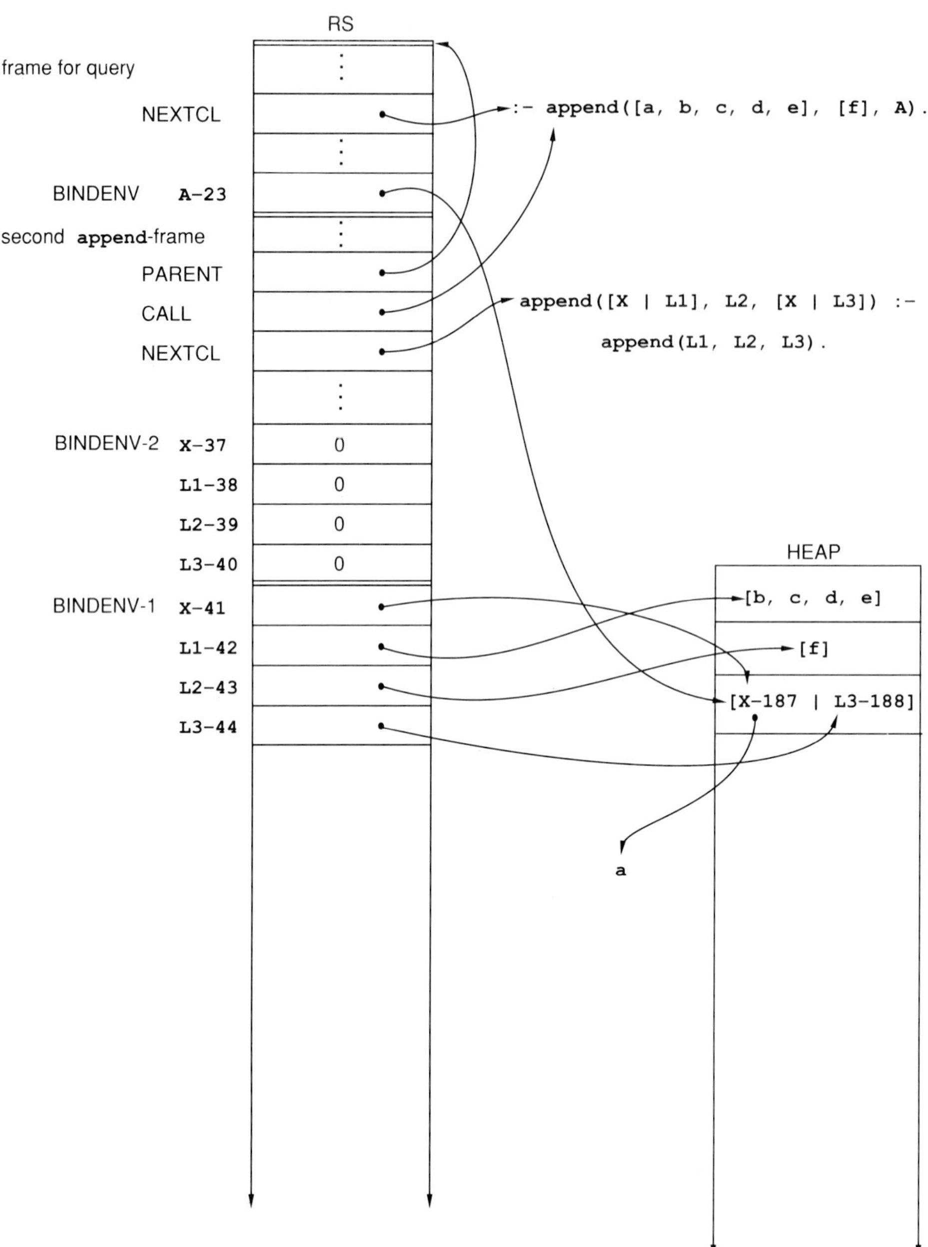
RS
frame for query
NEXTCL
:- append([a, b, c, d, e], [f], A).
BINDENV A-23
second append-frame
PARENT
CALL
NEXTCL
append([X | L1], L2, [X | L3]) :-
append(L1, L2, L3).
BINDENV-2 X-37 0
L1-38 0
L2-39 0
L3-40 0
HEAP
BINDENV-1 X-41
L1-42
L2-43
L3-44
[b, c, d, e]
[f]
[X-187 | L3-188]
a

Figure 11.9

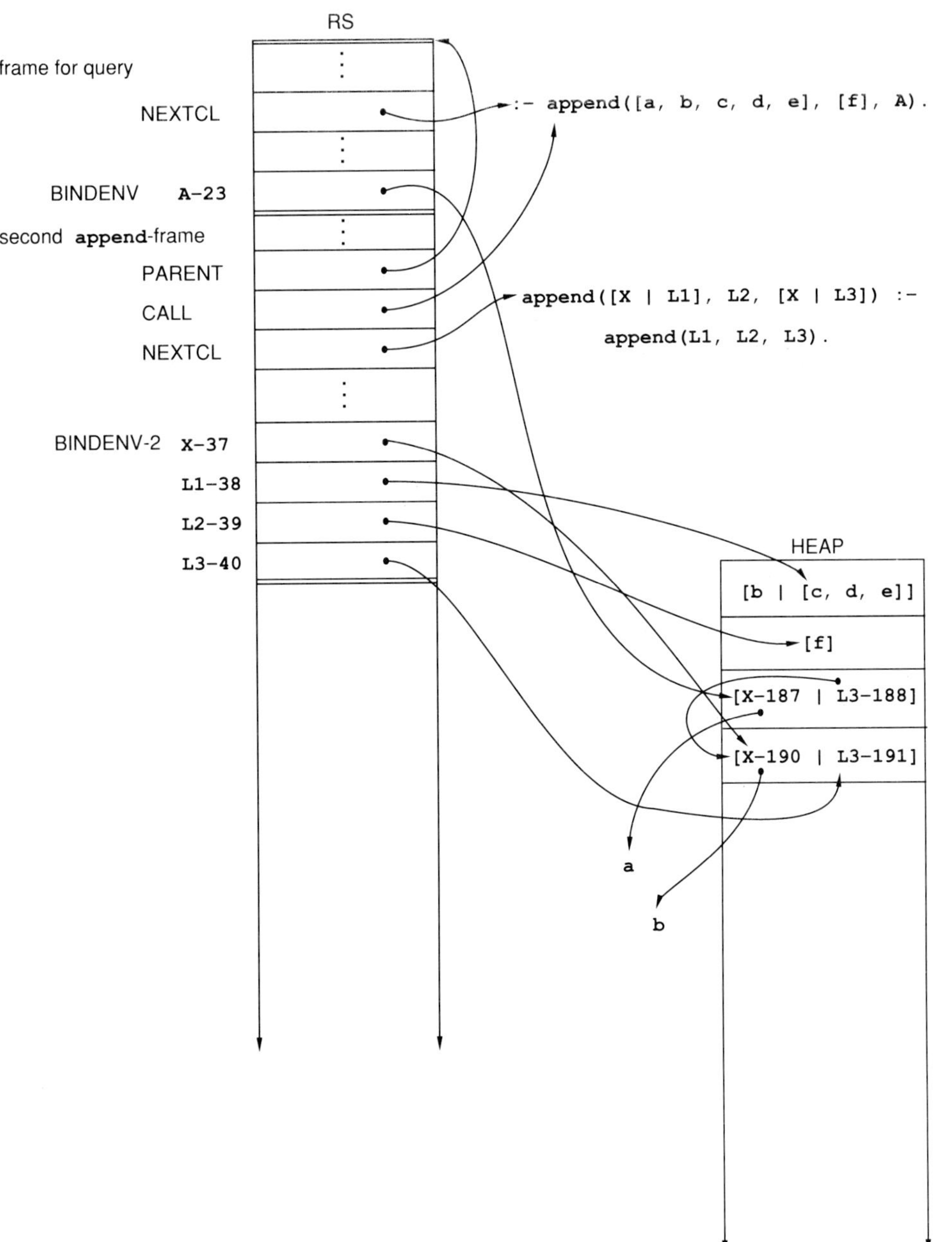
RS
frame for query
NEXTCL
BINDENV A-23
second append-frame
PARENT
CALL
NEXTCL
BINDENV-2 X-37
L1-38
L2-39
L3-40
:- append([a, b, c, d, e], [f], A).
append([X | L1], L2, [X | L3]) :-
append(L1, L2, L3).
HEAP
[b | [c, d, e]]
[f]
[X-187 | L3-188]
[X-190 | L3-191]
a
b

Figure 11.10

HEAP), since **L1-38** has to point to the tail of the list, and the interpreter does not copy terms that have already been copied to the heap. Observe the reuse of new variables **X-37**, **L1-38**, **L2-39**, and **L3-40** caused no problems, since there are no references to those variables. Also, in this instance the order of BINDENV-1 and BINDENV-2 on the stack did not matter, but it can make a difference. (See Exercise 11.17.) This space reclamation can be made to work with last calls in general, but the overhead is probably only worthwhile with tail recursion.

11.8. Compiling Prolog

How can we even think of compiling a language such as Prolog that is so obviously interpreted and requires so much storage management? Consider how we might progress from an interpreter to a compiler for a more traditional language, such as Pascal. Suppose we want to convert the interpreter to a code generator. When evaluating a single arithmetic expression, the interpreter branches to certain segments of machine code to perform the operations in the expression. It will execute the same sequence of machine instructions every time it evaluates the expression. Why not modify the interpreter so that, instead of executing the machine instructions for the operations, it writes those instructions to a buffer as compiled code. (We are glossing over some storage allocation issues, but this view of compiling is a reasonable first cut.)

For a sequence of expressions, we can just stick the buffered instructions together. When evaluating any kind of conditional statement, however, the interpreter does not always perform the same sequence of machine instructions. For such statements, the compiler must emit code to make the appropriate test and execute the proper alternative at run time. We must consider all sequences of instructions that the interpreter might execute and include each sequence and the correct branching instructions. For a procedure call, we could have the compiler emit the code that gets executed during the evaluation of that procedure (an in-line expansion). However, this approach is not space efficient, especially for recursion. The compiler can instead emit code to branch to and return from the code emitted from that procedure. (The Prolog compiler we describe will actually do some in-line expansion.)

Now consider a Prolog clause, say:

```
p(X, a, Y) :- q(X, Z), r(Z, Y).
```

Let's view this clause as a program and identify the sequential and control parts of its interpretation. At the top level the major pieces are:

1. allocate space for new variables,
2. call *match* on the head and whatever the goal is,
3. branch to **q**,
4. branch to **r**, and
5. free the allocated space before returning.

A sequence of machine instructions for steps 1 and 5 seems feasible, but we cannot expand the calls for 2, 3, and 4 in line, since any of them can be recursive. But some things in each call, such as dereferencing variables, happen the same way each time. A Prolog compiler might produce code to dereference the variables **X** and **Z** before the call to **q**, rather than doing them one at a time in a call to **match**. This strategy reverses the Procrastination Principle, since it does work eagerly that might not be needed later. (**Z** will never be dereferenced in the interpreted case if **X** fails to unify with the corresponding argument.) For dereferencing, the downside of procrastination weighs heavily. In the interpreter, **X** will be dereferenced for every **q**-clause tried against the **q**-goal. Furthermore, most calls have only a few arguments to dereference, so dereferencing all of them before matching is not much added overhead. It is hard to construct a realistic example where eager dereferencing does not pay off.

It also turns out that the call to *match* in step 2 is not totally unconstrained. We know something about the form of one argument to that call (the head of the clause). For example, since the second argument of the head is **a**, there are only two possible terms in the goal with which it could unify: another **a** or an unbound variable.

The compilation of Prolog can be viewed as specializing the nonrecursive interpreter to each predicate in a Prolog program. For each clause C in a predicate, we can determine in advance many of the assignments and branches the interpreter will make when C is the value of CURCL. In particular, the routines in the interpreter—*match, coppyapplyrepls, nextgoal, restore8*—can be specialized to such a degree for a particular clause that their effect can be captured with a small number of machine instructions. The goal is to do enough preanalysis of the interpreter vis-à-vis each clause that we can dispense with record representations of clauses altogether: all the information in a clause will be captured by its specialized version of the interpreter.

As an example of this strategy, consider the *match* routine. Suppose we have a clause C with head:

```
p(X, b, f(a, Y), X, g(h(X)))
```

and we want a specialized version of *match* where C's head is fixed as one of the literals. That version of *match* will be used when C is CURCL. We can determine the values of many of *match*'s variables and which way some **if**-statements will branch knowing just this one parameter. Let's analyze what happens in *match* when:

```
p(X, b, f(a, Y), X, g(h(X)))
```

is the first parameter. The first argument of this literal, **X**, can have no binding when *match* begins. Thus that variable can be bound to whatever is the first argument of the goal literal without even looking at that argument of the goal. For the second argument, **b**, matching will succeed only if the corresponding argument is either an unbound variable or **b**. For **f(a, Y)**, matching succeeds if the third argument of the goal is an unbound variable or a term with function symbol **f/2** whose first argument matches **a** and whose second argument can be anything (since the corresponding argument is the first appearance of **Y**). For the fourth argument, which is the second occurrence of **X**, we can make no decisions, because we do not know how the first occurrence of **X** was bound. For the fifth argument, we can say a little about the possibilities for the corresponding argument of the goal literal, but, again, we have no information in advance on the value of **X**.

The following pseudocode description of the matching process has the preceding literal as the first parameter. We use GOAL for the other parameter with a list of integers to reference arguments and subarguments. Thus GOAL.2 is the second argument of GOAL, and GOAL.5.1 is the first argument of the fifth argument of GOAL.

```
1. bind X to GOAL.1;

2. if unbound(GOAL.2) then bind GOAL.2 to b
   else if GOAL.2 = b then {do nothing}
   else fail;

3. if unbound(GOAL.3) then bind GOAL.3 to f(a, Y)
   else if structsym(GOAL.3) = f/2 then
     begin
       if unbound(GOAL.3.1) then bind GOAL.3.1 to a
       else if GOAL.3.1 = a then {do nothing}
       else fail;
       bind Y to GOAL.3.2
     end
   else fail;

4. match(X, GOAL.4);

5. if unbound(GOAL.5) then bind GOAL.5 to g(h(X))
   else if structsym(GOAL.5) = g/1 then
       if unbound(GOAL.5.1) then bind GOAL.5.1 to h(X)
       else if structsym(GOAL.5.1) = h/1 then match(X, GOAL.5.1.1)
       else fail
   else fail;
```

For arguments with function symbols, we are unwinding the recursive calls to *match* and putting them in line (steps 3 and 5). Also in step 5, we have omitted the occurs-check for the bindings of GOAL.5 and GOAL.5.1.

With this specialized version of *match,* we no longer need the head to clause C, because it is used only for matching. This code takes more space than the corresponding clause head, but we expect it to run faster than a call to *match* because of the binding and branching decisions done in advance.

We will use other techniques in compilation to speed execution of a clause. By keeping the values of GOAL.1 through GOAL.5 available in registers, we will be able to save on memory accesses. In some cases, using registers saves space, because no slot in the binding environment is needed for certain variables. Each literal in the body of a clause will be translated into code to set up these registers and create the values they reference. Also the work that *nextgoal* does in setting up a new stack frame, as well as the undoing that *restore* does, will be part of the code for a clause.

Going back to the specialized code for matching, consider the fragment:

bind GOAL.3 to **f(a, Y)**

This fragment actually represents a call to *copyapplyrepls* to make a copy of **f(a, Y)** on the heap under the current binding environment. In the interpreter the term being copied is located in the Prolog program. Usually compilers do not retain the original source program after they finish emitting machine code. But if our Prolog compiler discarded the original clauses, where would *copyapplyrepls* find a term to copy? Rather than having a structure for **f(a, Y)** that *copyapplyrepls* copies, we can just include code for a specialized version of that routine, too—code that builds the structure **f(a, Y)** on the heap. Observe that the specialized *match* code either builds **f(a, Y)** on the heap (and points GOAL.3 to it) or examines GOAL.3 to see if it matches **f(a, Y)**. It will turn out that the code for building **f(a, Y)** will be structured like the code for matching **f(a, Y)**, and we will exploit that common structure.

The final aspect of compiling we will consider is the last call optimization. The use of registers and choice points will make the ideas of that optimization more widely applicable. We can "link out" a clause when its final literal is *first* called after the rest of the clause is completed. Further, the optimization works for any clause in a predicate, not just the last, and we can reclaim space early for any clause, not just a tail-recursive clause.

We hope that our strategy of translating parts of clauses into straight-line machine code sequences by partial in-line expansion of interpreter routines makes compiling Prolog seem a more likely process. We present Prolog compiling techniques mostly by example. We start with a simple case—deterministic Datalog clauses—and then deal with nondeterminism and terms. First, however, we describe the "machine language" the Prolog compiler will generate.

11.8.1. *The Warren Prolog Engine*

For an actual Prolog compiler that generates code for an existing computer—say, a VAX—a clause is ultimately translated to instructions in VAX machine language. Most compilers for traditional languages first generate instructions in an intermediate language. A second phase follows in which the intermediate language program is translated into machine (or *native)* code. The intermediate language is midway between the source language and the target machine language, often resembling an assembly language. When going from source language to intermediate code, the compiler decomposes high-level control constructs (**if-then-else**, **while**, procedure call and return) into sequences of simple control operations (tests and jumps). It also decomposes complex expressions into sequences of single operations.

However, the mapping of labels and variables to storage locations is left to the intermediate-code-to-machine-instruction phase.

We view the intermediate language as the machine language of a sophisticated virtual machine that is specially designed to execute programs in the source language efficiently. Our intermediate code is the machine language for a virtual machine designed by D. H. D. Warren, which we will call the WPE (for Warren Prolog Engine). We describe compilation of Prolog programs into WPE instructions, but we do not discuss how to generate native machine code (for example, VAX instructions) from the intermediate (WPE) code. It should be clear from the description of the WPE instructions that each can be translated into just a few machine instructions and calls to library routines.

The WPE is designed so that the "specialized" versions of interpreter routines can be expressed in few instructions. For example, the fragment of matching pseudocode:

if unbound(GOAL.2) **then** bind GOAL.2 to **b**
else if GOAL.2 = **b** **then** {do nothing}
else fail;

that matches a goal argument to the constant **b** is realized with the single WPE instruction:

getCon r2, **b**

When translating a Prolog clause to WPE instructions, we will generate about one instruction per predicate, function, or constant symbol in the source. The translation of a clause in WPE instructions may take less space than the internal representation of clauses used by the interpreter. One way to save space for long-term storage of compiled Prolog is to store it as WPE instructions and do the final translation to native machine code when a clause is loaded into memory for use.

The WPE has a group of registers plus three stacks—the run-time stack, the copy heap, and the trail stack—and special instructions to manipulate these stacks. As before, the trail stack is used to unbind variables on backtracking, and the heap contains copy terms. All structured terms will be stored in the heap, with an n-ary term represented as a sequence of $n + 1$ words—one for the structure symbol (a reference to the symbol table) and n for the field values. The run-time stack is organized differently than before. It contains both *binding frames* to represent an instance of a clause and *choice points* to keep track of alternative clauses in a nondeterministic predicate and to support restoring of states on backtracking. Every clause (almost) will create a binding frame, but only some clauses will need a choice point. We describe choice points in more detail later. A binding frame contains:

1. a pointer to the parent's frame, the PARENT field
2. a RETURN field
3. bindings for new variables

The RETURN field is the analog to the CALL field in the nonrecursive interpreter. However, it points to the literal *after* the call literal (more precisely, to the WPE code for that literal). It is the point to which to return upon successful completion of the call literal. All the information on the call literal that is needed to make the call will be kept in registers of the virtual machine. Having a reference to the next literal in a clause body, rather than to the call literal, means that in the lazy-list representation of the remaining goals, we do not ignore the first element in a remainder list. Thus a chain of PARENT and RETURN values describes exactly the state of the goal list.

It is possible to design a Prolog virtual machine so that it uses exactly the frame format of the interpreter. The WPE, however, uses different data structures to take advantage of the von Neumann machine architecture and because of the importance of the last call optimization. In a von Neumann machine, copying a value from one memory location to another moves the value through a register. The WPE takes advantage of this property. Also, the last call optimization (whose most important instance is TRO) is extremely important to the space and time efficiency of Prolog programs. The WPE's use of registers and separate choice points and binding frames makes this optimization simple and efficient.

The WPE has a set of *numbered registers* that hold the arguments of the call (or goal) literal. These registers are designated r1, r2, r3, . . . in WPE instructions. By convention, register ri holds the ith argument of the call literal. We will assume that the virtual machine has enough numbered registers to hold all the arguments in any literal. In practice, the translated code may have to spill arguments into memory if there are not enough registers. An argument in a literal is either a constant, a structure, or a variable. If the argument is a constant, the register holds a symbol table reference. If the argument is a structure, the register contains a reference to the heap. For an unbound variable, the register points to the location of that variable in a binding frame or in the heap. If a variable is bound at the time of the call, however, it is dereferenced and its binding is put in the register. Obviously, tags or address ranges must be employed to discriminate the possible items in a register. The WPE also has a number of *special registers*. For the moment, we need only ENVREG, which points to the current binding frame. (The "ENV" is for "binding environment.") There is also an instruction counter, IC, which is incremented after each instruction. Because a clause is translated into WPE instructions, the IC determines the current clause being tried for the call literal.

11.8.2. *WPE Instructions*

We introduce WPE instructions as needed, while working through the translation of more and more complex examples. Most WPE instructions have two operands. An operand can be a register, a label, a symbol, or an integer. Predicate symbols in a Prolog program are transformed into labels for branching in WPE code. A label is indicated by a colon after a predicate name. One label is used for each clause in a predicate; all but the first are distinguished by numeric suffixes: **p:**, **p_2:**, **p_3:**, **p_4:**, and so forth. All other arguments—function symbols, constants, and variables—will be written symbolically in the examples. In the actual WPE code a function symbol or constant is a symbol table reference, and a Prolog variable is an offset into a binding frame. Note that a symbol table reference determines the arity of a function symbol, which we omit in example instructions. Integer operands are used to indicate the sizes for binding frames and choice points for allocating stack space.

As we said before, we start with deterministic Datalog programs. We look at WPE instuctions to put the arguments of a call literal into registers and to unify the head of a clause with them. Consider evaluation of the following program fragment:

```
:- p(a, W), s(W, b).

p(X, Z) :- q(X, Y), r(Y, Z).
```

For a call, the first n registers must be loaded with the n arguments of the call literal. For the call to **p** in the preceding query, we must load r1 with the constant **a** and r2 with the variable **W**. So r1 must contain a pointer to the symbol table entry for **a**, and r2 a pointer to the variable **W** in the current frame. After loading the registers, we are ready to call the **p**-clause to see if its head matches the call literal.

We use **p:** to label the sequence of WPE instructions that represents the **p**-clause. When executed, these instructions first carry out the unification of the clause head with the call literal in the registers. The following WPE instructions carry out the register loading and the unification of the clause with the call literal:

```
PROLOG SOURCE                              WPE MACHINE CODE
:- p(a, W), s(W, b).                       putCon   r1, a
                                           putVar   r2, W
                                           call     p:
                                           .
                                           .
                                           .
p(X, Z) :- q(X, Y), r(Y, Z).          p:   .
                                           .
                                           .
                                           getVar   r1, X
                                           getVar   r2, Z
                                           .
                                           .
                                           .
```

The putCon r1, **a** instruction loads the symbol table index for the constant **a** into r1. The putVar r2, **W** instruction initializes the instance of variable **W** in the current frame to be unbound and loads a pointer to it into r2. This pointer is calculated by adding the displacement of the variable within the binding frame to ENVREG.

Once these instructions execute, the registers contain the arguments of **p(a, W)**. The *call* instruction then branches to the address of the code for the clause for the **p**-clause. The instructions at **p:** are responsible for unifying the goal in the registers with the head of the clause. (We will shortly consider the instruction that creates a new frame for the **p**-clause.) The instruction getVar r1, **X** unifies the variable **X** in the new binding frame with whatever is in r1 by storing the contents of r1 into the variable **X**. This instruction does not check the binding for **X**. It can be used here because **X** is known to be free at the point the instruction executes. Similarly, we use the same instruction for the second argument in the head, because **Z** can be determined to be free at execution time.

This simple example gives a sketch of how the WPE executes the basic part of a Prolog program, the unification. There are, of course, a great many more details.

11.8.3. *Allocating Binding Frames*

Getting a little more detailed, we now describe exactly how the WPE allocates frames and manipulates their fields and the global registers. To keep the discussion simple, we continue to assume the predicates are deterministic. Recall that a binding frame has the following fields:

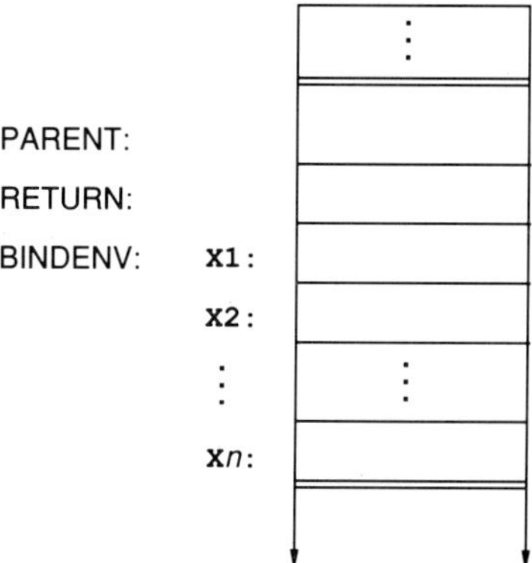

PARENT is the pointer to the frame of the caller. RETURN is the next literal to work on if the call literal for this frame is satisfied. Actually, it is the address of the WPE instructions to return to when the clause for this frame is finished. A global register, RETREG, holds the return address while a new binding frame is being constructed. BINDENV is the location of the new variables in the frame. Let's look in more detail at the example of the last section, paying particular attention to how the frame stack is managed:

PROLOG SOURCE	WPE MACHINE CODE		
`:- p(a, W), s(W, b).`		putCon	r1, **a**
		putVar	r2, **W**
		call	**p**:, 3
	rt: .		
	.		
	.		

```
p(X, Z) :- q(X, Y), r(Y, Z).    p: alloc
                                   getVar    r1, X
                                   getVar    r2, Z
                                   .
                                   .
                                   .
```

In the code for the call literal **p(a, W)** the code to construct the goal in the argument registers comes first. The *call* instruction loads the address of the following instruction (here rt:) into RETREG. This address is one more than the value of the instruction counter, IC. IC is then set to the target of the call, the location labeled by **p:**. The second operand for *call* indicates the number of words in the calling frame. In this case it is 3: 1 for PARENT, 1 for RETURN, and 1 for the only variable, **W**. Contrast this sequence to a procedure call in a traditional language, in which a procedure allocates stack space for *itself* upon entry, rather than letting the procedures it calls advance the top of the stack. This delayed allocation is the Procrastination Principle in the extreme. The advantage of this delay, which will be evident later, is that it allows facts to execute without pushing or popping a binding frame. The work for the frame is delayed forever.

The first instruction at **p:** is *alloc* (for allocate). This instruction is responsible for constructing a new binding frame on the run-time stack. It must increment ENVREG by the size of the previous frame. The WPE can find that size by using the address in RETREG to find the *call* instruction and extract its second operand (here 3). We are using the return point both for control and as an address for passing an argument. The old value of ENVREG is stored in the PARENT field of the new frame, and the contents of RETREG go into the RETURN field. The frame stack is then ready for the instructions that do the unification. Notice we do not have to clear the slots in BINDENV of the new frame because of the behavior of the subsequent *getVar* instructions.

11.8.4. *A Complete Datalog Example*

We consider the following complete (deterministic) Datalog example to see in more detail how variables are handled—both in loading the call arguments into the registers and in the unification performed by the instructions for the head of a clause:

```
PROLOG SOURCE          WPE MACHINE CODE

p(X, c, Y) :-          p: alloc
    q(X, Z, a),           getVar    r1, X
    r(Z, b, Y).           getCon    r2, c
                          getVar    r3, Y
                          putVal    r1, X
                          putVar    r2, Z
                          putCon    r3, a
                          call      q:, 5
```

```
                        rt1:  putVal    r1, Z
                              putCon    r2, b
                              putVal    r3, Y
                              call      r:, 5
                        rt2:  dealloc
                              proceed

q(A, b, A).               q:  alloc
                              getVar    r1, A
                              getCon    r2, b
                              getVal    r3, A
                              dealloc
                              proceed

r(a, b, a).               r:  getCon    r1, a
                              getCon    r2, b
                              getCon    r3, a
                              proceed
```

Consider the code for the first clause. When control is transferred to **p:**, r1, r2, and r3 will contain the arguments of the goal literal (which has main predicate symbol **p**). Also ENVREG will contain the caller's frame address, and RETREG will contain the address of the instruction after the call, the location to which to return. The *alloc* instruction calculates the location of the new frame by looking back to the call and sets the PARENT and RETURN fields in the new frame.

The next sequence of instructions performs the unification of the head of the **p**-clause with the call literal represented by the registers. When executed, the *getVar* simply stores what is in its register argument into its variable argument. There is no need to initialize any new variables; *getVar* takes care of each at the first occurrence. The *getCon* instruction, used here for matching the second argument, translates the constant **c** in the head. This *getCon* instruction unifies the constant **c** with whatever is in r2. That is, if r2 contains (or dereferences to) a variable, it sets that variable to **c**; if it contains a **c**, *getCon* makes no changes; if r2 contains anything else, *getCon* fails. (We will discuss failure later, along with nondeterminism.) The third argument is handled by the getVar r3, **Y** instruction, since it is also a first occurrence of a variable.

Those instructions translate the head of the clause. The next four instructions construct the goal **q(X, Z, a)** and call it. Each argument is put into a register. The instruction putVal r1, **X** loads the value of **X** into the indicated register. A *putVal* is used instead of a *putVar,* since this argument is not the first occurrence of the variable **X** in the clause, so **X** will be bound to a value. Next, *putVar* is used for **Z**, since this occurrence is the first for **Z**. The *putVar* initializes **Z** (in the current binding frame) to unbound and points r2 to it. The putCon r3, **a** simply puts the constant **a** into r3. The next instruction calls the clause for **q**. The second argument is 5, because this frame has two standard fields (PARENT and RETURN), and three variables: **X**, **Y**, and **Z**. If the call succeeds, control will pass back to the code for this clause at rt1:. This label is not necessary, because *call* sets RETREG using IC, the instruction counter.

The next four instructions set up the arguments of the **r**-goal in the registers and call the code for the clause for **r**. The two instructions referring to variables are both *putVal* instructions, since in each case the variable has occurred before. The call is to **r:**, again with an offset of 5. If the second call succeeds, we resume at rt2:. The *dealloc* instruction restores whatever frame called the **p**-clause as the top of the stack by loading ENVREG and RETREG from the PARENT and RETURN fields of the current frame. The binding frame for the caller of the **p**-clause is now the current frame. The *proceed* instruction simply branches to the address in RETREG. (The reader might wonder why the *call, alloc, dealloc,* and *proceed* instructions are broken up this way, when it might seem better to combine their functions and have fewer instructions. Bear with us; future optimizations will take advantage of this particular formulation.)

The code for the clause for **q** should now be understandable. The only new instruction is getVal r3, **A** used for the third argument. Note that this **A** is not the first occurrence, so we use a *Val*-type instruction to accommodate the binding for **A**. The *getVal* instruction must call the general unification routine, since it must handle any combination of items in r3 and variable **A**. Note that *getVal* is the only instruction (so far) that must do a general unification. All the others are simple special cases. The other thing to note is that this clause has no body, so there are no *call* instructions; it simply returns after the instructions that unify the head.

Finally, consider the code for the ground fact for **r**. This literal has no variables in it, and the clause does not call any other clauses (being a fact), so it does not need to allocate a binding frame for itself. The ENVREG and RETREG are simply left alone, and the *proceed* just branches back to the caller, after the constants are checked against the registers.

11.8.5. *Temporary Variables*

Ground facts need no binding frames, since they have no variables to instantiate. This optimization is quite different from others we have seen. Is there any other space we can save in a binding frame? In this section we consider cases where a variable in a clause need not have space allocated on the run-time stack. Avoiding that allocation may save pushing a frame, or it will at least cut down on the number of WPE instructions in the translation of a clause. In our example consider the fact **q(A, b, A)**, which is not ground. Can we get away without a binding frame for it, too? The answer is yes, if an instruction can use a register to get a value for its second operand, rather than consulting memory. Instead of storing the value to memory and then immediately fetching it back from memory, we use it directly from the register. Here is a translation of this fact:

PROLOG SOURCE		WPE MACHINE CODE	
q(A, b, A).	**q:**	getCon	r2, **b**
		getTVal	r3, r1
		proceed	

The *getCon* instruction unifies r2 with the constant **b**. The instruction getTVal r3, r1 is new. The 'T' stands for "temporary," indicating that the second operand is a register, and that the corresponding variable needs no space on the stack. All work concerning **A** can be carried out by register manipulation. (See Exercise 11.8.) The effect of the instruction is the same as for *getVal,* differing only in where it gets its second operand. Here it unifies the contents of r3 and r1. There remain no variables whose values need to be stored on the stack, so this fact needs no binding frame. We again dispense with frame manipulation, and leave the return point and the caller's PARENT pointer peacefully in their registers. A fact never needs a frame, because its variables are never used after unification in solving subgoal literals.

If a variable occurs only once in fact, it does not need any instructions at all. For example, a fact whose arguments are distinct variables is translated as just a *proceed.* A variable that occurs exactly once in a clause is called *anonymous.* Note that an anonymous variable in the head of *any* clause requires no instruction, either.

Temporary variables are neat. Can we use them other than simply in facts? Yes. Consider **X** and **Y** in the clause:

```
p(a, Z, X, Y) :- q(Y, X, W), r(W).
```

A naive implementation would handle **X** and **Y** in the head with:

```
getVar   r3, X
getVar   r4, Y
```

and then translate **Y** and **X** in the first subgoal literal as:

```
putVal  X, r1
putVal  Y, r2
```

X and **Y** are not used again after the first call. Storing the values of **X** and **Y** to memory and then loading them back into registers immediately is inefficient. They can both be temporary variables, handled through register manipulation:

PROLOG SOURCE	WPE MACHINE CODE
`p(a, Z, X, Y) :-`	`p: alloc`
`    q(Y, X, W), r(W).`	`   getCon    r1, a`
	`   putTVal   r1, r4`
	`   putTVal   r2, r3`
	`   putVar    r3, W`
	`   call      q:, 3`
	`   putVal    r1, W`
	`   call      r:, 3`
	`   dealloc`
	`   proceed`

Consider "getting" the arguments for the head of this clause. The *getCon* matches the first argument of the call with the constant **a**. The second argument of the head, **Z**, is an anonymous variable and can simply be ignored, as described earlier. The third and fourth arguments, the **X** and **Y**, can be temporary variables.

The reason **X** and **Y** can be temporary is that they have occurrences only in the head and the first literal of the body of the clause. In such a case a variable is used only to connect the value passed in from the call to the value passed out for the first literal. It is not needed after this function is fulfilled. Hence we use a register to hold the value for this short time. If **X** or **Y** appeared in the second literal, they would require space in the binding frame.

For this clause we let r3 be the register that holds the temporary variable **X** and let r4 be the register for temporary variable **Y** (since that is where they already are). There is no need for a *get*-type instruction for these arguments, since they are first occurrences. (If **X** or **Y** were repeated in the head, *getTVal* instructions would be required for the second and subsequent occurrences.) Next we must load the arguments for the call to **q**. The values of the variables **X** and **Y** must be moved to the correct registers preparatory to the call. The *putTVal* instruction simply moves the contents of its second operand register to its first operand register. The two *putTVal* instructions move **Y** and **X** to r1 and r2, respectively. The **W** is handled by a *putVar* instruction.

We must be careful to avoid register collisions. Consider the clause:

PROLOG SOURCE		WPE MACHINE CODE	
p(X, Y) :- q(Y, X).	**p:**	alloc	
		putTVal	r3, r1 % save **X**
		putTVal	r1, r2
		putTVal	r2, r3
		call	**q:**, 2
		dealloc	
		proceed	

Here we had to swap the values of two registers, so we moved the value of **X** to r3 to avoid losing it.

11.8.6. *Nondeterminism*

Up to this point we have considered only deterministic Datalog programs. That simplification allowed us to ignore heap management and backtracking altogether. Notice that in previous translations we always pop binding frames on success. Consider how frames are allocated, accessed, and freed. The current frame is always referenced by ENVREG, which in the deterministic case is always the top frame on the stack of frames. We do not need a separate top-of-stack pointer. Whenever a new frame is needed, the *alloc* instruction is used to obtain it. An *alloc* calculates the top of the run-time stack from ENVREG and the second argument to *call.*

To support backtracking, the WPE needs several data structures and global registers:

1. the TRAIL stack, to hold the addresses of variables to unbind on backtracking
2. TRREG, a register that contains the current top of TRAIL
3. the HEAP, which we will need later to store copy terms
4. HREG, a register that always holds the current top of HEAP

5. BREG, a register that always points to the top choice point on the run-time stack. (The "B" is for "backtrack.")

A *choice point* is a record that saves the current state of the WPE processor. It is used to allow the processor to restore an earlier state when it must backtrack. A choice point is stored on the run-time stack, along with the binding frames we have used before. To recreate a state, we must restore all registers as they were in that state, in addition to undoing bindings in the run-time stack. Thus a choice point contains a field for each register of the WPE, plus the next alternative clause:

NEXTCL:	the address of next clause to try on backtracking
CENVREG:	the current value of the ENVREG
CRETREG:	the current value of the RETREG
CTRREG:	the current value of the TRREG
CHREG:	the current value of the HREG
CBREG:	the current value of the BREG
CR1:	the current value of r1
CR2:	the current value of r2
.	
.	
.	
CR*n*:	the current value of r*n*

The choice point contains the contents of *n* registers, where *n* is the number of arguments in the current call literal. Therefore, the size of a choice point is variable. The number of registers to store will be an operand of every WPE instruction that manipulates choice points.

To recreate the state of the run-time stack, all the *get*-type instructions just described must log any changes to variables. Whenever a variable is bound, the address of that variable is pushed onto TRAIL and TRREG is incremented.

Consider WPE code for a predicate with more than one clause, and think about what its instructions do:

PROLOG SOURCE		WPE MACHINE CODE
p(a, Y) :- q(...), ...	**p:**	tryMeElse 2, **p_2:**
		alloc
		getCon r1, **a**
		.
		.
		.
p(b, Y) :- q(...), ...	**p_2:**	retryMeElse 2, **p_3:**
		alloc
		getCon r1, **b**
		.
		.
		.

```
p(c, Y) :- q(...), ...     p_3: retryMeElse 2, p_4:
                                 alloc
                                 getCon  r1, c
                                 .
                                 .
                                 .

p(d, Y) :- q(...), ...     p_4: trustMeElseFail 2
                                 alloc
                                 getCon  r1, d
                                 .
                                 .
                                 .
```

To handle multiple clauses in a predicate, we add *try*-type instructions before the code for each clause. These instructions manipulate choice points.

The tryMeElse 2, **p_2**: instruction is the first instruction executed when the predicate **p** is called. It lays down a choice point so that, on failure, the current processor state can be reestablished, and control can be passed to the second clause for this predicate. This instruction pushes a choice point on top of the run-time stack, storing all the register values discussed earlier. It stores them in reverse of the order listed, with the argument registers first. The first operand of the *tryMeElse* instruction determines how many argument registers are to be stored; the second operand is the value used to fill the NEXTCL field of the choice point. This instruction also sets the backtrack register, BREG, to point to the word beyond the last field in the choice point record, which is the convention for referencing choice points. Figure 11.11 shows the layout of a binding frame and a choice point just after pushing the choice point.

There is one problem yet to solve: How is the top of the run-time stack determined? Recall that the *alloc* instruction finds the top of the run-time stack by computing the size of the current frame from the *call* instruction, which is accessed through RETREG. The *tryMeElse* instruction can do the same. There is, however, a complication: Now that the frame stack can contain choice points, a choice point may be on the top of the run-time stack. To determine the top of the stack, *tryMeElse* must first determine whether a frame or a choice point is on top. It does so by calculating the address of the end of the current frame (just as *alloc* does) and then comparing that address with the current value of BREG. The value that is larger (closer to the top of the run-time stack) is the top of the stack. The *alloc* instruction must also use this method to determine the current top of the stack.

We have seen how a choice point is pushed onto the stack. The other aspect of nondeterminism is backtracking upon failure. In the deterministic case we could just halt and reject the query if matching ever failed. Now, whenever matching fails, a fail operation is performed. The fail operation is very simple; it uses BREG to find the address of the top choice point and simply branches to the location stored in the NEXTCL field of that choice point. That location will be the address of a *retryMeElse* or *trustMeElseFail* instruction that is the beginning of the next clause

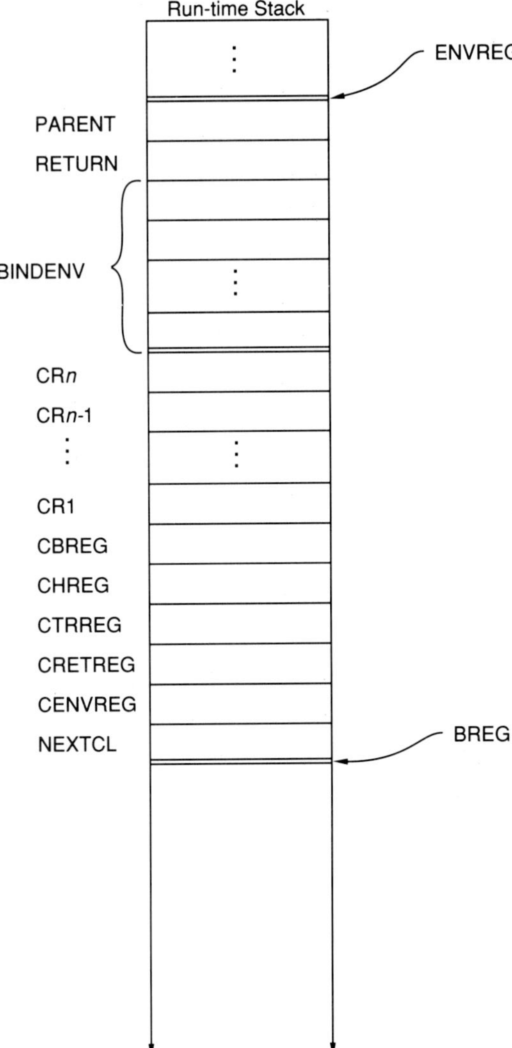

Figure 11.11

to try. The fail operation does not restore the state of computation—that is left to the *retryMeElse* or *trustMeElseFail* instruction.

Middle clauses for a predicate (not the first and not the last) start with a *retryMeElse* instruction. This instruction can be executed only as the result of a fail operation. It uses the choice point referenced by BREG to restore all the registers, except BREG, to their states when the choice point was laid down. The BREG register continues to reference the current choice point. Its first operand indicates how many numbered registers to restore. Its second operand is used to reset the

NEXTCL field of the choice point in preparation for the next failure. Also, the *retryMeElse* instruction must use the trail stack to free all the variables bound since this choice point was originally laid down, before CTRREG is used to restore TRREG. Those variables correspond to entries in the trail stack between the current value of TRREG (the current top of the trail stack) and the value of CTRREG in the choice point (the top of the stack when the choice point was initially laid down.)

The last clause (of two or more) for a predicate begins with a *trustMeElseFail* instruction. It restores the state using the choice point addressed through BREG, as for *retryMeElse,* then removes the choice point from the stack. It does so by restoring BREG to the value CBREG stored in the choice point. Control continues with the next instruction, in order to carry out the execution of the final clause. A subsequent failure will now result in the state of the previous choice point being restored, since all the choices for the current predicate have been exhausted.

In review, for a nondeterministic predicate, the first clause uses the *tryMeElse* instruction, which lays down a choice point. Middle clauses use *retryMeElse* instructions to restore the machine state using that choice point. The last clause uses *trustMeElseFail* to restore the state and remove the choice point. ("Trust me that there are no further alternatives.") Deterministic predicates—those with a single clause—still begin with an *alloc* instruction and do not lay down a choice point.

An added advantage of separating choice points from binding frames is that the deterministic frame optimization of Section 11.4 falls out for free. The next binding frame is allocated after the binding frame making the call, or after the last choice point, whichever is closer to the top of the stack. Any frame above both the calling frame and the last choice point must be completed, so it is okay to reuse its space (as long as we are observing our precautions on the way pointers go in the run-time stack). Note that the frame for the last clause in a nondeterministic predicate will be properly reclaimed on completion, because *trustMeElseFail* removes the choice point for the predicate before that frame is laid down.

EXAMPLE 11.5: Consider the following fragment of a Prolog program:

```
u(X) :- v(X).
u(X) :- q(X), m(X).
u(X) :- w(X).

q(Y) :- p(Y), r(Y).

p(Z) :- s(Z), n(Z).
p(Z) :- t(Z), n(Z).

n(a).
t(a).

r(W) :- k(W), h(W).
```

Suppose we are at the point of trying the **u(X) :- q(X), m(X).** clause. Then the top of the stack looks like:

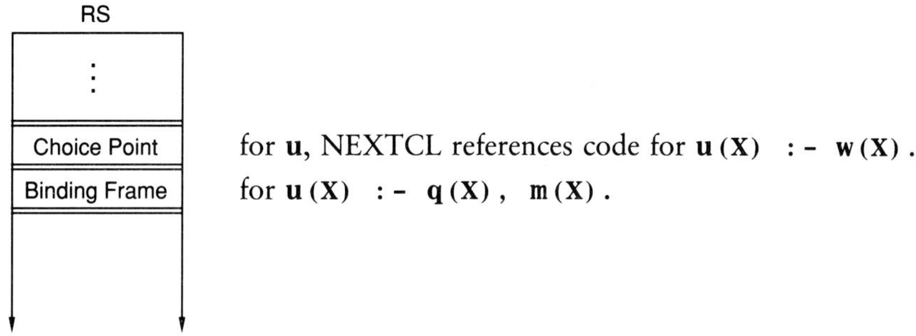

The WPE code for **u(X) :- q(X), m(X).** will call the code for **q(Y) :- p(Y), r(Y).**, which only allocates a binding frame. That code calls the first clause for **p**, which lays down a choice point and allocates a binding frame for **p(Z) :- s(Z).**:

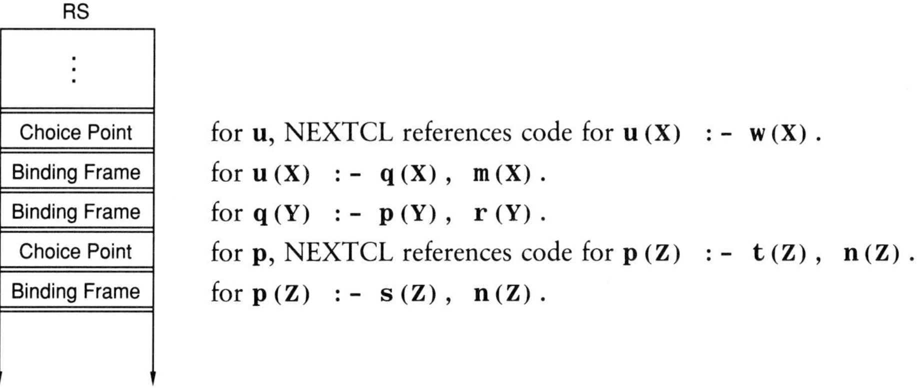

So far, no frames have completed, so no space is reclaimed. The first **p**-clause fails since there is no **s**-clause, and the second **p**-clause removes the choice point before allocating a frame:

RS

Choice Point — for **u**, NEXTCL reference code for **u(X) :- w(X).**

Binding Frame — for **u(X) :- q(X), m(X).**

Binding Frame — for **q(Y) :- p(Y), r(Y).**

Binding Frame — for **p(Z) :- t(Z), n(Z).**

The goals **t(Z)** and **n(Z)** will be satisfied without allocating any new frames (because **t(a)** and **n(a)** are facts). Once **n(Z)** is satisfied, the frame for the **p**-clause is completed. The next call is **r(Y)**, which invokes the code for **r(W) :- k(W), h(W).** That clause will allocate a frame just after the call frame, over the frame for **p(Z) :- t(Z), n(Z).**:

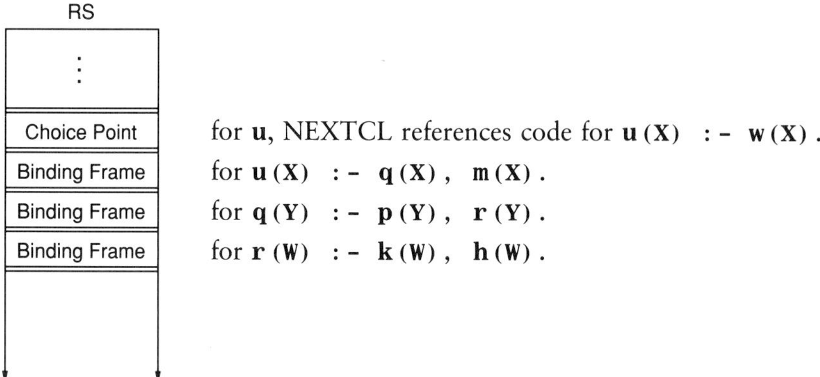

Assume the **r**-clause succeeds. Then both its frame and the **q**-frame are completed. Any clause for the next call, **m(X)**, will allocate its frame over the **q**-frame, since the choice point for the **p**-predicate has been removed. □

We reconsider a couple of previous implementation issues in light of having split choice points off from binding frames. In the nonrecursive interpreter we noted that variables in frames after LASTBACK do not need to be trailed. Here variables in binding frames after the last choice point need not go onto trail. Since choice points get removed from the stack when a call is on the last clause, a binding frame that was beneath a choice point can be uncovered before it is removed on backtracking. Any entries in TRAIL containing its variables can be reclaimed at that point.

Cut is much harder to implement with separate choice points and binding frames. Since choice points get removed from the stack early, we cannot easily determine which choice point goes with which binding frame. Thus it is difficult to locate choice points before the parent of the "cut" frame to cut back to. Two solutions are used in practice. One is to tag a binding frame with a bit that tells if the previous choice point is its choice point. Then a "cut" frame can determine whether to remove a choice point or cut back to it. The other is to pass information on choice points from a parent clause down to a "cut" frame. This solution requires determining which clauses can be the parent clause to a clause with a cut in it. A possible parent clause must pass down information on a choice point.

11.8.7. *Terms in Clauses*

We have not introduced any instructions to manipulate the heap thus far, because we have not yet considered terms. We now move from Datalog to Prolog. After translating clauses to WPE code, we discard them. Instead of using terms in the program for unification, the WPE code constructs terms as needed. All structure records are allocated on the heap, using HREG to find the top. The question is how and when to build structures.

11.8.7.1 Terms in the Body We first treat terms that appear in literals in a clause body. These terms will require *put*-type instructions. Consider an example:

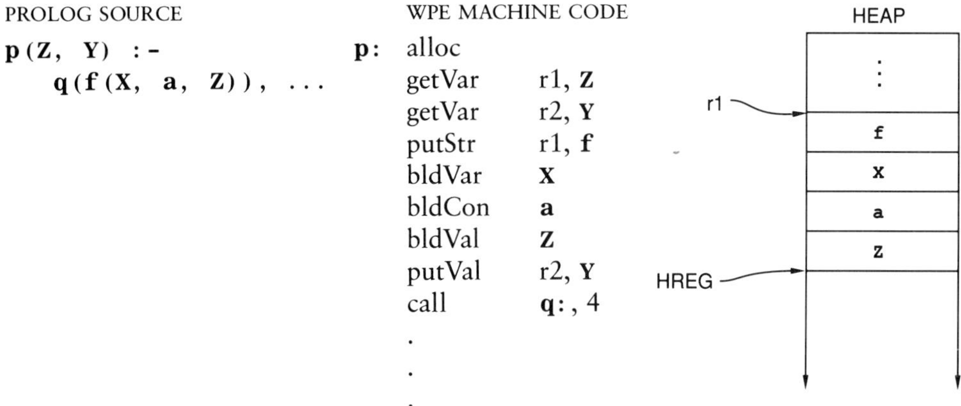

We have seen the *getVar* instructions for the head earlier. In preparation for calling **q**, we want to make r1 reference a structure record with structure symbol **f** and three fields—the first being **X**, the second being the constant **a**, and the third being **Z**. The putStr r1, **f** instruction pushes the symbol table reference for the **f** structure symbol onto the heap and sets r1 to point to that location in the heap. This instruction lays down the first of the four words needed to represent the structure record in the heap. The next instructions complete the record.

The bldVar **X** instruction pushes the variable **X** (from the current frame) onto the top of the heap, thereby adding the first field of the record. It is a *Var*-type instruction because this occurrence of **X** is the first in the clause, so **X** is known to be a free variable. Recall that to prevent dangling references when overwriting a completed frame, we must have no pointers from the heap to the run-time stack. Therefore, the *bldVar* instruction makes this word on the heap a free variable and points the new variable **X** to it.

The second argument is the constant **a**, and bldCon **a** simply adds the symbol table reference for the constant **a** onto the heap.

The bldVal **Z** instruction adds the the third argument. This instruction must push a word onto the top of the heap that represents the value of the variable **Z**. (We are dereferencing variables further than *copyapplyrepls* does in the interpreter when creating a copy term.) We might be tempted simply to move the current value of **Z** in the current frame to the top of the heap. However, we must be careful of the direction of the pointers. If **Z** currently points to a free variable located in some frame in the local stack, such a move will create a pointer from the heap to the local stack. (Oops!) Instead *bldVal* must first dereference the current value of **Z**. If it is a free variable **W**, *bldVal* pushes a free variable **W1** onto the top of the heap, points **W** to **W1**, and records the binding of **W** on the trail stack. If **Z** does not dereference to a variable, *bldVal* simply pushes its value onto the heap.

The final complication comes from nested structures. It is critical that the $n + 1$ instructions that build a structure record for an n-ary term be contiguous, since each one simply pushes a word onto the heap. Nested structures would cause a problem if we tried to construct them inline. Nested structures are therefore "flattened" by moving subrecords out to the front:

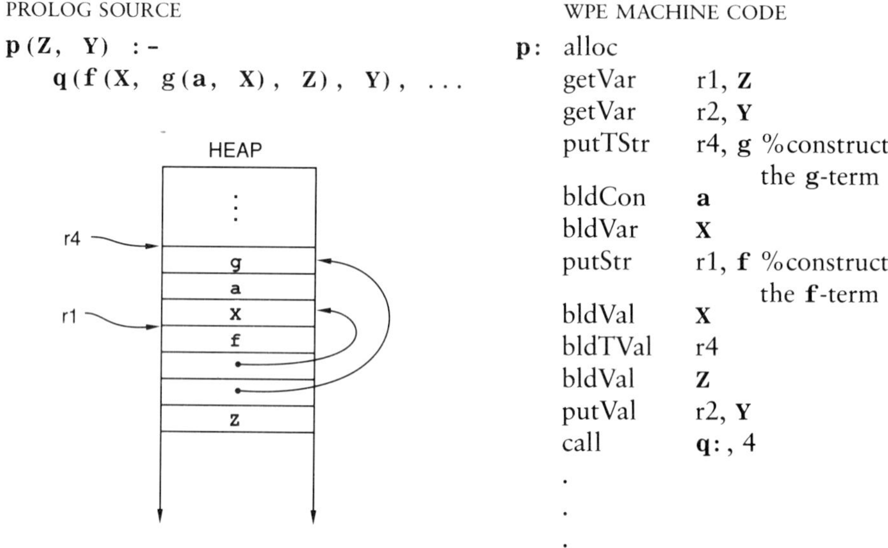

We have treated this clause as though it were something like:

```
p(Z, Y) :- Temp = g(a, X), q(f(X, Temp, Z), Y), ...
```

in which records are nested only one level deep. One new instruction is putTStr r4, **g**, which pushes a reference to the **g** structure symbol onto the heap and puts a pointer to it in r4. Again, the "T" is for "temporary." We can think of r4 as being a temporary variable (corresponding to the variable **Temp** in the flattened form of the clause). The next two instructions push the two fields of the **g**-record onto the heap. When we need this substructure for the second field of the **f**-record, we use the bldTVal r4 instruction, which simply pushes the contents of r4 onto the heap. Structures nested to arbitrary depth can be handled this same way. Note in this example the first use of **X** in the WPE code corresponds to the second occurrence in the clause. It is the order of use in the WPE code that determines whether a *Var*- or *Val*-type instruction is used. Thus the *bldVar* instruction is used for the **X** in **g**, because that **X** is the first one encountered when executing the code. The **X** that appears as the first argument of the **f**-term is translated by a *bldVal,* because the location for it on the heap must reference the variable already on the heap.

11.8.7.2. Terms in the Head The treatment of terms in the heads of clauses is a little more complicated. Again, we proceed by example:

PROLOG SOURCE		WPE MACHINE CODE	
p(X, f(a, X, Y), b) :- ...	**p:**	alloc	
		getVar	r1, **X**
		getStr	r2, **f**
		uniCon	**a**
		uniVal	**X**
		uniVar	**Y**
		getCon	r3, **b**
		.	
		.	
		.	

The *getVar* and *getCon* instructions for the first and third arguments of the head literal are familiar. The new instructions handle the **f** structure record. Consider what r2 might contain when this clause is called: a reference to a free variable, a constant, or a structure record. If r2 dereferences to a free variable, the code must build a record structure on the heap and bind that variable to it. If r2 references a constant or a record structure with a structure symbol other than **f**, unification fails. However, if r2 references an **f**-record, we must perform the unification on the fields of that record structure. To handle all these cases, the WPE needs two more registers: MODE_FLAG and SREG. The MODE_FLAG register holds a bit that indicates *read-mode* or *write-mode.* These modes will color the interpretation of *uni*-type instructions, which we explain further on. The SREG register is used to sequence through fields in a structure record. Since all structure records are on the heap, SREG holds an index into the heap.

The getStr r2, **f** instruction first dereferences r2. If the value is an unbound variable, the instruction sets the MODE_FLAG to *write-mode,* pushes a reference to structure symbol **f** onto the heap, and points the variable to it. If r2 dereferences to an **f**-record, *getStr* sets MODE_FLAG to *read-mode* and sets SREG to point to the first field of that record structure. If neither of those conditions holds, *getStr* performs the fail operation.

The uniCon **a** instruction does different things depending on the setting of MODE_FLAG. If MODE_FLAG is in *write-mode, uniCon* acts just like a *bldCon* instruction, pushing the symbol table reference for **a** onto the heap. If MODE_FLAG is *read-mode, uniCon* "unifies" the field pointed to by SREG with **a**. If the unification succeeds, SREG is incremented. Unification succeeds if the field SREG indexes dereferences to a variable, in which case that variable is bound to **a** and trailed, or if it dereferences to **a**. In any other case a fail is generated.

The uniVal **X** instruction also has two possible effects, depending on MODE_FLAG. For *write-mode, uniVal* has the effect of a *bldVal,* pushing the value of **X** onto the heap (or creating a new variable on the heap and pointing **X** to it, if **X** is unbound). For *read-mode, uniVal* functions like a *getVal* instruction with arguments **X** and SREG. Since **X** might already be bound, a call to the general unification routine is made with the values referenced by **X** and SREG.

The uniVar **Y** instruction acts as *bldVar* for *write-mode,* and as a getVar **X**, SREG for *read-mode,* binding local variable **Y** to whatever the field indexed by SREG dereferences to.

One last problem is nested terms in the *head* of a clause. Nested structures in the head involve the same problems as nested structures in literals in the body. Because of the way SREG is incremented, we must process all the fields of a structure one after the other; that is, all the *uni*-type instructions for the same record must come one after the other. The solution is to "flatten" nested structures so that we do not have to process nested structures directly. It turns out that we already have all the necessary WPE instructions for flattening. For example, the clause:

```
p(f(X, g(Y, a), d)) :- q(X, Y).
```

would be treated as the equivalent clause:

```
p(f(X, Temp, d)) :- Temp = g(Y, a), q(X, Y).
```

Thus the code generated for the following fact is:

PROLOG SOURCE		WPE MACHINE CODE		
p(f(X, g(Y, a), d), c).	**p:**	getStr	r1, **f**	
		uniTVar	r3	% **X** is r3
		uniTVar	r4	% **Temp** is r4
		uniCon	**d**	
		getStr	r4, **g**	% now nested structure
		uniTVar	r5	% **Y** is r5
		uniCon	**a**	
		getCon	**c**, 2	
		proceed		

(See Exercises 11.19 and 11.22.)

11.8.8. *Final Literal Optimization*

Recall the last call optimization from Section 11.6: If we have a clause such as:

```
p(X, Y, Z) :- q(X, Y), r(Y, Z).
```

that is the last clause for predicate **p** *and* we are about to consider the last alternative clause for the final literal (the last call of **r(Y, Z)**) *and* the clause is completed up to the last literal (no alternatives for **q(X, Y)**) *then* we can link around the frame of the **p**-clause. We know that if **r(Y, Z)** succeeds, control will ultimately pass to the caller of **p**, and also that there is no possibility of backtracking into this clause. The last clause for **r** can proceed or backtrack to wherever the **p**-clause would proceed or backtrack. We could not link around the frame for the **p**-clause on any other call for **r(Y, Z)**, since the possibility still exists of backtracking to one of the literals in that clause, in which case bindings in the frame are needed. Also recall that the complication of reclaiming the frame early seemed worthwhile only when predicate was tail recursive (TRO).

The use of registers and choice points in the WPE makes the last call optimization applicable in more cases and easier to apply. Further, we will always be able to reclaim the binding frame for a clause early. The optimization will apply on the *first* call to the final literal of *any* clause if the rest of the clause is completed. We call this optimization the "final literal" optimization.

Earlier we had to wait for the last call of the last literal, because we needed bindings for that literal on backtracking. Now, at the call to **r(Y, Z)**, the value of **Y** and **Z** go into registers. If **r** is a nondeterministic predicate, its code creates a choice point to save the values of these registers. Once these values are in registers, we no longer need the frame for the **p**-clause to keep the bindings for **Y** and **Z**. Also, since continuation information for success in a binding frame is separated from alternative clauses for failure in a choice point, we can link around the binding frame once we call the final literal on any clause. In the interpreter we could do so only for the last clause in a predicate, because stack frames held NEXTCL information for alternatives. Furthermore, with the interpreter, we reclaimed a frame early only for a tail-recursive predicate. With the WPE, whenever a clause is eligible for the final literal optimization, we can reclaim its binding frame early. Having registers means we can extract all the information from that frame needed for matching before we have to allocate any new frames.

The way the WPE manages the run-time stack makes the control flow for the final literal optimization particularly easy to implement. *Whenever* the code for the **p**-clause makes a call to **r(Y, Z)**, it lets the code for the **r**-predicate think the call came from the caller for **p**. If the **p**-clause is *not* completed up to the last literal, there will be a choice point somewhere above the frame for **p**. The code for **r** will allocate its frame after the choice point and the frame for **p** is preserved. If the **p**-clause is completed up to **r(Y, Z)**, there are no choice points after the **p**-frame, and **r** can overwrite its frame over the **p**-frame. The only trickiness in the final literal optimization for the WPE comes in making sure nobody tries to use local variables in the **p**-frame after it has been overwritten.

Once more we proceed by example, starting with Datalog clauses:

PROLOG SOURCE		WPE MACHINE CODE	
p(X, Y, Z) :- q(X, Z),	**p:**	alloc	
r(X, Y).		getVar	r1, **X**
		getVar	r2, **Y**
		putTVal	r2, r3 % **Z** is temp in r3
		call	**q:**, 4
		putVal	r1, **X**
		putVal	r2, **Y**
		dealloc	
		exec	**r:**

Everything is familiar up through loading the arguments for the call to **r**. (Recall that since **Z** occurs only in the head and the first literal of the body, it can be temporary.) After they are loaded, instead of calling and deallocating on return, we deallocate the binding frame and then execute **r**. The *exec* instruction is simply a branch. Since *dealloc* sets the ENVREG and RETREG registers to the values for the caller, and *exec* does not modify them, **r** will be entered as though called by the caller of **p**. We must pay special attention to variables **X** and **Y**. The problem is that the **p**-frame might be popped early from the run-time stack. We must be sure in that case that variables **X** and **Y** will not be needed. That is, no subgoal of **r (X, Y)** will try to bind to **X** or **Y**. The **p**-frame will be popped early only if it is on the top of the local stack, so no references to **X** or **Y** exist at the point of the call to **r**. There are no references from farther out in the run-time stack (because there is no "farther out"), and our variable-binding discipline prevents other references. The only place pointers could come from is the register contents we are passing down to **r**. We must be sure that neither register we are passing to **r** points into (or through) the binding frame for **p**. As long as we are careful to make the *put*-type instructions dereference their arguments before loading the registers, we can be sure that neither r1 nor r2 can point to **X** or **Y**. **X** and **Y** both appear in the head and are bound by *getVar* instructions. Thus there are three possible cases for **X** (or for **Y**):

1. It dereferences to a variable, which must be in the heap or a binding frame deeper in the run-time stack.
2. It dereferences to a constant.
3. It dereferences to a structure.

In no case will r1 reference a variable in the binding frame for **p**. For this clause the given translation works.

Now consider another clause:

PROLOG SOURCE	WPE MACHINE CODE		
p(X, Y) :- q(Y, X, X).	**p:**	putTVal	r3, r1
		putTVal	r1, r2
		putTVal	r2, r3
		exec	**q:**

Both the variables are temporaries, and we need a little fancy footwork to keep from trashing a register that contains a needed value. Also note that since all variables are temporaries, there is no need for an *alloc* and *dealloc* at all. This clause simply shuffles the registers a little and branches on to **q**. Again, a little thought shows that the registers cannot contain pointers into the local frame (very little thought, since there is no local frame).

But consider the case in which not all the variables have their first occurrence in the head:

PROLOG SOURCE	WPE MACHINE CODE		
p(a, Z, X, Y) :- q(Y, X, W).	**p:**	alloc	% incorrect!
		getCon	r1, **a**
		putTVal	r1, r4
		putTVal	r2, r3
		putVar	r3, **W**
		dealloc	
		exec	**q:**

The code shown here comes from the code we used when we first considered a closely related clause before. It has been modified to do an *exec* instead of a final *call*. We have left in the *alloc* and *dealloc* instructions, since variable **W** requires space in a binding frame.

This code will *not* work. When it branches to **q**, r3 contains a pointer to the unbound variable **W** in the binding frame. If the **p**-frame is on top of the stack, then **q**'s frame will be allocated over it, and r3 may well point to garbage. What can we do? We need to create a variable for r3 to reference but not in the binding frame. We can put it on the heap! Everything on the heap stays until backtracking. So instead of the preceding code, we use the following:

```
PROLOG SOURCE                          WPE MACHINE CODE
p(a, Z, X, Y) :- q(Y, X, W).       p:  getCon   r1, a
                                       putTVal  r1, r4
                                       putTVal  r2, r3
                                       putTVar  r3
                                       exec     q:
```

The change is that we introduce a *putTVar* instruction for variable **W**. This instruction allocates a new variable on the heap and points its argument to it. Since there is no longer a need for a binding frame, we can eliminate the *alloc-dealloc* pair. With *putTVar* we can translate any clause with only one literal in its body into code that has only temporary variables and thus allocates no frame.

This example with a variable whose first occurrence is not in the head suggests another case to look at:

```
PROLOG SOURCE                          WPE MACHINE CODE
p(X, Y) :- q(X, Z), r(Z, Y).       p:  alloc     % incorrect
                                       getVar    r2, Y
                                       putVar    r2, Z
                                       call      q:, 4
                                       putVal    r1, Z
                                       putVal    r2, Y
                                       dealloc
                                       exec      r:
```

This version seems like the natural "optimized" code to generate for this clause: move the *dealloc* before the last *call*, and make that *call* an *exec*. But there may be a problem with bindings. We must be sure that no register can point into the binding frame when we branch to **r**. There is a possible scenario in which r1 will do so. **Z** is initialized to unbound by the *putVar* instruction. The call to **q** could bind **Z** to some value, but it may not. If it does not, when we load r1 using putVal r1, **Z** in preparation for the branch to **r**, r1 will contain a reference into the binding frame for **p**. This possibility makes **Z** an *unsafe* variable. The solution is a new instruction, *putUVal* (for "put unsafe value"). The corrected code is:

PROLOG SOURCE		WPE MACHINE CODE	
p(X, Y) :- q(X, Z), r(Z, Y).	**p:**	alloc	
		getVar	r2, **Y**
		putVar	r2, **Z**
		call	**q:**, 4
		putUVal	r1, **Z**
		putVal	r2, **Y**
		dealloc	
		exec	**r:**

The *putUVal* instruction dereferences the variable indicated by its second operand. If that variable does not dereference to an unbound variable in the current frame, *putUVal* acts just like a *putVal* instruction: It loads the indicated register with the binding of the variable. If the register is any unbound variable in the binding frame, or dereferences to an unbound variable in that frame, *putUVal* "globalizes" the variable and points its register to that. A variable is globalized by allocating a new variable on the heap and pointing the original variable to it. Thus a *putUVal* guarantees that the register it loads will not point into the local frame.

With these instructions we can now translate any Datalog program into an efficient program that incorporates the last literal optimization. The extension to Prolog with structure symbols is straightforward. Notice that a variable whose first occurrence is in the body, but as a field in a structure, cannot have a later unsafe occurrence. The variable will be put on the heap (by a *bldVar* instruction) and so cannot dereference to a pointer into the binding frame. (See Exercise 11.23.)

11.8.9. *Trimming Environments*

The final literal optimization allowed us (in some cases) to reclaim an entire frame from the local stack immediately before we branch to execute the last goal in the body of a clause. By looking a little more closely, we can reclaim portions of frames even earlier. However, we may have to reorder variables in the binding frame to do so.

Consider the following example:

```
p(A, D) :- q(A, B), r(B, C), s(C, D).
```

Notice that variable **B** will be allocated space in the frame. But after the call to r has been set up, that variable is no longer needed. So if we are careful about the order in which we put variables in the frame, we might be able to trim off the variable **B** before we call **r**. We generate the following code:

PROLOG SOURCE		WPE MACHINE CODE		
p(A, D) :-	**p:**	alloc		
q(A, B), r(B, C),		getVar	r2, 2	% **D** is first in frame
s(C, D)		putVar	r2, 4	% **B** is last in frame
		call	**q:**, 5	% space for **D, C, B**
		putUVal	r1, 4	% **B** to r1

```
putVar    r2, 3    % C is second in frame
call      r:, 4    % space for D, C
putVal    r1, 3    % C to r1
putVal    r2, 2    % D to r2
dealloc
exec      s:
```

Notice we are using offsets into the binding frames in place of variable names to indicate the exact placement of variables in the frame. Although **B** appears before **D** in the clause, we place it last in the frame, so we can trim its binding before the call to **r**.

Now would be a good time to reread the introductory remarks at the beginning of Section 11.7. We have arrived at a succinct compiled version of what initially seemed a language amenable only to interpretation. To get long straight-line sequences of machine instructions, we reached down into the clauses being called and pulled out some operations we knew were going to happen, or were very likely to happen, such as variable dereferencing. We also did some symbolic evaluation of the *match* function to remove tests for which we can foresee the outcome, such as matching to an unbound variable. Some work got pushed from calling literal down to called clause, such as allocating a binding frame, when it was possible that the work could be avoided in some circumstances. The advantage of the copy-on-use representation for terms should be fairly clear. Any binding of a variable will fit in a single register. The copy-on-use approach does not really need the source code to copy terms. We can include code to build terms on the heap as needed, and the same code works for unifying terms with a switch set. A structure-sharing representation of terms would require us to retain the source program, or at least its terms, for reference.

If we were to look at just the compiled code, we would not be able to recognize the mechanism of a Horn-clause refutation procedure. We hope that the gradual development from naive interpreter through optimized recursive interpreter to nonrecursive interpreter and finally to compiled code has made evident some connections between the two.

11.9. EXERCISES

11.1. Write the procedure *nextgoal* for the nonrecursive interpreter *establish7* in Section 11.1.

11.2. Starting from the nonrecursive interpreter *establish7*, describe how to fold TRAIL and HEAP into the frame stack along with BINDENV.

11.3. Show that when a frame becomes completed (Section 11.4), all frames above it on the frame stack are completed.

11.4. Show the state of the heap and the state of the BINDENV fields (for the query and for the **p**-clause) in the frame stack after the literal **p** has been called (and before **q** is called), for the following program fragment:

```
:- p(a, W, U), ...

p(X, Y, f(X, Y)) :- q(...).
```

Assume the interpreter has the changes described in Section 11.5. Explain the details of how *copyapplyrepls* must handle variables in copy terms to ensure that there are no forward pointers in the run-time stack or any heap-to-stack pointers. Show how it behaves in the case of the example in Figure 11.5 if term **h(X33, U31)** must go on the heap and **U31** has previously been bound to **Y33**.

11.5. Consider the structure-sharing implementation of a nonrecursive interpreter with just a run-time stack: Each BINDENV entry is a molecule, consisting of a program term and a pointer to a frame whose BINDENV portion is used to dereference variables in that term. Show the state of the frame stack (2 frames) after **p** has been called (and before it returns) in the following program segment:

```
:- p(A, B, f(C), a), ...

p(X, f(Y), Y, X).
```

In order to be able to remove the completed frame for **p**, we must ensure that no pointers point into this frame from deeper in the frame stack. Explain why this constraint is violated in your configuration. Show that by moving variables **Y** and **C** to a stack of bindings (COMBA in Section 11.5.1) that remain until the frame is backtracked, pointers can be arranged to satisfy this constraint.

11.6. Show how a common variable can cause a reference that prevents releasing frames early, either in the head of a clause or in the body.

11.7. Modify the representation of clauses in structure sharing to number private and common variables separately. Modify *match* to make the pointers go the right way.

11.8. Show that in structure sharing with private and common variables, a molecule never needs to reference both a PRIVENV and a COMENV for the same term in the program.

11.9. In structure sharing with private and common variables, consider the clause head:

```
p(f(Y)) :- ...
```

Normally **Y** must be treated as a common variable. However, if we know that whenever the predicate **p** is called (perhaps through a declaration **p(+X)**), the argument will always be a nonvariable, **Y** can be treated as a private variable and placed in the PRIVENV. Explain why.

11.10. Give a routine for a version of *match* (appropriate for "filtering" possible clauses as discussed in Section 11.6) that assumes all unbound variables are distinct and that does not need to construct new bindings. It should, however, use existing bindings.

11.11. Compare the following hash functions on symbols for indexing to a 4-bit hash value.

i. high-order 4 bits of first character (ASCII)
ii. low-order 4 bits of first character
iii. length of symbol mod 16
iv. symbol table index mod 16

11.12. How do **assert** and **retract** work with indexing?

11.13. Other data structures can be used for creating indexes on arguments of clause heads. Describe how binary trees could be used, and compare them to the hash tables described in the chapter.

11.14. Backtracking reclaims space in the heap, but records in the heap can become inaccessible on forward execution. Garbage collection is the process of reclaiming space in the heap that is no longer accessible, before backtracking. Discuss the difficulties of implementing a garbage collector, and outline an algorithm. Explain how it would operate on the term **[b|c, d, e]** in Figure 11.10.

11.15. Consider the following definition of two predicates: **length/2** and **length/3**.

```
length(L, N) :- length(L, N, 0).
length([], N, N).
length([_|L], N, M) :- M1 is M + 1, length(L, N, M1).
```

length/3 is tail-recursive, and the tail recursion optimization of Section 11.7 applies. At a recursive call, explain how one frame overwrites the previous one. Write a Pascal procedure to calculate the length of a list using a while loop and a counter. Compare the executions (and the variables) of the Pascal program and the Prolog program (with the TRO).

11.16. Explain why the following tail-recursive program requires special care when moving a frame for the TRO.

```
length([], N, N).
length([_|L], N, M) :- M2 = M1, M1 is M + 1, length(L, N, M2).
```

11.17. Give an example to show why BINDENV-2 must be above BINDENV-1 during unification in the TRO.

11.18. For fact **q(A, b, A).**, show that no other variable can point to **A** as the result of any unification.

11.19. Give the WPE code for the clause:

```
p(f(X)) :- r(X, Y).
```

You will need a new instruction for translating **X**. Call it *uniTVar* (with a single register operand) and explain its operation.

11.20. Generate the WPE code for the following clause:

```
length(L, N) :- length(L, N, 0).
```

You should need only two instructions!

11.21. Consider compiling the following clause:

```
p(A, B, C, D) :- q(B, C, D, A).
```

The best code to generate is to move (using *putTVal*) to a temporary register, move each of r2–r4 down by one, and then move the temporary to r4. We can represent such a register-shuffling problem by a list of pairs of source and target registers. The problem here is described by the list:

```
[move(1, 4), move(2, 1), move(3, 2), move(4, 3)].
```

Of course, if made one after the other, these moves will lose the contents of r4. A solution is described by a list of moves that, when carried out in order, do the correct shuffling. A solution list for the preceding problem list is:

```
[move(1, 5), move(2, 1), move(3, 2), move(4, 3), move(5, 4)].
```

Write a Prolog predicate **genMoves(ProbList, SolnList)** that, when given any problem list, generates a solution list. Does your definition work if the same source register is moved to multiple targets?

11.22. Discuss how to compile the '=' predicate. Consider optimizations that can be done at compile time for the various cases <variable> = <variable>, <variable> = <term>, and <term> = <term>. Compare the instruction generated by your optimizations to that generated for nested terms, as described in Section 11.8.7.

11.23. Give the WPE translation for:

```
p(X) :- q(f(X)), r(Y).
```

and show why **Y** cannot be unsafe.

11.24. Consider how indexing might be added to a compiler. We would add new instructions to the WPE:

```
try    n, targetaddr
retry  n, targetaddr
trust  n, targetaddr
```

which are similar to the instructions *tryMeElse, retryMeElse,* and *trustMeElseFail,* except that the second operand is the address of the clause code and the following instruction is the address to branch to on failure. We also add an instruction:

```
branchOnBound r, hashtableaddr
```

where *r* is a register number and *hashtableaddr* is the address of a hash table. The *branchOnBound* instruction checks to see if the value in register *r* is a variable. If so, it does nothing (and the next instruction will be executed next). If it is not a variable, the instruction hashes the main structure symbol, adds that value to *hashtableaddr,* and puts the word at that address into the instruction counter (that is, it branches to the address retrieved from the hash table). Show the WPE program that includes indexing using these instructions for the Prolog program of Example 11.4.

11.25. Many Prolog systems simply fail if a predicate is called for which there are no clauses. Explain what WPE code a Prolog compiler should generate to handle this situation.

11.26. Notice the asymmetry between how terms in the head and the body of a clause are treated in compilation. Body terms always go in the heap, even if they are not needed after matching for bindings. For example, recall the membership predicate:

```
member(X, [X|L]).
member(X, [Y|L]) :- member(X, L).
```

If **L** were a list of pairs of the form:

```
[pair(1, 7), pair(3, 5), pair(5, 4)]
```

then a goal of the form **member(pair(3, 5), L)** would build a copy term on the heap, but no variable would be bound to that pair after unification. Any program with terms in the body of a clause can be converted to an equivalent program with terms only in the heads of clauses. The resulting program may end up with several "variants" of the same clause to handle different goals. For the preceding **member** predicate, the converted program would contain the following clauses:

```
pMember(X, Y, [pair(X, Y)|L]).
pMember(X, Y, [Z|L]) :- pMember(X, Y, L).
```

The goal **member(pair(3, 5), L)** in any clause body would be transformed into **pMember(3, 5, L)**, which has no terms.

a. Draw the state of the heap after executing each goal against its respective predicate, using the value of the list **L** given above.
b. Compare the translations of the two sets of clauses into WPE instructions. Note that *uni*-type instuctions are more expensive than *bld*-type instructions, because the former involve a test of MODE_FLAG.

11.27. By including an additional argument in which to pass the answer back, we can often rewrite a recursive predicate that is not tail recursive into a predicate that is tail recursive. For example, one definition of a predicate to compute factorial numbers is:

```
factorial(0, 1).
factorial(M, N) :- M1 is M - 1, factorial(M1, N1), N is N1 * M.
```

A tail recursive version of this predicate is:

```
factorial(M, N) :- tailFact(M, 1, N).
tailFact(0, R, R).
tailFact(M, P, R) :- P1 is M * P, M1 is M - 1,
                     tailFact(M1, P1, R).
```

Give tail-recursive definitions for the predicate **reverse(Front, Back)**, where **Back** is the list that is the reversal of the list **Front**, and for computing Fibonacci numbers. The following is a non-tail-recursive definition for Fibonacci numbers. Each number in the sequence is the sum of the previous two.

```
fib(0, 1).
fib(1, 1).
fib(M, N) :-
   M > 1, M1 is M - 1, M2 is M - 2, fib(M1, N1), fib(M2, N2),
   N is N1 + N2.
```

11.10. COMMENTS AND BIBLIOGRAPHY

At the outset it should be said that David H. D. Warren is the acknowledged master implementer of efficient Prolog systems. He led the first effort [11.1] to develop a Prolog compiler, the DEC-10 compiler. This system showed that Prolog could be implemented so that Prolog programs could compete with LISP programs in efficiency [11.2], and in some cases, even surpass it [11.3]. The importance of that achievement cannot be overestimated; without such an existence proof, Prolog would have remained simply a curiosity. He also introduced the use of mode declarations as compiler directives.

The next significant advance in Prolog implementations was also made by D. H. D. Warren in the design of what is now known as the "Warren Abstract Machine" or WAM [11.4], upon which our WPE instruction set is based. This architecture shows how to map Prolog elegantly onto a von Neumann register machine. It also provides a design for how Prolog might be implemented directly in hardware [11.5].

Campbell has edited a collection of papers [3.2] that deal with various issues in implementing Prolog, including the important feature of garbage collecting the heap. Other implementation papers can be found in the logic programming bibliographies of Balbin and Lecot [11.6] and Poe et al. [11.7].

A promising future step in obtaining very efficient implementations of logic programs is the area of compiler optimizations based on global flow analysis [11.8–11.11]. Through a static analysis of a complete Prolog program we can extract information about how certain predicates will be used and what predicates are determinate. This information can then be used by the compiler to transform the program into a more efficient program and to compile it to more efficient machine code.

11.1. D. H. D. Warren, *Applied Logic—Its Use and Implementation as a Programming Tool,* Ph.D. thesis, University of Edinburgh, Scotland, 1977.

11.2. D. H. D. Warren, L. M. Pereira, and F. Pereira, PROLOG—The language and its implementation compared with LISP, *Proc. ACM Symposium on Artificial Intelligence and Programming Languages,* issued as *SIGPLAN Notices 12*:8, and *SIGART Newsletter,* no. 64, August 1977, 109–15.

11.3. D. H. D. Warren, An improved Prolog implementation which optimises tail recursion, *Proc. Logic Programming Workshop,* Debrecen, Hungary, July 1980, 1–11.

11.4. D. H. D. Warren, An abstract Prolog instruction set, Report 309, Artificial Intelligence Center, SRI International, Menlo Park, CA, October 1983.

11.5. E. Tick and D. H. D. Warren, Towards a pipelined Prolog processor, *Proc. 1984 Int. Symposium on Logic Programming,* Atlantic City, N.J., February 1984, 29–40.

11.6. I. Balbin and K. Lecot, *Logic Programming: a Classified Bibliography,* Wildgrass Books, Victoria, Australia, 1985.

11.7. M. D. Poe, R. Nasr, J. Potter, and J. Slinn, Bibliography on Prolog and logic programming, *Journal of Logic Programming 1*:1, June 1984, 81–99.

11.8. C. S. Mellish, Some global optimizations for a Prolog compiler, *Journal of Logic Programming 2*:1, April 1985, 43–66.

11.9. S. K. Debray, Register allocation in a Prolog machine, *Proc. Third Symposium on Logic Programming,* Salt Lake City, UT, 1986, 267–75.

11.10. S. K. Debray and D. S. Warren, Automatic mode inference for Prolog programs, *Proc. Third Symposium on Logic Programming,* Salt Lake City, UT, 1986, 78–88.

11.11. S. K. Debray and D. S. Warren, Detection and optimization of functional computations in Prolog, *Proc. Third International Conference on Logic Programming,* London, July 1986.

12

An Example

In this chapter we develop an extended program in Prolog. The program uses some of the techniques presented in Chapter 8 and illustrates several areas in which Prolog is a particularly apt language: parsing, code generation and transformation, and database querying.

The example is the implementation of PIQUE, a query language for relational databases developed at Stony Brook and Oregon Graduate Center. We saw in Chapter 4 that Datalog can easily express queries against relational databases. PIQUE is a stronger language than most relational query languages. It uses some additional database scheme information to infer connections among classes of entities in the database. The database user is thus spared from having to specify certain logical connections, or joins, in a query.

12.1. Universal Scheme Query Languages

PIQUE is an example of a *universal scheme query language*. "Universal scheme" means that the user can visualize a database as a single relation of (possibly partial) tuples over a relation scheme that includes all the *attributes* (field names from the database). This view is in contrast to the usual situation of seeing many relations in the database with no single relation containing all the attributes.

If a particular database can be visualized as a single relation (not all can), why not actually store the database as such? There are two principal reasons. First, a single relation may be highly redundant in the information it stores. Second, having such a representation can preclude storing information about entities to which not all attributes apply.

EXAMPLE 12.1: Consider storing information on conference attendees in relational format. Say the conference is on programming languages. We are interested in the following attributes. (We use short names to make later relational expressions less cluttered.)

NM: name of a registrant
AF: institution to which registrant is affiliated
MB: membership in sponsoring societies; can be 'ACM', 'IEEE', or 'none'
RG: time of registration; can be 'early' or 'late'
RT: rate for the conference; depends on membership and registration time
TU: name of tutorial for which a registrant signed up; can be 'logic', for logic programming, 'appl', for applicative and functional languages, or 'oop', for object-oriented languages □

Representing this information over a single relation with the scheme *NM AF MB RG RT TU* has its drawbacks. First, there will be redundant information on rates, since they are determined by membership and registration time. Thus we can split off the attributes *MB RG RT* to form a separate relation. Second, we may have partial information in some cases, or attributes that do not apply. Note that with a relation on *MB RG RT*, we can record a particular rate even if no one has registered with that rate. Suppose also that a registrant may have multiple affiliations or may choose not to attend any tutorials. These possibilities call for representing the information in at least four relations.

EXAMPLE 12.2: We can break the single relation scheme for the registration database into four relations that are better suited to partial information and multiple occurrences of attribute values. In PIQUE, relation schemes must be unique, so we distinguish relations solely by their schemes.

r(NM AF)
r(NM TU)
r(NM MB RG)
r(MB RG RT)

Figure 12.1 diagrams these relation schemes. The following is a sample state of the database over these relations.

r(NM	AF)
M. Adams	U. of New Jersey
N. Bailey	Compco
O. Chu	Intercorp
P. Dritz	U. of New Jersey
R. Fellows	Intercorp
S. Goff	Carmel College

r(NM	TU)
N. Bailey	logic
N. Bailey	oop
O. Chu	logic
Q. Easton	oop
S. Goff	oop

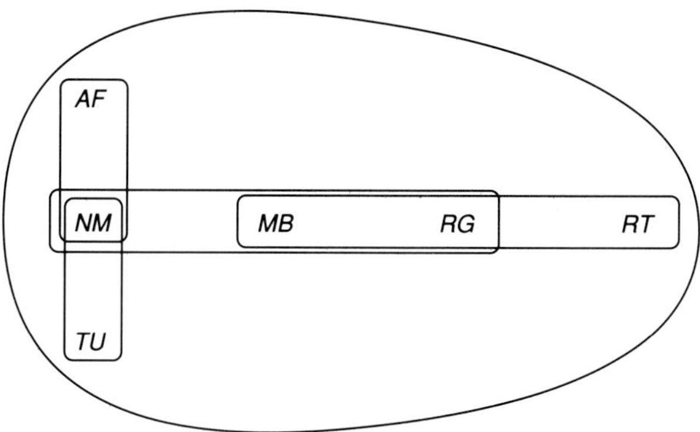

Figure 12.1

r(NM MB RG)

NM	MB	RG
M. Adams	ACM	early
N. Bailey	ACM	early
O. Chu	ACM	late
P. Dritz	IEEE	early
Q. Easton	IEEE	early
R. Fellows	none	early
S. Goff	none	late
T. Horn	none	late

r(MB RG RT)

MB	RG	RT
ACM	early	150
IEEE	early	160
none	early	175
ACM	late	200
IEEE	late	210
none	late	225

Notice we include a rate <IEEE late 210>, although no one has registered at that rate yet. However, there is no convenient place to store the tutorial <appl> that no one has signed up for yet. □

In the PIQUE data model the schemes of stored relations are called *associations,* and associations are permitted that are subschemes of other associations. (Most formal treatments of the relational model exclude this possibility.) However, there is a semantic constraint between an association R and a subassociation S, called the *containment condition*. The S-part of every tuple in $r(R)$ must be in $r(S)$:

$$\pi_S(r(R)) \subseteq r(S).$$

Recall that $\pi_S(r(R))$ is the projection of R onto the attributes S—that is, the values in the S columns of all the tuples in R. The subassociation provides a range of legal values for the larger association, in a sense.

Having the set of associations in a PIQUE database scheme closed under intersection is not essential, but it does offer semantic and computational advantages.

EXAMPLE 12.3: We add associations *NM* and *MB RG* to our database scheme, because they are intersections of other associations. We also choose to add an association *TU* to keep a list of the possible tutorial topics. The states of the relations on these additional associations are as follows:

r(NM)
M. Adams
N. Bailey
O. Chu
P. Dritz
Q. Easton
R. Fellows
S. Goff
T. Horn

r(TU)
appl
logic
oop

r(MB	RG)
ACM	early
IEEE	early
none	early
ACM	late
IEEE	late
none	late

□

In addition to a set **A** of associations, a PIQUE database scheme must have a set of *objects*, **O**, which indicate the natural connections among sets of attributes. Objects determine what joins to make among the association relations in order to connect particular attributes. The database designer supplies the objects on the basis of what he or she sees as natural connections.

EXAMPLE 12.4: The objects we add for the registration database are *NM MB RG RT, NM MB RG TU, NM AF MB RG*, and *NM AF MB RG RT TU*. These objects are diagrammed in Figure 12.2. □

The set **A** of associations is automatically included in the set of objects **O**, since if the attributes we want to connect lie in the same association, we want the relation for that association to connect them.

EXAMPLE 12.5: The PIQUE scheme for our further examples will be:

A = {NM, TU, MB RG, NM AF, NM TU, NM MB RG, MB RG RT}

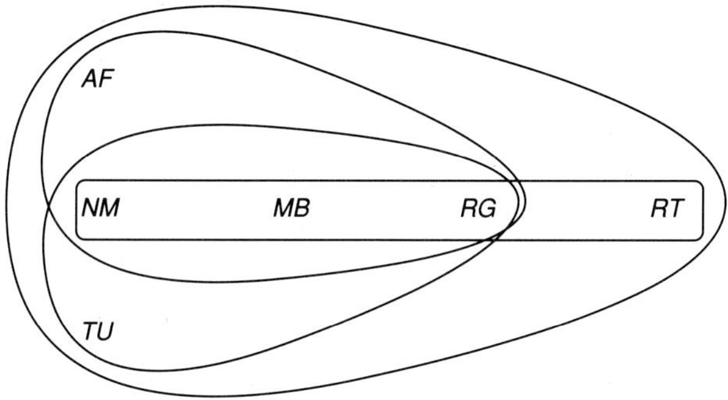

Figure 12.2

and

$$\mathbf{O} = \mathbf{A} \cup \{\text{NM MB RG RT, NM MB RG TU, NM AF MB RG, NM AF MB RG RT TU}\}. \ \square$$

We use the association relations to determine a derived relation $\tilde{r}(W)$ over each object W. That relation is formed by joining together the relations for all associations contained in W. That is:

$$\tilde{r}(W) = \mathop{\bowtie}_{R \in A,\ R \subseteq W} r(R).$$

EXAMPLE 12.6: For the registration database:

$$\tilde{r}(\text{NM MB RG RT}) = r(\text{NM}) \bowtie r(\text{MB RG}) \bowtie r(\text{NM MB RG}) \bowtie r(\text{MB RG RT}),$$

which yields:

r(NM	MB	RG	RT)
M. Adams	ACM	early	150
N. Bailey	ACM	early	150
O. Chu	ACM	late	200
P. Dritz	IEEE	early	160
Q. Easton	IEEE	early	160
R. Fellows	none	early	175
S. Goff	none	late	225
T. Horn	none	late	225 □

The containment condition allows the formula for $\tilde{r}(W)$ to be simplified. For associations R and S with $S \subseteq R$, the containment condition guarantees that $r(S) \bowtie r(R) = r(R)$. Thus, to compute $\tilde{r}(W)$, we need only take the *maximal* associations in W. An association R contained in object W is maximal relative to W if there is no association R' strictly containing R and contained in W.

EXAMPLE 12.7: The expression from the last example, for $\tilde{r}$(NM MB RG RT), simplifies to:

r(NM MB RG) $\bowtie$ r(MB RG RT). □

A corollary is that $\tilde{r}(R) = r(R)$ for any association R. Hence we dispense with the tilde in the remainder of the chapter.

We are almost finished with the formal part of the development. When processing a query in PIQUE, we determine the set of attributes X that appear in the query and then define a relation over those attributes. We call that relation the *connection* for X and denote it $[X]$. We compute $[X]$ by projecting $r(W)$ onto X for every object W that contains X, and then combining the results. The formula for a connection is thus:

$$[X] = \bigcup_{W \in O,\ X \subseteq W} \pi_X(r(W)).$$

EXAMPLE 12.8: Suppose we want the connection between names and rates: [NM RT]. Its formula is:

$\pi_{NM\ RT}(r(\text{NM MB RT RG})) \cup \pi_{NM\ RT}(r(\text{NM AF MB RG RT TU}))$. □

For simplifying the connection formula there is a rule similar to the one for formulas for object relations. We need only take the union over *minimal* objects. An object W containing X is minimal relative to X if there is no object W' strictly contained in W and containing X. This simplification follows from the result that:

$\pi_X(r(W)) \supseteq \pi_X(r(V))$

for any object $V \supseteq W$.

EXAMPLE 12.9: We can simplify [NM RT] to:

$\pi_{NM\ RT}(r(\text{NM MB RG RT}))$,

which evaluates to:

r(NM	RT)
M. Adams	150
N. Bailey	150
O. Chu	200
P. Dritz	160
Q. Easton	160
R. Fellows	175
S. Goff	225
T. Horn	225 □

There has been much debate on whether connections as defined here are a reasonable way to compute joins automatically for naive users, particularly when $[X]$ takes its values from multiple object relations. While it is certainly possible to conjure up examples where connections give counterintuitive results, connections seem a reasonable idea when the set of associations is produced from the normalization of a single initial relation scheme.

12.2. The PIQUE Query Language

The connections as defined in the last section take care of joining relations in our system, but we still need a way to specify selection conditions and Boolean combinations of those conditions. The version of PIQUE presented here is a simplified version of the original definition.

The simplest form for a PIQUE query is:

retrieve <list> **where** <condition>.

The <list> is just a sequence of attributes, separated by commas, that we want to appear in the result of the query. The <condition> is a sequence of selections of the form (<attr> <comp> <attr>) or (<attr> <comp> <const>), connected by '*'s. Here <attr> is an attribute, <comp> is a comparator appropriate to the attribute, and <const> is a constant.

EXAMPLE 12.10: A query to get the name and affiliation for all registrants who belong to ACM and registered early is:

retrieve NM, AF **where** (MB = 'ACM') * (RG = 'early'). □

A query in this form is processed in two steps. First, we compute the *mention set*, denoted *men*, for the query, which is the set of all the attributes that appear in the query. Then we compute [*men*] and restrict it by applying the selection conditions from the <condition> part of the query. We finally project the result onto the <list> given in the query.

EXAMPLE 12.11: For the query in the last example, we get the expression:

$$\pi_{NM\ AF}(\sigma_{MB = \text{'ACM'}, RG = \text{'early'}}([\text{NM AF MB RG}])).$$

Since the value of [NM AF MB RG] is:

NM	AF	MB	RG
M. Adams	U. of New Jersey	ACM	early
N. Bailey	Compco	ACM	early
O. Chu	Intercorp	ACM	late
P. Dritz	U. of New Jersey	IEEE	early
R. Fellows	Intercorp	none	early
S. Goff	Carmel College	none	late

the value of the whole query is:

r(

NM	AF
M. Adams	U. of New Jersey
N. Bailey	Compco

□

Queries involving **and**, **or**, and **not** are translated into queries in simpler form connected with intersection, union, and difference, respectively. Here is the translation for each logical connective:

retrieve <list> **where** <condition1> **and** <condition2> ≡
  (**retrieve** <list> **where** <condition1>) ∩
  (**retrieve** <list> **where** <condition2>)

retrieve <list> **where** <condition1> **or** <condition2> ≡
  (**retrieve** <list> **where** <condition1>) ∪
  (**retrieve** <list> **where** <condition2>)

retrieve <list> **where not** <condition> ≡
  (**retrieve** <list>) −
  (**retrieve** <list> **where** <condition>)

When a query is reduced to a combination of simple queries, *men* is computed for each simple query separately.

EXAMPLE 12.12: To find all people who are members of ACM and who registered late or early, and to find their rates, we use:

retrieve NM, RT **where** (MB = 'ACM') **and** ((RG = 'early') **or** (RG = 'late')).

This query is equivalent to:

retrieve NM, RT **where** (MB = 'ACM') ∩
  (**retrieve** NM, RT **where** (RG = 'early') ∪
  retrieve NM, RT **where** (RG = 'late')).

The expression for this query is:

$$\pi_{NM\ RT}(\sigma_{MB = \text{'ACM'}}([\text{NM MB RT}])) \cap (\pi_{NM\ RT}(\sigma_{RG = \text{'early'}}([\text{NM RG RT}])) \cup \pi_{NM\ RT}(\sigma_{RG = \text{'late'}}([\text{NM RG RT}]))).$$

Since [NM MB RT] is:

(NM	MB	RT)
M. Adams	ACM	150
N. Bailey	ACM	150
O. Chu	ACM	200
P. Dritz	IEEE	160
Q. Easton	IEEE	160
R. Fellows	none	175
S. Goff	none	225
T. Horn	none	225

and [NM RG RT] is:

(NM	RG	RT)
M. Adams	early	150
N. Bailey	early	150

O. Chu	late	200
P. Dritz	early	160
Q. Easton	early	160
R. Fellows	early	175
S. Goff	late	225
T. Horn	late	225

the value of the query is the intersection of:

(NM	RT)
M. Adams	150
N. Bailey	150
O. Chu	200

with the union of:

(NM	RT)
M. Adams	150
N. Bailey	150
P. Dritz	160
Q. Easton	160
R. Fellows	175

and:

(NM	RT)
O. Chu	200
S. Goff	225
T. Horn	225

The result is:

(NM	RT)
M. Adams	150
N. Bailey	150
O. Chu	200 □

EXAMPLE 12.13: To find all people who signed up for both the logic programming and the object-oriented languages tutorials, we use the query:

retrieve NM **where** (TU = 'logic') **and** (TU = 'oop').

The expression for this query is:

$$\pi_{NM}(\sigma_{TU=\text{'logic'}}([\text{NM TU}])) \cap \pi_{NM}(\sigma_{TU=\text{'object'}}([\text{NM TU}]))$$

whose value is:

(NM)
N. Bailey

Note this answer is different from the one for:

retrieve NM **where** (TU = 'logic') * (TU = 'object').

The '*' means that the two conditions hold in a single tuple in the (imagined) universal relation. Since no tuple can have two different values in the single NM field, the value of this query will always be the empty relation, regardless of the database state. The **and** allows the conditions to hold in different tuples. □

EXAMPLE 12.14: To find the names and affiliations of all people who did not sign up for the logic programming tutorial, we use:

retrieve NM, AF **where not** (TU = 'logic').

(This query assumes we are interested only in people with affiliations.) The expression for this query is:

$$[NM\ AF] - (\pi_{NM\ AF}(\sigma_{TU='logic'}([NM\ AF\ TU]))).$$

The value of this query is the difference of:

NM	AF
M. Adams	U. of New Jersey
N. Bailey	Compco
O. Chu	Intercorp
P. Dritz	U. of New Jersey
R. Fellows	Intercorp
S. Goff	Carmel College

with:

NM	AF
N. Bailey	Compco
O. Chu	Intercorp

which is:

NM	AF
M. Adams	U. of New Jersey
P. Dritz	U. of New Jersey
R. Fellows	Intercorp
S. Goff	Carmel College

This query gives a different result from:

retrieve NM, AF **where** (TU ≠ 'logic')

whose value is only:

NM	AF
N. Bailey	Compco
S. Goff	Carmel College

since it is computed over [NM AF TU] and includes in its answer only people with both an affiliation *and* a tutorial. □

These examples conclude the introduction of the PIQUE language. We turn now to representing PIQUE databases and processing PIQUE queries in Prolog.

12.3. Implementing PIQUE in Prolog

We now consider how to implement PIQUE in Prolog. There are two major aspects to the system: the representation of the database scheme and data, and the PIQUE query processor. The query processor consists of several components, shown in Figure 12.3: a scanner, parser, translator, query optimizer, and query evaluator. The scanner (a.k.a. lexical analyzer) takes as input a sequence of characters and groups them together to produce a sequence of tokens as output. The parser takes this sequence of tokens and produces an abstract syntax tree for the query. An abstract syntax tree is a data structure representing the implicit syntactic structure of the query. The translator takes the abstract syntax tree and produces a Prolog goal list that can be run against the database to answer the query. The query optimizer takes a Prolog goal list as input and produces an improved goal list as output. The output goal list gives the same answer as the input list but is expected to be more efficient. The query evaluator takes a Prolog goal list and evaluates it against the database. In our system the implementation of the evaluator is trivial. Since we use the Prolog system as the evaluator, we merely **call** the goal list. The remainder of the chapter discusses the database and each of these components in turn.

12.3.1. *Representing the Database Scheme and Data*

The query processor needs information about the database. It must be able to determine the attributes and their types, the associations and objects, and, of course, what data is in the database. Here we specify how this information is stored as Prolog facts.

First, the Prolog program must contain information concerning the attributes of the PIQUE database scheme. For this purpose, there is a binary predicate **attr**, which contains a fact for each attribute, giving the attribute name and whether it is a string or a number.

EXAMPLE 12.15: For the conference database, there were six attributes: NM AF MB RG RT TU, so the Prolog program includes the following facts:

```
/* attr(Attr, Type) for attribute Attr in the scheme
if values of that attribute are drawn from Type. */
```

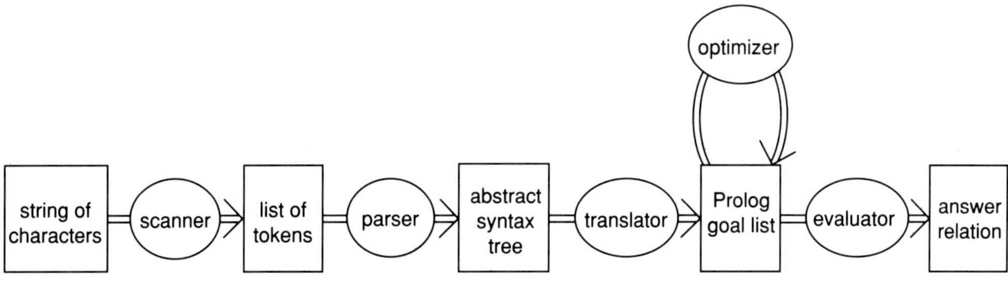

Figure 12.3

```
attr('NM', string).
attr('AF', string).
attr('MB', string).
attr('RG', string).
attr('RT', number).
attr('TU', string).
```

Note that the attribute names are constants, not variables, so they must be quoted. □

Second, we must store the actual data in the database. For each association there is one predicate.

EXAMPLE 12.16: For the conference database just described, there were seven associations:

A = {NM, TU, MB RG, NM AF, NM TU, NM MB RG, MB RG RT}

so the Prolog program will have seven predicates for the association relations—call them **r1**, **r2**, . . ., **r7**—which contain the following facts:

```
/* r(NM, AF) */

r1('M. Adams', 'U. of New Jersey').
r1('N. Bailey', 'Compco').
r1('O. Chu', 'Intercorp').
r1('P. Dritz', 'U. of New Jersey').
r1('R. Fellows', 'Intercorp').
r1('S. Goff', 'Carmel College').


/* r(NM, TU) */

r2('N. Bailey', logic).
r2('N. Bailey', oop).
r2('O. Chu', logic).
r2('Q. Easton', oop).
r2('S. Goff', oop).


/* r(NM, MB, RG) */

r3('M. Adams', 'ACM', early).
r3('N. Bailey', 'ACM', early).
r3('O. Chu', 'ACM', late).
r3('P. Dritz', 'IEEE', early).
r3('Q. Easton', 'IEEE', early).
r3('R. Fellows', none, early).
r3('S. Goff', none, late).
r3('T. Horn', none, late).
```

```
/* r(MB, RG, RT) */

r4('ACM', early, 150).
r4('IEEE', early, 160).
r4(none, early, 175).
r4('ACM', late, 200).
r4('IEEE', late, 210).
r4(none, late, 225).


/* r(NM) */

r5('M. Adams').
r5('N. Bailey').
r5('O. Chu').
r5('P. Dritz').
r5('Q. Easton').
r5('R. Fellows').
r5('S. Goff').
r5('T. Horn').


/* r(TU) */

r6(appl).
r6(logic).
r6(oop).
```

```
/* r(MB, RG) */

r7('ACM', early).
r7('IEEE', early).
r7('none', early).
r7('ACM', late).
r7('IEEE', late).
r7('none', late). □
```

The Prolog program must also have scheme information that gives the attributes for each association and tells what Prolog predicate holds the relations for the association. The predicate **assn** provides this information. The first field gives the Prolog predicate name that stores the data, and the second field contains the list of attributes in the association.

EXAMPLE 12.17: For the example database, the Prolog program contains the following facts:

```
/* assn(Predicate, ListOfAttributes). */

assn(r1, ['NM', 'AF']).
assn(r2, ['NM', 'TU']).
assn(r3, ['NM', 'MB', 'RG']).
assn(r4, ['MB', 'RG', 'RT']).
assn(r5, ['NM']).
assn(r6, ['TU']).
assn(r7, ['MB', 'RG']). □
```

The final scheme information concerns objects. We include a unary predicate **obj** that is true of a list of attributes if that list represents an object. Since every association is an object and its attributes are available from **assn**, we need not store **obj** facts for them again. A single rule for the **obj** predicate can define all associations as objects.

EXAMPLE 12.18: The **obj** predicate for the example database has the following definition:

```
obj(['NM', 'MB', 'RG', 'RT']).
obj(['NM', 'NB', 'RG', 'TU']).
obj(['NM', 'AF', 'MB', 'RG']).
obj(['NM', 'AF', 'MB', 'RG', 'RT', 'TU']).
obj(Obj) :- assn(_Rel, Obj).
```

(We use the convention that a variable occurring only once in a predicate should begin with an underscore.) □

The predicates just described store the scheme and data of the database, but there is other information derived from the scheme that the query processor needs. We discuss predicates for the derived information next.

Several simple set manipulation routines are needed. A list of attributes without duplicates will represent a set. Recall the conventions on mode declarations from Chapter 8: a '+' means the argument is always bound on a call to the predicate, a '–' means the argument is never bound on a call, and a '?' means it could be either way. The first two set predicates check membership and inclusion.

```
/* memberChk(+Elmt, ?List) if Elmt appears in list List. */

memberChk(X, [X|_]) :- !.
memberChk(X, [_|L]) :- memberChk(X, L).


/* subset(+List1, +List2) if every element of List1 is in List2. */

subset([], _).
subset([E|S1], S2) :- memberChk(E, S2), subset(S1, S2).


/* subsetOfOne(+S, +Set) if S is a subset of one of the sets in
Set. */

subsetOfOne(X, [S|_]) :- subset(X, S), !.
subsetOfOne(X, [_|Sets]) :- subsetOfOne(X, Sets).


/* supersetOfOne(+S, +Set) if S is a superset of one of the sets
in Set. */

supersetOfOne(X, [S|_]) :- subset(S,X), !.
supersetOfOne(X, [_|Sets]) :- supersetOfOne(X, Sets).
```

Since we will always call **memberChk** with the first argument bound, we can add a cut to the first clause for efficiency. This cut causes the call to become deterministic when the element is found in the list. This addition not only allows the deterministic optimizations of the interpreter to take effect but also ensures that a failure back into this predicate will not search the rest of the list. However, the presence of the cut means that **memberChk** cannot be used with the first argument unbound to generate all members of a list nondeterministically (which is why it is called **memberChk**, not **member**). The second argument to **memberChk** (indicated by **?List**) can be a list whose tail is a variable, and then **memberChk** will insert an element, if necessary.

Recall that the definition of connection requires that, given an object, we find the set of maximal associations contained in that object. The predicate **maximalAssns** does this determination. The main predicate it uses is **maxSets**, which scans through a list of sets and selects all the sets that are not subsets of others in the list. For efficiency, **maxSets** compares a set not with all sets prior to it in the list but only with those earlier sets already determined to be maximal. **SomeMax** accumulates maximal sets discovered so far in **Set**. **AllMax** is used simply to pass the value of

SomeMax in the final call back to the initial call. Note that by passing down a logical variable, a single unification at the bottom sets the value for all higher routines. This is similar to passing a **var** parameter down in Pascal.

```
/* maximalAssns(+Obj, ?MaxAssns) if MaxAssns is a list of the
maximal associations in the object Obj. */

maximalAssns(Obj, MaxAssns) :-
      bagof(Assn, subassoc(Assn, Obj), Assns),
      maxSets(Assns, [], MaxAssns).


/* subassoc(?Assn, +Obj) if Assn is an association that is a
subset of Obj, used for generating Assn. */

subassoc(Assn, Obj) :-
      assn(_Rel, Assn), subset(Assn, Obj).


/* maxSets(+Set, +SomeMax, ?AllMax) if Set is an arbitrary list
of sets, SomeMax is a list of maximal sets wrt itself and Set
(i.e. none of those sets properly contain any in SomeMax),
and AllMax is a list of maximal sets of Set + SomeMax. */

maxSets([], AllMax, AllMax).
maxSets([Set|Sets], SomeMax, AllMax) :-
      (\+ subsetOfOne(Set, Sets), \+ subsetOfOne(Set, SomeMax))
          -> maxSets(Sets, [Set|SomeMax], AllMax)
          ;  maxSets(Sets, SomeMax, AllMax).
```

EXAMPLE 12.19: For the example database, the following goal returns the maximal associations of the indicated object.

```
:- maximalAssns(['NM', 'MB', 'RG', 'RT'], Max).

 Max = [['MB', 'RG', 'RT'], ['NM', 'MB', 'RG']] ;

 no □
```

A related operation, which is necessary to compute the connection of an arbitrary set of attributes X, is to find the minimal objects containing X. We might be tempted to use negation and the preceding clauses, but this approach is doomed to failure, since (among other things) superset is not the negation of subset. The following clauses define predicates to find minimal objects, and exactly parallel the earlier ones:

```
/* minimalObjs(+X, ?MinObjs) if MinObjs is the list of minimal
objects that contain the set X. */
```

```
minimalObjs(X, MinObjs) :-
      bagof(Obj, containingObj(X, Obj), Containing),
      minSets(Containing, [], MinObjs).


/* containingObj(+X, ?Obj) if Obj is an object containing X;
used for generating Obj. */

containingObj(X, Obj) :-
      obj(Obj), subset(X, Obj).


/* minSets(+Set, +SomeMin, ?AllMin) if Set is an arbitrary list
of sets, SomeMin is a list of minimal sets wrt itself and Set
(i.e.  none of those sets are properly contained in any in SomeMin),
and AllMin is a list of minimal sets of Set + SomeMin. */

minSets([], SomeMin, SomeMin).
minSets([Set|Sets], SomeMin, AllMin) :-
      \+ superset_of_one(Set, Sets), \+ superset_of_one(Set, SomeMin)
         -> minSets(Sets, [Set|SomeMin], AllMin)
         ;  minSets(Sets, SomeMin, AllMin).
```

These predicates are used in the query translator component.

EXAMPLE 12.20: Consider the call:

```
:- minSets([[1, 2], [1, 2, 3], [4, 5], [5]], [], As).
```

[1, 2] is not a superset of any set in the rest of the list **[1, 2, 3], [4, 5], [5]]** or any set in '**[]**', so the computation takes the then branch and calls:

```
minSets([[1, 2, 3], [4, 5], [5]], [[1, 2]], As).
```

Here **[1, 2, 3]** is a superset of **[1, 2]**, so we take the else branch and call:

```
minSets([[4, 5], [5]], [[1, 2]], As).
```

Now **[4, 5]** is a superset of **[5]**, so we again take the else branch:

```
minSets([[5]], [[1, 2]], As)
```

that results in the call:

```
minSets([], [[5], [1, 2]], As)
```

which succeeds, binding **As** to **[[5], [1, 2]]**. □

12.3.2. *PIQUE Scanner*

Having finished with data, database scheme, and derived scheme information, we turn to the components of the query processor, beginning with the scanner for PIQUE. The job of the PIQUE scanner is to take as input the sequence of characters that make up a query and produce as output the corresponding sequence of meaningful tokens. A scanner normally reads the characters one at a time directly from an input device, and we could write our scanner to do that. (See Exercise 12.2.) However, for simplicity and purity, we assume that the characters that make up the query have already been read into a list of ASCII codes. Thus the scanner will be given a list of integers representing the codes of the input characters. We can use double-quoted strings to test our scanner since they are translated by the Prolog reader into lists of ASCII codes.

The main loop of the scanner, **tokenize**, repeatedly calls **nextToken** to construct all the tokens. The predicate **nextToken** looks at the sequence of characters and, based on the first character, decides what kind of token to scan off the list next. It uses the difference list technique of Section 7.5.2 to represent the prefix of the character sequence it recognizes as the token.

```
/* tokenize(+Chars, -Tokens) if Tokens is the list of tokens
represented by the list of ascii integers in Chars. */

tokenize([], []).
tokenize(Chars, [Token|Tokens]) :-
      nextToken(Chars, CharsLeft, Token),
      tokenize(CharsLeft, Tokens).


/* nextToken(+Chars, -CharsLeft, -Token) if the difference list
Chars-CharsLeft consists of the ascii integers that make up the
token represented in Token. */

nextToken(Chars, CharsLeft, Token) :- Chars = [C|R],
      (space(C) -> nextToken(R, CharsLeft, Token)
       ; alpha(C) -> scanAtom(Chars, CharsLeft, IdChars),
           name(Ident, IdChars),
           identOrKey(Ident, Token)
       ; numer(C) -> Token = number(Value),
           scanNumber(0, Chars, CharsLeft, Value)
       ; quote(C) -> Token = string(String),
           scanString(R, CharsLeft, Str),
           name(String, Str)
       ; delimit(C) -> Token = delim(D),
           name(D, [C]),
           CharsLeft = R
       ; spec(C) -> Token = special(Tok),
           scanSpecial(Chars, CharsLeft, Special),
           name(Tok, Special)
       ; fail
      ).
```

The predicate **tokenize** is a simple loop and can be quite efficient because it is tail recursive. Of course, to gain this efficiency, **nextToken** must be deterministic. The predicate **nextToken** constructs a token from the first characters in its input. A token is represented as a term with main structure symbol identifying the kind of token: **keyword**, **ident**, **number**, **string**, **delim**, or **special**. Each of these structure symbols is unary, and the single field value, which is always an atomic Prolog data object, further identifies the token.

Predicate **nextToken** determines the type of the token by using one of six predicates that classify characters: **space**, **alpha**, **numer**, **quote**, **delimit**, or **spec**. Depending on that character, it uses a particular predicate to construct the appropriate token. The declarative reading is a nested if-statement: "if the next character is a space character, then the token is the **nextToken** of the remainder of the character sequence; else if the next character is alphabetic, find characters that make up the atom, convert the characters to an atom, and determine whether it is a keyword or an identifier; else if . . . ." The **Chars** = **[C|R]** goal is included in the body, rather than using **[C|R]** as the first argument in the head, because we also need the value of **Chars** to pass to the scanning predicates. Notice that the final ; **fail** is unnecessary.

The **nextToken** predicate is deterministic (and tail-recursive when it calls itself to skip spaces). The determinism is critical to the efficiency of this predicate and is achieved by using the '->' construct. Recall that this construct contains an implicit cut. Were we to use multiple clauses to define **nextToken**, we would need to use explicit cuts to achieve the same effect. Note that the cuts would be necessary for efficiency, even though the predicate really is deterministic and only one clause can succeed. This need for cuts is because the determinism of **nextToken** would not be detected by the compiler (unless it did some rather sophisticated optimizations), so it could not take advantage of the tail-recursion in **tokenize**.

The predicates that classify the characters are straightforward. Note the use of CProlog notation for the ASCII codes for characters as integers. Recall that '**0'***c*' is the integer ASCII code for character *c*.

```
/* space(?C) if C is the ascii number for a white space character. */

space(0' ).
space(9).    /* tab */
space(10).   /* nl */


/* numer(+C) if C is the ascii number for a digit. */

numer(C) :- C >= 0'0, C =< 0'9.


/* alpha(+C) if C is the ascii number for an alphabetic character
or _. */

alpha(C) :- C >= 0'A, C =< 0'Z, !.
alpha(C) :- C >= 0'a, C =< 0'z, !.
alpha(0'_).
```

```
/* quote(?C) if C is the ascii number for the single quote. */

quote(0'').


/* delimit(?C) if C is the ascii number for a delimiter. */

delimit(0',).
delimit(0'().
delimit(0')).


/* spec(+C) if C is the ascii number for a special character. */

spec(C) :- C > 0' , \+ delimit(C), \+ alpha(C), \+ numer(C),
         \+ space(C), \+ quote(C).
```

The predicates that scan off the particular types of tokens use the difference-list technique to represent the characters matched. These predicates follow.

```
/* scanAtom(+Str, ?Rest, ?Ident) if the difference list Str - Rest
represents the longest identifier or keyword starting Str. */

scanAtom([C|R], Left, [C|Res]) :-
     (alpha(C) ; numer(C)), !, scanAtom(R, Left, Res).
scanAtom(Chars, Chars, []).


/* identOrKey(+Ident, ?Token) if Ident is an atom and Token is the
token (ident or keyword) for that atom. */

identOrKey(Keyword, keyword(Keyword)) :- keyword(Keyword), !.
identOrKey(Ident, ident(Ident)).


/* keyword(?Key) if Key is a keyword. */

keyword(retrieve).
keyword(where).
keyword(and).
keyword(or).
keyword(not).


/* scanNumber(+Num, +String, ?Rest, ?Value) if the difference list
String-Rest is the (longest) list of ascii numbers for a sequence of
digits, and Value is the integer resulting from concatenating Num
and those digits. */

scanNumber(Num, [Next|R], Left, Res) :-
     numer(Next), !,
```

```
        NewNum is (Num * 10) + Next - 0'0,
        scanNumber(NewNum, R, Left, Res).
scanNumber(Num, String, String, Num).


/* scanString(+Str, ?Rest, ?String) if the difference list Str - Rest
represents the shortest initial segment of Str terminating in a quote,
and String is that list of integers, not including the quote. */

scanString([], [], []) :- write('Error: unclosed string constant'), nl.
scanString([C|R], R, []) :- quote(C), !.
scanString([C|R], Left, [C|Res]) :- scanString(R, Left, Res).


/* scanSpecial(+String, ?Rest, ?SpList) if the difference list
String - Rest is the list SpList, and is the longest such list. */

scanSpecial([], [], []).
scanSpecial([C|R], [C|R], []) :- \+ special(C).
scanSpecial([C|R], Left, [C|Res]) :-
        special(C),
        scanSpecial(R, Left, Res).
```

Consider the definition of **scanAtom**. The order of the clauses is critical because we are searching for the longest initial string that can be an identifier. The cut is necessary so that backtracking does not find all initial substrings of the longest string. The same effect could be achieved by using the '->' construct and rewriting the clauses. The definition of **identOrKey** also uses a cut (instead of '->' or '\+') for this same purpose—to make the clauses mutually exclusive. Predicates **scanNumber** and **scanString** use a cut, whereas **scanSpecial** uses '\+'. The choice here is somewhat arbitrary: the '->' is probably the most efficient, the cut is often the easiest for the (initial) programmer, and the '\+' is the most pure.

EXAMPLE 12.21: The scanner processes the following query to give the indicated results:

```
:- tokenize("retrieve NM, AF where (RT > 160)", Tokens).

Tokens = [keyword(retrieve), ident('NM'), delim(','), ident('AF'),
       keyword(where), delim('('), ident('RT'), special(>),
       number(160), delim(')')] ;

no □
```

12.3.3. *PIQUE Parser*

In this section we give a parser of PIQUE queries. The input is a list of tokens as produced by **tokenize**. The output is a tree structure, called an abstract syntax

<query> → **retrieve** <retrieve_list> **where** <compound-condition>

<retrieve-list> → attr <retrieve-list-tail>

<retrieve-list-tail> → , attr <retrieve-list-tail>
<retrieve-list-tail> → ϵ

<compound-condition> → <and-condition> <compound-tail>

<compound-tail> → **or** <compound-condition>
<compound-tail> → ϵ

<and-condition> → <condition> <and-tail>

<and-tail> → **and** <and-condition>
<and-tail> → ϵ

<condition> → <simple-cond> <condition-tail>
<condition> → **not** <condition>
<condition> → (<compound-condition>)

<simple-cond> → (attr comparator <attr-or-const>)

<attr-or-const> → attr | string | number

<condition-tail> → * <simple-cond> <condition-tail>
<condition-tail> → ϵ

Figure 12.4

tree (AST). The parser is based directly on the context-free grammar for PIQUE given in Figure 12.4.

We have taken care in this grammar to avoid left recursion, since we want to use Prolog's depth-first evaluation strategy to parse it. These rules can be translated directly into Prolog clauses. We use a difference list to represent the input token stream. Many Prolog systems have a special syntax, called DCGs (for Definite Clause Grammars), that supports the writing of parsers such as this one. Given input representing context-free grammar productions, these systems automatically put in the variables for the input difference list. We will simply write the actual Prolog clauses ourselves—one clause for each production. For each nonterminal in the grammar, there is a predicate; for each rule in the grammar, there is a corresponding Prolog clause. The first two arguments of each predicate are the difference list representing the grammatical element scanned by the nonterminal. The third argument is the abstract syntax tree constructed during the parse.

The general form of the AST is **`retrieve(RetList, CompCond)`**. **`RetList`** is a list of the retrieval attributes, enclosed in **`attr`** terms, such as:

```
[attr('NM'), attr('AF')]
```

The **CompCond**, which captures the selection condition, can either be a simple list of comparisons, or a tree of such lists, built up of **and (Cond, Conj)**, **or (Cond, Dis)**, and **not(Cond)** subterms. Sequences of **and** and **or** terms string out to the right:

```
and(Cond1, and(Cond2, and(Cond3, Cond4)))
```

Each comparison in a list of conditions is represented as a **comp(Comparator, Attr, AttrOrConst)** term, which gives the comparator, an attribute, and another attribute or a constant. For example:

```
comp(>, attr('RT'), number(160))
```

The parser code is:

```
/* <query> --> retrieve <retrieve-list> where <compound-condition> */

query([keyword(retrieve)|Tokens], Left, retrieve(List, CompCond)) :-
      retrieveList(Tokens, [keyword(where)|Rem1], List),
      CompoundCondition(Rem1, Left, CompCond).


/* <retrieve-list> --> Attr <retrieve-list-tail> */

retrieveList([ident(Attr)|Tokens], Left, [attr(Attr)|List]) :-
      attr(Attr, _Type), retrieveListTail(Tokens, Left, List).


/* <retrieve-list-tail> --> , Attr <retrieve-list-tail> */
/* <retrieve-list-tail> --> */

retrieveListTail([delim(','), ident(Attr)|Tokens],
                 Left, [attr(Attr)|List]) :-
      !, attr(Attr, _Type), retrieveListTail(Tokens, Left, List).
retrieveListTail(Tokens, Tokens, []).


/* <compound-condition> --> <and-condition> <compound-tail> */

CompoundCondition(Tokens, Left, CompCond) :-
      andCondition(Tokens, Some, Cond),
      compoundTail(Some, Left, Dis),
      (Dis = []
          -> CompCond = Cond
          ;  CompCond = or(Cond, Dis)
      ).
```

```
/* <compound-tail> --> or <compound-condition> */
/* <compound-tail> -->  */

compoundTail([keyword(or)|Tokens], Left, Cond) :- !,
      compoundCondition(Tokens, Left, Cond).
compoundTail(Tokens, Tokens, []).

/* <and-condition> --> <condition> <and-tail> */

andCondition(Tokens, Left, AndCond) :-
      condition(Tokens, Some, Cond), andTail(Some, Left, Conj),
      (Conj = []
          -> AndCond = Cond
          ;  AndCond = and(Cond, Conj)
      ).

/* <and-tail> --> and <and-condition> */
/* <and-tail> --> */

andTail([keyword(and)|Tokens], Left, Conj) :- !,
      andCondition(Tokens, Left, Conj).
andTail(Tokens, Tokens, []).

/* <condition> --> <simple-cond> <condition-tail> */
/* <condition> --> not <condition> */
/* <condition> --> ( <compound-condition> ) */

condition(Tokens, Left, [Condition|Conditions]) :-
      simpleCond(Tokens, Mid, Condition),
      conditionTail(Mid, Left, Conditions).
condition([keyword(not)|Tokens], Left, not(Cond)) :-
      condition(Tokens, Left, Cond).
condition([delim('(')|Tokens], Left, Cond) :-
      compoundCondition(Tokens, [delim(')')|Left], Cond).

/* <simple-cond> --> ( ident comparator <attr-or-const> ) */

simpleCond([delim('('), ident(Attr), special(Comparator)|Tokens],
                  Left, comp(SComp, attr(Attr), AorC)) :-
      attr(Attr, Type),
      comparator(Comparator, Type, SComp),
      attrOrConst(Tokens, [delim(')')|Left], AorC, Type).

comparator(=, _, =).
comparator(<, number, <).
comparator(<=, number, =<).
comparator(<>, number, =\=).
comparator(>, number, >).
comparator(>=, number, >=).
```

```
comparator(<, string, @<).
comparator(<=, string, @=<).
comparator(<>, string, \==).
comparator(>, string, @>).
comparator(>=, string, @>=).

/* <attr-or-const> --> ident | string | number */

attrOrConst([ident(Attr)|Left], Left, attr(Attr), Type) :-
      attr(Attr, Type).
attrOrConst([string(Const)|Left], Left, string(Const), string).
attrOrConst([number(Num)|Left], Left, number(Num), number).

/* <condition-tail> --> * <simple-cond> <condition-tail> */
/* <condition-tail> --> */

conditionTail([special(*)|Tokens], Left, [Condition|Conditions]) :-
      !,
      simpleCond(Tokens, Mid, Condition),
      conditionTail(Mid, Left, Conditions).
conditionTail(Tokens, Tokens, []).
```

The predicate **attrOrConst** has a fourth argument, which is the type of the attribute or constant parsed. This argument is used to check that the types of the operands of a comparator agree. The ternary predicate **comparator** checks that an operator is a legal comparison operator and translates it to the corresponding evaluable Prolog comparison. We could actually use the term-comparison operators (the ones with @) for numeric as well as string comparisons, but it is cleaner (and slightly more efficient) to use the evaluable numeric comparisons for comparing numbers. The parser checks (using the database scheme predicate **attr**) that an identifier is indeed an attribute in the database. For the simple PIQUE grammar, that check could go in the scanner, since the only identifiers that are not keywords must be attributes. In a more general language this kind of checking would need context that is available only in the parser, so this check seems more appropriate in the parser.

This parser does no error diagnosis or error recovery; it simply fails when it discovers an error. In a system intended for real use, a better treatment of errors would be mandatory.

Notice that the first clause for each nonterminal includes a cut. The cuts could be omitted, since if the first clause applies, the second cannot. These cuts are only for efficiency; they make the parser more deterministic.

EXAMPLE 12.22: Consider the scanning and parsing of the following query.

```
| ?- tokenize("retrieve NM, AF where (RT > 160)", Tokens),
      query(Tokens, [], Ast).

Tokens = [keyword(retrieve), ident('NM'), delim(','), ident('AF'),
      keyword(where), delim('('), ident('RT'), special(>),
      number(160), delim(')')],
```

```
Ast = retrieve([attr('NM'), attr('AF')],
      [comp(>, attr('RT'), number(160))]) ;

no □
```

12.3.4. *PIQUE Translator*

The next component of the PIQUE query processor is the translator. It transforms the abstract syntax tree generated by the parser into a Prolog goal list that when evaluated (by **call**) produces the answers to the original query. We start with simple queries only and treat compound queries later. Recall that the first step in analyzing a query is to determine its mention set—the set of all attributes mentioned in the query. The following predicate **mention** computes the mention set of any subportion of an abstract syntax tree. It can be understood as an "extender" of mention sets: given an abstract syntax tree and a mention set, it extends the mention set to include all attributes mentioned in the tree. Notice the test to avoid adding an attribute to the mention set if it is already there.

```
/* mention(+Ast, +AlreadyMen, ?MenSet) if MenSet is the union of
AlreadyMen and the mention set of abstract syntax tree Ast. */

mention(retrieve(List, Cond), Msi, Mso) :-
      mention(List, Msi, Msm),
      mention(Cond, Msm, Mso).

mention([], Ms, Ms).
mention([A|B], Msi, Mso) :-
      mention(A, Msi, Msm),
      mention(B, Msm, Mso).

mention(comp(_Comp, A, AorC), Msi, Mso) :-
      mention(A, Msi, Msm),
      mention(AorC, Msm, Mso).

mention(string(_), Ms, Ms).
mention(number(_), Ms, Ms).
mention(attr(Attr), Msi, Mso) :-
      memberChk(Attr, Msi)
          -> Mso = Msi
          ;  Mso = [Attr|Msi].
```

EXAMPLE 12.23: Consider the computation of the mention set for the query from the last example. Here and elsewhere we omit some of the variable bindings in the answer.

```
:- tokenize("retrieve NM, AF where (RT > 160)", Tokens),
      query(Tokens, [], Ast), mention(Ast, [], MenSet).
```

```
Ast = retrieve([attr('NM'), attr('AF')],
      [comp(>, attr('RT'), number(160))]),
MenSet = ['RT', 'AF', 'NM'] □
```

The next step in translation is to compute the connection for the mention set. We will represent the connection as a Prolog goal list, which in general is a disjunction (union) of conjunctions (joins) of subgoals. That is, the connection will be (in general) a structure with main structure symbol ';'; each argument of which is a structure with main structure symbol ','. Each lowest-level subfield of one of these structures is a single literal for a database predicate. When the query gets evaluated, the projections needed in the connection are handled by specifying which variables should have their bindings returned as part of the answer.

EXAMPLE 12.24: The relational algebra formula for the connection [RT NM] is:

$$\pi_{NM\ RT}(r(\text{NM MB RG}) \bowtie r(\text{MB RG RT})).$$

The representation for this formula is:

```
',' (r3(_NM, _MB, _RG), r4(_MB, _RG, _RT))
```

which in operator notation (used from here on) is:

```
r3(_NM, _MB, _RG), r4(_MB, _RG, _RT) □
```

In the example database scheme there is no set of attributes whose connection requires a union. The objects are closed under intersection, which guarantees a single minimal object relation for any connection. For a union to arise, two objects must have an intersection that is not an object.

EXAMPLE 12.25: Consider a PIQUE database scheme over the attributes A, B, C, and D, with associations:

$$\mathbf{A} = \{\text{A, B, C, D, A B, A C, B D, C D}\}$$

and objects:

$$\mathbf{O} = \mathbf{A} \cup \{\text{A B D, A C D}\}.$$

(See Figure 12.5.) The formula for the connection [A D] is:

$$\pi_{A\ D}(r(A\ B) \bowtie r(B\ D)) \cup \pi_{A\ D}(r(A\ C) \bowtie r(C\ D))$$

which as a Prolog goal list is:

```
rAB(_A, _B), rBD(_B, _D); rAC(_A, _C), rCD(_C, _D) □
```

In the last two examples we used variable names to indicate the relationship between variables and attributes; when generating a variable in Prolog, however, we have no control over the variable names. We need another way to associate

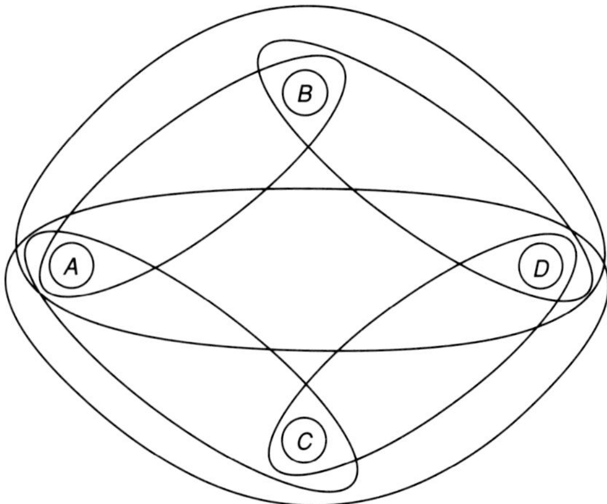

Figure 12.5

variables with attributes. We maintain a list of pairs; each pair associates an attribute name and a variable. We use the function symbol '/' to build pairs, which appear in operator notation.

EXAMPLE 12.26: The connection for [RT NM] could be represented by the goal:

```
r3(_1501, _1081, _1148), r4(_1081, _1148, _1242)
```

and the list:

```
['MB'/_1081, 'RG'/_1148, 'RT'/_1242, 'NM'/_1501]
```
□

The code to compute a connection expression follows.

```
/* connection(+AttrSet, ?Connection, ?AVList) if Connection is the Prolog
goal that represents the connection for the attributes of AttrSet, and
AVList associates the variables in Connection with attribute names. */

connection(AttrSet, Connection, AVList) :-
      minimalObjs(AttrSet, Objs), /* get covering minimal objects */
      connectionExpr(Objs, Connection, AVList).


/* connectionExpr(+Objects, ?Connection, ?AVList) if Connection (with
attribute list AVList) is the goal for the connection of the objects
in Objects. */

connectionExpr([Obj|Objs], Connection, AVList) :-
      maximalAssns(Obj, MaxAssns),
```

```
        joinExpr(MaxAssns, JoinExpr, AVList),
        (Objs = []
            -> Connection = JoinExpr
            ;  Connection = (JoinExpr; Connections),
               connectionExpr(Objs, Connections, AVList)
        ).

/* joinExpr(+Assns, ?Goal, ?AVList) if Goal (with attribute list
AVList) is the expression for the join of the associations in Assns. */

joinExpr([Assn|Assns], Goals, AVList) :-
        attrVarList(Assn, VarList, AVList),
        assn(Rel, Assn),
        Goal =.. [Rel|VarList],
        (Assns = []
            -> Goals = Goal
            ;  Goals = (Goal, Subgoals),
               joinExpr(Assns, Subgoals, AVList)
        ).

/* attrVarList(+Attrlist, ?VarList, ?AVList) if each pair of the ith
attribute in Attrlist and ith variable in VarList is a pair in
AVList. */

attrVarList([], [], _).
attrVarList([Attr|Attrs], [Var|Vars], AVList) :-
        memberChk(Attr / Var, AVList), !,
        attrVarList(Attrs, Vars, AVList).
```

The predicate **connection** uses **minimalObjs**, which we defined in Section 12.3.1, to find the minimal objects that cover the set of attributes of the mention set. It then constructs the connection expression from those objects. For each object, **connectionExpr** finds the set of maximal associations and then constructs the join expression for those associations. Each join expression becomes a disjunct in the final expression for the connection.

The predicate **joinExpr** constructs a basic goal for each association. It uses **attrVarList** to get the list of variables for the attributes of the association (where do the new variables come from?), finds the name of the predicate in the database, and uses '=..' to construct a Prolog goal. We keep **AVList** as an "open-tailed" list: It always has a variable as its "last" tail. With such a list **memberChk** never fails: if the element being sought is on the list, then the unification associates the variables as we desire; if the element is not on the list, it is added. This behavior is exactly what we need here. This technique is useful for processing other data structures with symbol-table-like behavior.

Thus **connection** returns a goal list representing a disjunction of join expressions and an open-tailed list of attribute-variable pairs. This predicate uses the list to make variables in joined relations agree, but it is also passed out for use by the selection condition.

EXAMPLE 12.27: Continuing with the same PIQUE query, we now pass the mention set on to **connection** to compute the Prolog goal list that represents the connection. This predicate also returns a list that tells us which variables represent which attributes.

```
:- tokenize("retrieve NM, AF where (RT > 160)", Tokens),
      query(Tokens, [], Ast), mention(Ast, [], MenSet),
      connection(MenSet, Connection, AVList).

Ast = retrieve([attr('NM'), attr('AF')],
      [comp(>, attr('RT'), number(160))]),
MenSet = ['RT', 'AF', 'NM'],
Connection = r4(_9793, _9860, _9954), r3(_10213, _9793, _9860),
      r2(_10213, _10808), r1(_10213, _11266),
AVList = ['MB'/_9793, 'RG'/_9860, 'RT'/_9954, 'NM'/_10213,
      'TU'/_10808, 'AF'/_11266|_11445] □
```

The final major step in translating a simple query is to convert the comparisons in the selection condition into a conjunction of Prolog goals. Note the use of the attribute-variable list to get the proper variables to use in the selection.

```
/* selectGoal(+CondList, ?Goals, ?AVList) if Goals is the Prolog
equivalent of the Ast condition list in CondList, and AVList
associates attributes and variables. */

selectGoal([], true, _).
selectGoal([Cond|Conds], SelGoal, AVList) :-
      selectCmp(Cond, SelSub1, AVList),
      selectGoal(Conds, SelSub2, AVList),
      conjoin(SelSub1, SelSub2, SelGoal).


/* conjoin(+Goal1, +Goal2, ?Conjuntion) if Conjunction is the
(simplified) conjunction of Goal1 and Goal2. */

conjoin(true, G1, G1) :- !.
conjoin(G1, true, G1) :- !.
conjoin(G1, G2, (G1, G2)).


/* selectCmp(+AstComp, ?Goal, ?AVList) if Goal is the Prolog goal for the
Ast comparison of AstComp, where AVList associates attributes and
variables. */

selectCmp(comp(Comp, Attr, AorC), Sel, AVList) :-
      fldVal(Attr, Var, AVList),
      fldVal(AorC, Fld, AVList),
      Sel =.. [Comp, Var, Fld].
```

```
/* fldVal(+AorC, ?Val, ?AVList) if Val is the Prolog term that
represents the value of the attribute or (typed) constant AorC,
and AVList associates attributes and variables. */

fldVal(attr(A), V, AVList) :- memberChk(A = V, AVList).
fldVal(number(A), A, _).
fldVal(string(A), A, _).
```

The predicate **selectGoal** converts a list of AST conditions, which compare attributes with attributes or constants, into a conjunction of Prolog comparison goals. It uses **selectCmp** to convert each condition. The predicate **conjoin** is used to simplify the conjunction when a component of the selection condition is **true**. Here **true** shows up only at the tail of a conjunction, but later optimizations can introduce it at other places. The predicate **selectCmp** uses **fldVal** to convert the attributes to variables and typed constants to their Prolog equivalents, and then uses '`=..`' to construct the Prolog comparison goal. Note that **fldVal** works relative to a list of attribute-variable bindings passed to it (or will build such a list if necessary).

EXAMPLE 12.28: Taking one more step in the running example:

```
:- tokenize("retrieve NM, AF where (RT > 160)", Tokens),
      query(Tokens, [], Ast), mention(Ast, [], MenSet),
      connection(MenSet, Connection, AVList),
      Ast = retrieve(List, Cond),
      selectGoal(Cond, SelGoal, AVList).

MenSet = ['RT', 'AF', 'NM'],
Connection = r4(_10049, _10116, _10210), r3(_10469, _10049, _10116),
      r2(_10469, _11064), r1(_10469, _11522),
AVList = ['MB'/_10049, 'RG'/_10116, 'RT'/_10210, 'NM'/_10469,
      'TU'/_11064, 'AF'/_11522|_11701],
List = [attr('NM'), attr('AF')],
Cond = [comp(>, attr('RT'), number(160))],
SelGoal = _10210>160
```

Notice that we had to deconstruct the AST to pull out the selection list to pass to **selectGoal**. □

EXAMPLE 12.29: Consider another PIQUE query, which has a slightly more complex selection condition:

```
| ?- tokenize("retrieve NM, AF where (MB = 'ACM') * (RG = 'early')",
     Tokens), query(Tokens, [], Ast), mention(Ast, [], MenSet),
     connection(MenSet, Connection, AVList),
     Ast = retrieve(List, Cond), selectGoal(Cond, SelGoal, AVList).
```

```
Ast = retrieve([attr('NM'), attr('AF')],
      [comp(=, attr('MB'), string('ACM')),
      comp(=, attr('RG'), string(early))]),
MenSet = ['RG', 'MB', 'AF', 'NM'],
Connection = r3(_13640, _13707, _13801), r1(_13640, _14127),
AVList = ['NM'/_13640, 'MB'/_13707, 'RG'/_13801, 'AF'/_14127|_14252],
List = [attr('NM'), attr('AF')],
Cond = [comp(=, attr('MB'), string('ACM')),
      comp(=, attr('RG'), string(early))],
SelGoal = _13707='ACM', _13801=early □
```

All that remains to handle simple queries is to put the pieces together to construct a single goal list. The predicates **translate** and **translateSub** do this construction.

```
/* translate(+Ast, -RetVars, -Goal): if calling Goal then printing
RetVars gives the correct result for the PIQUE query that has Ast
as abstract syntax tree. */

translate(retrieve(List, Cond), RetVars, Goal) :-
      mention(List, [], RetrSet),
      translateSub(Cond, RetrSet, RetVars, Goal).

/* translateSub(+CondAst, +RetrSet, -RetVars, -Goal): if RetVars
from Goal is the Prolog equivalent of the PIQUE query with RetrSet
as the retrieve set and CondAst as the condition.  */

translateSub(SimpCond, RetrSet, RetVars, Goal) :-
      mention(SimpCond, RetrSet, MentionSet),
      /* get the mention set */
      connection(MentionSet, Connection, AVList),
      /* get goal for connection */
      selectGoal(SimpCond, SelGoal, AVList),
      /* translate selections */
      attrVarList(RetrSet, RetVarsR, AVList),
      /* get the retrieve vars */
      reverse(RetVarsR, RetVars, []),
      /* put them back in order */
      conjoin(Connection, SelGoal, Goal).

/* reverse a list */
reverse([], L, L).
reverse([X|L1], L2, L3) :- reverse(L1, L2, [X|L3]).
```

The predicate **translate** is the top-level translation predicate. Given an abstract syntax tree, it produces a list of variables for the retrieval attributes and a Prolog goal list. Notice that the database projection is, in effect, done by returning the list of answer variables. Agreement on the variables among the retrieve list, the connection, and the selection condition is obtained by sharing **AVList**. The translation predicate first computes the mention set of the retrieve list and then calls **translateSub** to construct the Prolog goal list for the connection and selection condition. (We separate out **translateSub** in preparation for a later extension.)

The predicate **translateSub** computes the mention set of the whole query, starting from the mention set of the retrieve list, gets the connection for that mention set, and gets the selection goal list—all by using predicates defined previously. It then uses **attrVarList** to get the variables of the retrieve set, uses reverse to put them in the right order (since **mention** lists them in reverse order from how they appear in the query), and finally conjoins the connection goal list and the selection goal list to produce the final query. These lists must be conjoined in the order given, since the predicates in the selection condition need bound variables in general. A later optimization interleaves goals from the connection goal list and the selection condition goal list. The result is our first complete PIQUE query processor (for simple queries).

EXAMPLE 12.30: We now can produce the entire goal list for the example query.

```
:- tokenize("retrieve NM, AF where (RT > 160)", Tokens),
      query(Tokens, [], Ast), translate(Ast, Retlist, Goal).

Ast = retrieve([attr('NM'), attr('AF')],
      [comp(>, attr('RT'), number(160))]),
Retlist = [_10086, _11139],
Goal = (r4(_9666, _9733, _9827), r3(_10086, _9666, _9733),
      r2(_10086, _10681), r1(_10086, _11139)), _9827>160 □
```

The goal list constructed from a PIQUE query can actually be called in Prolog to produce the answer. The following simple predicates put together the predicates we have developed and display the results of evaluating a query. The predicate **evalQuery** calls the goal list repeatedly until there are no more answers.

```
/* evalPique(+String) scans, parses, translates and evaluates a
PIQUE query */

evalPique(String) :-
      tokenize(String, Tokens),
      query(Tokens, [], Ast),
      translate(Ast, RetVars, Goal),
      evalQuery(RetVars, Goal).


/* evalQuery(?Vars, ?Goal) calls Goal and prints out Vars for
each success. */

evalQuery(Vars, Goal) :-
      nl,
      call(Goal),
```

```
      write(Vars), nl,
      fail.
evalQuery(_, _).
```

EXAMPLE 12.31: Finally, we can evaluate the example query and find out the names and affiliations of the poor souls who have to pay exorbitant rates to attend the conference.

```
:- evalPique("retrieve NM, AF where (RT > 160)").

[O. Chu, Intercorp]
[S. Goff, Carmel College]
```
□

12.3.5. *Optimizations of Simple Queries*

Before extending the translator to handle compound queries, we consider a couple of ways to optimize the Prolog query that **translate** generates. While generating a Prolog goal list for a query, we paid no attention to the cost of evaluating it. The generated goal list may be very inefficient, and there may be more efficient ways to compute the desired answers. That is, there may be another equivalent Prolog goal list that computes the same answers with much less work than the one generated by **translate**.

EXAMPLE 12.32: Consider the translation of the following PIQUE query:

```
:- tokenize("retrieve NM, AF where (MB = 'ACM') * (RG = 'early')",
      Tokens),  query(Tokens, [], Ast), translate(Ast, RetList, Goal).

Ast = retrieve([attr('NM'), attr('AF')],
      [comp(=, attr('MB'), string('ACM')), comp(=, attr('RG'),
      string(early))]),
RetList = [_11519, _12006],
Goal = (r3(_11519, _11586, _11680), r1(_11519, _12006)),
      _11586='ACM', _11680=early
```

Examine the goal list produced. No Prolog programmer would write such a goal (even ignoring the odd association of the ',' operator). Two predicates are called with all variables unbound, and later some of those variables are explicitly equated to the constants 'ACM' and **early**. Putting the constants directly into the **r3**-literal is clearly more efficient. Not only does it allow the possibility of an indexed retrieval from **r3**, but more importantly, it may greatly reduce the number of tuples that must be retrieved from **r1**. □

For any equality comparison with a constant, we simply need to replace all occurrences of the variable by the constant in the goal list. If two attributes are equated in a comparison, we should replace one by the other in the goal list. Simply unifying the terms that are equated during construction of the goal list gives the desired replacement in either case. When building a selection condition, in **selectCmp**, rather than returning a Prolog term for an equality, we should unify the two operands then and there. The following new code for **selectCmp** incorporates the change. This optimization is similar to the strategy of "pushing selections through joins" in relational algebra expressions.

```
/* selectCmp(+AstComp, ?Goal, ?AVList) if Goal is the Prolog goal
for the Ast comparison of AstComp, where AVList associates attributes
and variables. If the comparison in an =, unify and return true. */

/* The first clause here is an optimization, unify operands of
equality in goal.  Note that the cut is necessary. */

selectCmp(comp(=, Attr, AorC), true, AVList) :- !,
      fldVal(Attr, Var, AVList),
      fldVal(AorC, Var, AVList).
selectCmp(comp(Comp, Attr, AorC), Sel, AVList) :-
      fldVal(Attr, Var, AVList),
      fldVal(AorC, Fld, AVList),
      Sel =.. [Comp, Var, Fld].
```

The comparison operator is first checked to see if it is '=', and, if so, the operands are unified, and the condition **true** is returned. Now the predicate **conjoin** used in **selectGoal** has more cases to simplify.

EXAMPLE 12.33: The following goal list is generated for the query from the previous example by the improved translator.

```
:- tokenize("retrieve NM, AF where (MB = 'ACM') * (RG = 'early')",
      Tokens), query(Tokens, [], Ast), translate(Ast, RetList, Goal).

Ast = retrieve([attr('NM'), attr('AF')],
      [comp(=, attr('MB'), string('ACM')), comp(=, attr('RG'),
      string(early))]),
RetList = [_11519, _12006],
Goal = r3(_11519, 'ACM', early), r1(_11519, _12006)
```

The translator now generates a more efficient goal list. □

The problem of equality comparisons raises a more general issue. One way of looking at the equality problem is that the equality comparison check could be made at the beginning of the goal list. (There is not much difference in doing the check at translation time or at the beginning of the goal list during evaluation.) Other comparisons can also be made earlier in the goal list. However, unlike equality, the other comparisons cannot provide bindings, so they must wait until the variables they use are bound.

EXAMPLE 12.34: Consider again the PIQUE query used earlier:

```
:- tokenize("retrieve NM, AF where (RT > 160)", Tokens),
     query(Tokens, [], Ast), translate(Ast, RetList, Goal).
```

```
Ast = retrieve([attr('NM'), attr('AF')],
      [comp(>, attr('RT'), number(160))]),
RetList = [_10086, _11139],
Goal = (r4(_9666, _9733, _9827), r3(_10086, _9666, _9733),
      r2(_10086, _10681), r1(_10086, _11139)), _9827>160
```

In the goal list generated for this query, the comparison **_9827>160** is done last, even though the variable **_9827** is bound by the very first subgoal: **r4(_9666, _9733, _9827)**. It is almost always more efficient to do the comparison immediately after that first goal, rather than waiting until the entire 4-way join is completed. Tuples for **r4** that do not pass the selection condition are filtered out earlier, saving time wasted on joining such tuples with tuples from the other relations. □

The general optimization problem here is conjunctive goal reordering: given a conjunction of goals, find the order for these goals that is most efficiently executed with Prolog's evaluation strategy. Of course, the best order is dependent on the state of the database. If one of the relations is empty, putting any goal corresponding to this relation first gives minimal search time. The "optimizations" covered here are expected to improve efficiency in most cases but can actually increase time on some database states. In the remainder of this section we will develop and implement a simple strategy for goal reordering. The equality optimization applies to any goal list generated as the translation of a simple query. The optimization we cover next applies only if no disjunction (union) is needed in the connection. That is, the goal list for the query is a straight conjunction.

The strategy is a "greedy" one: given a goal list, choose the cheapest (least expected time) goal to do next. Remove that goal from further consideration, and repeat the process on the remaining goals: choose the cheapest one to do next; delete that one from the list; choose the cheapest remaining goal to do; and so forth. Information about what variables will be bound at run time guides the choice of the cheapest next goal. The larger the number of variables bound, the cheaper we expect the goal will be, because we expect fewer matches for the goal. Of course, evaluating a goal against a database relation binds all its unbound variables, and these new bindings figure in choosing the goal to do next. We must treat evaluable predicates for comparisons specially, since they must have all variables bound before a call. We must maintain a list of the variables appearing in a goal list that are bound to constants when the goal list is executed, and update this list after each goal is removed. The top-level predicates for conjunction reordering follow:

```
/* optConj(+Goals, ?Opt) if Opt is a re-ordering of the conjunction
Goals, hopefully improved. */
```

```
optConj(true, true) :- !.
optConj(Goals, Opt) :-
      listify(Goals, GoalList),
      optConj(GoalList, [], OptList),
      conjify(OptList, Opt).


/* listify(+Conj, -List) if Conj is a (comma list) conjunction of
goals and List is the corresponding list of goals. */

listify((true,B), L) :- !, listify(B, L).
listify((A, true), L) :- !, listify(A, L).
listify((A,B), L) :- !, listify(A, L1), listify(B, L2),
      append(L1, L2, L).
listify(A, [A]).

/* conjify(+List, -Conj) if List is a list of goals and Conj is
the corresponding comma-list of goals. */

conjify([A], A) :- !.
conjify([A|L], (A, C)) :- conjify(L, C).
```

The predicate **optConj/2** begins the process. It turns the conjunction (a "comma" list) of goals into a standard list using **listify**, flattening and simplifying it in the process. This transformation is done because it is easier (and more efficient) to manipulate standard lists than comma lists, since standard lists are terminated with a '[]'. Next **optConj/2** uses **optConj/3** to reorder the standard list of goals under the assumption that no variables are initially bound. It then turns the reordered standard list of goals back into a conjunction with **conjify**.

```
/* optConj(+GoalList, +BndVars, ?OptList) if OptList is a re-ordering
of GoalList, under the assumption that all variables in the list
BndVars will be bound at the time GoalList will be executed. */

optConj([], _BndVars, []).
optConj(Goals, BndVars, [BestGoal|OptRest]) :-
      rate(Goals, BndVars, Ratings),
      best(Goals, Ratings, _BestRating, BestGoal),
      deleteId(BestGoal, Goals, Remaining),
      addVars(BestGoal, BndVars, NbndVars),
      optConj(Remaining, NbndVars, OptRest).
```

Predicate **optConj/3** first gives each goal a rating that estimates how good it would be as the first goal to evaluate. Then it chooses the goal that has the best rating to do first and deletes it from the list of goals left to do. It then adds all the variables in the chosen goal to the list of bound variables. (Assuming those variables are bound uses the property that, when a goal against any database relation is evaluated, all variables in the query become bound. This assumption is not true in general logic programs, since there can be universal variables in clauses, and so some goals may return unbound variables.) Finally, **optConj/3** loops to choose the next best goal and so on until no goals are left.

The **best**, **deleteId**, and **addVars** predicates are straightforward:

```
/* best(+GoalList, +NumList, ?BestGoal, ?BestNum) if GoalList is
a list of goals, NumList is a parallel list of numbers, BestNum
is the maximum number in NumList, and BestGoal is the corresponding
goal in GoalList. */

best([], [],0, []).
best([G|Gs], [R|Rs], Br, Bg) :-
      best(Gs, Rs, Sbr, Sbg),
      (R >= Sbr
          -> Br = R, Bg = G
          ;  Br = Sbr, Bg = Sbg
      ).


/* deleteId(+Goal, +GoalList, ?Remainder) if deleting Goal from GoalList
gives Remainder.  Note that == must be used since Goal has variables and
they should not be unified but tested for identity. */

deleteId(X, [Y|R], R) :- X == Y, !.
deleteId(X, [Y|R], [Y|S]) :- deleteId(X, R, S).


/* addVars(+Goal, +VarList, -NVarList) if NVarList is the result of
adding all variables in Goal to VarList (without making duplicates).
(Note constants are functors of arity 0.) */

addVars(_ = _, List, List) :- !.
addVars(Lit, List, NewList) :-
      functor(Lit, _Fn, Arity),
      addVars(Arity, Lit, List, NewList).


/* addVars(+Argno, +Lit, +List, -NewList) if Newlist is the result of
adding all variables in the term Lit that are at or earlier than position
Argno to List. */

addVars(0, _, L, L) :- !.
addVars(ArgNo, Lit, List, NewList) :-
      NArgNo is ArgNo - 1,
      arg(ArgNo, Lit, Arg),
      (memberId(Arg, List)
          -> addVars(NArgNo, Lit, List, NewList)
          ;  addVars(NArgNo, Lit, [Arg|List], NewList)
      ).
```

```
/* memberId(+X, +L) if L contains a term identical to X (not just
unifiable with X). */

memberId(X, [Y|_]) :- X == Y, !.
memberId(X, [_|R]) :- memberId(X, R).
```

The predicate **best** estimates the cheapest goal left on the list (recursively) and returns it if it is better than the first goal. This predicate could be made tail recursive by adding another argument. The definition is deterministic, hence all the space will be reclaimed when it returns anyway; also the lists involved are short, so this definition will do. The predicate **deleteId** must use '==' to do the comparison rather than simple unification, because we need to find the goal in the list that is identical, variables and all, to the one we seek. Two goals that are not identical could unify. The predicate **addVars** uses **functor** and **arg** to get the variables out of the goal and uses **memberId** to check whether they are already in the list of bound variables. Notice that **addVars** must be careful of equality goals, because they may not bind any variables. (A more careful treatment could be given, but equality goals will not appear in translations from PIQUE queries anyway; they have been eliminated by an earlier optimization.) Since these predicates involve metaprogramming in which the data objects represent parts of Prolog programs, we must be very careful with variables.

We now describe how to rate each goal. Each goal is given an initial rating based only on the number of variables that will be bound if the goal is executed next. In general, each bound argument place can be thought of as providing a selection on the relation, and the more selects, the fewer tuples that will get through. And the more restrictions earlier in the evaluation of the query, the faster it will execute. The more argument places bound, the better, so we take that number as the basic component of the initial rating. (Alternatively, we could use the percentage of argument places bound.) If all the argument places are bound, the goal is simply a filter, since it does not bind any new variables, and it is an excellent goal to do next. Such a goal has a bonus added to its rating. This special case actually is an instance of a more general phenomenon—a goal that is bound on a *key* of the relation. A relation can have only one tuple with any set of values on its key attributes. If a goal is bound on a key, it can succeed in only one way, so it also is an excellent goal to do next. Since the database scheme does not have information on keys available, we cannot detect this situation. Similarly, if a goal has an argument position bound for which there is an index, it may also be a good goal to execute next. (See Exercise 12.12.)

There is another reason, apart from the preceding considerations, to evaluate a particular goal next. If the goal binds a lot of variables used in subsequent goals, those goals will have high ratings. We take this effect into account, essentially as a tie-breaker. A goal's rating includes a fraction of the sum of the initial ratings of all other goals under the assumption that the goal is evaluated first.

The following clauses define this rating scheme:

```
/* rate(+Goals, +BndVars, ?Ratings) if Ratings is list of ratings
corresponding to the list of goals Goals, under the assumption that the
variables in BndVars will be bound when each goal is evaluated. */
```

```
rate([], _, []).
rate(Goals, BndVars, Ratings) :-
      rateA(Goals, BndVars, ARatings),
      rateB(Goals, [], BndVars, ARatings, Ratings).

/* rateA(+Lits, +BndVars, ?Ratings) if Ratings is the list of simple
ratings of Lits under the assumption of variables in BndVars being
bound. This rating depends only on the single rated goal and which
variables are bound. */

rateA([], _, []).
rateA([Lit|Goals], BndVars, [R|Rs]) :-
      functor(Lit, Fn, Arity),
      numberBnd(Arity, Lit, BndVars, R1),
      bonus(Fn, Arity, R1, R),
      rateA(Goals, BndVars, Rs).


/* numberBnd(+ArgNo, +Lit, +BndVars, ?Num) if Num is the number of
variables in Lit (with argument positions less than or equal to
position ArgNo) that are also in BndVars. */

numberBnd(0, _Lit, _BndVars,0).
numberBnd(ArgNo, Lit, BndVars, R) :-
      ArgNo > 0,
      arg(ArgNo, Lit, Arg),
      ((nonvar(Arg); memberId(Arg, BndVars)) -> Inc = 1; Inc = 0),
      NArgNo is ArgNo - 1,
      numberBnd(NArgNo, Lit, BndVars, Rr),
      R is Rr + Inc.


/* bonus(+Predsym, +Arity, +Nbound, ?Rating) if the Rating is the
rating for a literal for predicate Predsym/Arity win Nbound argument
places bound. */

bonus(=, 2, _, 100) :- !.
bonus(Cmp, 2, NBound, Rate) :- comparator(_, _, Cmp), !,
      (NBound =:= 2 -> Rate = 15; Rate = -10).
bonus(_, Arity, NBound, Rate) :-
      (NBound =:= Arity
          -> Rate is NBound + 10
          ;  Rate is NBound).


/* rateB(+LitsToRate, +OtherLits, +BndVars, +ARatings, -Ratings) if
LitsToRate is a list of goals to rate, OtherLits are other literals
in the goal, BndVars is the list of variables that will be bound at
execution time, ARatings are the simple A-ratings of the LitsToRate,
and Ratings is the list of final ratings. */

rateB([], _D, _BndVars, [], []).
rateB([Goal|Gs], Done, BndVars, [Ar|Ars], [R|Rs]) :-
```

```
        append(Done, Gs, OtherGoals),
        addVars(Goal, BndVars, NbndVars),
        rateA(OtherGoals, NbndVars, NRatings),
        sum(NRatings, Br),
        R is 100 * Ar + Br,
        rateB(Gs, [Goal|Done], BndVars, Ars, Rs).


/* sum(+NumList, ?Sum) if Sum is the sum of numbers in NumList. */

sum([],0).
sum([N|R], S) :- sum(R, M), S is N + M.
```

The predicate **rate** computes the list of ratings for a goal list by first generating the initial ratings with **rateA** and then adding in secondary ratings based on improvement in other goals using **rateB**. The predicate computes the initial ratings by using **numberBnd** to count the number of bound variables and using **bonus** to add in the bonus for having all argument positions bound. Notice that **bonus** handles the complication with evaluable predicates. Equality goals can always be executed very cheaply and should be done as soon as possible, so they are given a high bonus. Comparison predicates cannot be evaluated until all arguments are bound, so they get a negative bonus for any unbound arguments. If all arguments of a comparison goal are bound, it is given a bonus because it does not involve a database access and is very cheap to execute. The predicate **rateB** uses **rateA** to compute the rating of each other goal under the assumption that a goal is executed first and adds the sum of those ratings to 100 times the initial rating of the goal.

EXAMPLE 12.35: The translator can now optimize the running example:

```
:- tokenize("retrieve NM, AF where (RT > 160)", Tokens),
        query(Tokens, [], Ast), translate(Ast, RetList, Goal),
        optConj(Goal, OptGoal).

RetList = [_9915, _10968],
Goal = (r4(_9495, _9562, _9656), r3(_9915, _9495, _9562),
        r2(_9915, _10510), r1(_9915, _10968)), _9656>160,
OptGoal = r4(_9495, _9562, _9656), _9656>160,
        r3(_9915, _9495, _9562), r2(_9915, _10510), r1(_9915, _10968)
```

The **r4** goal is chosen first because it allows the comparison to be done next. The comparison is done second. The next two goals are chosen on the basis of numbers of bound variables. □

EXAMPLE 12.36: We developed the conjunction optimizer in the context of database queries, but it actually can be applied to most any Prolog goal list. The optimizer makes the assumption that, when successfully completed, any goal will bind all its arguments, but this assumption is often fulfilled, or almost fulfilled, by Prolog programs. (Evaluable predicates can cause problems when the assumption is violated.) Consider the map-coloring example from Section 4.6, using the map shown in Figure 4.1. Recall that the **next** predicate is true of pairs of colors that are different, and so can be next to each other. The coloring problem can be solved by executing a large conjunction of **next** goals that says which regions are adjacent. The conjunction reorderer can optimize this goal list as well:

```
:- optConj((next(CR1, CR2), next(CR1, CR3), next(CR1, CR5),
       next(CR1, CR6), next(CR2, CR3), next(CR2, CR4), next(CR2, CR5),
       next(CR2, CR6), next(CR3, CR4), next(CR3, CR6),
       next(CR5, CR6)), Opt).

Opt = next(CR1, CR2), next(CR1, CR3), next(CR2, CR3), next(CR1, CR6),
      next(CR2, CR6), next(CR3, CR6), next(CR1, CR5), next(CR2, CR5),
      next(CR5, CR6), next(CR2, CR4), next(CR3, CR4)
```

All the goals have the same initial rating, because all variables are unbound. The goal **next(CR1, CR2)** is chosen first because **CR1** and **CR2** appear most frequently in other goals. The goal **next(CR2, CR3)** moves up in order because its variables are bound after the first two goals. □

12.3.6. *Compound Queries*

The translator so far works only on simple PIQUE queries. This section extends the translation predicates to handle complex queries involving '**and**', '**or**', and '**not**'. The only predicate that we need to change is **translateSub**. It must handle complex conditions. Extensions of Prolog programs are not always this easy. (We separated **translate** and **translateSub** in the earlier development in anticipation of this extension.) But Prolog programs often extend to handle more cases simply by adding clauses. The new **translateSub** clauses and the one new predicate we need follow:

```
/* translateSub(+CondAst, +RetrSet, -RetVars, -Goal): if RetVars from
Goal is the Prolog equivalent of the PIQUE query with RetrSet as the
retrieve set and CondAst as the condition. */

translateSub(not(Cond), RetrSet, RetVars, (Goal1, \+ (Goal2))) :- !,
      translateSub([], RetrSet, RetVars, Goal1),
      translateSub(Cond, RetrSet, RetVars, Goal2).

translateSub(and(C1, C2), RetrSet, RetVars, (Goal1, Goal2)) :- !,
      translateSub(C1, RetrSet, RetVars, Goal1),
      translateSub(C2, RetrSet, RetVars, Goal2).

translateSub(or(C1, C2), RetrSet, NewVars, ((Eq1, Goal1);
    (Eq2, Goal2))) :- !,
      translateSub(C1, RetrSet, RetVars1, Goal1),
      translateSub(C2, RetrSet, RetVars2, Goal2),
      newVars(RetVars1, RetVars2, Eq1, Eq2, NewVars).
```

```
translateSub(SimpCond, RetrSet, RetVars, Goal) :- /* same as before */
      mention(SimpCond, RetrSet, MentionSet),
      /* get the mention set */
      connection(MentionSet, Connection, AVList),
      /* get goal for connection */
      selectGoal(SimpCond, SelGoal, AVList),
      /* translate selections */
      attrVarList(RetrSet, RetVarsR, AVList),
      /* get the retrieve vars */
      reverse(RetVarsR, RetVars, []),
      /* put them back in order */
      conjoin(Connection, SelGoal, Goal).


/* newVars(+VarList1, +VarList2, -EqGoal1, -EqGoal2, -NewVarList) if
VarList and VarList2 are parallel lists of variables, NewVarList is a
parallel list of new variables, and EqGoal1 is a conjunction of
equalities equating pairwise the variables of VarList1 and NewVarList,
and EqGoal2 is the same for VarList2 and NewVarList. */

newVars([V1], [V2], N = V1, N = V2, [N]) :- !.
newVars([V1|V1s], [V2|V2s], (N = V1, Eq1), (N = V2, Eq2), [N|Ns]) :-
      newVars(V1s, V2s, Eq1, Eq2, Ns).
```

Consider the translation of a query involving '**not**'. Recall that the definition of the semantics of such a query is:

retrieve <list> **where not** <condition> ≡
    (**retrieve** <list>) − (**retrieve** <list> **where** <condition>)

We use **translateSub** recursively to translate the two subqueries. They use the same retrieve set and so return the same list of variables. Using the same **RetVars** in the two calls to **translateSub** makes the variables the same in the resulting query. The set difference operator can be effected in Prolog by using conjunction and negation-as-failure ('\+').

A compound goal involving '**and**' is handled similarly. Here we want the intersection of the two subqueries, so we use the conjunction of their translations. Again, we simply pass in the same **RetVars**, the list of variables the query will return its answers in, to both recursive calls of **translateSub**. Thus they both use the same variables in the separate goal lists.

We now come to the clause that handles '**or**'. The Prolog operator to use for union is '**;**', but there is a subtle problem with variables. We might be tempted simply to share the retrieve variable list between the two subqueries, as we did in the previous two cases. But this approach can lead to trouble. Consider what might happen. The goal list for one subquery might be **(r(X, Y), X = 10)** with retrieve variables **[X, Y]**. This goal list will be optimized by evaluating equality at translation time to the goal list **r(10, Y)** with retrieve "variables" **[10, Y]**. This optimization is fine for this goal list in isolation, but say we disjoin it with another subgoal, **r(U, V), V = 20**, with retrieve variables **[U, V]**. That goal list is optimized to **r(U, 20)** with retrieve variables **[U, 20]**. Were we to share the retrieve list, we would get `(r(10, 20); r(10, 20))` with retrieve variables `[10, 20]`, which is incorrect. The selection on the first argument being **10** should not apply to the second subquery, and the selection of the second argument to be **20** should not apply to the first subquery. The resulting query does not compute the union of the two separate subqueries. We must be more careful and construct a new list of variables for the retrieve set of the compound query. For each subquery we build a goal that equates (at query evaluation time) the new variables with the retrieve variables of the subquery. For this example, we introduce new retrieve variables `[N1, N2]` and construct the goal list:

```
(N1 = 10, N2 = Y, r(10, Y); N1 = U, N2 = 20, r(U, 20))
```

This query computes the union of the subqueries correctly. Notice that the **translateSub** clause for 'or' compound queries does not share the retrieve variable list but uses **newVars** to construct the two conjunctions of equations, which are then prepended to the subqueries before they are disjoined.

EXAMPLE 12.37: Consider a simple compound query involving '**and**' and its translation:

```
:- tokenize("retrieve NM where (TU = 'logic') and (TU = 'oop')",
     Tokens), query(Tokens, [], Ast), translate(Ast, RetVars, Goal).

RetVars = [_10440],
Goal = r2(_10440, logic), r2(_10440, oop)
```
□

EXAMPLE 12.38: The following compound query involves '**not**'.

```
:- tokenize("retrieve NM, AF where not (TU = 'logic')", Tokens),
     query(Tokens, [], Ast), translate(Ast, RetVars, Goal).

Ast = retrieve([attr('NM'), attr('AF')],
      not([comp(=, attr('TU'), string(logic))])),
RetVars = [_10226, _10293],
Goal = r1(_10226, _10293), \+ (r4(_12017, _12084, _12178),
      r3(_10226, _12017, _12084), r2(_10226,logic),
      r1(_10226, _10293))
```

This use of negation-as-failure is sound, even though there are unbound variables in its scope. No unbound variable in the scope of the '\+' also appears outside its scope. □

EXAMPLE 12.39: For a compound query involving 'or', consider:

```
:- tokenize("retrieve NM, MB where (MB = 'ACM') or (MB = 'IEEE')",
     Tokens), query(Tokens, [], Ast), translate(Ast, RetVars, Goal).

RetVars = [_14434, _14480],
Goal = (_14434=_11503, _14480='ACM'), r3(_11503, 'ACM', _11664);
           (_14434=_13578, _14480='IEEE'), r3(_13578, 'IEEE', _13739)
```

Had we not constructed the new retrieve variable list, the construction of the query would have failed, because the two constants do not unify. □

EXAMPLE 12.40: As a final example that shows a more complicated compound query, consider the following:

```
:- tokenize("retrieve NM, RT where (MB = 'ACM') and
      ((RG = 'early') or (RG='late'))", Tokens),
      query(Tokens, [], Ast), translate(Ast, RetVars, Goal).

RetVars = [_15621, _15362],
Goal = (r4('ACM', _15268, _15362), r3(_15621, 'ACM', _15268)),
      ((_15621=_18181, _15362=_17922), r4(_17761, early, _17922),
      r3(_18181, _17761, early); (_15621=_20701, _15362=_20442),
      r4(_20281, late, _20442), r3(_20701, _20281, late))
```
□

This section completes the query processor for PIQUE. Other optimizations involving common subexpressions and independent subgoals are left as Exercises 12.16 and 12.18.

12.3.7. *Programming in Prolog*

As a retrospective on implementing the database query processor in Prolog, let's consider what was easy to do and what was hard. The scanner was relatively easy once we settled on the system structure. The parser was very easy, given the grammar; the Prolog parser is a trivial transformation of the formal grammar, so the only difficulty there is in devising the correct grammar.

Developing the translator and optimizer components was more difficult, but that is to be expected because they are conceptually more complex. Consider how we went about this task. We first wrote a simple version of the translator that handled only a part of the full language, the simple queries. We were able to get that working and test that indeed it was generating the correct goals. That could be tested very easily simply by **call**-ing the generated goal. It was (relatively) easy to get up and running a simple version—a version that had the correct basic structure of the final system. Then we elaborated on that program. We added optimizations, step by step, checking at each point that the program still had the correct behavior and still worked on all the test examples we had generated earlier in the development process. At each point we had a program we could test to see if the design was correct. There was no point at which we had to do a lot of design work without being able to test it out by running it.

After we had developed the optimizer to a certain point, we went back and extended the translator to handle compound queries. This required adding just a few simple clauses. All the basic functionality was there already; we simply had to arrange to combine it appropriately. Actually, as noted at that time, we (the authors) had looked ahead and knew that we would need certain functions put together in a certain way, and so we presented the predicates that way at the beginning. The separation of the predicates **translate** and **translateSub** is the prime example of this. When actually developing the code for presentation, we did not separate them; we had just a single predicate that performed both functions. But when we had to expand the translator to handle compound queries later in the chapter, we went back and found that the old **translate** had to be divided. And it was trivial to do. Rearranging the decomposition of a problem into predicates and subpredicates is a constant problem in developing systems. Logic programs seem to make that a much easier process.

Once the proper decomposition of **translate** was made, elaborating the program simply meant adding more clauses to handle the new cases. It is a general property of logic programs that to extend a program to handle a new situation that was not handled before requires the addition of new clauses. Old clauses need not change. This property makes it very easy in logic programs to begin with a simple prototype and then extend and elaborate it into a full and complete system.

The program developed in this chapter is clearly not a full industrial-strength query processor. It could, however, form the basis for one and be elaborated into one. At some point the elaboration would most likely include replacing the use of Prolog's internal database to store all the relations with an external disk storage system. This might involve interfacing to an existing database system or might involve developing a new system written in a lower-level language. But the structure (and harness) set up by the Prolog program will continue to be usable through that entire development process.

Logic programming is a practical tool that can help significantly in the development of large and complex software systems that solve real problems.

12.4. EXERCISES

12.1. Write a Prolog predicate that checks that a PIQUE database is consistent—that is, that it satisfies the containment conditions.

12.2. Convert the scanner to read from an input stream, using **get0**, instead of using a list of ASCII codes as input.

12.3. Enhance the scanner to handle source comments.

12.4. The parser simply fails if there is a syntax error in the query it is given. Since you can anticipate under what circumstances certain calls will fail, you can add default final clauses to those parsing predicates to print out useful error messages when it is about to fail. (You may need cuts in the other clauses to keep from printing out errors.) Extend the parser in the text to include some error checking. A complete treatment of error handling in a parser is extremely complicated. Discuss the problems you encountered, and give syntax errors that your extended parser does not handle well. Explain why it does not.

12.5. Rewrite the predicate **selectGoal** to make it tail recursive.

12.6. A database programmer using Prolog may want to be able to use a PIQUE query to define a new Prolog predicate, which can be used later. For example, the programmer might want to define **earlyACM(NM, AF)** as the relation defined by the query:

retrieve NM, AF **where** (MB = 'ACM') * (RG = 'early').

Add to the PIQUE syntax a way to specify such a command, and modify the Prolog PIQUE processor to define the indicated predicate when it processes such a command.

12.7. Modify **evalPique** to print the answer to a query as a table, with left-justified columns for strings and right-justified columns for numbers, and an attribute name at the head of each column.

12.8. Run the translator, including equation optimization through unification, on the query:

retrieve NM **where** (TU = 'logic') * (TU = 'oop').

What happens?

12.9. Write a single predicate, without cuts, that replaces **listify** and **conjify**—that is, works in both directions. At first, assume that the input is a simple right associative conjunction and perform no simplifications. Then add the simplifications that are done in listify. What happens?

12.10. The reordering optimizer is inefficient because it recomputes **rateA** unnecessarily, since **rate** calls it and then calls **rateB**, which calls **rateA**. Change the optimizer so that **rateA** is not recomputed.

12.11. In the reordering optimizer, if we really use the look-ahead rating, **rateB**, only as a tie breaker, we only need to compute it for the goals that have the best **rateA**, not all the goals, as **optConj** does. Rewrite **optConj** to incorporate this change.

12.12. The goal-reordering algorithm could be improved if it had more information concerning the relations.
   a. It could use information about keys in base relations. Devise a way to represent key information in the scheme, and revise the **optConj** predicate to take it into account.
   b. Base relations may have indexes on certain attributes, which make it faster to retrieve tuples given values on the indexed attributes. (This is especially true if the base relation is too big to be stored entirely in memory.) Devise a way to represent information on the existence of indexes in the database scheme and revise **optConj** to use it during optimization.

12.13. Many Prolog predicates are written so that they expect their first arguments bound and bind their last arguments. Extend the optimizer to take this tendency into account.

12.14. Devise a database and query for which **optConj** produces a suboptimal ordering.

12.15. The translator and optimizer given here work directly on Prolog goals—

variables and all. This means that the definitions cannot be pure because they have to use metapredicates, such as **var**, '==', and so forth, that are sensitive to whether a term is currently a variable or not. An alternative for writing such programs is to:

1. turn all variables into distinct ground terms that represent the variables,
2. process the goal list as a ground term, and
3. turn the ground terms representing variables back into actual variables in the result.

a. Define a predicate **numberVars(+Term, +VIn, -VOut)** that takes an arbitrary term **Term** and replaces the variables in it with terms of a special form: **vble(*n*)**, where *n* is an integer. Each distinct variable is replaced by a **vble**-term with a distinct integer. **VIn** and **VOut** are integers and all integers used in **vble**-terms are between **VIn** and **VOut**.
b. Define a predicate **unnumberVars(+NumTerm, -UnTerm)** that takes a closed term **NumTerm** with **vble**-terms for "variables" and produces a term with those **vble**-terms replaced by real logical variables.
c. Discuss the pros and cons of using such predicates when manipulating Prolog terms in the optimization phase.

12.16. Construct a predicate to optimize goal lists produced by the PIQUE translator to eliminate common subexpressions. For example:

```
r1(X, Y), r2(Y, Z), X > 50, r1(X, Y), r2(Y, Z), Z < 30
```

simplifies to:

```
r1(X, Y), r2(Y, Z), X > 50, Z < 30
```

Such a goal list can arise from a compound query with an '**and**' connective.

12.17. What new optimizations could be made assuming a predicate **materialize(GoalList, Format)** that finds all answers for **GoalList** and **assert**s them (temporarily) as facts in the database using a term **Format** as a template to give a predicate name for the facts and an order for the variables? An example use of **materialize** is:

```
materialize((r1(X, Y), r2(Y, Z)), temp12(X, Z))
```

The translation of a PIQUE query may now contain **materialize** goals.

12.18. Two goals in a goal list are *independent* if at the time the first goal is encountered during evaluation it shares no unbound variables with the second goal. Should the second goal fail, there is no point in retrying the first goal, since nothing will change for the second goal and it will fail again. In the goal list from Example 12.29:

```
Goal = (r4(_9666, _9733, _9827), r3(_10086, _9666, _9733),
    r2(_10086, _10681), r1(_10086, _11139)), _9827>160
```

the **r2** and **r1** goals are independent. The notion of independence generalizes easily to groups of goals. Construct an optimizer that modifies a goal list to avoid unnecessary backtracking through independent groups of goals. You may need to add rules to the Prolog program temporarily before evaluating the modified goal list.

12.5. COMMENTS AND BIBLIOGRAPHY

The example of this chapter gives an idea of how Prolog can be used to solve a real problem. The Association-Object Data Model, whose query language we implemented here, was developed and explained in several works [12.1–12.5].

D. H. D. Warren [12.6] presents another approach to using Prolog to optimize database queries expressed in Prolog. Giannesini and Cohen [12.7] discuss a different formulation of grammars in Prolog that is amenable to grammatical modifications and verifying properties of grammars.

For more information on database query processing, see Maier [4.2] or the collection by Kim, Reiner, and Batory [12.8].

12.1. D. Maier and D. S. Warren, Specifying connections for a universal relation scheme database, *Proc. ACM-SIGMOD Int. Conference on Management of Data,* Orlando, FL, June 1982, 1–7.

12.2. D. Maier, D. Rozenshtein, S. Salveter, J. Stein, and D. S. Warren, Toward logical data independence: A relational query language without relations, *Proc. ACM-SIGMOD Int. Conference on Management of Data,* Orlando, FL, June 1982, 51–60.

12.3. D. Rozenshtein, *Query and Role Playing in the Association-Object Data Model,* Ph.D. thesis, State University of New York at Stony Brook, 1983.

12.4. D. Maier, D. Rozenshtein, and D. S. Warren, Window functions, in *Advances in Computing Research,* vol. 3: *The Theory of Databases,* P. C. Kanellakis and F. P. Preparata (eds.), JAI Press Inc., London, 1986, 213–46.

12.5. J. Stein, *Constraints in the Association-Object Data Model,* Ph.D. thesis, State University of New York at Stony Brook, 1987.

12.6. D. H. D. Warren, Efficient processing of interactive relational database queries expressed in logic, *Proc. 7th VLDB Conference,* Cannes, 1981, 272–81.

12.7. F. Giannesini and J. Cohen, Parser generation and grammar manipulations using Prolog's infinite trees, *Journal of Logic Programming* 1:3, October 1984, 253–65.

12.8. W. Kim, D. S. Reiner, and D. S. Batory (eds.), *Query Processing in Database Systems,* Springer-Verlag, New York, 1985.

Appendix: Possible Course Projects

This book may be used as the main text for an upper-level undergraduate course or an introductory-level graduate course. If it is to involve a programming component, the course can take one of two directions. One direction emphasizes the theory and use of logic programming systems and includes programming in Prolog. The other path emphasizes the theory and implementation of a logic programming system. This appendix outlines these two courses and discusses programming projects for each.

Theory and Use of Logic Programming

The first type of course emphasizes the theory and use of programming in logic. It requires that the students have access to a Prolog interpreter or compiler and a manual for the available Prolog system. A secondary text, such as *Programming in Prolog* by Clocksin and Mellish, might be recommended for the students. This course would cover Chapters 1, 2, 4, 5, 7, 8, 9, and 12. Programming assignments would require that the students write programs in Prolog. Some of these programs could be taken from the exercises at the end of each chapter.

One difficulty with this approach is that there are not many interesting projects that can be written in pure Proplog, the language of Chapters 1 and 2. The first project could be to write a Proplog program to help in an identification problem, along the lines of the fabric example of Chapter 1. For example, there are several books on how to identify plants, trees, birds, mushrooms, diseases, and so forth, which the students could use for reference. Then a nonprogramming assignment could be given for Chapter 2.

Another possibility is for the instructor to write a simple Proplog interpreter, in Prolog, that would allow the Proplog programmer to supply weights to clauses to help guide the search. Then the project could be made more interesting by having the students use this more complicated system. This project would have more of the flavor of an AI problem of diagnosis.

A possible programming assignment in Datalog involves language recognition, as discussed at the beginning of Chapter 7. The assignment could be to write a recognizer for a subset of Pascal. Alternatively, the language could be a data retrieval language such as the one introduced in Chapter 12. The final project might then extend the language recognizer to a full system that interprets the language. If the language were a subset of Pascal, the final project would be a simple Pascal interpreter written in Prolog. If the language were the data retrieval language of Chapter 12, the final project would implement the full system from Chapter 12, with some enhancements or modifications, such as those suggested in the exercises for Chapter 12.

Another possibility for a final project is to have the students write logic program interpreters in Prolog. For example, they could write a breadth-first or best-first interpreter for Prolog programs, or a bottom-up interpreter for Datalog programs.

Implementation of Logic Programming Systems

The second possible emphasis of a course based on this book is the theory and implementation of a Prolog interpreter. Such a course would emphasize Chapters 3, 6, 10, and 11 and would spend less time on Chapters 7, 8, and 12. The programming projects would be written in Pascal, or some other high-level procedural language, and would involve the implementation of a Prolog interpreter.

There are a variety of ways such a Prolog implementation project could be developed. The instructor probably will have to provide a parser to construct the internal representation of the clauses. One approach is to have the students program a sequence of interpreters following the development in the book. An alternative is for the instructor to provide a simple interpreter and have the students make modifications to implement suggested optimizations.

The one aspect of the code given in the text that does not translate directly into a high-level typed language is the implementation of structure records. It would be nice to use the type system of the implementation language directly, but Pascal, for one, is not this flexible. The simplest solution is to allocate these records as a sequence of words from an array. The first word of the sequence would contain the index of the structure symbol in the symbol table, and the subsequent words would contain indices of the values of the fields. The program would determine the number of fields by using the arity field of the symbol table record indexed by the first word of the sequence. A package of routines to manipulate records represented this way might be provided by the instructor.

A variant on this organization is to have the students program their interpreters in teams, dividing up the matching, copying, and other routines.

Index

Prolog predicates are given in **monospace**; Pascal routines and WPE instructions are listed in *italics*.

abstract syntax tree 498–99
accumulated substitution 233, 238, 258, 388
addtolist 23
Aho, A. V. 165–66
alloc 452, 456, 458
and 4, 47, 55, 58, 59, 173
anonymous variable 455
$answer pseudoliteral 141
answers 140–42, 372–74
apply 134, 229–30, 385
Apt, K. 105–6
arg 331–33, 428
arg 282, 385
argument 128
argument 136
arithmetic predicate 153, 259–61, 323–25
arity 176
arity 282
asnumber 259
asref 259
assert 337–41, 345, 428
asserta 337–38
assertz 338, 340–41
association 481, 491
  maximal 483, 492
association-object data model 526
associative law 59, 187
AST. *See* abstract syntax tree
atom 171, 175
atom 328–30, 428
atomic formula. *See* atom
attribute 153, 479

backtrack point 425–27, 462
backtrack register 457
backward chaining. *See* top-down interpreter

bagof 334, 336–37, 428
Balbin, I. 477
Bancilhon, F. 263
base, Herbrand. *See* Herbrand base
  of a clause set 66
  of a functional formula 354
  of a predicate formula 180
  of a program 51, 168, 349
  of a propositional formula 57–58
  proposition 40
Batory, D. S. 526
binary resolution 201–2, 204, 209, 213–15, 371
binary resolvent 201–2, 425
binding array 251–58, 403–9, 424–25
binding environment 425, 432–33
binding frame 417, 448–49, 451–52, 470–71
Blair, H. 105–6
bldCon 463
bldTVal 464
bldVal 463–64
bldVar 463
bottom-up interpreter 17–24, 94, 258, 262, 409
bound variable 178
Bowen, K. A. 345
Boyer, R. S. 415
Boyle, J. 106
branchOnBound 475
breadth-first search 33, 78, 93–95, 258, 409
Bruynooghe, M. 262–63
bucket 435
Burnham, W. D. 345

call literal 420
call 318–20, 428
call 450, 452
Campbell, J. A. 117, 477
cardinality of a set 102
CDB. *See* completed database
center clause 73, 209

Chang, C.-L. 105, 222
character constant 317
character string, representation 317
choice point 417, 448, 457
Clark, K. L. 105–6, 263, 312
clausal form 191, 361
clausal formula 60, 64
clause 3, 64, 128, 190
  body 4
  head 4
  Horn. *See* Horn clause
  indexing. *See* indexing
  representation 21–23, 227–28, 383
  semantics 171, 350
  unit. *See* unit clause
clause set 64, 191
Clocksin, W. F. 345
closed formula 178
closed-world assumption 95
Codd, E. F. 165
Cohen, J. 526
collision 435
Colmeraur, A. 312
comma list 514
common variable 432
commutative law 59, 187
comparison predicate 151–52, 325, 330–31
complementary literals 65
complete deduction procedure 63
completed database 96
completed frame 431, 460
compose 231–32, 387
composition, of substitutions 197–99, 236–40, 389–90
Con$_f$ 179
concat 23, 229–30, 234
concatenation, of goal lists 235
  of lists 287–90
concatenation, lazy. *See* lazy concatenation
conj 59, 61–62
conjunctive form 59–60, 64, 190
connection 484, 492, 504–5
constant 128
constant mapping 179–180
containment condition 481
contraction step 77, 375, 411
control predicate 320–23, 326–27
copy 229, 384
copyapply2 234, 236, 388
copyapplyrepls 237, 389–90, 431–32, 447
copyapplyrepls6 408
copycat 30–31, 91
copycat2 134
copycompose 234, 388–89
copy on use, for code 243
  for terms 394, 399–403, 404, 409, 415, 471
copystruct 384–85
copy term 400, 431
current input stream 315
current output stream 315
cut 320–23, 427–28, 462
CWA. *See* closed-world assumption

database 16
database scheme, PIQUE 489–91
Davis, M. 220, 222–23
Davis and Putnam method 220, 222
DCG. *See* definite clause grammar
dealloc 454
Debray, S. K. 477
decision procedure 217
declarative semantics 45
deduction procedure 63
deductive database 165
deep-copy on use 413
definite clause 81
definite clause grammar 499
demo 41–42
demonstration DAG 19
demonstration tree 17, 19–24, 25–30, 94
DeMorgan's laws 59–60, 187
depth-first search 32–33, 78, 92–94, 216, 258, 409, 411–12
  staged 409, 412
deref 237–40, 389–90, 394
deref5cu 399–400
deref5ss 395–99
deref6 252–53
deref6cu 404
deref6ss 403–4
dereferencing 238, 252–53, 389–90, 393–94, 403–4
derefopt 240
deterministic frame 429–33, 460
Dietrich, S. 263
difference 156–57, 159–60
difference list 293–96
distributive law 60, 187
domain 167, 179, 353
  of a program 168, 349

elimdupl 91, 93
empty list 287, 290
environment register 449
establish 107, 109, 111, 133–34, 141–42, 147–49, 152–53, 215–17, 280
establish1 229–32, 384–88
establish2 233–35, 388–89
establish3 236–40, 389–90
establish4 241–43, 391–92
establish5 245–49, 393–94
establish6 256–57, 259–60, 407–9, 417–18
establish7 422–24
establish8 426–28
establishbu 22–24, 53–54, 94
establishtd 29–33, 94, 95–97, 107
establishtdn 97
evaluable predicate 151–53, 160, 258–61, 313, 427–28
evaluation function 354
exec 467

exhaustive propositions 56
existential quantifier 175
extension step 77, 374, 411

fact 3
  semantics 50–51, 145, 170, 350
factor 204
factoring 204, 371
fail 319–20
failure node 67–68, 368
failure tree 68, 368
falsifying truth assignment 51
file 315
final literal optimization 466–70
findfirst 281–84, 385–88
first 108–9, 111, 229
first5 245–46, 393
formula, predicate. *See* predicate formula
  propositional. *See* propositional formula
  universal. *See* universal formula
formula tree 57
forward chaining. *See* bottom-up interpreter
forward reference 430–31
frame. *See* binding frame
framed literal 77, 374, 411
framelength 427
free variable 178
full resolution 202–4, 214, 371
Fun_f 353
functional logic, semantics 353–57
function mapping 353
function symbol 352–53. *See also* record name
functor 331–33, 428

Gallaire, H. 106, 166
Gallier, J. 105
Garey, M. R. 105
generalized Proplog program 98
generate and test 151, 303–6
gensym 339
get0 317, 428
getCon 453, 465
getStr 465
getTVal 454–55
getVal 454
getVar 451
Giannesini, F. 526
globalized variable 432, 470
global variable. *See* common variable
goal clause 82
goal list, semanatics 172
goal reordering 513
grammar, Datalog 168–69
  definite clause 499
  functional logic 353
  PIQUE 499
  predicate logic 174–75
  Prolog 349
  Proplog 47–48
  propositional logic 56

Gray, P. 165–66
Green, C. C. 222–23
ground instance 128
ground literal 145

Hall, A. R. 345
halt 319–20
hashing 435–37
Hayes, J. 345
Hayes, P. 105–6
headless clause 82–85
heap 407–8, 425, 431–32, 440–44, 463–64
  register 456
Henschen, L. 105, 222–23, 263
Herbrand base 192, 365
Herbrand interpretation 192–94, 347–48, 364–66
Herbrand model 167, 194, 364
Herbrand's Theorem 194–95, 366–68
Herbrand universe 167, 192, 364
Hewitt, C. 312
Hogger, C. J. 312
Horn clause 78, 81, 209, 376

idempotent substitution 197
if 4, 47, 55, 79–81, 191–92
if-then-else 327
implementing function 260
implication form 80, 209
implies 62
independent goals 525–26
indexing 108–9, 228, 433–37
inference node 69
inference rule 62–63
infinite term 312
input clause 83
input resolution 79, 82–94
  completeness 85–87
input/output predicate 314–17
instance, clause 128, 201
  ground. *See* ground instance
instance 134, 229, 235, 243
instantiation 128, 170, 182, 194, 350
instruction counter 449
interpretation 50. *See also* structure
interpreter 16
intersect 156–57, 159
is 324–25, 427
isempty 108, 111, 229
isempty5 245, 393
isnumber 259
is_satisfiable 62

Johnson, D. S. 105
join 155–56, 159
Joseph, M. L. 44

Kanellakis, P. C. 526
Kanoui, H. 312
key, of a relation 516
Kifer, M. 263

Kim, W. 526
Königs Lemma 368
Kowalski, R. A. 44, 105–6, 312, 345

Lassez, J.-L. 223
last call optimization 437–44, 447, 466
lazy concatenation 109
lazy list 109, 244, 392, 410–11, 420
lconcat_rest 112, 245–46, 393
Lecot, K. 477
Lee, R. C.-T. 105, 222
left recursive rule 310
left vine 83
leftwards node 85
lexical analyzer. *See* scanner
lexical convention 315
lexical rule 47
Li, D. 165–66
Lifting Lemma 205–8
linear resolution 73–74
list
  constructor 287, 290
  processing 287
  syntax 290, 316–17
literal 60, 128
  negative 79
  positive 79
  representation 226, 381–83
Lloyd, J. 380
local substitution 225, 243–45, 393–94, 420
  representation 249–51, 403
local variable. *See* private variable
logic, definition 46
logical equivalence 59–60, 186, 357
logical implication 52–54, 61–62, 71, 171–72, 186, 351–52, 357–60
logical variable 128, 170, 408–9
logically_implies 53–54
Loveland, D. W. 105–6
Lowering Lemma 208, 222
Lozinskii, E. L. 263
lrest 112
lrest5 245–46
Lusk, E. 106

Maher, M. J. 223
Maier, D. 165–66, 263, 526
Manna, Z. 105–6
Marriott, K. G. 223
Martelli, A. 380
match 134–38, 200–202, 229–32, 240–42, 253–55, 280–81, 370–71, 440, 445–47
match1 281–82, 385–88, 390–91
match4 241–43, 391–92
match5 246–47, 393–94
match5cu 400–402
match5ss 395
match6 255–56, 258–59, 404–7
match8 427
matching function 134–38, 229–32, 280–84. *See also* unification
matching literals 201
matrix 189, 361
McKay, D. 263
meaning function 51, 57–59, 79, 170–72, 182–85, 350–52, 356–57
Mellish, C. S. 345, 415, 477
Meltzer, B. 223, 415
member 23
Mendelson, E. 104–5
mention set 485, 503–4
metaprogramming predicate 327–34
mgu. *See* most general unifier
Michie, D. 223, 345, 415
minimal model 97–99, 104–5
minimal truth assignment 96
Minker, J. 106, 166
mode declaration 314
mode flag 465
model 51, 59, 96–99, 171, 185, 351, 356
  Herbrand. *See* Herbrand model
  minimal. *See* minimal model
model elimination 75–78, 105, 374–76, 409–12, 415
  completeness 411–12
molecule 244–45, 392–93, 433
Montanari, U. 380
Moore, J. 415
most general unifier 197, 199–200, 223, 370
mutually exclusive propositions 56
MYCIN 44

Naish, L. 345
name 331–32, 428
Naqvi, S. 263
Nasr, R. 477
natural join. *See* join
negation-as-failure 97, 105, 147–51, 322–23
negative literal 79
newcopy 237–38, 385
new variable 249
newvars 246, 249, 395, 401
newvars6 255–56, 407, 427
nextgoal 424, 431
Nilsson, M. 117
Nilsson, N. J. 105–6, 222
nl 315
nondeterminism 429, 431, 456–62
nonrecursive interpreter 417–24
nonvar 328–29
not 55, 58, 173
not 97, 147–51, 160
NP-complete 105
number, representation 151, 258
number 328, 330
number 428
numvars 251

object 482, 491
  minimal 484, 493
occurs check 284, 371, 415
open formula 178

open-tailed list 506
operand, of WPE instruction 449–50
operator notation 316
or 55, 58, 59, 173, 326–27
or-tree 91. *See also* search tree
Overbeek, R. 106
overflow area 435

Pao, Y. H. 345
parser, in Datalog 269–74
  PIQUE 498–503
  Proplog 47–50
  recursive-descent 48, 117
parsing, English 294–96
Pasero, R. 312
Pereira, F. 345, 477
Pereira, L. M. 477
PIQUE 479–88
Plaisted, D. A. 415
Planner 312
Poe, M. D. 477
positive literal 79
positive unit resolution 103, 105
Potter, J. 477
predicate 140, 145
  definition 128
  evaluable. *See* evaluable predicate
  factor 175
  formula 174–75
  name. *See* predicate symbol
  symbol 128, 176, 226
  term 175
  unit 175
predicate logic, semantics 178–85
predsym 134, 229, 231
prefix 189, 361
prenex form 189, 360–61
Preparata, F. P. 526
printvine 91–92
private variable 432
probing 435
procedural system 33
proceed 454
Procrastination Principle 114, 116, 131, 233, 236
progenitor 75–76, 374
program term 400
program variable 249
project 155, 158
proposition 3, 50
  base 40
propositional factor 56
  symbol 47–48, 108
  term 56
  unit 56
propositional formula 56
  semantics 57–59
Przymusinski, T. C. 105–6
put 317, 428
putCon 450
Putnam, H. 220, 222–23
putStr 463
putTStr 464
putTVal 456
putTVar 469
putUVal 469–70
putVal 453
putVar 450

quantification 167, 173–74
quantifier 176
  binding variable occurrences 178
  equivalences 187–89
  existential. *See* existential quantifier
  semantics 183
  universal. *See* universal quantifier
query language 153–60, 479
  completeness 158
query optimization 511–19
query processing 153, 489

Ramakrishnan, R. 263
rconcat 237
read 315–17, 319–20, 428
read mode 465
record 275
  name 275, 286
  semantics 286
recursion 142–44, 160, 437
reduction step 77, 375, 411
refutation
  principle 63, 65
  procedure 63, 90, 202–3
  tree 71, 209–17
  vine 94, 212–17
refutation complete 66
register 449, 457
Reiner, D. S. 526
relation 153
  scheme 153
relational
  algebra 153–60, 165
  calculus 153
  database 153–60, 165, 479–85
  operator 154
relationally complete 158
repeat-fail loop 341
replacement 134, 369, 393–95
replacement list 236–37, 389–90, 403
resolution
  closure 65, 70
  completeness 66–72, 205–7, 372
  correctness 66, 205, 372
  DAG 72, 209–10
  full. *See* full resolution
  input. *See* input resolution
  linear. *See* linear resolution
  restrictions 72–78
  rule 63–65, 104, 201–4
  selected literal. *See* selected literal resolution
  soundness. *See* correctness
  step 65

resolution *continued*
  tree 71
  unit. *See* unit resolution
  vine 83
resolvedf 92
resolvedf2 93–94
resolvent 65, 201
  binary. *See* binary resolvent
rest 108, 229
restore 255–56, 408
restore8 426–27
retract 338–41, 428
retryMeElse 458–60
return register 451
Robinson, J. A. 104–5, 222
Roussel, P. 312
Rozenshtein, D. 526
rule 3
  semantics 50–51, 146, 170, 350
run-time stack 420–25, 448–49

Saccà, D. 263
Sagiv, Y. 263
Salveter, S. 526
satisfaction equivalence 360
satisfiable
  clause set 66, 68, 71
  formula 61–62, 185, 356
  Horn clause set 87–89
satisfied 23–24
satisfying truth assignment 51
scanner 47
  PIQUE 495–98
Scheme, relation. *See* relation scheme
scope, of a quantifier 176
search, breadth-first. *See* breadth-first search
  depth-first. *See* depth-first search
  strategy 32–33, 63, 90
  tree 17, 32, 94
select 154–55, 158
selected literal 74
selected literal resolution 74–75, 83, 89–90, 209, 257, 374
selection condition 154
semantic tree 67, 366–68
semidecidable problem 217
sentence. *See* closed formula, proposition
sentential operator 55, 79
Separability Lemma 90
set
  manipulation 492
  predicate 334–37
setof 334–36, 345, 428
Shapiro, E. 345
Shapiro, S. 263
Shoenfield, J. 380
Shortliffe, E. H. 44
side clause 73, 83, 209
Skolem function 361–64
Skolemized formula 362
Slinn, J. 477
SL resolution. *See* selected literal resolution
Smazola 301
  Grand 306
sorting 307
soundness 45
statement 3
Stein, J. 526
Sterling, L. 345
Stickel, M. E. 409, 412, 415
stratifiable program 99, 105
structure 181, 185, 355
  manipulation predicates 331–34
  symbol 281, 382
structure sharing
  for code 225, 243–45, 392–94, 409
  for terms 394–99, 402–4, 409, 415, 432–33
subformula 57
substitution 134–38, 196–99, 223, 369–71, 395–96
  accumulated. *See* accumulated substitution
  local. *See* local substitution
symbol table 49–50, 108–9, 226, 249–51, 381–83

tail recursion optimization 437, 439–44
Tarnlund, S.-A. 263, 312
tautology 61
temporary variable 454–56, 468–69
term 175, 275
  representation 226, 315, 381–83, 462–66
  testing predicates 328–30
theorem prover 55. *See also* deduction procedure
Tick, E. 477
token 47
top-down interpreter 17, 25–33, 94, 107–8, 116, 133–38, 262, 279–84, 384–88, 409
trail
  register 456
  stack 253, 405, 425, 432
transitive closure 165, 296–99
translator, PIQUE 503–11
trimming environments 470–71
TRO. *See* tail recursion optimization
true 326
trustMeElseFail 458–60
truth assignment 50–54, 58, 67, 167, 170–71, 180–81, 350–52, 355
  minimal 96
truth table 61–62
tryMeElse 458
tuple 153

Ullman, J. D. 165–66, 263
uniCon 465
unifiable atoms 370
unificaction 168, 201, 222, 258, 370–71
unifier 197, 199–200, 370
  most general. *See* most general unifier
unify 215
union 156–57, 159

unit clause 3, 94
unit resolution 94, 222
  positive 103
uniTVar 466
univ 331, 333–34, 428
uniVal 465
uniVar 465
universal
  formula 167, 190, 361, 366
  quantifier 175
universal scheme query language 479
universe. *See* domain
unsafe variable 469
unsatisfiable. *See* satisfiable
update predicate 337–41

valid formula 61–62, 66, 185, 356
valid 62
van Emden, M. H. 262–63
van Heijenoort 222–23
var 328–29, 428

variable, logical. *See* logical variable
variable 231, 249
Vieille, L. 263
vine 73, 83
  properly ordered 89
violates 284, 371, 387
violates4 392
violates5 397

Walker, A. 105–6
Warren Abstract Machine 476–77
Warren, D. H. D. 262–63, 345, 448, 476–77, 526
Warren, D. S. 262–63, 345, 477, 526
Warren Prolog Engine 447–51
Wos, L. 105–6, 222–23
WPE. *See* Warren Prolog Engine
write 315–17, 428
write mode 465

Zaniolo, C. 263